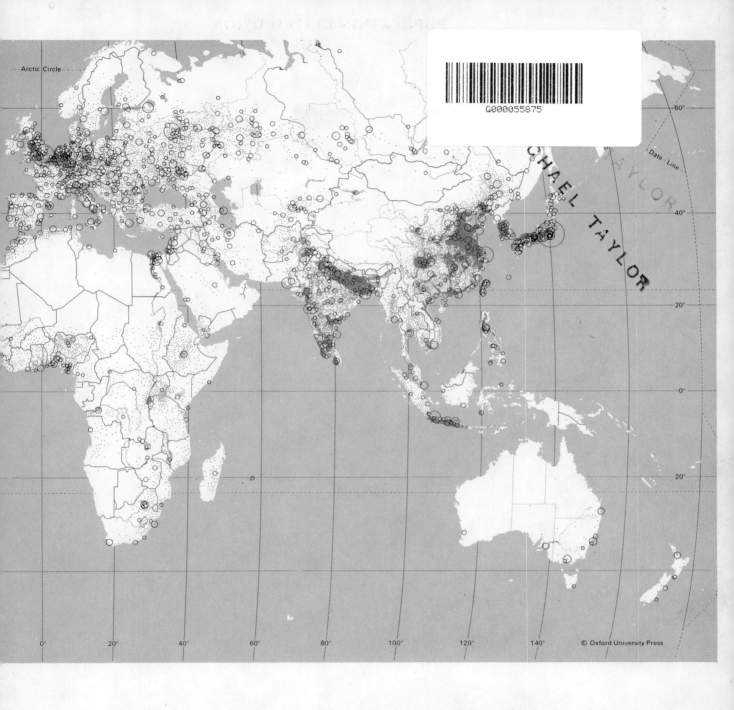

G000055875

PHILIP-PINES	PARAGUAY	TURKEY	POLAND	U.S.S.R.	SOUTH AFRICA	MEXICO	TAIWAN	SWEDEN	GERMANY F.R.	FRANCE	IRAQ	U.A.R.	BRAZIL	ISRAEL	U.S.A.	NETHER-LANDS	U.K.	JAPAN	CANADA	ARGENTINA	AUSTRALIA
27 088	1 817	31 391	29 776	208 827	15 994	34 923	13 383	7 766	53 977	46 520	8 262	25 984	70 119	2 183	179 323	11 462	52 709	98 275	18 238	23 031	11 541
116	5	42	102	11	15	23	365	17	233	91	19	31	10	129	21	375	226	270	2	8	2
15	17	19	23	24	27	28	29	31	32	34	34	35	36	41	45	47	49	50	52	57	63
1 402	305	2 052	1 261	6 507	1 153	3 353	1 155	1 262	2 191	7 369	1 745	4 220	5 383	390	11 410	1 048	7 914	11 005	2 437	7 000	2 445

THE GEOGRAPHY OF ECONOMIC ACTIVITY

McGRAW-HILL SERIES IN GEOGRAPHY

Edward J. Taaffe and John W. Webb, Consulting Editors

The Geography of Economic Activity
Third Edition

Richard S. Thoman

Department of Geography
California State University
Hayward

Peter B. Corbin

International Resource and Development Research, Incorporated
Cambridge, Massachusetts

McGraw-Hill Book Company

New York   St. Louis   San Francisco   Düsseldorf   Johannesburg   Kuala Lumpur
London   Mexico   Montreal   New Delhi   Panama   Paris   São Paulo   Singapore
Sydney   Tokyo   Toronto

THE GEOGRAPHY OF ECONOMIC ACTIVITY

1 2 3 4 5 6 7 8 9 0   FLBP   7 9 8 7 6 5 4

This book was set in Century Schoolbook by York Graphic Services, Inc. The editors were Janis Yates, Helen Greenberg, and Susan Gamer; the designer was Merrill Haber; the production supervisor was Joe Campanella. New cartography was done by Harry Scott.
The printer was Federated Lithographers-Printers, Inc.; the binder, The Book Press, Inc.

Library of Congress Cataloging in Publication Data

Thoman, Richard S   date
    The geography of economic activity.

    (The McGraw-Hill series in geography)
    1. Geography, Economic.   I. Corbin, Peter B., joint author.   II. Title.
HF1025.T47   1974   330.9   74-5756
ISBN 0-07-064207-9

Contents

Preface

Like its predecessors, this third edition of **The Geography of Economic Activity** is an introduction to economic geography, written mainly for the student who has had little or no access to geography since childhood. It is designed to provide both an insight into the field of economic geography and a better understanding of the complex and tense world in which we live. More important, it should provide a preliminary view of regional planning, a process which now appears inevitable and which should affect profoundly the lives of all readers of this book. Both authors have been active in this process and write from practical as well as academic experience.

Economic geography has ties to both economics and geography. It exists mainly because of a need to recognize and understand the location and functional linkages of economic activity in a world that varies conspicuously from place to place in both human and natural features. Traditionally, conclusions in the field have been drawn mainly from inductive observation of actual features, or from numerical reports like census data. During the past quarter century, another viewpoint has received emphasis in both scholarly and applied efforts, especially in economic and urban geography. This viewpoint, which relies heavily upon theory and deductive reasoning, now has been accepted by most geographers as an added dimension to traditional scholarship.

It is important to present both of these viewpoints to the beginning student. But how can this best be done? Inasmuch as Professor Thoman's views and approach emphasize historical-inductive-institutional reasoning, and Dr. Corbin's thinking is more in tune with the theoretical-deductive school, we decided that each author should be free to present his ideas in specific chapters, pointing out which methods and concepts are shared, which are distinctive, and how they eventually merge, especially in the recommendation of regional plans.

In the Introduction, we set down, in broad terms, the definition of economic geography, including its relationships to the human and physical environments. Part 1, mainly at the global level of observation, emphasizes classifications and patterns pertaining to both the physical and the human environments that are generally accepted as important for understanding today's real world. In Part 2 we look more closely at the field of economic geography—at concepts and methods held in common by the historical-inductive-institutional approach and the theoretical-deductive approach, and at those concepts and methods which are not necessarily shared. In Part 3, using the United States as a laboratory and commenting briefly on Canada and other selected areas, we consider the location of specific primary, secondary, and tertiary stages of economic activity, offering both historical-inductive-institutional and theoretical-deductive explanations for these respective locations and resultant functional patterns. In sequential chapters, we begin with a different primary activity—agriculture, commercial grazing, forest products industries, commercial fishing, and mining—and move into selected secondary and tertiary activities, offering both types of explanation for the location and other salient features of each stage. Finally, in Part 4, we move to the all-important aspect of regional planning, in which economic geography can play so important a role.

As is explained in more detail in the accompanying instructor's manual by Professor Donald G. Holtgrieve, this book is designed for use in both single-term and full-year courses. Some teachers will wish to emphasize the world patterns or case studies, and will give particular attention to Parts 1 and 3. Others will wish to stress the methodology in Part 2, the regional planning in Part 4, or both. For those wishing to review the methodology, but lacking time for detailed presentation, Chapter 8 contains the concepts and methods shared by the two approaches, Chapter 9 a review of the historical-inductive-institutional approach, and Chapter 13 a summary of the theoretical-deductive approach that has been presented in more detail in Chapters 10 to 12.

We follow the precedent of previous editions in using Plates 2, 5, 6 and 8 of *Elements of Geography* by Vernon C. Finch, Glen T. Trewartha, Arthur H. Robinson, and Edwin H. Hammond (New York: McGraw-Hill Book Company, 1957) as models for Figures 2.3, 2.4, 2.7, and 5.1, and in making original maps of distribution of manufacturing (Part 3) from data supplied by the United States Bureau of the Census. Other figures from copyrighted or public sources are credited in the captions as these appear on specific pages.

The reader may find it advantageous to use both the glossary and the index in looking for meaning of terms and concepts. Expressions which are in general use in economic geography are in the glossary. More specialized or unique terms or concepts, explained in the text, may be found in the index. In some cases, both the glossary and the index may be helpful. A good dictionary is recommended for such words as ''plowing'' and ''harrowing,'' which the authors believe to be part of a student's vocabulary but which some students maintain are not common words in today's changing world.

In addition to a diligent staff at McGraw-Hill whose efforts have been both tireless and appreciated, the authors wish to express gratitude to two persons who have been of enormous assistance. Mr. Harry Scott, in preparing cartography not used in previous editions, has exceeded substantially the responsibilities normally associated with that role. Mrs. Evelyn Z. Thoman—researcher, typist, proofreader, index specialist, reviewer, and constant source of encouragement—has earned a commendation that cannot be adequately expressed here.

Richard S. Thoman
Peter B. Corbin

THE GEOGRAPHY OF ECONOMIC ACTIVITY

Introduction

The Field of Economic Geography

Economic geography is the study of (1) the location of economic activity and (2) some impacts and relationships affecting or affected by such location.

The activity with which economic geography is concerned includes *consumption, production,* and *exchange.*

Consumption. Consumption is the using up of goods and services.[1] Goods can be grouped into two categories: *consumer goods* and *producer goods*. The first are utilized mainly by individuals and include such items as food, shelter, clothing, and other commodities that directly satisfy human needs and wants. Since they are consumed by individuals, consumer goods are found in all societies, whether simple, complex, or somewhere in between. Producer goods, in contrast, are not consumed directly by individuals, but are used to facilitate production of consumer goods and other producer goods. These include such items as transportation equipment, industrial machinery, and other material that is used up in the act of further production. Currently, producer goods are found especially in societies using technically advanced tools and methods.

The total volume of consumption for any nation involves both consumer and producer goods over a given period, and for the entire world that volume necessarily includes all materials used up directly by the world's inhabitants, plus the wear and tear on the world's instruments of production.

Services as well as goods are consumed, especially in a modern economy. Many services, such as those of accounting departments of manufacturing plants, are associated with the production of goods, while others are associated with the exchange of goods. Technically, therefore, one may speak of producer and consumer services, although a distinction seldom is made in practice.

Production. Production is the provision of producer and consumer goods and services. We consider

---

[1] Unless otherwise noted, *consumption* is considered in the broadest sense to be synonymous with *disappearance* and includes waste as well as use.

3

here that three types of production exist: *primary,
secondary,* and *tertiary.*

Primary. Primary production is the taking of a
substance directly or indirectly from the physical setting (or, as it is sometimes called, the natural environment). The five primary activities customarily recognized are *agriculture, grazing, forest-products
industries, fishing and hunting,* and *mining and quarrying.*

Agriculture is here defined as the growing and raising under human supervision of plants and animals.
Besides the more common activities, it includes truck
gardening, planting and harvesting tree crops, planting
grasses and legumes regularly for either direct harvest
or pasture, and producing fish and game under human
supervision rather than in a wild habitat.

Grazing is here considered to be the use of natural
vegetation for animal forage, the animals being under
direct or indirect human supervision. In some places,
the natural vegetation used as forage may be reseeded
by man, but such reseeding is not done regularly.

Forest-products industries are here considered to
involve the gathering by man of every *natural* forest
product useful to him. Timber, naval stores, latex,
maple syrup, cinchona bark, carnauba wax, palm leaves,
quebracho extract, and numerous other commodities
are so gathered. As is true in the case of grazing, the
plant life in question is predominantly natural and not
planted regularly by man. The maintaining of a farm
woodlot, for example, is here considered agriculture
rather than a forest-products industry.

Fishing is here considered to consist of the taking
of marine life from water bodies and waterways. The
activity includes exploitation of water fauna which
have been raised artificially in fish hatcheries to replen-
ish dwindling natural supplies, but excludes the taking
of fish from regularly stocked farm ponds. Hunting is
the killing or capturing of undomesticated game.

Mining and quarrying involve the taking of mineral
and rock resources from nature, usually from the land.
However, some minerals are obtained from the earth's
water and air.

Secondary. Secondary production is manufacturing, including creation of energy and also including
construction of buildings. This activity involves the
changing of individual materials, or the combining of
different materials, into more useful or desirable products. The form of the original materials is therefore
changed in the manufacturing process, and their value
usually is increased. We consider here that manufacturing involves handicraft activities as well as factory
production.

Tertiary. Tertiary production is commercial output of services rather than goods. Some tertiary activities, such as transportation or retail and wholesale
trade, exist for the purpose of transferring or selling the
goods produced by primary and secondary production.
Other tertiary activities, such as the professions, government activities, and personal services, exist because of
a high degree of efficiency in primary and secondary
production: In economies where, because of efficient
technology and high capital investment, a large volume
of production of goods is possible with a comparatively
small number of primary and secondary employees, it
is also possible for a very large number of workers to
be engaged in tertiary activities. In other economies
where primary and secondary production are not so
active, there are fewer opportunities in the tertiary
activities.

One geographer has suggested that a new term,
quaternary activities, be used to designate those tertiary activities for which much education or training
is required and which therefore contribute much to an
economy, in terms of both critical decisions and value
of services.[2] However, this term has not yet been fully
accepted.

Exchange. Most goods and services must be
moved from places of production to those of consumption. Such movement usually involves a change in ownership or control (trade) and a physical transfer (transportation) of those goods. In this movement, there is
no further production of the goods; only further
services are needed. Both transportation and trade increase the value of goods and services, and this is reflected in higher costs to the ultimate consumer, unless
government subsidies or other artificial forces are introduced.

[2] See Jean Gottman, *Megalopolis,* The Twentieth Century
Fund, New York, 1961, pp. 576–577.

These economic activities of consumption, production, and exchange do not exist in abstract space, but are located somewhere on the earth's surface. Once located, they have an impact upon both the physical setting and the human environment of their respective vicinities, and many also have an impact upon one another—regardless of whether they are located close together or a substantial distance apart. The field of economic geography is especially concerned with (1) why such economic activity is located where it is; (2) the nature of the impact of such activity upon its vicinity, including the natural environment, and the impact of the vicinity and the natural environment upon the activity; and (3) the relationships between that particular activity and other activities located elsewhere in the vicinity, the region, the country, or the world. Inasmuch as the location, the vicinity impact, and the interactivity relationships involve human decision, economic geography can also be considered an inquiry into spatial aspects of human perception and behavior as these relate to the aforementioned economic activities, impacts, and relationships.

Interactions of Man, Culture, and Nature

Although the entire surface of the earth is potentially useful, economic activity is found only in certain places. Why? One set of reasons must involve the various conditions, both positive and negative, afforded by the cultural and natural environments. At present, for example, man cannot grow corn commercially in the open oceans. Although technology is enabling man to reduce and even nullify many obstacles once thought unconquerable, he has *not* conquered nature. (After all, nature is the *universe,* not this tiny earth!) Because of his technological and other cultural advances, man *can* carry on a variety of economic activities in places currently unused for such activities. He could, for example, encourage certain types of agriculture into higher latitudes and altitudes than those currently under heaviest production. However, if he did so, these newly cultivated areas would be in competition with areas more favorably endowed by nature (unless demand for the products of the newly cultivated areas rose or was protected by tariffs, quotas, or other artificial means), and very possibly they would not survive such competition. *Economic feasibility* thus reduces further the number and extent of places where, in terms of *natural and cultural possibility,* a given type of economic activity may be carried on. Within the more restricted realm of economic feasibility, human beings select the actual sites—*of economic reality*—for the economic activity they maintain at any given time (p. 15). Logically, these actual sites should be located within the general realm of economic feasibility.

Thus, in economic geography, we always have three general realms to consider in assessing the location, impacts, and functional relationships of economic activity: (1) the realm of natural and cultural possibility, (2) the realm of economic feasibility, and (3) the realm of economic reality. None of these realms is static; changes in the size of each depend mainly upon advances in human technology and capital—and specific decisions—and can result in an expansion (or contraction) of any or all of the three realms. Theoretically, the only ultimate barrier to the expansion of each realm is the actual size of the earth's surface. With increases in technological and economic efficiency, man could expand each realm until it filled the entire world. Initially, the realm of natural and cultural possibility would be expanded to the worldly limits, then the realm of economic feasibility, and finally the realm of economic reality.

Whether this action would be wise is another important question associated with economic geography—a question which will reappear later in this chapter when we consider regional planning and the conservation of both the cultural and the natural environments.

Approaches

Many different attempts and general approaches have been made toward gaining a better insight into understanding the location, impact, and relationships of economic activity, but two have emerged as especially

On the following pages are illustrations of the primary, secondary, and tertiary activities. One picture (usually at the top of the page) shows each activity in a technically advanced economy that has benefited from the Industrial Revolution, and another shows the same activity in a developing economy that has not benefited very much to date from that revolution. Note the large number of people usually shown at work in the developing economies (revealing labor-intensive conditions), and the large amount of machinery in the technically advanced economies (revealing capital-intensive conditions).

Top left: Harvesting tomatoes in California. (Council of California Growers)

Below: Plowing an experimental farm near Saha in Egypt. (International Cooperation Administration)

Right: Mechanized harvesting of timber in Ontario, Canada. (Government of Ontario)

Below: Cutting timber in Sierra Leone. (British Information Services)

Above: Range cattle around a pond in Nebraska. (U.S. Forest Service)

Below: Bedouins and livestock at a water hole near Turaif, Saudi Arabia. (Exxon)

Top right: Fishing near the coast of British Columbia. (National Film Board of Canada)

Below: Natives fishing in northern Nigeria. (British Information Services)

Above: Stripping iron ore with power equipment in the Hull-Rust-Mahoning Mine near North Hibbing, Minnesota. (Exxon)

Left: Hand stripping of tin ore at the Pengal Mine in northern Nigeria. (British Information Services)

Fitting the engines and rear axles to automobile bodies in the United States. (General Motors Corporation)

Below: Making a harp in Rangoon, Burma. (Miller Services Ltd)

Left: Retail trade in a U.S. department store. Note the charge account invitation. (Miller Services Ltd.)

Below: The Sunday market in Cuzco, Peru. (Exxon)

relevant to the present day. We should say at the outset that the two are not mutually exclusive, but contain a significant degree of overlap, as we shall explain in detail in the second part of this book.

The institutional approach. One of these approaches, which in this book we shall call the *institutional approach,* emphasizes the importance of a historical record and of such institutions as business organizations, government, legal regulations, and a very wide range of still other institutions which condition human thought and behavior pertinent to our subject matter in economic geography. Scholars using this approach almost invariably also make use of *inductive reasoning*—the observation of details and the classification of such details into categories or groups—in order to discover what such details have in common and thus to arrive at universal principles or truths.

The theoretical approach. A second way of understanding the subject matter of economic geography, which its adherents usually call the *theoretical* or *deductive* approach, resembles rather closely the methods of the pure scientist. In brief, this approach begins, like its institutional counterpart, with observation of a set of details and proceeds through simple measurement and classification of these details into groups or categories for a specific purpose. At this point, however, the theoretical approach follows the methodology of the pure sciences: It postulates possible theoretical explanation of the details and categories, carefully noting the assumptions by which postulation is removed from the reality that is the actual world. This approach relies rather heavily upon the assumption that human behavior, whether or not man is aware of it, is sufficiently logical as to form an integral part of a spatial order. Like the institutional geographer, the theoretical geographer recognizes the importance of culture and of nature in understanding the location, impacts, and relationships of economic activity, but he tends to view these as features that modify an otherwise logical theoretical model. Perhaps more than the institutional approach, the theoretical approach views the world as a huge man-land *system* which functions in a sufficiently logical way as to produce a *spatial structure* on the earth's surface.[3] This system, like the human body, is considered to be made up of a series of subsystems and to be the result of interaction of a series of natural and cultural processes. Geography's overriding problem, according to this school of thought, is to understand the complex man-land system, and the resulting spatial structure, through analysis of the subsystems and their interrelationships. Economic geography's role in the overall discipline is to understand those systems related to the location, impacts, and relationships of economic activity—again as a spatial structure, or orderly and predictable arrangement.

Overlap and Distinctions

It is important to note here that the institutional and theoretical approaches seek essentially the same objectives: the understanding of (1) the current location of economic activity, (2) the impacts of that activity upon the natural and human environments and the impacts of the natural and human environments upon the activity, and (3) the relationships among economic activities. *However, a major difference between the two approaches is the degree of confidence placed in the logic of human behavior.* Adherents of the institutional approach believe that because location is but one result of many human decisions which are made by individuals or by representatives of governments, corporations, unions, churches, universities, or other organizations, and because those decisions are not always similar, a thorough understanding of the resulting spatial pattern is not obtainable without careful study of separate institutional and historical backgrounds. Adherents of the theoretical approach, while aware of the importance of historical background and of institutions in decision making, tend to place a greater degree of emphasis upon the present geometric configuration and relationships, upon spatial structure as this can be evaluated through statistical analysis, and such adherents believe that this spatial structure can be explained by specific theories and models.

[3] See especially *The Science of Geography,* Report of the Ad Hoc Committee on Geography, Earth Sciences Division, National Academy of Sciences–National Research Council Publication 1277, Washington, 1965.

While stressing once again that the two approaches overlap, and sometimes merge, and that they are not the only approaches in geography today, the authors of this book not only will present, but also will represent, the two viewpoints—the senior author the institutional, and the junior author the theoretical. Throughout the book, we shall carry on a friendly discussion as we examine the definition, the theory, and the practice of economic geography—and, especially in the section on regional planning, we shall emphasize the importance of both approaches to the discipline.

Levels of Observation (Scale)

The subject matter and accompanying problems in economic geography can be observed at different *levels* or *scales* that range from local to global. A *local* level of observation or scale may involve a city block, the immediate neighborhood, the community, or even a metropolitan area. At some point not specifically defined, the local level or scale gives way to a *regional* perspective, which may include one extremely large metropolitan place and its tributary urban region, a number of smaller urban places and their tributary regions, or both. It may include a sizable amount of purely rural territory, with no urban places. Frequently, regions intersect state or provincial boundaries, including portions but not all of several states or provinces.

At still higher levels of observation or scale, the perspective may include an entire nation, or even several nations at *national* or *international* levels of observation. Finally, it may include the entire earth, in what usually is called the *worldwide* or *global* level of observation or scale.

Problems or questions in economic geography usually can be examined profitably at the different levels of observation or scale. The reader will note that, in this book, the level of observation will range significantly with different types of questions and problems. The beginning student, as well as the experienced specialist, may well ask repeatedly, as each new question is encountered:

1 What is the level of observation or scale at which the question or problem is viewed?

2 If more than one level of observation or scale is involved, what are the relationships, if any, between the levels and between the answers that are found for each level?

Economic Geography and Planning

Through economic geography we seek to *understand* the present location of economic activity and its impacts and relationships. However, in these days of rapidly advancing technology, accompanied by increasing populations and varying degrees of intelligence in using our human resources and our natural environment, it no longer is adequate for us merely to understand. We must now *plan* the location of such activity in an intelligent and rational manner. If our past has been one of coincidence and accident mixed with rational thought, our future must be one of rational thought prevailing over coincidence and accident. We are at a critical point in the history of mankind, and the next half century may well be the period in which human beings decide whether they will live intelligently on the earth, in harmony with the natural environment and in pursuit of a higher quality of life, or surrender to internal forces of greed and mismanagement that can cause erosion and decay.

Although economic activity is certainly not the whole of human activity, we must not underestimate its importance. Without a well-located, smoothly functioning economy, we will not have sufficient capital to finance the finer works in the arts, far-reaching measures to conserve our natural environment, or other aspects of a quality of life that is now recognized as an important objective of mankind. Nor is economic geography concerned with location alone: As we have already mentioned, each unit of such activity has an impact upon the natural and cultural environments of its immediate vicinity, and those natural and cultural environments also have an impact upon that activity.

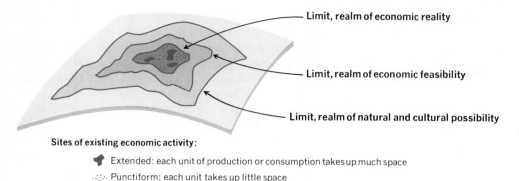

Sites of existing economic activity:

Extended: each unit of production or consumption takes up much space

Punctiform: each unit takes up little space

Realms of locational and functional relationships in economic activity.

Finally, economic activity may have an impact upon other economic activity, whether located close at hand or some distance away.

In planning, we move from understanding these aspects of economic geography to planning them in an intelligent way. Understanding is a necessary prerequisite to planning, but our efforts should not end with understanding alone. Nearly a half century ago, after the Great Depression of 1933, our economist colleagues intensified their efforts in economic policy. A major problem then was that of "boom-and-bust" periods of monetary inflation and depression. Several years of prosperity would be followed by several years of sudden economic catastrophe.

The stock market crash of 1929, followed by the Great Depression of the 1930s in the United States, was a climax period in this series of boom-and-bust cycles. Since that time, through regulation of economic levers, governments have avoided the excesses of boom-and-bust, so that we have enjoyed relative economic stability for a period of forty years.

However, in our use of space on this earth, we have allowed the boom-and-bust, freewheeling forces to continue. True, we have had some metropolitan planning and other urban planning—and, in some areas, even rural planning—but all these efforts have not been very effective, especially in the United States. We have now reached a point in time when we must view space on this earth, and the physical and cultural environments, in much the same manner as the economists regarded the fluctuating economy prior to the 1930s. We must think in terms of removing the excesses of extreme misuse of space and of the natural and cultural environments and use space and the natural and human environments much more intelligently.

For this reason, the last part of this book involves regional planning. *Both authors have been very active in a regional planning program for the province of Ontario in Canada,* where substantial progress is being made in reaching certain planning objectives. Although these efforts will be described at some length in Part 4, we wish to emphasize at this point that such objectives, like those in economic geography, recognize (1) the importance of location of economic activity, (2) the impacts of such activity on the natural and cultural environments and the impacts of those environments upon such activity, and (3) the relationships between and among various units of economic activity. In short, the main transition from economic geography to planning, especially regional planning, is from the idea of *understanding* to the idea of *planning*.

Book Format

The format of this book is designed to furnish the reader with, on the one hand, an insight into the breadth and complexity of the field of economic geography and, on the other, a grasp of some of the methods and approaches used in solving specific problems. Accordingly, Part 1 is a generalized review of key aspects of the field presented at the global level of observation or scale. The rapid or uneven growth of population; the changing conditions from rural to urban, and at the same time the persistence of rural agrarianism in many areas; the meaning of the term *development* and its measures; the importance of the natural environment; and the kinds and locations of consumption, production, trade, and transportation—all these are presented briefly in Part 1.

In Part 2, we examine approaches to economic geography, emphasizing the institutional-inductive approach and the theoretical-deductive approach and indicating the complementarity of the two approaches.

In Part 3, we select commodities, most of which originate in primary activity, and carry these through stages of processing and exchange to their ultimate destinations. For each stage, we offer both institutional-inductive and theoretical-deductive explanations. This is done in detail for the United States and by suggestion for certain other areas.

Finally, in Part 4, we reach the all-important question of planning, especially regional planning. Here we seek to make a transition, on the basis of our knowledge and experience in both economic geography and the planning process, from understanding to planning. We examine the nature of the planning process and consider its application in three different parts of the world—the province of Ontario in Canada, the Tennessee Valley Authority of the United States, and the Greater London area of the United Kingdom.

PART 1
The Existing Environments
The Real World

This part is an appraisal of selected features from the cultural and natural environments that are important in economic geography, presented at the global level of observation, or scale. The methods used are description, simple measurement, classification, and qualitative or subjective analysis. The purpose of this part is to provide a general background for more specific information given in Parts 2, 3, and 4.

Chapter 1

The Demographic, Political, and Cultural Environments

In an assessment of the location and functional relationships of economic activity, sheer numbers, growth rates, and distribution of people are very important considerations, as are the political units governing those people and other aspects of the cultures through which their thoughts and actions are filtered.

Population

The number, rate of increase or decrease, and distribution of people are important within economic geography in some ways which can be understood and rationalized. People plus purchasing power account for consumption of goods and services. People must produce to live, and hence there exist production, trade, and transportation. More and more people live in urban places and create *urban patterns of occupance*. Those who remain away from such places create *rural patterns of occupance*. All these concepts, which are treated in this chapter and later ones, have been studied, and some answers are known.

However, the wholes of the populations may be greater than the sums of their parts. Human beings are multidimensional—and the complexities of this truth are not fully understood. Is urbanization desirable—and, if so, what are the optimum sizes of urban units created for specific purposes? Is there an optimum population size and density? An optimum growth rate? These and other vexing, sometimes irrational, questions will arise again in this book, especially in Part 4.

There are now some 4 billion people in this world. At current natural increase rates, there will probably be between 6 and 7 billion by the year 2000. The world's billions are only now beginning to reap the harvest of centuries of "fertility investment"; the momentum of demographic change, like other momentums, begins with almost imperceptible sluggishness, intensifies slowly but gradually over long periods of time, and finally bursts into fruition almost all at once. We are now at the bursting point (Fig. 1.1). The recent popular accounts of a looming population explosion are not overly dramatic when trends are viewed in perspective.

To persistently increasing numbers may be added the uneven distribution of mankind over the face of the

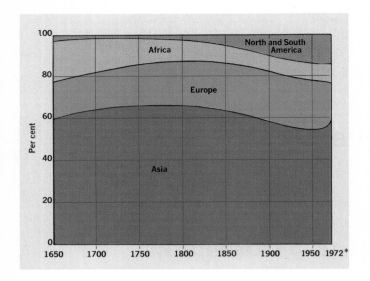

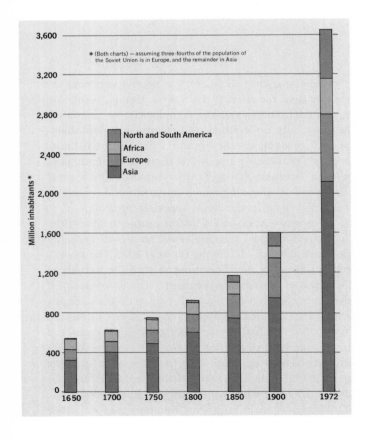

earth. Man has crowded into the choicest locations, preferring these to the tolerable but not so favorable areas and shunning the excessively cold or hot or dry or wet or mountainous lands. Moreover, the locations that have been favored by nature are unevenly populated. Many older civilizations, notably some Asian cultures that have not been so active in colonization, tend to experience increasing population pressures. Even in Europe, where emigration has been heavy, population densities are high. Conversely, most of the territory colonized from Europe has not yet reached the density felt in Asia and Europe. Today, over four-fifths of the world's residents are in the Eastern Hemisphere. More than five-sixths live north of the equator. Nearly three-fifths reside in the six largest nations—China, India, the Soviet Union, the United States, Indonesia, and Japan. Approximately two-fifths are jammed into China and India alone. Over one-seventh are in Europe (excluding the Soviet Union). Obviously, under such circumstances the world's needs and wants, and the means of satisfying them, are numerous and unevenly distributed. However, concern with man-land balance is by no means restricted to our times, but is traceable at least to the late eighteenth century and the writings of Malthus.

The Malthusian Doctrine

The essence of the doctrine. In 1798, when the world's population totaled slightly over 900 million, Thomas Robert Malthus, an English economist and ordained minister, published a book-length treatise entitled *An Essay on the Principle of Population as It Affects the Future Improvement of Society.* From the time of its appearance, the Malthusian doctrine has consistently provoked controversy in both scholarly and popular literature. Basically, Malthus stated in this and revised versions of his work that populations tend to increase at a geometric rate much faster than their means of support, which increase only at an arithmetic rate. If not held in preventive check by war, vice, or,

Figure 1.1 Growth of the world's population, in numbers and per cent. Unless quick action is taken, the population explosion is just beginning—especially in the world's economically deprived areas.

preferably, moral restraint, numbers of people come to exceed the productive capacities of the land. Malnutrition, exposure to the elements, disease, and other agents of decimation then begin to take their respective tolls. Finally outright famine, the most efficient reaper of them all, stalks the countryside until the man-land balance is restored.

Demographic conditions in Malthus's time. Malthus wrote at the early dawn of an industrial and scientific age that was to render some of his major assumptions obsolescent, even obsolete. He could not possibly have foreseen some of the effects of that age, especially those which (1) increasingly enlightened mankind as to nature's potential of endowment for human use and (2) permitted man to gain control over his own potential for human reproduction. To Malthus, "land" was mainly agricultural acres fertilized, under optimum conditions, by natural manures. Advanced agricultural practices were then largely unknown, and the factory had not yet come to dominate the English landscape. Small wonder that he was concerned that the 16 million inhabitants of the United Kingdom of his day might become excessive! (One can only conjecture what his reaction would have been had he been informed prophetically that this population, despite wholesale emigration to other continents, would experience more than a threefold increase in less than a century and a half!) His basic principle, therefore, that populations invariably outgrow their means of subsistence, now is recognized as invalid. Man's increased efficiency in utilizing nature and in controlling his own rate of reproduction as well as other forces has offset Malthus's extreme predictions. And yet the principle still sheds light on man-land ratios in countries that have been affected only slightly, if at all, by the industrial revolution.

Post-Malthusian population trends. The 900 million people inhabiting the earth when Malthus published his treatise were distributed about as unevenly as the population is today. Over 85 per cent were in Asia (including Asian Russia) and Europe, with the former alone accounting for approximately two-thirds of the world's total (Fig. 1.1). In the years that followed, the population of Europe grew rapidly in association with the embryonic industrial revolution. Furthermore, millions of emigrants left Europe in response to new opportunities beckoning from across the oceans. As a result of this population growth and emigration, Europeans living at home and abroad made up a higher percentage of the world's population than previously. By 1900, Asia contained only about 57 per cent of the world's people, and Europe slightly over 25 per cent. The remainder were accounted for chiefly by recent immigrants to the Americas and by a rather rapidly growing native population in Africa.

The twentieth century witnessed a slowing down of population growth in Europe (although the records of individual nations vary sharply) and a speeding up in certain other areas, notably Asia. The major gains have been most dramatic in lands sometimes classified as "developing" or "less developed"[1]—lands along the eastern and southern rim of Asia, in Africa, and in Latin America. The most serious aspects of these increases are their recency and their scope. They are now in process and show no indication of abating. They are so dynamic that even conservative estimates declare that the population of Asia (excluding the Soviet Union) will more than double within the next half century. If these predictions are fulfilled, as they may well be, the proportion of the world's people in Asia will be even higher than the current 57 per cent. The same predictions apply to most other less developed regions in varying degrees.

These trends are illustrated in Figure 1.1, showing current annual rates of population growth. The world average, it will be noted, is about 2 per cent per year. Most countries with highly efficient economies—in Europe and its offshoots—have rates of population increase considerably below the world average. In the United States and Canada, growth rates were at the world average until recently, but are declining. Most countries in which economic output is low have high rates of increase—some of them as high as 3 per cent per year or over.

These increases, although foreboding, are interesting in view of the Malthusian doctrine. It is well known that the hardships of misery, disease, malnutrition, and

[1] We shall have much more to say about less developed and advanced countries in the next two chapters and in others.

periodic famine have long been active in less developed lands, and many scholars have assumed, apparently correctly, that these were preventing overwhelming increases in population there. In recent years, well-known techniques and instruments of combating diseases and other bodily infirmities have been applied to the inhabitants of some less developed lands with almost instantaneous results. These techniques include the use of efficient insecticides, vaccines, drugs, antibiotics, and similar preventives. In a surprisingly large number of less developed lands where these means have been used, death rates have declined, whereas birth rates have not. As a result, natural increases in population have been almost appalling and now constitute problems of major importance for many young and comparatively unstable countries. The problems focus basically upon a simply worded and yet difficult question: How are the new mouths to be fed and the new bodies to be clothed adequately in order to keep the Malthusian famine from coming forth to stalk the countrysides?

The answer to this question of man-land ratio is not easily found in practice, but approaches to it are possible. We should not forget that two variables are involved: (1) the sizes and rates of growth of populations and (2) the amount and rate of growth of production. Most existing plans for improving the lot of the world's poorer, overpopulated areas concentrate upon increasing production. Less than a portion of 1 per cent of most budgets is allocated to slowing the rate of population growth. Birth control is an obvious answer. Birth control is comparatively inexpensive and, for the individual as well as for society as a whole, policies can be flexible. Japan has shown that population increases can be slowed. Faced with the reality of a small national territory following World War II, that nation

Figure 1.2 Population and labor force relationships in selected countries. Data for some nations are official estimates only. Both the estimated and reported figures are complicated because women and children are counted in labor forces of some countries but not in others, unemployed or underemployed persons may or may not be included, and some people work in at least two occupations. The labor forces of many developing countries probably are larger than shown here.

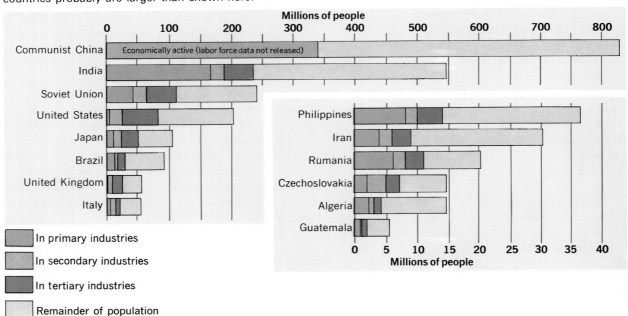

decreased its rate of population growth to slightly less than 1 per cent per year, compared with a world average of slightly over 2 per cent. Yet the growth rate of Japan's population—and that of any other group adopting birth control—can be easily increased once again if a need arises. Recently, the population growth rate of the United States has declined, mainly because of new means of prevention.

Labor force. Primary, secondary, and tertiary production and tertiary exchange are carried on by a *labor force* that normally employs at least 35 per cent of a nation's population. For some countries, it may be 40 per cent or even slightly more. (These figures vary from country to country partly because of differences in employment practices and partly because there does not exist a standardized, internally accepted definition of the term *labor force,* so that some countries include younger ages, more part-time workers, etc., than others. See Figures 1.2 and 1.3.)

Countries differ not only in the relative percentages of their populations actually in their labor forces but also in the structure of their labor forces. Nations emphasizing heavy consumption of inanimate energy, mechanized production, and specialized labor skills tend to produce enough goods so that over one-half of their labor forces need not be engaged in actual production of commodities, but can devote full time to services. Those nations in which animate energy and hand methods still dominate in production tend to have only a few personnel in tertiary occupations, and each productive worker is more or less a jack-of-all-trades, providing his own services as well as his own goods.

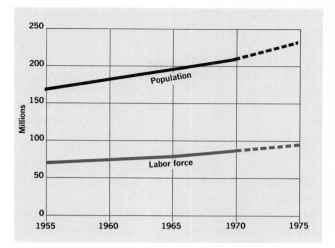

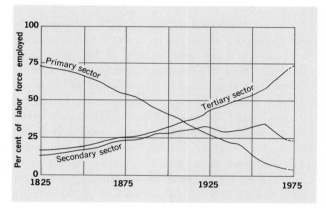

Figure 1.3 Population and labor force projections for the United States, which is fast becoming a country dominated by tertiary employment.

Rural and Urban Occupance

Most human beings reside, worship, work, market their produce, purchase their desired commodities, and play in a manner peculiar to their own culture. They lay out transportation and communications routes within and among the buildings, fields, and other artifacts of life and livelihood. They set down arbitrary property and political boundary lines which serve as a framework for these artifacts. In short, when man lives in an area, he establishes a *pattern of occupance* there.

Although occupance patterns vary throughout the world, all can be classified into *rural* and *urban* types. This is usually done rather arbitrarily, by law, by decision of some executive agency of the government, or by both. Since this action is almost invariably taken at the national level, there is an appreciable difference among nations concerning the definition of rural and urban. In the United States, urban units are incorporated places of 2,500 or more inhabitants (with certain exceptions that do not fit this classification easily and yet are obviously urban). This is a moderate definition as compared with others: Canada regards as urban all places of 1,000 or more population; Egypt, all primary towns of provinces and districts; Italy, all places with less than one-half of their population employed in agriculture; Belgium, communities of 5,000 or more residents; the Netherlands, municipalities of 20,000 or more; and Japan, municipalities of 30,000 or more. Because of such disparities, demographers and other scholars are increasingly using the population size of urban units for both local study and international comparison, regardless of domestic classifications.

Historical urbanization. One of the most interesting aspects of urbanization is its recency. Rather conclusive evidence indicates that very few sizable cities existed before the classical ages and that even the Greek and Roman cities were few in comparison with the number that exist today. Indeed, one authority, Prof. Kingsley Davis, estimates that as late as the beginning of the nineteenth century, less than 2½ per cent of the world's people were living in cities of 20,000 or more, and less than 2 per cent in cities of 100,000 or more (Table 1.1). With the Industrial Age, however, came the urbanization of much of Europe, marked by the mushrooming of cities not only on the Continent itself but also in outlying European offshoots. Urban percentages of total populations approximately doubled each succeeding half century for the world as a whole and multiplied even faster where machines became commonplace. By the mid-twentieth century, over one-fifth of the world's people lived in cities of 20,000 or more, and over one-eighth lived in metropolises of at least 100,000.

Current urbanization. If we consider the year 1950 to mark a separation between historical and current urbanization, we can say that three significant characteristics of present-day urbanization are that (1) it is still increasing at an extremely rapid rate, (2) it is still concentrated in European or Europeanized areas, and (3) it is, however, shifting slightly in relative importance from Europe to Asia and other heretofore predominantly rural areas.

Increasingly rapid pace. The rapid pace of urbanization, especially into larger urban units, is shown in Table 1.1, notably in projections of 1970 to the year 2000. In 1970, nearly one-fourth of the world's people

TABLE 1.1
PER CENT OF THE WORLD'S POPULATION LIVING IN CITIES OF VARYING SIZE, 1800–2000

Year	Cities of 20,000 or more	Cities of 100,000 or more	Cities of 1,000,000 or more
1800	2.4	1.7	
1850	4.3	2.3	
1900	9.2	5.5	
1950	20.9	13.1	
1970		23.8	12.4
1980		28.4	15.8
1990		33.5	19.8
2000		39.0	24.4

Sources: For data up to 1950, Kingsley Davis, ''The Origin and Growth of Urbanization in the World,'' *The American Journal of Sociology,* **60**:433, 1955; for later data, Kingsley Davis, *World Urbanization 1950–1970,* vol. II, *Analysis of Trends, Relationships and Development,* University of California at Berkeley, Population Monograph Series, no. 9, 1972, p. 123. The data for 1970 and projections to 2000 are one of a set of generally similar reported and projected percentages for respective years. For more details, see the latter source.

lived in cities of 100,000 or more, and approximately one-eighth lived in cities of 1 million or more. By the year 2000, as shown in the table, nearly 40 per cent will be in cities of 100,000 or more, and nearly 25 per cent in cities of 1 million or more. The reader will note that recorded and projected population figures for the twentieth century show that cities of 100,000 or more increased, or will increase, their total share of overall population from 5.5 to 39 per cent! When we keep in mind that the population of the world was approximately 1.6 billion in 1900 and is estimated to be between 6 and 7 billion by the year 2000, the enormity of this shift of population into large urban places becomes apparent. Its impact on individual countries is shown in Figure 1.4.

European culture. Table 1.2 indicates that Australia–New Zealand, North America, and Europe—all of them essentially products of European culture—were the leaders in both 1950 and 1970 in degree of urbanization and are still continuing to change to urban conditions. The Soviet Union, Latin America, Asia, Africa, and Oceania other than Australia–New Zealand are less urbanized, but the Soviet Union is in marked change.

Increased urbanization in traditionally agrarian countries.

However, as is shown in Table 1.2, the pace of urbanization is increasing in traditionally agrarian countries and therefore is a worldwide phenomenon. This increase is sobering because a means of support for many of the newly arrived urban immigrants is not always available. In other words, the factories, retail and wholesale trade organizations, etc., which provide the key economic support for most cities

are not always established in sufficient quantity and quality to provide livelihood for the growing urban populations. Professor Davis has estimated that all countries now usually classified as less developed have more people living in cities than all countries usually classified as technically advanced. Furthermore, in many traditionally agrarian countries, the urban immigrants have moved to the cities not so much because cities *attract* as because countrysides *repel*. There is no longer room for them in many rural areas, and since emigration to other countries is almost impossible because of immigration quotas set up by nations to which they might go, their only alternative is the city or town

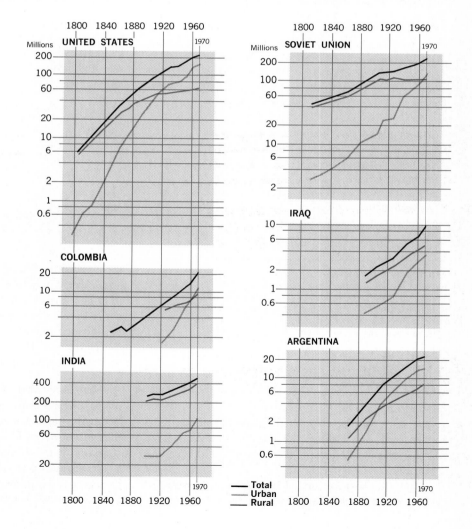

Figure 1.4 Trends in urban, rural, and total population in selected nations. The graph is on a semilogarithmic scale. Note the rise of urban populations of all countries, whether technically advanced or developing. Keep in mind, however, that each country has its own definition of "urban."

TABLE 1.2
WORLD URBANIZATION, 1950–1970:
INDICES OF URBANIZATION IN
CONTINENTAL AREAS, 1950 AND 1970*

| Continental area | | Percentages | | |
| | | | Urban | |
	Rural	Total urban	Town	City
1950				
Australia–New Zealand	30.0	70.0	20.6	49.4
North America	37.2	63.8	20.5	43.3
Europe	46.6	53.4	21.9	31.4
U.S.S.R.	57.5	42.5	21.6	20.8
Latin America	59.7	40.3	20.5	19.9
Asia	84.6	15.4	6.6	8.9
Africa	86.2	13.8	8.9	6.5
Oceania	95.1	4.9	4.9	—
1970*				
Australia–New Zealand	15.7	84.3	23.1	61.1
North America	24.9	75.1	17.7	57.4
Europe	37.0	63.0	24.1	38.9
U.S.S.R.	37.7	62.3	30.9	31.4
Latin America	45.6	54.4	20.9	33.5
Asia	74.6	25.4	9.7	15.7
Africa	78.2	21.8	10.6	11.2
Oceania	92.2	7.8	7.8	—

*Estimate by Kingsley Davis.
Source: Kingsley Davis, *World Urbanization 1950–1970,* vol. II, *Analysis of Trends, Relationships and Development,* University of California at Berkeley, Population Monograph Series, no. 9, 1972, p. 170. The classification "urban" is according to each country's definition and hence varies from country to country.

of their own country. Here too there is no real place for them, and as a group they become a problem of the greatest magnitude. This new "enforced urbanization" is especially characteristic of the rimlands of southern and eastern Asia, where the rural populations have grown beyond the means of support under existing conditions.

Not all urbanization of less developed areas, of course, is enforced. The growth of modern domestic industries in many such areas, notably of food-processing and textile plants, has meant the need for labor. Such factories as these are comparatively new to less developed areas. Doubtless they will receive close attention as a solution to both the problem of jobless city residents and that of general scarcity of commodities with which to supply life's basic economic needs in such areas.

Countries

The Pattern of Political Units

As was suggested in the Introduction, the earth's land surface is organized politically into a hierarchy of political units—both domestic and nondomestic—ranging in size and level of authority from the hamlet and the tribe to the largest nation. The hierarchy is seldom rigidly defined; i.e., seldom does one level of unit have absolute authority over another. (Witness the perennial controversy over federal versus states' rights in the United States and over federal-provincial rights in Canada!) Nor is the hierarchy consistent throughout the world's many areas. One form of this hierarchy might be as shown in the diagram at the top of the opposite page.

Except for nomadic tribes (and not all tribes are nomadic by any means), all these political units are sedentary and occupy specific areas of the earth's surface. Considered as a whole, the units are numerous, and a world map of all would be complex indeed. Each unit has jurisdiction over certain functions of significance in economic geography, but we shall focus mainly on only the highest level of the political units and the most coarse of the political patterns—that of nations and their nondomestic affiliates.

Number and distribution. Over 140 sovereign nations and a host of subordinate states, cities, and territorial dependencies provide political administration for the world's billions. Independent nations range from the tiny Vatican city-state, with slightly more than 1,000 inhabitants, to China, with a reported population of nearly 850 million. Most nations contain more than 1 million and fewer than 60 million inhabitants.

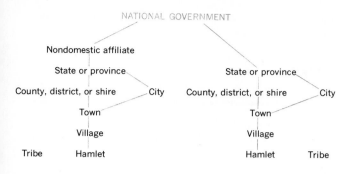

NATIONAL GOVERNMENT

Political units are composed of people—of the same 4 billion people already stated to be very unevenly distributed over the earth's surface. The pattern of political units is also uneven, and its irregularities do not coincide with those of population distribution. When, therefore, the patterns of population distribution and political units are combined, there appears all too often a compartmentalization in which some nations, such as Libya, are essentially devoid of population, while others, such as Belgium and the Netherlands, are almost unidentifiable portions of large population clusters, and still others, such as Canada and Australia, are lopsided imbalances of heavy population on the one side and wide-open spaces on the other. (See map on inside front cover.)

Effect on consumption and production. Government policy is intricately interwoven with economic activity. The kind and degree of government jurisdiction and/or influence varies from almost total control in certain Communist countries to an ambiguous but very important assertion in economies championing private enterprise. It affects consumption as well as production, especially by regulation of taxes and by other monetary means, but also by direct decrees that become most conspicuous in time of war. All levels of government are involved, although in differing ways. We shall elaborate upon the role of government in consumption and production at appropriate places in later chapters, but its importance in an assessment of economic geography should be appreciated.

Effect on exchange. A nation tends to be self-oriented. Except when there is aggression from the

outside, a nation's existence depends upon the wishes of its citizens and/or its administrators, all of whom tend to place their own country's welfare above that of other countries. Hence a national boundary line, which appears unimpressive on a map and which is often unfenced on the earth's surface, can be a serious barrier to otherwise unhindered movement of *commodities, currency,* and *people* and, under extreme conditions, to *communication.* The major obstacles encountered at a political border include import, transit, and export tariffs; quotas; disease inspection (of both commodities and people); currency control; and immigration laws. These usually, but not always, restrict or limit *incoming* commodities and people and *outgoing* currency. Whatever the restriction, it is usually intended to benefit the nation that has brought it into being.

However, the division of the world's people into political units may or may not hinder their efforts toward economic cooperation, since a political boundary line is no stronger an obstacle than may be decreed by participating governments. If, therefore, a nation follows a policy of complete cooperation with all other political units, the "barrier effect" of its boundary lines is minimized. If, on the other hand, the policy is of selective cooperation or of some form of isolation, the boundary obstacles may become almost insurmountable. In practice, the economic policies of political units range from almost complete isolationism to almost unrestricted cooperation, and the complexity of the world's economic geography is thereby increased.

Still more intricacy is added by the existence of nonindependent political units with subordinate political and economic status. In international affairs, colonies and other absolute dependencies obey the decrees of their respective mother countries, and quasi-independent political units follow their mother countries' guidance.

Effective and Outlying Areas

Populations are unevenly distributed, not only for the world as a whole, but also for individual countries. Most political units are composed of one or more *effective areas* and one or more *outlying areas.* The former are invariably highly populated and are usually highly urbanized.[2] Together with their immediate fringe territories, they enclose the portion of a political unit where things are happening—where the basic decisions are being made for the entire unit. The outlying areas, outnumbered in population and usually outdistanced in technical, social, and artistic development, are weaker in voice, regardless of the type of government in power. Their chief contribution to decision making tends to be that of a brake; they are usually opposed to change, notably drastic change.

It is generally erroneous, therefore, to think of the pattern of political units in the traditional sense, as shown on the back-end of this book. Instead, if one wishes to be realistic, he should visualize the pattern of effective areas of the world on the front-end map. This pattern, interestingly, is even less uniform in distribution than that of the political units themselves.[3]

A very few nations, very small, very intensively populated, like Belgium and the Netherlands, do not exhibit effective-area–outlying-area relationships when viewed on a global scale, but even these break down into such components when the scale is enlarged.

The significance of effective areas to economic geography is enormous. Regardless of the scale of political units—whether nations and overseas dependencies, component states, provinces, districts, counties, townships, cities, villages, or hamlets—an effective area is usually discernible. Effective areas, therefore, are the mainsprings of consumption, production, and exchange for each political unit in question.

Cultures

We mentioned in the Introduction that economic activity is one aspect of culture, and we have defined culture as a recognizable way of life among a group of people—as a summary of what that group believes to be of positive and negative importance, including its objectives, problems, and achievements.

This concept, and the distinction between "culture" and "cultures," can best be made by specialists in cultural geography. Professors J. E. Spencer and William L. Thomas have set down a definition and a distinction as follows:

> The word *culture* has long enjoyed wide currency. There is culture in the sense of tillage or cultivation; there is culture meaning the possession of standards of value, discrimination, and good taste, and implying good breeding, refinement, and learning. There is culture in the simple ethnographic sense, referring to any particular body of beliefs, habits, practices, and technologies possessed by a discrete human population. However, culture has a broader, all-inclusive connotation. Culture is the distillate of total human experience; its possession not only distinguishes man from other living forms but, indeed, sets him apart as a unique evolutionary product. As a "culture bearer," able to communicate his cumulative experience, man is the first species capable of consciously and deliberately altering the course of his own evolution.
>
> Through this shareable, transmissible, progressively transformable tradition, human organization achieved a new means of evolution. Man's intelligence has enabled him to penetrate and occupy all parts of the earth's surface, even though as an animal he is not physiologically equipped to do so. By qualitative increases in social organization and in adapting invented techniques to productive ends, man has made pieces of organized living matter and varieties of inanimate matter serve his own ends and has enabled a quantitative increase in his numbers. His own creation, culture, has done for him what genetic mechanisms have afforded other animals. His registration and transmittal of human

---

[2] The reader can easily see that functional regions (p. 131) would be vital portions of most effective areas as defined above, especially for highly urbanized nations. However, there are rural nations that contain clustered populations but lack such a focal point. An oasis in the desert may attract many rural dwellers, organized only loosely, if at all, but clustered because land in the oasis is productive, whereas the land beyond is sterile for lack of water. Focality—certainly urban focality—may be lacking in such an oasis, and yet it may contain the majority of a nation's population; it may be, in other words, the population's effective area in terms of actual political, economic, social, and religious functions. For this reason, the term *effective area* is preferable to *functional* or *nodal region* for global concentrations of people and human activity.

[3] In reality, of course, there is a transition from heavy population density at the cores of the effective areas to almost a vacuum in the most distant outlying reaches. We have classified this transition rather crudely into effective areas and outlying areas, largely for emphasis. Had we desired, we could easily have provided several classifications, graduating them by level of intensity—by, for example, specific population per square mile.

experience has continuously accumulated an un-limited number of complex ideas and techniques and organized them permanently in collective human memory.

A clear distinction must be made between culture as a collective body and cultures, the parts of the totality. The splitting and branching of man over the earth gave rise to individual cultures. These "cultures"—the technico-mental systems developed as ways of life by the many partially isolated fragments of mankind—gradually came into existence through the unique experiences in space and time of various population groups. But cultures never became completely isolated; they have remained parts of the whole. Through human activity, they have penetrated, metamorphosed, borrowed from, and absorbed one another. Although there is an evolutionary aspect to the growth of individual cultures, like evolution in general, certain traits or trait complexes may fall into disuse, be forgotten, and require relearning. An industrial society obviously knows more than a gathering and collecting society about the physical laws of matter, and certainly uses more complicated techniques of processing materials. Yet the former has forgotten much about the resources, relationships, and processing techniques that the latter knew, and sometimes claims initial discovery for some of the things it has actually relearned or borrowed.[4]

Two points concerning the above discussion are especially relevant to economic geography. One, which we discussed briefly in the Introduction, is that economic geography is a key topic in both culture and cultures. Inasmuch as consumption, production, and exchange are activities which all men everywhere engage in daily, nuances of these activities are very much a part of the overall intelligence, or culture, which Professors Spencer and Thomas state have enabled man to penetrate and occupy all parts of the earth. On the other hand, different groups, both large and small, in various parts of the world each have their own set of mores, folkways, and other distinct qualities—in short, their own culture—which affects consumption, production, and exchange.

The subject matter of economic geography is also a means by which cultures change. An excellent illustration is the factory, which, originating in Western Europe, has been transferred by diffusion to many other parts of the world. The Communist countries adopted the factory as a mainstay of their economic planning and utilized it intensively. Most of the less developed areas regard the factory as a means of increasing their output and hastening their transition toward development. More recently, in the tertiary activities, the supermarket also has been adopted increasingly for retailing merchandise in cultures which once resisted it because it was considered too mechanical and too deficient in the personal qualities thought necessary for over-the-counter exchange.

People, Countries, and Cultures in Economic Geography

It is impossible, of course, to do justice in a brief space to any topic with which this chapter is concerned. However, it would be highly inappropriate to omit any of these from a treatment of economic geography—particularly in a section on the real world. In Part 2, where we shall explain theory, the student should keep in mind that every theory is valid only within its own set of assumptions. Sooner or later, it must be reapplied to the real world, and in that real world each of us plays different roles—whether as consumer, producer, doer, thinker, decision maker, or many others. What counts in the final analysis is our individual and group *values,* what we believe to be important. Our economic decisions, our social decisions, our political decisions, and still other decisions emanate from these values. And these values are all a part of the real world.

The noted economist Gunnar Myrdal has put it well in his book entitled *The Challenge of World Poverty.*[5] He states that economic and social theory, while useful, can lead to "blind alleys" in which professors spend much time attempting to seek answers to their

---

[4]J. E. Spencer and William L. Thomas, *Introducing Cultural Geography,* John Wiley & Sons, Inc., New York, 1973, p. 19.

[5]Gunnar Myrdal, *The Challenge of World Poverty,* Pantheon Books, a division of Random House, Inc., New York, 1970.

own predetermined hypotheses. He states further that in this real world, political and social conditions do exist and need to be recognized, certainly in any meaningful efforts at improvement. Corruption, for example, is one of several considerations which is not usually accounted for in political or economic theory. Mr. Myrdal states that differences in climate and other aspects of the natural environment are very real and may result in differences in both physical and mental activity which are not as yet fully understood. In the final analysis, the objectives of the social sciences should be—those of us who are idealists believe they are—to improve the real world. This being so, we should not lose sight of that world.

Chapter 2

The Natural
(Physical and Biological)
Environment

Human thinking follows cycles. At one time, geography was considered to be mainly earth science. Then our methods changed to focus on man-land relationships, sometimes using regions as a way of classifying such relationships. Some current geographers believe that geography, notably economic geography, is concerned prevailingly with the location and linkages of economic activity, and not particularly with the natural environment.

Both authors of this book believe that the natural environment deserves critical attention by geographers, including economic geographers. Understanding the location and linkage relationships of economic activity includes the critical idea that such activity is part of the physical as well as the human setting—the natural as well as the demographic environment. When we shift the emphasis from understanding to planning, as we do in Part 4 of this book, we find that the physical environment retains its importance—indeed, may become more important in this age of attention to appropriate measures of conservation and ecological balance.

We have indicated that the natural environment

may receive an impact from the location of economic activity in a given area and also may exert either positive or negative influence upon the location of such activity. The natural environment is especially important to economic geography in two respects: (1) *It is a storehouse of certain source materials that will be consumed ultimately by man, and* (2) *it provides certain physical and biological conditions within and on which man's consumption, production, and exchange occur.* A consideration of the location of an economic activity, and its functional relationships with other economic activities, would be incomplete if it did not take these important environmental aspects into account.

In recognition of the importance of ecology in economic geography, here defined as impacts of economic activity on the natural environment and reciprocal impacts of the natural environment upon economic activity, this chapter treats selected physical features so that they will appear to the reader as something more than mere amorphous, fuzzy thoughts. They are shown as classifications, many of which have stood the test of time and have not yet been superseded. They are world patterns of exploitable minerals, climate, and biotic and soil resources. Although landforms are also important features of the natural environment with respect to the location of economic activity, their impact is not so apparent at the global level of observation as at national, regional, and local levels.

Minerals

Formation

Of the 106 elements now known, 92 are natural and are found in the earth's crust, water, or air.[1] Table 2.1 contains an estimate of the elements dominating the earth's crust and their approximate percentages. Eight, it will be noted, are outstanding.

Of the more than 1,600 minerals now recognized, only about 50 are classified as rock-making. Most of the remainder, while occurring in rocks, are injected into crevasses, fissures, etc. Rock structure is so complex that it would be difficult to relate specific minerals to specific rock types. Most of the metallic minerals, however, appear to be related directly or indirectly to igneous rocks.

Table 2.1 emphasizes the very small percentage of the earth's crust that most single elements constitute. Elements, it will be remembered, make up minerals. Most minerals, too, are poorly represented in that crust—so poorly, in fact, that the exploitation of certain desired minerals may be commercially unfeasible at a given time. The actual degree of concentration necessary depends upon the substance being sought; for example, shallow ores containing less than 1 per cent of metallic copper now are mined profitably, whereas materials containing 20 per cent or less of iron now are generally considered too lean for exploitation. Until quite recently, iron compounds of less than 50 per cent metal were not considered commercially exploitable, but technological advance has made possible the use of poorer ores.

Although the total geologic history of natural ele-

[1] The remainder are man-made.

TABLE 2.1

COMPOSITION OF THE EARTH'S CRUST BY DOMINANT ELEMENTS*

Element	Percentage
Oxygen (O)	46.710
Silicon (Si)	27.690
Aluminum (Al)	8.070
Iron (Fe)	5.050
Calcium (Ca)	3.650
Sodium (Na)	2.750
Potassium (K)	2.580
Magnesium (Mg)	2.080
Percentage of eight dominant elements	98.580
Titanium (Ti)	0.589
Hydrogen (H)	0.140
Phosphorus (P)	0.130
Carbon (C)	0.094
Manganese (Mn)	0.090
Sulfur (S)	0.082
Barium (Ba)	0.050
Chlorine (Cl)	0.045
Chromium (Cr)	0.035
Fluorine (F)	0.029
Zirconium (Zr)	0.025
Nickel (Ni)	0.019
Strontium (Sr)	0.018
Vanadium (V)	0.016
Cerium (Ce), Yttrium (Y)	0.014
Copper (Cu)	0.010
Uranium (U)	0.008
Tungsten (W)	0.005
Lithium (Li)	0.004
Zinc (Zn)	0.004
Columbium (Cb), Tantalum (Ta)	0.003
Hafnium (Hf)	0.003
Thorium (Th)	0.002
Lead (Pb)	0.002
Cobalt (Co)	0.001
Boron (B)	0.001
Glucinum (Gl) [Beryllium (Be)]	0.001
Total	100.000

*The table shows only the thirty-five leading elements in the earth's crust, including sea and air. The percentage of all other elements would be very low—for each, less than that of glucinum.
Source: Amended from E. B. Branson and W. A. Tarr (rev. by C. C. Branson and W. D. Keller), *Introduction to Geology,* 3d ed., McGraw-Hill Book Company, New York, 1952, p. 8.

ments can never be known, certain processes of concentration now are understood. Some of these processes occur in the absence of water, and others result from water action. Those involving water appear to be responsible for a majority of minerals now being exploited. Both surface and subsurface water must be considered, and the latter may have been either rising or sinking at the time it acted upon the mineral in question. Coal was deposited by surface water as a sediment and was subsequently covered. It thus occurs today as a layer, or stratum, however altered by rock deformation. In contrast, most of the metallic minerals have been removed from their original igneous rocks by either surface or subsurface waters and now occur as deposits in small and large fissures and holes or even in tiny interstices between the grains of some porous rocks.

The few and simplified illustrations of the preceding paragraph are intended to emphasize a highly important aspect of the natural occurrence of minerals—namely, that they do not exist as a uniform blanket throughout the earth's crust, but are very unevenly distributed, both horizontally and vertically. The reader should never lose sight of this point. Some social scientists "take the natural environment as given"— assume, for purposes of theoretical calculation, that nature's bounty is uniformly distributed. This is simply not true, whether we are concerned with soils, vegetation, animal life, minerals, or other natural features. As suggested in Figures 2.1 and 2.2, minerals are particu-

Figure 2.1 A hypothetical view of the three basic rock types and some overlying landforms. The rock structure may or may not affect the orientation of the landforms. The volcanic cone, already above the heights of the other mountains, may rise even higher if the volcano remains active. Metamorphic rock, shown here in an irregular stratum, might well be less concentrated, and it might also occur around the magma because of heat and pressure there. Some of the relatively unaltered igneous rock has been uncovered by erosion and, at the right of the drawing, now lies at the land surface. Note variations in form and structure of rock strata. Before removal by water (Fig. 2.2), many types of minerals originally occurred in igneous rocks.

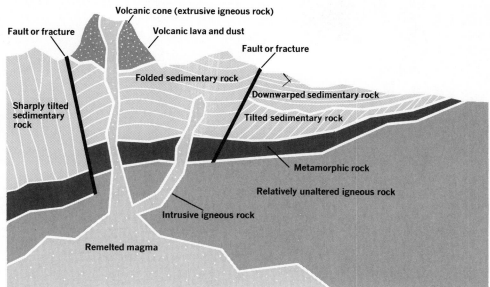

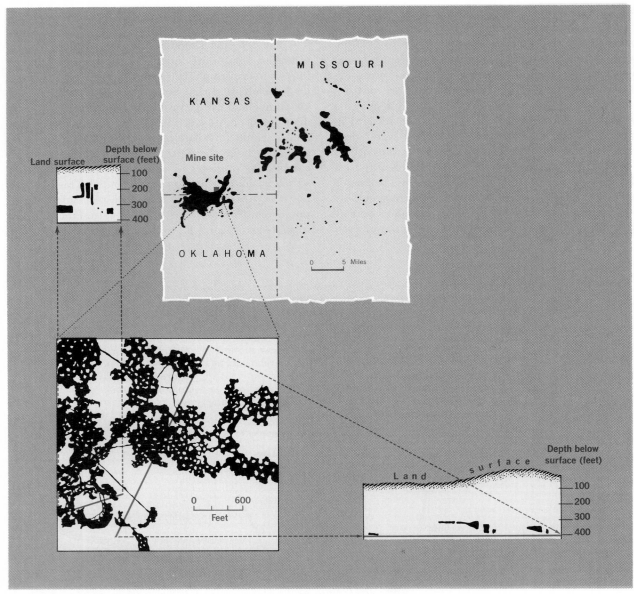

Figure 2.2 Water-deposited zinc and lead ore in the tri-state district of Missouri, Kansas, and Oklahoma. The upper map shows where most mining has taken place. The lower map shows the extent of underground mining in one of the most actively exploited mines. The cross sections, in which the vertical scale is exaggerated, show different levels of tunneling. The ore has been deposited by underground water into a porous limestone that dips gently downward toward the northwest. Local geologists disagree as to whether the water was rising or sinking when the ore was deposited. The water tended to carve horizontal circles or arcs, leaving the ore in these.

larly erratic in their distribution—in localities, in states, in nations, in continents, and in the world.

Patterns of Exploitation

Areas of unusually heavy mineral exploitation are shown in Figure 5.3, page 75. Nations in North America and Europe, including the Soviet Union and a few other countries, have actively exploited local reserves, whether on the coasts or inland. In other continents, however, the areas of exploitation tend to fringe sea-coasts—to be oriented, in other words, to ocean shipping lanes which connect them with technically advanced societies.

Climate

Climate is unique among the natural environmental features emphasized in this book in that it is an intangible. The term *climate* refers to a series of changes within the atmosphere and involves also, although mainly in gaseous form, moisture contributions to and from the hydrosphere. In other words, climate is a summary (usually taken over a minimum period of one year) of day-to-day weather conditions, the basic elements being (1) *temperature,* (2) *humidity* (including precipitation), (3) *pressure* (weight), and (4) *winds.* These four basic ingredients are constantly changing, both absolutely and relatively, and their changes result in changes of weather and climate—the former on a short-term basis and the latter on a very long-term basis.

Classification and Distribution

The relationships among the four basic elements of a climate, although constantly changing, are well enough systematized to permit general classification. Most of the accepted classifications are based on averages, means, ranges, and seasonal rhythms of temperature and humidity, the two elements of weather and climate that appear to be most directly critical for man and his activities.

Before attempting a study of a specific climate classification, the reader should be aware of the existence of an orderly pattern of global distribution—of an arrangement which tends to repeat itself from continent to continent. Regardless of hemispheres, a climate which occupies a certain position in one continent will tend to be found in an analogous position in all other continents. This is due chiefly to the fact that the climatic elements are affected, directly or indirectly, by a number of climatic *controls* (incoming solar radiation, wind currents, ocean currents, etc.) which, for the most part, are themselves in orderly arrangement and which have global influence.

Exceptions to the orderly pattern of climates do exist, and these are likewise traceable to climatic controls—but usually to controls that are not in repetitious arrangement. Outstanding among such controls are landform features, which often interrupt the functioning of controls responsible for orderly climatic patterns and hence either void entirely or restrict severely the normal area of a climate's distribution. They are influential over all the climatic elements. Land masses that are extraordinarily large, like those found especially in the northern portion of the Eastern Hemisphere (where Europe, Asia, and northern Africa tend to heat up and cool off as a single unit), may interfere directly and severely with temperatures and indirectly with pressures, winds, and precipitation. Landforms situated wholly or partially within the high latitudes, such as Antarctica, Eurasia, and North America, are characterized by cold, even frigid, climates not found elsewhere except at very high altitudes. Landforms of prominent elevation, including nearly all major mountain systems and plateaus, not only reach into cooler temperatures but also cause air to rise and often to precipitate moisture. Consequently, the windward slopes of such landforms are often wet, and the leeward slopes dry.

A classification of thirteen climate types, separated on the basis of temperature and humidity, is presented in Figure 2.3.

Tropical rain forest. The tropical rain-forest climate occupies continental interiors of low to moderate elevation along the equator and reaches discontinuously outward to include a few western coasts and several eastern coasts, of which some are as distant as the Tropic of Cancer and the Tropic of Capricorn (Fig.

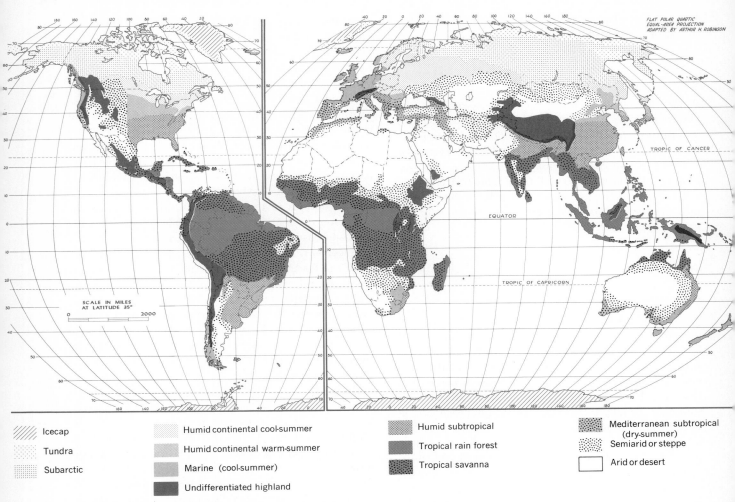

Icecap

Tundra

Subarctic

Humid continental cool-summer

Humid continental warm-summer

Marine (cool-summer)

Undifferentiated highland

Humid subtropical

Tropical rain forest

Tropical savanna

Mediterranean subtropical (dry-summer)

Semiarid or steppe

Arid or desert

Figure 2.3 The world pattern of climates. (After the Koeppen system, modified by Trewartha.)

2.3). It dominates the Amazon River basin of South America and the Congo River basin of Africa, includes the major islands of Indonesia, and sends offshoots from each of these tropical areas toward the subtropical latitudes.

As its name implies, tropical rain-forest climate has temperatures which never drop to the freezing point, but maintain a monotonous regularity, day by day and year by year. The temperatures of the strictly equatorial locations usually range between 75 and 80°F, with the range increasing with the latitude. The four seasons

scarcely exist as such. In the very low latitudes, temperatures tend to be highest during the months of March to May and September to November, for at these times the noonday sun is directly overhead, and the incoming solar radiation is at its maximum effectiveness along the equator. During the remainder of the year, the noonday sun is perpendicular to the earth's surface at places either to the north or to the south, and the equatorial temperatures decline slightly. On about June 22, the noonday sun is directly over the Tropic of Cancer, and on approximately December 22 it is over the Tropic of Capricorn. Equatorial locations thus tend to experience a dual temperature maximum, with the highest readings during the vernal and autumnal equinoxes and the lowest during the summer and winter solstices.

The precipitation of tropical rain-forest climate is heavy and regular, amounting to at least 60 inches, and sometimes exceeding 200 inches, each year. Daily thundershowers are common, and there is no pronounced dry season. Hurricanes (also called *typhoons*) seldom occur between lat 5°N and S, but they may strike the eastern coasts reaching beyond those latitudes.

Tropical savanna. Situated on either side of tropical rain-forest climate is the tropical savanna climate, which extends rather continuously to lat 15°N and S and fragmentally to the Tropics of Cancer and Capricorn (Fig. 2.3). Except where interrupted by prominent landforms, tropical savanna climate occupies major areas in South America, Africa, and southeastern Asia; portions of the coastal sections of Australia, Madagascar, Java, Ceylon, and Hispaniola; and all Cuba, as well as numerous smaller islands.

Although temperatures of tropical savanna climate fall into the same classification as those of tropical rain-forest climate, they tend to be slightly cooler and to have a more pronounced annual range than in the very low latitudes.

The distinguishing feature of tropical savanna climate is the seasonality of its precipitation, which, although ranging from approximately 30 to 60 inches a year, is concentrated within the summer months. Winters are pronouncedly dry. Hurricanes may strike all eastern coasts in this climate except along the shore of the Atlantic Ocean south of the equator. Here, for reasons not yet fully understood, none occurs in any climate type.

Humid subtropical. Moving still farther toward the middle latitudes, one finds the eastern portions of continents occupied by humid subtropical climate, which usually extends latitudinally from the vicinity of the Tropic of Cancer to approximately lat 40°N and from the vicinity of the Tropic of Capricorn to approximately lat 40°S. Excellent examples are found in the southeastern United States, in southeastern Asia, and

in Uruguay and its neighbors in South America, with smaller examples along the eastern fringes of Australia and South Africa and in the Adriatic and Balkan countries of Europe. Like the two tropical climates, it is largely in orderly arrangement, the only major exceptions being the European fragments, which are due mainly to local causes. Frost may be expected in this climate, the frequency and severity increasing with latitude. As implied in the term *subtropical*, however, the growing season is still long, and temperatures, even in winter, are not harshly cold (Fig. 2.3).

Precipitation in this climate is quite regular and heavy, amounting usually to 40 to 70 inches per year. There is no distinctly dry season. Hurricanes and related storms occur, with greatest frequency and intensity in early autumn and spring.

Mediterranean subtropical. Continental western coasts that are within lat 30 to 40°N or S are generally under mediterranean subtropical climate. This climate is developed most adequately along the Mediterranean Sea, for that large indentation is the "western coast" of a land complex which includes Europe, Asia, and Africa north of the equator. This climate is found also on the two "western coasts" of Australia and in southern Africa, central Chile, and southern California.

The distinguishing aspect of this climate is its precipitation, but not so much the annual amount, which ranges from 5 to 30 inches, as its seasonality. Nearly all the precipitation occurs during the winter months; summers are deficient in rainfall—indeed, often completely arid. Few hurricanes occur on continental west coasts and are virtually absent in areas dominated by this type of climate.

The temperatures are moderate, not greatly unlike those of humid subtropical climate.

Marine. Most regions of marine climate are located poleward from mediterranean subtropical climate, but a few are poleward and/or upslope from humid subtropical climate. Throughout most of the world, this climate is restricted by mountains to narrow strips, usually along western coasts, and to offshore islands. In northwestern Europe, however, it reaches southward to an alpine system appreciably removed from the Atlantic Ocean and eastward to the colder continental climates of the remainder of the Eurasian continental plain.

Marine temperatures are cool in both summer and winter, and the growing season, often upward of 180 days, is surprisingly long in consideration of the high latitudes (40 to 60°N and S).

Except along the very humid slopes of certain mountains, average annual precipitation ranges generally between 25 and 30 inches, with no specific season of drought or deficiency.

Humid continental warm-summer. The large size and high latitudinal extent of Eurasia and North America result in three climates not found in the Southern Hemisphere—the humid continental warm-summer, the humid continental cool-summer, and the subarctic.

In the United States and in southeastern Asia, the humid continental climate is immediately north of the humid subtropical climate. In the Balkan countries of Europe, it is east of the humid subtropical climate.

As its name implies, this climate is rather moist, with precipitation usually in the range of 25 to 45 inches annually. Summers are ordinarily but not necessarily the times of highest precipitation, and there is no specific dry season. Temperatures vary markedly during the course of a year in response not only to the march of the seasons but also to the pronounced summer heating and subsequent winter chilling of the land masses. This is true despite the fact that all three major regions of this climate type are adjacent to oceans or seas; for westerly winds, which prevail in these latitudes, tend to carry continental influences to the east.[2] The winter season is sufficiently cold and long that the frost-free period ranges from 150 to 180 days.

Humid continental cool-summer. This climate is distinguished from its southern neighbor, the humid continental warm-summer climate, especially by cooler temperatures and a shorter growing season (120 to 150

days) and by a slightly reduced precipitation. Its harsher temperature and humidity conditions mark the northern limit of effective agriculture at current levels of science and technology.

Subarctic. On the poleward margins of the humid continental cool-summer climate of the Northern Hemisphere is an extensive area of subarctic climate. Annual precipitation is low, frequently totaling less than 20 inches. Rates of evaporation in these cool temperatures are retarded, however, and so the climate is considered moist. In some areas there is a summer maximum of precipitation, and in others a winter maximum, but no season is noteworthily deficient in moisture. Summers are short, and the average annual temperatures are not high. An erratic growing season of 60 to 90 days renders agriculture almost impossible.

Tundra and icecap. These climates are found in the very high latitudes, with the icecap climate covering the sizable land masses of Greenland and Antarctica, and the tundra climate fringing most land masses that reach into these latitudes. Both are very cold and are usually low in precipitation. However, evaporation is retarded to the extent that these climates are classified as humid rather than arid.

Arid, or desert. The world contains a surprisingly consistent tier of subtropical deserts that enclose central and western portions of continents, generally between lat 20 and 30°N or S. The most prominent of these are the Sahara, the Arabian, and the Thar Deserts, which constitute the "west central" portion of the Eurasian–northern African land complex; the desert in western Australia; the Kalahari Desert of South Africa; the Atacama Desert of Chile (an extension of which, because of local conditions, reaches northward through coastal Peru almost to the equator); and the Sonora and related deserts of North America.

Other deserts are due mainly to their situation on the leeward margins of prominent landforms. These include particularly the Turkestan Desert east of the Caspian Sea in the Soviet Union, the Tarim River basin and Gobi Desert of western China, the desert in central Iran, and the Patagonian Desert of Argentina.

Average annual temperatures in the subtropical

---

[2] An exception can be noted during the summer season of southeastern Asia, where a persistent sea-to-land monsoon develops during the warm season; however, the moisture and moderate temperatures of this wind are altered as it passes over the mountains of southern China, Korea, and Japan, and it approaches the humid continental warm-summer climate as a rather hot, drying airflow.

deserts are warm or hot and in the middle-latitude deserts are alternately very hot and very cold. Precipitation seldom exceeds 10 inches per year.

Semiarid, or steppe. Semiarid, or steppe, climates represent a transition from deserts to more humid conditions and consequently are found almost invariably along the outer margins of deserts. Their causes and their global distribution are so similar to those of deserts that further elaboration is unnecessary. They are distinguished from deserts primarily on the basis of precipitation, which tends to range from 10 inches in the cooler areas, where evaporation is somewhat retarded, to 25 inches in areas of very active evaporation.

Undifferentiated highland. Temperatures decrease with elevation at an average rate of 3.3°F per 1,000 feet if air is stagnant or moving horizontally and usually at a higher rate if air is rising. Higher landforms, therefore, have cooler temperatures than lower elevations.

Precipitation is also affected by prominent landforms, which tend to have moist conditions on slopes facing a prevailing wind and dry conditions on their leeward slopes.

Because of the marked impact of landform elevation, the climates of prominent landforms are classified in a specific category known as *undifferentiated highland climate*. The lower margins of this climate are almost indistinguishable from the climates of the surrounding countrysides, but with ascent the temperatures are lower, and the precipitation may or may not alter, depending upon local conditions. In reality, therefore, the undifferentiated highland climate represents a catchall climate—a generalization for a host of tiny, vertically aligned climate zones which are too small to be viewed with understanding on a world map. Where moisture is adequate, there is a tendency for such climates to be arranged in a series of consecutive tiers, not unlike the latitudinal arrangement of the world's moist climates. Thus, for example, if one were to move up the eastern Andes in Ecuador, he might be able to pass through successive zones corresponding to the humid subtropical, humid continental, subarctic, and tundra climates, respectively.

Flora

Botanical life can be said to be either *macroscopic* or *microscopic*—either visible or invisible to the naked eye. Most microscopic plant life is not of major concern to the beginning student of economic geography, as it does not appear to have a direct association with man's efforts to gain a livelihood or with other aspects of man's economies. In contrast, the macroscopic flora of both land and water, especially the former, is of decided interest because it is used extensively to satisfy human needs and wants. Ranging in size and complexity downward from trees, this and antecedent vegetation once covered the earth's land surface, except the cold and dry portions. Despite its removal in large amounts by man, much remains to the present day. Maritime plant life, on the other hand, tends to be restricted to upper water levels that are accessible to sunlight, with the larger, rooted forms growing along the continental shelves and other shallows, and the smaller forms floating freely in water. As yet, man has seen fit to exploit only a small amount of the known maritime plant life, which remains more or less as it would have been if man had not existed.

Land Flora

Land vegetation has been classified in three groups: (1) forests, (2) grasses, and (3) shrubs and tundras (Fig. 2.4). Although there are many exceptions, forests tend to be found where climates and soils (especially soils) are moist, grasses where climates and soils are moist to dry, and shrubs and tundras (respectively) where climates and soils are very dry or cold.

Forests. Forests, the most widespread of the three groups, extend discontinuously from lat 70°N southward to the tips of all continents and major islands except polar Antarctica. In northern Anglo-America and Eurasia, they reach without serious interruption from the Pacific to the Atlantic Oceans. Moreover, they are found on most high landforms, regardless of the vegetation below. Today, despite man's exploitation,

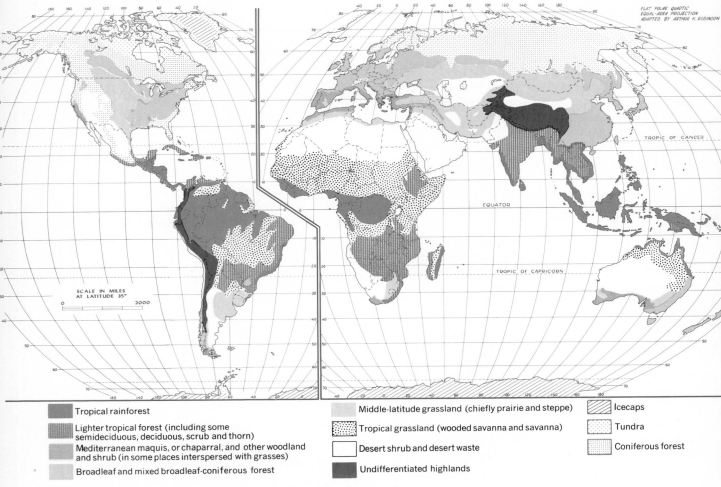

■ Tropical rainforest	▨ Middle-latitude grassland (chiefly prairie and steppe)	▨ Icecaps
▦ Lighter tropical forest (including some semideciduous, deciduous, scrub and thorn)	▨ Tropical grassland (wooded savanna and savanna)	▨ Tundra
▨ Mediterranean maquis, or chaparral, and other woodland and shrub (in some places interspersed with grasses)	□ Desert shrub and desert waste	▨ Coniferous forest
▨ Broadleaf and mixed broadleaf-coniferous forest	■ Undifferentiated highlands	

Figure 2.4 The world distribution of original natural vegetation.

they occupy over one-fourth of the earth's total land surface (Fig. 2.5 and Table 2.2).[3]

Low-latitude forests. The world's tree life is characteristically subdivided into two categories—the low-latitude and the middle-latitude forests. These, in turn, are usually classified into broadleaf-evergreen, deciduous, and narrowleaf-evergreen varieties.

[3] A recent world land-use estimate by the Food and Agriculture Organization of the United Nations is as follows: barren land, 48 per cent; forests, 27 per cent; grasslands, 15 per cent; cropland, 10 per cent.

In the low latitudes are dense stands of broadleaf evergreens containing a wide range of types, frequently more than sixteen per acre. They have been classified mainly by their Latin designations and are not well known in popular terminology. Some appear to be close cousins of mahogany, teak, and ebony trees that flourish in slightly higher latitudes. Also the palm tree is usually present in one form or another. They are called *broadleaf evergreens* because, in these mild regions, they are never without foliage, which consists of broad, flat leaves. In many cases a changing of leaves occurs,

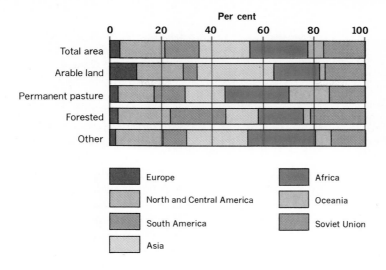

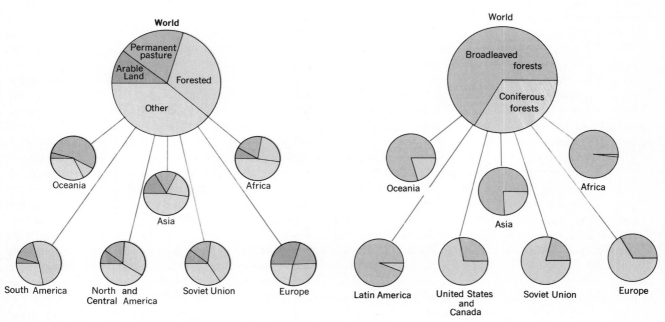

Figure 2.5 Gross land use in the world and major divisions, and distribution of the world's forests by major division.

TABLE 2.2
WORLD FOREST RESERVES,
(IN MILLIONS OF ACRES)

Nation or group	Total forests	Accessible forests	Inaccessible forests
U.S.S.R.	1,835.0	1,050.2	784.8
Brazil	1,186.3	296.5	889.8
Canada	845.1	321.7	523.4
United States	777.1	450.0	327.1
Total	4,643.5	2,118.4	2,525.1
Europe (excluding U.S.S.R.)	335.1	327.6	7.5
Other areas	4,503.4	2,037.4	2,466.0
World total	9,482.0	4,483.4	4,998.6

Source: World Forest Resources, United Nations, Food and Agriculture Organization, Rome, 1955, pp. 60–68.

but it is on a continuous basis, so that the trees are never bare. A forest like this, usually referred to as a *selva* or *tropical rain forest,* reaches average heights of 150 to 180 feet, and some trees exceed 200 feet. Not all growth is this tall, however, for the selva is a multilevel forest with shorter trees, shrubs, and parasitic jungle growth notably present along clearings, waterways, and other places where breaks appear in the umbrellalike canopies of the tallest trees. In slightly higher elevations, these forests merge into related varieties of trees which, despite their cooler habitat, remain evergreen.

With a few important exceptions, the wood of the selva is hard and difficult to work, the other products are in only moderate demand, and the locations are appreciably inaccessible. For these reasons, the selva has been exploited only preliminarily, except by the overcrowded populations of the older civilizations in the mainland sections of southeastern Asia. The tropical rain forest may therefore be considered a reserve of potentially useful timber which will be tapped if dwindling reserves in other areas make such action necessary. It is an extensive reserve, accounting for about one-half of the world's existing timber resources classified as productive or capable of exploitation.

Also in the low latitudes are a few semideciduous and deciduous trees which apparently shed their leaves because of regular or sporadic drought. These are erratically distributed from the selva approximately to the Tropics of Cancer and Capricorn, usually merging into low-latitude grasses. Their height and luxuriance decrease latitudinally with decreasing moisture and range from conditions resembling those of the tropical rain forest to isolated, single, stunted trees. These trees are best developed where adjacent to the selva.

Fringing either the low-latitude deciduous trees or the tropical rain forest are erratically distributed stands of scrub or thorn forest, a series of plants that manage to exist in the drier sections of the tropics. Being drought-resistant, most of these have a minimum of foliage, are quite woody and thorny, seldom reach more than 5 or 6 feet in height, and are restricted in commercial utilization essentially to grazing.

Middle-latitude forests. Ideally, the latitudinal arrangement of the world's forests would appear to be that of a transition from broadleaf-evergreen to deciduous to narrowleaf-evergreen trees with increasing distance from the equator. In fact, where moisture permits, this distribution is recognizable, but with a major exception: Notably in the southeastern United States between lat 25 and 35°N (and extending even farther northward within the higher elevations of the Appalachian Mountains) is a prodigious growth of pine and associated narrowleaf softwoods that reproduce themselves by bearing and shedding cones and hence are called *coniferous.* Analogous varieties appear in corresponding positions (the eastern section of continents roughly between lat 25 and 35°N or S) in South America, Africa, Australia, and Asia, but their stands are usually more sparse and more liberally sprinkled with deciduous trees. They are blessings to the regions possessing them, for they can be utilized intensively for a wide variety of purposes; since they grow in relatively mild temperatures and under plentiful supplies of moisture, they replace themselves more quickly than the evergreens of the higher latitudes. If man continues to cut timber with his current prodigious energy, these forests, especially in the United States, may well become the chief source areas of the softwoods.

Beyond these stands of subtropical coniferous trees are middle-latitude broadleaf forests that occupy ex-

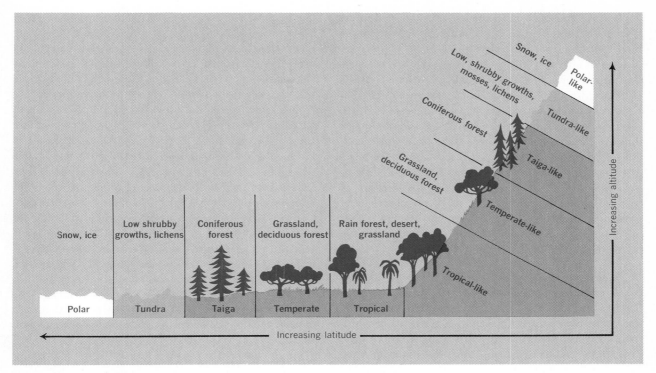

Figure 2.6 Vegetational transition and general correlation between latitude and altitude. The subtropical coniferous forests, not present in all continents, are not shown. (After Paul B. Weisz, *The Science of Biology*, 3d ed., McGraw-Hill Book Company, New York, 1967, pp. 224–225.)

tensive areas of the east central United States, north central and southeastern Canada, northern Europe, west central and east central Asia, and coastal strips of southeastern Australia and southern Chile, as well as a small district in southeastern Brazil. These include a large number of specific types, of which the more common varieties are oak, hickory, chestnut, elm, cottonwood, poplar, ash, walnut, beech, birch, and maple. Most are deciduous, shedding their leaves annually because of seasonal cold. The reserves of these middle-latitude broadleaf forests have been decimated by man to a greater degree than any other group—not because they are so desirable, for they are mostly hardwoods and are not so suitable for most of man's purposes as the softwoods, but because they, like the American Indian, once occupied a territory that expanding populations found very much to their liking. It will be noted that of the world's three major clusters of population,

those of Anglo-America and Europe lie almost wholly within this deciduous belt, as does the northern part of the agglomeration in southeastern Asia. Today, these trees constitute only 14 per cent of the productive timber reserves of the world.

High-latitude and high-altitude forests. Still farther poleward and upslope (as temperatures decrease with higher altitude as well as latitude) are the most widespread stands of coniferous softwoods (Figs. 2.4 and 2.6). This is "Christmas tree" vegetation—pine, spruce, fir, cedar, larch, hemlock. Most of these trees are not only narrowleaf but also shortleaf evergreens. The largest stands are in the Soviet Union, Canada, Alaska, and Fennoscandia. Each forest projects southward, particularly along the higher landforms, where temperatures are cooler. In contrast, the Southern Hemisphere is essentially devoid of extensive forests that are exclusively coniferous, except in the intermediate and upper reaches of the uplands. The coniferous forests of the high latitudes and altitudes are the most extensively utilized of all, especially along their equatorward margin. Their reserves have been depleted rather seriously, emphatically so in Anglo-America, where man has not yet experienced the need to achieve a proper cut-growth ratio. Even in Eurasia, where man has exploited forests for a longer period of time, there are nations which have not yet learned through the sometimes disastrous expedient of trial and error that forest depletion can be costly—and that these critical resources, existing as they do under rather cool climates, do not tend to reproduce themselves rapidly in polar reaches of the middle latitudes. Today, coniferous trees constitute 36 per cent of the world's productive timber reserves.

Mediterranean vegetation. Continental western coasts between approximately lat 30 and 40° in either hemisphere tend to be characterized by a vegetation known as *chaparral* or *maquis*—a series of drought-resistant vegetative types which are smaller than most trees, taller than many shrubs, and more luxuriant than most scrub or thorn forests. Rather surprisingly, the majority of these are broadleaf evergreens successfully withstanding the dry summers of their habitats by resistances other than the shedding of leaves. They are usually quite sparse in stand and may be interspersed with some grasses. Their significance in economic geography lies primarily in their supply of a few gathered commodities and in the limited pasture they provide for animals, notably goats, which are sufficiently agile to take advantage of them. They also are used as fuel.

Grasslands. The majority of natural grasslands may be classified into four broad categories: savanna, prairie, steppe grasses, and alpine meadows. The first is restricted almost entirely to the low latitudes, the second and third to the middle latitudes, and the fourth to mountains. Each of the first three categories occupies enough space to be shown on a world map (Fig. 2.4), the first as a distinct area, and the other two in combination. Alpine meadows usually are found in small amounts at high elevations.

Savanna grasses. The savanna grasses fringe the low-latitude forests of all continents but Asia, where semideciduous trees tend to replace them. They are reedy plants resembling sorghums and reach heights of 4 to 12 feet. The tallest varieties tend to be found in the more copious moistures of the low latitudes, fringing the semideciduous forests and occasionally the tropical rain forest. They do not tend to form a compact turf, but exist as individual plants. Although perennials, they wither, and their stalks die during the dry winters of tropical savanna climate and send forth new shoots when the spring rains come. Their direct economic significance to man is chiefly that of providing forage for grazing purposes—forage which approaches adequacy during the wet season but becomes brittle and difficult, even dangerous, to graze during the dry period, for it tends to inflict rather severe lacerations upon animals' internal tissues. Savanna grasses are very widespread, occupying a total area approximately equal to that occupied by the world's steppelands. Occasionally, varieties of intermediate height are interspersed with stands of such trees as the acacia, resulting in a parklike landscape.

Prairie grasses. Originally occupying extensive regions of Anglo-America and Latin America and noteworthy territory in European Russia, central Manchuria, the Hungarian basin, and the Transvaal–Orange Free State sections of the Republic of South Africa, prairie grasses have been appreciably removed by man. The climates under which they thrive are excellent for a wide selection of man's crops, and so they are being obliterated. They are thin-stemmed, turfed, and thick in stand. Under optimum environmental conditions, they may reach heights exceeding 10 feet. In less favorable habitats, notably where moisture is reduced, they may be only a few inches tall. They are usually perennials, but being located in the middle latitudes, they freeze down in winter and send up new growth in the spring. Only in Latin America are large virgin stands still in existence.

Steppe grasses. Steppe grasses usually fringe middle-latitude deserts, providing a transition from them to the more luxuriant vegetation. (Most of the low-latitude climates, where steppe grasses might be expected, have some form of shrub or thorn forest.) Some are turfed, like the prairie varieties, but are only a few inches in height. Others are tufted and somewhat taller, perhaps as much as a foot high. They occupy approximately as much of the world's total grassland area as the savannas and much more area than the prairies. They have found widest expression in central Asia, with smaller but prominent representations in North America, South America, Africa, and Australia. Their direct economic significance to man is chiefly in the grazing industry, although their soils tend to be fertile for many crops if irrigation water is available.

Alpine meadows. In most mountainous and other upland regions, zones of grasses reach above the timberline and merge into the tundra. These grasses are usually quite short, turfed, and capable of existing under the erratic high-landform weather and climate conditions, which may change quickly and drastically. It is their good fortune to occur where man usually does not desire to plant crops, and their sole contacts with human civilization usually take place under either the watchful eyes of the shepherd or the awed eyes of the tourist.

Desert shrublands; tundras. The transitions from warm to very cold climates and from moist to very dry climates are marked by corresponding gradations from tall, thick, intricate vegetation to that which is short, sparse, and of relatively simple pattern. This last stage is reached in both arid and frigid regions. Most of the world's arid deserts—in contrast to the implications of many motion pictures—are rocky and are at least sprinkled with types of drought-resistant bush, shrub, or cactus, all of which are termed *xerophytes*. Most of these either have the capacity to resist transpiration (the releasing of moisture by plants in a manner generally similar to perspiration in some animals), and thus are able to conserve their meager water supply, or else pass very quickly through the flowering and reproduction cycle after an uncommon bit of precipitation, remaining as dormant seeds for the coming hours, days, months, or even years until the moisture reappears.

The tundras, here interpreted as including only the mosses and lichens of the very high altitudes and latitudes, are even more stunted than the desert bushes, but they tend to constitute somewhat more of a carpet than the desert plants. Both categories offer very limited grazing possibilities, and the tundras provide some peat for fuel; generally, both are of little current use to mankind.

Regions and vertical zones of transition. Attention has been focused upon certain core types of plants so that the reader can envision their distribution. It is perhaps unnecessary to explain that these classifications, like all such categorizations, are somewhat arbitrary, that in reality each region merges gradually into its neighboring area, and that often the merging is so subtle that their dividing lines are drawn somewhat subjectively. This is true of vertical as well as horizontal merging; anyone familiar with high mountain country, for example, knows that the term *timberline* usually denotes a myth and that *timber zone* would be a more accurate description for the increasingly stubby tree growth that tries valiantly to extend itself upward into the alpine meadows.

Water Flora

Although the flora of the earth's water bodies clings to the peripheries of continents and therefore has been, throughout human history, accessible to man, it does not play a direct, vital role in many of man's efforts to gain a livelihood. Botanical water life either has been carried by waterways to the larger repositories or is indigenous; it is either floating or rooted. The floating plants, being mobile, cannot be grouped satisfactorily into areas of prevailing types, as is possible with land vegetation. The rooted plant life of water, while varied, does not appear to exhibit the marked physical differences from place to place that are apparent in the distribution of plant life upon the lithosphere. For both types, photosynthesis is necessary, and both therefore exist at depths sufficiently shallow to receive sunlight—generally less than 1,500 feet. Within this limitation, the floating varieties, especially the microscopic and tiny plankton, move about rather freely, but are most numerous along coastal shallows and river mouths. Most botanical water life is classified further as (1) algae, which do not flower and essentially have no well-defined, rigid structure, and (2) the maritime groups that do possess such characteristics. Algae include very small, sometimes microscopic plant life as well as larger flora, of which some is rooted and some is floating. Certain of the larger varieties are sources of iodine, the principal item of economic significance derived directly by man from marine botanical forms. Far more important is tiny plant life, which is the food for a substantial portion of the earth's marine and freshwater fish.

Recently, some water flora has become a serious liability in man's relationship with his natural environment. In freshwater lakes and streams, particularly the Great Lakes of North America, certain algae, fertilized by untreated and treated sewage from cities, thrive. Passing through their life cycle rapidly, they flourish in the early spring, die, sink, and decompose. Oxygen and other elements necessary for marine life are removed from the water in the decomposition process, and the lakes thus become "dead water."

Soils

Most of the continental platforms which stand above prevailing water level (and do not, therefore, include continental shelves) are surfaced with a cover of *soil,* the medium through which land flora is joined, physically and physiologically, with the earth's land surface. Soil, in other words, is the loose land-surface material in which vegetation can grow. Genetically, soil is the result of a slow admixing of critical organic and other materials traceable mainly to surface life, with equally necessary minerals and other materials originating in subsurface rock strata. The mixing is carried on through the chemical and mechanical action of underground and surface water and air and through the activities of myriads of microscopic and macroscopic plants and animals, including the roots of vegetation growing at any particular place. Also very important to this mixing are the slope and the rock makeup of the land on which the soil is being formed, as these influence markedly the degree and rate of chemical and mechanical weathering, erosion, and deposition. Climate is significant both directly and indirectly, as it sets temperature and moisture limits to certain types of plant life, provides the precipitation responsible for

much of the water action, and acts in diverse other ways. Indeed, there appears to be a general association between the broad climate, vegetation, and soil regions of the world, particularly where soils have developed in the places where they are now found.

Essential Soil Elements and Properties

Minerals. Soils are composed of minerals, organic matter, water, and air. At least half their bulk is derived from minerals, and their composition is appreciably a reflection of the makeup of the underlying *parent materials*—the uppermost layer or layers of rocks. Since almost 98 per cent of the earth's rock structure is composed of eight elements in combination with one another and with other elements (Table 2.1), these eight tend to predominate in the mineralized portions of the earth's soils, although they differ a great deal in relative amounts from place to place. The remaining mineral accumulation in soils is made up of all other elements.

Most plants require sixteen elements for normal growth—carbon, hydrogen, oxygen, nitrogen, phosphorus, sulfur, potassium, calcium, magnesium, iron, manganese, zinc, copper, molybdenum, boron, and chlorine. All are obtained from the soil except carbon, hydrogen, and oxygen, which come mainly from water and air. Nine of the basic sixteen elements are classified as *macronutrients* and must be present in the soil in comparatively substantial quantities for most plant growth. The remaining seven—iron, manganese, zinc, copper, molybdenum, boron, and chlorine—are *micronutrients* (sometimes called *trace elements*) and need be present only in small quantities for normal vegetative growth.

Of the eight abundant elements in the earth's crust and hence in soil minerals, silicon and aluminum are of no apparent value to plant growth. Sodium appears to be equally unnecessary for the development of flora, but it is vital for some of the animals which graze on it. All the other abundant crustal elements are macronutrients except iron, which is a micronutrient.

Organic materials. Contributions to soil from flora and fauna include organic remains ranging in stage of decomposition from tissues of newly expired life to a more degraded, blackish, spongy, absorbent substance called *humus.* In total, organic contributions make up a comparatively small fraction of an average soil, but are a source of nitrogen, calcium, potassium, phosphorus, and sulfur for living plants. Humus also fosters plant growth in various other ways.

Water and air. The amount of water and air in a soil differs sharply from place to place and depends not only upon their being readily available but also upon the degree to which the nature of a soil permits their penetration. Under optimum conditions, they may constitute nearly half the total bulk (pore space included) of a soil.

Fundamental properties. Both the mineral and the organic constituents weather and decompose chemically and mechanically until some grains of each pass through the submicroscopic size, eventually becoming *colloids.* Although not yet fully understood, colloids are believed to be forms through which certain elements, especially the soluble salts and some organic chemicals, pass into the roots of vegetative life. They are somewhat adhesive and may help larger soil particles stick together into aggregates known as *floccules.*

The sizes of particles making up a soil determine its *texture.* Fine-textured soils tend to be made up of clay, coarse textures of sand, and intermediate textures of loam, which is a combination of clay and sand. Silts are also of intermediate texture.

The arrangement of a soil's particles constitutes its *structure,* which is dependent largely upon the shape and uniformity of individual soil grains and upon the capacity of such grains to form floccules. If the particles are long and thin, for example, they may be tightly packed, with few or no pores for air and water; if all the particles are roughly circular, the situation will be markedly different. The amount of humus in a soil is also a significant determinant of its structure.

Soil texture and structure are interrelated. In combination they are vital to a soil's compactness and permeability. Both, especially texture, are at least partially responsible for a soil's *tilth,* or crumbly reaction to a plow. Fine-textured soils tend to form clods, and coarse soils tend to crumble when tilled.

The *color* of soils ranges from black to white and includes yellow, red, rust, brown, and gray. Color may be an indication of other soil qualities, such as acidity, alkalinity, or humus content, but its significance varies so sharply with each soil that generalizations must be made cautiously.

The *fertility* of a soil refers to its content of nutrients. Its *productivity* refers to its capacity to yield specific crops under definite conditions of climate and cultivation. These two terms are frequently misused as synonyms.

Classification of Soils

One of several soil classifications involves *orders, groups,* and many finer subdivisions. A different but overlapping classification involves soil *acidity* and *alkalinity.* We are interested chiefly in soil groups, but we can understand these better by first examining soil orders and soil acidity and alkalinity. The three recognized orders are *zonal, intrazonal,* and *azonal* soils.

Zonal soils. Most soils can be categorized into horizontal zones, which generally coincide with areas of climate and natural vegetation. Thus, an area or zone with a certain climate and natural vegetation tends also to contain soil characteristics which normally accompany that particular climate and its associated plant life. Such soils are known as *zonal* soils. Invariably, they have formed in the places where they now exist. With the passing of time, they have developed vertical profiles, or series of vertically arranged *horizons,* which have been recognized as indicated in Table 2.3.

Intrazonal and azonal soils. *Intrazonal* soils, while usually evidencing at least the suggestion of a profile, tend to be dominated by soil-forming factors other than climate and natural vegetation. *Azonal* soils do not have well-developed profiles. They frequently are composed of alluvium, silt, sand, or other materials which recently have been deposited by wind, water, or ice. It is difficult to generalize concerning either of these soil orders because each varies markedly from place to place. However, neither order contains a very large portion of the world's soils.

TABLE 2.3

THE ZONAL-SOIL PROFILE

Horizon	Position and depth	Description
A	From surface downward; usually not more than 15 inches	Zone of leaching (chemical withdrawal) and eluviation (mechanical withdrawal) of materials; usually organic, especially in upper portions; organic matter increasingly decomposed with depth
B	Just beneath horizon A; usually base is no deeper than 36 inches	Zone of illuviation (accumulation); materials from both horizon A and horizon C find their way to horizon B
C	Just beneath horizon B; usually base is no deeper than 8 feet	Zone of altered parent materials moving up from below to horizon B
D	Just beneath horizon C	Zone of unaltered parent materials, usually bedrock

Pedalfers, pedocals, and neutral soils. Some soils are dominated by weak acids derived partially from organic life and partially from chemical reaction of water with solid ingredients. Such soils are notably present under moist conditions. They are called *pedalfers* because of their high content of aluminum (Al) and iron (Fe)—a content resulting from the resistance of these two elements to the acid and water action which removes many other elements. To the economic geographer, the significant point about the pedalfers is that they are acid. They exist chiefly in wet areas and cool areas. Other soils, found notably under dry conditions, are termed *pedocals* because of their high content of calcium (Ca) and other alkaline, or nonacid, elements. They exist chiefly in arid and semiarid areas. Still other soils are neutral—that is, neither predominantly acid nor alkaline in chemical reaction. These are usually encountered where moist and dry climates meet.

Ideally a soil should not be excessively acid or nonacid for the growth of most crops. The very acid soils are especially unfavorable. The highly pedocalic soils, however, can be made to produce without too much cost if proper drainage systems accompany their necessary irrigation.

Association with vegetation. All luxuriant forests are rooted in pedalferic soils. All desert plants and essentially all short grasses are rooted in pedocalic soils. The tallest of the grasses, usually mixed with trees, tend to exist in soils that are pedalferic, whether in the low or middle latitudes. The transition to pedocalic soils is usually found where grasses are of intermediate height, interrupted by tree growth only along the waterways.

The association of vegetation with soils is particularly important in two respects: (1) The vegetative type suggests the degree of moisture in a given climate, and this moisture, in turn, is an active agent in affecting the amount of soluble ingredients and in maintaining the current plant life of a soil, and (2) different forms of plant life contribute humus to the soil in sharply varying amounts and ways that affect very markedly the qualities of their respective underlying soils.

Association with trees. The roots of most trees pass through the more active portion of a soil into horizon C and perhaps even horizon D, for such roots are necessary not only for sustenance but also for support. They are usually sizable in diameter and tubular. When the trees eventually die, they decompose slowly, adding only a small amount of their humus to the soil. Moreover, being tubular, they provide channels of easy access by which water and air can enter the soil and thereby hasten the process of pedalferization. Humus contributions from the part of the tree above the soil are limited to the annual leaf fall, if the tree cover is deciduous, or to a rather consistent but light accumulation of individual leaves, if it is evergreen. In either case, the leaves drop only to the surface of the ground, and the humus must enter the soil through slow processes of chemical and mechanical change, during which time it is subjected to continuous oxidation and erosion from surface air and water. Tree life cannot be considered, therefore, the best of the possible natural vegetational forms for direct soil maintenance. Still another comparative liability is indirect: Trees do not generally attract the larger herbivorous animals or the carnivorous animals that feed upon them. Forest soils have thus not benefited from the humus of the manures and decomposing carcasses that accompany such life.

Association with grasses and xerophytes. Grasses are generally the best sources of soil humus. Their roots are numerous but thin. When they die, the entire roots decompose quickly into organic soil accumulation. The amount of annual humus contribution from the stalk section varies, of course, with the height of the plants, but it usually exceeds the leaf drop from most trees. Most grasses occur where the stems and leaves wither and die each year, because of either frost or drought, thus returning more humus to the soil than is true of at least evergreen trees. Finally, the grasses attract large animals and benefit by their presence. In contrast, xerophytes add little humus to the highly pedocalic soils in which they occur.

Soil Groups: Association with Climate and Vegetation

Soil orders are subclassified into groups on the basis of depth, color, organic content, acidity and alkalinity, and still other properties. Such groups are mainly subdivisions of zonal soils, described above. They are shown in Table 2.4, compared with broad regions of climate and natural vegetation in Table 2.5, and mapped in Figure 2.7.

Red and yellow soils. The red and yellow soils, one of the most widespread of the soil groups, are found under the trees of the tropics and subtropics where moisture is copious. These soils are badly leached (i.e., their soluble materials have been largely removed by chemical weathering and erosion), they do not contain much humus, and they may be regarded as generally unproductive. Occasionally, where underlying parent materials provide consistently good supplies of minerals, as in some volcanic and some limestone areas, they are more productive—as indeed are other soils underlain by such materials.

TABLE 2.4

CLASSIFICATION OF SELECTED SOIL GROUPS BY ACIDITY AND ALKALINITY

Pedalfers (acid)	Transitional or essentially neutral	Pedocals (alkaline)
Red and yellow soils		
Gray-brown forest soils (including podzolics)		
Prairie soils	Prairie-chernozem soils	Chernozem soils
Podzol soils		Brown steppe soils
Tundras		Arid-desert soils (sierozems)

Gray-brown forest soils. These are found largely in Anglo-America, Europe, and eastern Asia, with traces in the Southern Hemisphere. They underlie deciduous hardwoods, are moderately leached, have the richest humus accumulations, and are the most productive of the forest soils. Some, notably in higher latitudes, have podzol tendencies (discussed below) and are termed *podzolic.*

Podzol soils. The podzol soils (ashen soils) are most extensively distributed in the Soviet Union and Canada. Found under narrowleaf, shortleaf coniferous vegetation (often called *taiga*), they are ash gray in color, quite acid, shallow, lacking in humus, and comparatively unproductive. Unlike the warmer soils, which owe their acidity to high rainfall, the podzols are acid largely because of retarded evaporation and drainage in cool climates where not much precipitation actually falls and where the subsoils are usually frozen in winter.

Tundra soils. Occupying cold areas of *permafrost* (permanently frozen subsoils), these soils are usually intrazonal and even azonal, for they are frozen solidly in winter and are marshy in summer because the frozen subsoils restrict drainage.

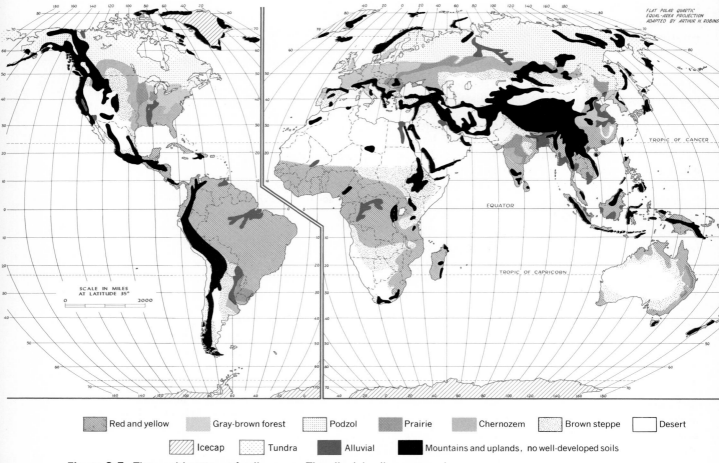

Red and yellow	Gray-brown forest	Podzol	Prairie	Chernozem	Brown steppe	Desert
Icecap	Tundra	Alluvial	Mountains and uplands, no well-developed soils			

Figure 2.7 The world pattern of soil groups. The alluvial soils are azonal. The soil groups shown here are more generalized than in some classifications.

Prairie soils. The most naturally fertile soils are the prairie-chernozem-steppe soils, often mapped and discussed as the *black soils*. This general title applies aptly to the prairies and the chernozems but not so aptly to the steppe varieties, which are brown rather than black in color. They mark the transition from the pedalfers to the pedocals, with the prairies being the least acid of the pedalfers, and the chernozem and steppe soils—notably the chernozems—the least alkaline of the pedocals.

The prairie soils are deep, black, waxy, rich in humus, and productive. They are among the world's most highly prized soils.

Chernozem soils. Generally like the prairies, except that their overlying grasses are shorter and their chemical reaction is slightly alkaline rather than acid, the chernozems (black soils) are also among the best in agricultural productivity. However, lack of ready availability of water at all times is a problem in the utilization of some chernozems—a problem that becomes increasingly acute with transition to drier soils.

TABLE 2.5

ASSOCIATIONS BETWEEN THE WORLD'S CLIMATES,
NATURAL VEGETATION, AND SOIL GROUPS

Climate	Natural vegetation	Soil group
Tropical rain forest	Tropical rain forest	Red and yellow
Tropical savanna	Transition from tropical rain forest to semideciduous trees to tall savanna grasses to short savanna grasses	Transition from red and yellow to prairie to chernozem
Humid subtropical	Prevailingly deciduous hardwoods, replaced in some areas, especially the United States, by longleaf, narrowleaf conifers	Red and yellow; mostly red under deciduous trees, and yellow under conifers
Mediterranean subtropical	Chaparral, maquis	Transported (because of coincidental location of most such climates in or near mountains)
Marine	Middle-latitude deciduous trees, sometimes mixed with shortleaf, narrowleaf conifers	Where occurring in mountains, soils are transported as in mediterranean climates, above; where plains prevail in this climate, as in Europe, soils are gray-brown forest, becoming more podzolic with higher latitude as conifers increase in proportion of vegetative cover
Humid continental warm-summer	Primarily middle-latitude deciduous trees in moist portions, transiting to prairie grasses in drier sections	Mainly gray-brown forest soils where under trees, and prairie soils under grasses
Humid continental cool-summer	Mixed deciduous forest and shortleaf, narrowleaf conifers, transiting to prairie grasses on drier margins	Gray-brown (podzolic) transiting to true podzols in higher latitudes and to prairie and prairie-chernozem soils on drier margins
Subarctic	Shortleaf, narrowleaf conifers (taiga)	Podzol
Tundra	Tundra	Tundra
Icecap	None	None
Semiarid, or steppe	Steppe grasses, transiting to prairie grasses in wetter sections and to drought-resistant (xerophytic) types on drier margins	Brown steppe, transiting to chernozem on wetter margins and to desert (sierozem) on drier margins
Arid, or desert	Drought-resistant (xerophytic) types	Desert (sierozem)

Brown steppe soils. Deprived of the prodigious humus accumulations that give color and high fertility to the prairies and chernozems, the brown steppe soils are nonetheless able to produce efficiently if utilized scientifically—especially where irrigation water and proper drainage or the growth of drought-resistant crops is feasible.

Desert soils. Although generally rich in alkaline elements and somewhat poor in humus, desert (sierozem, or white soil) lands can be made to produce under careful management. The availability of water, however, is a severe restriction, as may be also the superfluity of some salts, the removal of which sometimes becomes troublesome—two major problems that arise in attempts to utilize such soils.

A New Soil Classification

The soil classification discussed above reflects long-term relationships between climate, natural vegetation and wildlife, underlying parent materials, and soil. It does not reflect accurately current conditions of soils which have been cultivated and hence have been subjected to a mutation of the initial ecological relationships. During this century, and especially during the past twenty-five years, the United States government has developed a new soil classification, sometimes called the *Seventh Approximation,* based essentially on chemical composition, acidity, organic content, structure and texture, and thickness of topsoil. In other words, the classification depends heavily upon identifiable features, rather than a historical association with climate, natural vegetation and wildlife, and parent materials.

Figure 2.8 The Seventh Soil Approximation of the United States. This classification is based on identifiable features of current soil orders, rather than on historical interpretation. For further explanation, see Paul W. Mausel, "An Introductory Approach to Soils in Geography Instruction," *Journal of Geography,* vol. 61, no. 1, 1970, pp. 30–36.

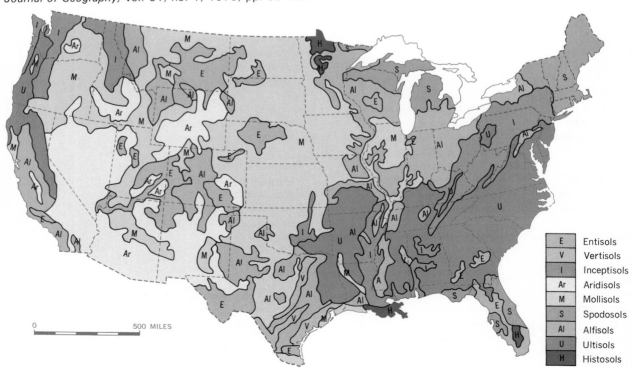

E	Entisols
V	Vertisols
I	Inceptisols
Ar	Aridisols
M	Mollisols
S	Spodosols
Al	Alfisols
U	Ultisols
H	Histosols

0   500 MILES

That classification and explanation are shown in Figure 2.8. It is not yet available for areas outside the United States, but is used increasingly within this country.

Fauna

Animals are more mobile than plants, and their natural life zones are not so well defined. Moreover, man has removed the wild fauna from lands he now occupies intensively, and the animals of outlying areas are of little economic interest other than to small numbers of primitive or quasi-primitive societies. The number of people dependent upon hunting game is very small.

Zoological water life is much more important to man and may become even vital as human populations increase. As on land, the tiniest forms are microscopic and unicellular, often indistinguishable from their botanical counterparts. More than on land, these small forms constitute the food supply for many larger forms of life which man exploits. Of the more than forty thousand known categories of fish, over one thousand have been designated as commercial.

Chapter 3

The Economic Environment: Levels of Development

If economics is the study of gaining a livelihood—or of allocation of key resources—an economy provides for livelihoods and for allocation of resources. We noted preliminarily in the Introduction that not all the world's economies are functioning at the same level of efficiency in providing for livelihoods or for allocation of resources. In this chapter we shall examine the meaning and process of economic development, as well as some global patterns.

History and Economic Development

The historical sequence of economic change from such primitive activities as hunting and gathering to agriculture, to manufacturing, and then to commercial production of services, is well known. According to one school of thought, the development of economies can be viewed as a series of historical stages, with each stage more advanced than its predecessor. The noted economist and historian W. W. Rostow recognizes five developmental stages in historical time: (1) the traditional

society, (2) preconditions for takeoff, (3) the takeoff, (4) the drive to maturity, and (5) the age of high mass consumption.[1]

The *traditional society,* as its name implies, has existed in an area for a long time. Its values are largely inherited, and many of its customs have outlived their usefulness. This society may be governed in one of several possible ways, but whatever its organization, the society is no longer capable of increasing output per person, so that hand-to-mouth living is the rule rather than the exception. This stage may last for an indefinite period of time.

Preconditions for takeoff may be introduced by an invasion from the outside or by an awakening from within. New ideas, usually heralded by new leaders, begin to take root. These ideas gradually develop beneath the mantle of the still dominant traditional

[1] See especially W. W. Rostow, *The Process of Economic Growth,* Oxford University Press, Fair Lawn, N.J., 1960; and W. W. Rostow, *The Stages of Economic Growth,* Cambridge University Press, New York, 1960.

group. This stage may last a long time—possibly over a century.

With *takeoff* comes a sudden eruption of new forces that have been building during the preconditions period. New capital and technology, which have been developing slowly, quickly come to the forefront. Secondary and tertiary production may become more active. New transportation and communications facilities are constructed. All this activity usually means that the new group of leaders, whose power has grown during the preconditions period, have at last become dominant. The actual takeoff period usually is very short, lasting thirty years or less.

The *drive to maturity,* which may last as long as sixty years, involves the maturing of an economy from its embryonic takeoff phase into full stature. Secondary and tertiary activities, and subdivisions of these activities, become numerous. New branches and subdivisions also may appear in primary production.

High mass consumption, the final stage, is self-explanatory; enough goods and services exist to satisfy all needs and many wants. Beyond high mass consumption, Rostow suggests, are such noneconomic objectives as better appreciation of art and music.

Whether or not we accept the Rostow argument or any other specific theory concerned with the historical evolution of economic activity, we do recognize the importance of historical influence on present-day economies. This importance is reflected in the criteria by which we measure underdevelopment as well as in the classifications we devise, as will be seen in the discussion to follow.

Classification by Level of Economic Development

Although the task of making an inventory of the world's economic geography is by no means complete, enough information exists to classify areas into at least two developmental levels: (1) those which are economically and technically advanced and (2) those which are economically and technically less developed. The classification can be broken down into still more groupings, but these two have become familiar and serve to emphasize the basic ideas. Furthermore, precise data on

a number of countries are lacking, and additional breakdowns would involve considerable guessing.

Definition and reservations. Now that we have some terminology, what is the meaning of our terms? The clue lies in the word *developed,* which is implied in the first category (economically and technically advanced) and stated in the second. What is a developed economy? Basically, it is one in which the human and natural resources of an area are being used at a relatively high level of efficiency at a given time. In addition, now that regional and national planning are widely recognized, the term is used increasingly to mean the establishment of social, political, economic, and conservation goals and the implementation of such goals. If we accept these definitions, however, we need to understand three important reservations.

First, economic or technical advance does not necessarily imply *cultural* advance. Each reader of this book doubtless can call to mind some person who is a "whiz" at mechanics or finance but who knows precious little about, let us say, the humanities or philosophy. So it is with cultures. Some emphasize specialized knowledge, whereas others place a premium on broader objectives.

Second, developmental potential varies from place to place. If all economies, both large and small, were fully developed, they would yield unequal incomes per person. Among the outstanding differences in potential is that of land, or natural environment. One area may contain a wide range of natural resources, and another almost none. Such inequities appear not only among different countries but also in different areas of a single country. There may be "pocket areas" of underdevelopment in technically advanced countries and pocket areas of technical advance in less developed countries.

Third, as we noted above, developmental levels change with time. If the people of an area awaken to the need for economic development and are able to attract capital, improve technology, increase efficiency of labor, and otherwise increase production relative to population, the area may move toward, or even into, a condition of technical advance. Conversely, an area may decline for one of a number of reasons.

The criteria. A number of criteria have been employed to determine level of economic development.[2] Of these, three generalize the results rather satisfactorily. The first indicates percentage of an area's labor force in agriculture, the second shows consumption of electric energy per inhabitant, and the third reveals per capita income. The first thus reflects the extent to which the labor force of an economy has moved away from primary production and toward secondary and tertiary production. It thus indicates historical trends. The second measures the efficiency with which modern forms of energy are being put to use. The third shows the ultimate result of any change in man-production ratio—namely, the actual income per person.

Labor force in agriculture. With allowance for exceptional circumstances, the degree of technical advance increases with decline in importance of agriculture in a country's labor force. Countries with very small portions of their working forces in agriculture and other primary activities thus are considered the more technically advanced. Available data on this subject are shown in Figure 3.1. The reader probably is not surprised to find that the United States and Canada, much of northern Europe, Australia, and New Zealand have small portions of their respective labor forces in agriculture. Uruguay and Argentina, frequently considered agricultural countries, also actually have comparatively few employed in agriculture, as has Israel. A second group, more oriented to agriculture but still below the average for all reporting countries, contains much of central and southern Europe, Iceland, the Soviet Union, and Japan, plus various nations in the rest of the world. Data for countries with more than the world average of their labor forces in agriculture are far less complete. However, it is clear that some of Latin

America is at a level immediately below the average, whereas many parts of Africa and Asia have large portions of their working forces in agriculture. Three of the world's largest nations—China, India, and Indonesia—have over 65 per cent of their labor forces in agriculture.

Per capita energy consumption. Figure 3.2 emphasizes the large amount of energy available to technically advanced nations, especially the United States, Canada, Sweden, Denmark, Belgium, Czechoslovakia, and East Germany. (The favorable position of East Germany is due partially to the loss of population. Kuwait is included because of revenues from petroleum sales.) The second highest category includes the remaining countries of northern Europe plus Italy, several countries of eastern Europe, the Soviet Union, Australia, New Zealand, Japan, Israel, and isolated countries elsewhere. (Commercial consumption is included as part of the total; thus, Venezuelan refineries "consume" much petroleum, as does a refinery in Aden, even though many of the products eventually will be exported.) Most countries, however, are at or below the world average—even Uruguay, Argentina, and Chile, all of which are above the average for reporting countries in most measures of this kind.

Per capita income. Many of the basic patterns of the two preceding indices appear again in Figure 3.3. The United States, Canada, central and northern Europe, the Soviet Union, Australia, and New Zealand—all have high incomes per person. Most of the remaining countries of Europe, Japan, Israel, South Africa, Uruguay, Argentina, Colombia, Venezuela, Panama, Costa Rica, Mexico, Cuba, Jamaica, and Puerto Rico are at the world average or above. Of the remaining countries for which information is available, those in Latin America are near the world averages, and those in Africa and eastern and southern Asia are in one of the two lowest categories.

The classification. Keeping in mind the importance of historical development of economies and remembering the three reservations stated earlier about the term development, we are in a position to derive a map of technically advanced and less developed coun-

[2] Including per capita indices of freight and passenger traffic, transportation-route distance, motor vehicles owned, telephones used, domestic and international mail flows, newspaper circulation, energy consumed and produced, foreign trade, urbanization, cultivated land, per-unit area indices of crop yields on cultivated land, population density, transportation-route mileage, total population, birth and death rates, and infant mortality rates. This list is indicative rather than complete. See especially Norton S. Ginsburg (ed.), *Atlas of Economic Development,* The University of Chicago Press, Chicago, 1961. Professor Brian J. L. Berry, using multivariate analysis, has combined these numerous criteria into a few patterns which can be mapped. See especially, pp. 110–119 in Ginsburg's work.

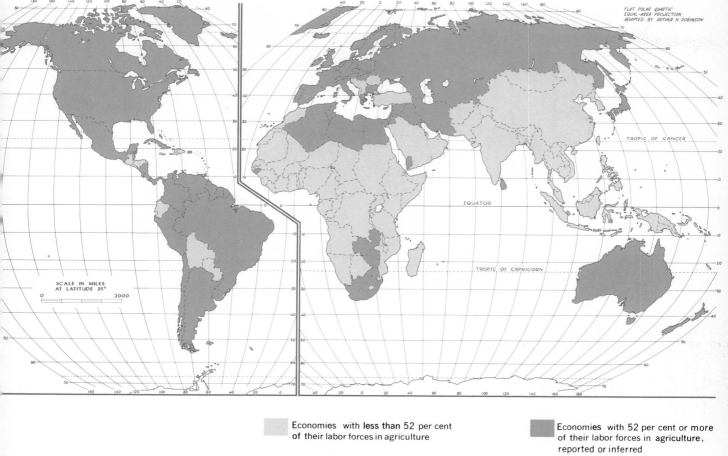

Figure 3.1 Classification of economies by per cent of labor force in agriculture. See also Table 5.1.

Economies with **less than** 52 per cent of their labor forces in agriculture

Economies with 52 per cent or **more** of their labor forces in agriculture, reported or inferred

tries. This is shown in Figure 3.4. It has been constructed on the basis of percentages of labor force in agriculture and adjusted by per capita energy consumption and per capita national income. By now it should contain few surprises. Most of the world's technically advanced countries are in northern Europe and in other areas that have been affected by European cultural heritage, especially the industrial revolution that began in Europe more than two centuries ago. Japan, although disassociated from direct European ties and impacts experienced by other countries in the technically advanced group, has been very successful both in adapting the industrial revolution to its production needs and

in reducing the rate of population growth so as to maintain a balanced population-productivity ratio. All in all, slightly less than 30 per cent of the world's population lives in these technically advanced countries.

The less developed countries, partially because of the large number of people represented and partially because of their widespread distribution over the face of the earth, represent very diverse cultural backgrounds and natural conditions. Some are pushing zealously toward technical advancement and by some measurements have achieved this status. However, the majority have not changed their traditional ways of living, including economic conditions, very much.

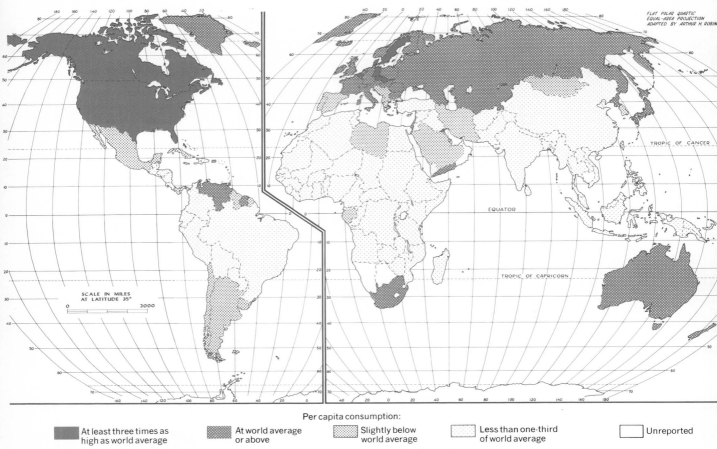

Per capita consumption:

| At least three times as high as world average | At world average or above | Slightly below world average | Less than one-third of world average | Unreported |

Figure 3.2 Classification of economies by per capita consumption of inanimate energy.

Technically advanced economies. At least twelve features may be observed in most technically advanced economies: (1) comparatively small allocation of labor force to agriculture; (2) energy available in large amounts at low cost per unit; (3) high levels of per capita gross national production and income; (4) high levels of per capita consumption; (5) relatively low rates of population growth; (6) modern, complex facilities for transportation, communication, and exchange; (7) a substantial amount of capital for investment; (8) urbanization based on production as well as exchange; (9) diversified manufacturing that accounts for an important share of the labor force; (10) numerous tertiary occupations; (11) specialization of both physical and mental labor and surpluses of both goods and services; and (12) a highly developed technology that includes ample media and methods for experiment. A thirteenth, differential regional development within a given country, is found in both technically advanced and less developed economies, but especially in the former. The first three, it will be noted, are the criteria by which we constructed Figures 3.1 to 3.3. We shall now assess the remainder.

High per capita consumption. This is the fifth of the Rostow stages of economic development, and

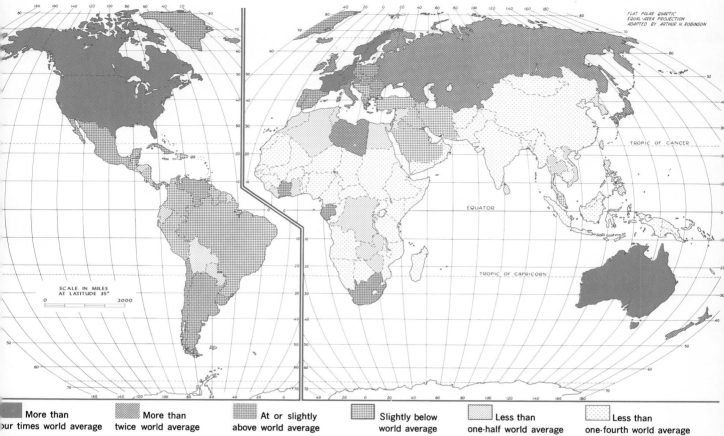

Figure 3.3 Classification of economies by per capita gross domestic products (per capita gross domestic income).

More than
our times world average

More than
twice world average

At or slightly
above world average

Slightly below
world average

Less than
one-half world average

Less than
one-fourth world average

hence it indicates rather substantial progress toward the ultimate goal. Certainly the reader who lives in the United States, Canada, northwestern Europe, or any of the other countries whose economies are classified as technically advanced is well aware of the high level of per capita consumption in his country. Individuals living in certain technically advanced economies have well over fifty times as much money to spend each year as individuals in certain less developed economies. Such a statement does not give adequate consideration to varying price levels among nations and does not make allowances for goods produced at home in many less developed economies, but it nonetheless serves to illus-

trate our point. We shall have more to say concerning per capita consumption in Chapter 4.

Slow population growth. We have seen in Figure 1.1 that rates of population growth in most technically advanced areas are low. The usual explanation is the "standard-of-living effect"; that is, when people attain a certain standard of living, they desire fewer children in order to give those children (and themselves) as many advantages as possible. To a degree this has happened in Europe and, more recently, in the United States and Canada. However, South Africa, Australia, and some other developed countries exhibit rates of pop-

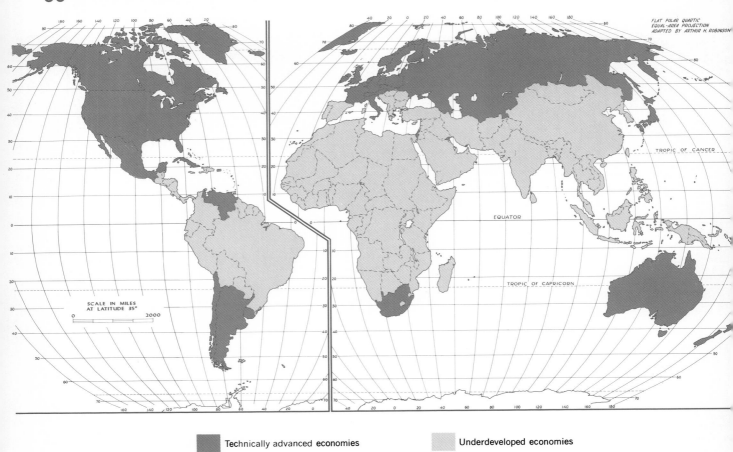

| Technically advanced economies | Underdeveloped economies |

Figure 3.4 The world's technically advanced and underdeveloped economies, based on review of Figures 3.1, 3.2, and 3.3, plus existing literature.

ulation growth higher than might be expected. South Africa and Australia have encouraged immigration, and their rates thus have been raised. There is a definite tendency for higher standards of living to be associated positively with lower rates of population growth.

Transportation, communication, and exchange.
These facilities have been described as "lumpy" in that they involve heavy investment which usually is of no value until an entire project is completed. Building a railroad line between two points, for example, involves constant investment while construction is going on; yet the line is of no value until it reaches the second point and actually begins to haul freight and passengers. The presence or absence of efficient transportation, communication, and exchange facilities therefore can be considered a good index of the degree to which an area is developed.

Investment capital. Capital may take the form of goods or money. Generating investment capital is one of the most difficult challenges of a development program. Such capital is not entirely a fixed amount, but involves also the capacity to borrow. Confidence in an economy therefore is as important as the existence of capital goods or money. A developed economy is based upon a superstructure of capital goods, especially producer goods, and is not deficient in either consumer goods or money. It is not uncommon for surplus capital from a well-developed economy to be applied to a development program or to selected aspects of such a program in a less developed economy.

Urbanization. We have shown in an earlier section that more and more of the world's people are going to be born or are being born in metropolitan areas, cities, and towns and that the vanguard of this trend can be found in technically advanced economies. Before the industrial revolution, such cities as existed usually depended largely upon surrounding countrysides for existence; they were mainly exchange centers, housing a few artisans who provided the "something extra" for the lucky who could afford to buy their wares. Modern cities in technically advanced lands are still exchange centers—retail and wholesale trade accounts for a sizable portion of the labor force in many large and small urban units in such lands—but they also generate a large measure of their own production. Such production, of course, comes appreciably from the many factories, large and small, which chambers of commerce seek as eagerly as miners of the old West once sought gold—and for the same general reason.

Diversified manufacturing. It has been said that a dynamic economy must be active in the production of primary metals (notably iron and steel), chemicals, textiles, and food. These are certainly prerequisite materials upon which further output is based. The output of fabricated products, transportation equipment, buildings, etc., is based upon primary metals; an almost innumerable and rapidly growing list of diverse items are based upon chemicals; the output of apparel, upholstery, and related fabrics and nonfabrics is based upon textiles; and human existence itself is dependent upon the production of food. Perhaps we should add to this list the growing electronics industry, which, in all its ramifications, is assuming a pronounced importance in modern industrial output. An economy deficient in any of these industries would find competition difficult with an economy containing a complement.[3]

These five, however, are but the foundation industries. Upon them rest a marked number and variety of specialized activities, each of which has a definite destiny to fulfill in a modern economy. Individual factories may specialize, but a truly competitive economy in today's scheme of things must have a diversified manufacturing structure.

Numerous tertiary occupations. A recheck of Figure 1.2 will indicate the extent to which tertiary, or service, occupations characterize technically advanced economies. The resident of a technically advanced country sometimes takes for granted the number or variety of services available for himself, his family, and even his dog.

Specialization. The presence of tertiary activities is made possible largely through specialization and consequent surplus production in primary and secondary activities. Once brought into existence, tertiary activities themselves have become highly specialized. The trend, which is continuing, is based on the very simple idea that a specialist can do a job better and, in the long run, less expensively (especially when aided by a machine) than the generalist can. So that jack-of-all-trades, the "Jonathan Jo" of A. A. Milne's whimsical child's verse, is disappearing in technically advanced countries, but is very much present in the less developed societies.

Technology and experimentation. The importance of the first of these terms is shown by the fact that we are speaking of countries that are or are not technically advanced. Modern production is based upon demonstrated results—whether in factories, on farms, in transportation, in clerical offices, or in any of a sizable list of additional economic ingredients. Although the chemical and electronic industries lead in this respect, most dynamic industries reinvest substantial portions of their gross returns in research. The net result is a continuous change in methods and tools—an unceasing adoption of something just a little bit better. Assuming general stability in an economy, we may take the pace of such change as an indication of the degree to which that economy is vibrant and strong and intends to remain so.

Internal regional differences. Both technically advanced and less developed countries may have inter-

---

[3] To those who think otherwise, particularly in respect to food industries, and who cite the United Kingdom as an example, we answer: (1) Although that country imports much food, it processes a large quantity of that food domestically, and (2) lack of adequate domestic food supply *has* been a handicap in the United Kingdom's recent ability to compete.

nal regions with economic conditions quite different from those of the entire country. Many technically advanced countries are becoming increasingly concerned with their slow-growth regions—regions of economic stress, development areas, redevelopment areas, or whatever they may be called. As more people move into cities, more and more of the countryside may be regarded as neglected. The United States has classified one-third of its total land area, containing over one-fifth of its population, as in need of redevelopment. There is a fine point of consideration here: We ought not to confuse areas experiencing *temporary stress* with areas which never have been developed very fully and may lack developmental potential.

Less developed economies. As a generalization, we can look for conditions in less developed economies that are the reverse of those discussed above. With respect to the last point, we may find an internal range of regional economic development in less developed as well as in technically advanced countries.

Why not, then, merely reverse the adverse conditions that hamper less developed countries? Or, stated differently, is economic growth a process that can be activated at any time and in any place? This question raises others. Are less developed areas merely places that have been bypassed in such a process, or series of processes, of economic advance? If such a process exists, is it merely economic, or is it broader; does it include other cultural considerations? Can the past experience of technically advanced nations be applied without fundamental change to improving less developed areas?

No universally accepted answers exist. Some people believe ardently in process: just plug an economy into a process formula, and progress will occur. Others believe that if such a process exists, it is so general that knowledge of it will provide only general guidelines for planning in a specific area. We consider here that the marks of process are distinguishable but that individual less developed areas are confronted with conditions and problems that either (1) did not exist in countries now classified as technically advanced when, during the past two centuries, they were emerging from underdeveloped circumstances or (2) were not so important then as now. Some of these conditions and problems are *economic dualism, cultural dualism or pluralism, differing atti-*

tudes toward achievement, very high man-land ratios, and dependence upon a world market over which each less developed country has little control.

Economic dualism. Many less developed countries have technically advanced and peasant economic sectors that function almost independently of one another. The technically advanced sector may or may not be financed or controlled from abroad, but it is highly oriented to the world marketplace. It usually involves agriculture or mining, but may include other activities. It is administered efficiently, employing specific amounts of labor for specific amounts of capital investment. The peasant sector, on the other hand, usually has evolved slowly over the centuries, under indigent cultures. Its capital investment comes from domestic sources. Its markets are mainly domestic. In short, its full cycle—investment, consumption, and production, and exchange—is domestic. Its use of labor, frequently in family agriculture, may be inefficient, so that a given amount of land may be called upon to support as many people as are in an extended family. Underemployment and unemployment usually exist in this sector.

The technically advanced and underdeveloped sectors do have one important relationship with each other: The advanced sector depends upon the peasant sector for most of its labor. Because of high rates of population growth, that supply usually is so abundant that wages, even in the technically advanced sector, remain low. To the degree that economic advance involves integration of various sectors into a smoothly functioning economy—and history has recorded this to be a high degree—the presence of two or more dissimilar sectors within a country is a barrier to such advance.

Cultural dualism or pluralism. This problem, sometimes referred to as *sociological dualism* or *pluralism,* results from the presence within a country of a substantial number of representatives of two or more cultures. Barriers of custom, language, religion, and other cultural traits, sometimes accompanied by intercultural frictions, may be serious obstacles to economic advance in such a country.

Two questions may arise in the reader's mind at this point: (1) Why separate economic dualism from cultural dualism or pluralism? (2) Did not cultural pluralism exist in parts of Europe in the early phases of the industrial revolution there, so that European experience can be used in treating this problem in countries still less developed?

Concerning the first question, the answer is "yes—but." An economy is part of a culture. However, one school of thought holds that economic conditions are so important in the cause and cure of underdevelopment that only these need be given serious consideration. A second school holds that the reverse is true—that many schemes for economic development have failed because other cultural considerations were neglected. It is the authors' belief that both approaches have merit. The basic causes of underdevelopment are economic. Yet the planner who gives insufficient attention to cultural attitudes and beliefs may fail to implement his economic objectives. Also, the development of an area ultimately extends beyond economic objectives to such goals as appreciation by many people of art, music, literature, and other noneconomic components of a culture. Thus, while economic objectives are paramount in the early stages of a country's advance, existing noneconomic aspects of a culture or cultures must be given close attention by economic planners. Meanwhile, broader, noneconomic goals are logical ultimate objectives of any plan for development. Economic development is but a means to an end.

Concerning the second question, it is true that cultural differences did exist prior to this century and that European experience can be helpful. However, most countries involved in the European industrial revolution were very small, and their experience will be of somewhat limited value to large less developed countries, such as India, where cultural pluralism is especially serious.

Differing attitudes toward achievement. A major problem in many less developed areas is the lack of a desire on the part of the people to achieve, or to "get ahead." This desire, in turn, frequently is stimulated by hope of material gain. It is a fact that some people in less developed countries will seek employment, sometimes far from home, but give that employment up after they have saved a bit of money. They then return home and stay there until the money is gone, at which time they look for work again. We would be overgeneralizing if we were to imply that this problem is extremely serious in all less developed countries; it is not. Nor is the problem confined to less developed areas; some residents of technically advanced countries have little desire to achieve. However, the problem is sufficiently grave that developing a desire to achieve is given serious consideration by many planners and consultants who are responsible for attempting to improve conditions in less developed areas.

High man-land ratios and rates of population growth. We mentioned previously that population sizes and rates of growth are particularly high in some less developed areas. Here is a major difference between many less developed economies of today and those of two centuries ago in Europe and elsewhere that since have become technically advanced. Nor have most less developed areas done much to slow this rate of growth. Instead, they have concentrated on increasing production—all too frequently, agricultural production—so that they are merely feeding the additional mouths, and not always doing this very well. Domestic financing of producer goods thus is difficult if not impossible, so that economic conditions in many less developed countries are not improving as much as they would if the rates of population growth were slowed.

Heavy dependence upon world markets. It is not uncommon for less developed countries to depend heavily upon sales into world markets as a source of national income. This dependence frequently narrows to income available from one or two products—and these products usually stem from agriculture or mining. The principal buyers of products from less developed countries are technically advanced nations. To a substantial degree, the world markets are "buyer's markets"; demand is more limited than supply, certainly potential supply. During the past century, suppliers of certain commodities have made several attempts to form combines and thereby regulate both prices and the volume of movement. These invariably have failed because buyers have found alternative sources of supply. The majority of less developed lands are thus caught up in a financial eddy from which they derive substantial revenue but over which they have little control.

Chapter 4

The Economic Environment: Structures and Patterns of Consumption

The Introduction to this book contains the statement that consumption is *a* basic stimulant, if not *the* basic stimulant, to economic activity. We are born with the desire—in fact, the need—to consume food and water. As we mature, that desire includes want as well, and especially in the more complex economies, it involves social as well as individual needs and wants. However, consumption does not result from desire alone, but from *demand,* which is desire plus purchasing power. In commercial economies, that purchasing power can be measured in terms of *gross national product,* which is the sum of all goods produced and services rendered in a given economy. In subsistence economies, where use of currency and cost accounting is not so active, such measurement must consist of estimates rather than calculations.

Nevertheless, we can benefit from examining the geographic distribution of consumption throughout the world, its internal structure within specific nations and economies, and its role in technically advanced and less developed lands. Unfortunately, we are not yet able to secure detailed inventories of consumption on a worldwide basis. Most appraisals are based instead upon income, which indicates general capacity to consume. Even data on income are reported reliably for only about one-half of the world's countries and for less than one-half its population; we must depend upon estimates for coverage of the remaining economies, nearly all of which are usually classified as underdeveloped. Even so, some interesting implications and indications can be discovered.

Uneven Global Distribution

At this stage of our reasoning, we are interested in *absolute,* or *aggregate,* consumption, both in the entire world and in its individual component economies. It does not matter for the time being whether the commodities supplying this consumption to any specific economy are domestic or imported. Lacking complete inventories on such consumption, we can approximate it roughly by multiplying per capita income (here interpreted as equaling per capita gross domestic product—GDP) by total population, thus obtaining potential consuming capacity at any given time. The results of one such approximation are shown in Table 4.1.

TABLE 4.1

ESTIMATED CONSUMING CAPACITIES OF SELECTED
BLOCS AND NATIONS

Bloc or country	Population (in millions)	Per capita GDP (in U.S. dollars)	Index of consuming capacity (per capita GDP multiplied by total population, in billions)
EEC (original six only; excluding new members and associate members)*	189.3	2,560	484.5
United States*	204.8	4,734	969.6
Japan*	103.4	1,911	197.6
West Germany*	61.5	3,034	186.7
France*	50.8	2,901	147.3
United Kingdom*	55.7	2,128	118.5
Italy*	53.7	1,727	92.7
Canada*	21.4	3,676	78.7
India	539.4	91	49.1
Australia*	12.5	2,916	36.6
Brazil	95.3	362	34.5
Mexico*	50.5	668	33.8
Sweden*	8.0	4,055	32.6
Netherlands*	13.0	2,353	30.6
Belgium*	9.7	2,633	25.5
Argentina*	23.4	1,053	24.6
Switzerland*	6.3	3,135	19.7
South Africa*	20.7	838	17.3
Denmark*	4.9	3,141	15.4
Philippines	38.5	361	13.9
Turkey	35.2	363	12.8
New Zealand*	2.8	2,188	6.1
Peru	13.6	398	5.4
Israel*	2.9	1,836	5.3
Ecuador	6.1	270	1.6
Uganda	9.8	131	1.3
Honduras	2.6	277	0.71
Paraguay	2.4	249	0.60
Iceland*	0.20	2,387	0.48

Note: Communist nations are not included in the source for GDP. However, per capita GDP has been estimated at $1,000 per year in the Soviet Union and at $100 in China. Multiply these by recent populations of each country (241.7 million for the Soviet Union and 850 million for China) results in a consuming-capacity index of 241.7 for the Soviet Union and 85.0 for China.

*Technically advanced nations or blocs.

Source: Several sources for population as of 1971 or closest year. Figures for per capita GDP, calculated at factor cost and official exchange rates, are from *Yearbook of National Accounts Statistics, 1971,* United Nations, New York, 1973, vol. 3, pp. 3–7. Gross domestic product is a conservative measurement when applied to technically advanced countries in that it excludes net receipts from abroad. If calculated by gross national product, the table would indicate even greater differences between per capita incomes in the leading technically advanced countries and those in other countries.

Although the table must be interpreted cautiously, especially in that it does not allow for differences in purchasing power among economies, it nonetheless contains two very important implications for economic geographers: (1) Aggregate consuming capacity depends upon total population as well as upon per capita income, and (2) technically advanced nations, notably the United States, dominate as potential consumers.

The importance of total population as well as per capita consumption is indicated by the positions of specific countries, especially those of the twenty leaders shown in the table. The United States, with a high per capita income as well as a large population, unquestionably is in the forefront. Most of the other leading nations have at least moderately high per capita incomes and populations. However, China and India have per capita incomes of $100 or less a year and yet, because of their large populations, possess high aggregate demand. Mexico, Brazil, and Turkey are also prominent in consuming capacity, because of either large populations or relatively high per capita incomes. On the other hand, Canada, Australia, Sweden, Belgium, the Netherlands, and Switzerland have comparatively small populations but are among the leaders in aggregate consuming capacity because of their high per capita incomes.

The dominance of technically advanced nations in aggregate consumption is indicated by the marked differences in the indices of consuming capacity between technically advanced and less developed nations as shown in Table 4.1. Lacking complete data, we cannot be certain just how much of the world's total consumption is accounted for by the technically advanced group. However, if we assume that the average per capita income for the world is $600 per year—a generous figure in view of the data shown in Table 4.1 and the fact that most nations not in the table are less developed—the index number for the 3.7 billion world inhabitants in 1970 would be about 2220. The three leading technically advanced blocs and nations—the United States, the European Economic Community (EEC), and the Soviet Union—would account for over three-fourths of that capacity, and the United States alone for about 44 per cent.

The world's technically advanced nations thus can be visualized as Gargantuan consumers. Their domestic economies supply part of, but not all, the commodities that they consume, and they are substantial importers. (Some, of course, are also substantial exporters.) A marked decrease in their capacities to consume would result in a slowing down of production, not only at home, but also in dependent economies that export to them and receive imports from them.

The relation of United States consumption to the well-being of its own and other economies can scarcely be overemphasized. This one nation's capacity to consume is so high that, despite its outstanding ability to supply most of that consumption from domestic output, it is still the world leader in international trade. The statement has been made that when the United States sneezes, the world catches pneumonia. Until the volume of consumption becomes more evenly distributed throughout the world, the markets of the United States and other technically advanced nations, most of them in the non-Communist realm of political and economic influence, will continue to be key considerations in the functioning of the world's economies.

However, Western Europe and Japan have moved into a position of prominence in consumption, and the Soviet Union and Eastern Europe are becoming increasingly active. As can be seen in Table 4.1, the consuming capacity of the EEC bloc is nearly one-fourth of the world total. With an industrial structure effectively rebuilt since World War II and a rising level of living, Western Europe offers every evidence of embarking upon a policy of high mass consumption without precedent there, although with a resemblance to the high mass consumption in the United States and Canada. Japan's increase in level of living since World War II has been even more striking; this one country probably accounts for nearly 9 per cent of the world's consuming capacity. The Soviet Union, now that its economy rests firmly on a manufacturing base, is making consumer goods available in increasing numbers to its inhabitants, and some of the countries in Eastern Europe are following a similar course. All in all, the Soviet Union probably accounts for more than one-tenth of all consuming capacity today, and Eastern Europe for one-twentieth.

Another view of volume and trends in consuming capacity is not so satisfactory. The world's less developed economies have not increased their absolute consuming capacity since World War II nearly so much as the technically advanced countries. Although there have been some exceptions, one of the truly pressing problems of our time is the widening gap in consuming capacity between the world's technically advanced and less developed economies.

Structures (Sectors)

So far, we have examined overall capacities to consume, but not structures or sectors (classifications by income, age, nationality, etc.). We stated in the Introduction that *structural* (or *sectoral*) and *spatial* (or *pattern*) relationships *exist* and are *reciprocal.* Components of a structure or sector are not abstract; they are located somewhere on earth. Spatial patterns, in turn, are not autonomous or free-floating, but very much related to their respective structures or sectors. This is true not only of consumption but also of essentially all features studied in economic geography.

Consumption varies among cultures, nations, and societies, not only in volume but also in structure. Particularly conspicuous in this context are differences in emphasis upon producer as compared with consumer goods and upon personal expenditures for necessities as compared with luxuries.

In this Industrial Age, a nation that consumes in large volume usually must first produce in large volume—and modern production requires expensive capital equipment. A substantial share of consumption therefore involves producer goods, notably in the technically advanced countries where such goods are concentrated. Less developed countries tend to spend higher shares of their incomes on consumer goods.

However, proportionate expenditures for producer goods within a given economy are only moderately high if that economy enjoys the benefits of past capital accumulation, preferably over a long period. It is when a less developed economy decides to become more advanced, technically and economically, that an extraordinary percentage of national income must be diverted to producer goods, especially if that economy is unable to attract substantial amounts of foreign currency in the form of direct investment, loans, or other aid. This is one important reason why less developed economies find the transition period to technical advance so difficult.

The two-thirds of the world's people living under conditions of technical and economic underdevelopment, and some living under conditions of technical advance as well, think not so much in terms of producer and consumer goods as in terms of how to get enough to eat each day. Such thinking has been generalized by the German statistician Engel into a so-called *law of consumption,* which states that poorer families and societies tend to spend a much higher percentage of their respective incomes on food than more wealthy individuals and groups. The law is applicable to lower-income groups in technically advanced countries as well as to less developed societies, but is reflected particularly in national statistics of the latter. Figure 4.1 tends to substantiate Engel's law on a global scale.

Despite their relatively high percentage of income spent on food, over one-half of the world's people do

Figure 4.1 Percentage of per capita income spent for food, housing, clothing, and other purposes in selected countries. The figures include estimated income for agricultural products consumed on farms. The figure can be considered a documentation of Engel's law of consumption. Note that housing, especially, receives a much smaller share of income in underdeveloped than in technically advanced nations.

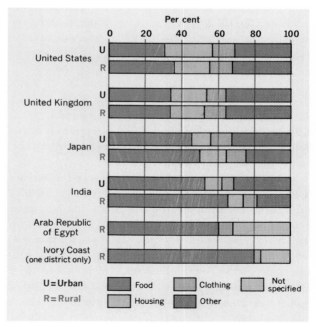

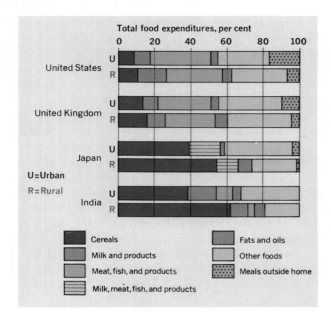

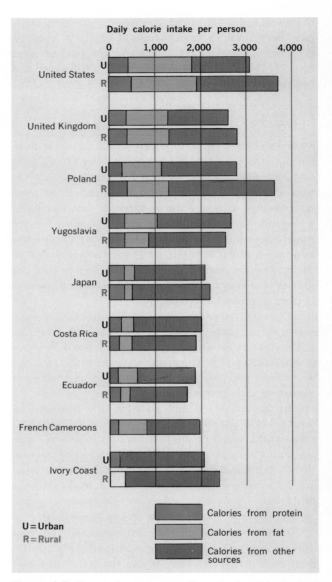

not get as many as 2,250 calories daily, and an additional one-sixth live on fewer than 2,750. Only one-third—essentially the same one-third that live in technically advanced societies—take in as many as 2,750 calories daily, the lowest amount considered necessary to maintain minimum health in an average twenty-five-year-old (Fig. 4.2).

Patterns

Furthermore, the structures of consumption show different patterns when mapped on a worldwide scale. Figure 4.2 shows the differences in overall calorie intake, and Figure 4.3 shows dietary patterns.

Consumption in technically advanced countries tends not only to be large in volume but also to involve substantial amounts of producer goods and consumer luxuries. Aggregate consumption in less developed countries varies markedly with total population and tends to involve fewer producer goods and more consumer necessities, especially food. Exceptions to these generalizations are most numerous and pronounced in economies in which efforts are being made to move from less developed conditions to higher levels of livelihood.

Figure 4.2 Proportionate expenditure for food, including home-produced food, and per capita calorie intake in selected countries. Note the high percentage spent on milk in India, where milk and its products are scarce. Note also the high percentage of expenditures for cereals in India and Japan. In the longer graph, data for rural Ecuador and the Ivory Coast are from only one village in each country. (After the State of Food and Agriculture, various issues.)

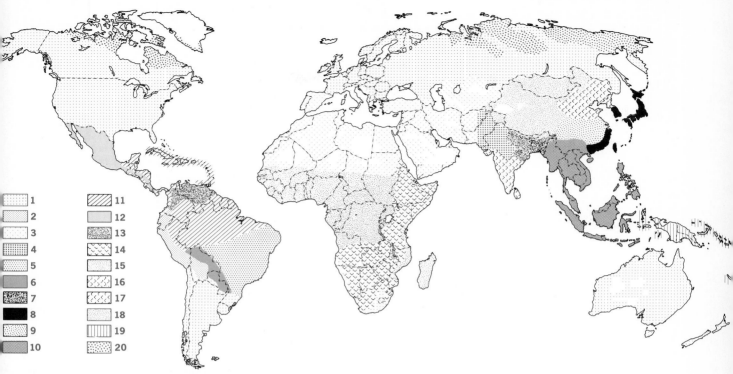

Figure 4.3 World dietary patterns

Major source(s) of calories*	Important source(s) of protein†
1 Wheat, potato, sugar, meat, fats and oils	Beef, pork, mutton, dairy products
2 Wheat, millet and sorghum, barley, rice	Dry beans, dry peas, chick-peas, lentils
3 Wheat, maize, barley, rice, fats and oils	Beef, pork, mutton, dry beans, dry broad beans, chick-peas
4 Wheat, maize, barley, potato	Dry beans
5 Wheat, maize, rice, sugar	Beef, dry beans
6 Wheat, maize, cassava	Beef, dry beans
7 Rice	Dry beans, dry peas
8 Rice, wheat	Fish, soybeans
9 Rice, maize, sweet potato	Pork, fish, soybeans, peanuts
10 Rice, maize, sweet potato, coconuts, cassava	Fish, soybeans, peanuts, dry beans
11 Rice, maize, bananas, yams, cassava, sugar	Dry beans, dry peas
12 Maize	Dry beans
13 Maize, wheat, potato	Beef, dry beans

Continues on page 70.

Figure 4.3 Continued

Major source(s) of calories*	Important source(s) of protein†
14 Maize, millet, and sorghum	Dry beans, dry peas, dry broad beans, chick-peas, lentils
15 Millet and sorghum, maize, rice, yams, cocoyams, sweet potato, cassava, bananas	Dry beans, dry peas, peanuts
16 Millet and sorghum, rice, cassava, coconuts	Fish, dry beans, lentils, peanuts
17 Millet and sorghum, wheat, maize, potato	Pork, mutton, soybeans, peanuts
18 Barley	Dairy products, mutton, goat
19 Cassava, yams, taro, bananas, coconuts	Fish, pork
20 Animal fats, wheat	Fish, local game animals

*Major sources derived from starchy staples and other sources where applicable.
† In addition to protein derived from grains. (After Herbert G. Kariel, ''A Proposed Classification of Diet,'' *Annals of the Association of American Geographers,* vol. 56, 1966, pp. 74–75.

Underconsumption and Underproduction

For technically advanced lands, the Industrial Age is fast becoming an age of automation. Production and exchange are increasingly carried on by electronically controlled machines and decreasingly by physical and mental labor of human beings. But there is no such thing as push-button consumption—at least, not of most consumer goods. Yet consumption is a major stimulant to economies, and should it decline in technically advanced countries, the productive machinery soon would become glutted by mechanically produced merchandise. The fear of underconsumption is thus more or less constant in some technically advanced societies. Man there virtually has been returned to the Garden of Eden, where his major task in life is to consume. Now, however, unless he harvests all the fruit, the orchard will sicken and perhaps die.

Less developed countries, in contrast, are faced with the sobering possibility of continued underproduction. For them, a major problem is not how to keep consumption at a sufficiently high rate to maintain or expand production but how to produce enough—even enough food—to meet life's minimum requirements. For them, the Malthusian doctrine has real meaning.

Chapter 5

The Economic Environment: Structures and Patterns of Production

In the two preceding chapters we emphasized levels of economic development in the world, and structures and patterns of consumption, both viewed with particular attention to the worldwide scene. In this chapter we shall retain our global perspective in an examination of structures (or sectors) and patterns of production.

Structures (Sectors)

Although the complex process of production necessarily involves a wide range of structures and different levels of observation, we shall emphasize here the global perspective and the sectoral classifications of primary, secondary, and tertiary activities which were presented initially in the Introduction. Because the concept of a quaternary activity has not yet been sufficiently widely accepted to merit individual classification in census data, it will not be included in this chapter.

Although not all countries have conducted thorough census inventories, and therefore a full range of data are not yet available, a careful estimate of the allocation of the world's labor force is contained in Table 5.1. Well over one-half of the world's labor force is engaged in agriculture and grazing, with only an estimated 1 per cent involved in grazing. The other primary activities, like grazing, employ very small proportions of the world's labor force—generally at or below 1 per cent each. Over one-fourth of the world's labor force is involved in tertiary occupations, and nearly 20 per cent in manufacturing and construction. Possibly the figure for agriculture is low because the countries which have not furnished data tend to rely heavily on agriculture.

Among the technically advanced nations are Canada, the United States, the United Kingdom, and France. Here, agriculture began to decline as the predominant component of the labor force in the last century, and it has continued to decline since that time. At present, only 7 per cent of the labor force in Canada is engaged in agriculture, 4.2 per cent in the United States, 3 per cent in the United Kingdom, and 8.6 per cent in France. Manufacturing has accounted for a

TABLE 5.1
ALLOCATION OF THE WORLD'S
LABOR FORCE*

Productive occupations	Per cent
Agriculture and grazing†	51.9
Manufacturing and handicrafts	19.4
Minerals extraction and quarrying	1.0
Fishing and hunting	0.5
Forest-products industries	0.5
All other occupations	26.7
Total	100.0

*The world's labor force is here considered to amount to 40 per cent of its population.
† Data on grazing are not separated from those on agriculture in source materials; however, it seems unlikely that the grazing labor force amounts to more than 1 per cent of the world's total labor force. A substantial portion of persons in many developing countries are reported as "looking for work" and are not included in the above breakdown.

consistently high proportion of employment in these four countries in the past century, but has begun to decline slightly, at least in relative terms. Clearly, the tertiary, or service, activities are the key group for future employment in these and other technically advanced countries.

Meanwhile, agriculture is still a mainstay of support for countries in early stages of development. In India, for example, the proportion of the labor force devoted to agriculture is still very high—over 70 per cent of the labor force. The importance of the secondary, and especially of the tertiary, activities is correspondingly reduced. Also, many people are seeking work in most developing countries—but in vain.

In countries on the threshold of technical advance, such as Mexico and Yugoslavia, agriculture accounts for a high but relatively declining share of productive employment, and secondary and tertiary activities are rising.

Urbanism is not so predominant in less developed economies as in technically advanced ones (pp. 23 to 26), and most rural people in less developed places are farmers, not "rural nonfarm" dwellers.

Primary Activities

Patterns

The patterns of world production range markedly. Some, particularly agriculture and grazing, which require large amounts of space for each unit of production, can be mapped globally, as is shown in Figure 5.1. (For comparison, note also Fig. 5.2, showing frost-free days.) All the other primary occupations, and the secondary and tertiary occupations, tend to occupy very small individual sites per unit of production, and any global map of their distribution necessarily is even more generalized than a map of agricultural and grazing types and regions. Nevertheless, we can show the areas of mineral exploitation (Fig. 5.3) and of fishing (Fig. 5.4). Forest-products industries are known to be especially intensive in the area once occupied by middle-latitude mixed forest and high-latitude evergreens (Fig. 5.5), especially where large urban markets are not far removed.

Agricultural Types and Regions

The portion of the earth's surface devoted to agriculture has been subdivided into a number of regions on the basis of types of practice. One such classification is shown in Figure 5.1. It involves mainly three criteria: (1) the degree of commercialization, or tendency to exchange finished products; (2) the type of crop or combination of crops and animals; and (3) the intensity of land use. Eight types and their regional expressions are to be considered here: (1) primitive-subsistence agriculture, shifting and sedentary; (2) intensive-subsistence agriculture; (3) plantation agriculture; (4) mediterranean agriculture; (5) commercial grain farming; (6) commercial crop and livestock farming; (7) commercial dairy farming; and (8) commercial gardening and fruit culture. These eight types provide livelihood for well over one-half of the world's labor force. Two other types and regions, nomadic herding and livestock ranching, provide livelihood for an additional 1 per cent. These, however, are grazing rather than agriculture.

Primitive-subsistence agriculture, shifting and sedentary. The criterion characterizing this type of

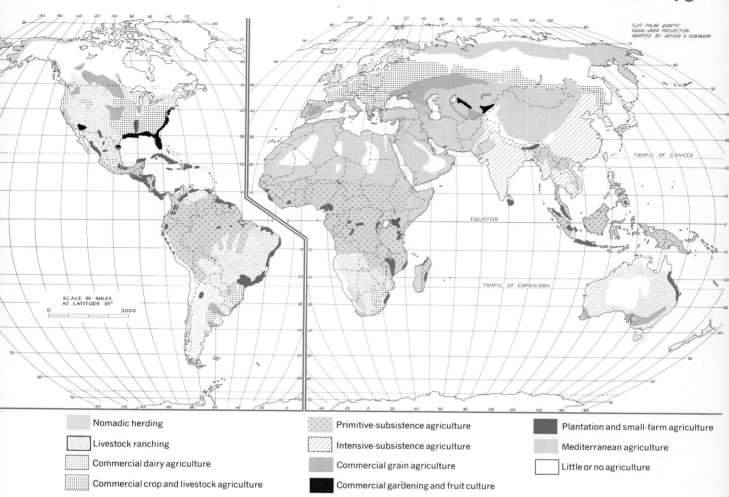

Figure 5.1 Types of agricultural and pastoral land use and their world distribution. Some important areas of commercial production, such as commercial gardening and fruit culture, do not appear on this highly generalized map because they occupy very little land, especially near large urban concentrations in Europe and North America. Commercial dairy agriculture also exists in many places too small to be shown here.

agriculture is that it is primarily a rather crude production for subsistence, and few of its harvested crops enter either the domestic or world markets.

Production structure and methods. As the name implies, this is a hand-to-mouth, simple agriculture. To the degree that farms are surveyed and identified, their

sizes tend to be small (Fig. 5.6). The tools range in complexity from a stick in a human hand to an animal-drawn plow. In very elementary cultures, planting is done in existing forest clearings, usually by gouging holes in the ground with a stick and inserting seeds among endemic shorter types of vegetation. In some areas the taller trees are burned or hacked away in

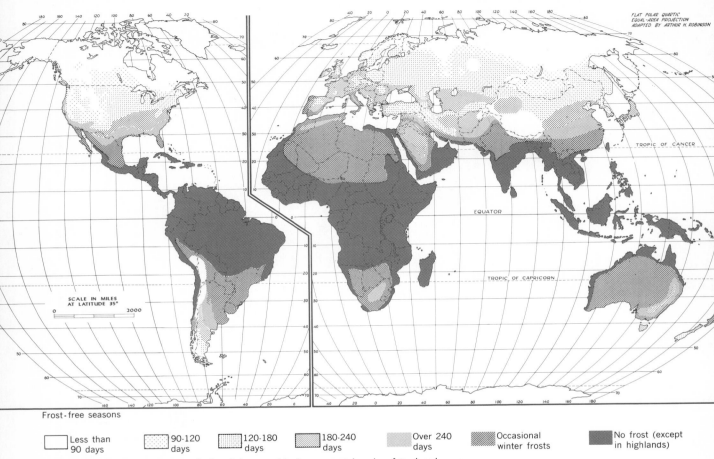

Frost-free seasons

☐ Less than 90 days   ▦ 90-120 days   ▦ 120-180 days   ▦ 180-240 days   ▦ Over 240 days   ▦ Occasional winter frosts   ▦ No frost (except in highlands)

Figure 5.2 Frost-free periods of the world. At current levels of technology, agriculture is not usually practical where the frost-free period is less than 90 days. Note the large portions of Canada and the Soviet Union thereby restricted from present-day agriculture. Except where irrigation is possible, little agriculture is carried on in very dry areas. Subfreezing temperatures and aridity thus are the principal natural constraints to agriculture.

small clearings; these are abandoned when the soil becomes depleted after only a few years' use, and the cultivators move to new clearings and new homes. In yet other areas, the fields are permanently cleared but are rotated, so that one field may lie fallow for a year or two. In still other areas, the fields are planted and harvested continuously, but their yields remain low. Fertilization in the modern sense is rare throughout regions of this type of agriculture, and market exchange is usually limited to small amounts of produce ex-

changed in local bazaars. Only a trickle of their products reaches the world markets. In a few places, usually under foreign encouragement, some crops are planted for commercial harvest. These include palm trees planted for their coconuts or palm oil and cacao trees which yield cocoa. However, most crops are consumed domestically, including the harvests from such well-known plants as corn (or maize), sorghums, dry (or upland) rice, cassava (or manioc), beans, peas, peanuts, and varieties of squash and melons. Animals, found

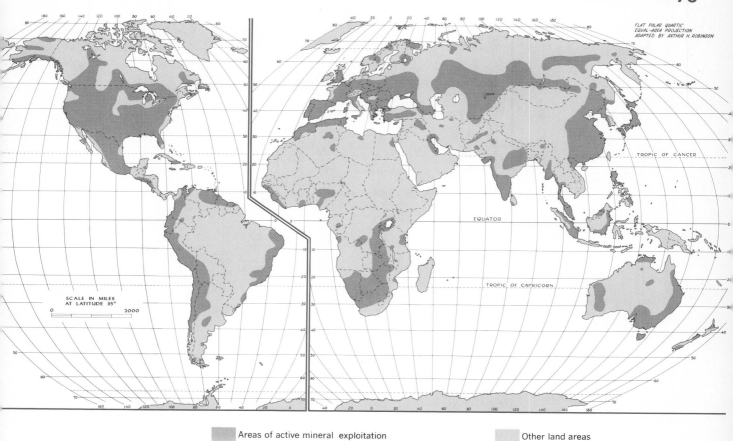

Areas of active mineral exploitation   Other land areas

Figure 5.3 Major areas of active mineral extraction. Note that technically advanced lands have been and are being thoroughly worked. The developing areas are not yet so fully exploited, and activity there tends to be near coasts from which ships can carry their mineral products to the technically advanced countries.

principally among the more culturally advanced of the small but numerous societies in regions of subsistence agriculture, are mostly sheep, goats, and cattle and are located in semiarid lands rather than forests. The uplands and mountains, particularly in Latin America, are the habitat of the llama and alpaca as well as more familiar species.

World distribution. Primitive-subsistence agriculture is found extensively throughout the tropical and some of the subtropical portions of all landforms in the low latitudes. As a general classification, it en-

compasses more of the earth's surface than any other agricultural type. In terms of land actually cultivated, however, it is comparatively unimportant; only a small fraction of the world's tilled land is situated in areas of primitive-subsistence agriculture.

Association with populations. The occupance of regions of subsistence agriculture is prevailingly sparse and rural. It contains small pockets, however, of rather heavy population density, usually in coastal locations and in some mountain and upland valleys. Some of these pockets are experiencing a rather marked popula-

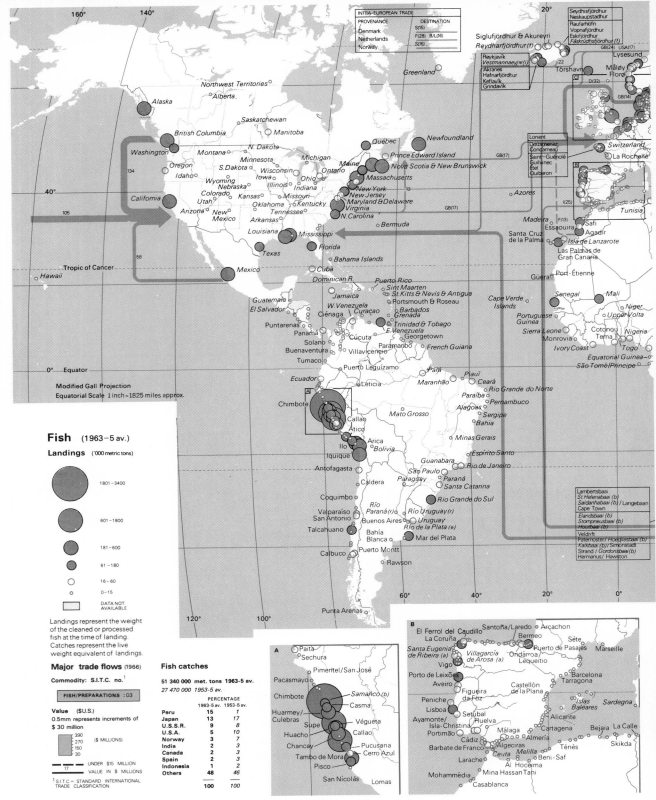

Figure 5.4 World catch of all marine life. (After *Oxford Economic Atlas*, 4th ed., p. 27.)

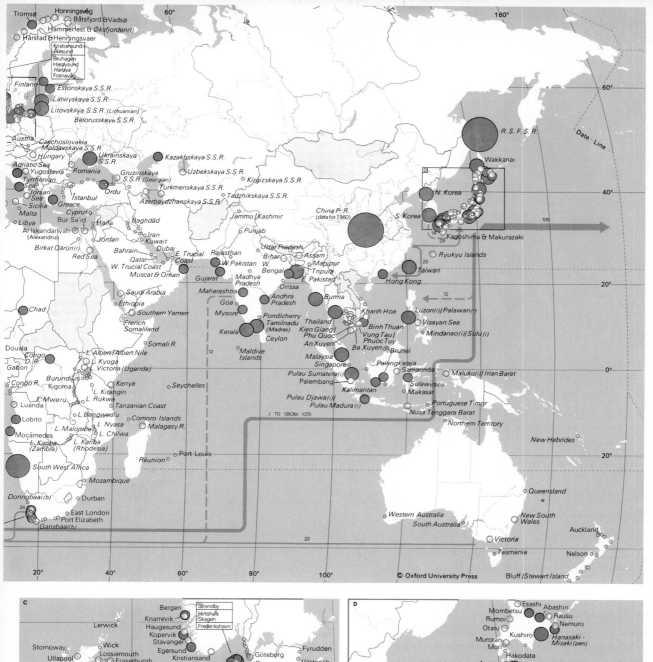
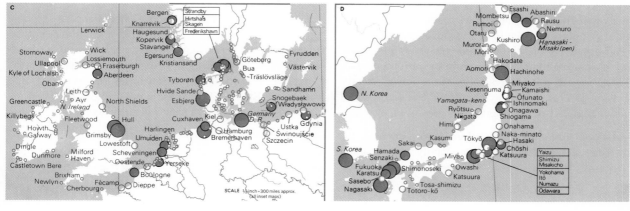

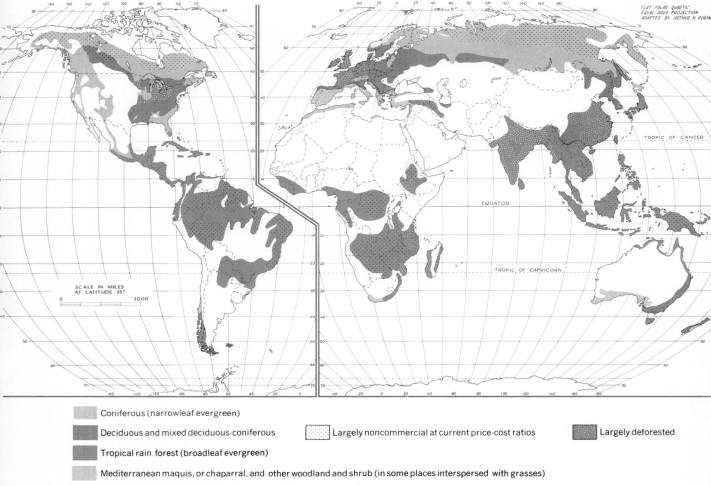

Coniferous (narrowleaf evergreen)

Deciduous and mixed deciduous-coniferous

Tropical rain forest (broadleaf evergreen)

Mediterranean maquis, or chaparral, and other woodland and shrub (in some places interspersed with grasses)

Largely noncommercial at current price-cost ratios

Largely deforested

Figure 5.5 World distribution of primeval forests, present-day commercial forests, and deforested areas.

tion growth that is coincident with, and a part of, the general population growth of less developed lands. In the more sparsely populated areas, the growth does not seem to be pronounced, although information on some of these areas is not always complete. Country-to-city migration is also apparent, chiefly in the same small effective areas of dense population pressure.

Association with political units and economies.
Only a few political units are essentially encompassed by regions of primitive-subsistence agriculture. The

most conspicuous examples are Zaïre, People's Republic of the Congo, the Central African Republic, and a number of countries along the tropical coast of western Africa; Guyana, Surinam, and French Guiana in South America; and Malaysia in southeastern Asia. Portions of Brazil, Ethiopia, Indonesia, and still other countries extend into this type of agricultural region.

Natural environmental and cultural associations. This type of agriculture is found mainly in tropical rain-forest climate along with tropical rain-forest

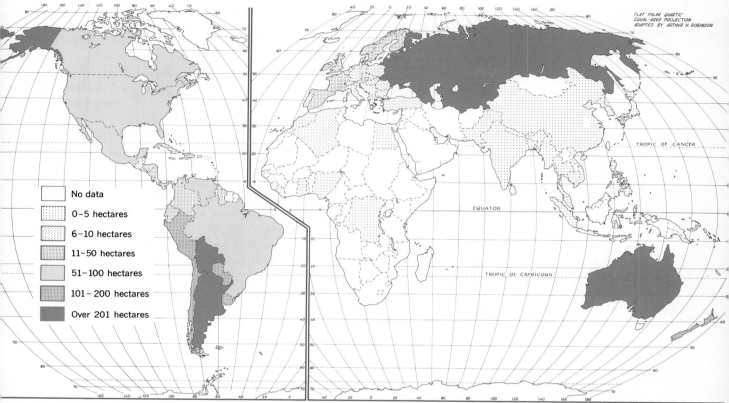

Figure 5.6 Size of farm. Sizes shown on this map are national averages; substantial variations within each country may be concealed. One hectare equals 2.471 acres. (After David Grigg, ''The Geography of Farm Size: A Preliminary Survey,'' *Economic Geography*, **42**:205–235, 1966.)

vegetation on red and yellow soils. It extends especially into the tropical savanna climate, along with associated tropical savanna vegetational and soil types. Notably in Latin America, it reaches also into undifferentiated highland climate, and in Africa into low-latitude semiarid as well as undifferentiated highland climates. It is found in all categories of landforms, although it is best developed where well-drained flat land exists. Its growing season is free of frost except in higher elevations (Figs. 5.1 and 5.2).

Inasmuch as this type of agriculture is so widely distributed, it necessarily involves many societies of differing cultures. In both hemispheres, these societies tend to be small and aloof from more intricate civilizations as well as from one another. A substantial number are tribally organized. Most of the waking hours of individuals are spent in livelihood activities, of which agriculture is the most complex; other activities include crude forest-products industries, hunting, fishing, and grazing.

Intensive-subsistence agriculture. This classification, like primitive-subsistence agriculture, is based chiefly on the comparatively small exchange of finished products, which tend to be fashioned at home mainly for home consumption. As the name implies, intensive-subsistence agriculture differs from primitive-subsistence agriculture principally in the intensity of its land use—in the necessity to utilize all possible land for agricultural purposes and to wring the maximum yield from every piece of land. Yet for centuries the methods of these regions, surprisingly, were rather crude, and the yields were as low as those of regions considered more primitive. Within the past decade, however, some remarkable improvements have been made in yield per acre, sometimes through use of better strains of wheat, rice, corn, and other products and sometimes through fertilization.

Production structure and methods. The emphasis here is upon food, which is produced most efficiently by raising crops that man can consume directly. Where animals are present, they tend to be used for draft purposes, to be scavengers, or to be homeless "mavericks" protected by religious beliefs. The crops are mainly grains and vegetables. Paddy rice predominates in most areas where it can be grown, and these areas extend discontinuously from central and southern Japan and Korea equatorward to the warmest margins of regions of intensive-subsistence agriculture. In places where fields cannot be flooded, dry or upland rice is grown. The significance of rice to regions of this type of agriculture is apparent in the fact that about 85 per cent of all the world's rice is produced here. Most of the world's international trade in rice is in reality a coastwise movement along eastern and southern Asia. Wheat, corn, barley, sorghum, millet, and some oats tend to be grown actively where rice does not thrive, their areas of growth overlapping somewhat with those of rice. Nongrain crops include soybeans (mainly in northern China and all of Korea), peanuts (in southern India and northern China), sugarcane (in India, southern· China, and Pakistan), sesame seed, rapeseed, tobacco, tea, many garden vegetables, and some fruits.

These regions also grow fibers, notably cotton (in western India, northeastern China, upper Pakistan, and the Nile flood plain and delta of Egypt), jute (in the Ganges-Brahmaputra delta of Bangladesh and India), silk (in central and southern Japan and coastal and central China), and hemp (in northern China and southern Japan). These regions dominate the world exports of jute and silk and also contribute other fibers (on a smaller scale) to world markets.

Animals and poultry tend to be distributed unevenly in accordance with cultural (usually religious) belief as well as economic utility. Swine and poultry abound as scavengers in China, but are virtually non-

existent in India and in areas dominated by the Moslem faith. India probably contains more cattle than any other nation; estimates place the total at between one-fifth and one-third of that of the entire world. Except for draft purposes, however, most of these animals are of little use to man; they are protected from slaughter by religious beliefs and social mores. Sheep and goats are found in significant numbers in the regions of intensive-subsistence agriculture, most prominently in India.

In non-Communist lands, holdings tend to be small, seldom exceeding 5 acres per farm owner, and generally of even lesser size (Fig. 5.6). The poorer families, especially the landless workers, have benefited during this century from a number of land-reform programs, wherein efforts are made to bring more land into production and to redistribute some land heretofore controlled by large landowners, many of them absentee landlords. Because of the heavy populations, however, it does not seem that such measures will permanently solve the problem of small holdings.

The ownership of land in most Communist countries is being assumed by the national governments, although a form of token redistribution among the landless sometimes precedes this appropriation. The actual working of the land tends to be done mainly by groups of farm families organized into collectives varying in accordance with land productivity and with the amount of land generally available. Whether this type of agricultural organization will result in generally higher yields remains yet to be demonstrated. It does not appear likely, however, that any type of organization will alleviate completely the heavy man-land ratio of these regions.

Traditionally, yields per acre have been low in most areas practicing intensive-subsistence agriculture. As recently as 1960, wheat yields in India averaged only 10 bushels per acre, and in China only 16 bushels per acre, as compared with 18 bushels per acre in the United States and 35 bushels per acre in intensively farmed France. However, in the 1960s and early 1970s, yields per acre increased dramatically, especially in Pakistan and India but also in other parts of eastern and southern Asia. China may also have experienced this increase. Between 1960 and 1970, the index of agricultural production for Pakistan rose from 100 to 165, and that for India rose to 140. Both wheat and rice were involved primarily in these increases. New strains of wheat and rice, and more effective fertilization and farming methods, were largely responsible for these increases.

World distribution. Intensive-subsistence agriculture is concentrated in eastern and southern Asia, where it covers practically all cultivated land. Included are most of Bangladesh, India, China, and Japan and part of Pakistan, Burma, Thailand, Cambodia, North Vietnam, South Vietnam, and South Korea. A few tiny representations of this type of land use are found elsewhere, primarily in the Eastern Hemisphere; the most conspicuous is the Nile River delta of Egypt. Unlike regions where primitive-subsistence agriculture prevails, the regions of intensive-subsistence agriculture include large amounts of land actually cultivated. India alone contains nearly one-sixth of the world's total cultivated land, and China contains an additional one-twelfth. The amount held by other nations in this category is much smaller, but aggregately is worthy of note. All in all, intensive-subsistence regions account for about 30 per cent of the world's cultivated land.

Association with populations. Approximately one-half of the world's people live in the regions of intensive-subsistence agriculture. The heavily populated effective areas of China, India, and Japan, as well as those of smaller nations, are farmed largely by intensive-subsistence practices.

Association with political units and economies. Nearly all countries characterized by intensive-subsistence agriculture are politically sovereign, and most received their independence only after World War II. (Japan stands out in many ways as an exception.) Their economies tend to be less developed and exhibit a low propensity to exchange. Because of their heavy population pressures, however, their aggregate market potential is high (Table 4.1).

Natural environmental and cultural associations. This type of agriculture (concentrated in southeastern Asia) is best developed under tropical and subtropical climates, where the growing seasons are long. Smaller appendages extend northward from these locations along the Pacific coast to northern China, Korea, and Japan. Intensive-subsistence agriculture is carried on in tropical rain-forest, tropical savanna, humid subtropical, and humid continental climates, together with their associated vegetational and soil types. Nearly all

these regions are influenced by the Asian monsoons and hence experience rather pronounced summer-rain–winter-drought precipitation conditions (although the winters are moist in some sections, particularly southern China and Japan). Occasionally a moisture deficiency occurs in summer, especially in northern China and in India, causing crop failure and famine. Because of the high population pressures, all usable land is cultivated, regardless of landform.

Not all climates of southern and eastern Asia favor this agriculture. The regions of intensive-subsistence agriculture are bordered on the Asian interior by territory that is either too high or too dry to permit this type of land use at current technological levels.

Cultural as well as natural patterns are considerations especially important to this type of agriculture. The various natural conditions where intensive-subsistence agriculture occurs are roughly duplicated elsewhere—for example, along the southern, eastern, and northern sections of North America. However, intensive-subsistence agriculture is not found conspicuously in the North American counterparts of the Asian climates. The reasons for this, while partially attributable to the much lighter population pressure in North America as compared with that in southeastern Asia, appear also to be partially cultural. Thus, comparing agriculture in eastern Asia to that in eastern North America, we find striking examples of similar natural conditions that have been used very differently under the guiding rules and laws of differing cultures.

Plantation agriculture. For want of better nomenclature, the term *plantation* is used in this book to denote sizable tracts of agricultural land owned by private individuals or corporations and operated directly or indirectly by a centralized management. Some degree of specialization in both labor and harvested crops usually exists, and most of the crops are sold in the world markets. The labor tends to be done by either hired workers or tenants. Agricultural methods and tools tend to be more technically advanced than in most smaller farming operations. The classification of regions of plantation agriculture is therefore based upon the size of holding, the mode of ownership, the mode of operation, and the degree of commercialization.

Production structure and methods. Plantation agriculture is mainly a commercial venture initiated by individual owners and operators. Usually, it involves the growth of commodities for sale in markets where those commodities cannot be grown because of adverse climatic and/or other natural environmental features. Sugar, cotton, bananas, coffee, rubber, copra, tobacco, and tea head the list of such commodities; some items of lesser significance are rice, cinchona, sisal, henequen, hemp, peanuts, palm oil and kernels, cacao, gutta-percha, and the once-prized spices. Of the eight leaders, four are tree crops.

The plantations are usually owned by Europeans or descendants of Europeans, who may or may not reside on the plantations or even in the country where the plantations are situated. They are usually managed by Europeans or highly trusted non-Europeans (often partly European in extraction), and most of the labor is non-European. European or Europeanized control over management is retained where (1) rigid time schedules of production have to be met, (2) complex farming practices and tools are utilized, and/or (3) heavy financial investment is necessary. Nearly all plantations must contend with at least one of these specifications.

Plantation laborers usually are hired help or tenant farmers. Where there is hired help, management tends to be more centralized, since control over laborers is direct. Where the tenant system dominates, decisions as to specific land use are sometimes left to the tenant, as long as these decisions do not alter the general directives of the landowner. Control by the landowner is often maintained not only through leasing arrangements but also through ownership of harvesting machinery or preliminary milling equipment.

The mechanization of agriculture has influenced plantations, although the nature and extent vary with the crops produced and with the attitudes and financial reserves of the owners. The major effects are the reduction of the degree of dependence on human labor and the possible enlargement of operating units. The planting and cultivating operations usually are more easily mechanized than harvesting is. Many plantations have been slow to mechanize, partly because of the very cheap labor already at their disposal.

World distribution. The majority of the world's plantation regions are situated in the low latitudes, and only a few are located poleward of the Tropic of Cancer or the Tropic of Capricorn. Notably in the southeastern United States, however, this type of agriculture extends conspicuously but erratically as far north as lat 35°. Like primitive-subsistence farming, plantation agriculture is found in both hemispheres; indeed, plantation districts frequently appear on a map as islands of intense commercial activity surrounded by great areas of subsistence agriculture.

Association with populations. Unlike regions dominated by the two forms of subsistence agriculture discussed previously, plantation districts do not occupy large portions of the earth's land surface. Instead, they appear as rather small but distinctive splotches, surrounded by other types of livelihood (Fig. 5.1). Plantation agriculture therefore does not provide livelihood for people distributed over wide areas, as do primitive-subsistence and intensive-subsistence agricultures.

More often that not, plantation districts coincide with areas of moderate or even heavy population density. To some extent, the plantations create such population clusters, since they provide employment for many workers who live on the plantations or in the vicinity. Yet in some instances it appears quite likely that such population clusters would exist even if there were no plantations, for all forms of agriculture are oriented to good land.

Association with political units and economies. Plantations, especially those in the low latitudes, tend to be located in less developed economies (compare Figs. 5.1 and 3.4). In Latin America and southeastern Asia, most of the political units that are associated with such factors are independent, and several in Africa either are currently self-governing or are about to become so. Most of the Latin American political units have been sovereign for over a century, but most of the Asian and African units are just beginning to assume the responsibilities of self-government. The emotions involved in the struggles for independence may affect plantation agriculture adversely in Asia and Africa, and the question of whether, and in what form, plantations will survive has not yet been answered. Notably in southeastern Asia, plantations are being broken up into subsistence tracts. Commercial plantations controlled from the United Kingdom tend to be located primarily in countries which comprised the British Commonwealth. Foreign enterprises of other European nations are also located mainly in the current or former political or economic affiliates of those nations. The United States has focused especially on Caribbean America, an area within the dollar currency bloc.

Natural environmental and cultural associations. Most plantations are situated within tropical savanna, humid subtropical, or tropical rain-forest climates, with their associated vegetation and soils. Where certain crops require yearlong cool temperatures, the intermediate and lower reaches of undifferentiated highland climates are also utilized. Flat, fertile, well-drained land, at the varying elevations needed to grow crop specialties, is preferred by plantation owners and managers.

Culturally, the plantation is a European product—although paradoxically, few plantations exist in Europe today. In areas where Europeans have migrated in substantial numbers, plantations can be considered a part of present-day domestic cultural patterns. This is generally true of plantations in the United States, Latin America, and Australia. Notably in Africa and southeastern Asia, however, the plantations represent injections of European culture into indigenous ways of life. In some areas the plantations represent an injection of one type of Europeanized culture into another.

Mediterranean agriculture. Areas dominated by mediterranean climate have evolved a rather distinctive mode of land use. This classification, the only one to be designated on the basis of its associated climate, is in reality a classification based mainly on land utilization.

Production structure and methods. Mediterranean agriculture reflects mediterranean climate. Generally found in this type of agricultural region are (1) crops which yield early in the season, having reached maturity through utilization of winter and early spring precipitation; (2) crops which withstand the dry summers without requiring irrigation; and (3) crops which benefit from irrigation water created by melting snow in nearby mountains or from water that has been delayed in its initial flow by the vegetation in the catchment basins of these highlands. Grains, notably wheat, dominate the first category; three crops—olives, dates,

and cork oak—together with some drought resistant vines prevail in the second; and a wide variety of garden vegetables and fruits make up the third. The intensity of land use and allocation of land among the three categories vary not only with such natural environmental conditions as amount and annual distribution of precipitation but also with such economic factors as size and accessibility of domestic and foreign markets. In the Northern Hemisphere, the mediterranean climate regions supply fruit and vegetable to thickly settled manufacturing regions located within a feasible range of transportation. In the Southern Hemisphere, where populations are more sparse and accessible markets are correspondingly smaller, less land is devoted to truck gardening.

In addition to crops, most mediterranean landscapes contain animals. More often than not, the animals are subordinate in significance to crops. Beef and beef-dairy cattle are present especially in Chile, California, and parts of southern Europe. Sheep and goats are the most numerous around the Mediterranean Sea and in Australia and Africa. Swine are found chiefly in southern Europe.

World distribution. Like its associated climate, mediterranean agriculture is found on continental western fringes generally between lat 30 and 40°N and S. It is most extensive along the arable margins of the Mediterranean Sea, which is the "western fringe" of the Eurasian-African land mass, and is found also in the southwestern United States, central Chile, the southernmost tip of Africa, and the western fringes of Australia.

Association with populations. It has been suggested that the Garden of Eden may have existed in this type of climate. If so, it is not surprising that the garden was attractive to man. Throughout the world, mediterranean climate tends to overlie small but rather dense population clusters which border the sea on one side and extend up the uplands and mountains on the other. In the United States, pronounced migrations to this climate from other parts of the nation have occurred during the past thirty years, so that California now has the largest population of all the states.

Association with political units and economies. Mediterranean agriculture is found almost entirely in political units that are independent and in economies at a high or moderate level of technical advance. Only in northern Africa and the Middle East is this type of agriculture associated with less developed economies (although Chile, in South America, is sometimes classified as less developed).

Natural environmental and cultural associations. The mediterranean climate throughout the world tends to be near low or high mountains. Since the seasonal distribution of precipitation in this climate is that of winter moisture and summer deficiency, the uplands and mountains play a role in land use by capturing much of the winter snow and not releasing it as running water until the following summer, at which time it is most welcome for irrigation purposes. Although these regions contain populations that are native or of native-European mixture, they are for the most part dominated by European cultures. Only in parts of the Middle East and in northern Africa do non-European peoples tend to be in control of political units and economies, and even here, chiefly because of the petroleum riches being extracted by European and United States interests and because of Europe's strategic location in the world, European influence (including some from the Soviet Union) is felt.

Commercial grain farming. This type of agricultural region is distinguished mainly by the type of crop produced and by the degree to which that crop enters into commercial markets, usually world markets. The comparatively few sizable regions engaging in this type of agriculture tend to specialize in the production of one particular grain crop, growing it almost entirely for commercial markets.

Production structure and methods. Like plantations, commercial grain farms are large, financed by high capital investment, specialized as to crops produced, and centrally managed.

In non-Communist countries, commercial grain farms tend to differ from plantations chiefly in that (1) their land valuation per acre tends to be lower than that of plantations, and so cultivation on grain farms is designed to achieve a high yield per worker, with only secondary emphasis placed upon yield per acre; (2) their yield per worker is maximized through the use of ma-

chines; and (3) they are usually owner-operated, and most of the labor is supplied by members of the owner's family or a few hired hands.

Wheat is outstanding among crops grown in commercial-grain-farming regions. Corn, oats, and barley are noteworthy. Since the crops from commercial grain farms are raised mainly for sale, few animals are maintained on such farms.

Communist nations have no plantations as such, and so comparison between their commercial grain farms and plantations is not possible. Commercial grain farming in Communist nations is restricted mostly to the Soviet Union, where it is conducted primarily on collective farms.

World distribution. Regions of commercial grain farming are prominent in the middle latitudes of central and western North America and of central Asia, and they appear in patches in the middle latitudes of South America and Australia (Fig. 5.1).

Association with populations. Commercial grain farming involves the utilization of machines, much land, and few people. Consequently, it is usually found where populations tend to be sparse, except in such areas as effective Argentina, effective Uruguay, and the effective area of the Soviet Union, where commercial grain farming overlaps other productive activities, particularly manufacturing.

Association with political units and economies. The technically advanced economies with commercial grain farms can be divided into two categories: (1) those in which grain is a major component of exports and hence vital to the country's commercial life and (2) those in which grain as an export crop is not so predominant because of (*a*) a major domestic demand for it and (*b*) competition from other types of farming. Canada, Australia, and Argentina are leading examples of the first category. Large in physical area, containing climates well suited to growing grain, and yet small in aggregate population, these countries depend on grain as an export. The United States and the Soviet Union are the main examples of the second category. Their large domestic populations consume much of the grain directly or indirectly, and hence exports of the grain, while large, are not so vital to their economic well-being as is true of Canada, Australia, and Argentina.

Natural environmental and cultural associations. Most commercial grain farming is found in semi-arid climate, with its associated vegetational and soil types, although such farming extends into peripheral climates and conditions. In Argentina and Uruguay commercial grain farming takes place almost completely in humid subtropical climate. As with farm land generally, flat land is desired, but since these crops are raised almost entirely without irrigation, other land can be used. In the Palouse country of eastern Washington, for example, rather sharply undulating hills are used.

If one assumes that the Soviet Union has now "Europeanized" Soviet Central Asia, it can be stated that all areas of commercial grain farming are associated with the European cultural heritage. However, no sizable areas of commercial grain farming are found in Europe itself, except in European Russia.

Commercial crop and livestock farming. This type of agricultural region is defined principally on the basis of the variety, intermixture, and commercial nature of its crop and animal products.

Production structure and methods. This is an agriculture with diversification, rotation of crops, and high yield. Methods and tools used in these regions are among the most advanced of all agricultural regions, and efforts are made to achieve both a high yield per person and a high yield per acre, particularly in Europe. Such achievement means use of commercial fertilizers as well as animal manures, careful rotation of crops and pastures, wise use of animals, and use of modern machinery. Crops include the grains (corn, wheat, oats, rye, barley), root crops (potatoes, sugar beets, garden vegetables), fruits (apples, peaches, pears, etc.), vines (particularly in Europe), fibers (notably flax), and diverse other crops (soybeans, alfalfa, clover, linseed, buckwheat, etc.). Animals are raised as well (particularly swine, beef and dairy cattle, and sheep). This is a commercially oriented production with some subsistence characteristics showing through the commercial veneer. A farmer in such regions usually sells most of his crops and/or animals, but not too many of these enter into the world markets; nearly all are in heavy domestic demand.

World distribution. Commercial crop and live-stock farming is found almost entirely in the middle latitudes. Nearly all nations with commercial crop and livestock farming are technically advanced, and most are situated in North America or Eurasia.

Association with populations. This type of agriculture is located beside or near three vast urban complexes of the Northern Hemisphere—in Western Europe, the Soviet Union, and the United States—plus small areas in the Southern Hemisphere. It includes some 700 million people and thus ranks second only to intensive-subsistence agriculture in this respect. However, unlike populations who live in areas of intensive-subsistence agriculture, most inhabitants of regions of commercial crop and livestock farming are city dwellers who are only indirectly, if at all, oriented to agriculture—except in one vital sense: They must eat, be clothed, be housed, and otherwise be provided with need and want satisfaction that stems, in part, from agriculture.

Association with political units and economies. We have noted that this type of agriculture prevails in technically advanced nations and is most widespread in the Northern Hemisphere. The Soviet Union, the United States, and Western Europe each contains large representations, with smaller portions found in Canada, Mexico, Brazil, Argentina, the Union of South Africa, Rhodesia, and the far northeastern part of China.

Natural environmental and cultural associations. The climates most frequently associated with crop and livestock farming are the humid continental warm-summer, humid continental cool-summer, marine, humid subtropical, and subarctic. The core climates of the group with respect to specific regions of crop and livestock farming tend to be the humid continental warm-summer and the marine, and the others tend to be peripheral.

The main cultural influences affecting crop and livestock farming, like those affecting plantation agriculture, mediterranean agriculture, and commercial grain farming, have been derived, sometimes with modifications, from Europe.

Commercial dairy farming. This is a relatively intensive type of agriculture usually found in places where many crops will not mature fully but will mature

enough for dairy feed. Climates associated with this agriculture are the cooler portions of humid continental, marine, or undifferentiated highland climates. Since milk and milk products are the chief items for sale—many of which are quickly perishable—places of production tend to be close to markets. The area of dairy farming in North America is within, and generally north of, the continent's cluster of manufacturing cities; the two areas in Europe are on either side of Europe's manufacturing districts; and the area in Australia is around and between the major cities. Some dairying, as in much of New Zealand and part of Australia, produces more than local markets can consume, and hence much butter and cheese and related less perishable products are made specifically for more distant market places. Thus dairy farming is a technically advanced occupation producing for markets where high levels of living prevail. Except in Europe, most commerce in milk and milk products is domestic. In Europe, however, such commerce is more international in character, chiefly because a number of small nations constitute the areas of supply and demand.

Commercial gardening and fruit culture. This is an intensive type of farming, utilizing advanced methods and tools for growing high-value produce for sale chiefly in urban markets located within a feasible transportation range. The produce consists of a wide range of truck-garden vegetables and middle-latitude as well as low-latitude fruits. Such agriculture is most conspicuous along the fringes of the Atlantic and Pacific Oceans and the Gulf of Mexico in the United States, and is found elsewhere in places too small to appear satisfactorily on a global map. These smaller places, too, are generally accessible to urban markets and are located mostly in Europe, Argentina, and Australia. Commercial gardening and fruit culture are found mainly in technically advanced economies rooted in European civilizations, and, partly because of produce perishability, their location as well as their extensiveness tend to be closely associated with markets; the natural environment is a secondary but still important consideration. Indeed, many such tracts, well located to markets, often receive much attention and financial investment toward overcoming adverse natural environmental features. Specific techniques include the use of greenhouses, the supplying of plant nutrients by chemical means, and the use of irrigating water in humid as well as dry climates to overcome any temporary moisture deficiency. These techniques, plus canning, refrigeration, and other methods of food preservation, have been useful in reducing adverse effects of harvest seasonality, which is a major natural environmental constraint to the geographic distribution of this type of farming.

Technically advanced and less developed conditions. Of the eight agricultural types discussed, the first two prevail in less developed economies, and the last five in technically advanced economies (Figs. 5.1 and 3.4). One, plantation agriculture, occurs chiefly in less developed areas, but is to a great extent a transplant of technically advanced conditions which affect only the plantation districts and not surrounding native economies. Most plantations depend upon international markets, not domestic ones. Six types of farming associated with technical advance account for the majority of agricultural commodities entering into international trade.

Trends in Agriculture

Structure. We noted earlier in this chapter the changing structure of the agricultural population of the world. In the past quarter century, agricultural employment has declined sharply in countries which either are on the threshold of active development or have recently reached that status, according to most classifications. For example, in 1950 agriculture was responsible for 73 per cent of all employment in Yugoslavia, whereas in 1965 that figure was only 47 per cent; in the Soviet Union, the percentages changed from 50 to 32 in that same period, and in Spain from 48 to 35. In the more developed economies, where agriculture already ranked low as a source of livelihood, its decline continued, but at a slower rate than in the intermediately developed economies. For the less developed countries, however, agriculture has remained a strong mainstay of livelihood. In India, where over one-sixth of the world's people are found, agriculture continued to support, in 1965, the same 70 per cent of all productive workers that it had in 1950.

Finally, the range of total national employment in agriculture is interesting. In the United Kingdom, only 3 per cent of the working population is engaged in agriculture, and in the United States, only 4.2 per cent. In contrast, in Uganda, 91 per cent of all employed workers are in agriculture.

Pattern and location. *Global patterns.* The primary changes in volume of land used in agriculture have occurred in the developing regions of the world. Latin America is the most important of these large blocs, but the Middle East, Africa, and the Far East all have added substantially to their acreages. In contrast, the overall status in the developed portion of the world has been essentially the same for the past twenty years. Substantial increases in the Soviet Union have been offset by essentially equally large withdrawals in North America. All in all, between 1948 and 1968, there was an increase of about 16 per cent in the acreage responsible for the world's twelve major crops.

There are now more than 3 billion acres of cultivated land in the world, or just slightly less than 1 acre for each person. An additional 5 acres per inhabitant are estimated to be either too cold or too arid for utilization at current levels of technology. Yet another 4 acres cannot be used effectively either because the terrain is too rough or because the soils and associated top-surface conditions will not respond to attempts at cultivation. This leaves somewhat fewer than 3 acres per existing inhabitant on the earth which could be utilized. These are located mainly in the tropical rain-forest, tropical savanna, humid subtropical, marine, and humid continental warm-summer and cool-summer climates (Fig. 2.3).

Regional patterns: size of producing unit. An interesting trend in the pattern and location of agriculture involves the size of farm. A recent world generalization is shown in Figure 5.6, which gives classifications of size only and does not reflect some interesting trends responsible for the respective sizes. In Canada, the United States, and much of Western Europe, the size of producing units has been increasing as more capital has been substituted for labor, and economies of scale are sought to increase both per-acre and per-person output. Because private ownership is the pri-

mary form of land tenure, this has meant, literally, more acres owned per person or farm. In the centrally planned countries, most of the land is now owned by the state and operated in cooperatives, under varying actual names which change from time to time. Each cooperative involves a substantial number of families and workers. In Mexico, most of the agricultural land is also owned by the state, but a prevailing form of land tenure is the *ejido,* also a cooperative—but one in which the individual has the permanent right to work a given plot of land as long as productivity remains at a certain level. The creation of the *ejidos* in Mexico is one manifestation of a widespread land-reform movement that is found throughout much of the less developed world—a movement in which land is being taken from large landowners and made available, in the form of outright ownership, the right to work, or cooperatives, to large numbers of heretofore landless persons. The results of these experiments are not yet fully known. However, they appear to have been at least political successes in many of the countries where they have been initiated.

Functioning. Despite the fact that agriculture has not experienced a dramatic increase in overall acreage, it has remained sufficiently efficient as to its functioning process so that total agricultural production is increasing at a rate generally equal to, and in some cases slightly greater than, that of population growth. In the period 1956–1968, the average annual increase in agricultural production for the world as a whole was 2.7 per cent, compared with an overall population increase of slightly over 2 per cent per year. Interestingly enough, this percentage was shared equally by the developed countries and the developing countries. (However, the reader should note that the agricultural output of developed countries was at a much higher rate in the period 1956–1958; therefore, the absolute volume of production increase in the developed world has been substantial.)

Although the substitution of capital for labor and the intensive utilization of technology now characterize the developed countries more than the developing ones, it is interesting to note that in the twenty years between 1948 and 1968, the number of tractors used in

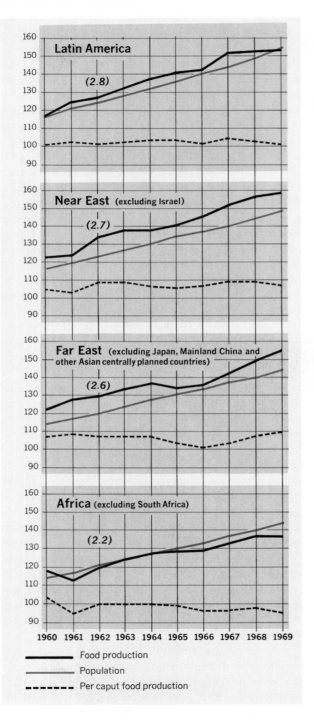

Food production

Population

Per caput food production

agriculture increased at an annual rate of 9 per cent for the developing countries, compared with 5 per cent for the developed countries. Similarly, the average of the developing countries as to annual rate of increase in the consumption of fertilizer was almost twice as large as that of the developed countries. However, for both tractors and fertilizer, the developing countries' rate of growth is calculated from a very low 1948 figure, whereas that for the developed countries was much higher. Also important in the late 1960s was the "green revolution"—the dramatic increases in yields of wheat and rice in certain less developed areas through the use of newly developed strains.

Despite these increases in productivity, Figure 5.7 shows that the ratio of growth in food supply is still precarious in the developing nations in comparison with population growth. In Africa, population expansion exceeded the rate of food output for essentially the whole decade of 1960, and in Latin America a similar condition began to appear in the late 1960s.

Structure, Pattern, and Trends in Other Primary Activities

We have indicated earlier (p. 72) that primary activities other than agriculture account for approximately 3 per cent of the world's labor force. About 1 per cent of this group is in grazing, 1 per cent in minerals extraction and quarrying, and 0.5 per cent each in forest-products industries, and fishing and hunting (Table 5.1).

Figure 5.1 shows that grazing occupies substantial amounts of land surface. Grazing can be divided into two categories: nomadic herding and commercial live-stock ranching. The first is more closely associated with the less developed economies, and the second with the more developed economies. As the names imply, the first is essentially a subsistence activity, and the second is appreciably commercial. The actual number of people engaged in both is declining—in nomadic herding be-cause of a gradual shift from this way of life into seden-tary conditions, and in commercial livestock ranching because of the increasing size of producing units and

Figure 5.7 Trends in agricultural production and popula-tion in the world's developing areas. (After Food and Agriculture Organization *Yearbook,* 1970, p. 130.)

the concomitant decline in the number of people actually earning their livelihood this way. Productivity per person and per acre are essentially constant in nomadic herding, but are rising rather dramatically in commercial livestock ranching.

In mining and quarrying, forest-products industries, and fishing, there is a definite trend toward substitution of capital for labor and an effort to increase economies of scale and output per person. For all three activities, this trend is accompanied by efforts aimed at pushing the first stage of manufacture to or toward the actual site of raw-material procurement, grinding that material into a semifinished product, removing a maximum amount of waste at the site of the raw material, and shipping the desired goods immediately toward the more efficient manufacturing operation that is located nearer markets, usually at, or in the vicinity of, large urban places. The average annual increase in mining output in the period 1956–1968 was about 9 per cent, that of forest products was somewhat less than 2 per cent, and that of fishing was slightly less than 7 per cent. In all three activities, there has been a tendency to utilize lower-quality raw material. There is also a definite danger, especially in mining and fishing, that expected rates of consumption may be excessive in view of fixed reserves (in the case of mining) or annual natural increase (in the case of fishery products).

Secondary and Tertiary Activities

Structure

We have seen in Table 5.1 that tertiary activity provides a livelihood for more than one-fourth of the world's people, and secondary activity for nearly one-fifth. It is clear from the discussion earlier in this chapter that these activities are more in evidence in the developed portions of the world than in the developing portions. In many of the more developed economies, manufacturing has reached a relative zenith of importance, especially when considered in terms of employment, and is beginning to give way to tertiary activity. In Canada, for example, the per cent of all employed workers en-

gaged in manufacturing declined from 24 in 1961 to 22.7 in 1970. In the United States, the decline in that decade was from 31 to 26 per cent. This trend is not yet so pronounced in other manufacturing areas of the world, but is beginning to be evident in some parts of Western Europe. Inasmuch as there is also a decline in employment in primary industries within the more developed areas, we can infer that tertiary activities will become more important there. Of these tertiary activities, retail and wholesale trade have retained their relative positions throughout the 1960s in the United States and Canada and have increased slightly in most countries of Western Europe. The major gains have taken place in the provision of professional services within the more developed countries—government, education, health, and other institutions which provide services that an increasingly affluent society considers necessary.

If we consider development to be a process, and (measured by employment) the ratio of primary to secondary to tertiary activities to be an important part of that process, we see emerging from the historical record a series of important events. First is the emergence of primary activities—at the outset, the exploitative and the extractive activities, soon followed by agriculture. At an intermediate stage of development come the early forms of manufacturing. At a more mature stage, when primary and secondary activities have found their relative levels in the overall economic systems, we see the ultimate emergence of the tertiary activities, many of which are designed to serve human wants rather than needs. Inasmuch as these wants are endless, we can expect the relative importance of the tertiary sector to increase, subject only to the constraints of a capacity to finance them. That capacity, in turn, depends appreciably upon the absolute and relative efficiency of an economy's primary and secondary production in supporting the important, but not always vital, contributions of those tertiary activities which cater to wants rather than needs.

Patterns, Location, and Functioning

Secondary and tertiary activity occupy very small sites relative to value of capital investment, level of employment, and output (p. 15). Further, they usually are found within or near urban units—especially very large urban

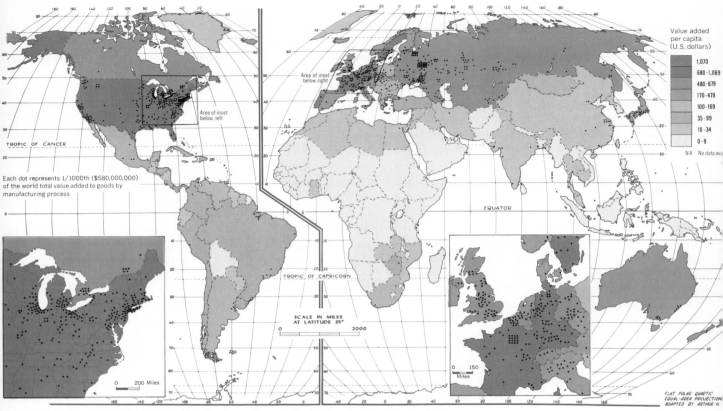

Figure 5.8 World distribution of manufacturing (generalized). (After *Encyclopaedia Britannica*.)

units. Therefore, it is impossible to treat adequately the location of these activities, and their aggregate locational patterns, in this global perspective. That for manufacturing is shown, in generalized form, in Figure 5.8. That for tertiary activities, the establishments of which tend to be smaller and even more numerous than those of manufacturing, can be visualized in a distribution of the world's population and urban places (back end-paper map). A more satisfactory treatment of these activities must await examination at a larger-scale level of observation. In Chapter 8, we shall appraise, in a pragmatic way, some of the locational tendencies of both manufacturing and services. In Part 2, we shall reopen this question, both pragmatically and theoretically. Finally, in Part 3, we shall examine, by the case-study technique, the successive stages through which these goods and services are forwarded in moving from production to ultimate consumption.

Chapter 6

The Economic Environment: Structures and Patterns of Trade

Trade exists either because localized demand for materials exceeds (or is expected to exceed) the possibilities of the localized supply or because the supply exceeds the demand. This demand-supply imbalance, in turn, may be due to differences among human beings, their cultures, or the particular features of their natural environment. For example, insulin is purchased by a person with diabetes because it is a bodily necessity; here the demand is due to a unique human deficiency. Rice is a staple among foods and an imported commodity in most of the larger nations of the Far East; here the demand is in large measure cultural—the result of a developed taste for this particular food. It may well be in part natural, for rice grows well in this area of the world. The Asian trade in rice is due to an excess of demand over supply in the importing nations. This excess is partly ascribable to essentially human factors —to the high natural increases in those nations—but is due also to cultural and natural factors, for man has not yet utilized nature efficiently enough in this part of the world to produce rice in quantities that are adequate for domestic consumption—and who is to say whether the limitations to his production are entirely natural, cultural, or human? Certainly higher yields per acre and per person could be achieved with known methods that are used elsewhere, but how can these be purchased or otherwise made available? And assuming that they were utilized to the utmost, would the production even then be adequate, especially when the high natural increases in population are considered?

If enough space were available, we could add many other examples to those of rice and insulin, and we should arrive eventually at the same impasse in our efforts to seek a precise cause of trade. Suffice it to say that the very many and pronounced differences among human beings, their cultures, and their respective shares of the earth's natural features appear to be indirectly responsible for trade. The direct cause was stated in the last paragraph: the excesses of localized demand (desire plus purchasing power) over localized supply of, or of supply over demand for, the commodities traded. These excesses, it should be emphasized, have deep roots in the past.

The resulting commerce may be considered at several levels of classification: First, there is trade between individuals; this is too detailed, and each transaction too trivial, to be of much service to our examination. Second, there is exchange of goods between market centers and their trading areas and between ports and their hinterlands; this is of appreciable interest to us. Finally, there is trade among nations, and this is of decided interest to us. All three levels, but particularly the last two, are best developed and organized in technically advanced nations, and the generalizations that follow are applicable only loosely to less developed nations. The appropriateness of their application increases with degree of technical advancement.

In Part 2, especially in Chapter 13, we shall inquire into theoretical explanations of trade. Here in Part 1, which is devoted to the real world, we are examining current trading conditions and trends.

Market Centers and Trading areas: Ports and Hinterlands

Almost all urbanized settlements are trading centers for their resident populations and for the people living in adjacent countrysides. Of course, they usually contain other activities, like manufacturing, which are important to their welfare but which need not be emphasized in this discussion of trade. In a few places of specialized effort, such as political capitals, resorts, and mining and university towns, the trade may be restricted essentially to the population of the urbanized settlement itself, but exceptions like these are rare. Generally, each urban settlement, large or small, has its own trading area which is a composite of all the trading territories served by individual firms located in that settlement.

Hierarchical Arrangement of Settlements

The size, distinguishing features, and complexity of each trading area tend to vary in accordance with the size of the market center with which it shares an interdependence. Moreover, trading centers and areas are in a recognizable hierarchical order, with the territory of each included also with the territories of the larger

units. Thus the market and supply areas of hamlets are encompassed by those of villages; those of villages, by those of small towns; those of small towns, by those of large towns; those of large towns, by those of cities; and those of cities, by those of metropolises.[1] In practice, the hierarchy cannot always be readily distinguished, but its presence is very real. A major reason for its existence is the fact that not all goods and services are available from all sizes of settlements, and persons seeking a particular type of good or service necessarily will go to the urbanized unit where it can be had. In other words, nearly every settlement in the hierarchy offers all the goods and services obtainable from all settlements of a lower level, plus certain specialties that cannot be found in those smaller settlements.

Villages and hamlets. These smallest of market centers, often as much rural as urban, are the most numerous, and their trading areas are correspondingly the smallest. Usually they offer only retail trade, and this only in the most regularly consumed commodities —groceries, gasoline, drugs, commonplace hardware, etc. Often these are all sold from the same store. The facilities for accommodating surplus goods from the surrounding countrysides are equally parsimonious, for markets in such small settlements cannot compete satisfactorily with those of towns, which almost always are not far away. Villages and hamlets are thus essentially market centers of convenience upon which nearby residents can depend for life's daily necessities.

Towns. In addition to the simple retailing services operating in competition with those of the villages and hamlets, the towns offer more highly specialized retailing possibilities as well as the more elementary types of wholesaling outlets and certain professional and trade services. Thus it is possible not only to obtain a wider selection of food, gasoline, drugs, hardware, etc., but also to "shop around" among the small but numerous clothing and shoe stores, ten-cent stores, appliance

---

[1] The terms *village, town, city,* etc., are used here to designate increasing size and complexity of urbanized settlements and not to refer to their political organization or administration. Rural villages of certain cultures are chiefly residential and do not fit easily into the above classification.

stores, bakeries, automobile dealers, farm-machinery distributors, and a variety of other outlets. Not infrequently (notably in the United States), coast-to-coast retail organizations are represented, but, except for food supermarkets, their stores are usually rather modest. The wholesale firms tend to be those servicing the numerous retail outlets of the nearby villages and rural routes, with petroleum products and groceries among the leading commodities so handled. Service firms specializing in cleaning, laundering, shoe repairing, automobile repairing, etc., are well represented in towns, as are the legal and medical professions.

Towns are often market as well as supply centers. Official or unofficial marketplaces usually are set aside in towns for exchange of fresh produce from the country, and some of the retail establishments also purchase such produce for local resale. In areas of grain production, grain elevators are frequently the tallest structures in the town's skyline, except, perhaps, for the water tanks. Flour mills, hay mills, sugar refineries, canneries, milk-processing plants, and stockyards are still other marketing outlets found in towns of varying size.

Cities and metropolitan areas. The largest urbanized settlements, like the intermediate and the smallest, dominate the retail trade of their respective adjacent countrysides, but unlike the smallest and in a manner only suggested by settlements of intermediate size and activity, they are influential in trade that is removed—sometimes far removed—from their actual locations. These largest urban agglomerations are the places to go for commodities that simply cannot be obtained otherwise, as well as for a much wider selection of the more ubiquitous goods. These commodities are dispensed sometimes from huge establishments like Macy's and Gimbels, sometimes from offices like those in the Empire State Building, and sometimes from a rolltop desk in a building on the waterfront.

The retail influence of urban agglomerations is very real, but wholesaling activities are the functions which truly extend the overall impact of the larger urban units to other parts of a country and to other countries. Reaching beyond the retail-trade areas of these units are wholesale territories—first, contiguous areas that are consistently dominated by the urban units which

core them and, second, twilight zones of competition between the wholesale territories of two or more cities or metropolises. Beyond these twilight zones the impact of the largest urban units is reduced to tentacles which, reaching to almost every settlement—perhaps in the form of branch stores, regional headquarters, or traveling salesmen—are constant reminders of the presence and prestige of the world's largest urban agglomerations.

Other equally dynamic ties act to gather in surplus commodities from different portions of a given country or from different countries so that they can be made available for redistribution. The market-center-trading-area bonds between these largest, or urban, units and their outlying associates thus make possible reciprocity of impact, whether outlying associates be in adjacent, contiguous retail- and wholesale-trade territories or in the form of individual contacts from positions well beyond the outer margins of those territories.

Ports and hinterlands. Merged into, and yet distinguishable from, the market-center–trading-area relationships are connections between ports and *hinterlands*. A hinterland differs from a trading area in being oriented to the incoming and outgoing foreign and coastwise shipping of a port, rather than to the retail-wholesale features of an urbanized settlement. Of course, many ports are also market centers and possess both trading areas and hinterlands, although the two usually do not precisely overlap. The ports in question may be water ports or airports, but almost invariably they are the former and in most cases are seaports.

Continuous and discontinuous hinterlands. Just as trading centers have their contiguous trading areas and their more distant, less distinctive trading territories, so do seaports lay claim to *continuous* and *discontinuous* hinterlands. The former are more or less generally recognized as being clearly oriented to their adjacent seaports. The latter are the more nebulous areas, beyond all continuous hinterlands, to which no seaport can lay exclusive claim and in which all vie for commerce. Discontinuous hinterlands are found more often in large nations—the Middle West of the United States (Fig. 6.1), the Urals region and the eastern portion of the effective territory of the Soviet Union, the

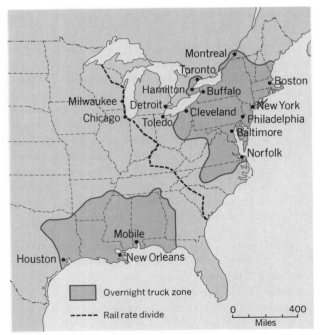

Figure 6.1 Hinterlands of selected ports in the United States, and the truck-rail rate divides between New York and New Orleans. (After Donald J. Patton, "General Cargo Hinterlands of New York, Philadelphia, Baltimore and New Orleans," *Annals of the Association of American Geographers,* **48**:436–455, 1958, and James B. Kenyon, "Elements in Inter-Port Competition in the United States," *Economic Geography,* **46**:1–24, 1970).

central portion of the peninsula of India. Some examples may be found also in nations of intermediate size: In West Germany, the discontinuous hinterland is the southernmost reaches of the country, north of the Alps; in Sweden, it is in the heart of that country's effective territory. For the commerce of these uncommitted, nebulously delimited discontinuous hinterlands, the major seaports are always in particularly active competition.

International Trade

Trade among nations is better known to most of us than trade within nations because detailed records have long been kept and are frequently published in popular as well as scholarly journals. This trade is also functionally organized in a manner generally resembling that of internal trade, but at a higher level of observation. Its focal points tend to be the world's more developed economies, particularly the effective areas of northwestern Europe and eastern North America, from which trade-route linkages reach out to other parts of the world, concentrating upon the functionally or nodally organized, regional arrangements within those other areas. International trade thus exhibits patterns that by now should not be new to the readers of this book: marked activity in the more dynamic sections of the developed nations, with other countries participating more or less in direct proportion to their propensities and capacities to exchange.

Background, Structure, and Patterns

Background. Trade among nations may be said to antedate nations themselves because this type of exchange took place between individuals and groups so long ago as to have been in existence when pictorial and written records came into being. However, modern, international trade on a global scale is scarcely more than a century old.[2] This century can be divided into three periods: 1865–1914, when a truly worldwide trade was established; 1915–1939, when there were both fluctuation and consistency; and the near-quarter century from 1940 to the present, during which there has been readjustment and pronounced growth. In the first period, particularly because of the dynamic political colonization based in Western Europe, which depended in large measure upon the economic industrial revolution that also had its emergence in Western Europe, international trade achieved global status. It also grew rapidly, increasing from slightly less than 5 billion dollars in 1867–1868 to nearly five times that figure by 1913. The next period, which essentially separated the two world wars, was both inconsistent and consistent. International trade rose rapidly until 1929, declined sharply in the Depression years of the early 1930s, and rose again in the late 1930s to 25 billion dollars annually (measured in 1938 dollars). In the third period, there was again a fluctuation as the key trading nations adjusted from wartime to peacetime conditions. Political and economic colonialism collapsed as a strong force in international trade throughout much of the then developing world and was replaced by numerous, usually small, politically independent countries which, even today, have not yet found a clear long-term focus in international trade. Meanwhile, the centrally planned economies emerged as strong trading nations, although not necessarily as a bloc. Most important of all, the European Economic Community and the Euro-

pean Free Trade Association were established and, in the early 1970s, merged embryonically into a larger European Economic Community. The ultimate result of these changing forces was a rapid growth in world trade which, by 1970, had increased by nearly twelve times its 1938 level when measured by current prices, and by nearly five times that level when measured by 1938 prices.

Structure. Measured by value, the structure or composition of modern international trade can be broken into six categories. Miscellaneous manufactured commodities account for nearly one-fourth of the total, and manufactured machinery and transport equipment are responsible for nearly an additional one-fourth. Almost one-fifth involves food, beverages, and tobacco, and slightly less than one-seventh is made up of crude bulk materials other than fuel. Mineral fuels and related materials make up nearly one-tenth, and chemicals the small remainder. If our measuring unit were tonnage, rather than value, these figures would be sharply altered. The crude materials, mineral fuels, and food, beverages, and tobacco—all products of primary industry—would be responsible for a much higher percentage than the semifinished and finished materials.

Pattern. Current patterns of world trade are summarized in Figures 6.2 to 6.5. The developed market economies now account for over 70 per cent of both exports and imports; the less developed, noncentrally planned countries account for approximately 18 per cent; and the centrally planned economies account for the remainder. Of individual trading blocs, the new and enlarged European Common Market is without peer, being responsible for well over one-third of all exports and imports. Among single nations, the United States is now responsible for slightly more than 13 per cent of all exports and for nearly as high a percentage of imports. Japan, Canada, and the Soviet Union, with shares of world trade ranging above or below 5 per cent, are other major trading nations on the world scene, besides those found in the European Common Market.

Roles of Selected Nations

The trade of the world's leading trading blocs and nations, and of their leading trading partners, is shown

[2] See especially Richard S. Thoman and E. C. Conkling, *The Geography of International Trade*, Prentice-Hall, Inc., Englewood Cliffs, N.J., 1967.

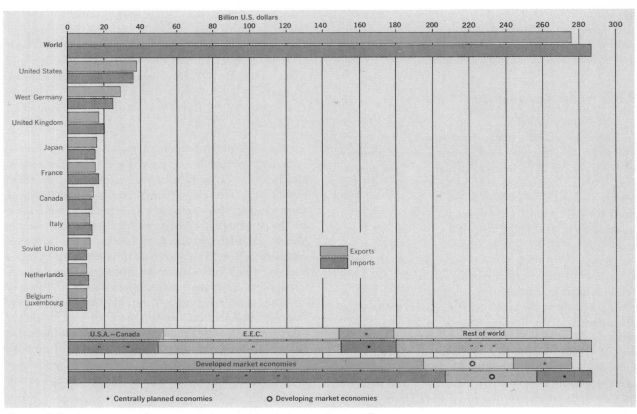

Figure 6.2 Exports and imports of the world, of the leading trading countries, and of various groupings of countries. Note the dominant positions in world trade held by the United States and Canada, and the European Economic Community. The excess of imports over exports is due to cost of transportation. (United Nations *Yearbook of International Trade Statistics.*)

in Figures 6.3 to 6.5. The maps and associated legends are self-explanatory. The plight of the world's less developed economies is no where better reflected than in their meager participation, especially on a per capita basis, in this international trade.

Impact of Government Policy

Whereas trade between and among individuals and, to a degree, between and among cities and their trading areas is relatively unaffected by government action, international trade is very much affected by such ac-

tion. This is due largely to the fact that international trade is one of the main expressions on the international scene of the internal viewpoints and policies of any political unit. Thus a country may adopt a protectionist policy and, through various measures, inhibit or restrict the flow of all trade or that of selected commodities. On the other hand, the same country may adopt a freer trade policy and encourage all trade or trade of selected commodities. Paradoxically, the historical records of most countries do not show consistency in this regard; instead there is a tendency for cycles to exist, swinging to and away from free trade and protectionism.

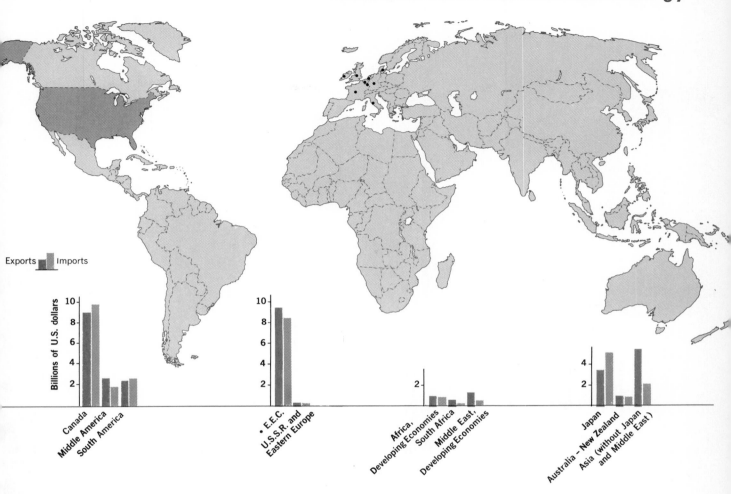

Figure 6.3 Exports and imports of the United States.

Tariffs and related controls. One of the most important influences by political units upon the volume and direction of world trade is exerted through such devices as *quotas, exchange controls, compensations, tariffs,* and *trade agreements*. Quotas may involve specific limitations by governments with respect to both the amounts of designated commodities which can be legally imported or exported and the nations to or from which they can be shipped. The next two are more indirect: Exchange controls are tools through which is made known the unwillingness of a country to accept, or permit its merchants to accept, more than specified amounts of the currency of other nations. Com-

pensations, in contrast, are subsidy arrangements for the encouragement or discouragement of certain trade by governments making such aid available. Except during periods of emergency and other extraordinary times, however, the aggregate effect of these tools of trade control is not so pronounced as that of tariffs, which are assessments levied by governments upon commodities entering or leaving their areas of jurisdiction,[3] and of trade agreements, which are designed for purposes

[3] More specifically, the word *tariff* refers to schedules of specific duties, and the word *customs* to the total import assessments. However, we are using the word *tariff* as a synonym for *customs,* in accordance with increasingly common practice.

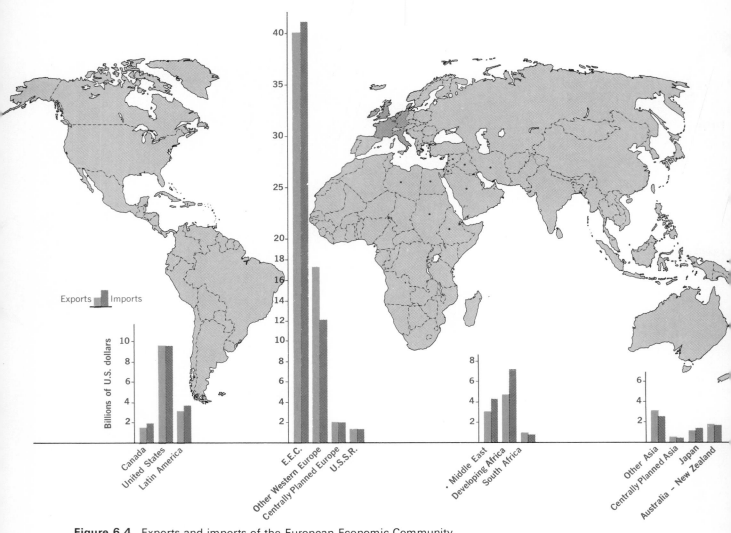

Figure 6.4 Exports and imports of the European Economic Community.

suggested by the term itself. All these various means of channeling trade overlap in actual practice, but we shall be particularly interested in the last two.

Tariff classification. Tariffs may be considered from several points of view. When weighed as to purpose, they are divisible into *protective* and *revenue* classifications; the former are designed to protect a home industry from foreign competition, and the latter are designed to yield taxes to the government responsible for the tariff. Applied to commodity movement, tariffs

are either *import* or *export* measures—i.e., levied upon either incoming or outgoing merchandise. Considered as to actual duties, tariffs may be *specific,* wherein an exact sum per unit is levied upon the merchandise in question; *ad valorem,* wherein the levy is in terms of per cent of the value of that merchandise; or *compound,* wherein some type of combination of the specific and of the ad valorem duties is employed.

Tariffs and more developed market economies. The tariffs of developed market economies are essen-

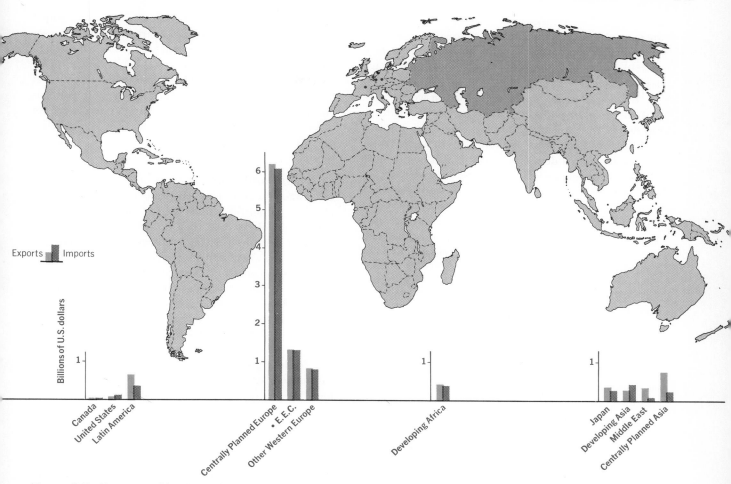

Figure 6.5 Exports and imports of the Soviet Union.

tially all import measures, and their levels have varied with both time and place. They stand today at heights that can best be generalized as more than moderately restrictive. This is true not only of the United States and Canada but also of many nations in northwestern Europe and some in outlying areas.

The United States and Canada. Beginning with the time of its inception and climaxing in the Hawley-Smoot Tariff of 1930, the United States formalized a tariff policy which, while fluctuating, trended toward increasingly high protective barriers. During the past quarter century, however, the nation has reversed that

trend; whereas in 1932 the total duty collections amounted to nearly 20 per cent of all imports and almost 60 per cent of all dutiable imports, they now amount to approximately 9 per cent of all imports and 14 per cent of all dutiable imports. These figures evidence a decline in United States tariffs that is not generally known. Indeed, tariffs of this country rank beneath those of most other leading commercial nations, including many Western European countries, which long have been advocating freer trade on a worldwide basis. The existing measures, some of them still high, are applicable chiefly to foreign products which might compete with domestic manufacturing and agriculture. In some cases the tariff decline represents an apparent rather than a real concession, inasmuch as quotas and/or other control measures have been substituted in order to check the inward flow of undesired goods.

Canada occupies a pivotal position in world trade. Not only is it an important trading nation, but it also has active trade relationships with the United States, the European Economic Community (Common Market), and Japan, and is developing still more ties. Its tariff policies, although varied, tend to be somewhat analogous to those of the United States. Some efforts have been made toward trade agreements between the two countries to offset some of the excessive tariff measures each maintains toward the other. These agreements have met with varied degrees of success and approval from the two countries.

Western Europe. Prior to the advent of the European Common Market, the tariff policies of Western Europe varied among the several nations involved, with the lowest duties prevailing in the north, intermediate rates in the latitudinal center, and the highest measures in the south. These tariff measures tended to be highest on manufactured commodities in the industrial north and upon agricultural produce in the south.

The efforts of the Common Market, which we shall describe in greater detail shortly, have been to remove all tariff and related measures among member nations and to adopt a common posture toward all commodities originating from outside the Market itself. We shall examine this question in further detail later in this chapter under Trade Agreements.

Other developed market economies. The tariff policies of the remaining developed economies vary sharply inasmuch as many of these are important producers of primary products and at the same time are attempting to develop secondary industry. Import tariff measures tend to be designed to protect key industries in the primary and secondary sectors. In addition, a number levy export tariffs on primary goods leaving the country and also on some exports of secondary products.

Less developed countries. The trade of most less developed nations is rather light, and many of their governments are only relatively youthful, having gained independence within the past quarter century. Consequently, tariff policies frequently are not yet discernible. Such tariffs as do exist are chiefly revenue measures assessed against outgoing mineral and agricultural products purchased by the more developed countries and upon imported luxuries. In Latin America, where independence is not a recent occurrence, such duties are often responsible for 25 to 50 per cent of all revenues received by the respective governments.

Tariffs and centrally planned economies. Trade is a monopoly of national governments in the centrally planned nations. Tariffs therefore do not assume the importance there that they do in other areas of the world. In certain of the more active trading economies of this group where adjustments must be made between world market price and domestic price of specified commodities, a form of tariff is employed. Measures similar to quotas also are used occasionally. However, these are difficult to isolate in trading statistics, and their importance is difficult to assess.

Trade agreements and organizations. ***Traditional agreements.*** Trade agreements traditionally have been more or less documented "gentlemen's agreements" executed bilaterally, with each interested nation entering into a number of such relationships with different nations as partners. Almost invariably they involve mutually satisfactory policy concessions agreed upon by nations participating in a given agreement. Where negotiated under the protective umbrella of an affiliation like a currency bloc or a loose political confederation, they usually are completed with maximum ease and finesse. However, they have been employed as well where no such affiliations are involved. More recently, they have tended to be multilateral, as is evidenced particularly by the General Agreement on Tariffs and Trade.

The General Agreement on Tariffs and Trade (GATT). On January 1, 1948, there came into being the General Agreement on Tariffs and Trade, an international body intended to reduce and stabilize tariffs and to provide a means of continuous consultation on trading problems. In addition, GATT favors the abolition of quota restrictions, with certain exceptions which are noted in the agreement itself. By 1970, the membership in GATT had reached seventy eight, plus countries that were participating under selected additional arrangements. All in all, they are responsible for over 85 per cent of international trade. Less developed countries make up a majority of GATT members, and increased attention is now being accorded to the viewpoint of such countries and their needs in the international trading scene. GATT has sponsored a number of international conferences designed to reduce tariffs and other import restrictions and also has served to facilitate payments and settle complaints.

The Organization for Economic Co-Operation and Development. In 1947, twelve European nations formed a group called the Organization for European Economic Co-Operation. In 1961, that group was enlarged to include Canada and the United States, and its name changed to the Organization for Economic Co-Operation and Development. At present, member countries are Austria, Belgium, Canada, Denmark, Finland, France, Greece, Iceland, the Irish Republic, Italy, Japan, Luxembourg, the Netherlands, Norway, Portugal, Spain, Sweden, Switzerland, Turkey, the United Kingdom, the United States, and West Germany. Australia and Yugoslavia have a special status and are active in certain functions. The primary objectives of this organization are to maintain a high level of economic growth and employment, and a corresponding high standard of living, in the member countries; to promote economic expansion in member as well as nonmember countries; and to contribute to the expansion of world trade on a multilateral, nondiscriminatory basis. Their interest reaches beyond their own member countries to include assistance to the less developed countries.

The European Economic Community. In contrast to the two organizations discussed above, the European Economic Community is an effort at complete integration of component members into a larger economic unit. Membership includes Belgium, France, Italy, Luxembourg, the Netherlands, West Germany, Denmark, the Irish Republic, and the United Kingdom. The EEC came into being on January 1, 1958, and at that time comprised only the first six members listed above. The three additional members were added in

1972. In addition, Greece and Turkey are associated with the Community, as are eighteen African former colonies of various full members.

Despite growing pains, the European Economic Community has achieved a remarkable degree of success. In the period 1971–1974, an independent revenue system for the entire Community is being phased in, so that the Community will function increasingly as a single unit. A common currency is being adopted, as are common license plates for automobiles. In the most recent major series of GATT conferences, the Community negotiated as a single unit, and not as individual governments. Efforts now are being taken toward political union.

Impact of government action. The net result of the various efforts of national governments has been more or less in accordance with the intent of such action. Where the effort has been toward cooperation, the success of the European Economic Community indicates that such cooperation is possible. On a smaller scale, in Latin America, the Central American Common Market, with membership from El Salvador, Guatemala, Honduras, Nicaragua, and Costa Rica, has also been successful in increasing a measure of internal cooperation. The Latin American Free Trade Association, involving Argentina, Bolivia, Brazil, Chile, Colombia, Ecuador, Mexico, Paraguay, Peru, Uruguay, and Venezuela has not been quite so successful. It is important to note that international organizations of this nature almost invariably are dedicated to overcoming protectionist tendencies in international trade. Where changes from this trend have occurred, they have been the results of actions by individual nations, usually in a time of temporary emotional stress.

Measurement of trade. *Balance of trade.* Individual countries are very sensitive to three measures of their international trade. The first is *balance of trade.* Basically, a country's balance of trade is the difference between the money value of that country's merchandise imports and exports. A balance is considered favorable when a country enjoys a surplus of exports over imports, and unfavorable when imports exceed exports. Most countries seek a favorable balance —but do not always succeed.

Balance of payments. The balance of trade is one important aspect of a country's *balance of payments,* which is the difference between the total payments made to foreign nations and the total receipts from foreign nations over a specified period of time. These payments include gold, all merchandise and services, expenditures of tourists and other travelers, and returns from the lending or exchange value of currency.

Terms of trade. Although less explicit, the idea of *terms of trade* is used to apply to the total conditions under which a nation carries on its foreign trade, including balance of trade, balance of payments, and individual prices of specific commodities. If the terms of trade are favorable to a given country, that country's position and potential in world trade are advantageous. If not, the reverse is true.

Trends and the Future

International trade is important not only as a linkage among specific countries but also as a source of livelihood. Its linkage aspects have been discussed in the immediately preceding pages. In brief, it is rising in importance, particularly with regard to the more developed economies. Technically, as nations are subsumed into larger customs unions, it may appear to decline, simply because it is reported on the basis of larger units—a larger "geographic mesh." In fact, however, it merely transfers its status from international to internal trade, as described at the beginning of this chapter. However classified, the future of international trade appears to be favorable in terms of overall growth.

Trade is also an important consideration in livelihood. It accounts for an estimated 10 per cent of the world's labor force and for as much as 20 per cent of the labor force of the more active commercial nations. It supports far more people than any of the world's lesser primary activities—minerals extraction, fishing, forest-products industries, and grazing—and is responsible for over one-half as many as are engaged in manufacturing.

However, with respect to the future of individual countries, current trends in international trade reveal one extremely important adverse feature. This relates to terms of trade and to the less developed economies. In brief, the terms of trade are turning increasingly against the less developed economies, mainly because such economies are not yet capable of producing many of the goods and services required in the secondary and tertiary activities and must import these. In return, they offer to the world market their own primary materials. Whereas prices of primary materials have risen very slowly, those for secondary and tertiary goods and services have risen dramatically. Thus many of the less developed countries are forced to pay an increasingly large price differential between their imported necessities and their exported surpluses. This grim fact, coupled with an increasing gap throughout the world between per capita income in the less developed economies and that in the more developed economies, merits serious attention on the part of anyone sincerely concerned with the geography of economic activity. Unless this growing gap can be narrowed—indeed, eliminated—the long-range chances for world stability are very, very poor.

Chapter 7

The Economic Environment: Structures and Patterns of Transportation and Communication

Today's volume of consumption, production, and trade would have been impossible without large-scale transportation and communication. Particularly vital is commodity movement, which is as important to the functioning of the world's economies as the flow of blood through the human body. The principal interest of economic geographers in transportation and communication lies in their impact—in time and cost conditions and variations, as these affect the movement of goods, people and their services, and messages. We shall examine that impact in greater detail in Part 2.

In this chapter, we shall focus attention on the actual media of transportation in order to understand more fully the discussions which are to follow. By way of illustration, in Figure 7.1 point C represents the place of consumption of a given commodity or service, whereas P is the site of production, and the intervening arrow shows the *linkage* relationship which results from efforts at P to supply the demand at C. Linkage is shown here as a straight line. However, when translated to the earth's surface, the actual movement of goods, people and services, or messages may follow rather

circuitous routes and may be subjected to numerous interruptions, changes from one transportation or communication medium to another, or temporary placement in warehouses. Furthermore, the location, on the earth's surface, of C and P may be affected by the kind of transport media serving both places, as well as by the time-cost impact.

The media under consideration are ocean vessels; lake vessels; inland waterway, coastwise, and intercoastal craft; railway trains; motor vehicles; pipelines; airways; and such elementary transportation forms as direct human or animal drayage or porterage. We shall also take a look at other forms of transport now on the drawing board—some practical and possibly on the threshold of adoption, and others more exotic and requiring more experimentation.

Of the media now in existence, the ocean vessel and the railway train are the leading carriers. The ocean vessel is probably responsible for about one-half, and the railway train for about one-third, of the ton-mileage (weight multiplied by distance) of the world's freight. In terms of tonnage alone, the railway train is the

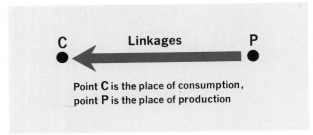

Figure 7.1 Abstract concept of production, consumption, linkages. A linkage denotes flow, rather than route.

world's prime mover, carrying approximately two-thirds of the weight of all cargo.

Whether in terms of quantity, quality, or efficiency of operation, the world's more developed economies are served more effectively by transportation and communication media than the less developed economies. From the viewpoint of the individual person or firm, this means wider range of choice among specific carriers or types of carrier and a good possibility of substitution of one type for another in emergency situations. As a matter of policy from the viewpoint of national, regional, state, or local economies, this signifies not only internal strength in provision of linkage relationships but also an important contribution to the economy itself. In the United States, for example, the transportation industry contributes between 15 and 20 per cent of that country's gross national product each year. Conversely, the less developed countries, which are forced to compete on an equal basis in the world's marketplace with the more developed economies as well as with one another, are in a comparatively disadvantageous position—a position which is worsening rather than improving.

Comparative Costs

Because of the wide variety of carriers and of goods and people which are carried, it is impossible to generalize meaningfully on relative and absolute costs among transportation and communication media. However, insight is provided if we examine a specific commodity in a specific area. In Figure 7.2, we see the costs of transporting oil within Europe by various media. From the illustration, three points are clear:

1 Not all carriers are equally equipped to transport this particular commodity for all possible distances. Road transport is essentially the only form of local delivery, and international tankers become the principal means of transport when the length of haul exceeds 1,000 miles.

2 There is a range of cost, with the highest charges shown in motor-truck delivery, followed by railways, coastal watercraft, and small-diameter pipelines and extending through the larger inland watercraft, the larger-diameter pipelines, and down to the maximum efficiencies of ocean tankers reaching or exceeding 150,000 deadweight tons. Note that the greatest range lies within the pipelines, where costs are nearly 2 cents per ton-mile for the very small-diameter lines and less than $\frac{1}{10}$ of 1 cent for large-diameter lines.

3 For all carriers, costs per ton-mile decline with longer distances, up to the maximum range which can be served efficiently by that particular type of carrier, in competition with other types. The most striking increase in efficiency with distance is in coastwise watercraft, and the least dramatic is in pipelines, whatever the diameter of the line.

Not shown in the illustration, for obvious reasons, are costs of transporting bulk commodities in the Great Lakes of North America or by aircraft, animal drayage, and human porter. Estimates elsewhere place these figures at approximately $\frac{1}{10}$ of 1 cent per ton-mile for a Great Lakes vessel, 15 cents per ton-mile for aircraft, 30 cents per ton-mile for animal and wagon or cart, and as high as $1 per ton-mile for human porter.

Again, the reader is cautioned that all the data shown above are somewhat generalized; however, they do provide a measurement which can be taken as a guideline of understanding for much of the remainder of this chapter.

Water Transportation

Water not only supports the weight of its carriers but also is relatively frictionless. Moreover, its routes usually need little if any artificial maintenance. Transportation media utilizing water thus are comparatively

Figure 7.2 Comparative costs of transporting oil by different media. ''Bridging'' means long haul in truck transport. ''Mty'' refers to carrying capacities, in metric tons, of pipelines with different diameters. ''Dwt'' is deadweight tonnage of ocean vessels (footnote 1, below). The entire graph is based on conditions in Western Europe. (After Michael E. Hubbard, *Economics of Transporting Oil to and within Europe,* Maclaren and Sons, Ltd., London, 1967, p. 78. Reprinted by permission.)

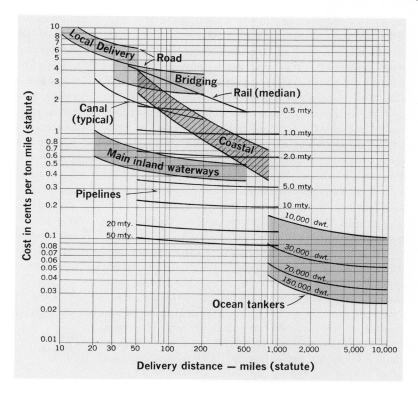

inexpensive to operate, particularly when heavy, bulky merchandise is the cargo.

Although economical, the water carrier also is comparatively slow and hence tends to specialize in liquid or solid-bulk cargoes or other merchandise for which rapid delivery is not a must. This is particularly true of inland-waterway and coastal craft, which are in constant competition with faster but more costly overland media that are attractive to shippers of perishable commodities and package cargo. Ocean-crossing vessels, on the other hand, are free from such competition and hence haul appreciably larger quantities of semifinished and finished commodities. All water craft are in competition with the embryonically developed air-freighting services, but the volume of commerce handled by the latter is as yet very small.

Transoceanic Shipping

The carriers. The world's merchant fleet involves nearly fifty thousand vessels which are larger than 100 gross registered tons,[1] and these aggregate a grand total of 247 million gross registered tons. Nearly 60 per cent of these (here considered by actual number of vessels) are no larger than 2,000 gross registered tons each, and as a rule they do not venture into the open seas. Almost another 30 per cent are registered at between 2,000 and 8,000 gross tons, and only the remainder, slightly ex-

[1] Ship tonnages are variously designated as follows: *gross tonnage,* used in official registries of ownership, signifies the total capacity of a ship measured in per-ton units of 100 cubic feet, less certain authorized deductions; *net tonnage,* used to admit and clear ships in harbors and to assess dues, etc., involves the same measuring unit as gross tonnage but provides also for the subtraction of space occupied by quarters for the captain, crew, passengers, etc., and thus depicts the actual carrying capacity of a ship; *measurement tonnage,* used to assign space to shippers, is arrived at in a manner generally like that used in reaching net tonnage, except that the measuring unit is 40 cubic feet; *displacement tonnage,* expressed in either long tons (2,240 pounds) or metric tons (2,205 pounds), refers to the weight of water which a vessel displaces and may pertain to an unloaded ship plus weight of crew (displacement light) or a fully loaded ship, including fuel (displacement loaded); *deadweight tonnage* designates the cargo-carrying capacity of a ship and is expressed in either long or metric tons.

ceeding 10 per cent, are in the class of distinctly large ships which range from 8,000 to 200,000 or more gross registered tons. In 1972, there existed a total of 164 vessels with individual gross registered tonnage exceeding 100,000 (or about 200,000 deadweight tons). Of these, 162 were tankers and 2 were ore-bulk-oil carriers.

The increase in size of the world's merchant fleet has been dramatic, nearly doubling in the decade 1960–1970. This is particularly true of tanker fleets, the average annual increases of which now account for more than half of the world total. As of 1972, nearly 40 per cent of all merchant-fleet tonnage involved tanker vessels, whereas 38 per cent involved nonbulk vessels, and 22 per cent were carriers of ore and bulk other than petroleum or its products.

Besides increased utilization of large tankers and other bulk carriers, an extremely important recent technological development in the world's transoceanic shipping has been the advent of the *container ship*, a vessel designed especially to carry containers which measure 8 feet by 8 feet by 10 to 40 feet. Each ship can carry between 1,000 and 2,000 containers. Some of the new vessels accommodate both containers and other cargo, including automobiles and containers which have their own wheels (roll-on, roll-off cargo). Once in a port, the containers are shifted from ship to dockside by cranes designed especially for that purpose. In addition, attention is now being given to increasing the number of roll-on, roll-off vehicles.

The growth in the use of container vessels has been phenomenal. In 1966, five shipping lines offered container services. By 1967, this number had increased to 38, serving more than 100 ports. One year later, the number had increased to 88, serving more than 200 ports. The actual number of container ships rose from 50 in 1968 to more than 300 in 1970. It has been estimated that by 1980, 60 per cent of ordinary nonbulk, dry cargo—mostly semifinished and finished products—will move by container vessel.

The advantage of the container vessel over the ordinary ship is to be found particularly in increased speed and reduced costs. Container vessels now being built will have a cruising speed of 35 knots per hour, as compared with present cruising speeds of 20 to 24 knots. The principal saving of time, however, is in the port itself, where the ship is very rapidly unloaded and reloaded and sent back out to sea. Nine ships with average carrying capacities of 1,300 containers each can replace eighty conventional ships in the North Atlantic run because of the increased efficiency in operation.

Figure 7.3 shows the impact of containerization upon port-to-port cost for an ordinary-sized dry-cargo vessel, a large dry-cargo vessel, an ordinary-sized container ship, and a large container ship. The reader can easily see the enormous decline in the overall cost in container versus package-cargo vessel and also recognize that most of this decline is in loading and unloading, which accounts for nearly one-half of the total operating costs of the vessel. This decline is offset somewhat by the costs of packing and unpacking the container and the costs of the containers themselves, but even when these are included, savings are about one-third to one-fourth of the operating revenues of conventional vessels.

The terminals. Ships load and unload at *ports*, wherein are found the necessary facilities for such oper-

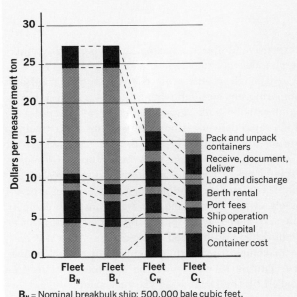

Figure 7.3 Impact of containerization on ocean shipping. (Reprinted by permission of the National Ports Council.)

B_N = Nominal breakbulk ship: 500,000 bale cubic feet, 17 knots speed

B_L = Large breakbulk ship: 700,000 bale cubic feet, 17 knots speed

C_N = Nominal container ship: 455 containers, 19.5 knots speed

C_L = Large container ship: 910 containers, 19.5 knots speed

HAVANA, CUBA

Coastal (natural)

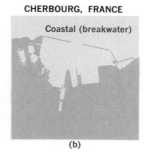

(a)

CHERBOURG, FRANCE

Coastal (breakwater)

(b)

BOMBAY, INDIA

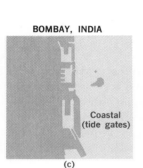

Coastal
(tide gates)

(c)

JACKSONVILLE, UNITED STATES

River (natural)

(d)

BREMEN, WEST GERMANY

River (basin)

(e)

BREMERHAVEN, WEST GERMANY

River (tide gates)

(f)

BRUGES, BELGIUM

Canal or lake

(g)

RAS TANURA, SAUDI ARABIA

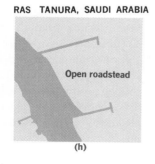

Open roadstead

(h)

ations. Although only a few ports forward and receive most of the world's commerce, there are nearly 6,500 ports in the world today accessible to oceangoing ships. Port facilities necessarily include, of course, some means of accepting the cargo. The simplest ports possess small-boat service to and from the ship and precious little else. From this crude stage of development, the world's port facilities range upward in completeness and complexity, until ultimately they entail the intricate systems of piers, wharves, sheds, warehouses, tank farms, grain elevators, dry docks, dauphins for midstream tie-ups, fixed and floating cranes, towage, lighterage and stevedoring arrangements, ship repairing and chandlering services, and the associated constant activities of a leading seaport.

Most ports are located in *natural harbors,* which are the crucial places along coastlines where natural conditions favor the putting in of water craft. A coastal indentation that combines ice-free, naturally deep water with freedom from obstruction and protection from extremes of weather is considered to be an excellent site for harbor development. An additional amenity is the contiguous presence of an inland-waterway or lowland-overland route by which a hinterland can be easily reached. The port-harbor types of the world have been classified as natural, coastal, tide-gate coastal, natural river, artificial river, tide-gate river, canal or lake, and open roadstead, as is shown in Figure 7.4. Obviously, their specific port-harbor associations vary,

Figure 7.4 Harbor types. A natural coastal harbor is sheltered from wind and open water by location on a shoreline indentation. A breakwater coastal harbor lies behind a man-made barrier that provides shelter from wind and open water. The tide-gate coastal harbor keeps water at a constant level by locks, regardless of rise and fall in tides. A natural river harbor is like a natural coastal harbor except that it is located on a river; its port facilities, however, frequently are parallel to the waterway on which it lies. In a river-basin harbor, slips for vessels are dug into the river banks or floodplain, usually obliquely or at a right angle to the trend of the river. A tide-gate river harbor is like a tide-gate coastal harbor except that it is located on a river. A canal or lake harbor usually is artificial rather than natural and may be connected to open water by an artificial waterway. The facilities of an open-roadstead port reach into the water as jetties; under these circumstances, there is essentially no natural harbor, and cargo may be carried between ship and shore in boats. (After drawings in *World Port Index,* Washington, D.C., 1953.)

but their function is inevitably the movement, with or without accompanying storage, of cargo.

Despite the spate of seaports, most of the world's commerce is transmitted through only a comparatively small number of major terminals. These are clustered particularly in Western Europe, which still remains the major focus of world trade. Its principal corollary is in eastern North America, extending from Canada through the Caribbean. Port activity is also intense in certain sections of eastern and southern Asia, particularly Japan, and is increasing markedly both in Japan and in the Soviet Union. Seaports of the less developed nations, in contrast, are much fewer in number and more conspicuously separated from one another, with each serving its own specific hinterland. In many cases, a less developed nation possesses only one port, with the nation its hinterland.

The routes. Although the potentialities for roaming are vast, the world's shipping follows rather well-defined channels. Most vessels operate regularly between leading ports, having been attracted there by active demand and supply conditions of the hinterlands of those ports. Where possible, they follow the *great circle route*—the shortest distance between two points on the earth's surface—deviating from this route only where markets or natural conditions necessitate their doing so. The resultant traffic lanes can be grouped in five broad and overlapping patterns: the North Atlantic routes, which extend between the dynamic manufacturing and commercial regions of eastern North America and Europe; the inter-American routes, which connect the United States, Canada, and Alaska with one another and with the Latin American nations, notably in Caribbean America; the Latin American–European routes, which are especially pronounced between southern Latin America and Europe; the European-African-Asian routes, which, separating at Gibraltar, not only serve the Mediterranean Sea and the Indian Ocean, the China Sea, the Sea of Japan, and the Pacific Ocean but also reach ports along the western, southern, and eastern coasts of Africa; and the Pacific Ocean routes from Asia and Oceania to the Americas. At the time of this writing, the important routes which formerly focused upon the Suez Canal have been at least temporarily discontinued because the canal itself is now out of operation.

Complemented by smaller trading routes which cross the Pacific Ocean and which fill other instances of the overall pattern, these routes basically connect the technically advanced areas of Europe and North America with one another and with outstanding less developed nations, as well as with outstanding more developed areas. Most of these routes benefit substantially from man-made or man-improved waterways: The North Atlantic routes now project into the Great Lakes by way of the improved St. Lawrence Seaway, and the Panama and Suez Canals, when operating, are crucial focuses, respectively, of the inter-American and European-American-Asian routes.

Ownership and operational policies. The world's merchant fleet essentially is owned by governments, corporations and companies, other institutions, or individual citizens of technically advanced nations. This ownership may or may not be reflected in flag registration because some owners prefer to register their vessels under flags of nations other than the ones of which they are citizens. Currently, about 15 per cent of all gross registered tonnage of merchant vessels is under the flag of Liberia, 12 per cent under that of Japan, 11 per cent under that of the United Kingdom, somewhat less than 9 per cent under that of Norway, slightly less than 7 per cent under that of the United States, almost as many under that of the Soviet Union, and about 5 per cent under that of Greece. Most of the remainder are registered under flags of countries in northwestern Europe, in which the Federal Republic of Germany, Italy, France, the Netherlands, and Sweden are especially important. Of the leaders, all but Liberia and Greece are technically advanced. The prominent position of these two countries, as well as that of Panama, results from the fact that they permit the shipowning citizens of other nations to take advantage of certain exemptions and inducements of their laws by registering under their flags.

When examined by schedules of operations, the world's nonmilitary freight-carrying fleets may be subdivided into *liners, tramps,* and *private carriers.* Liners maintain regularly scheduled service for passengers, passengers and cargo, or cargo only. They are particularly numerous on the North Atlantic trade routes, but also offer direct service to nearly every active seaport, with transshipment to smaller coastwise vessels of goods destined for smaller ports. They usually are the largest and fastest civilian ships in existence and, when carrying merchandise, tend to haul the more expensive goods which can stand their higher freighting charges and which are attracted to their faster service. This is the service wherein container ships are so rapidly coming to the fore.

Tramp ships do not maintain regular schedules and carry whatever cargo is available at any port of call—usually bulk freight that is low in value. Compared with liners, they tend to be older, smaller, more uncertain in schedule, and willing to carry almost any legitimate cargo if the time at which that cargo should arrive is not a crucial factor.

A neat distinction between tramp and liner shipping is perhaps somewhat misleading, for some companies keep their ships of intermediate age, size, and speed on a standby basis, sometimes using them in liner services and sometimes sending them out on tramping junkets.

Private carriers are used primarily by large manufacturing concerns to deliver raw materials, fuel, or finished products. They are particularly numerous in association with corporations and companies of the United States that refine petroleum or produce industrial metals. Many are tankers.

Trends. A century ago nearly all the world's ships were sailing craft. Then came the steamship, which for over fifty years burned coal and now largely consumes fuel oil from petroleum. It is augmented today by the internal-combustion engine, which also burns petroleum products. Indeed, the majority of new vessels have internal-combustion engines. The fuel of tomorrow, already well past the initial stages of experimentation, is nuclear power. The increasing efficiency of fuel consumption will aid both liner and tramp shipping to the extent that longer uninterrupted hauls of heavier loads will be possible and few delays will be attributable to the putting in of a vessel to a port for refueling. Concomitantly, this same increase in efficiency will mean a decline in much of the bulk-cargo traffic, for the fuels being delivered to strategically located refueling points—the fuels which may be replaced by long-lasting, mobile nuclear power sources—constitute significant quantities of such traffic.

As stated previously, ships are increasing in size and versatility of use. We have emphasized the sharply rising importance of the container vessel. In addition, both the tanker, a semihollow liquid carrier, and the combination passenger-cargo vessel are comparatively new to the world's merchant marine. Tankers are particularly effective cargo carriers, for their cargoes can be pumped mechanically off and on the ship and can automatically fill every cubic inch of the hold without human aid. Consequently, tankers carry not only petroleum but also other materials which can be reduced to liquid, like latex and sulfur, and goods normally canned or bottled, like fruit juices or wines. The most important trend in tanker construction is toward larger size and computerized operation, with crews correspondingly reduced. Now on the drawing boards are almost fully automated vessels with carrying capacities of 500,000 deadweight tons.

The trends in operational policies are toward more regularly scheduled liner service, with special attention to container operations and to combined passenger-freight vessels, whether such vessels are tankers or dry-cargo carriers. Another trend is toward diversification of ownership; at the turn of the century, the Union Jack of the United Kingdom flew over approximately one-half of the tonnage of the world's merchant fleet. Today, even though dominated by relatively few nations, that fleet is of much more varied nationality, Scandinavia, Europe, and the Soviet Union having emerged into notable prominence. That this trend is continuing is emphasized in a comparison of current flag registry with that of even a decade ago, when about 21 per cent of all gross registered tonnage of merchant vessels was under the flag of the United States, 15 per cent under that of the United Kingdom, 10 per cent under that of Liberia, 8 per cent under that of Norway, and the remainder under the flags of Western European countries, Greece, Panama, and the Soviet Union. Two major changes are apparent. First, Japan, Norway, and the Soviet Union have engaged in rapid shipbuilding, so that the number of vessels under their control is now substantially greater than was true in the early 1960s. Second, Liberia and Greece have sharply increased their relative positions, whereas Panama has declined relatively, as the leading less developed nations of flag registry. As we have seen, these three countries allow foreign owners to register under their respective flags, and their high reported positions are due more to international politics than to economics.

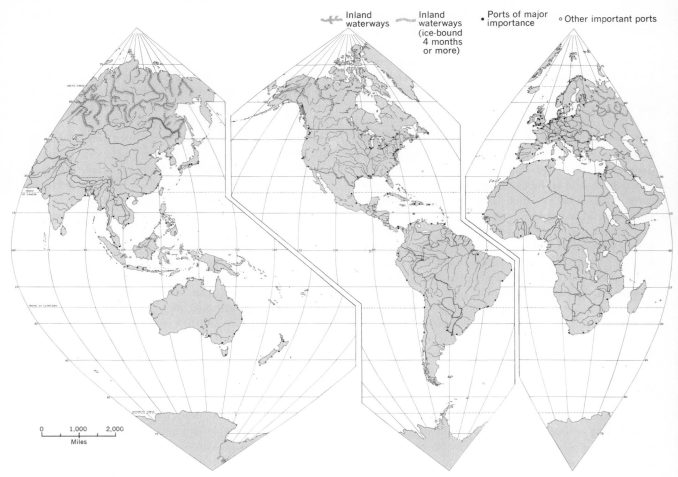

Inland waterways — Inland waterways (ice-bound 4 months or more) • Ports of major importance ○ Other important ports

Figure 7.5 The world's leading ports, inland water routes, and sea lanes. No ocean traffic is moving through the Suez Canal at present, and the future of the canal is in doubt because it will not be able to accommodate the larger supertankers without drastic new construction and enlargement. Even Egypt now has a pipeline bypassing the Suez Canal. If the canal becomes operative, its rate structure will need to be partially subsidized by Egypt to compete with alternative routes, especially that around the southern tip of South Africa; with supertankers, the longer voyage now is economically feasible because of their huge cargo carrying capacity. See also Figs. 18.14 and 20.2. (After *Encyclopaedia Britannica*.)

Inland-Waterway and Coastal Shipping

The carriers. Except for lake vessels, inland-waterway craft are quite small. They are seldom able to carry more than 3,000 deadweight tons. Most carry even less. Notably in North America and in some areas of northwestern Europe, the actual carriers are shallow-draft barges laced together, either in single-file arrangement or in pairs, and towed by tugboats. Indeed, when timber is moved, the barges may be dispensed with, and the tugs merely pull the log cargo made up into large rafts. Inland-waterway or coastal craft sel-

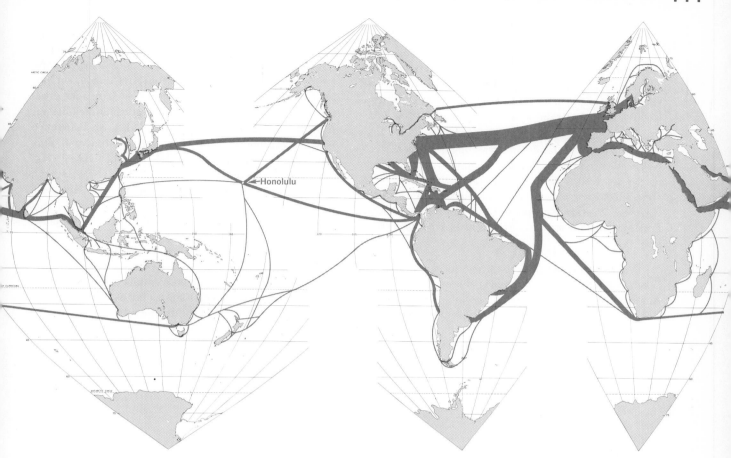

dom draw more than 6 or 7 feet of water, and hence they generally do not require channels deeper than 9 feet. In contrast, most lake carriers are larger, sometimes carrying more than 20,000 deadweight tons. Those of the Great Lakes of North America were until recently built to specifications necessitating a 20-foot channel depth, but with the deepening of those channels to 27 feet as part of the program of the Great Lakes–St. Lawrence Seaway, ships drawing 25 feet of water may pass through them with ease. Some experiments and preliminary trials are now being conducted in which barges, like containers (p. 106), are loaded on overseas carriers. Other efforts are being directed toward utilization of large seagoing barges pulled by tugs.

The terminals. Inland-waterway and coastal carriers specialize in bulk freight, and their terminal facili-

ties reflect such specialization. More often than not, those facilities are incorporated into the overall structure of a major port, where inland and coastwise carriers meet with transoceanic shipping for transshipment purposes. Where such terminals are not combined with active seaport facilities, as was true along the western margin of Lake Superior before the advent of the Great Lakes–St. Lawrence Seaway, they are predominantly geared to bulk transfer and hence are dominated by gravity chutes, loading shovels, grain elevators, pumping gear, and other trappings for loading and unloading such merchandise.

The routes. In the world patterns of inland and coastal shipping, the technically advanced lands are once again very conspicuous (Fig. 7.5). The routes in Europe are both very numerous and very actively used.

The routes of the United States (Alaska excepted) and of European Russia are moderately numerous and moderately utilized. The routes of eastern and southern Asia are moderately numerous but very actively used. The routes of the very high and low latitudes are used lightly except in eastern and southern Asia. Of all continents, only Australia is without inland routes.

Operation. Inland-waterway operation is perhaps best understood when studied regionally, for the commerce involved is mainly domestic or regional. We are concerned here chiefly with the activities of North America, Western Europe, the Soviet Union and Eastern Europe, southeastern Asia, South America, Africa, and Australia.

North America. Three categories of inland and coastal shipping are particularly discernible in North America, the first two involving oceangoing vessels: (1) Great Lakes–St. Lawrence shipping, (2) coastwise and intercoastal oceangoing traffic, and (3) inland and intracoastal movements.

If we define the Great Lakes–St. Lawrence shipping lane as that section of the Great Lakes–St. Lawrence Seaway which can be traversed by lake vessels, we find that this lane extends from Duluth and Superior in the United States, and Thunder Bay in Canada, on the west, to Seven Islands, at the lower St. Lawrence estuary in Quebec, on the east. The lane thus includes all five Great Lakes, plus the Great Lakes–St. Lawrence Seaway extending from Kingston to Montreal, plus much of the estuary of the St. Lawrence River (Fig. 7.6). Before the completion of the St. Lawrence Seaway, vessels could traverse only the Great Lakes themselves. The primary function of lake vessels then was to carry iron ore and grain from the western Lake Superior ports to the lower lake ports and to return coal and some petroleum products. The St. Lawrence Seaway, which was designed to allow oceangoing vessels into the Great Lakes, instead allowed the lake vessels to move into the St. Lawrence and downstream as far as Seven Islands. The reason for this is found in the relative dimensions of the vessels: A laker, drawing 26 feet of water or less, may carry more than 20,000 deadweight tons. Such lake

Figure 7.6 The Great Lakes–St. Lawrence Seaway. The main map shows only the St. Lawrence River, the navigable channel of which has been constructed and is maintained by both the United States and Canada. The inset shows the entire Great Lakes–St. Lawrence Seaway. The small segments connecting the Great Lakes have been deepened and are maintained by the United States alone. The channel depth of the entire Seaway is 27 feet. At Montreal, the water is deeper. Less than three-fourths of the world's merchant shipping vessels can move up the entire Seaway as far as Chicago, Duluth, or Thunder Bay. The remaining one-fourth involves vessels too large for the Seaway—vessels which carry the lion's share of the world's international trade.

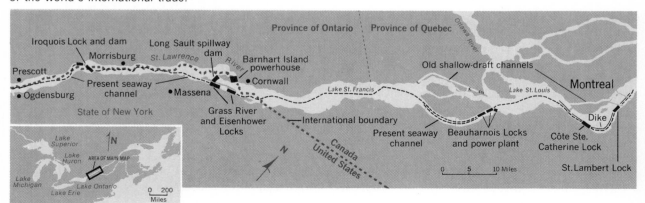

vessels look more or less like oversized cigars; they are very long and shallow and need little internal structuring to survive the comparatively mild storms of the Great Lakes and upper St. Lawrence River. In contrast, ocean ships, which must be built to survive open-sea conditions, are shorter and stronger. As a result, the largest ocean vessel which can navigate the St. Lawrence Seaway cannot carry more than 12,000 deadweight tons. For this reason, the lake vessel has penetrated as far seaward as possible.

Despite the enlargement of the Great Lakes route with the addition of the St. Lawrence Seaway, more than three-fourths of all tonnage in the overall Great Lakes–St. Lawrence system remains within the Great Lakes proper. As in the past, this movement is largely of iron ore and grain from Duluth and Superior and other western lakehead ports down to the lower lake ports of Chicago, Detroit, Cleveland, Buffalo, and similar destinations. The reverse flow is largely coal and petroleum products moving northward. Of the segment which now stretches through the Welland Canal and St. Lawrence River, the primary movement is westbound iron ore from Labrador and eastbound coal, grain, soybeans, and manufactured iron and steel goods—a substantial share for transshipment at either Montreal or Seven Islands (Sept-Isles) to oceangoing carriers.

An interesting aspect of most Great Lakes ports, notably so if they are not oriented to overseas commerce, is that either their respective shipments heavily exceed their receipts or their respective receipts heavily exceed their shipments. Thus shipments dominate overall commerce of ports on Lake Superior, and receipts dominate most of the ports on Lakes Michigan, Erie, and Ontario. A major exception is Toledo, where heavy movements of coal from Appalachia are forwarded both to the northwest by the Great Lakes shipping lanes and to the northeast via the St. Lawrence River.

The coastwise and intercoastal oceangoing commerce is found mainly along the Atlantic and Gulf Coasts of the United States and involves primarily the movement of petroleum from Texas and Louisiana seaports and of Appalachian coal transshipped at Hampton Roads and smaller eastern ports to the fuel-hungry and populous northeastern states. Along the

Pacific Coast, petroleum from southern California to the far northwest of the United States constitutes a movement of secondary significance. Finally, a decreasing quantity of bulk goods moves between the two coasts via the Panama Canal.

The active inland and intracoastal shipping lanes, usually no more than 9 feet deep and dominated by smaller craft, are also situated chiefly within the United States (Fig. 7.5). The major traffic is along such waterways as the Mississippi, the Illinois (plus its connections to Chicago), the Ohio, and the Tennessee Rivers and along the Gulf Intracoastal Waterway from Mobile to Corpus Christi and Houston. Petroleum and coal are overwhelmingly predominant among the freighted commodities. Petroleum products are also important along the New York State Barge Canal, together with some grain.

Western Europe. The European coastline is largely submergent, so that the oceans and seas have encroached upon the land, and the resultant large and small peninsulas and indentations are conducive to coastwise shipping. Such sizable and relatively constant rivers as the Rhine, the Danube, and the Elbe Rivers, interconnected and augmented by lesser rivers and by a series of canals, add to the possibilities of such shipping. Much of the commerce of Europe, therefore, is waterborne—the coastwise cargoes in small craft of 3,000 deadweight tons or less and the river and canal cargoes in units of progressively shallower draft and carrying capacity as the upstream segments of waterways are approached. Many of the riverboats as well as ocean vessels are individually owned carriers, which along some routes are more prevalent than barges. Specific freight includes coal, iron ore, petroleum, grain, sand and gravel, fertilizers, and other bulk freight as well as a very limited amount of package cargo.

The Soviet Union and Eastern Europe. The sphere of influence of the Soviet Union now orients much of the commerce of Eastern Europe toward the Soviet Union. Its presence has meant a rearrangement of most of the traffic lanes of the northern portion of Eastern Europe, which before the last war looked appreciably to such westward-trending arteries as the Elbe River, the Mittelland Canal, and the complementary overland routes for trade outlets. The effects of this sphere of influence have not been quite so drastic in south central Europe, which traditionally has looked eastward toward the Black Sea via the Danube River route, but even here some change of orientation has occurred.

Although there are fewer inland waterways in the Soviet Union proper than in Western Europe, they usually are quite long. The interconnected system involving the Volga and Don Rivers and Lakes Ladoga and Onega is of outstanding significance, for it allows water craft to reach the White, Black, Baltic, or Caspian Seas from any point along its length, including the capital city of Moscow. The final splice within this system was added with the completion of the Volga-Don Canal in 1952, thus providing for interchange between the Volga River–Caspian Sea routes and those of the Don River, Black Sea, and associated waterways. The lion's share, possibly as much as 85 per cent, of the river commerce of the Soviet Union travels over this system— including the 50 per cent of the nation's total which moves over the Volga River alone—with most of the remainder accounted for by the northward-flowing rivers of European and Asian Russia. The commerce is made up largely of timber in the far north and of coal, petroleum, grain, iron ore, and fish in the central and southern regions. Essentially all rivers are frozen in winter for at least four months, and those in the far north for a much longer time.

Coastwise commerce is limited chiefly to the Black and Caspian Seas and to the summer runs along the fringes of the Soviet Arctic. Intercoastal shipping is of little importance, partially because of the distance involved. Such shipping is virtually overseas commerce; the distance from Odessa to Vladivostok via the Suez Canal is almost as great as that between the same two ports via the Panama Canal.

The outlying areas. The small-craft shipping of much of southeastern Asia, Latin America, Africa, and Australia is very much a matter of coastwise vessel movement. Such activity is pronounced within the island nations of Japan, the Philippines, and Indonesia and is equally or even more active along the rim of Asia's mainland from China to Pakistan. It is definitely reduced in intensity, although very much present, along the coasts of continents in the Southern Hemisphere.

The inland-waterway movement, while less conspicuous than coastwise shipping, is evident. Ocean vessels of intermediate size reach Hankow on the Yangtze River of China, and much smaller shipping continues upstream to Chungking. Small native craft shuttle between Rangoon and Mandalay on the Irrawaddy River of Burma. Similar navigation occurs on a number of natural waterways of this general portion of Asia and in Africa, the more actively used being the lower Ganges and Brahmaputra, the Mahanadi, the Kistna, and the Cauvery Rivers in India; the Indus in Pakistan; and segments of the Nile in Egypt and Sudan and of the Congo, the Niger, and smaller rivers in Africa. In South America, the most frequently utilized waterways are the Magdalena, the lower Orinoco, the main stream and several tributaries of the Amazon, and the lower Paraná-Paraguay-Plata. Navigation is interrupted by rapids on some rivers, notably those in Africa and the Magdalena River in South America.

Ownership and trends. Most inland-waterway and coastwise commerce is transported by craft belonging to the country wherein the goods are being moved. In centrally planned nations, its capital equipment, like that of all other transportation and production, is essentially state-owned. In the United States, it is essentially all privately owned. In the remaining areas the ownership varies, with a tendency for predominance of state ownership in many European political units and in the more technically advanced of the less developed nations.

In the past quarter century, the amount of inland-waterway and coastwise shipping has not increased in general proportion to the increase in world productivity or to that of transoceanic commerce. This is partially because the pipeline, a strong competitor of the small water carrier, has come to be a significant mover of liquid and gaseous materials, and even slurried solids. For example, a pipeline has been proposed to carry iron ore slurry from the Mesabi Range in Minnesota directly to Chicago. Cost of transport: $3.66 to $3.97 per long ton, compared with $4.08 (rail-lake vessel) or $5.60 (all rail). (See U.S. Bureau of Mines Information Circular 8512, 1971.) Also important has been the substitution of petroleum and gas for coal, and other changes in technology.

Overland Transportation

The Railways

A century and a half ago the railway was virtually unknown. A century ago it had established itself as a major carrier. Today, although having suffered in competition with other carriers, notably the truck and the pipeline, it remains the world's prime mover of commodity tonnages.

The carriers. Diesel locomotives have gained almost complete supremacy in the United States and Canada and are increasing in importance in Western Europe. Electric motors are used particularly in Switzerland, Sweden, Italy, the Netherlands, Norway, and Austria and to a noteworthy degree in Japan, Brazil, and the Soviet Union. In many less developed areas, steam engines continue to be important. Freight cars, especially numerous in technically advanced countries, vary among nations as to size and load carried: The typical freight-car shipment in the United States and Canada ranges from 25 to 80 tons (average: 64.3 tons); in the United Kingdom the average size is 9 tons; in Denmark, 12 tons; in France, 16 tons; and in Portugal, 9 tons.

The terminals. Trains, like ships, are loaded and unloaded, and therefore many of their individual terminals are more or less miniature versions of those in seaports. Their terminal facilities are not usually so concentrated as those of seaports, however, because the freight cars can be shunted more effectively than ships to individual warehouses. Unlike vessels, trains are made up of a series of individual carrying units and must be broken up periodically so that the freight-car components can be forwarded to new trains or sidings. At critical junctions, usually key cities, *classification yards* exist for the purpose of breaking and re-forming trains. Once found close to civic centers, these facilities are now being constructed predominantly in suburbs, often at the crossings of main lines entering urbanized areas and belt lines which, circling those areas, provide railway facilities to manufacturing plants and other industries that have shifted to the suburbs. This is particularly true in the United States.

The routes. The world's railways are as unevenly distributed as the levels of its technical advancement and its populations. Tightly woven networks exist in the most active and populous areas of Noth America and Europe, and each sends tentacles in all directions toward either the oceans or empty countrysides. Away from these nodes, railway development has been much more erratic (Fig. 7.7).

There are more than 7 million miles of railway trackage in the world. Of this total, 28 per cent is in the United States, over 11 per cent is in the Soviet Union, more than 10 per cent is in the nine countries of the European Economic Community, and nearly 6 per cent is in Canada.

North America. The United States and the effective territory of Canada are so thoroughly crisscrossed with railway lines that only the most isolated outreaches are beyond easy accessibility (Fig. 7.7). These two nations rank first and third, respectively, among all nations when appraised by trackage, with nearly 210,000 miles of main lines in the United States, amounting to more than four times the total in Canada (and nearly three times that in the second-ranking Soviet Union). But even such dense networks do not reveal the intensity of traffic they make possible, for many lines are double-tracked and/or equipped with centralized traffic-control systems for maximizing the use of individual tracks by dispatching trains accurately. The outlying areas of North America—Alaska, northern Canada, the intermontane west of Canada and the United States, and Caribbean America—are places of isolated lines rather than networks, and the monotonous regularity of such lines is broken only by an occasional junction point or an even more infrequent node marking the presence of a population cluster and productive industry.

Western Europe. The network of rail lines in northwestern Europe is even more closely woven in its densely settled core districts than is true in most corresponding core districts of North America, for in Europe the motor vehicle and the pipeline, while active, do not offer the degree of competition to railways that is found in the United States and Canada. From those densely tracked districts, European lines extend toward the Arctic north, the Soviet Union, and the Mediterranean Sea.

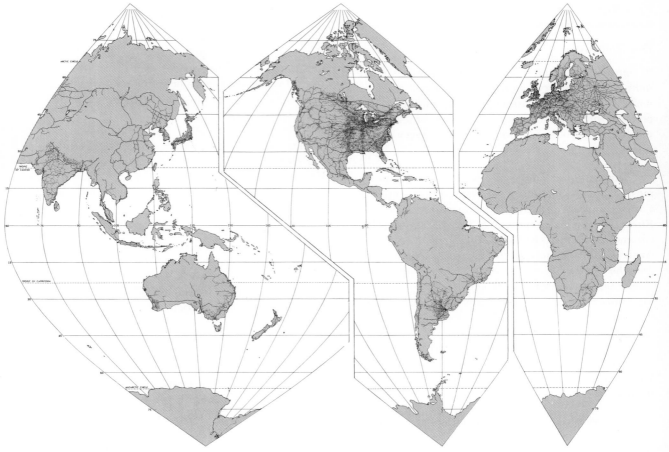

Figure 7.7 The world's railroad lines. (After *Encyclopaedia Britannica.*)

The Soviet Union and Eastern Europe. The Soviet satellite countries along Russia's western perimeter represent transitions from the northwestern European network to the less dense but extensive system of the Soviet Union. The three most industrially advanced of these—East Germany, Poland, and Czechoslovakia—contain much more trackage than their more rural southern neighbors, but in all these countries, as in the Soviet Union, the railway is the foremost freight carrier.

Most railways in the Soviet Union are west of the Ural Mountains. From this area of concentration, tracks stretch as individual lines or as a series of lines toward the north, the south, and particularly the Asian east. Here, in the rapidly developing portion of the effective territory of the Soviet Union, relatively new tracks have been constructed among the Urals and Kuznets industrial districts, the Karaganda coal fields, the Irkutsk industrial district, and the agricultural oases and cities along the southern fringe of Soviet Central Asia. Probably the best known of the many Russian railroads is the Trans-Siberian, winding for over 5,000 miles from Moscow to Vladivostok on the Pacific coast. Along this and parallel routes, the Soviet Union's effective area is slowly being extended eastward.

Other areas of the world. Railway development in places other than the three most technically advanced areas reflects closely the past influence of Europe. In Latin America, the Union of South Africa, and Australia, the railroads were direct cultural implants by Europeans or their descendants. In India, where an effective network exists, and in most of Africa and much of southeastern Asia, where the lines are more sporadic and tend to serve key seaports, many of the railroads were constructed in an earlier time by the colonialist nations (and hence are excellent evidence that the impact of colonialism upon areas where it now prevails or once prevailed is certainly not entirely disadvantageous). Japan industrialized and constructed its railways only after quasi-enforced contact with the Occidental world in the form of Admiral Perry's heralded visit there. China's early railroads were built chiefly by European capital, and many of the later ones, notably in Manchuria, were built by Japan when China was under Japanese control. Korea's numerous railroads also were constructed largely by the Japanese. Turkey's railroads were initiated through the efforts and financial backing of German, French, and British firms, as were others in the Middle East and czarist Russia. The direct and indirect influence of Europe upon the world is probably in no way more effectively, thoroughly, and clearly attested than in the current pattern of the railway lines.

Among outlying nations, the technically advanced but commercially oriented countries display route patterns suggesting commodity movement between ocean port and hinterland. Argentina, the Union of South Africa, and Australia are striking examples (Fig. 7.7). Interestingly, the less developed areas evidence generally similar route patterns—but the individual lines, often constructed by foreign interests for exploitation and homeward shipment of mineral or agricultural resources, are fewer in number. Only in Japan, India, and Korea do nationwide networks prevail in these outlying areas, and these owe their existence to conditions indicated earlier in this chapter.

New railway lines. The world as a whole appears to be experiencing a slight retrenchment in total railway lines. Most of this retrenchment involves feeder lines of technically advanced lands such as the United States—lines which are suffering in competition with motor vehicles and other forms of transport. Notably

in centrally planned nations, however, the railroad trackage is increasing. Besides new lines in the Soviet Union and in some of its European neighbors, railways are being added in China and peripheral Asian nations. In China, these lines are especially important in that they provide better liaison between the country's effective and outlying areas.

The critical importance of gauge. Because the world's railway lines have developed at different times and under different conditions, their specifications vary. One of the most critical of such specifications is gauge—the distance between the rails. Where tracks of differing gauges meet, usually at political borders, entire trainloads of merchandise must be transferred, for the simple reason that the rolling stock of one gauge cannot be accommodated by track of a different gauge. Occasionally, but not often, a third rail is added to a railway bed so that trains of at least two gauges can utilize the same route.

There are many gauges, but the most common are *standard* (4 feet 8½ inches), *broad* (at least 5 feet, and in some cases wider), and *narrow* (comprising many different gauges, the most common being meter gauge, which is 3 feet 3⅜ inches, and a gauge in most former British colonies of 3 feet 6 inches).

Most of North America—notably the United States, Canada, and Mexico—is dominated by the standard gauge. The same gauge is found in most of Western Europe, except in Spain and Portugal, where the prevailing gauge is 5 feet 6½ inches; in Ireland, where it is 5 feet 3 inches; and in the Austrian Alps, where a narrow as well as a standard gauge is extensively employed. The broad gauge of 5 feet is accepted throughout the Soviet Union, but not in many of its neighbors.

In the more outlying areas, however, the gauges are much more varied. That of Argentina is mainly broad (5 feet 6 inches), but some of the trackage is also meter. In Brazil, Chile, Ecuador, Bolivia, and the southern sections of Caribbean America the gauge is meter, and in Peru and Uruguay it is mostly standard. In Egypt, Morocco, and the Asian nations of the Middle East the gauge is principally standard, as it is in China and Korea. In central and southern Africa it is chiefly narrow (3 feet 6 inches). In India it is partly broad (5 feet

6 inches), partly narrow, and partly meter. Along the Asian rim from Burma to Japan it is mainly meter (except, of course, for China). In Australia it is broad (5 feet 3 inches), standard, and narrow, and in New Zealand it is narrow.

The most persistent uniformity of gauge and the highest measure of railroading versatility are found, with some exceptions, in the most technically advanced nations. Perhaps one day we shall have a plan farsighted enough to provide for complete uniformity of gauge throughout the land areas of the world.

Operational policies, ownership, and trends. Despite the extensiveness of its trackage, the railroad train is mainly a short-haul carrier when compared with the ocean vessel. In large nations like the Soviet Union, Canada, and the United States, its average haul is less than 400 miles, and in the small countries of northwestern Europe, only 75 to 150 miles. The operational policies and trends vary with ownership. Government-owned railroads predominate in all centrally planned nations; in nearly all of Europe; in most of southeastern Asia, Australia, and New Zealand; and in such separated countries as the Union of South Africa, Morocco, Algeria, Tunisia, Argentina, Colombia, and Mexico, and in the state of Alaska. Government ownership is present but not always predominant in Canada, Brazil, Chile, Portugal, Switzerland, and Greece. Among the more developed lands, only in the United States are essentially all lines privately owned.

In most of the world's political units the railroad train is an important carrier of passengers as well as freight, and hence the lines assume a multi-use status. However, in much of Europe, in Canada, and particularly in the United States, the automobile accounts for a substantial share of the passenger traffic—in the United States for over 85 per cent of all its nonlocal passenger miles. Moreover, in these same nations the motor truck and the pipeline are offering new and serious competition in freight commerce. Therefore, the most notable trends in overall policies of railway freight haulage are apparent in the United States, where the railway companies are encountering increasing competition from other media and where many private lines are attempting to remain competitive by (1) abandoning passenger service; (2) relinquishing uneconomical

feeder lines that carry freight; (3) operating subsidiary trucking companies, the trucks replacing rail runs in certain areas and being hauled on flat cars ("piggyback") in joint rail-highway operations; and (4) charging slightly higher rates. Despite all these operational changes, however, the immediate future of railroads in the United States—particularly of the short-haul railroads in the Northeast that now cope with still added competition from ships on the Great Lakes–St. Lawrence Seaway—does not appear to offer promise of continued overwhelming dominance in freight movement. Only slightly more than one-half of the domestic intercity freight of the United States now is carried by rail. As recently as 1928, nearly four-fifths moved by rail.

However, one may well ask whether the long-term future of railroads may not be brighter. As the economy expands, more goods and people will need to be carried. Can the nation afford continued investment in costly highways and air terminals, when railroad tracks already exist and are not being used to capacity? A benefit-cost assessment would appear to be necessary—and soon!

The government-owned railroads of the world will probably continue into the foreseeable future at their present or even higher relative positions. Since they are subsidized, they will carry what needs to be carried—people, package freight, bulk goods—where other carriers are not more effective. This is especially true of the centrally planned economies.

The Highways

Except in some less developed countries, the motor vehicle is a vital necessity for the local deliveries in most cities and towns, and during the past quarter century it has begun to compete actively for intercity freight (Fig. 7.8). Known road mileage in the world is more than fifteen times the amount of railroad trackage. The United States accounts for 32 per cent of this total, the European Economic Community for over 12 per cent, and the Soviet Union for nearly 8 per cent. In the United States, over 20 per cent of the ton-mile freight movement is by truck. In Europe the figure is not so high, but is increasing. Even in the Soviet Union, where the construction of motor vehicles and roads has

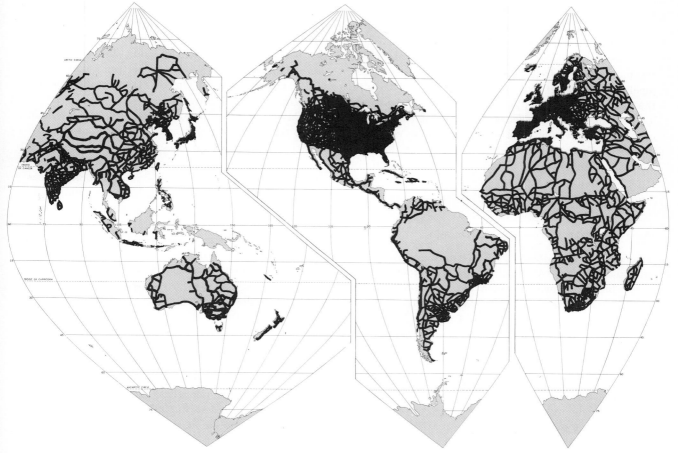

Figure 7.8 The world's motorable roads. Areas within 25 miles of motorable roads are shown. (After *Encyclopaedia Britannica.*)

not been emphasized as much as railways, the truck accounts for a substantial per cent of the ton-mileage of all freight.

It appears, therefore, that throughout the world and particularly in more developed economies that are not centrally planned, the motor truck will become a serious competitor for the high-value, low-bulk type of commerce that moves between, as well as within, urban units.

The Pipelines

Pipelines serve (1) to transport liquids and gases the entire distance from the sources of raw materials to

markets, (2) to carry liquids from the sources of raw materials to ports of shipment, and (3) to carry liquids from receiving ports to ultimate markets. At present, they are used overwhelmingly to transfer petroleum and its products and natural gas, but they offer promise of conveying diverse other materials that are liquefied or can be carried in suspension. Currently, pipelines range downward from 48 inches in diameter. Once constructed, they are comparatively simple to maintain—indeed, they are quasi-automatic in operation.

Pipeline networks are well developed in the United States and are more than noteworthy in the Middle East, the Soviet Union, Canada, Europe, and Venezuela. In the United States, where they had been well established by the outbreak of the last war and received much more attention during that war when many coastwise tankers were sunk by German submarines, they are now responsible for over 20 per cent of the ton-mileage of all freight. Among the other areas with pipelines, the Soviet Union is like the United States in that its network is chiefly one of internal development. The Middle East and Venezuela are important areas of pipeline movement from supply sources to seaports; in Europe the movement is from seaports to the interior; and Canada is an area of both internal supply (from the mountain west to the east) and supply from seaports to markets.

Pack Animals, Porters, and Drayage

In the most technically advanced nations, the draft animal is rapidly disappearing, and the human porter is all but unknown. (Reasonable facsimiles of the human porter are to be seen, paradoxically, in such busy places as the garment district of New York City, where, in the heart of Manhattan Island, they unconcernedly push racks of dresses down streets already choked with vehicle traffic!) In many less developed economies, however, as well as in some economies that are quite accomplished technically, the horse and wagon, the ox and cart, the dog team, the pack animal—yak, camel, alpaca, llama, even the sheep and goat—are still actively employed in transportation. Although information concerning them is meager and although they are a part of the passing scene, such animate forms as these are not to be overlooked in the total evaluation of transportation.

Air Transportation

Especially during the past decade, the airplane has become an important carrier of both people and high-value merchandise. In the United States, over 10 per cent of all passengers now travel by air. The number of passenger miles (passengers multiplied by miles of each trip) is increasing at an average rate of about 2 per cent each year in this country. Although the movement of goods by air is still insignificant when measured by tonnage—amounting to less than 1 per cent of the world's total tonnage of freight moved—it more than quadrupled during the 1960s even when considered in this way. When measured by value, its importance is more than striking: In 1970, 14 per cent of the value of all exports from the United States, and 8 per cent of all imports, moved by air.

Current policies of using larger aircraft should enhance the role of air transport. This increased importance will be especially effective in two ways. First, more goods as well as passengers will move by air, and this medium of transportation should become increasingly significant. Second, the airport, involving movement of freight as well as passengers, will come to resemble the seaport, as to total array of facilities, much more than is now the case. This trend, in turn, will affect the geography of economic activity, as to both site and general location. Careful attention is now being accorded the sites of new airports, particularly the larger airports serving metropolitan areas, not only regarding traditional aspects such as availability of flat land for takeoff and landing and freedom from climatic and other natural environmental constraints, but also concerning the role of the airport in the development of the region of which the metropolitan airport is a part. The geographic location of the modern airport increasingly resembles that of a seaport which is relieved of its shoreline locational restrictions. In other words, the same locational guidelines can be applied to both, except that the airport is free of a coastline constraint. The network of future airports will be distributed increasingly in terms of their capacities to serve the needs and wants of man.

Trends in Transportation

We are at the threshold of some very important technological innovations in transportation that can significantly affect both economic geography and planning. With regard to movement of persons, some developments are past the pilot-test stage and are well on the way to general acceptance. Trains moving at 125 miles per hour now are operating, but these may soon become replaced by land vehicles which, although using wheels for slower speeds, actually move without wheels to achieve speeds up to 300 miles per hour. One version

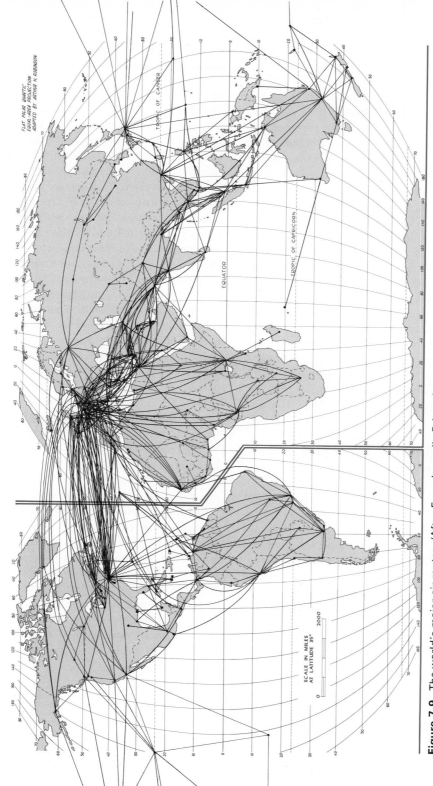

Figure 7.9 The world's major air routes. (After *Encyclopaedia Britannica* and information from The American Geographical Society.)

depends upon a cushion of air to separate it from a guiding rail. Another, which now appears the front-runner, depends upon reverse magnetism to lift the vehicle from its guiding rail, and is propelled by a modern version of an electric motor. Speeds this high, if not offset by stations being located too closely together, can allow commuting to work from distances of 200 miles. (They allow for faster time, but do not necessarily reduce cost, and therefore probably would need to be publicly subsidized if adopted into common use.)

A new aspect of air travel also may exist by the turn of the century. This is the hyperplane, which actually is a two-stage vehicle modeled after today's rockets. The lower stage—the booster—would be very much like a current 747. Riding "piggyback" on it would be a second, rocket-powered aircraft, in which passengers are carried. The booster plane would rise, with its rocket-and-passenger load, to current flying heights. Then, after being "aimed" by the booster, the rocket plane would take off, reaching suborbital speeds of up to 15,000 miles per hour. It would fly in a high arc and descend to its destination. The hyperplane would be practical for distances exceeding 3,000 miles, but not less. Those distant places would be within one and one-half hours' flying time from the point of takeoff. Places less than 3,000 miles away, being reached by traditional aircraft, would be more distant, when measured by travel time (but *not* when measured by travel costs) than places reached by hyperplane!

Technological changes affecting movement of goods pertain to savings in costs rather than time. These involve especially larger units of transportation—supertankers, railway cars, trucks, pipelines, and aircraft. They thus should reduce the transport cost constraints on the location and efficient functioning of economic activity, just as innovations in passenger movement will yield savings in time. The net effect of current technological changes, and those expected within the remainder of this century, should be to provide man with greater freedom of choice in locating economic activities.

Communication

Communication facilities are important in the geography of economic activity in three critical ways. First of all, they facilitate the knowledge of demand and supply for goods and services, whether applicable to needs or wants, and hence contribute enormously to the efficient functioning of the world's economies. Second, communication is increasingly employed as a substitute for transportation. To a degree, this is true at all levels of development. In many of the world's frontier areas of both developed and less developed economies, communication is utilized to the maximum degree as a substitute for actual movement of people and services. Shortwave sets long have been used in such areas, not only to remain in day-to-day contact but also to provide educational and health services. Nearer the world's metropolitan areas, there is an increased tendency to substitute communication for transportation. This has been traditionally the case with telephone and radio, but with the advent of computers, television, and new means of color video presentation, it is increasingly possible to communicate one's needs and wants rather than make journeys. The suggestion has been made that a substantial decentralization of both economic and political activity from the cores of urban centers can be facilitated by this type of substitution. (A major technological liability, however, is the relative ease with which such communication can be intercepted by various technical listening devices.)

Certainly one of the most important and increasing contributions of communication is the role of this medium in the assessment of the physical setting. Through satellites and remote sensing devices, plus varieties of photographic film, it is now possible to survey, with a remarkable degree of accuracy, not only the atmosphere of the earth but also its surface and subsurface—and, indeed, the surfaces of the moon and Mars as well. The importance of communication to this aspect of the geography of economic activity is only now beginning to be appreciated.

PART 2
Approaches to Economic Geography

We indicated in the Preface and in the Introduction the important aspects of approach, method, and information to be discussed in Part 2. There are numerous approaches to the field of economic geography. Two, however, can be distinctly recognized: the historical-institutional-inductive approach and the theoretical-deductive approach. In this book, the senior author presents the first viewpoint, and the junior author the second. Both authors' views are incorporated in the sections where the approaches are synthesized. Chapter 8 contains the methods and concepts common to both approaches, Chapter 9 gives a further elaboration of the historical-institutional-inductive approach, and Chapters 10 to 13 provide a further elaboration of the theoretical-deductive approach.

The reader will note that methods and concepts common to both approaches already have been applied in Part 1. The approaches themselves will be applied in Parts 3 and 4.

Chapter 8

Methods and Concepts Common to the Institutional and Theoretical Approaches

We mentioned previously that the institutional and theoretical approaches to economic geography are not mutually exclusive, but overlapping. In this chapter we shall note first the overlap in methods and second the overlap in certain basic concepts.

Methods

Description

Whatever its validity, an idea is of very little value until it is communicated. Some form of description usually is a necessary first step in such communication. For the sciences and many of the arts, this description almost always is in the form of the written or spoken word. For certain of the arts, it may be in terms of music, color, form, or other means not requiring the written or spoken word.

As the first step in analysis, description is extremely important to both the institutional approach and the theoretical approach. It is important because it involves a clear grasp of what is being described, as well as the transfer of that grasp to the reader or the listener. Considerable mental discipline is required to carry out successful description, and the experienced observer frequently passes initial judgment on the quality of a research effort on the basis of its descriptive aspects. This is true for two reasons. First, the description lays the groundwork for the more advanced argument, and the reader or listener can quickly appraise the incisiveness of the author's or the speaker's thinking on the basis of how effectively that groundwork is laid. The description may be concerned with the subjects, objects, or methods of study, and usually it involves all three. Second, because it does lay the groundwork for the remainder of the study, the description normally comes early in the study, and the reader or listener's first contact with the research effort is by way of its description section.

Measurement

As we all know, the weakness of simple description is lack of precision. Numbers, statistics, and mathematical techniques and methods lend precision to analysis, provided the translation of qualitative, and sometimes philosophical, terms into numbers has been done correctly.

Perhaps the most valuable of all the simple numerical tabulations is census information. All the world's more developed economies, and most of the developing ones, gather information periodically about their populations, economies, societies, and an ever-widening range of additional considerations in the form of census tabulations which are published under selected headings. In the United States, census information, gathered at the beginning of each decade, is available concerning population and related characteristics. In addition, at regular intervals that do not necessarily coincide with the decennial census periods, census data are gathered for agriculture, manufacturing, wholesaling, retailing, transportation, and still other activities. These are published under standardized headings, with each subgroup a further breakdown and more detailed articulation of the specific topic under consideration.[1] The United Nations also has a classification of census information involving all members, to the extent that each wishes to send such information in a code somewhat similar to that of the United States and other countries. At some future date, which optimally will be as early as possible, all the countries of the world may agree upon standardized census headings so that numerical comparisons between different countries will be possible.

In addition to regular census information, a wide range of numerical data are available from public and private sources, and of course can be obtained by the researcher in independent field work. The strong and increasing emphasis placed upon measurement indicates its importance to work not only in geography but also in other disciplines and in the daily operations of essentially all economic activities. The advent of the computer increases the potential for measurement and for the use of analytical techniques, which usually begin with simple measurement and then carry forward into procedures which are much more complex.

[1] U.S. Office of Management and Budget, *Standard Industrial Classification Manual, 1972,* 1972.

Classification

Classification logically follows some, and precedes other, description and measurement. Usually, classification also follows, rather than precedes, definition of a research objective. Many of the classifications which have been presented in earlier chapters of this book were adapted from such research efforts. For example, Figure 2.3, the map of climatic regions, is a generalization of a very refined classification wherein climate is inferred from vegetational association and expressed through specific measurements of temperature and precipitation. Similarly, classifications of soils and natural vegetation are drawn from research efforts with very specific purposes, and some of these have also been initially expressed in numerical terms. There have been many efforts to classify levels of development, and in this book we have used three, expressed numerically, to arrive at a specific classification of development (Fig. 3.4): (1) per cent of the labor force in agriculture (Fig. 3.1), (2) per capita consumption of energy (Fig. 3.2), and (3) per capita gross domestic product (Fig. 3.3).

The importance of both measurement and classification to research is that they assist in *resolving form into structure.* When we look about us, we see a myriad of natural and human features interposed in what at first appears to be a haphazard array. However, by measuring according to specific criteria, usually with a specific purpose in mind, man has been able to classify many of these criteria into groups that can be viewed structurally or sectorally (usually by tables or graphs) or spatially (usually by maps). Especially during the past decade, we have become very sensitive to the interrelationships of structure (or sectors) and space. We understand that, for example, primary, secondary, and tertiary activities can be shown in a table or graph as sectors—say, per cent of labor force of a given country or of the world found in each sector. However, this picture is incomplete without a map expression of the spatial distributions and the linkages of these sectors. Both the graph and the map are, in effect, classifications which have some meaning in themselves but much more meaning when considered in terms of their reciprocal relationships. In brief, structures (sectors) affect space, and space affects structures (sectors). Proponents of both the institutional and the theoretical approaches to geography are increasingly aware of this important consideration.

Concepts

The primary differences between the institutional and the theoretical approaches to economic geography are in methods, as explained above, rather than concepts. Neither approach considers the concepts of the other to be wholly invalid, although there may exist differences in emphasis. A number of concepts in economic geography are considered important by both approaches, and we shall examine these.

Site and Relative Location

Although geography has evolved into a complicated and refined discipline, it is still concerned basically with location and the implications of location. The first and necessary aspect is the fact of location. A city, country, mountain range, manufacturing area, or other cultural or natural feature is situated where it is and nowhere else. In simple descriptive terms, this is the geography which most of us teethed upon (and which too many people consider the whole of geography even today!). The absolute fact of location is, however, one important aspect of geography. As a student from Iran said recently in a tone of desperation to his instructor at a United States university, "How can I discuss the problems of my country in any intelligent way with students of your country when most of them think Iran is in South America?"

Site. The absolute fact of location, in which a feature is shown on a map, involves not only position but also site. The site of a feature extends to its natural as well as its cultural implications and involves a series of *vertical relationships* that are more relative than absolute (glossary). These include a full spectrum of geologic, soil, water, social, economic, political, and other aspects with which that feature may be associated. In economic geography, only those aspects become meaningful which contribute in some way to the location and functioning of economic activity in relative as well as absolute terms.

Relative location. If there were only one feature with which geography were concerned, very possibly our assessment would be a very simple one and would always be in absolute terms, However, geography is concerned with a myriad of features, both natural and cultural, in a myriad of locations. Furthermore, these features are not inert, but are constantly interrelating with one another, both vertically and horizontally. For this reason, relative location becomes an extremely important consideration in geography, and especially in economic geography. With change in time, in this age of rapidly altering technology, the positions of each of the features, both near and far, relative to one another, may be altered dramatically.

All this may be illustrated by a case study of New York City. The absolute fact of New York's location is that it is to be found in a coordinate position of lat 40° 45′N and long 74°W. However, in a relative sense with respect to selected natural features, New York is on the Atlantic seaboard of the continent of North America, at the mouth of the Hudson River, and at the southern outreach of the Hudson–Mohawk–Lake Champlain lowland. With respect to selected economic features, New York is on the eastern margin of the United States–Canadian manufacturing belt and is situated comfortably at a break-of-bulk position (transfer point from land to sea) on the North Atlantic shipping route between that manufacturing belt and concentrations of manufacturing and markets in Western Europe and elsewhere.

This relative location is not static, but must be continually reassessed with the passing of time and changes in technology, economics, societies, political conditions, human values, and even aspects of the natural environment. Success of the airplane in moving people over long distances has caused New York to decline sharply as a passenger embarkation and debarkation center. Completion of the Great Lakes–St. Lawrence Seaway has meant a reassessment of New York's freight-haul relationships with its normal hinterland. The rise of New Orleans as a more active seaport, a rise due not so much to changing technology as to the dynamic energy of a few key leaders, has also caused a reassessment of New York's relationships with its trading area, especially that portion situated in the western portion of the manufacturing belt.

In this capsule evaluation we have not, of course, begun to analyze the full absolute and relative implications of New York's location. We have, however, suggested some of these implications of the geography of economic activity for this particular place.

Regions and Margins

If, for any undefined area in the world, or in the entire world, we were merely to describe the absolute and relative site and locational aspects of the area, we would be engaging in the descriptive stage of a research effort. In attempting to understand more clearly both the absolute and the relative aspects of location, the geographer has classified these aspects into *regions. A region is a portion of the earth which has been delimited on the basis of one or more unifying criteria.* A region may be very small or very large; no limiting criteria have yet been generally accepted. Now that more data are available and are manageable because of the computer, it is increasingly possible to use a number of criteria in classifying regions.

The homogeneous region. Geographers, especially, long have recognized the homogeneous region, which is identifiable on the basis of one or more *static criteria* (Fig. 8.1). By *static,* we mean inert, or at least considered in an inert sense. The homogeneous region may be delimited on the basis of either a natural or a cultural criterion or on the basis of a combination of criteria. It may be as small as a city block or as large as the Rocky Mountain–Andean cordillera. It may involve cities as settlement features (but not, as we shall see in the next section, as nodes of dynamic activity); groups of manufacturing areas such as the manufacturing belt of the northeastern United States and southeastern Canada (again, considered as settlement features); farming types such as are mapped in Figure 5.1 and described at length in Chapter 5; and regional subdivisions of climate, natural vegetation, or soils, such as are mapped in Figures 2.3, 2.4, and 2.7 and described in Chapter 2. (For still other examples, see Figs. 2.8 and 5.2 to 5.6.) These homogeneous regions are not mutually exclusive, but are overlapping. Furthermore, each region may be subdivided into smaller regions or aggregated into larger ones, if such action is

necessary because of the need for different levels of observation.

The advantage of the homogeneous region is that it allows man to see more clearly the general similarities and differences of the features with which geographers are concerned. The homogeneous region is an especially useful device not only for understanding the complexity of the earth's surface but also for comparing man's uses of different parts of the earth with one another and also against a theoretically optimum standard and pattern of utilization.

The functional region. Whereas the homogeneous region has been known to geographers for centuries, the importance of the functional region has been recognized only in the twentieth century and is only now coming to be appreciated fully. The functional region, as its name implies, is related to the spatial implications of human activity (Fig. 8.2). Indeed, the utility of the functional region is confined almost entirely to human activity and is scarcely applicable to the natural environment as such. Inasmuch as human beings make decisions in central headquarters and transmit those decisions by way of transportation and communication routes to areas affected by such headquarters, the functional region almost invariably takes the form of a central node, with spiderlike arteries reaching out to the area affected. A simple concept of such a region is a farmstead relative to the farm itself, with the routes to and from the fields comprising the connecting linkages to the affected area. Various sizes of cities and metropolitan areas, and their trading areas, are important functional regions, as we shall emphasize in the next section. A political capital has ties over its sovereign political unit. Figure 8.2 shows these and other illustrations. (For other examples, see Figs. 6.1, 12.19, and 25.1.) Again, we should note that levels of observation will reveal different sizes and types of functional regions.

Importance of Urbanization

In an age when so many people throughout the world are moving to urban units, especially to large metropolitan areas, we can scarcely overemphasize the importance of the functional region, as expressed in urbanization, to modern economic geography. As we shall see in Part 4, this type of region is equally important to the planning process.

The urban hierarchy. We have noted in Chapter 6 the relationships between market centers and their trading areas and their ports and hinterlands. These relationships are one aspect of an *urban hierarchy,* which long as been recognized but which has been refined in modern theoretical research efforts; it will be described at some length in Chapter 12. The important point about the urban hierarchy is that, especially with respect to retail and wholesale trade, there is a tendency for a "pecking order" to be established among urban units, with the largest ones dominating the next largest, and these the next largest, etc. (Figs. 8.3 and 12.19). This domination affects not only the internal structures of the various sizes of urban units but also their relative locations and spacing, especially with respect to the larger units. This is true particularly of retail and wholesale functions performed by the various sizes of urban units. In the large metropolitan areas, a full range of functions, no matter how specialized, is to be found, from a corner grocery store to a highly specialized medical clinic. At intermediate levels of urban units, the number of functions decreases, with the type of functions almost invariably becoming more general and less specialized with decreasing size of urban unit (Fig. 8.3). If the size and location of urban units were to depend entirely upon the retail and wholesale trade of a region which is not affected by outside influence, we would logically expect a regular spacing of different sizes of urban units in the hierarchy (see especially pp. 189 to 195). However, the injection of manufacturing, government activity, universities, and other important aspects of urban economies often alters the real pattern substantially.

Urban-regional relationships. The importance of urbanization extends far beyond the concept of the city itself to include regional relationships. Indeed, modern research and planning, particularly in the more developed areas, seldom envisage regional relationships in isolation, but particularly as an area is affected by, and affects, urban units. Thus, the functional region is playing an increasingly important role in both research and planning.

Importance of Energy

Both the institutional approach and the theoretical approach to economic geography recognize that understanding the role of energy is essential to understanding the present location and function of economic activity and to predicting or planning its future location and impact. Interestingly, the importance of energy does not lie so much in the actual location of its sources of supply because these are decreasingly significant in attracting manufacturing and other types of economic activity. (For example, coalfields once attracted blast furnaces, but this is no longer the case.) The importance of energy to economic geography lies in the reverse consideration: Being available in increasing quantities and becoming increasingly easy to transport and hence ubiquitous, easily available energy allows man an increasingly wide range of choice in either the concentration or dispersal of his economic activities. A historical summary of sources and utilization of energy is shown in Table 8.1. In the entire world, energy consumption is increasing at a rate slightly exceeding 5 per cent per year, compared with an average world population growth of slightly less than 2 per cent annually.

Locational Tendencies and Relationships of Primary, Secondary, and Tertiary Activity

The institutional and theoretical approaches also hold in common the concept of certain locational tendencies in production. In assessing these tendencies, it is recognized that primary, secondary, and tertiary activity—and, indeed, components of each—have their own locational requirements. The reader will note that the cost and/or time of delivering a good or service is an extremely important consideration affecting the location of almost all types of economic activity, and especially manufacturing.

Sometimes these locational requirements are imposed by nature: All the lesser primary activities—minerals extraction, fishing and hunting, forest-products industries, and grazing—are necessarily located at sites where raw materials occur naturally.

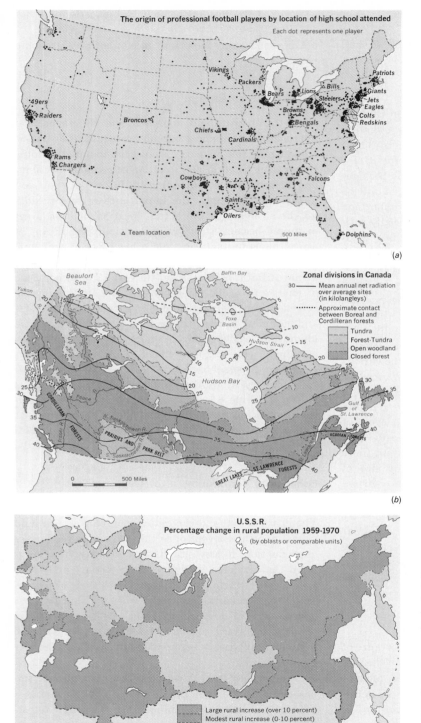

Figure 8.1a,b,c Different types of homogeneous regions, viewed at the national level of observation. Figure 8.1a shows places of origin of professional football players, by location of high school. The dots show places, not linkages. However, if we were to draw a line connecting the dots to the teams where the players now are, we could call this map a dynamic, or functional, pattern. (See Fig. 8.2.) Figure 8.1b shows forest categories as homogeneous regions, over which are superimposed isolines of mean annual net radiation, plus a line showing contact between boreal and cordilleran forests. Figure 8.1c shows change in rural population of the Soviet Union between 1959 and 1970, by categories of intensity. (Adapted from sources in the *Geographical Review*.)

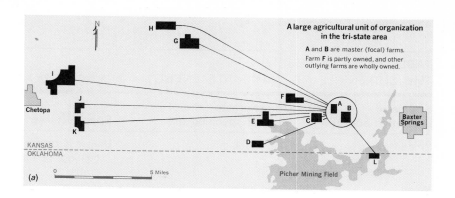

A large agricultural unit of organization in the tri-state area

A and B are master (focal) farms.
Farm F is partly owned, and other outlying farms are wholly owned.

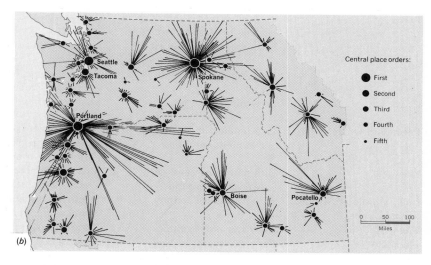

Central place orders:

● First
● Second
• Third
· Fourth
· Fifth

Figure 8.2a,b,c Different types of functional or nodal regions, viewed at local and regional levels of observation. Figure 8.2*a* shows a local area and indicates the number of fields and farms actually operated from farmsteads at A and B in Kansas and Oklahoma. Figure 8.2*b* shows different sizes of urban centers, or central places, and the lines, called *desire lines,* show the trips rural people make to those places over a period of time. (Reprinted from *Economic Geography*.) Figure 8.2*c* shows the market areas of a single wholesaling company in Maine. On the left, the functional regions are shown by boundaries around their peripheries, rather than by desire lines. On the right, schematic arrow designs show the general distribution of tonnage flows from each of two warehouses of the company. The irregular solid line on both maps shows the approximate boundary between the areas served by each of the two warehouses. In contrast to the static conditions shown in Figure 8.1, these regions all show linkages, usually focused on nodal centers.

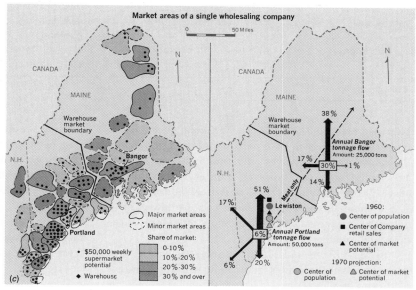

Market areas of a single wholesaling company

Major market areas
Minor market areas

◆ $50,000 weekly supermarket potential
◆ Warehouse

Share of market:
0-10%
10%-20%
20%-30%
30% and over

Annual Bangor tonnage flow
Amount: 25,000 tons

Annual Portland tonnage flow
Amount: 50,000 tons

1960:
● Center of population
■ Center of Company retail sales
▲ Center of market potential

1970 projection:
● Center of population
△ Center of market potential

TABLE 8.1
THE CHRONICLE OF INANIMATE ENERGY

Source of inanimate energy	Approximate time of earliest specified use	Specified use
Wood	Prehistoric	Domestic cooking and space heating; perhaps handicrafts
Wood	Early historic	Handicrafts
Wind	Early historic	Transportation
Water	Perhaps early historic; certainly in classical antiquity	Handicrafts and crude mills
Coal	Early thirteenth century	Space heating and domestic cooking
Coal	Early eighteenth century	Steam engines for factories; coke for metalworking
Coal	Early nineteenth century	Steam engines for transportation
Petroleum	Late nineteenth and early twentieth centuries	Space heating and lighting; domestic cooking; motors for transportation
Electricity	Late nineteenth and early twentieth centuries	Motors for factory machines and transportation*
Coal, petroleum, wood, natural gas	Early twentieth century	Electricity generation in thermoelectric units
Water	Early twentieth century	Electricity generation
Electricity	Early twentieth century	Metal processing; space heating and lighting; domestic cooking
Natural gas	Early twentieth century	Space heating; domestic cooking
Nuclear energy	Mid-twentieth century	Electricity generation and specialized uses

*Experimentally.

The very existence of such occupations depends upon exploiting resources in their natural habitats, and man's choice of location involves only which sites to exploit. As we shall soon see, however, man is now exploiting lower-quality sources in these activities, and his range of site choice is thereby increased because low-quality natural resources are found in more numerous sites than high-quality materials.

In agriculture and manufacturing (especially the latter), however, nature's limitations are not quite so rigid, and man exercises more freedom of choice in locating these activities. Wherever he enjoys such freedom, he gives *relative costs* serious consideration in the making of his locational decisions, for his stimulus to production tends to be the maximization of profit. Such costs may be divided further into *procurement, processing,* and *distribution* costs—costs of obtaining the necessary ingredients, of combining them, and of making them available for consumption. The first and last of these involve costs of transportation.[2] We have noted

[2] See especially E. M. Hoover, *The Location of Economic Activity,* McGraw-Hill Book Company, New York, 1948.

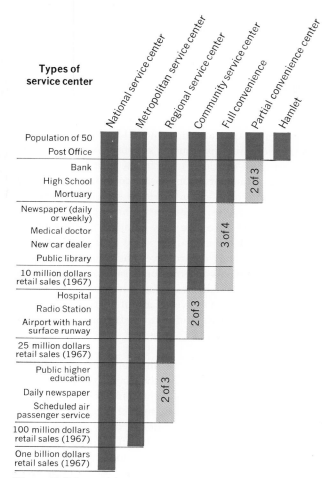

Figure 8.3 A graphic representation of an urban hierarchy. Each larger urban size usually offers all the functions in the smaller sizes, plus additional, more specialized activity. (Neil C. Gustafson et al., *Recent Trends/Future Prospects: A Look at Upper Midwest Population Changes,* Upper Midwest Council, Minneapolis, 1973, p. 41.)

seen, however, a substantial portion of this activity, especially wholesaling and some retailing, has close ties with secondary activity and may locate with respect to, although not necessarily in the vicinity of, secondary industry. In general, however, tertiary activity is oriented to large and dense populations—and hence to urban systems and networks.

Agriculture. Three aspects of agriculture are particularly important to an understanding of its current location: (1) It requires comparatively large amounts of permanently used ground for efficient production; (2) as a general occupation, it is somewhat restricted in location by a number of natural environmental features; and (3) it is partially subsistence and partially commercial in nature, with locational considerations meriting particular attention where commercialism is very evident or predominant. It is further affected by government policy which is generally of a quasi-political nature and hence less susceptible to logical analysis. Finally, technological change is important—again, especially in commercial agriculture.

Areal dispersedness. Certainly in comparison with manufacturing or minerals extraction, agriculture requires an extensive area of land surface for its production. As shown in Figure 5.1, it encompasses a substantial part of the earth's entire surface. Even individual production units (farms, etc.) are much larger than their counterparts in manufacturing. Consequently, considerations involving agricultural production must necessarily involve sizable areas (Fig. 5.6). In addition, more attention can be given to the global location of the subordinate aspects of agriculture than is possible with other productive activities. In Figure 5.1, for example, we can distinguish eight categories of agricultural land use and can plot each successfully on a world map. By way of comparison, entire manufacturing plants are only a series of scattered points on the same map, with the size of each point exaggerated beyond reality to make it visible.

Significance of the natural environment. Among the various ways of gaining a livelihood, agriculture represents an intermediate stage of man's independence of nature. It is not so rigidly oriented to nature as the other four primary activities, which must

that even in rigidly planned economies, where maximization of profits is not a major objective, careful attention is given to relative costs in making decisions about location.

Except for sites of natural beauty or sites that have other attractive qualities which are important to the tourist industry, the natural environment imposes few direct constraints upon tertiary activity. As we have be carried on at the precise source of raw materials. On the other hand, it is not so unhindered by nature as many components of manufacturing, for which the natural environment constitutes only a secondary consideration in matters of location. The limitations placed upon agriculture by nature are not so apparent in the obtainment of raw materials (seeds, shoots, etc., containing the potential of crop and animal growth), labor, nonhuman energy, or entrepreneurship because these are all quite mobile. The critical agents of agricultural production, however—notably climates and soils—do involve certain restrictions upon agricultural location. Of these, climate is the more important, for man has not yet been able completely to overcome certain absolute minimum temperature and moisture requirements of most domesticated animals and plants. The site requirements, too, are significant. For example, agriculture seldom thrives away from level, well-drained land.

Partial orientation to markets. Areas of subsistence agriculture tend to involve more or less spontaneous local use of natural conditions by inhabitants. In areas of commercial or commercial-subsistence agriculture, however, strategically located markets tend to affect the uses of the land, particularly in that they provide for areas of whole or partial crop or animal specialization. How this is done is explained more thoroughly in Part 2 of this book. At this point in our discussion, it is sufficient to understand that transportation costs from the farm to the market are especially significant.

Manufacturing. Manufacturing involves the further processing of materials received from the primary activities (except in such comparatively rare instances as the taking of nitrogen directly from the air—instances wherein it provides its own raw materials). Unlike primary or tertiary activity, that processing may be a large-scale, multistage operation, with raw or semifinished materials advancing from one manufacturing stage to another. The several stages, and the factories in which they are housed, may be located close together or may be separated by thousands of miles. Also, the size of the physical site for manufacturing is usually very small, especially in comparison with agriculture and grazing, whereas the value in capital investment

and the value of final product, as well as labor cost, are all very high relative to the acreage of ground occupied. Finally, manufacturing does not have the direct, sensitive relationship with the natural environment that is found in the primary activities, and its location is less affected by natural vicissitudes.

Freight rates and the orientation of manufacturing. Since they are the principal ingredients of both procurement and distribution expenses, transportation costs are vital considerations in the location of manufacturing. Transportation costs, to shippers, depend upon *freight rates*—upon intricate systems of arriving at shipping charges. These rates, having evolved over long periods of time, are very complex and are under various jurisdictions. Usually some regulatory governmental agency has control over the domestic rates of a country, whereas international rates are commonly arrived at through shipping conferences—periodic meetings of representatives of all interested carriers. As they affect the location of manufacturing, freight rates may be summarized as follows:

1 Charges for generating and terminating traffic—terminal charges incurred at the freight yards, stations, and warehouses—usually represent very significant costs of shipment. Generally, such charges are lower on a per-unit basis in large, dynamic traffic centers handling much cargo. Because of this feature and because of the additional reduction in per-unit freighting costs between terminals where large, continuous traffic flows are involved, the shipping costs along routes of heavy traffic are often lower than those between a major and an outlying terminal or those between two outlying terminals.

2 Considerations such as value (implied in the stage of manufacture), weight, and bulk of commodity enter actively into freight-rate computations.

3 Freight rates tend to be established on a zonal basis and hence are not always directly proportional to distance. Thus, for illustration, two different urban places, one substantially closer than the other to a traffic-generating or traffic-terminating center, may ship goods to, or receive goods from, that center at precisely the same rate if they are classified in the same shipment zone. This is an important consideration in the location of many manufacturing activities.

4 It is a common practice, notably among railroads in the United States, to permit in-transit freight-rate privileges, wherein a raw material destined for a given market can be halted and processed at any feasible point along the route and then reshipped at the original through rate, provided no backhaul is involved. Because rates on raw materials are generally lower than those on finished products, in-transit privileges may result in marked savings for some manufacturers. This, too, is a critical factor in influencing the location of certain types of manufacturing.

5 The size of shipment also is important, especially from the standpoint of the individual shipper. In railway movement, for example, carload rates are cheaper than less-than-carload rates for individual shipments because the latter involve placing several different shipments into a single freight car—an operation involving extra handling and recording costs.

6 Competition among the different types of carriers, and among the different firms or other organizations of any single type, is always a major consideration in setting freight rates.

7 Sometimes, in order to equalize the opportunity for competition among the various traffic centers, freight rates are adjusted rather arbitrarily by regulatory bodies. As a result, rates from a common trade area to a moderately active terminal city may be made lower than those to a very dynamic terminus with more frequent and speedy service. The shipper thus can choose between paying a slightly lower rate for slower movement of his goods and paying a higher rate which assures him of more rapid service.

Although all these features are given careful attention by those responsible for locating manufacturing plants, the magnetism of commercial cities is outstandingly important. Because freight costs between dynamic centers of traffic generation and termination often are lower than those to, or between, smaller towns, manufacturers are prone to take advantage of such economies. The result is a tendency for manufacturing to concentrate in the vicinities of these large *break-of-bulk* cities—places where cargo is transferred from ship to land transportation or to railway trains, where it is broken up and re-formed, where it is transferred from rail to truck, or where a similar break occurs in the normal flow of cargo movement. In recent years, the suburbs of such break-of-bulk centers have been important as manufacturing sites, offering prime service without inner-city congestion. Not infrequently, such centers are components of major manufacturing clusters or districts, and the freight-rate advantage is only one added attraction to location there.

Orientation tendencies of manufacturing. *Toward raw materials.* Some manufacturing tends to be situated near raw materials. This is particularly true of industries or stages of industries which either result in a pronounced decrease in the bulk or the weight of raw materials or enable the preservation of otherwise perishable commodities. Were they located elsewhere, either procurement would be impossible because of spoilage, or its costs would be excessively high because of the large amounts of worthless materials being transported. The milling and sometimes the smelting of low-grade ores, the sawing of lumber, the ginning of cotton, the extraction of sugar from both beets and cane, and the canning of many varieties of fruits and vegetables are good examples of such industries. Orientation to raw materials may or may not be associated with the fact that raw materials constitute significant percentages of the value of finished products.

Toward energy. In the early stages of the industrial revolution, coal was the major source of inanimate power. Man's ability to process his raw materials was then comparatively inefficient (with a high ratio of energy to raw materials required), and it was cheaper to move the raw materials to the energy. The better coal deposits thus marked many sites of intensive manufacturing. This was especially true of heavy industry in Europe and in Europeanized sections of the globe. Today, however, with the increase in the efficiency of processing and the concomitant increase in the mobility of power—including the substitution of liquid and gaseous fuels for coal in many areas—manufacturing tends to be less power-oriented than in the past. Nevertheless, the sites of many industrial districts remain near the coal seams that once were vital and still are important to their continued operation. A few industries are power-oriented even today. For example, the electrolytic processes in refining aluminum require very large amounts of electricity. Hence aluminum producers locate near power sites.

Toward labor. The world's handicraft industries, carried on mainly in households, are rather pronouncedly labor-oriented. In the past, and to a degree in the present, some manufacturing of technically advanced societies must give labor serious consideration. Some factories, requiring only a minimum of skills (such as small textile plants and shoe plants), tend to locate where a surplus of female labor might exist—in some mining areas, for example, where family incomes are low and work for the normal breadwinner cannot be counted upon. Certain other firms making diverse products appear to have moved to areas of moderate urbanization, where labor unions are not so powerful as they are in the larger cities.

Modern manufacturing, however, appears to be decreasingly labor-oriented. This is due appreciably to the growing mobility of labor, which may migrate long distances in response to both seasonal and permanent offers of employment. It is due also to the automation, or quasi automation, of some industrial plants. Although labor is a major factor for certain industries, it is on the whole less costly to manufacturing than raw materials. (See Part 3, Approach and Methods.)

Toward markets. Agglomerations of people, especially urban dwellers, signify markets. Historically, past and present capital cities of many European nations, attracting populations to serve their governmental and other service functions, have been excellent examples of such markets, stimulating local manufacturing even though other manufacturing requisites may not be at hand. Most of the present-day or one-time European capitals—London, Paris, Berlin, Vienna, Warsaw, Moscow, and Leningrad, to name a few—have thriving diversified manufacturing that is, or once was, in large measure oriented toward markets. In this industrial age, with the earth's rapidly growing populations migrating to the cities in higher and higher numbers, urban markets are becoming more important.

Certain types of manufacturing, designed particularly to provide daily consumer necessities, are present in so many of the earth's cities and towns—particularly those of Europe and of Europeanized regions—that they have come to be known as *ubiquitous industries.* These process the milk and its products, bake the bread, and—in this twentieth century—prepare the soft drinks for local populations. They are invariably market-oriented.

Where stages of manufacture exist, or where one industry uses the by-products of another, the location of such industries in proximity may result in a saving of transportation costs—a saving that is often all the more pronounced if the end-product market is also in proximity. Many agglomerated industries are, therefore, located in areas of dense urban populations—in consumer market areas. Since the end products of manufacture are of relatively high value and since they often require extraordinarily large amounts of space in shipment because of their unwieldy shapes, they may command high freight rates when transported over long distances. A tendency therefore exists for the final stages of multistage manufacturing to be oriented to the market areas, just as the early stages are somewhat oriented toward raw materials. Much of the agglomerated manufacturing in market regions is thus comprised of plants devoted to the later stages of processing.

Toward quality of life. Especially within the past two decades, a new type of economic activity has appeared which sometimes is difficult to classify distinctly as either secondary or tertiary. This is a highly technical, very sophisticated type of activity, usually involving production or use of the computer. The ratio of capital to labor in such industries is very high, and such employees as do exist either are very well trained and educated or are technicians trained for specified purposes. For such activities, it sometimes is important to locate within a cluster of generally similar activities, partly because of the need to exchange information frequently and partly because of the ease of servicing the complicated capital equipment when it is so clustered. Not infrequently, the wider territory served by such firms can be reached through communication rather than transportation routes, and therefore it is possible for such firms to locate in a place to which they are attracted because of the overall quality of life in the specific vicinity.

As the various locational constraints are being reduced by new inventions and innovations, this tendency toward taking the quality of life into consideration is also being shared by other, more traditional activities. Hence such amenities as climate, recreational features, and access become extremely important locational and functional considerations—and in some instances may outweigh the traditional ones.

Markets, raw materials, energy, labor, and people. As societies and economies become increasingly clustered in districts of high densities of habitation and land use, it becomes correspondingly difficult to distinguish one specific orientation of a manufacturing plant or industry. If present in an area of large population, such an enterprise is assured a market for its consumer goods and many of its producer goods. Increasingly, with the reuse of various commodities (such as wastepaper, which is manufactured into newsprint, other low-grade papers, and cardboard, and new and old scrap iron, copper, lead, aluminum, and other metals which are remelted into raw-material form), many of the raw materials now come from these heavily populated clusters—from areas once regarded wholly as markets. Energy, increasingly mobile, may be obtained from firms in the market areas—firms which act also to supply the fuel needs of resident populations. Labor, too, may be obtained from these populations. In short, much modern manufacturing appears to be oriented to urban areas of dense population, rather than to any of the specific locational considerations.

Footloose industries. For some manufacturing industries, no specific advantages in procurement, processing, and distribution costs are gained as a result of location near raw materials, energy, labor, or markets. These are usually called *footloose industries.* Often their special position results from the fact that while their processing makes full use of raw materials initially present in commodities (so that little weight or bulk is lost in manufacture), they can benefit by using the in-transit freight-rate privilege and hence can process their raw materials at any point along the route between the raw materials and the market without incurring increased freight costs. If no other locational factor is worthy of serious attention, they tend to be located with respect to terminal facilities and hence are found frequently in break-of-bulk centers. These industries are extremely important to regional planning, inasmuch as some can be located in widely different combinations of demographic, cultural, political, economic, and natural environmental conditions.

Tertiary activities. Traditionally applied to manufacturing, the term *footloose* recently has been considered with respect to some tertiary activities. By and large, tertiary activities tend to be located with regard to two important considerations: (1) markets for their services and goods—in other words, the general distribution of people, especially in large urban places—and (2) selected aspects of the natural environment. Because most tertiary activities make services available to people, the first of these criteria obviously is the more important in assessing the location of tertiary activity. The second criterion applies specifically to government agencies responsible for natural environmental assistance, regulation, and control, such as departments of forestry, mines, and agriculture. Regardless of density

Figure 8.4 Public estimate of profits, and actual profits, in business organizations of the United States. (*Business Week.*)

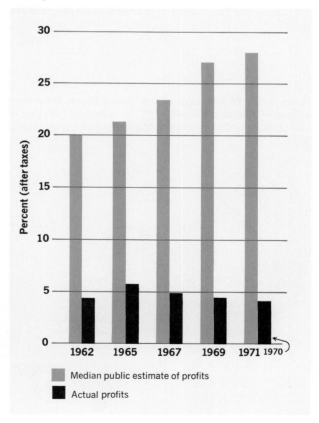

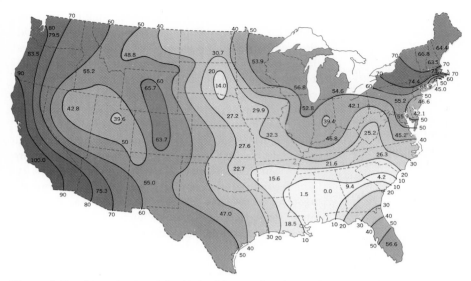

Figure 8.5a Mental map of the United States showing residential preferences of California students. (P. R. Gould, *On Mental Maps,* Michigan Inter-University Community of Mathematical Geographers, vol. 9, 1966, Fig. 2.)

Figure 8.5b Mental map of the United States showing residential preferences of Alabama students. (P. R. Gould, *On Mental Maps,* Michigan Inter-University Community of Mathematical Geographers, vol. 9, 1966, Fig. 5.)

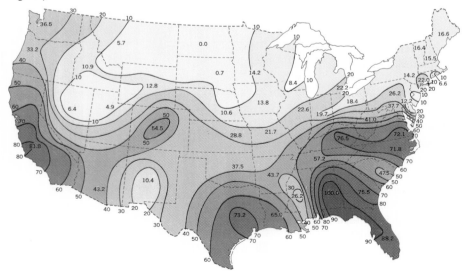

of population, such agencies must have jurisdictional responsibility for a given amount of *space,* including the resources within that space. However, certain tertiary activities are not governed so specifically by either of these two locational forces that they must be considered oriented to one or the other. Such an activity also can be considered footloose and, like its counterpart in secondary activity, not strongly oriented to any locational pull. By and large, however, because of the propensity for serving large numbers of people, the tertiary activities tend to be located in various large and small urban places, with the more specialized being found in the larger urban places. For the tertiary activities, particularly, communication may play an extremely important role in both location and functioning. In a significant and growing number of instances, communication is being substituted for transportation as a means in the efficient location and functioning of these activities. This important aspect of substitution of one flow medium for another must be given careful consideration in assessing current conditions and trends of this activity.

Importance of Change

Both the institutional approach and the theoretical approach to geography recognize that geographic conditions are not static, but are constantly experiencing change—in some cases, rapid change. This change is associated especially with man and his works, but also exists in the natural environment. Understanding technological change, involving not only new inventions but also new methods and procedures, is especially important in understanding the location and functioning of economic activity. An increasingly significant consideration is change in human values—what is considered important and unimportant. We shall have more to say about this in the next section.

Importance of Perception of the Environment

A comparatively new school of thought in geography, which is relevant to economic geography and which affects both the institutional and the theoretical approaches, involves perception by man of his cultural and natural environments. In other words, this school is interested in what human beings think is true, as compared with what is actually true as determined scientifically. Perception may differ substantially from measured fact, as is shown in Figure 8.4, where actual corporate profits are compared with a cross section of popular concept of those profits.

Geographic research to date in this area has concentrated especially on discerning human reactions to floods—on both a short-term and a long-term basis. When flood warnings come many individuals do not perceive the danger, and do not react in time to save their property, and sometimes themselves, from inevitable destruction. Once a flood has passed, they tend to move back and rebuild in exactly the same way as previously, despite admonitions of improved ways of rebuilding.

Still another concept of the perception of the environment involves students' perception of living preferences in the United States (Fig. 8.5).

If the social sciences truly exist for the purpose of assisting societies, then it is extremely important to understand the conditions not only as the scientist measures and otherwise understands them but also as members of societies perceive them to be. This dimension is important to understanding present conditions, but it is vital to the planning of future conditions, especially in democracies, where individuals have an effective voice in general planning procedures.

Chapter 9

The Institutional-
Historical-Inductive
Approach

Some years ago, the noted writer Arthur Koestler, in an introduction to *The Yogi and the Commissar,* said:

> I like to imagine an instrument which would enable us to break up patterns of social behaviour as the physicist breaks up a beam of rays. Looking through this sociological spectroscope we would see spread out under the diffraction grating the rainbow-coloured spectrum of all possible human attitudes to life. The whole distressing muddle would become neat, clear and comprehensive.
>
> On one end of the spectrum, obviously on the infrared end, we would see the Commissar. The Commissar believes in Change from Without. He believes that all the pests of humanity, including constipation and the Oedipus complex, can and will be cured by Revolution, that is, by a radical reorganization of the system of production and distribution of goods; that this end justifies the use of all means, including violence, ruse, treachery and poison; that logical reasoning is an unfailing compass and the Universe a kind of very large clockwork in which a very large number of electrons once set into motion will forever revolve in their predictable orbits; and that whosoever believes in anything else is an escapist. This end of the spectrum has the lowest frequency of vibrations and is, in a way, the coarsest component of the beam; but it conveys the maximum amount of heat.
>
> On the other end of the spectrum, where the waves become so short and of such high frequency that the eye no longer sees them, colourless, warmthless but all-penetrating, crouches the Yogi, melting away in the ultra-violet. He has no objection to calling the universe a clockwork, but he thinks that it could be called, with about the same amount of truth, a musical-box or a fishpond. He believes that the End is unpredictable and that the Means alone count. He rejects violence under any circumstances. He believes that logical reasoning gradually loses its compass value as the mind approaches the magnetic pole of Truth or the Absolute, which alone matters. He believes that nothing can be improved by exterior organisation and everything by the individual effort from within; and that whosoever believes in anything else is an escapist.[1]

[1]Arthur Koestler, *The Yogi and the Commissar,* The Macmillan Company, New York, 1945, pp. 3–4.

Although this quotation is not directly applicable to the two approaches to economic geography, it contains overtones which are surprisingly close to the mark. The theoretical-deductive approach is "Commissarish" in that it does generally accept the proposition that reasoning is an unfailing compass, and the universe a kind of very large clockwork in which a very large number of electrons, once set into motion, will forever revolve in their predictable orbits. Many adherents of this approach also think that whosoever believes in anything else is an escapist. The institutional-inductive approach is definitely "Yogaish" in that adherents have no objection to calling the universe a clockwork, but they do believe that it could be called, with about the same amount of truth, a music box or a fishpond. Many also believe that logical reasoning gradually loses its compass value as the mind approaches the magnetic pole of Truth and that ends are unpredictable. Some think that whosoever believes in anything else is an escapist.

The same general idea has been expressed more recently by a sociologist:

There are two distinctive, legitimate approaches to the study of human activity. One establishes patterns and trends of behaviour through the use of census data, without ever talking to the people under study. The other . . . begins with an individual, his hopes, fears, problems, solutions, and the habitual associations of his daily round of life. . . . Both approaches have their advantages and perils. . . . The census approach forces the investigator to produce an ideal model of society, against which existing practices are evaluated. This tends to produce a reification of the model; behaviour is judged as though the reification were real life. This is legitimate as long as one goes along with the model and does not ask about possible alternatives. . . . With the individual interview approach, however, the respondent sets the criteria against which he evaluates his life. His model may be as unrealistic as [the other], but at least it is not imposed. This approach is true to life but is restricted to life experiences and does not introduce broader and more theoretical alternatives. The individual describes his life, taking into account his ideal model and the social restrictions within which he lives. The two approaches ask different questions of

different materials and so raise different issues. Each throws light on the state of man.[2]

The basic difference between the two points of view is that of emphasis. The viewpoint of Koestler's Commissar, like that of Lucas's census approach, is that there exists an overriding order in human relationships, and in man's association with his physical environment, which must be sought. Any deviations from this order are just that—deviations. Koestler's Yogi and Lucas's individual emphasize the unique. They maintain that while there may be some universality, it results from the aggregation of individual or unique viewpoints, and not necessarily from deviation from any kind of universal model. At first glance, this difference may appear to be superficial and even unimportant, but with increased study and insight, one recognizes it as extremely important. As we shall see in later chapters, it is significant not only in understanding current conditions but also in attempting to predict and plan the future.

Let us look more closely at the institutional-historical-inductive approach, which emphasizes the importance of unique features, and the theoretical-deductive approach, which emphasizes the dominance of universal features, in man's day-to-day existence and his future.

The Institutional Approach

Human Wills and Institutions

The most distinctive aspect of the institutional approach to economic geography and to other disciplines is the conviction on the part of its adherents that human beings are separate, distinct entities who do not always think, act, or react in ways which are completely predictable. In other words, they can be understood, at least in part, by following the approach of the Yogi rather than that of the Commissar. This includes un-

[2] Abstracted from Rex A. Lucas, *Minetown, Milltown, Railtown: Life in Canadian Communities of Single Industry*, University of Toronto Press, Toronto, 1971, p. X.

derstanding the location and function of economic activity, with which economic geography is particularly concerned.

Of course, the adherents of the institutional approach grant that certain tendencies can be isolated by studying group behavior, just as life expectancy can be generally foretold by insurance companies through the use of actuarial tables. These tendencies, however, are of maximum utility when large numbers of people are involved; they become decreasingly accurate with reduction in the number of people under consideration to the point where they are essentially useless in predicting the life-span of an individual. This can be done more effectively by studying his own unique background and existing health, the life-spans of his forebears, and other attributes which can be thoroughly assessed when attention is focused upon that person, only.

The basic argument of the institutional approach to economic geography, therefore, is that the pattern of location of economic activity is the result of a series of decisions by individuals. These individuals are not free of influence, but function within the institutions of the culture, society, political unit, and economy with which they are associated and with which, with allowance for change, their ancestors have been associated for a long period of time. For purposes of illustration, we can consider three sets of circumstances in which such decisions are made: those in which individuals act more or less alone, those in which managers or boards of directors of private companies and corporations act in behalf of their respective organizations, and those in which government representatives act in the interest of their particular groups.

Decisions by individuals. There is a saying that the Lord must love poor people because He made so many of them. Although not all individuals making more or less unilateral decisions affecting economic activity are necessarily poor, the majority are not wealthy, and they are very numerous. However, their overall decisions do not affect a very large share of the world's economic activity. Indeed, most have decision-making authority only over their own personal effects,

including, in some cases, their own residences. A smaller number may have decision-making authority over various sizes of farms, manufacturing establishments, or trading places. Even these, however, do not have absolute freedom in decision making, but are subject to the laws of the political units in which they live, to customs, and to reactions of other people around them.

Because so many people are involved in this group of decision makers, we can gain some understanding of them through the actuarial approach—through the gathering of statistics about farm sizes, capital and labor investment, locations regarding markets, crop and animal specialties, etc. However, even these conditions vary with cultural heritage, so that it is difficult to generalize meaningfully about an area as large as, for example, eastern and southern Asia.

In summary, decisions by individuals are not subject to the same degree of discipline and internal organizational rules and regulations that characterize corporate and governmental decisions. Hence these decisions tend to be somewhat unique and uninhibited, although they are influenced by different cultural and natural conditions. Because so many people are involved in these decisions, it is possible to understand them in general terms by processing data about them which can be gathered and analyzed and by studying them firsthand in qualitative but analytical research.

Decisions by boards of directors. These decisions are particularly important in economic geography for three reasons. First, corporations tend to control economic activities of substantial value which may occupy substantial amounts of space. Second, such decisions—including those affecting location of economic activity—tend to be made by groups rather than individuals, although final ratification may be up to an individual. Third, the decisions are within the context of a corporation's own rules and regulations, which aggregately constitute still another filter of influence, over and above the cultural and natural conditions that affect individual decisions, as described in the preceding section.

The net result of such decisions is that they are made to promote the best interests of the corporation.

If the corporation is producing more than a single product and, as is frequently the case, if the products are totally unrelated in economic function, the locational decisions may reflect such policy. It would be naïve, therefore, for the economic geographer to examine the actual location of, say, specific units of production and distribution and arrive at conclusions about their true locational decisions without first understanding thoroughly the policies and decision-making processes of the respective corporations.

Decisions by government. Like the private corporation, various governmental decision-making bodies also function within the context of their own working rules and regulations. Also as within private corporations, those rules and regulations have been created because they reflect the real or imagined best interests of the organizations. Those best interests are not always identical: The objectives of local or municipal government may be quite different from those of state or provincial government, and these, in turn, may vary markedly from those of national government. By and large, the major function of government with respect to the location and functioning of economic activity is that of regulation, whether by ownership, decree, or incentive.

Interaction of individual, corporate, and governmental decisions. In attempting to understand the location and functioning of economic activity, the economic geographer is confronted not with a single set of decisions but with an interaction of these various decisions, each made within the context of its own rules and regulations and overall cultural and natural conditions. Adherents of the institutional approach to economic geography maintain that if the objective of the discipline is true understanding of existing location, such understanding is impossible without a thorough knowledge of these rules and regulations and of the cultural and natural conditions.

Historical Background

Until now we have considered decision making within the context of cultural and natural conditions, but only at a given time. However, the pattern of economic activity that exists on the earth's surface is not the product of current decision making, nor of that of the last decade or even the last century. It is, instead, the precipitate of a series of decisions, under changing cultural and natural conditions. In this process of change, the present location of a farm, mine, factory, or other economic activity may be quite illogical in view of current conditions, but quite logical against a background of conditions of the period in which the activity was located in the place where it still may be found. Thus, to the complexity of understanding cultural and natural conditions of a given time and place is added the need to understand cultural and natural conditions of past times and places, if we are to appreciate fully the present role and functioning of economic activity.

Area Specialization

A quality which tends to distinguish the institutional-inductive approach from the theoretical-deductive approach is specialization by experts in specific areas of the world. This quality is a logical result of the belief of the institutional-inductive adherent that there are unique aspects of geography and that these are as important as the universal aspects, which are of primary concern to the theoretical geographer. Area specialization particularly emphasizes *knowledge of languages* common to a given area. By way of careful study of languages and literature, as well as customs, folkways, mores, laws, patterns of occupance, landforms, soils, natural vegetation, climate, and—most important—the interrelationships between and among these and still other features, the institutional geographer arrives at preliminary conclusions. He or she then examines both the similarities of this particular area or activity to other areas or activities (universal qualities) and the differences (unique qualities). Research of this kind yields a very valuable insight, however unmeasurable, into the nature of human beings and activities in a given area, and the relationships among different activities and areas, including ecological implications.

Comparison with the Theoretical-Deductive Approach

The institutional geographer arrives at conclusions by reviewing all available literature, usually augmenting such an effort by field work. In economic geography, he or she is especially sensitive to production and transportation costs, whether measured in money or time. The final work may appear less precise than that of a theoretical-deductive expert, but it may also approximate more closely the reality of existing conditions.

In addition to noting the importance of the costs and time involved in producing and transporting goods and services, the institutional geographer is sensitive, as is the theoretical geographer, to the magnetic attraction of large numbers of people, whether for purposes of consumption, production, or exchange and distribution of goods and services. However, unlike the theoretical geographer, he has found it difficult to arrive at specific and neat weights to assign to the roles of these large numbers of people to economic activity. Are they more important as consumers? As resources of labor supply? As sources of used products which are recycled in the form of semiprocessed materials and enter again into the manufacturing process? As a saving in transportation costs, since they are clustered so tightly together and hence encourage both consumption and production to be closely associated geographically?

Here we see at once the strengths and weaknesses of the institutional-inductive approach. On the one hand, it draws its conclusions from a careful assessment of existing conditions, rather than from a theoretical model which is an artificial creation and which is always removed from reality by way of a set of limiting assumptions, as we shall see in succeeding chapters. The approach places a strong emphasis upon the unique aspects, as well as the universal aspects, of human and natural conditions, hence it arrives very cautiously at generalizations, which may be somewhat weak. Adherents of this approach also are very sensitive to the fact that decision making involves the full spectrum of human interest—religious, political, social, economic, conservational, and still other factors. These adherents find it difficult to "slice off" economic activity as such and provide explicit reasons for the location of that activity, when, in fact, decisions concerning the location of economic activity are very much related to a myriad of other decisions.

Adherents of the institutional approach therefore tend to develop generalizations rather than laws, and tendencies rather than predictions. Their methods involve primarily careful single judgments, first expressed by individual scholars and then, by means of the written word and public meetings, brought under critical review. Some aspects of the institutional-inductive approach, particularly those dealing in historical economic geography, which is very similar to history, may be appropriately considered art more than science. However, the institutional approach is an extremely important aspect of learning; it is a channel to truth so distinctive that it will continue to be utilized. Like the Yogi, it crouches in the colorless, warmthless, but all-penetrating ultraviolet end of the spectrum of human behavior. It is not nearly so "flashy" as the theoretical approach and usually makes somewhat parsimonious use of computers and other costly gadgets, but its results are those of careful thought and will continue to be used profitably in geographic research.

Basic Principles

In summary, we can say that the institutional-historical-inductive approach to economic geography rests on seven basic principles, no one of which can be disregarded in a full interpretation:

1 Economic geography is not a distinct discipline so much as an emphasis upon the location and functioning of economic activity—the livelihood aspects—of the overall discipline of geography.

2 Its distinctive qualities therefore result largely from past and present human decisions in a reciprocal relationship with past and present cultural and physical environmental conditions.

3 Some of these qualities—whether man-made or of the physical environment—are so cyclic in time and so repetitive over the surface of the earth that their change can be called a *process* (a succession of causally related events which, in some form, may be repeated) and their spatial patterns can be classified, measured, and perhaps one day predicted. These are called *universal qualities.*

4 Other qualities are sufficiently individual, whether because of an unparalleled aspect of a given culture, a given person, or a given feature in the physical environment, that they are more or less *unique.* Their change over time may well be a succession of essentially unrelated events rather than a process, and their occurrence in space is sufficiently unique that they cannot be easily classified, measured, or assessed by a model. Instead, they must be assessed by scholars in a subjective manner.

5 A careful study of historical background and a thorough analysis of both cultural and physical environmental conditions as they relate to that background constitute a necessary step in the evaluation of both universal and unique qualities.

6 Although the time and cost implications in movement of people and goods are important in economic geography, *they are not always governing considerations* in any given situation or in the field as a whole because (1) human values of time and cost may vary from person to person, place to place, and culture to culture and (2) even within the context of a given set of human values, decision makers do not have a universally conceived rationale of behavior. There usually is as wide a range of opinion among experts adhering to a given approach as among the so-called uninformed.

7 In arriving at a truly objective position concerning past, present, and future location and functioning of economic activity, it is necessary to judge in relative rather than absolute terms and to speak of tendencies rather than laws. Human beings are more than cogs in a wheel, and do not fit neatly into laws.

Chapter 10

The Theoretical Approach: Basic Concepts

The Nature of Geographic Theory

The Scientific Method

Let us dispense at the outset with the popular notion that some subject matter is scientific while other subject matter is not. In university curricula and elsewhere, a distinction is often made between science subjects and arts subjects, producing the idea that some subjects are scientific because they deal with "scientific" subject matter. That is, science becomes defined by the subject matter it studies. We shall show rather, that science is better defined as a *method of study,* somewhat strictly defined but unrelated to subject matter per se. Therefore, any subject matter becomes science if studied with the scientific method. For example, we may study fine art scientifically if we, first, make some *observations;* second, order those observations into some kind of *classification;* and third, using logic, try to *explain* the relationships we observe. Finally, we may use the knowledge thus gained to proceed to the final stage of the scientific method: prediction. Some art critics employ the scientific method in their evaluation of an artist's work. For example, they may use the principles of psychology to explain color and form produced on the canvas and to predict these from a knowledge of the artist's background of development.

We have stated that science is a method and shown that this method involves observation, classification, explanation, and prediction. Let us now look at each component.

Observation. Observation is the process of obtaining information through any of our senses; that is, we may see, hear, touch, taste, or smell things. We say that any such observation is an *empirical observation,* contrasted with derived knowledge obtained through reasoning. The economic geographer may make either *quantitative* or *qualitative* observations of different geographic characteristics. For example, he is concerned with such quantitative information as population densities, rental value of land and factory space, the transportation system, heights of buildings, and width of streets. He is also concerned with such qualitative aspects of urban regions as the poor quality of housing and public facilities or the beauty of city buildings and parks. Note that the economic geographer need not be in an urban area to make empirical observations about it. He can obtain his information from a variety of *census publications, land-use maps, municipal tax assessment records,* and many other sources. Although it is second hand to him, empirical observations have been made to obtain that data, and it remains empirical by translation to maps or tables. However, we can readily see that quantitative empirical data can be more easily and precisely passed on than qualitative descriptive data, which can easily become distorted.

Classification. We must then put this wide range of observations into some useful classification. The scientific process requires us to proceed in an orderly way to a given objective. Obviously, the way we classify our data will, in part, depend upon our objectives. For example, when we try to explain the different forms of land use in a region, it is often useful and economical to place these forms into a manageable number of classes. A first approximation may be a fivefold classification of commercial, industrial, agricultural, recreational, and residential land uses. Or if we need more detailed categories, additional forms can be added and then broken down into subclasses. In studying a region's labor force, we may wish to classify workers as primary, secondary, and tertiary. At a more detailed level, tertiary workers can be broken down to include those engaged in wholesaling, retailing, transportation, commerce, and government services. What are the basic ideas involved in all classifications?

First, we must clearly state the variables on which the classification is based, and the classification must be exhaustive and exclusive. At a simple level, we may go back to our land-use classification of commercial, industrial, agricultural, recreational, and residential land and add a further class of *low-price land.* Obviously, this last would not be a logical class. Our classification is based on the various types of use, while low-price land is based on monetary value and is a subdivision of all five land uses, not a logically separate class. The same rationale holds in the case of our occupational groups when we add a further group—say,

high-income workers—which is based on a monetary variable. Therefore, our first requirement is that all classes in our classification have a common characteristic.

Second, our classification should be detailed enough to fit our objective. For example, it would be of little value to use the occupational breakdown mentioned if we were attempting to explain the types of residences of secretaries working in the city's central business district. We would need to develop the breakdown much further, including, for example, not only those employed by firms in the tertiary sector but also, *within* that group, those employed by legal firms, travel agencies, banks, and head offices of petroleum companies or airlines. Hence, the detail of our classification is determined by both available empirical information and the problem to which we are applying the scientific method. (See also Chap. 8, p. 126.)

Explanation. Having made observations and ordered them into a classification, we must formulate an explanation in order to solve the problem. The explanatory stage in the scientific method is in many ways the most elevated part of the process. It is also the most difficult, and very often what passes for scientific research actually avoids or omits this necessary stage. Many books have been written on the nature of scientific explanation, and it is still debated among philosophers. However, we shall try to state clearly the generally accepted features of explanation and to point out the misconceptions held even by many professors.

First, our explanation must be logical. That is, we must follow a rigorous, formal argument in our reasoning (see the section on models). Second, it is important to realize that generally there is no *single* explanation for any question; what evolves is a very personal consensus between the person posing a problem and the person solving it. To stress the relative nature of explanation, let us develop an example. If a child, on seeing a red automobile, poses the question to its parent, "Why is that car red?", the child's problem may be solved by the statement, "Because the car is painted red." For a high school student posing the same question, such a reply would be considered witty but in no way adequate. An appropriate or acceptable explanation to him would probably involve some reference to fashion in automobile colors and to the psychology of the individual who purchased that type of automobile. If the question were posed by a university student in marketing research, the explanation which satisfied the high school student would again probably be inadequate. He would require some reference to marketing research data on income and pricing and to the psychology of color in relation to demand. What we are stressing, therefore, is that explanation becomes increasingly detailed as the knowledge of the questioner increases. *An explanation is complete when the person to whom it is given has no further questions.* What satisfies the child would not be acceptable to a university student or to his professor.

Let us go back to the original question posed by the child and the explanation given by the parent. You will say that the parent has not answered the question, at least in your opinion. If you look more closely, you will see that you hold this opinion because the answer merely restates the child's question in another way: it observes that the car is painted red, just as the child has already observed. We call such an explanation a *tautology* or a *tautological explanation*. While in this case the tautological nature of the explanation is easy to see, a long, complicated question "solved" by a long, complicated explanation may involve a tautology difficult to catch. Hence, our explanations must be logical and not tautological, and as most geographical problems are locational problems, *our explanations will therefore involve logical locational reasoning.*

In our locational explanations we must use *locational variables*. We may define a locational variable in any particular case as *a variable which is relevant to our problem and which varies spatially.* For example, if a tax is the same for a firm wherever it locates in a given state, it may be a relevant factor in explaining a firm's costs; it is not relevant in explaining the firm's location, for the tax is the same wherever the firm locates in that state. That is, the tax is not a spatial *variable* but a spatial *constant*.

If the foregoing observation seems somewhat platitudinous, let us emphasize how few researchers recognize its implications and how often, in appraising researchers' proposals, one may observe a large amount of time and money devoted to collecting information on variables which are constant throughout the area when such research seeks to find optimum or best locations. Hence, we must be careful not to waste time and money by researching such variables or confusing our reasoning by their introduction.

Prediction. Finally, our scientific method will prove most useful if we can, with the knowledge gained so far, make some predictions about the future. We shall come back to the problems associated with prediction, but at the moment let us identify two basic types of prediction. First, if we make predictions in the form of what will definitely happen, admitting no other possible outcome, we say that the prediction is in a *deterministic* form. On the other hand, if we predict what will probably happen, allowing for doubt, we speak of a *probabilistic* prediction. In urban areas at the present time there is much concern with air pollution. We can study weather patterns, the emission of pollutants into the atmosphere from a city's industries, and the relationships between the two in order to predict how much pollution the people of the city will have to endure on some future day. As we cannot say with absolute certainty what weather conditions will prevail on that day, we shall have to calculate the probability of different weather conditions existing, and hence our prediction about the degree of air pollution will also be in the form of a set of outcomes ranked in order of probability. In the deterministic explanation we may know from long observation the number of automobiles entering a city at a given time of day on a given route, we may know the number of lanes on that route, and we may be able to predict how long it will take a person to drive a given distance on that route at that time. This prediction we may present in the form of a deterministic statement admitting no possibility of error.

It is useful to distinguish between the two basic types of probability: (1) *subjective probability,* in which predictions are made with the fear of possible error, and (2) *objective probability,* in which predictions are made in terms of estimates of their likelihood of being true, while using rational methods or empirical observations to predict that likelihood. The latter type of probability statements are usually presented in quantitative terms, and we refer to this type of probability as *mathematical probability.*

Buridan's ass.[1] We have introduced the notion of deterministic results or predictions and the notion of probabilistic predictions. In the case of deterministic results, all our observations were known and not permitted to change. The important factors were knowns or givens. In the probabilistic case, we had observed the important factors, but the values of these were not all known; that is, we did not know what the weather would be like on a particular day, although we could say with some certainty what it most probably would be like. Our predictions regarding a particular day could be stated only in probabilistic terms. This distinction is useful to us in many aspects of geographic theory, and it is therefore important to do a bit of preparatory work on it at this stage.

We are all aware of the usefulness of probability statements. They are part of our everyday conversation and thinking. The answer to the question, "What grade will you get in this course?" could quite possibly be, "I have a fifty-fifty chance of an A or a B." While your knowledge of course requirements and your previous academic performance may tell you that these two grades are the only reasonable possibilities, you may not get either one. There may still be an element of chance outside your reasoned calculations. The professor may be in a bad mood, and when he looks at the curve he has prepared, he may draw the line between B's and C's to your disadvantage. We recognize such random chance elements as being part of reality, just as we recognize that we have a fifty-fifty chance of calling the toss of a coin correctly.

We must now introduce the problem of indeterminacy a little more formally. Acceptance and use of the idea of indeterminacy and probability are quite new in our thinking, as is illustrated by the case of Buridan's ass. The medieval philosophers posed the problem: Given a mule in a stall with two bundles of hay at equal distances from each nostril, which bundle will it bite first? This, they said, could not be determined, leading them to the absurd conclusion that the mule would not be able to decide and thus would die of starvation.

Obviously, it is hard to believe that an animal, however foolish, would die of starvation with food a foot away from its mouth. We can reason better now, however, nearly seven hundred years later.

Let us pose a similar situation relevant to economic geography. A girl invites her boyfriend to her apartment for a steak dinner. However, she discovers that she lives an equal distance from two supermarkets which sell equally good meat at equally high prices. To which supermarket should she go? This cannot be determined. We may, along with the medieval philosophers, deduce that she goes to neither and that her boyfriend arrives in the evening to find that she has bought no food because she could not decide which supermarket to go to. On the other hand, we have the concept of probability and can say that there is a 50 per cent chance that she will go to one and a 50 per cent chance that she will go to the other.

This classical problem of Buridan's ass probably arose as a refutation of Buridan's theory of the will, which stated that in a case of *symmetrical preference*—that is, where two things are equally desirable—reason cannot provide a basis for selection. We have a distinct problem in theory here when we attempt to develop our models of spatial structure and spatial movement in geographic areas. Let us see how the words of an authority on the works of Jean Buridan can aid us in solving this problem: "There is almost no discussion in modern literature of the logical issues involved in resolving the problem of Buridan's Ass; that is, of reasoned choice in the absence of preference."[2]

Let us follow Rescher in our analysis of the problem, which we may think of as containing two distinct but closely related aspects: choice in the case of *symmetrical knowledge,* and choice in the case of *symmetrical preference.* We shall deal with choice in the case of symmetrical knowledge first.

Assume that an individual can purchase meat from two stores. One sells good meat and the other poor meat, but he does not know which sells which. Preference is not involved here, only lack of information. All he knows about both stores is their location, and thus the information he has about them is perfectly sym-

---

[1] Jean Buridan (*ca.* 1295–1356) was a French philosopher and scientist who became a successful professor of philosophy and eventually a rector in Paris, where he had studied philosophy with William of Occam.

[2] Nicholas Rescher, *The Encyclopedia of Philosophy,* pp. 427–429.

metrical. There is no basis for a reasoned choice of one over the other. However, if he is reasonable, he must choose between them, and therefore he must select randomly.

There are three courses open to him which are mutually exclusive and cover all possibilities:

1 He may by some means decide to favor store A over store B.

2 He may by some means decide to favor store B over store A.

3 He may choose randomly, that is, be completely impartial as between store A and store B.

Any of these choices yields the same expectation of gain. On the basis of the information he has, it is just as probable that store A sells the good meat as it is that store B does. Thus there is a 50 per cent chance of success associated with adopting any of the three procedures. But that is on the basis of *expected success.* On the basis of *reason,* however, he must choose alternative 3 because there is no known reason for him to favor store A or store B. Therefore, he cannot rationally select either alternative 1 or alternative 2. Hence, in a condition of symmetrical knowledge, random choice is the only rational course of action.

Let us now deal with choice in the case of symmetrical preference, that is, the case in which two things seem equally good to us. These may be two apartments, two supermarkets, or two jobs. Here our knowledge makes us regard them as equally desirable because every reason for which we like one applies equally to the other. Our knowledge of both is identical. Obviously, we have here a special case within the symmetrical-knowledge case, and here, too, there is no rational basis for making any choice or decision. The only rationally justifiable course of action is alternative 3, which is random choice.

Now we can see that our spatial theories and models, which must logically involve randomness in human spatial behavior, cannot be deterministic. They will be probability models. However, we shall see that when we deal with very large numbers of people, actions in the aggregate enable us to treat what are probabilities at the scale of the individual in a deterministic framework.

Necessary and sufficient conditions. Not only must we show economy in our selection of variables to explain location, being careful in observing that we do not allow spatial constants to enter into our explanations, but we must also distinguish relevant from irrelevant variables in other ways. An important distinction here is that between *necessary* and *sufficient conditions,* or *necessary* and *sufficient explanatory variables.* This is a ticklish distinction, and the reader should not be discouraged if he does not master it at one reading. Many professors have to think twice, if not three times, when using this distinction in their arguments. We may distinguish necessary as opposed to sufficient conditions in the following way: An event will not necessarily take place if necessary conditions are fulfilled, but it will not take place if these conditions are not fulfilled. On the other hand, if sufficient conditions are fulfilled, an event will take place.

Putting the distinction into a locational framework within the field of economic geography, we might analyze all those factors which are necessary for the existence of retail stores—for example, their nearness to a certain number of people, their easy access, and enough money in the hands of the people to enable them to buy the goods which the stores sell. On investigating all retail outlets in a city, we may find that these conditions are fulfilled in every case. Then we can say that these are the necessary conditions for retail-store location. However, if some other researcher points out an area in which these conditions exist but in which there are no retail outlets, we may feel that we have a logical problem. The situation is easily resolved, however, by stating that the variables we have isolated are the necessary conditions for retail-store location (nowhere is there an example of a store located where these conditions do not exist), but that they are not sufficient conditions (since we have discovered them in locations where there are no stores). Obviously, we need some further factor to explain our store location over and above, or in addition to, our necessary conditions. Most probably, such a factor would be an entrepreneur's decision to locate his store at a particular point. Hence in this case we can say only that the conditions are necessary for the existence of a retail store but that they are not sufficient to produce a retail store.

We pointed out that (1) necessary conditions must

be fulfilled in order for something to occur in a particular place and (2) if we find that the particular thing we are investigating exists in every case where those conditions exist, then we have reason to think we have covered all the conditions necessary to explain its location. We may say we have isolated both the necessary and sufficient conditions for its existence.

We then went on to say that sometimes we may isolate a set of conditions which are always present when a particular thing is found to exist at some location, but that we may find instances in which all those conditions exist but in which the thing we are investigating does not occur. In such a case, although we may have been successful in isolating the necessary conditions, they are not sufficient conditions, and we need something more. This distinction is parallel to the elementary logical proposition which states: All men have beards; A has a beard; therefore A is a man. We know this is not true since there are such things as bearded ladies. Therefore, in order for A to be a man, he must have a beard (a necessary condition), but merely growing hair on a face does not make a man; hence, the beard is not a sufficient condition.

We can see how useful this distinction is when we are analyzing the reasons why things are located where they are. It aids the completeness of our theory in that *not only does it explain why things are located where they are, but it also can help to explain why things are not located where they are not.* When geographers talk about the factors of location and spend time studying an industry in terms of its requirements, they are usually producing a study of the *necessary conditions* for that industry to locate where it is. Seldom do they go on to show places in which all those requirements are met but in which no representative plant of the industry is located. If they did, they would find that, at that stage, they had not succeeded in isolating *all* the conditions—that they had succeeded only in isolating those conditions which were necessary to explain the location but which were not sufficient. If they do study further and observe all those factors which occur where the industry is located and if there exists no collection of these factors where the industry is not located, then they have succeeded in isolating or explaining the conditions which are both necessary and sufficient. We cannot afford to be slipshod in our development of

logical explanations, and hence, when handling many locational variables, we must take pains to distinguish which locational variables constitute necessary conditions, which constitute sufficient conditions, and which constitute both necessary and sufficient conditions.

Finally, let us reemphasize that a condition may be necessary but not sufficient, or sufficient but not necessary. It is *necessary* that a building have a certain density of population nearby for it to be a retail store, but it may have that density of population and be the city jail. It is *sufficient* that the building be run by a single proprietor and carry retail goods for sale, but it can be a retail store without a single proprietor—for example, it may be run by a large corporation.

The Structure of Theory

Hypothesis. When we attempt to produce a logical explanation of a geographic feature using scientific procedures, we have to make an educated guess as to the things we shall need to produce that explanation and the relationships that may reasonably be expected to exist between them. This initial idea, or educated guess, we term a *hypothesis.* In common parlance, what is barely an idea, educated guess, or hypothesis is often termed a *theory.* A theory has three necessary parts: (1) a hypothesis, (2) a set of assumptions or premises, and (3) the resulting postulates. These three components of theory are linked together by the formal procedure of logical reasoning. We have already noted what a hypothesis is, and so let us now deal with the remaining two components.

Assumptions. When he makes assumptions as a necessary part of his theory, the scientist usually attempts to make them as close to the real world as he can. This is true when he is using the theory to explain directly a problem in the real world, or to provide a direct solution to a problem in the real world. He may not, however, be directly concerned with answering any pressing real-world problem at all, but merely contributing to the development of the theory of the discipline in which he practices. Or he may feel that the direct approach is very difficult and not economical in the long run, and so he may decide on an indirect approach and make assumptions that are very far from the real world. It is important to realize that the scientist is unconstrained in this respect. He may make any assumptions he chooses which may, directly or indirectly, sooner or later result in a useful theory. For example, he may assume that all ghettos in the city are occupied by high-income whites, that all low-income workers are high-income workers, or that all men are women and all women are men. The assumptions or premises he uses are "if" statements implying that each assumption is preceded by "if this be so."

Weak and strong assumptions. An assumption which is a simple statement about reality and which is observed and accepted to be true by everyone is said to be an *axiom* or *axiomatic*. For example, we need not stress as an assumption the fact that the great majority of the central-city labor force have to travel to work in the morning and travel home at night. This is axiomatic in terms of our movement analysis of urban populations. Let us now distinguish between what are commonly termed *weak assumptions* and those which are termed *strong assumptions;* this distinction will be very useful in helping us decide whether we are being efficient in developing our theory.

A *weak assumption* is one which achieves the greatest generality; in other words, it is one which requires the fewest qualifications in terms of its application to what we know to be true in the real world. Hence, an assumption which constitutes an axiom is the weakest of all assumptions, since it requires little or no qualification in order to be proved true. It asserts that which we already know. For example, we may assume that all living people in the city breathe. This is a very weak assumption; no qualifications would be necessary. If, on the other hand, in an analysis of urban pollution, we wished to estimate the volume of particulate matter inhaled by the urban population, we might assume that the volume of air inhaled by an individual was dependent only on his occupational group. This would be a very strong assumption since it would require many qualifications; in fact, occupational group may not be relevant at all. Therefore, the more particular we are in the assumptions we make, the stronger our assumptions become; that is, the more detailed the conditions we wish to assume, the more qualifications they require, and hence the stronger the assumptions.

In geographic spatial theories, many basic assumptions are implicitly made but not explicitly stated. One such assumption in geographic movement theory is the *law of minimum effort,* commonly termed *lex parsimoniae.* This law states that if an individual wishes to travel from point A to point B, he will take the easiest, fastest, or least costly route according to whether he is considering comfort, speed, or expense. Of course, there are many instances in which no such law is followed. For example, a student may take a very roundabout route to buy a beer in the hope that he will meet a girlfriend. (In this case, however, he has deviated from what we call a single-purpose trip!) In fact, most people can readily think of instances in which they did not abide by *lex parsimoniae*—for example, finding their way around a city with which they were not familiar. On the other hand, we may say that most people, most of the time, tend to follow the law of minimum effort in their movement. In any case, in deriving assumptions on which to base our theory, we are looking for the most general statements we can make, and in order to get rid of a basic assumption, we must demonstrate that another basic assumption which is to take its place is more general. (Students sometimes take circuitous routes, but this would hardly entitle us to throw out *lex parsimoniae* and adopt in its place a law of maximum effort, which would state: If a person wishes to go from point A to point B, he will select the most expensive way, the longest way, or the most difficult way!)

Postulates. We have begun to know a great deal about the nature of assumptions on which to base our theory. Postulates are the final outputs of theory. They are the results we obtain from having made our assumptions and having applied strict, logical reasoning to them.

We may construct a simple theory as follows: If we assume, first, that individuals in the city travel mainly from home to work in the morning and from work to home in the evening (a basic assumption of our movement model) and, second, that the capacity of the means of transportation remains constant during the day, then our logical postulate is that there are two periods of traffic congestion in all cities—one in the morning and the other in the evening. This postulate will be true as long as no factor enters to contradict our assumptions. For example, if a heavy snowfall prohibits commuting, our theory will no longer apply. While this point may seem obvious, we can vouch that such misunderstanding—although at a far more intricate and sophisticated level—lies at the basis of a great many professional arguments both in the literature and in advanced seminars in universities. That is, professors and graduate students contradict the postulates of a particular theory by delightedly giving examples which do not apply to the assumptions on which the theory is based. Now we can take care of this wasteful and foolish argument by stating that when we have made our assumptions, we hold constant every other factor which might become relevant to the theory. For example, in our previous illustration, we hold the weather constant in the sense that we assume normal weather conditions, and our theory does not allow any phenomenal snowfall to invalidate it. This way of closing up our theory to relate only to our assumptions is done formally by introducing the concept of *ceteris paribus,* meaning "if everything else remains the same" or "all other things being held constant."

We start off our theory, then, by saying that, if we assume A, B, and C, then, *ceteris paribus,* D and E will result. Obviously, our *lex parsimoniae* assumption on movement, when applied to a student leaving his dormitory to buy a beer, tells us that he will, *ceteris paribus,* buy the beer at the nearest bar. In this case, *ceteris paribus* obviously will not take care of the case in which a bar twice as far away as the other offers better beer than can be obtained anywhere else or the case of the student whose real purpose in going out is to walk past the girls' dormitory, which is three blocks in the opposite direction. Our theories must remain very simple and can involve only the most mundane events.

Occam's razor.[3] We now come to a very important principle, which must always govern our theories and which our theorists must always observe. This is the principle of Occam's razor, which in essence says that *the assumptions upon which we base our theory must always be the weakest in form and the fewest in number necessary to explain the observed phenomenon.*

[3]William of Occam, an English philosopher of the early fourteenth century, is said to have dissected problems as with a razor.

It is really a general principle of efficiency to be observed in scientific theory.

If, say, we can arrive at a postulate or a logical finding by making three very simple assumptions and if someone else can obtain that same postulate or finding by making only two of those assumptions or two different but equally simple assumptions, then we must, by observing the principle of Occam's razor, prefer the latter theory. Likewise, if two theories both require the same number of assumptions to obtain the same postulate but the assumptions of one theory are strong while those of the other are weak, we must accept the theory using the weak assumptions.

Objectivity. Theorists often do not observe the principle of scientific objectivity, but rather become very emotional about their own pet theories, regarding them affectionately. Hence, they tend to preserve their own theories and defend them against others. While this is acceptable in the case of theories based on the same number of assumptions, the weakness or strength of which is the same, it is not acceptable in the case of theories which differ in these two respects. Occam's razor cuts off excessive requirements in theory formulation. It requires the scientist to be economical and efficient in developing his theory; the razor must always be observed.

The processes of induction and deduction. At one stage in the development of scientific investigation, a simple distinction was made between the processes of deduction, on the one hand, and those of induction, on the other. *Deduction* was simply the process of logical reasoning from a set of assumptions. The logical reasoning itself was termed *deductive reasoning.* It produced deductive results or deductive postulates which could be later checked with events in the real world. *Induction,* on the other hand, was a process involving the collection of facts and *demonstration* of the relationships between those facts. On that basis, induction is sometimes considered an empirical process, while deduction is considered more abstract.

While this distinction may still be useful to assist our thinking at the elementary level, it is far more complicated at the advanced level than was formerly thought. This is largely the result of more rigorous thinking concerning what is assumed to be involved in the inductive process. It is maintained, for example, that we cannot just collect facts about observed processes, since there is probably an infinite number of facts which could be collected about any one process. It is argued, therefore, that we must start with some form of deduced relationships in mind which will tell us which facts are important to collect. That is, *all scientific investigation begins, to some extent at least, with a form of deductive hypothesis.* On the other hand, in testing a purely deductive hypothesis, we must obtain facts from the real world, and hence the inductive process is involved in any meaningful development of deductive theory. However, we shall keep these two processes clearly in mind, not as two distinct, separate, and exclusive processes, as was formerly done, but as processes which are both involved in almost all scientific investigation but which may receive different emphasis. We shall remember that one scientific study may be more inductive than another or, alternatively, more deductive than another.

Evaluating Models

In this section we shall develop some clear-cut ideas concerning models since they are increasingly applied to problems in geographic analysis. We need to know what constitutes a model, what models are used for, how models relate to the real world, and on what bases we may judge the value of a model.

What a model is. First, a model constitutes a formal statement of a theory. This statement may be in the form of words, mathematical notation, a diagram or graph, or a physical model.

We have previously noted that a hypothesis is not a theory; a hypothesis constitutes what might be described as an educated guess or idea, while a theory is far more formally structured. We have seen that the structure of theory involves assumptions, logical reasoning, and postulates. Since a model is a formal representation of a theory, it too will consist of those basic elements. As we have said, a model may be presented in various forms, although in many cases very complete or comprehensive models will involve all or several of those forms. For example, an economic model of New

York City might consist of an entire book using words, mathematical notations, and graphs and diagrams. An urban model of Boston could include textual material, mathematical equations, maps, graphs and diagrams, and also miniature physical representations of buildings, highways, and the Charles River.

These are examples of very comprehensive and complicated models; the great majority of models, however, are statements of relationships between just two variables, for example, a simple two-variable model showing the relationship between the number of trips people make to a given shopping center and their distance from it. This model would be summarized in a simple graph with distance on the horizontal axis and number of trips on the vertical axis. This is shown in Figure 10.1. A written explanation would normally accompany this graph. In addition, if a line were drawn connecting the various points—as shown—this could be expressed in mathematical notation. Denoting number of trips by Z and distance by $D,$ we could express the

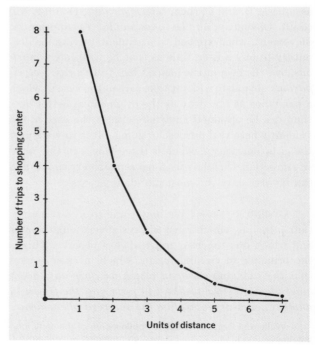

Fig. 10.1 Trip frequency or elementary interaction model.

model as

$$Z = a \cdot D^{-1}$$

where a is the number of trips starting from the origin and D^{-1} is the rate at which trips terminate with distance. Our model tells us that for any unit in distance from the origin, the number of trips made declines by 1 over D, for example, ½, ⅓, and ¼ where distance is two units, three units, and so on.

Use of models. Many professors maintain very strictly that the purpose of scientific investigation is to help us to understand the real world. The models that we construct, since they are formal statements of theories which are developed by scientific investigation, must apply to the real world and specifically help us solve the problems that confront us. They argue that in order for our models to do this, our assumptions must be *realistic*—that is, as close as we can make them to what we observe in the real world—and that our postulates, which we derive from those assumptions, must be useful in helping us solve problems and predict events in the real world.

We doubt that present-day scientists would contend that we can ever fully understand reality. Many professors in our own discipline, however, contend that geography is the study of reality, of the world as it exists. They have been associated with the development of geography largely as a descriptive and fact-recording discipline concerning various regions of the world. As it is clearly impossible to describe all the facts about any region, it has been argued that their main concern is with those things which show significant variation from place to place. Hence, geography has been largely an empirical discipline concerned with recording facts about distributions which show some spatial variation.

Models are approximations to reality. Let us go a step further and observe that we can never describe all differences that exist since all things, at least at the human scale, are very different. Even the pencils which students use to take lecture notes vary in detail, as do the pieces of chalk used by professors. Since we accept that we can never fully describe, much less fully understand, reality in its entirety, and since we have already observed that the first principle of the scientist and of scientific inquiry is to be efficient and economical, we

cannot afford to adopt this all-inclusive descriptive approach to our work. We must get as close to reality as we can with the limited budget at our command, a budget consisting of our ability and the available time and equipment. We must use our ingenuity in adopting that method which will enable us to go as far as possible, within these constraints, toward understanding reality. Then if we continue our inquiry, we may build on that knowledge and go a little further. We use our ingenuity to discover the best ways to sneak up on reality, knowing that although we shall never fully understand everything, the more ingenious and persistent we are, the closer we shall come to reality and the clearer our brief glimpse of it will be. Hence, let us formally state that *scientific inquiry involves a series of successive approximations to reality.*

Now we shall return to the argument of those who state that our assumptions must be as realistic as possible, that our postulates must aid directly in solving our problems, and that by testing our models in the real world, we can achieve the aim of science, namely, to predict events in the real world.

We have identified scientific inquiry as a series of successive approximations to reality, and we have noted that later developments build on earlier findings. It often happens that a problem has been observed, or a relationship hypothesized, which has not been investigated before. The problems that confront us now in our environment—while they may, in some respects, have counterparts in medieval and ancient times—are very much new. They are problems of our day, and hence much of the scientific inquiry developed to study new relationships and solve new problems may be simplistic. It represents the early stages of scientific inquiry upon which later research has to be based. It has to start from simple assumptions and produce incomplete or partial results. It cannot possibly provide complete and ultimate answers to these new, complicated problems. We cannot, therefore, reject such inquiry as being too simplistic and very far removed from reality merely because it does not enable us to predict everything in our new problem environment.

Evaluation. The argument which says that our theories and models must be of direct use in problem solving may be called the *utilitarian argument* since it holds that a theory must be judged in terms of its usefulness in predicting the real world. We all know of cases in which a theory has been expounded, only to be ignored as being of little use and then later revived and judged generally to be of the greatest importance in terms of application. Newton's law of gravity, while meaningful to a handful of research physicists for several hundred years, became of much greater direct utility only when orbital spacecraft were developed. No doubt, the utility of the theory of relativity will not become apparent for many decades. In our own discipline, the work of Walter Christaller on central-place theory was of little direct significance until the 1950s, when debate surrounding it generated its reemergence, and it is now only in the seventies that many planning authorities are introducing Christallerian concepts into planning our spatial economic environments (pp. 361 to 370). The point here is that just because we cannot see the immediate usefulness of a model, we must not unconditionally reject it. We must attempt to be liberal in our judgments, for what we deem useless now may later be considered very valuable, and we ourselves may in the future be criticized for short-sightedness.

Models are also judged according to what may be called *heuristic criteria,* or the value of a model in instructing a student or other researcher in how a problem may be investigated. That is, the model may serve to show the student what things are important and how he should bring them together. Theoretical models are a very efficient way of doing this. They may not answer our everyday problems and they may be very far removed from reality, but they may, on the other hand, be of great heuristic value in that they can serve to point up the types of factors which may be important and the nature of the relationships between them. For example, the concentric zonal theory of city structure (that cities grow in concentric zones of activity around key nodes or cores) may be considered very far removed from reality, and such a simple model could not be used to solve either urban land-use problems or pollution problems directly.

On the other hand, it certainly is a useful example of how the theory of urban structure may be approached at a very early stage in our successive approximations to the real world. It is something on which we may begin to build in order to proceed to a more realistic case. We may therefore note, in summarizing our argument so far, that our scientific theory should not be judged solely in terms of whether it applies to reality, whether it predicts the real world, or whether it is of direct and immediate use in solving real-world problems. The usefulness of things, if we are to consider this in our judgment, is not a very precise measure at all; in fact, when we set about thinking in a rigorous manner, it is very difficult to determine precisely what we mean by "usefulness," and certainly as scientists we would not say that *our* concept of usefulness should be universally accepted. We can therefore see that the idea of usefulness is very subjective and would require many limiting qualifications in order to become objective in a particular case.

How closely do models describe the real world? We can say that our models do not have to relate to the real world at all. As we have seen, we may make any assumptions we wish, and hence we may arrive at any conclusions in our theory. There is, in fact, only one principal rule which we have to follow: Our reasoning must be logical. In terms of our model, this means that our postulates must be logically derivable from our assumptions. If they are, the model may be judged sound. Whether it is a good model or not depends upon whether we are efficient and have strictly applied Occam's razor. This is somewhat the *ivory-tower view* of scientific theory, but it is necessary for the maximum ferment and evolution of ideas.

Basic Concepts in Theoretical Economic Geography

Isotropic Space and Anisotropic Space

Along with the development of concepts in any scientific discipline, there is a parallel development of a terminology, very often referred to as *jargon.* Critics deplore the use of jargon, but we must recognize that it is to some extent a necessary and inevitable result of the level of precision required in our thinking. We shall now introduce some of the more fundamental concepts in theoretical economic geography, together with the terminology in which they are necessarily explained, and we shall take great pains to state clearly and definitively the meanings of our terms.

Let us review briefly the meaning of a *definition,* which may be seen as representing a mean between two extremes—the extremes of the maximum amount of precision and the minimum amount of words. The first extreme tends to produce exceedingly long definitions constituting, in their fullest form, possibly an entire chapter of a book. The other extreme is brevity; perhaps two or three words may constitute a definitive statement or definition. The more rigorous we make a definition, the longer it tends to become; on the other hand, the more we pursue the objective of economy or brevity, the more vague the definition will be. Hence, in defining our terminology, we must attempt to obtain as much precision with as much economy as possible. The best definitions therefore represent a mean between the extremes of economy and precision.

The economic geographer, like many scientists in the other social science disciplines, can seldom experiment with phenomena in a laboratory. The economist, for example, in developing the analysis of demand and supply, is unable to proceed very far if he considers the multitude of factors which can possibly influence demand and supply in the real world. He therefore has to select those factors which he considers of first importance and assume all others to be held constant. He often introduces the *ceteris paribus* clause, "other things remaining the same." Economic geographers attempt to explain why things are located where they are, and in order to proceed with their analysis, they have to simplify the real world. We therefore introduce the concept of the *isotropic surface,* which we may at least initially consider to be a segment of the earth's surface which is the same in every part of its extent, or, undifferentiated over its entire extent.[4] This concept is derived from the mathematical concept of Euclidean 2-space, which is a flat, two-dimensional space, any unit of which is identical to any other unit. Euclidean space is the same as metric space. Space of a single dimension, that is, unidimensional space, consists of a straight line.

Two-dimensional space defines areas having both length and breadth, while three-dimensional space defines volume.[5] The real-world space in which we live is three dimensional—we are able to travel north, south, east, or west, and at least to a limited extent, to descend or ascend.

It is important to realize that the simplest space in which we are able to develop our theory is Euclidean 2-space, and specifically Euclidean 2-space of the *isotropic surface.*

If we wish to complicate the surface by placing things on it—a river, a city boundary, a factory, or a residential neighborhood—the surface is no longer isotropical, and we then define it as an *anisotropical surface.* Therefore, as we mentioned earlier, the scientific process may be considered to consist of successive approximations to reality, and hence we may view the assumption of an isotropic surface to be the simplest of all assumptions and also the furthest removed from the real world. The more anisotropic we allow our surface to become, that is, the more complicated we make it, the closer it will be to the real world.

The isotropic surface is therefore the geographer's laboratory. It is a controlled situation to which he may add factors at will to produce anisotropic conditions in order to trace through the effects of their introduction. Likewise, he can trace the spatial effects of removing various factors he has introduced and various combinations of different values of factors. This is the controlled space designed for us for the development of geographic theory.

We do not look for isotropic surfaces in the real world because they do not exist there. An individual who discards a model based on the concept of isotropic space because he can find no isotropic surface in the real world has missed the point. A parallel situation exists in economics. The economist does not throw out the entire theory of perfect competition because he cannot discover an ideal, perfectly competitive market. Rather, he uses the perfect-competition model or concept to attempt to understand the nature and direction

[4] The term *isotropic* is derived from the Greek *isos,* meaning "equal," and *tropus,* meaning "surface." The introduction of this term to our discipline and the useful application of the concept are due to Professor Hagerstrand.

[5] We are familiar with these dimensions in everyday life, since we are constantly confronted with distances, areas, and solid objects which have volume. We are perhaps less familiar with space that has more than three dimensions. In the mathematics of vector spaces, however, the scientist may introduce as many dimensions as he deems necessary or convenient to use.

of various influences upon that model, and he hopes that by introducing complications into such a simple case, he will come closer to understanding the immense complexities of competition in the real world.

Geographic Space and Its Measurements

The economic geographer must be familiar with many types of space and distortions of space in order to comprehend the complex spatial distributions that characterize the economic environment. As we have seen, the simplest space of geographic theory is two-dimensional Euclidean space, or metric space.[6] It is Newtonian space, ordered on axes which are fixed, and all elements in the space are located with respect to those axes. The earth's grid is an example of such a system. We locate the cities of Boston, New York, and Philadelphia in degrees of latitude and longitude, that is, with respect to the parallel and meridian axes.

In many of the problems which confront us, the ordering of objects by such a reference system tells us very little about important aspects of their location in the real world. The economic geographer is more concerned with the location of things with respect to one another than he is with their location with respect to the earth's grid based on the positions of the equator, the poles, and, conventionally, the meridian of Greenwich, England. For example, a housewife could locate precisely the position of her house in degrees, minutes, and seconds, but she is far more concerned with its position relative to shopping facilities, work, etc. Likewise, for business firms the absolute position of Boston is normally of very little importance, but its location with respect to New York, Toronto, and Montreal may be of great significance. (See also Chap. 8, pp. 127 to 128.)

Operational space. As position in Euclidean space is unimportant, the dimension measured on our absolute scale of miles is often very insignificant in the

---

[6]We may formally define *metric space* as a set T such that to each pair x, y of its points there is associated a nonnegative real number $\rho(x,y)$, called their *distance,* which satisfies three conditions:

1 $\rho(x,y) = 0$ if, and only if, $x = y$
2 $\rho(x,y) = \rho(y,x)$
3 $\rho(x,y) + \rho(y,z) \geqslant \rho(x,z)$

The function $\rho(x,y)$ is said to be a metric for T.

---

real world. Position becomes important only if it correlates closely with or signifies the length of time it takes to travel those miles or the costs incurred. Distance or space measured in terms of time or cost is called *operational space* because only space measured in these terms is important in geographic analysis. In the spatial economic environment it does not matter how many miles a residential suburb lies from the center of a city; what is significant is how rapidly an individual can get to work or, even more important, how rapidly he can get home from work. It is not how far Boston is from New York that matters, but how much it costs a student to go home for vacation.

Basically, then, we must consider two main dimensions of operational space: *cost space* and *time space.* The earth space in which we live is one of infinite variety, and no two areas are precisely the same. Not only do we move through this space ourselves, but we also send information through it by telephone and mail and buy and sell commodities which have to be transported through it. Therefore, we do not have the benefit of a single time space or a single cost space. Our operational space is complicated by the many different modes by which movement through space takes place. We may visit a friend by automobile, train, plane, or a combination of these. We may travel as an individual, as a family, as a member of a club, or as an employee of an airline. Thus there is not a single cost space or a single time space, but as many as there are types and modes of interaction. In reality, however, only a limited range of possible modes will be relevant in any particular type of movement. Only one of the dimensions of time or cost will be relevant in a particular choice of mode; either the time constraint or the cost constraint will apply. (See also Chap. 8, pp. 129 to 139.)

We shall discover in the next section that only the isotropic space of our geographic laboratory is pure Euclidean space and that while we may *assume* that our operational space is also Euclidean space, *in the real world it is a far more complicated non-Euclidean space.* The operational space of the real world is greatly distorted.

It will be helpful to introduce one further concept here, that of an individual's *action space,* which we may define as that area throughout which an individual functions or interacts. In any normal day an individual may travel from home to work or college, go to a restaurant, and take in a movie. He has a relatively limited action space during a twenty-four-hour period, but over a week, a month, or a year, the action space increases. We are concerned with normal conditions over time; however, abnormal conditions, such as a heavy snowfall which restricts action space severely, may also be observed. Abnormal constraints produce abnormally constrained action spaces. Conversely, if the proverbial rich aunt gives her favorite nephew several thousand dollars at the end of the spring term and he chooses to visit Afghanistan, normal money constraints are removed, and he consequently has an abnormally expanded action space.

Space distortions and shape transformations. We have moved from the space of the isotropic surface to operational space on the time and cost dimensions. In our discussion we stressed that *miles do not matter.* Now we shall introduce some complications of cost space and time space which will enable us to get a little closer to reality.

We all have experienced higher costs of traveling a given distance in some cities than in others, and also higher costs in certain parts of a given city than in others. We have also experienced *costs per mile* which are high for the first 2 or 3 miles but which drop as travel distance increases. Fare stages are also a common feature of some forms of transportation; the fare does not alter at all over certain distances and then proceeds to jump to a new level after a given point has been reached. That is, the cost does not vary continuously over distance, and therefore the cost space is said to be *discontinuous.*

Before continuing with this discussion, let us introduce some further terms. We shall define *isochrone* as a line representing *equal travel time* from a given point. Hence, our travel-time space or travel-time surfaces will be represented as *isochronous surfaces.* We shall define *isotim* as a line representing *equal travel costs* from a given point, and thus our travel-cost space or surfaces will be represented by sets of isotims.

As we have pointed out, the real economic space environment is highly complicated, and we shall consider the types of complications under the headings *space distortion* and *space inversion.*

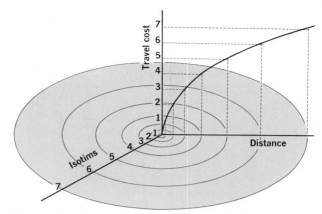

Fig. 10.2 Travel costs which vary over distance.

Space distortions on the cost and time dimensions. The simplest case of space distortion on the cost dimension is one in which unit costs of travel do not increase proportionately with distance. If we make a journey of 5 miles by bus and then another journey of 50 miles, the second journey is unlikely to cost us ten times as much. In other words, the extra miles we travel cost less per mile. Formally, we say that *the marginal cost of travel falls,* and the resulting graph or curve relating cost to distance is convex from above. This produces a progressive widening of the isotims, so that a unit of cost-distance in the outer parts of the travel area is greater than a unit of cost-distance closer to the origin (Fig. 10.2).

A similar distortion appears on the time-distance dimension, a distortion we have all experienced in a central city during the rush hour. A graph of travel time may look as shown in Figure 10.3. On the basis of the graph, one can see that the limits of the central city most likely end somewhere between isochrones 5 and 6, since after isochrone 5 has been reached, the rate of widening of the isochrones increases considerably.

In the case of taxi travel, the meter chops up distance into equal segments of cost space. Similar observations may be made in terms of any kind of fare-stage pricing by other means of transport (Fig. 10.4).

Space inversions on the distance and cost dimensions. We have all experienced the necessity of going past our destination and then backtracking some

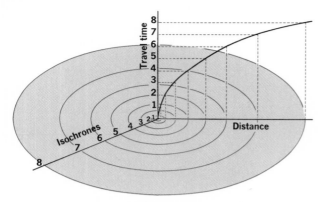

Fig. 10.3 Travel time which varies over distance.

distance in order to reach it. This often happens when we travel by air between two large cities and then drive back to a smaller town located close to the city where we landed. In Figure 10.5, although our final destination, town B, lies closer to our originating point, city A, in cost distance it appears as shown in Figure 10.6.

Fig. 10.4 Graphic presentation of discontinuous cost space.

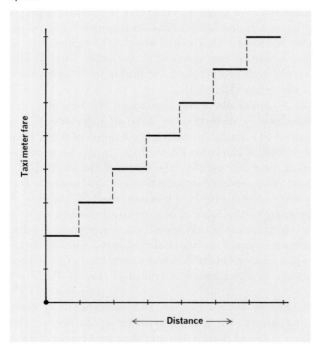

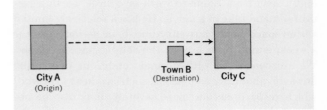

Fig. 10.5 Actual location in space.

We have two further examples of distortion on the distance dimension between cities and within the city. We may not, for example, be able to fly direct from Boston to Toronto, but may have to travel via New York. Under certain conditions, we may even have to travel from Toronto to Boston by flying via Montreal or Philadelphia. In each case the actual distance covered, the *operational distance,* between the two cities is far greater than the distance in the metric of our latitude-longitude system. Similarly, if we wish to visit a friend who lives in another part of the city, and if we are going to travel during the rush hour, it may take less time to go to the outskirts of the city and get on an expressway than to travel the shortest distance through the city. Again our operational distance is far greater than the actual distance, although in terms of the time involved, the circuitous route is far closer. Therefore, our isochronous surface inverts the actual distance surface.

We are all familiar with one-way street signs, which result in some interesting asymmetric distortions of space. In Figure 10.7, the distance from A to B is eight blocks, but the return distance from B to A is only four blocks. Finally, we may mention asymmetric distance on the cost dimension, the simplest example being a

Fig. 10.6 Transformation of actual location in space to operational space.

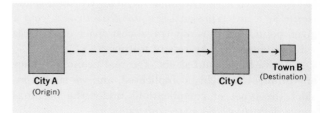

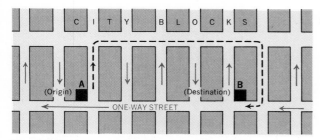

Fig. 10.7 An example of asymmetric urban space.

round-trip fare which is less than twice the cost of a single fare. Again the cost of going from A to B is less than that of going from B to A (assuming that the cost of travel from A to B has been incurred).

Shape transformations. Having shown how metric space becomes highly distorted by its transformation into operational space on the time and cost dimensions, and also having shown that miles do not matter, let us now try to understand how shapes of regions within cities based on distances can reveal complicated, irregular patterns and how, conversely, these shapes very often begin to reveal distinct regularities when they are transformed into operational dimensions. Even more importantly, as we are concerned with principles and theory, we may begin to understand how a circular market area in theory developed in the metric space of the isotropic surface can be identical with an amorphous market area in the real world since it may have been determined largely on a nondistance travel-time dimension (Fig. 10.8). We may also compare five trans-

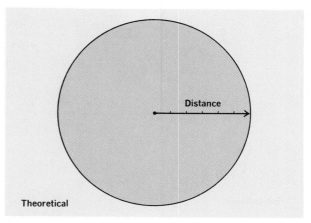

Fig. 10.9 Region's shape in theory on an isotropic surface.

formations of a region's shape, using the region's center as the origin or source of our calculations (Figs. 10.9 to 10.13).

We have introduced some of the complexities of the real world and have also demonstrated the principles upon which shape transformations occur as we move into different dimensions upon which we actually measure space. However, in order to develop our principles further, we shall go back as often as possible to the simple space of the isotropic surface. We should point out, though, that the reader has been introduced to an important field of advanced mathematics known as

Fig. 10.10 Region's shape in the real world. Actual political boundary of, say, a municipal city.

Fig. 10.8 Shape produced (left) by describing a line 3 miles from point A, and (right) by actually traveling from point A on ground transport.

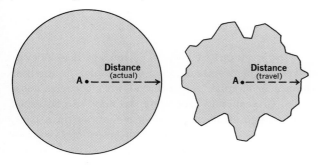

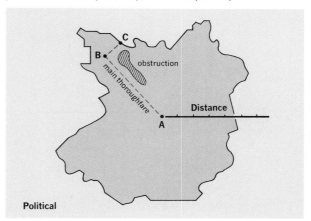

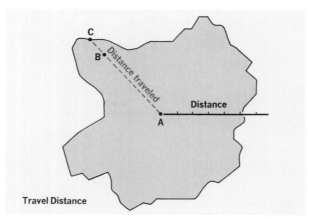

Fig. 10.11 Region's shape based on distance actually traveled on a highway network from a center to a representative set of points on the actual boundary.

topology. Some people call this new field of advanced mathematics "rubber-sheet geometry," and it is in this area of research that future geographers will be making significant contributions to our discipline.

Site and Situation

We have studied the concept of geographic space and the way in which we can move from our simplest Euclidean space in theory, the isotropic surface, to more complicated anisotropical space. We have also analyzed

Fig. 10.12 Region's shape based on least *cost* of traveling from the center to a representative set of points on an actual region boundary.

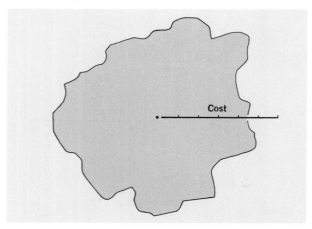

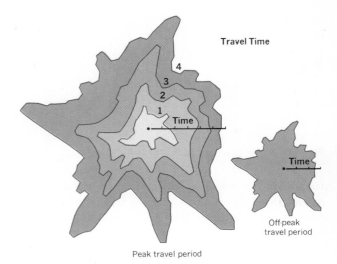

Fig. 10.13 Region's city shape based on travel *time* from the center to a representative set of points on the actual boundary.

the dimensional forms in which operational space was developed and the ways in which these dimensions of space assisted in the development of our theory. While the ideas of space are the most fundamental to our discipline, we must be familiar with several other basic concepts in order to build a good foundation for understanding the nature of geographic theory in economic geography. The first of these is the concept of *site* and *relative location.* If we asked an economist what concepts he considered most basic in elementary economic theory, he would most likely say "supply and demand." If we posed the same question to a geographer, he would most likely answer "site and situation."

Anything which is located on the earth's surface and which occupies some earth space has two important locational characteristics. The first of these is the space the thing occupies, which we discuss in terms of *site characteristics.* (See also Chap. 8, p. 127.)

The concept of site. This concept does not involve any constraints of size. For example, the smallest thing a geographer is concerned with occupies some space. In economic geography we may be concerned with a single residence or even a fountain in a park, or we may be concerned with an entire city, a city's region of influence occupying many hundreds of square miles, or a region of a country covering thousands of square miles. Whenever we think about the space occupied by a particular thing of geographic interest, we are conceptually thinking of its site, and site characteristics are defined in terms of the internal characteristics of the area occupied. In the case of a residence, the area it occupies may be on a bank or slope, and we would say that the site slopes. It may be in an area near a river, and thus be on a wet and foggy site, or near a factory that emits noxious fumes, in which case the fumes would be one of the site characteristics. As another example, a city may occupy a coastal or river site, a lowland level area, or an upland rocky area. All these characteristics, which are internal to the area occupied by a particular thing, are its *site characteristics.* Not only must they be seen as the physical geographic characteristics, but as all the *in situ* characteristics of the place we define. If the place is a city, the population densities, religions, prices of goods, city taxes, etc., are all defined as site characteristics.

   The concept of situation. The concept of situation refers to the spatial relationships which a particular space or place has with other places. Again taking the example of a residence, we shall be interested in how far it is from a shopping center, from a place of work, and from factories emitting pollutants. Each of these things will affect site characteristics, but they will not themselves *be* site characteristics. For example, the nearness to the factory will determine one site characteristic—namely, the amount of pollution actually in the site area—while the nearness of the site to a shopping center, a place of work, and the city center will affect its cost characteristics, such as the land rent or land purchase price. Each of these things is determined, then, by the situation of the residence and the same holds true in the case of a city. For example, the land value in a small city which is close to a larger city will be affected, as will perhaps the intensity of its atmospheric pollution. Now we see that *situation,* or *relative location,* as it is sometimes called, defines and is defined by the external relationships which a place has with other points on the earth's surface, and not by the internal characteristics of the space occupied, that is, its site. These are two analytically distinct things, and as we shall see, they are vitally important for our understanding analytically why things vary throughout space. However, as we pointed out, these two characteristics in the real world are not always distinct, but often are intimately related.

   We have seen that operational space changes as we change the cost and speed of movement. Therefore, we can see that if a city develops air transport or expressways or commuter railway to the next city, it actually moves closer to that city. Hence, as technological relationships improve connections, relative locations change. If jet speed to London from New York becomes twice as fast, London has moved to one-half the time distance it was from New York. Even in a site sense, London will probably change, as movement of goods between New York and London will affect prices, densities of populations may change as people change their residences between the two cities, and cultural exchange will produce *in situ* changes.

Space Systems

We have already touched upon the idea of a system in the section on functional regions (Chap. 8, p. 131); here, however, we shall look more closely into the system concept and its application to economic geography. At the same time, we shall introduce some terminology of system analysis.[7]

   We may define a *system* as a set of components which are interrelated in some way; that is, the components will have some kind of causal relationships with one another constituting an observably organized working *ensemble.* Any action by one component will bring about a response or reaction from another. We can all think of many examples of systems, from the telephone system to the transportation system in our city. In the case of the telephone system, telephone receivers are linked to other telephone receivers, and signals are transmitted over the system. In the case of an urban transportation system, various points of the city are linked by highways and railway lines, and goods and persons are transported over the network. We can also think about systems in which people are the components if they are linked together in some way. For example, we talk about the family system, in which the

[7] Webster defines a system as "an assemblage of objects united by some form of regular interaction or interdependence."

relationships are established by birth and marriage. On a larger scale, we may think of the electoral system in a city as consisting of components of the electorate and the elected representatives linked together by the expression of voting wishes and the responsibilities of the elected to carry out the wishes of the electorate.

We can see, then, that the term *system* is a very general one referring to a wide range of physical, administrative, and technological ensembles, and we must go somewhat further than this in order to arrive at a concept of system that will be useful in economic geography. First, let us distinguish between what are known as *open systems* and those which are defined as *closed systems*. An open system is a system in which the relationships between the components in the ensemble can be altered or influenced by other components. This means that the relationships cannot be fully determined by observing only the actions of the component parts. The human body is a system which is internally regulated to some degree, but is not closed since outside influences such as food, temperature, and air pollution can and do affect its internal operation. On the other hand, a telephone system within an office building which is not linked with the outside is a closed system since its operation is affected only by the use of its components. A city subway transportation system may be regarded as a closed system if there is no direct connection with other cities.

It is clear, therefore, that the distinction between open and closed systems is to some degree a matter of definition of the components and their relationships. If we define a system in terms of a few components between which the relationships are complex, we are defining an open system, since components other than those by which we define the system will be important in determining what happens in it. On the other hand, if we define all the components necessary to describe all relationships, we are beginning to define a *closed system*. That is, as we expand our system to include more and more components and their relationships, we begin to reduce more and more the number of outside determinants. We could, in the extreme, regard the universe, the earth, or the United States each as a closed system. We can detect here a very close parallel with our discussion of functional regions (p. 13).

Before defining a space system, let us familiarize ourselves with the concepts of *endogenous* and *exogenous* factors. As we shall see, a discussion of these terms will parallel what we have said so far about open and closed systems.

Endogenous factors are those factors which are themselves determined by the system; that is, they are completely within the system, and their values are determined by other components and their relationships in the system. Therefore, in a completely closed system all the factors we talk about whose values vary are defined as *endogenous variables*. In many biological systems, the size of each of the parts of the system is closely related to the size of all other parts. In the case of the human body, the length of the arms maintains a close relationship with the rest of the body as growth proceeds. Such growth relationships are termed *allometric growth*. This tendency for a mutually determining relationship to be maintained between the various parts of a system is considered to be endogenously determined.

Exogenous factors are factors outside the system which may affect it in some way. We may have a system which is largely defined as a closed system, in that it is generally free from outside influences, but in which, on occasion, an outside influence will have an effect. On the other hand, in the case of open systems we recognize that outside influences are operative all the while. That is, many factors are exogenous factors, or outside the system, and the values of many of the factors within the system are exogenously determined. For example, prices of certain goods within the city may be largely determined endogenously, that is, by factors within the city such as wages, rents, and the cost of power. If, however, the state imposes a sales tax on those goods, we have an exogenous factor influencing prices, which may normally be largely endogenously determined.

Let us now define a *space system*. We have begun to obtain some conceptual equipment and terminology about the system concept which will aid us in defining our space systems. In a sense, all systems are space systems if their components occupy space and the relationships are communicated over distance. A clock, for example is a closed mechanism or system which will occupy space, but traditionally geographers have not been concerned with the scale of system which a clock represents. Our scale of analysis has been at the regional level, with our regions ranging from continental regions down to city regions and regions within the city.

The space systems which we are interested in from the viewpoint of geographic analysis are those in which space is of first-order importance in the operations of the system. We have seen that the ideas of space associated with space-occupying elements have two perspectives: (1) the space actually occupied by a component, which we defined as the *site characteristics,* and (2) the relative locations or distance relationships these sites have with one another, which we called *situation characteristics.* These two elements then define our space system in terms of the area it actually occupies and the distances over which relationships are maintained. Where distances are so small that no time or cost is involved when one component communicates with another, such as in the clock, we would not define the system as a space system. On the other hand, a subway system involves time and cost in making contact from one terminal or station to another. We can see that this time and cost of connection or interaction between parts of the system and the maintenance of the network over which these communications are made is an essential, if not the most essential, characteristic of the system, and hence we call it a *space system.* Let us now attempt a formal definition of what we mean by a space system in geographic analysis. We define a space system as any *assemblage of objects united by some form of regular interaction or interdependence in which the space occupied by the component parts is significant and or the interaction between the component parts involving overcoming distance makes such interaction a first-order characteristic of the system.*

The Problem of Scale[8]

The problem of scale is a vexing one in geographic analysis, leading to much argument about the applicability of certain findings which tend to be logically irrelevant. The concept of scale is largely one involving generalization, and hence we may obtain some insights into the problem by looking at the nature of generalization per se. A *generalization* is a statement about a set

[8] See also the Introduction, page 14.

of things or events which tends to be true about that set but which may not, and logically need not, be true about any of the things or events individually. Now it is easy to see that an arithmetic average is a generalization stated in numerical form. We may say that the average height of co-eds in our university is 5 feet $2\frac{1}{2}$ inches, but we may search the university and not find one girl precisely that height. It would be illogical, however, to argue that the average was therefore false. It would be equally illogical to argue that the average was false if we happened to find a girl 7 feet tall. Although this may seem platitudinous, let us remember that one can neither contradict nor corroborate a generalization on the basis of a specific example. The only way we can contradict a generalization is by stating a more general generalization, that is, by making a general statement which applies to a greater number of cases or one to which there exist fewer examples to the contrary. In the case of our arithmetic average, 5 feet $2\frac{1}{2}$ inches may have been obtained from a 10 per cent sample of the height of co-eds, and we may not have included the "seven-footer." If we took a 20 per cent sample, we might find the average height—that is, our generalization—to be 5 feet $3\frac{1}{4}$ inches, and we could then advance this as a more general generalization. We have spent some time elaborating the above as it is surprising how much argument both in and out of universities consists of one person making general observations and another arguing from specific instances. Politicians are masters of such illogical argument involving completely different levels of generalization.

Let us now look at the problem of scale in geography. This is essentially the same as the problem of generalization, except that it involves the level of spatial generalization. The level of generalization in geography tends to vary directly with the size of the area with which we are dealing. If we work at the level of the continental United States, the findings we produce may not be true of any individual county or of any individual census tract in a city. We may generalize that the east side of a city is a manufacturing region, and we cannot argue that this is false because we have discovered no fewer than thirty residential buildings in that region.

Also, in the case of spatial generalization, the larger the region we cover, the greater the diversity of phenomena in the space, and hence our classifications of those phenomena tend to be at a higher level of generalization. For example, if we are studying an entire city, we may generalize land use into commercial, industrial, residential, and recreational classifications. That is, as the universe of phenomena expands, the classes into which we place those phenomena tend to be at a higher level of generalization. We group many different types of manufacturing into one class of land use on the map because of the economy of generalization. Often, however, we tacitly assume that all units are homogeneous in respect to things other than those covered in our classification. We must carefully guard against this. We may apply our general categories to things other than those we are classifying only when our classification fits closely the characteristics of those other things. For example, we may find that on the basis of a reasonable number of observations, our class of manufacturing land use correlates closely with, say, a high level of air pollution; our class of commercial land use, with less pollution; our class of residential land use, with less pollution; and our class of recrea-

tional land use, with least air pollution. In such a case we say that land use tends to be a reasonable *proxy variable* or *surrogate* for air pollution. The use of proxy variables is important in all the social sciences where data on one type of phenomena are unavailable or inaccessible in terms of cost or time required for procurement. Such instances involve second-degree generalizations.

Finally, let us make what are perhaps the most important observations about scale to be made in this section—those involving the scale at which we are working and the problems we are attempting to solve. It is obvious that if our observations are at one level of spatial generalization, such as the county level, we cannot hope to answer problems associated with another level—the census tract, for example. Similarly, if our available data are at the census-tract level, we cannot hope to solve problems at the city-block level or make predictions at the city-block level of spatial generalization. For each level or scale of area, there exist appropriate levels of generalization in our data; we cannot catch small fish with coarse nets.

Chapter 11

The Theoretical Approach: Spatial Order and Linkages, the Principle of Comparative Advantage, and Distance-Decay Functions

Perhaps the most important task of the economic geographer is that of explaining why particular types of production and consumption take place in particular areas and why goods move from various origins to various destinations. Although we have examined these concepts by broad definition and concept in Part 1, it now becomes necessary to assess them more rigorously.

Spatial Order and Linkages

The answers to questions of location and linkages involving economic activity are invariably to be found in differences in *factor distribution* and transportation cost. In economics, the *factors of production* are generally conceived to be natural resources or land, labor,

and capital. These differences provide the basic explanations for the territorial specialization of *spatial order,* the rational patterns of economic activity, which the geographer perceives in the economic environment he is seeking to understand. In other words, the differences account for the localized specialization of production (land use) and the movement of goods and persons between and among the specialized areas (linkages, or trade, or interaction; see Fig. 7.1, p. 104).

Types of advantages. The advantages which different regions may possess include the following, the first three of which are the factors of production as defined in economics:

Natural resources (land). These consist of climatic resources such as temperature, rainfall, sunshine, etc.; soils and vegetation resources; mineral resources; and topography influencing such things as port facilities and transportation. Sometimes, especially in economics, all of these resources are referred to as land. They play an important part in determining a region's production. (See Chap. 2.)

Supply of labor. Both quantitative and qualitative considerations are important. Regions may have a relative abundance of labor or a relative scarcity. Our use of the term *relative* here refers to the demand for the factor, in this case labor. Qualitative considerations refer to the skill and attitudes of the labor force, which are dependent on education, training, and cultural backgrounds.

Capital stock. Efficient production relies heavily on the available capital within the region for carrying out primary activities such as agriculture and mining; secondary activities, or manufacturing; and tertiary activities. Inhabitants of regions with high standards of living and high levels of production are able to save more easily and therefore can accumulate capital stock for specialization in the production of capital-intensive outputs. Although capital, as used here, includes money, it refers mainly to all investment (buildings, machinery, etc.) involved in production.

Prevailing power structure. Governments and other institutions tend to influence the production specialization of a region. Lists of strategic commodities, the accomplishment of long-range social objectives, subsidies, tariffs, and general regional planning will often contribute decisively to the determination of regional specialization. (For more details see Chap. 6, especially pp. 96 to 99; Chap. 8, pp. 141 to 143.)

Proximity to materials and markets. The factors noted above are internal to a particular region; they contribute to, and hence in part explain, the particular specialization which develops in a region. A further factor of vital importance is the relative location of the region or its situation relative to inputs (assembly costs) and outputs (marketing costs), which together determine the overall transportation costs faced by a region. (See also Chap. 7, p. 104, and Chap. 8, pp. 129 to 139.)

The Principle of Comparative Advantage

Inasmuch as both nations and subnational regions contain varying amounts of the three factors of production, different governmental and managerial outlooks and abilities, and different locations from materials and markets, it logically follows that some nations and/or regions possess advantages over others. Drawing upon this knowledge, David Ricardo formulated, in 1817, a *principle of comparative advantage,* which is especially useful in modern economic geography. We shall define this principle shortly. First, let us examine some other of its aspects, so that the definition will take on more meaning.

For the doctrine of comparative advantage to apply, it is necessary, of course, that the regions or areas of specialization be capable of interacting with one another. We can stipulate two basic requirements for specialization within the system of interaction. First, the things in which specialization takes place must be transferable, that is, economically capable of being transported between or among areas. Second, there must exist a surplus for export of the output in the area of specialization and demands for the specialized outputs in other areas.

Bilateral and multilateral trade. It is important to stress, however, that there is no necessary reason why regions specializing within the system should maintain symmetrical trading relations with each other. That is, region A could specialize in commodity X and export it to region B, but there is no need for region A to import anything at all from region B; rather, it could import its requirements from region C in the system. This lack of symmetry in trading relations often tends to perplex the student and result in politicians tacitly assuming that if their country imports from a given region or country, then for some reason—never made clear and certainly not an economic reason—that country should import equal amounts from them. When regions or countries import goods from, and export goods to, each other, we speak of *bilateral trade.* Sometimes agreements are reached between countries in the form of reciprocal trade agreements to balance the value of the imports and exports flowing beweeen them. However, by far the greater proportion of goods flowing between countries does not balance between each pair of countries. That is, bilateral balances are unusual. In the absence of restrictions on trade between countries, all that is required is that the goods imported by a country from many others balance, at least over a finite period of time, the value of its total exports. Hence, *multilateral trade* among countries is by far the most characteristic type and gives rise to a network of trade relations, in the form of goods moving among countries, which is extremely complicated and intricate. When we view trade flows at a lower level of observation or scale—that between or among regions within a country—we see interregional rather than international linkages. However, internal regions, as such, do not levy constraints like tariffs, quotas, or other regulations imposed by national governments (Chap. 6, pp. 96 to 101). Hence, trade between and among regions is multilateral.

Absolute and comparative advantage. Let us now look at the rationale behind the doctrine of comparative advantage. If a region can produce a product and market it more cheaply than a second region, we say that it has an *absolute advantage* in that particular line of production over the second region. It may happen that the second region can produce and market another product more cheaply than the first, in which case we say similarly that it has an absolute advantage in its particular line of production over the first region. In other words, if a region can produce something more efficiently than another, we say that it has an absolute advantage in that type of production.

Some regions are rich in a wide range of physical and human resources and can produce almost all goods more cheaply than other regions with which they are in contact. Similarly, some regions are very poor in resources—for example, regions in many underdeveloped countries—and as a result, they can produce little or nothing more cheaply than other regions. In this case, the developed region has an absolute advantage in all lines of production, while the underdeveloped region has an *absolute disadvantage* in everything.

When such a situation exists, what is the feasible economic answer to specialization? Will the rich region produce everything, and the poor region nothing? No; the answer is that *each region does the best it possibly can.* The rich region will specialize in producing those goods in which its absolute advantage is greatest, while the poor region will specialize in producing those goods in which its absolute disadvantage is least. The reason for this is that the resources of each region flow to those types of activities which are most efficient and therefore yield the greatest rewards in relation to internal factors of production—natural resources or land, labor, and capital.

As we have seen, a region may have absolute advantages in many or all types of production, while another region has absolute disadvantages in many or all types of production. That line of production in a region associated with the *greatest absolute advantage* over other regions is called its *comparative advantage.* Similarly, that line of production in a region with all disadvantages which represents its *least absolute disadvantage* is called its *comparative advantage.* This is the doctrine of comparative advantage.

Let us restate the doctrine: *The doctrine of comparative advantage states that a region will tend to specialize in producing those goods in which it has a comparative advantage, that is, those goods in which its absolute advantage is greatest or its absolute disadvantage is least.*

The reader is familiar with differences in soil fertility in agricultural areas which are related to concentrations of different crop types. Disregarding all other influences for the moment (let us say, *ceteris paribus*), a given crop will tend to be produced in areas where the soil is advantageous for that particular crop and then sold in other areas where the soil is not advantageous for that crop, but rather for some other crop. At a different level, the distinction may be made between agricultural land use and urban manufacturing land use, crops being sold in the city and manufactured products being sold in agricultural areas. At the elementary level, productive soil and relatively abundant space constitute the agricultural advantages, and technical knowledge and manpower constitute the urban advantages.

We may also use the doctrine to explain the specialization which exists between cities. For example, Cambridge, Massachusetts, tends to show a relatively high concentration of research outputs and educational facilities. If we marked off on a map that part of the urban area occupied by research institutions, it would reveal a different area of such specialization from that in, say, Mobile, Alabama. We may go on to further degrees of detail, using the doctrine to explain the relative specializations within a city in terms of manufacturing areas, commercial areas, and residential areas, and even specialization which may take place in a single street. We mention this because the doctrine of comparative advantage was first elaborated by economists to explain specialization between countries. Geographers, on the other hand, are concerned with spatial specialization at all regional scales, and the doctrine loses none of its explanatory power with variation in the size or scale of region.

Limitations to regional specialization. For any given region, we usually do not find complete specialization of production. Regions often produce part of their requirements and import the remainder from other areas. England imports wheat from the wheat regions of the United States and Canada, but also produces some wheat at home. The United States automobile industry produces many units for the domestic market, but also imports automobiles from Japan, West Germany, France, the United Kingdom, etc. While this is the general case with regional specialization, it does not invalidate what we have said about the doctrine of comparative advantage. What we have said so far stands firm in the *ceteris paribus* case. Now, however, we shall consider some limiting factors so that we may proceed a little closer to the complicated real world we seek to understand. We shall select only the main limitations and discuss them under the headings of *diminishing returns* and *transportation costs*.

Diminishing returns. If a region has a comparative advantage in a particular line of production, this does not necessarily mean that such an advantage will be maintained over all volumes of output in the short-run period of time. The resources or factors of production devoted to a particular activity are not capable of being increased with equal speed. Some, such as factory space, available land, and certain types of capital equipment, are relatively fixed in amount in the short-run period. Hence, in order to increase output, only those factors which are readily available can be increased, namely, the variable factors, such as labor or capital. If the region is producing its output most efficiently, i.e., at the least cost, then it must be combining the factors of production in the most efficient proportions. If, as output expands, all factors cannot be increased with equal ease, then the increased output must result in a less efficient combination of inputs. In other words, as more factors are introduced, then at some level of output the additional units produced by those factors will fall. It is this tendency toward diminishing returns in production which can put a ceiling on the amount of production of a commodity in a given region and hence limit the degree of its specialization.

Transportation costs. Limits to the spatial extent of the market. When we noted the types of advantages a region may possess, we introduced the advantage of proximity or location. In economic terms, these advantages translate into transportation costs. In discussing the effects of transportation on specialization, we shall first introduce two extreme situations, then the more realistic effects of transportation, and finally the interrelationships between site or *in situ* advantages and relative location or transportation advantages.

Extreme cases. We have pointed out that in order for specialization to occur according to the principle of comparative advantage, the regions which specialize must necessarily be in contact. If transportation cost between regions were so high that contact could not take place, then no specialization could result. Each region would have to produce everything it needed itself. Alternatively, if transportation costs were zero, then, *ceteris paribus*,[1] there would be complete regional specialization. Each region would produce only those goods in which it had a comparative advantage.

General case. More generally, transportation costs are positive, but permit the products of a region to be

[1] We have used the term *ceteris paribus* here so that we can dismiss such complications as diminishing returns and limited demand and observe the effect of transportation costs only.

transported to markets some distance from the producing region. At some given distance, however, the additional transport costs will so increase the cost of the good that the demand for the good at that given distance and at that given price will be zero.[2] This limit determines the spatial extent of the market. The quantity of the good demanded within the market area, however, will be less than the region could produce in terms of its available resources of land, labor, and capital. Given the prices of the product within the market area, however, those additional resources will obtain higher returns in some other lines of production and therefore will not move into the production of that region's specialized line of production. There are two principal reasons why the returns to factors of production will begin to fall as increased output occurs. First, as output increases while demand remains the same or increases less fast, the price of the product will fall, and therefore the returns to factors will tend to fall. For example, if prices fall, profits and wages tend also to fall. Second, a region's resources will be limited, and in order to obtain more resources in a given line of production, higher returns will have to be paid to encourage them to move into that line of production—for example, the payment of overtime rates above regular wage rates. In this way, a limit will be set on the specialization that occurs within a region.

Relations between advantages of site and situation. We may now note some relationships between the doctrine of comparative advantage and our concepts of site and situation. An area may have a comparative advantage for the production of a given commodity—such as providing housing, as in residential land use— for one or both of two reasons. Its advantages may be either *site advantages* or advantages of *relative location.* As we have seen, site advantages are defined by a site's internal characteristics, for example, a riverfront site for a city power plant. Relative-location advantages are defined in terms of the external relationships a site has with other areas. For example, the power-plant site may be well downstream near the main consuming centers, thus reducing the distances of power transmission.

[2] More precisely, at a price in which factor returns from producing that good fall below their opportunity costs or transfer earnings.

In order to clarify our concepts further, we may make the following distinction: Strictly speaking, site characteristics can affect only *in situ* advantages or production advantages, whereas relative-location advantages can affect only the movement of inputs (assembly costs) and outputs (distribution costs) and thus affect *in situ* production costs *indirectly.* In the case of residential land, site advantages affect only the utility obtained from actually occupying the residence or actually being on the site.

This distinction is of prime geographic significance. The two types of advantages may work together to reinforce the total advantages of an area for a particular use, they may work together to reinforce the disadvantages for a particular use, or they may work in opposite directions. Ghetto areas may have very bad site disadvantages in terms of the internal, physical, and social conditions for residential land use, but they may have great advantages of relative location in that they are close to downtown office blocks and restaurants offering employment and thus do not involve high costs of commuting to and from work. Similarly, where workers' residences are near gasworks, petroleum refineries, or chemical plants, the site disadvantages involving noxious fumes are endurable only because of the benefits of very low or zero commuting costs. A marshy area many miles from the city center would tend to have few advantages in terms of either site or location and may remain unused for urban purposes. If the relative location is changed, however, by the construction of a high-speed commuter rail through the region to the next city, this improved relative location may so improve the comparative advantage of the marsh that it becomes worthwhile to drain it, that is, alter its site character so that residential construction can be undertaken. Very steep slopes near the center of a city may possess such great advantages of relative location that flattening of the slopes to improve site qualities may be undertaken.

Where suburban expansion takes over agricultural land, the two forms of production, i.e., food and housing, may both require similar site characteristics such as flat, well-drained land; however, the advantage of relative location is greater for housing than it is for crop production. Hence, high prices will be paid for relatively small parcels of land for residential land use which will

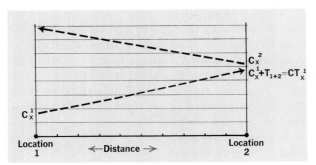

Fig. 11.1 Location 1 produces commodity *x* at a cost of C_x and can deliver *x* at location 2 at a cost of CT_x. This is below the cost of production at location 2, which is C_x^2.

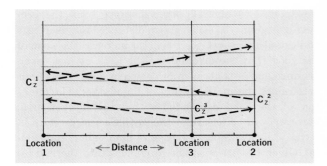

Fig. 11.3 $C_z =$ cost at each location. Location 3 has both a production-cost advantage and a relative-location advantage over the other two locations.

far exceed and therefore outbid the value in agricultural land use.

The comparative-advantage site-situation relationship may be summarized in Figures 11.1 to 11.3.

Figure 11.1, location 1 produces commodity *x* at a cost of C_x and can deliver *x* at location 2 at a cost of CT_x, which is below the cost of production at location 2, namely, C_x^2.

In Figure 11.2, the costs of production of *y* are equal at locations 1 and 2, but location 2 can sell *y* at location 3 at less than can location 1. Hence, location 2 has a relative-location advantage at location 3 over location 1.

In Figure 11.3, C_z represents the cost at each location. Location 3 has a production-cost advantage and a relative-location advantage over locations 1 and 2.

Fig. 11.2 The costs of production of *y* are equal at locations 1 and 2, but location 2 can sell *y* at location 3 at less cost than location 1 can. This fact gives location 2 a relative-location advantage at location 3 over location 1.

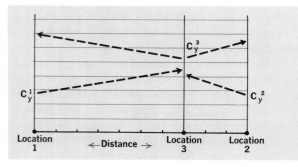

Distance-Decay Functions

Defining a Distance-Decay Function

An important basic concept and analytical tool in both theoretical and applied geography is the *distance-decay curve* or *function*. As we have already seen, distance is the fundamental geographic dimension, and the distance-decay curve specifies the relationship which a variable bears to distance. That is, we may measure the volume or quantity of any given variable at increasing distances from a specified reference point and plot those relationships on a graph. When we join the observations we have made by a line, we find that the values of the variable tend to decrease as distance increases. Let us be clear at the outset that not all things will decline with distance. Over a specified range we may find some variables remaining constant, while some may increase with distance. These relationships depend, of course, upon what we are measuring, but the most general situation we meet with in geography is that in which the variables we are interested in, namely, spatial variables, decrease with distance. Let us then define the distance-decay function as *a series of rectangular coordinates relating a given variable with distance and showing greater values of the spatial variable for any smaller distance than for any greater distance.* The origin or reference point from which we start will of course be a nodal point of the distribution we are studying. Very often in general analysis of urban structure, that reference point is the city center. Values for a variable selected, say, the number of office buildings, are plotted on a graph, with values of occurrence of the variable on the vertical axis and distance marked off on the horizontal axis. We may also select an individual's residence and plot the number of trips he makes to different shops, the visits he makes to friends, etc. If our final line or curve has no bumps in it—that is, if nowhere does the variable show a greater value at a greater distance than at a smaller distance—we say that the function is *monotonic decreasing.*

We have then a monotonic decreasing decay function, the simplest of all cases. If it is very flat, having a gentle slope, we may deduce that the variable we are measuring is not very sensitive to distance change because large changes in distance away from our selected origin result in only slight changes in the value of our variable. Alternatively, if the decay function is very steep, revealing large changes in the value of the variable with only small changes in distance, we may deduce that our variable is highly sensitive to distance. Let us introduce the term *spatial elasticity* in order to describe such relationships between a variable and distance, noting that the steeper the curve, the greater the change in the variable with distance, and hence the more elastic that variable is with respect to distance, or, in other words, the more responsive it is to distance. Alternatively, as we have noted, a flat distance-decay curve shows the variable to be relatively unresponsive to distance changes and hence spatially inelastic.

This situation of a monotonic decreasing decay curve, whether elastic or inelastic, constitutes a basic geographic model of the relationship of a spatial variable to distance. It is a very simple model and requires that we make assumptions in order for the relationship to be logically acceptable and also empirically verifiable. These assumptions are twofold. First, we must assume that the origin point from which we calculate the distance-decay curve is the origin point which exercises a dominant or at least a very significant influence in some way on the spatial distribution of the variable. That is, there must be a significant reason for the existence of a relationship between the variable and the origin. The second assumption is that the distribution is not invalidated by the nature of the surface over which the variable is distributed. Ideally, it would be the surface of our geographic laboratory, the isotropic

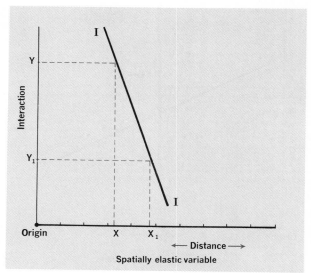

Fig. 11.4 A variable which changes rapidly over distance from a given origin is said to be spatially elastic.

surface. However, in our real-world situation we need to assume only that the surface is continuous and available for the distribution of our variable to occupy it. That is, the surface is not discontinuous, as it would be if we were measuring a land variable near the shore and out over the ocean or in the case of land areas prohibited by government or some agency from occupancy by our variable.

We may pursue the analysis of spatial elasticity a little further. The variable in Figure 11.4 is spatially elastic, while the variable in Figure 11.5 is spatially inelastic. This shows that for a given increase in distance X to X_1, the value of the variable falls off more in the case of the spatially elastic variable than in the case of the spatially inelastic variable, namely, Y to Y_1 when we compare the two figures.

We may examine the effect of a change in overcoming distance, say, a change in the cost or speed of travel. In general, effects of these changes will operate in the same direction. A reduction in interaction time will lower the constraints on the time budget and, *ceteris paribus,* enable a greater volume of interaction to take place at all given distances than previously. A reduction in interaction costs will, *ceteris paribus,* lower the constraints on the money budget and allow

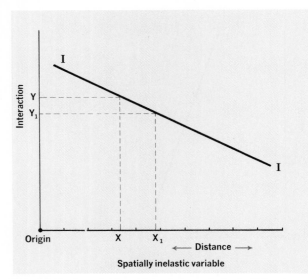

Fig. 11.5 A variable which shows relatively little change over distance from a given origin is said to be spatially inelastic.

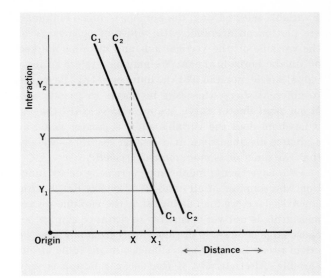

Fig. 11.7 The effect of a reduction in transport costs on a spatially elastic variable.

a greater volume of interaction to take place at all given distances. These situations are summarized in the graphs shown in Figure 11.6.

From our graphs we can deduce an interesting result which may be stated as follows: *The greater the*

spatial elasticity of a variable, that is, the more responsive it is to distance, the greater will be the effect of an increase in speed or a decrease in cost on the volume of interaction. This situation is summarized in Figures 11.7 and 11.8. In Figure 11.7, our variable has a high

Fig. 11.6 With a reduction in travel cost or travel time, we may expect the volume of interaction to increase.

Fig. 11.8 The effect of a reduction in transport costs on a spatially inelastic variable.

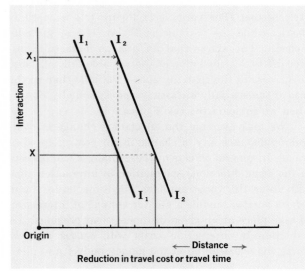

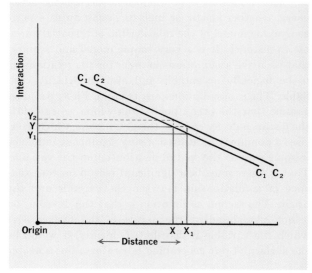

spatial elasticity, and the volume of interaction at distance X is Y. With a decrease in the cost (time) of interaction from C_1 to C_2, the volume of interaction at level Y increases in distance from terminating at X to terminating at X_1. We may also say that the volume of interaction terminating at X_1 was Y_1 before interaction costs were reduced to C_2 but that after interaction costs were reduced, the volume of interaction between the origin and X_1 rose from Y_1 to Y. Alternatively, in Figure 11.8, the variable has low spatial elasticity; it is relatively unresponsive to distance changes. With a decrease in cost of interaction, one can go from origin to X_1 for the same amount it previously cost to travel to X. Hence, the volume of interaction previously terminating at X now goes on to X_1; that is, the volume of interaction at X_1 before cost reduction was Y_1, and after cost reduction it rises to Y. Similarly, the amount of interaction at X rises from Y to Y_2.

Reasons for Distance-Decay

We have gone some way in defining the distance-decay function and have noted that it is one of the basic concepts in our discipline. Its construction was simple; we merely plotted from a selected origin a set of values at given distance intervals on a graph. We now must explain why things decay with distance. Answers to this question are still being sought in the field of theoretical geography, and so we must not be discontent if we cannot produce categoric or exhaustive answers.

In one sense we might say that there are as many reasons why things decay with distance as there are things which decay. That is, each thing which reveals distance-decay probably has some unique factors which will explain it. However, since we are concerned with the principles of our subject, we shall discuss several general classes of reasons that we hope will explain most distance-decay phenomena, at least as a first approximation. Then we may investigate specific factors which become important in particular cases, hoping to achieve a more complete explanation at the individual level of analysis.

First, however, we must introduce a further term. We shall call any factor which causes a variable to decay over distance, that is, anything which impedes the variable from having an even distribution throughout space, an *impedance factor*.

Economic reasons. For convenience, we may divide the economic reasons for distance-decay into two basic categories: (1) the cost of overcoming distance in terms of money and (2) the cost of overcoming distance in terms of time. Both of these increase with distance, and they are limited for any given use. Hence, as the money costs of interaction from a selected point increase, the observed values of a variable may be expected to decrease. Likewise, as the time required to interact from the point increases, the value of the variable will decrease. As we have stressed, in most cases both these factors will operate in the same direction, but only one of them will be relevant for any given location. For example, if we had an unlimited supply of money for a particular purpose, we would still have a limited time budget. On the other hand, if we had an unlimited supply of time, we would still operate under the constraints of a finite money budget. We can generalize these prevailing constraints to almost all phenomena, whether they be small firms sending out salesmen or buying different inputs, large corporations, government offices, military installations, etc.

Noneconomic reasons. The costs of overcoming the friction of distance, whether measured in time or money, are the basic economic reasons for distance-decay. However, if we could show examples of things decaying with distance while economic factors are held constant, it would be logical to assume that there must be other explanations. For example, if we plotted the number of letters going from a major city in the United States to all places within the United States, we would expect to see more letters going shorter distances than longer distances. (We must, of course, discount the influence of the size factor by comparing only cities of equal size.) Since the cost of sending first-class mail anywhere in the United States is constant, the distance-cost surface for United States mail is flat, showing no increase or decrease from any point. Therefore, because the cost of sending letters is constant, we cannot use it as an explanation for the fact that fewer letters are sent longer distances than shorter distances, and we must look elsewhere for a reason. Let us introduce the concept of *information*. The basic principle here is that we are far more likely to be familiar with our immediate neighborhood than with very distant places. We are also far more likely to know more people in the city where we live (unless, of course, we have just moved there) than people in other cities, and we are more likely to know more people in cities closer to ours than in cities further away. Just as we can extend our economic reasoning from introspection, that is, from an examination of our own time and money budgets, so we can extend our reasoning concerning mail and the location of our friends and other correspondents to a general principle in the urban space system. We may say, therefore, that the degree of knowledge about distant places and things tends to decrease as distance increases, and hence it may be purely a lack of knowledge which produces a distance-decay function.[3]

Intervening opportunities. We may add a fourth factor, namely, the existence of *intervening opportunities,* to the possible classes of explanation of distance-decay functions already discussed. Although the actual intervening-opportunities model will be dealt with later in this chapter, for completeness let us introduce the basic notion here as one of our reasons for distance-decay phenomena.

In the case of an individual traveling a given set of distances, the possibility that an intervening opportunity will occur before he completes any one of those distances increases as the distances increase. For example, if we decide to travel up to 5 miles in order to purchase a shirt, there will be some probability that we can get an equally satisfactory shirt closer than 5 miles. If we decide to travel up to 10 miles to purchase the shirt, our chances of finding one closer than 10 miles would be even greater, and so on with further increments in distance.

Given, then, the existence of the chances of obtaining satisfaction closer to our point of origin than at some given distance, and given also that those chances increase with distance, the chances that we will continue traveling to any point at a given distance will be less as the distance of that point from the origin increases. Hence, this alone would produce distance-decay functions.

[3] Economists may argue that knowledge itself, in that there is a cost associated with acquiring it, is just as much an economic reason for distance-decay as time or money cost. However, traditional economic theory at the elementary level is based firmly on the assumption of perfect knowledge, and work on the spatial variation of information is undertaken in many disciplines other than economics; hence it is classed here as a noneconomic factor.

Having discussed the reasons for distance-decay—namely, costs, information, and intervening opportunities—let us look at basic models that treat each of these.

The Gravity Model

One of the simplest models of human interaction is the *gravity model,* so called because interaction between, say, urban centers or other interaction points is assumed to vary directly with the size of the centers and to vary inversely with the distance separating them. In terms of size, which we have not yet discussed, the law of gravity tells us that the gravitational force exerted between two bodies is proportional to the product of their masses and inversely proportional to the square of the distance separating them. There is no general explanation of why this type of model should fit most human interaction, except for, as we have shown, the costs of overcoming distance—money costs, time costs, and inconvenience costs. We have also introduced other impedance factors such as the tendency for information to decrease with distance and the probability that intervening opportunities will occur as distance increases. However, there is no single general explanation for the gravity model, though there are, of course, individual explanations for individual types of interaction.

The gravity model tells us that if a small city and a large city are located an equal distance from the city in which we live, we would travel more often to the large city than to the small one; that is, if we decided to make a trip of a given distance from our city, there would be a greater chance of our selecting the large city as our destination. Let us generalize what we infer about our own spatial behavior to entire populations and say that the number of trips from a given center to each of a set of other centers will tend to be proportional to the product of their size and that of the originating center and inversely proportional to the distance separating each with the originating center. We know that such a statement must be based on some assumptions; most readers will be familiar with those assumptions or at least be able to guess what they might be.

First, we assume that the interactions we are comparing take place in homogeneous space, that is, that the space we are working with—time space, cost space, etc.—is homogeneous between the centers. It is no use showing that interaction between a given center and a smaller center is greater than that between the given center and a larger center if there are considerable barriers to interaction in the latter, for this would invalidate the comparative application of the model.

Second, we assume that our populations are the same in all cases, or, in other words, that we have a homogeneous universe. We assume that the interaction between two centers involves people or goods that are similar to those in two other places between which there is interaction. If this is not so, obviously our model will not predict interaction in both cases equally well. If one set of populations is more wealthy than the other, we may find that the gravity model underpredicts the amount of interaction, since people with more money tend to travel more, make more long-distance telephone calls, and generally maintain higher levels of interaction. This assumption of similarity of populations includes the idea that the cities between which the interactions take place vary only in size, since this is the only other variable in the model. For example, let us go back to our original case of a large city and a small city both an equal distance away from the city where we live; we said that we would be more likely to travel to the large city. This would not be so, however, if the small city held many more attractions for us and if severe pollution in the large city deterred us from visiting it. This would be the reverse of what we normally expect, namely, that larger cities offer more varied attractions than smaller ones, and hence we could not expect our general model to predict such a nongeneral case.

Let us develop the general notation for the simple gravity model. We shall designate the volume of interaction as I. The letters i and j are the centers between which the interaction takes place; that is, i is the origin, and j is the destination. We shall use D to designate distance, and M to designate the size of the center. Then,

$$I_{ij} = \frac{M_i \cdot M_j}{D_{ij}}$$

where I_{ij} is the interaction or movement between i and j; M_i and M_j are the size of centers i and j, respectively; and D_{ij} is the distance between i and j. This tells us that the volume of interaction between ij is inversely proportional to the distance separating them.

We have already said that the simple gravity model applies generally to interaction in homogeneous space in which there are no special circumstances producing variations and in which only the size of centers varies. This will not get us very far if we compare different *types of interaction* over *different modes*. Let us here define modes of interaction in terms of land, sea, and air; media, in terms of the particular form of land transport such as automobile, bus, and rail; and sea transport, in terms of cargo ship, passenger liner, etc. Let us also define types of interaction as physical movement of goods and persons, and nonphysical movement of such things as information.

We see that physical movement of people within the city and between cities is undertaken for many different reasons—they travel to school and to work, they go shopping, and they visit parents or friends on holidays. They use many different modes and media. The same is true in the case of the movement of different types of goods. Some are heavy, bulky, and costly to move, while others are light, compact, and involve low moving costs; thus the two types of goods will move via different modes and media. We shall therefore see that some movement in space will decline quickly with distance—that is, it is spatially elastic—and other types of movement will decline less quickly with distance—that is, it is spatially inelastic.

In Figures 11.9 and 11.10 we have two distance-decay curves of interaction produced by the gravity model. The steep curve in Figure 11.9 shows interaction falling off rapidly, and as we have already seen, we may deduce that movement is very costly and hence that the effect of distance on the volume of movement is very great. Figure 11.10 shows the opposite situation in terms of cost and the effect of distance. Now it is possible to produce a steeper or more gentle slope to the distance-decay curve; i.e., we can vary the importance of distance by placing an exponent on distance, or, in other words, by raising it to some power. Our model then becomes

$$I = \frac{M_i \cdot M_j}{D_{ij}{}^x}$$

The larger our exponent x, the more important distance is in influencing interaction, and the steeper our distance-decay curve—that is, the more elastic the interaction is with respect to distance. The smaller the expo-

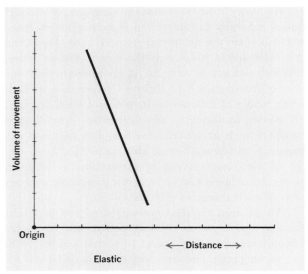

Fig. 11.9 Trip termination with a very high cost of movement (plotted on a semilogarithmic scale).

nent on distance, the less influence distance has on interaction, and the more inelastic interaction is with respect to distance.

It has been demonstrated that the gravity model can be produced by simple probability concepts. At any location in a system of interaction centers there will

Fig. 11.10 Trip termination with a low cost of movement (plotted on a semilogarithmic scale).

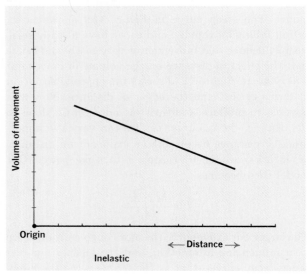

exist a number of interaction values—as many as there are points of interaction, each being calculated as in the simple gravity formula mentioned above. If the values produced by the gravity model at any given location are summed and each value is expressed as a proportion of that sum, then those values can be thought of as probabilities. That is, the probability that an interaction will occur between a given point and an origin point is proportional to the relative value of the gravity model produced by that origin point at the given point. For example, if two predicted values of interaction at a point are 7 and 3 from two points of interaction A and B, then the probabilities that an individual will travel to either are 70 and 30, respectively. This procedure may be generalized for any number of points of interaction as follows:

$$P_{ij} = \frac{I_j/D_{ij}{}^r}{\displaystyle\sum_{j=1}^{n} I_j/D_{ij}{}^r}$$

where P_{ij} = probability of interaction between a place at a given point i and a given point j

I_j = origin of interaction, point j

r = parameter of distance affecting a particular type of interaction

Therefore interaction values have been normalized and expressed as probabilities.

The Intervening-Opportunities Model

The intervening-opportunities model was first formulated in 1940 by the sociologist Samuel Stouffer, who was concerned with migration within the United States. He stressed that there was no deterministic relation between migration and distance as used in the gravity model, and he desired to introduce sociological variables. He said that the number of people migrating a given distance would be proportional not to the *size* of the population existing at that distance but to the number of *opportunities* existing at that distance. Further, he said that migrants would be constrained not by the distance separating them from those opportunities but by the number of other opportunities they had to pass up in order to get to them. For those opportunities which were passed up he used the term *inter-*

vening opportunities. He stated his hypothesis as follows: "The number of persons going a given distance is directly proportional to the number of opportunities at that distance and inversely proportional to the number of intervening opportunities." This is expressed in the following formula:

$$M = K\frac{\Delta x}{x}$$

where M is the number of migrants traveling a given distance, Δx is the number of opportunities at that distance, and x is the number of opportunities intervening between the origin and Δx. If we are measuring opportunities outward from a given center, they will be calculated as lying in distance bands or concentric circles outward from that center as shown in Figure 11.11. Intervening opportunities lying between the origin and x_n are therefore expressed as $x_1 + x_2 + \cdots + x_{n/2}$. Stouffer was concerned with explaining the number of migrants leaving a given place in the United States to go to any other place, and he considered that the number of jobs taken up by migrants would be a reasonably good approximation of the number of opportunities

Fig. 11.11 The spatial structure of the intervening opportunities model.

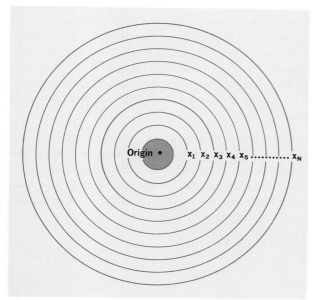

existing at that place. There are several criticisms of his original formulation which will not concern us here. The most basic is tautological definition of opportunities. Stouffer's model has been used by many workers, and good results have been obtained with it.

Let us make some observations concerning the model. First, we may note that the general structure of the gravity model and that of the intervening-opportunities model are similar in the sense that they involve both a direct and an inverse proportionality relationship. Second, there is some probability that the number of opportunities will increase with distance, and hence the intervening opportunities can, in certain cases, be collinear with distance in the gravity model. Third, there is also a probability that the number of opportunities at a given distance will vary directly with the size of the center existing at that distance and hence also vary directly with the size of the center as used in the gravity model. While the two models appear to have some simple structural similarities, however, they are very different. The gravity model is built on an isotropic-surface assumption. The intervening-opportunities model is built on the assumption of an anisotropic surface. Moreover, in a single test situation the two models invariably produce very different results. At this stage we may mention the work of Edward Ullman on interaction since it is directly related to the gravity and intervening-opportunities models. Ullman pointed out three necessary conditions for economic interaction between two places to occur. First, there must be *complementarity* between the two places, meaning that in one place there exists a demand for a good which is capable of being supplied by the other place. Second, there must be *transferability,* meaning that the good is capable of being economically transported between the two places. Third, there must be no *intervening opportunities* between the complementary places, i.e., no places closer to the original center that can supply the demand.

Let us continue the discussion of the intervening-opportunities model not only in terms of migrants but also in terms of movement in general. As we suggested, it can be used as a general explanation of distance-decay functions involving movement. Let us also introduce a probability parameter λ. We shall let this measure the probability that a given opportunity will *not* be passed up. Then the closer λ is to unity, the greater the probability that a given opportunity will not be passed up. For example, if λ = 0.5, there is a fifty-fifty chance that the opportunity will not be passed up; if λ = 0.75, there is a 75 per cent chance that the opportunity will not be passed up.

Several important factors tend to determine the value of λ.

Heterogeneity of opportunities. The first of these factors is the amount of variance between the opportunities, that is, how heterogeneous they are. For example, a traveler will pass up an opportunity only if he expects to increase his satisfaction by going farther. The more heterogeneous the various opportunities are, the more likely the traveler is to expect that he will benefit by traveling farther. If all opportunities are identical, that is, homogeneous, there is no reason to proceed beyond the nearest opportunity. Therefore, we may state that *where opportunities are homogeneous, λ = 1, and as opportunities become more heterogeneous, λ becomes smaller.*

Trip purpose. The second factor relates to the purpose of the trip. For example, it may be a single-purpose trip or a multipurpose trip. The single-purpose trip may be highly specific (mailing a letter) or very general (an unplanned evening out), and similarly with multipurpose trips. We can see that trip purpose is the mirror image of homogeneity or heterogeneity of opportunities. In the case of a highly specific trip purpose λ = 1, the traveler would not proceed beyond the first opportunity that satisfied his requirement. As the generality of the trip purpose increases, λ declines; we are more likely to pass up a given opportunity in the hope of doing better. Let us now state a relationship in rather formal language: *The heterogeneity of opportunities and the specificity of trip purpose are mutually determined. If we consider the maximum-opportunity heterogeneity to exist when all opportunities are different and the maximum specificity of trip purpose to exist when it can be satisfied by one category of opportunity only, then λ in both cases must be zero or 1.*

Density of opportunities. The gain to be derived from proceeding to a better opportunity must be balanced against the higher cost of getting there. The farther away the next opportunity is—that is, the greater the distance between opportunities—the less likely the traveler is to pass up a given opportunity. Therefore, given a fairly uniform distribution of opportunities, the lower the density of opportunities in general, the greater λ is likely to be. A decline in unit travel costs (in time or money) will mean that a more distant opportunity will seem more attractive. Therefore, one can expect λ to decline as transportation improves.

Accordingly, we would expect that within a given, fairly uniform area, trips with purposes tending toward fairly homogeneous destinations would exhibit a higher distance exponent than trips to heterogeneous destinations. Empirical results tend to corroborate this. Jobs tend to be heterogeneous, men's jobs more heterogeneous than women's, and so one would expect a fairly low distance exponent for work trips by men than by women. Social trips are made to visit households. A household chosen at random is unlikely to be a suitable destination for a given social trip, and so one would expect a very low distance exponent for social trips. On the other hand, mailboxes are fairly homogeneous. If we were to make a study of trips made for the purpose of posting letters, we would find a very high distance exponent. Grocery stores and supermarkets are generally homogeneous, as are public schools, and trips made to them tend to be associated with high distance exponents.

Conclusion. In general, then, λ will be a monotonically declining function of transportation cost, of the heterogeneity of trip purpose, of the number of opportunities passed up, and of the distance to the next opportunity and subsequent ones, or, in other words, the density of opportunities.

Chapter 12

The Theoretical Approach: Elementary Geographic Models of Spatial Structure

Spatial Structure and Rent

Spatial Structure. So far we have discussed the elements of theory, the concepts and measurements of space, and some of the basic concepts which constitute or underlie the geographic theory of economic regions. We shall now attempt to understand some of the simple models of the spatial structure of economic activities. First, let us state the meaning of spatial structure and then select the basic models we can use to approach an understanding or explanation of such structure.

By *spatial structure* we mean the pattern or set of spatial relationships which are maintained by different functional components of the space economy—in other words, their layout or plan. These components are perceivable space-occupying components performing different economic functions. Therefore, they have relative locations and occupy space, and hence our observations of them are in terms of land-use types. The land-use map reveals, then, both the *areas occupied* by different economic activities or functions and their *relative locations* with respect to one another.

As we emphasized in a previous chapter, the structural pattern observed will depend to some extent upon the degree of detail or level of generalization according to which we classify land use. If, for example, we use a simple fivefold classification of agricultural, residential, industrial, commercial, and recreational land uses, the spatial structure revealed will be somewhat more simplified than if we used a more detailed, tenfold classification. In fact, we may put forward the generalization that the more detailed land-use classifications we use, the more complicated the structure that is revealed will tend to be. That is, there is a different degree of spatial generalization involved.

The theory of economic geography is concerned with explaining how such structures come into being or what forces are operative to explain them. Obviously, as we become less general—that is, more detailed and particular—we discover more and more detailed, unique, or specific forces which will explain a given locational structure in the real world. At the beginning, however, let us attempt to isolate the force or forces operative at the general level and put them into a logical framework. If we follow such a course, it will become clear that we cannot understand locational structures until we understand the concept of *geographic rent*. To do this we must first understand *economic rent* because the economists to whom we owe much of our knowledge of the concept of rent have lumped geographic rent under the general heading of economic rent and have not concentrated to any significant extent on elaborating the theory in a spatial context. Let us therefore proceed step by step, defining each term as we go so that we may acquire a thorough knowledge of the important concept of geographic rent.

Contract rent. In everyday discussion *rent* usually refers to a payment we make for the right to use something, the title to, or ownership of, which belongs to someone else. In a modern economy one can rent a vast variety of things as a private person, from houses and apartments to cars and formal dress. Incorporated companies may rent anything from a factory or computer to a typewriter. A farmer may rent land, buildings, and machinery. All these rentable items have several things in common: A payment is made for their use, and they are rented for a given period, at the end of which they return to the owner's possession. Rentable items must therefore be durable and not consumed by the person renting them. One cannot rent a hamburger, for example. This type of rent we shall call *contract rent,* and we shall define it in terms of the common characteristics mentioned: *Contract rent is a periodic payment for the use of a durable item belonging to someone else.* While, as we have noted, a wide variety of durable items fall under that heading, rent still most commonly arises in the case of the ownership of space. In rural areas the most common type of rent is land rent, and even in the city the most common item rented is space, whether it be an apartment, office, or plot of land. It is in terms of land that the concept of economic rent first arose, and hence we shall look briefly at the early notions of rent in our quest for an understanding of geographic rent.

Ricardo's concept of economic rent. In 1817 David Ricardo elaborated a theory of economic rent. He considered economic rent to be the payment for the use of things which could not be produced. He pointed out that the rent yield of a unit of land is equal to the excess returns from using that land over the least fertile land. Let us assume that land which is just worthwhile cultivating yields zero rent. We call such land *marginal land,* since land that is less fertile is left uncultivated and land that is more fertile is all cultivated. Then, as we move to more and more fertile land, the economic rent (excess returns or profits) will be greater and greater; that is, the most fertile land will yield most rent over the least fertile or marginal land. Less fertile land will yield less rent over and above marginal land until the least fertile land cultivated, the marginal land, yields no rent.

Ricardo observed that if competition between land *users* were perfect, then the whole of that surplus (excess of returns or profits mentioned above) would be paid by the user of the land to the landlord. Hence, the user of the land would receive no extra profit because he was renting the more fertile piece of land. Each farmer would make just enough to live, whatever the fertility of the soil he cultivated, and the differential returns from fertility would be scooped off by the landlords. In this perfect-competition case, then, economic rents would be identical to contract rents.

Let us look at the logical process by which this situation arises. If farmer A's land, for example, produced 10 bushels of wheat per acre at $10 a bushel, equaling $100, and farmer B's land produced 5 bushels per acre at $10 a bushel, equaling $50, and if costs of cultivation including the farmers' living expenses worked out at $10 per acre, then the rent of farmer A's land would be $90 per acre, and that of farmer B's would be $40. If farmer A's rent were less than $90, say $80, then he would be receiving $10 over B's returns for doing the same work, that is, cultivating a unit of land. It would therefore pay B to offer A's landlord anything over $80 so that he could rent the land rather than A. This process of bidding up the contract rents on each parcel of land which yielded a surplus would continue until the condition were reached in which the surplus return from soil-fertility differences all went on to the landlords in the form of contract rents.

Now we have stated that rent in the Ricardian sense, or economic rent, is a surplus return of a more fertile piece of land over the least fertile. Therefore, all cultivated land yields a surplus.

We may also consider the economic rent of class

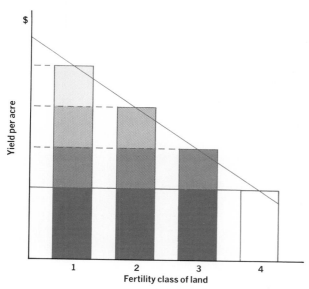

Fig. 12.1 Rent yields which differ with the fertility of land growing the same crop.

from the same crop grown on different classes of land to different crops grown on the same piece of land.

From Figure 12.2 we can see that there is a surplus yield from using the land for crop A over and above its next best alternative use and a surplus yield from using the land for crop B over the next lower alternative use, namely crop C. Thus, all land will be devoted to its most profitable use and will all be scooped off by the landowner. We might observe at this point that the term *transfer earnings* is sometimes used for this last concept, which we shall define as follows: *that surplus or excess return accruing to a particular use of a piece of land over its next best alternative use.*

Von Thünen's concept of geographic rent. At the same time Ricardo was developing his theory of rent, J. H. von Thünen was formulating a very similar concept. However, von Thünen approached the problem from a very different perspective, one that has rendered his ideas, although formulated in an agricultural context, of most significance to geographic analysis in general and to economic and urban analysis in particular. This reveals the generality of von Thünen's notions, and hence the usefulness and the ubiquity of the basic

1, most fertile land, over class 2, and so forth, and consider that surplus to be economic rent (Fig. 12.1). We need not necessarily use the zero rent yield of marginal land as the starting base for calculating economic rent. In fact, it often is more useful to know the surplus of class 2 land over class 3 land than over marginal land. Let us then define *economic rent* as the surplus yield of a piece of land over the next best piece of land.

Now just as we can study Ricardo's ideas on economic rent by comparing the differential fertility of land under one crop, that is, by holding the crop or land use constant and comparing different pieces of land, so also can we employ the same device holding a unit of land constant and varying its alternative uses. A given piece of land can be used for growing, let us say, three types of crop: A, B, and C (Fig. 12.2). Let us also say that crop A, yields 20 bushels per acre at $1 per bushel, crop B produces 20 bushels at 75 cents per bushel, and crop C produces 10 bushels at 50 cents per bushel. Then the yield of the land, which is the price times the quantity that can be sold will be 20 × 1.00, or $20 for A; 20 × .75, or $15 for B; and 10 × .50, or $5 for C. Now we can use a graph similar to that shown in Figure 12.1, leaving land yield or price times quantity on the vertical axis and merely changing the horizontal axis

Fig. 12.2 Rent yields which differ for different crops grown on land of the same fertility.

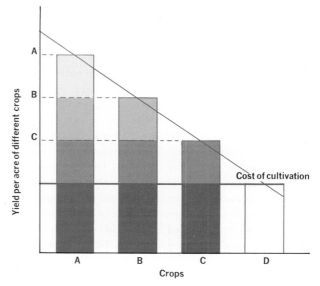

geographic variable of *distance,* in influencing not only agricultural structures but also all spatial economic systems.

Von Thünen owned an agricultural estate called Tellow, situated in northern Germany near Rostock. As an agricultural estate owner he was concerned with understanding the reasons for the variation in the spatial distribution of agricultural products. He observed that in the real world, there are countless explanations for such variations—differences in the slope of the land, in drainage and rainfall, and in soil fertility, for example. He therefore posed the following question: Even if such obvious differences affecting agricultural land use were removed, would there still be differences in agricultural land use which were not the product of randomness? That is, is there another, more fundamental or underlying cause which will explain such land-use variations?

In seeking to answer this question, von Thünen began by assuming the existence of a land area which was undifferentiated throughout, that is, a surface over which everything was held constant. This is our concept of an isotropic surface. As the reader will readily observe, von Thünen's approach at the outset was quite opposite to that of Ricardo. Ricardo used the differences in the natural fertility of the soil, which he referred to as "the inalienable and indestructible qualities of the soil," to explain the differences in the rent yield of land and hence, as the basis on which to elaborate his theory of rent. Von Thünen, on the other hand, assumed such differences away and, as we shall see, employed the geographic location of a piece of land as the basis on which to explain the regular variations in the rent yield of land and hence the differences in land use (Fig. 12.3).

We shall not elaborate the entire von Thünen theory (for a summary, see Fig. 12.3 and caption), but only those aspects essential for our understanding of his explanation of geographic rent. On the isotropic surface bounded by a wilderness, so that we need admit no exogenous or external influences, he assumed there existed a single market center to which all agricultural products traveled to be sold and from which all farmers' products were obtained. Given these basic assumptions, would there arise any differences in rent and agricultural land use? Under such conditions, the

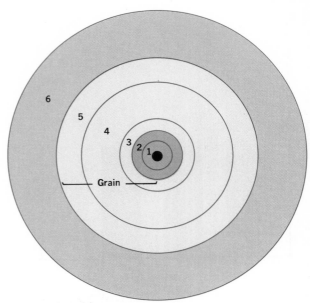

Figure 12.3 The von Thünen circles. The dot in the center is the city. Circle 1 encloses a district of intensive dairying (fluid milk) and truck gardening—both producers of perishable commodities. Circle 2 contains wood-cutting industries, necessarily close to market because a high demand existed within the city for wood and because slow and costly animals and wagons were the chief form of transport in the prerailway time of von Thünen. Circles 3, 4, and 5 surround crop-rotation systems, each of which involves grain. Intensity of land use decreases with increased distance from the central city. Circle 6 encloses a very extensive type of stock raising, with emphasis upon wool, butter, cheese (and some meat)—products which, in the main, can be preserved for long periods of time and can stand the cost of a long haul to market. Beyond is uncultivated land that can be cultivated if necessary. With increased size of the central city, the radius of each circle is extended, but the relative position of each remains the same.

only factor which would vary in the system would be the distance of a piece of land from the central market. We may measure distance in terms of the time spent in travel (the farmer's time budget), the payment made to a hauler or shipper (his money budget), or the effort he employs in carrying goods to the market (his energy budget). However we measure such costs, they will increase with distance from the market. For the purpose of keeping our exposition simple, we shall couch our arguments in terms of the money cost of movement.

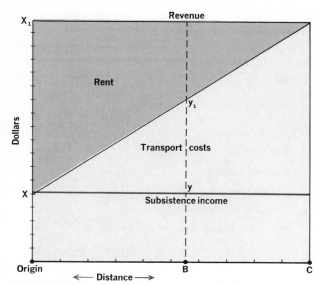

Fig. 12.4 Rent yields are reduced by increasing transport costs until they become zero at location C.

On our isotropic surface, where all land is equally fertile and all farmers are equally efficient, the physical productivity of the soil is constant throughout space. We assume also that all farmers at the market will receive the same price for their products. Hence, the revenue or income line for farmers (the market price times the amount they produce) will be a horizontal straight line. Now each farmer will require some level of income in order to survive; we shall designate this *subsistence* or *necessary income*[1] and measure it again in money terms, which will also appear as a horizontal line on our graph because no matter how far the farmer lives from the market, he will still require the same income to remain alive. Each farmer will have to pay to get his produce to the market, and so we must subtract this from his revenues. As distance increases, he has to pay more for shipment and hence has less revenue left. We shall represent this by the distance between the revenue line and the diagonal line, the costs of shipment

[1] If there were no alternative occupation for the farmer, that is, if he could be nothing but a farmer, the line would represent a subsistence-level income, a sufficient income to keep him alive. If there were alternatives open to him, the line would represent the amount of income necessary to retain him in that occupation, which would be that amount he could earn in the next best alternative occupation, his *transfer earnings*.

increasing as distance increases, with no costs at zero distance (Fig. 12.4).

We may now pursue our reasoning on geographic rent (Fig. 12.4). At distance OC (O meaning origin), all revenue above subsistence or necessary income goes into shipment costs. There is no excess yield over subsistence income on land, which is distance C from the market. Beyond that distance, shipment costs become too great for agricultural production to take place, and thus we have established, along with von Thünen, that even if land is equally fertile, it will not all be cultivated because an *external margin* of cultivation will be established beyond which it will not be profitable to cultivate. At zero distance from the market, that is, on land adjoining the market, the yield over subsistence is XX_1 dollars and at distance B from the market that excess is X_1y_1 dollars. Now we shall see that land at all distances less than the external margin of cultivation yield a surplus return over the subsistence or necessary income and that the differential increases, so that the excess is always greater for the piece of land closer to the market than for a piece of land further away. Let us also observe that at all points closer than C, the net income yield is greater than that required to keep the farmer alive or greater than that required to keep him producing as a farmer. We shall call this surplus the *geographic rent* and proceed to define geographic rent as *that surplus return accruing to a piece of land because of its more favorable location over another piece of land*. Therefore, rent at any location is

$$R = P \cdot Q - (Pc + Tc)$$

where R is the rent; $P \cdot Q$ is price times quantity of output, or the farmer's revenue; and Pc and Tc are production costs and transportation costs, respectively.

Now we shall have to show that in the ideal competitive situation, all geographic rent will be scooped off by the landlords, so that again geographic rent will, under our perfect-competition assumptions, be equal to contract rent. We shall see, then, that an identical argument to the one we employed in the case of economic rent in the Ricardian sense will apply here. Let us assume that the landlord at B charged the farmer less than the geographic rent yield at location B. Then farmers at that location would receive a net return greater than all other farmers. Hence, it is simple to reason that other farmers would compete for land at B, each offering the landlord a little more rent out of the extra return from that land in order to secure it for themselves, until eventually all the surplus would go to the landlord, and each farmer would again receive a net return equal to his necessary or subsistence return.

Summarizing what we have said so far concerning economic rent, we see that some land yields a return over and above the return on the other land, and we view this extra return as a *surplus*. While Ricardo emphasized differences in the natural fertility of soil as the most important factor producing such differences, von Thünen stressed the location of a piece of land relative to its market as the main factor producing such differences. We have elaborated the theory of economic rent in terms of the agricultural case because it was in that context that the notions were first derived. However, the reasoning applies equally well to urban land use as to agricultural land use, and we shall employ it to explain differences in land use in both these areas. Let us emphasize, however, that while economic rent in the case of land or space arises both from the differential fertility of the soil, which we recognize as a *site difference,* and from differences in relative position, that is, *relative location,* we shall find in the urban environment that far less can be explained in terms of site differences. We therefore arrive at the important proposition that *most of the economic rent which arises in urban regions is geographic rent, or the surplus revenue or advantage which a better location yields over a less good location.*

The isotropic model. Now that we understand the concept of rent, we may formulate a land-use model of a city or region in terms of a very simple structure. Let us reduce the amazing array of urban land uses to just three classes of use, namely, commercial, industrial, and residential. We shall see that such a simple classification results in a very simply structured city or region. We need not worry about this. All we need to show is that our model is logically rigorous and that it adequately demonstrates the method by which geographic rent theory explains the land-use structure of an area. The model itself and the results of it will be only first approximations to the complications of the actual or real-world region.

Let us follow the original work of E. S. Dunn quite closely and use a similar notation. We shall first define our variables and then conduct our analysis in those terms.

The variables are classified as follows:

Dependent variable:

R = rent per unit of land

Independent variable:

k = distance

Constants or parameters:

E = yield per unit of land

p = market price per unit of commodity

a = production cost per unit of commodity

f = transport rate per unit of distance for each commodity

$$R = E(p - a) - Efk$$

Therefore, R is a linear function of distance.

Our first land use has a very steep slope, (Fig. 12.5); the distance variable is of first importance in deter-

Fig. 12.5 Rent for land use requiring a high level of accessibility.

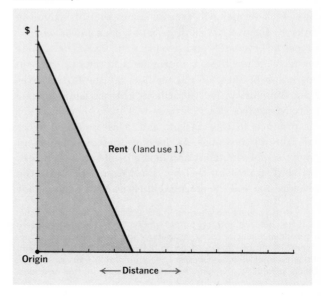

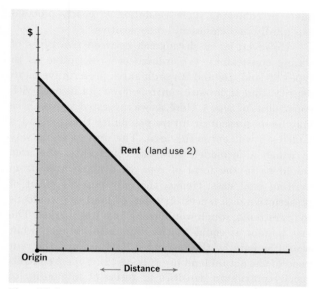

Fig. 12.6 Rent for land use requiring a medium level of accessibility.

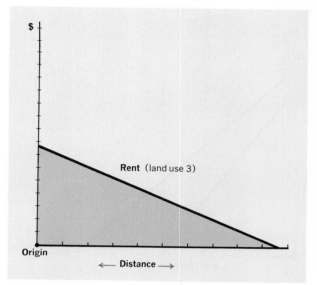

Fig. 12.7 Rent for land use for which accessibility has low priority.

mining its profitability, or rent yield. Stated in another way, we may say that as commercial land use moves away from the center of the city, its profitability decreases rapidly. Our second land use, industrial land use, differs from the first in two respects: First, it is a less profitable land use at the city center than commercial land use (the intercept on the ordinate axis is below that of our first land use), and, second, the slope of the rent function is less, indicating that it is less sensitive to distance or accessibility to the center (Fig. 12.6). Similar reasoning applies to our third land use (Fig. 12.7). Both the intercept at the center is lower and the slope of the rent function is less.

We may now place the three separate graphs of land uses together and produce Figure 12.8. At distance X, land use 2 yields a greater return than land use 1:

$$E_1(p_1 - a_1) - E_1 f k_1 < E_2(p_2 - a_2) - E_2 f k_2$$

At distance X_1,

$$E_2(p_2 - a_2) - E_2 f k_2 < E_3(p_3 - a_3) - E_3 f k_3$$

At distance X_3,

$$E_3(p_3 - a_3) - E_3 f k_3 = 0$$

That is, we have reached the margin beyond which the land use of our urban region ceases to be profitable.

Let us examine carefully why these changes in land use occur. We have pointed out that two conditions are necessary and that neither is by itself a sufficient condition. The first is that the rent yield at the center must be greater for one land use than another. That is, $R_1 > R_2$; or, more fully, $E_1(p_1 - a_1) > E_2(p_2 - a_2)$.

Fig. 12.8 The spatial distribution of land uses of different rent yields and accessibility priorities.

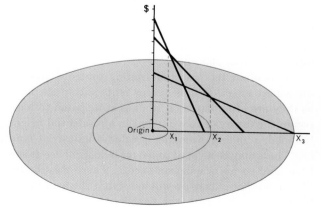

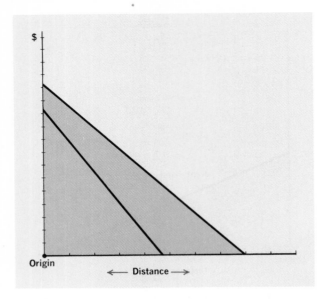

Fig. 12.9 The lower rent curve has a higher accessibility priority (slope) but a lower rent yield.

This condition is fulfilled in Figure 12.9, but we can see another condition is necessary: that the rent function for one industry must be steeper than that for the other, $-E_1f_1 > -E_2f_2$. This condition is fulfilled in Figure 12.10, but again we see that no land-use changes occur. In Figure 12.11, the two conditions are fulfilled, in terms of both the R intercept and the slope of the rent function, and hence at X distance from the origin, land use 1 can be logically revealed to give way to land use 2.

Rent and zoning. Let us look briefly at the effects of zoning regulations on urban rents. We shall not survey the problem fully at this stage; it is only one aspect of urban planning.

It is often the case that zoning controls have no immediate effect on land use or rents within the city, as they are often based on what is anticipated to happen in the future. It may be that in a residential neighborhood, a zoning ordinance precludes industrial land use. There may be no land zoned for industrial use at the time, and so no evacuation occurs. There may be no likelihood that industries will move into the area in the future. In such a case, the benefits to the urban tax-

payer in achieving such legislation (a costly process) can hardly be demonstrated as positive.

However, let us distinguish between two types of zoning constraints: (1) ordinances prescriptive as to types of land use and (2) ordinances prescriptive as to density, that is, lot-size controls. First, let us deal with constraints of type 1. Here, as we suggested above, there may be no present or future possibility that precluded land uses will enter the area. The only possible way in which a forbidden land use could enter the area would be in the form of rent yield above that from existing land uses. Hence, the only possible effect of prescriptive ordinances on types of land use would be to lower rents, which would result in a free market. The loss in rent is equal to the difference between what would be paid by the precluded land use and the rent yield of the actual land use (Fig. 12.12). Type 2 controls specify maximum densities in terms of minimum lot size. They too will have no effect if the market demand is for lots equal to the minimum lot size specified or larger. The operational effect and the value of legislation in such a case is equal to zero. Identical arguments apply in the case of maximum lot size. However, if a residential-location seeker has to buy more land than

Fig. 12.10 The lower rent curve has a lower accessibility priority (slope) and lower rent yield.

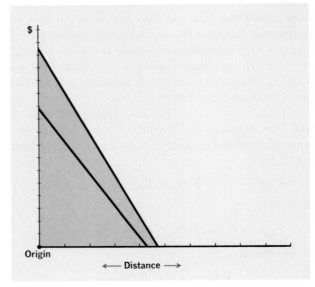

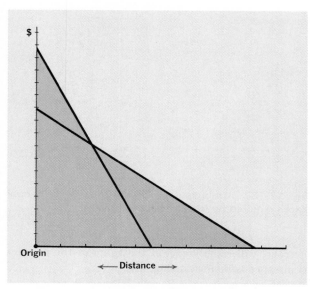

Fig. 12.11 The rent curve intersecting the other from above has the highest accessibility priority, but it will occupy the land only up to the point of intersection.

he desires, he will offer less per unit, and hence rents will be less. If he is constrained by a maximum lot size, he will get less land than he desires.

The Christallerian Model

Central-place theory. One of the most important models in economic geography is the central-place theory of Walter Christaller. In 1933, Christaller wrote *Die*

Fig. 12.12 The rent loss from precluding a profitable land use is shown by the shaded area.

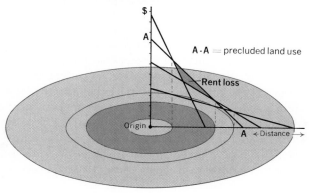

Zentralen Orte In Suddeutschland, or *Central Places in South Germany.* The work had practical implications and was meant to aid planning at that time in Germany. Basically, it was concerned with the urban hierarchy—with size and location of different categories of urban places. (See also Fig. 8.3, p. 133.) Since that time, central-place theory has established itself more and more as one of the most important sources of essential, basic principles of theoretical economic geography. Not only has central-place theory developed as a source of fundamental theoretical principles of spatial organization, but it is also being used more and more as a practical planning tool.

As with most models, the strength of the Christallerian framework stems from its simplicity and its generality. It has been observed that:

> Since the assumptions of the Christallerian framework have most relevance to service activities where the pull of raw materials tends to be minor and least relevance to basic industry oriented wholly or partially to localized raw materials, the Christallerian approach is most pertinent for the study of highly urbanized regions in which service activities dominate the economic structure.[2]

Assumptions of the Christallerian framework. Let us first look at the following list of assumptions and postulates and then discuss each in turn:

Assumptions
1. An isotropic surface
2. An even distribution of rural population
3. A triangular distribution of population centers
4. A marketing range for each function
5. A population threshold for a given function
6. Constant spatial behavioral parameters of the population

Postulates
1. A size hierarchy of central places
2. A functional hierarchy of central places
3. Market areas consisting of regular hexagons continuously covering the isotropic surface

[2]Walter Isard, *Location and Space Economy,* Cambridge, Mass., The M.I.T. Press, 1956.

4. Market areas for lower-level functions that are smaller and located completely or partially within the market areas for higher-level functions
5. Higher-order central places that are farther apart than lower-order central places

Assumption 1. An isotropic surface. We have already encountered the concept of an isotropic surface in various connections. The Christallerian assumption is that the surface is continuous and unbounded and that it is isotropic with respect to movement over it. That is, transportation cost is equal in all directions from any point on the surface. Hence, isochrones or isotims would be represented by equally spaced concentric circles from any point selected on the surface.

Assumption 2. An even distribution of rural population. The rural population is served by a set of central places which are evenly distributed across the isotropic surface. We shall see that all our assumptions remain consistent and that our postulates are all logically derivable from those assumptions—that as the density of rural population increases, the distance between central places of a given size decreases. Hence, when there is a very sparse rural population, central places will also be very sparse; in other words, the distance between central places will increase.

Assumption 3. A triangular distribution of population centers. The third characteristic of the central-place framework is a triangular distribution of central places. This distribution, we shall find, is necessary in order for all places or all populations to be served in the system. That is, our simple geometry requires, in terms of elementary two dimensions, a triangular distribution—i.e., A, not B (Fig. 12.13).

Assumption 4. A marketing range for each function. This assumption states that there is a maximum distance beyond which an individual will not travel for a given level of function. That distance will be directly correlated with the order of function offered; that is, people will travel shorter distances for low-level functions and longer distances for high-level functions. Hence, market areas for low-level functions will be small, while the market area for highest-level functions may constitute an entire country. Low-level functions are generally low-cost commodities, and hence the cost

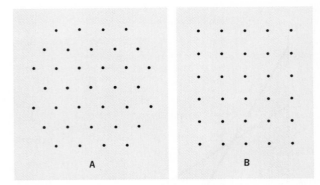

Fig. 12.13 Distribution A is the distribution of central places required by the Christallerian model.

of travel will rapidly exceed the value of the product as distance is increased (Fig. 8.3).

Assumption 5. A population threshold for a given function. According to this assumption, there is a minimum number of inhabitants below which a given level of function will not appear. That is, lower-level functions will require fewer inhabitants to support them than middle-order functions, and middle-order functions will require fewer inhabitants than the highest-level functions. It follows, therefore, from the population-threshold assumption that a higher-order center with a larger population will offer higher-level functions because it serves a larger rural population, but at the same time it will contain the necessary population to fulfill the threshold requirements of all lower-level functions. We can say, therefore, that functions are cumulative up to the highest-level function which a center has the population threshold to offer.

Assumption 6. Constant spatial behavioral parameters of the population. Our sixth and final assumption is that an individual develops no preferences for patronizing any given center over any other center, except that he will always patronize the nearest center offering a given level of service. This assumption therefore excludes the possibility of *multipurpose trips* in which an individual would pass up a smaller center nearby offering a given level of function in order to travel to a more distant, larger center to obtain several of the services offered.

Postulates of the Christallerian framework.

Postulate 1. A size hierarchy of central places. Our first postulate is that not all central places will be the same size. That is, it logically produces differences in the sizes of central places, from hamlets and villages through towns, to regional cities, and beyond. As we can order these from the lowest or smallest centers to the highest or largest centers, we refer to a *size hierarchy.* The Christallerian framework assumes the maximum number of different sizes of center to be seven. These are referred to as *orders of centers,* ranging from the smallest, or first-order center, to the largest, or seventh-order center, in a fully developed central-place system. While we may say that this is not a very startling finding, as everyone knows that central places are not all the same size, it is still necessary to explain simply and logically *why* this may be so. (See also Fig. 8.3.)

Postulate 2. A functional hierarchy of central places. This postulate states that the functions of central places become ordered into a hierarchy. Thus we can recognize low-level services, such as those we require every day; common services which are not highly specialized, such as most of the food contained in our regular diet; and high-level specialized services which we require at very infrequent intervals, such as hospital services. This postulate will be easily obtainable from Assumptions 4 and 5.

Postulate 3. Market areas consisting of regular hexagons continuously covering the isotropic surface. From Assumption 5 we may postulate that two centers of equal size would offer the same level of functions to their surrounding populations. Assumption 1 indicates that travel would be equal in all directions from any point. Consequently, market areas under this assumption and Assumption 2 would necessarily be circular. However, in order that none of the rural population lies outside the range of a given supplier, such as would occur in area A in Figure 12.14, market areas of nearest neighbors of the same size overlap. Within the "eye" of overlap is an area of competition, and we could generate on a probability basis the increasing likelihood that a given individual located in the eye would go to one area rather than the other. However, the Christallerian model is deterministic, and a right-angled bisector will divide the market area of the two nearest neigh-

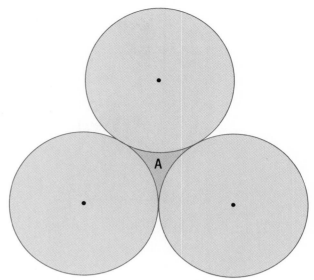

Fig. 12.14 Market areas of the three central places do not overlap; therefore, area A is not served.

bors down the center of the eye of overlap (Fig. 12.15). There is no probability involved since those neighbors fall in one market area or the other.[3] This occurs between all nearest neighbors of the same size, and hence we derive the hexagonal framework from the triangular distribution of central places (Fig. 12.16).

Postulates 4 and 5. Market areas for lower-level functions that are smaller and located completely or partially within the market areas for higher-level functions; higher-order central places that are farther apart than lower-order central places. We have also observed that market areas for higher-level functions will be large and hence contain within them market areas for lower-level functions. This is obtained from the range of a product and the population threshold, and is shown in the second-order system illustrated in Figure 12.17.

That centers of any given size will be farther apart than centers of any smaller size is derivable in the same way. Their maximum distance apart is determined by the maximum range of a given service. A second condi-

---

[3] If we assume that people are located on the line, we have the case of Buridan's ass to help us out. Similarly, as we shall see, if a person is located at the vertex of a hexagonal market area and equidistant from three central places, the case of Buridan's ass can provide us with a solution.

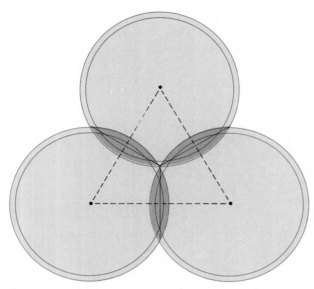

Fig. 12.15 The boundaries of the three centers' market areas are defined by bisectors of lines joining them.

Fig. 12.16 When bisectors of lines joining all adjacent central places are drawn, a hexagonal system of market areas emerges.

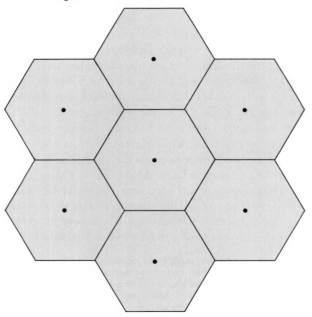

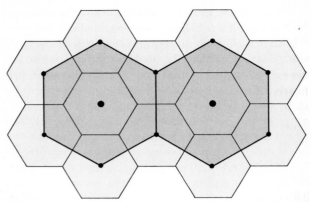

Fig. 12.17 A second-order system of market areas in Christaller's K = 3 or marketing system.

tion is that the given necessary minimum population which would support that service lie within the maximum range. Given a uniform density of rural population, the distance between central places of a given order would have:

1 A maximum distance determined by the maximum range of the highest-level function offered and minimum density of rural population. If centers were farther apart, an insufficient threshold of populations would reside within the necessary maximum distance or range.

2 A minimum distance is determined by the higher density of rural population which would produce the necessary population threshold. If the centers were farther apart than this minimum distance, then another center would develop between them so as to meet the minimum-distance requirement. This gives us the result, namely, that the system minimizes the number of central places subject to the constraints of the range of services and that all populations will be served. The density of population, or threshold constraint, enables central places to locate as far apart as possible without allowing an intermediate center of the same size to develop between them.

Christallerian theory and reality. Christaller's model has been criticized as too theoretical by many geographers. The first response to it was that the real world does not contain systems of central places with the perfect symmetry of the model and that it should therefore be thrown out. However, we no longer search for the ideal system in the real world because conditions in the real world are far more complicated than those required in the ideal system. Let us look at how "realistic" Christallerian theory actually is, at least that part of it to which we have been introduced so far.

Cities are not all the same size. This is verifiable wherever we look: India, Canada, Brazil, or Massachusetts. Larger cities are spaced farther apart than smaller ones. This is a generalization, to be sure, since there are such things as twin cities located very close together—Minneapolis and St. Paul, for example—but it holds in the majority of cases. The population threshold is an eminently realistic assumption. Seldom do we find symphony halls or stock exchanges located in villages or small towns. Market areas and the range of a good are two things related to the population threshold. We know from introspection that we will travel greater distances for certain goods than for others.

Therefore, what the critics of the model are really objecting to is not the essential or meaningful parts, but the inessential parts—the isotropic surface, the even distribution of rural population, the triangular distribution of central places, and market areas consisting of regular hexagons. We have emphasized that these are the simple conditions developed in our theoretical geographic laboratory and that they therefore do not apply in a similar way or produce the same results outside our theoretical laboratory. We do know, however, that if we use complicated real-world operational space rather than simple laboratory space, then, by employing topological transformations—or, rather, our "rubber-sheet geometry"—we can see how more realistic Christaller's model actually is.

The Christallerian and von Thünen models. Although Walter Christaller was the first to produce a comprehensive theory explaining consistently the distribution of settlements in the economic system, we find that many aspects of previous and later locational analysis can be integrated into it. For example, von Thünen's work may be viewed as a special single-center case of Christaller's marketing principle, and hence

much of the subsequent market-area analysis can be integrated with it. In the case of von Thünen, there is a maximum distance from the market that a particular crop can be grown (assuming, of course, that the market price of that crop is constant and that the transportation rate and unit cost of cultivation also remain constant). The reason why the particular crop is not grown at a greater distance is that some other land use becomes more profitable and can yield a higher rent. In this sense, then, the *range of a product* in the Christallerian model is the outer *margin of production* in the von Thünen model. We also saw in the von Thünen model that if the price of a product at the market decreases, then the area of its production will contract. The contraction of the area of production will take place along the least profitable outer margin. In this sense, then, the area of production constitutes a *threshold* of supply to support a given price level. If the area varies, the supply of the product will vary. Conversely, if the price of the product varies, say through increased demand, the area will vary, and so supply will increase. We have, therefore, both the *market range of a product* and the *threshold* concept in the von Thünen model; as we have seen, these are integral parts of the Christallerian model.

Christaller's pure systems. Christaller developed a series of central-place hierarchies which were "pure" systems. That is, the hierarchy or central-place system was analytically distinct or pure in that it was organized upon a single dominant principle. We may say that the system was so arranged as to achieve a dominant objective function such as to facilitate the *marketing* of goods and services or achieve orderly and effective *administrative control*. In this section we shall briefly review three such analytically distinct or pure systems.

Let us designate the number of smaller places dependent upon a central place of the next higher order as its *K value*. If, for example, a given central place served two other central places of the next lower order, we might say that its *K* value was equal to 2. Remember, however, that the given central place will serve its own population with the functions for which the smaller centers are dependent upon it. We must therefore add its own population to the number of places dependent upon it for those functions, and therefore the K value becomes 3, being comprised of two separate populations plus its own population. In the pure networks or systems of Christaller, that relation or dependency value is constant between all successive orders in the hierarchy. A seventh-order place will serve the entire system population with seventh-order functions since there are no other centers in the system large enough to offer seventh-order services. Hence, at the seventh-order level all places are dependent upon a single largest center. We may establish the number of places dependent upon another place of a given order in the fixed or pure system using the relationship $D_x = K^x$, where D is the number of dependent places, K is a constant representing the type of network, and x is the order in the hierarchy. Thus, a third-order place in a $K = 3$ system would have twenty-seven dependent places, and, similarly, a fourth-order place in the system would have eighty-one dependent places for fourth-order functions.

Three main systems with a fixed K relation which Christaller developed were $K = 3$, the marketing system; $K = 4$, the traffic system; and $K = 7$, the administrative system. The actual geometries produced by these pure systems are shown in Figures 12.18 to 12.20.

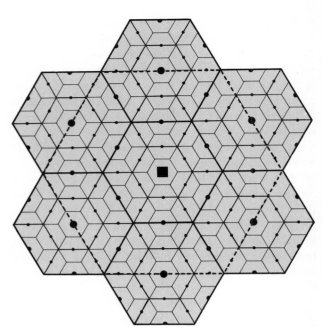

Fig. 12.19 Christaller's $K = 4$ network with centers up to the fourth order in the hierarchy.

Fig. 12.20 The arrangement of Christaller's $K = 7$ network (political principle) developed to the first order.

Fig. 12.18 Christaller's $K = 3$ network with centers up to the fifth order in the hierarchy.

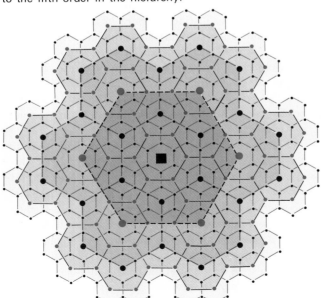

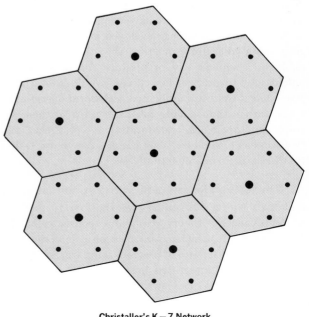

Christaller's K = 7 Network

In the case of the $K = 3$ network, the marketing system, the objective of the system is to maximize the supply of services. The reader will notice that all central places occur at the vertexes of the hexagonal market areas of the next higher-order center. Therefore, each center is equidistant from three larger centers of the next order. We assume that the population of a center is divided between three centers, so that a center will draw on one-third of the population of a center at the vertexes of its hexagonal market area. As there are six vertexes to the hexagon, and hence six surrounding centers, each contributing one-third of its population to the larger center, their combined populations total two centers. We shall add to this the center's own population and thus establish a total of three populations dependent upon it for its highest-level functions.

Just as the $K = 3$ system maximizes the number of central places, the $K = 4$ traffic system minimizes the cost of providing the transport network. Its objective, therefore, is to arrange the distribution of central places so that as many important places as possible lie on one traffic route between larger towns. The reader will notice that in the $K = 4$ system, central places are all located on the sides of the hexagonal market areas of the next higher-order center. They are therefore equidistant between two higher-order centers rather than three, and hence they are divided between two centers. Since there are six sides, or six dependent centers, the total populations dependent on the next higher-order center are six half populations, i.e., three plus the center's own population, totaling four—hence the $K = 4$ system.

Finally, in the $K = 7$ system, the administrative system, no central places occur on the boundaries of hexagons, and thus there is no division of central places. This is required by the system objective, namely, unequivocal administrative control, which would clearly not be achieved by the division of central places. This spatial organization is achieved by reorienting the hexagonal areas of each level of administrative control containing the central place within that area and six dependent central places. The $K = 7$ system has a progression of dependent central places of 1, 7, 49, 343, 2,401, etc., up to the seventh order.

While the logic of the Christallerian fixed K or pure systems is analytically useful, we find in reality that urban systems do not orient themselves towards a single objective, and often not even to a dominant objective. Hence, we find that actual systems are usually a mixture of these pure systems. The work of the economist August Losch moved in this direction.[4]

The Weberian Model

We have seen that the von Thünen model helps to explain why a particular piece of land will be used for a particular purpose by showing how it will be put to that use which yields the greatest profit, resulting in the highest rent or price being paid for it. We saw also that von Thünen first developed his theory in connection with agricultural land use. Second, we saw how Christaller developed his model to explain in a comprehensive way the geographic distribution of urban settlements. We now wish to discuss a model which will provide us with answers to a different question: At which point in an economic region will a manufacturing plant tend to locate? The reader will note that, whereas von Thünen and Christaller were concerned with land use in a regional perspective, Weber was interested in the location of a single plant.

This problem was tackled by Alfred Weber in his work entitled *The Theory of Industrial Location* (1909). Rather than trying to outline Weber's theory exhaustively, we shall attempt to isolate the more important concepts in order to obtain an elementary understanding of his logical explanatory model.

Transportation costs. Weber distinguishes between two types of transportation costs: *assembly costs* and *marketing costs*. Assembly costs are those costs incurred in transporting raw materials to the point of production, that is, transportation costs on inputs. Marketing costs are the costs incurred in transporting the commodity produced to the market.[5] One can see, then, that total transportation costs are merely the sum of assembly costs on raw materials and marketing costs on outputs; we must take both into account. If a plant

---

[4] August Losch, *The Economics of Location,* Yale University Press, 1954.

[5] It is important to remember throughout the general theoretical framework that transportation costs to the market or consumer may be treated as synonymous with the costs a consumer will incur to travel to the products. This latter is stressed in Christaller's model.

locates at the market, then total transportation costs will be equal to assembly costs, since marketing costs will necessarily be zero. The same reasoning applies if a plant locates at the point where a raw material occurs, provided that it is the only raw material used. If, however, a plant locates at neither the market point nor the raw-material point, both types of cost are incurred. The closer it is to the market, the greater the assembly costs, and the smaller the marketing costs. The closer it is to the raw material, the smaller the assembly costs, and the greater the marketing costs.

Transportation costs are determined not only by the distance covered but also by the transportation rate. We may define the transportation cost of movement as the transportation rate times the distance covered. If, for example, the rate of transporting a finished product was twice the rate of transporting a unit of raw material, then one could transport the finished product only half the distance he could transport the raw material for the same expenditure (Fig. 12.21).

Weber states that the two basic elements of transportation costs are weight and distance. The transportation rate, then, is the cost of moving one unit of "weight" of the product over one unit of distance. In practice there are many different rates, depending on whether the goods to be transported are bulky, perish-

Fig. 12.21 The isotims around the raw material point are twice as far apart as those around the market point, showing that the transport rate for raw material is half that of the finished product.

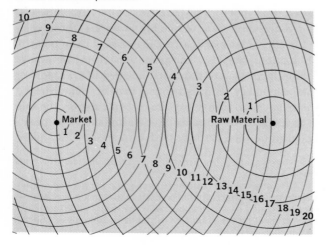

able, etc., as well as special agreed-upon rates. Mode and media of carrier are also significant (Chapter 7, pp. 104 to 122, especially Figure 7.2). Weber points out that geographical distances should not be measured by their geographical length but in proportion to the decreasing rate scale.

Raw materials. We must now discuss Weber's classification of raw-material inputs in the production process. He classified raw materials on two bases: (1) distribution and (2) whether they lose weight in the process of production. Weber pointed out that there are two extremes of raw-material distribution. A raw material can occur everywhere throughout an economic region or at one or several particular points in it. The first type of raw material he called *ubiquitous,* and the second he called *localized.*

As for his second basis for classification—whether or not the raw material loses weight in the process of production—Weber referred to those raw materials which enter into the finished product without any weight loss as *pure* raw materials, and to those which lose weight, having only part of their weight in the finished product, as *gross* raw materials.

It is interesting to think about the usefulness of these classifications when developing a logical model to determine a minimum-cost location. In the case of the first classification, we can see that only one of the types of raw material can in any way influence costs of location, and hence the point at which those costs are minimized. *Ubiquitous raw materials* can by definition be obtained anywhere, and therefore they cannot involve transportation costs to move them to the point of production. Thus we may reasonably assume that the cost of ubiquitous raw materials will be constant throughout a region. On the other hand, *localized raw materials* will involve no cost of transport only if the production point is located at their point of occurrence. As the production point is moved farther away from the localized raw material, costs of transporting it to that point will increase.

In the case of the *gross raw material* which loses weight in the process of manufacture, the closer we locate to it, the shorter the distance the excess weight will have to be transported. On the other hand (assuming that the raw material and the market are not at the same point), there is no advantage in locating closer to a *pure raw material* rather than farther away. For example, if the market is located at a point other than that where the gross raw material occurs, then anywhere we locate along a line joining the raw material and the market will involve the same transport cost. If we locate one unit of distance closer to the raw material, we will save one unit of transport costs (1 ton-mile) on the raw material. However, we will be moving one unit of distance away from the market, and therefore we will increase our cost of transport on the finished product by one unit of transport cost, or 1 ton-mile.

In the simplest case, therefore, we can see that ubiquitous and pure raw materials will have very little influence on the choice of location where that location aims at achieving the point of minimum transport cost. The raw materials of major importance are those which are localized and gross.

Let us now develop Weber's method of obtaining the point of minimum total transport costs. We can do this using a simple case in which we have one raw material that is localized and pure and one market at a location other than at the raw material. We also assume for simplicity that our region is isotropic with respect to transportation costs and that the transportation rate is a constant function of distance. We then draw concentric circles around each point, as shown in Figure 12.23. These concentric circles are lines of equal transport costs, or *isotims*. It is easy to see that the higher the transportation rate, the more rapidly transportation costs increase.

Two further terms need to be introduced and explained. The first of these is the *material index,* which specifies the relation between the weight of the localized raw materials and the weight of the product. Weber defines the index as the "proportion of weight of localized raw materials to the finished product." If coal was a raw material and there was no weight loss, so that 1 ton of coal produced 1 ton of finished product, then the material index would be 1. Similarly, if 2 tons of coal produced 1 ton of finished product (i.e., if there was weight loss), the material index would be 2:1 or MI = 2. The material index does not vary, regardless of how many tons of ubiquitous raw materials are included in the product.

The *locational weight* of a product is the *total* weight which has to be moved in the locational region—

that is, the movement not only of raw materials but also of the finished product. It is clear, then, that locational weight will be 1 plus the material index. If the MI = 0 (i.e., if only ubiquitous raw materials are used), the locational weight will be 1 (i.e., 1 + 0). If the MI = 0.5, the locational weight will be 1.5. The locational weight of an industry increases constantly with increases in the material index.

Weber makes the following general observations:

1 Generally, industries with high locational weights (high MI) will be pulled to raw-material orientations. Those with low locational weights (low MI) will be pulled to market orientations.

2 Pure materials never bind production to their locations.

Figure 12.22 A schematic view of Weber's theory of location for individual manufacturing establishments, or plants. Energy is here considered as one of two raw materials forming two points in the locational triangle, the third being markets. The initial position of the plant's regional location is at the point of minimum transport costs. This position is considered further regarding labor costs, and finally regarding agglomeration. (After Carl H. Cotterill, *Industrial Plant Location: Its Application to Zinc Smelting,* American Zinc, Lead, and Smelting Company, St. Louis, 1950, Fig. IV-1, p. 67)

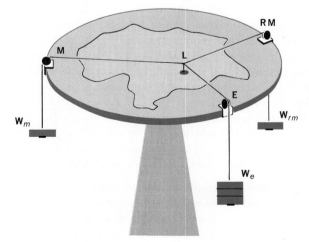

W = Weight of transported materials

M = Location of markets for plant's products

R M = Location of raw materials going into plant's products

E = Location of energy for plant

L = Location of point of minimum transportation costs

3 The greater the weight loss of the weight-losing raw materials, the stronger their pull on production to their deposits. Production will move all the way to a localized raw material if its material index is equal to, or greater than, the material index of all other localized raw materials plus the weight of the product.

Labor orientation and isodapanes. Let us now introduce the labor input and assume that labor varies in efficiency throughout our region—in terms of wage cost per unit of output, not level of wages. The attraction of efficient labor locations, Weber points out, is that of a *substitute* rather than an *alternative*. The question which is posed by differences in labor efficiency is therefore whether the industry will locate at the minimum-transport-cost location or move completely to the efficient labor location.

In developing this analysis, Weber introduced the concept of the *isodapane*. If a plant moves away from the point of minimum-transport costs, it must necessarily incur greater transport costs. The farther it moves away, the greater the difference will be over and above the minimum. We can locate all points which exceed the minimum-transport cost by an equal amount and join them by a curve or line. This line is termed an *isodapane. It is a line of equal total transportation costs above the minimum-transport cost.*

For labor to pull the plant away from the minimum-transport-cost location, the savings in labor cost must exceed (or at least equal) the additional costs above the minimum-transport cost. As we get farther away from the minimum, there will be an isodapane beyond which the increased transport costs cannot be offset by labor economies. This is Weber's *critical isodapane*. Within this isodapane, savings in labor costs offset the increased transportation costs; outside it they do not. Hence, within the critical isodapane firms will be labor-oriented; outside it they will be transport-cost-oriented.

Weberian agglomeration analysis. So far we have followed the Weberian method of determining the minimum-transportation-cost location, and we have gone through the procedures of deriving, in the case of the individual plant, the relevant isotims and isodapanes. In the case of secondary, or manufacturing, activities, however, seldom are locations determined by a firm in isolation. Decisions regarding the location of an individual firm usually involve consideration of the

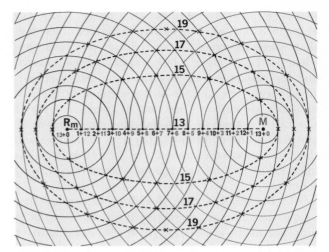

Fig. 12.23 Isodapanes of 15, 17, and 19 are constructed, showing that along those lines, cost of production exceeds the minimum cost of 13 by 2, 4, and 6 units, respectively. If 15 is a critical isodapane, then savings of labor costs within it will offset increased transport costs by up to 2 units inside the critical isodapane.

location of other firms. Considerations in such decisions include (1) labor economies, (2) the development of subsidiary industries and services, and (3) the development of infrastructure. In the case of the third economy of relative location we may distinguish between physical infrastructure such as roads, harbors, railway sidings, etc., and nonphysical infrastructure. The relevant types of nonphysical infrastructure include such items as the provision of insurance coverage, fire department services, police services, etc. Weber used the term *economies of agglomeration* to cover what we refer to as *external economies of scale*. These economies of agglomeration or concentration of industrial firms at a particular point provide advantages for firms to concentrate or locate together. The following analysis is designed to demonstrate an important principle: If several firms have minimum-transportation-cost locations at *different* points in the regional economy, then in order for them to locate at a single point of concentration, the economies achieved from agglomeration by each firm must be equal to or exceed the excess costs which they would incur over and above their minimum-transportation-cost location in each case.

We have outlined the rationale for developing isotims in the simple case, i.e., lines of equal transportation

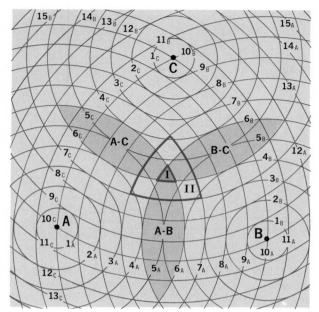

Fig. 12.24 For cost saving advantages from agglomeration equal to an increase of 6 units above their minimum costs, firms A, B, and C would be willing to locate in agglomeration triangle I, and for savings equal to 7 units in agglomeration, triangle II. If only two firms were to agglomerate, achieving a savings of 6 units, they would locate in an agglomeration eye shown by areas A–B, B–C, and A–C.

cost. We have also similarly constructed isodapanes, i.e., lines of equal total cost, assuming in this case that all costs other than transportation costs are constant throughout our region. Let us assume that we have three firms—A, B, and C—whose minimum-transportation-cost locations are as given as in Figure 12.26. Let us further assume that the isodapanes consist of concentric bands about each point that increase as each firm moves away from its minimum-transportation-cost location. Notice that the isodapanes in each case are equally spaced, indicating that the costs of production increase somewhat as each firm moves away from its minimum-cost location. Notice also that we are left with a triangular figure which is bounded by the sixth isodapane of every firm. We call this triangle the *agglomeration triangle,* and we logically deduce that, for the three firms to locate within that triangle rather than at their individual minimum-cost locations, the advantages of agglomeration must be greater than, or

at least equal to, six units of increased total transportation cost.

This is, of course, a very simple but nonetheless rigorous analysis. In order to show that our reasoning can provide solutions to more complex situations, let us complicate the analysis in two ways. First, we shall show the location and value of the agglomeration triangle in a case where the isodapanes are not equally spaced (Figure 12.26). Second, we shall introduce different-sized firms to show the effect of the stronger bargaining power of the large company when it agglomerates with smaller plants (Figure 12.25).

Fig. 12.25 If firms A, B, and C could achieve savings from agglomeration equal to 5 units above minimum costs, they would be willing to agglomerate in triangle I. If such savings were equal to 7 units, they would be willing to agglomerate in triangle II. If firm A were larger, with stronger bargaining power, it could pull both A and C into that section of triangle II closer to it, i.e., 3 and 4. If B were stronger than C, it could shift the agglomeration area to 4, where it increases its costs only to 6 units, whereas C increases by 7 and A (the strongest) still only 3 units.

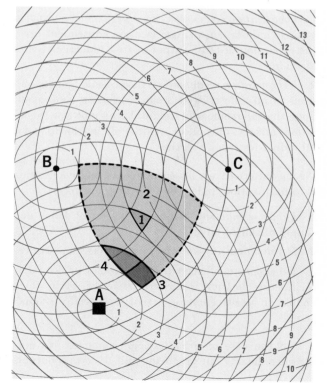

Economies of Relative Location

The Nature of Locational Economies

In this section we shall define the economic advantages which result when a plant or site has a *favorable relative location* with respect to other economic entities or activities. These are referred to as *internal economies of scale* by economists and as *scale-of-site economies* by geographers. The economies we are concerned with now have nothing to do with the size or scale of a particular operation; rather, they involve its relative location or its external relationships with other entities. Such economies have been referred to as *external economies of scale, economies of concentration, economies of spatial juxtaposition, economies of agglomeration,* and *economies of linkage.* As we can see, an amazing array of terms are applied to the advantages of relative location.

Isard, following Ohlin and Hoover, developed a twofold classification of economies resulting from the relative location of firms:

1 *Localization economies:* those realizable by firms in a single industry at a single location consequent upon the expansion of total output of that industry at that location

2 *Urbanization economies:* those realizable by all firms in all industries at a single location consequent upon the enlargement of the total economic size (population, income, output, or wealth) of that location for all industries taken together

We may alternatively list economies of relative location or concentration under the following headings:

1 *Labor economies:* localized division of labor and supply of skilled labor

2 *Development of subsidiary industries and services*

3 *Development of infrastructure:* social or economic facilities (education, highways, railways, etc.) which enable or assist economic activity, especially production

In the case of urbanization economies, we may consider the city our producing unit of certain outputs

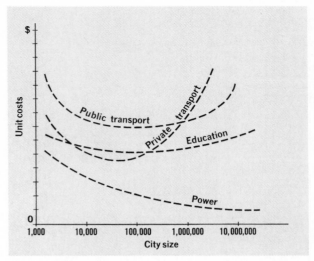

Fig. 12.26 Urban costs tend to fall with increasing city size and then rise. Note that the cost of certain urban services begins to rise at different levels of urban size.

of goods and services and relate the unit cost of those outputs with increasing scale of city size. A hypothetical set of cost-size relationships is given in Figure 12.26.

Interindustry Flow Matrix

Input-Output Tables

It is clear how difficult it is to deal with interdependence in a quantitative and rigorous way. Economists have not yet succeeded in measuring externalities successfully. However, one method generated to study industrial complex analysis involves the use of an input-output model which enables the researcher to follow the backward and forward linkages between industries or sectors within a given region.

While we have included this type of work in the theoretical section of the text, it is essentially no more than an empirical accounting system. In fact, its limitations are largely the result of the absence of theory associated with input-output or interindustry flow analysis. However, since it shows flows from sector to sector in a given economy, it provides an excellent means of assessing recent or current conditions, and even for comparing different economies as to internal sectoral flows. The technique was originated by Professor Leontief at Harvard University in the 1930s[10], but is it only in recent years that interest in it and extensions of its use have materialized. This has in no small measure resulted from the development of the digital computer, since massive quantities of data have to be processed by simple arithmetic and mathematical procedures.

The input-output table is so called because it constitutes a statement, in table form, of what inputs from

INPUT–OUTPUT TABLE

OUTPUTS	INPUTS			FINAL DEMAND	TOTAL OUTPUT
	PRIMARY	SECONDARY	TERTIARY		
PRIMARY	10 .20	15 .15	5 .05	20	50
SECONDARY	10 .20	25 .25	15 .15	50	100
TERTIARY	5 .10	15 .15	20 .20	60	100
VALUE ADDED	25 .50	45 .45	60 .60	= 130	

Sector flows are shown in this Interindustry Flow Table or Input–Output Table, in which the economy has been broken down into a simple three-sector system. Figures in color are in arbitrary value units, for example, billions of dollars. Across each row the figures show where the outputs of a sector go, that is, to its own and to other sectors (called *intermediate outputs*), plus its deliveries of *final products*. These add up to the sector's total output, given in the last column.

The inputs to each sector from other sectors are shown down each column. These inputs, together with the sector's *value added* (largely the cost of its labor inputs, wages, and profits), must be equal to the value of the sector's total output. The total final demand (130 value units) gives the *gross national product* of the system, which equals the total of *value-added* contribution of all sectors.

Input–output coefficients (small figures in corner boxes) show the value of inputs required from each source per dollar's worth of output. These are obtained by calculating the ratio of the value of inputs from any sector to the total output of a given sector. For example, the Primary Sector produces 50 units of value by obtaining 10 value units from itself and 10 from the secondary sector, giving an input–output coefficient of ·20, and 5 value units from the Tertiary Sector giving a coefficient of ·10. Finally, the sector's value added (labor input) is 25 value units, giving a coefficient of ·5. The input–output coefficients must, of course, equal one (1) for each sector.

any industry or sector in the table are required by an industry to produce a unit of output. Tables can be constructed at any level of aggregation or detail. The degree of detail in the table, or model, as it is often called, is limited by three things, namely, (1) the use to which the table is put, (2) the available data, and (3) the costs of computation. With very large, detailed models (over seventy or eighty sectors) costs (2) and (3) increase rapidly.

For the purpose of exposition we could construct a very aggregated or simple model of the economy containing only three sectors: primary, secondary, and tertiary. This table would tell us two things about each sector, namely, (1) where each sector obtained its inputs, for example, what inputs the primary sector required from the secondary and tertiary sectors, and (2) where the outputs of each sector go. For example, how much of the output of the primary sector went as inputs to the secondary and tertiary sectors? In the table the first of these bits of information (inputs from) is found by reading the values down the column under the heading "primary sector." The second set of information (outputs to) is obtained by reading across the row marked "primary sector." Thus, the table would specify in quantitative form all the relationships between our sectors.

However, so far the table has specified only the *intermediate demand* for inputs, since our primary industry would also send some of its outputs to consumers for their final use. Therefore, we need to add a further column on the extreme right of the table "final demand." In the terminology of input-output analysis, this column is called "final demand."

One further addition is required. We have in our table inputs to the primary sector from the secondary sector (e.g., machinery and appliances) and from the tertiary sector (e.g., finance and insurance). However, the primary sector requires labor inputs also. These are provided by households, and therefore, we will need an additional row marked "value added" to tell us the labor inputs to each of the three producing sectors.

This simple table would tell us many things. For example, if we have an increase in final demand, we can obtain increases in employment and increased expansion of other sectors. That is, we can trace impacts of demand in one sector through all other sectors. While in our example this may not seem significant, in a very detailed model the information on the nature of impacts is highly impressive. One difficulty in the input-output table concerns the entries of coefficients specifying the proportion of inputs from each sector for one unit of output. These coefficients are assumed to be constant relationships, but as we have seen, when we have increasing returns to scale, an increasing output may not require constant quantities or proportions of inputs. Moreover, these relations change over time.

Our final remarks on input-output should review several points which specify its usefulness in a spatial sense. First, we should observe that each industry or sector in the input-output table must be physically located in or distributed throughout space; hence, we can obtain important information from the table if it is coupled with a detailed distribution of the sectors. As linkages emerge between industries involving physical movement of goods we can obtain information on flows. Economists are attempting to link flows directly in the table by using gravity model formulations. Not only are input-output tables useful at very detailed levels of analysis of distributions, but multinational models give national impacts of changes in international imports and exports and interregional models give interregional flows. The interregional models have proved significant in the development of regional development planning.

Chapter 13

The Theoretical
Approach Reviewed

The three preceding chapters have been devoted to the theoretical approach in geography because this approach is rather new and not so well understood as the institutional approach. Realizing that some courses are too short for the exhaustive study presented in those chapters, we are presenting here a review of the basic ideas. The reader is urged, however, to refer to the longer discussion, including illustrations, and also to the Glossary for more details.

The Theoretical Approach: Basic Concepts

In this chapter, we examined geographical theory, particularly the scientific method, which involves observation, classification, explanation, and prediction. (See also Chap. 8, pp. 125 to 127.) Observation may involve any of our five senses and may be gained through field work or such library effort as examination of census publications, land use maps, and other sources of infor-

mation. Classification is a breaking down of this information into categories which can be understood. Explanation, which in science must be logical, is complete when the person to whom it is given has no further questions. Where an explanation merely restates the original question in another way, it may be called a *tautology,* or *tautological explanation.* Tautology, however, is not logic. In geography, logical explanation involves *locational variables*—aspects which are different from place to place. Spatial *constants,* which do not differ from place to place, do not assist in geographical explanation.

Finally, the scientific method involves prediction: either *deterministic,* in which we state definitely what will happen, or *probabilistic,* in which we indicate what will happen within a certain degree of probability. Inasmuch as our spatial theories involve human spatial behavior, most cannot be deterministic; instead, they will indicate a probability.

In choosing our variables, we must be aware of *necessary* and *sufficient conditions,* or *necessary* and *sufficient explanatory variables.* An event will not nec-

203

essarily take place if the required conditions are fulfilled, but it certainly will not take place if these conditions are unfulfilled. On the other hand, if sufficient conditions are fulfilled, an event will take place. If, for example, we analyze all factors necessary for the existence of retail stores and find that they are fulfilled in every case, we can say that all the required conditions for retail location exist. However, if we note that, despite these necessary conditions, there are no retail outlets, we lack the sufficient conditions—possibly the decision of a would-be manager to place his store there. But if such a store is at that location, the sufficient conditions have been fulfilled.

This careful logic helps us to understand not only why things are located where they are but also why things are not located where they are not.

Theory, which is part of science, involves (1) a hypothesis, (2) a set of assumptions, or premises, and (3) the resulting postulates. A *hypothesis* is an educated guess as to the things we need to produce an explanation and the relationship that might exist within that explanation. Assumptions are logical statements by which hypotheses may be removed from the myriad conflicting conditions in the real world, so that the subject of the explanation can be viewed more carefully. *Postulates,* which are the final outputs of theory, are the results we obtain from having made our assumptions and from having applied strict, logical reasoning to them. It is important always to apply to scientific inquiry a principle which in essence says that *the assumptions upon which we base our theories* must always be the weakest in form and the fewest in number necessary to explain fully the observed phenomena.

Logical reasoning is deductive reasoning (see pp. 153–154). It produces deductive results or deductive postulates, which can later be checked with events in the real world. All scientific investigation begins, to some extent at least, with a form of deductive hypothesis.

To understand theory, *models* frequently are employed. A model may take the form of words, a mathematical notation, a diagram or graph, or even a physical, tangible shape (Fig. 10.1). A model always constitutes a formal statement of a theory. Some very comprehensive models may involve many variables, but the great majority are statements of relationships between just two variables.

Since they are formal statements of theories developed by scientific investigation, and since scientific inquiry involves a series of successive approximations to reality, models do have some relationship to actual conditions. However, we should not reject the immediate usefulness of a model merely because it does not explain current reality. Very probably, a model or theory may not prove useful for a long period of time. Indeed, our models do not have to relate to the real world at all. Yet they must be logical—contain logical postulates which are drawn from logical assumptions.

Basic Concepts in Theoretical Economic Geography

Any geography student knows that the subject is concerned with space. However, a scientific study of geography need not be limited to the earth's actual surface but may well involve *isotropic space* and *anisotropic space*. Isotropic space is two-dimensional only. If we wish to complicate our two-dimensional surface by placing some things on it—but not necessarily all the earth's features—then we have anisotropic space. The isotropic surface is the scientific geographer's laboratory; he can increase its two dimensions by whatever factors are necessary to meet the assumptions and postulates of any theory.

Distance in geography, certainly in economic geography, may be considered in terms of operational space—in either a cost or a time dimension—and hence thought of as either *cost space* or *time space*. In the first instance, we refer to the cost of transporting a person or a thing a given distance, and in the second we refer to the time necessary for such transportation. Yet another dimension is an individual's *action space*—the area throughout which an individual functions, usually on a daily routine of going to work or school and returning home. Cost space, time space, and action space do not necessarily correspond with actual distance on the surface of the earth but vary with freight rates, fares, travel time, etc. This is an extremely important concept, one which differs from the usual idea that geography is concerned only with actual distances and conditions. Particularly in economic geography, we are much more concerned with cost space, time space, and operational space than with actual miles (Figs. 10.2 to 10.13).

Still other concepts in scientific geography (also in institutional geography; see Chap. 8, pp. 127 to 128) are *site* and *situation.* Site refers to the features in a place occupied by a particular thing of geographical interest, such as an area near a river which may have a wet and foggy site, or within a city which may have high population, varied religions, various prices of goods, city taxes, etc (see also vertical linkages; glossary). A situation refers to the spatial relationships which a particular place has with other places—the nearness to a city or to a factory, etc. Situation is relative location (also considered in terms of horizontal linkages; glossary), identified by the relationships a place has with other points on the earth's surface. These external relationships are very important and constantly changing, and affect sharply cost space, time space and action space, as mentioned above.

Space in scientific geography may be viewed as involving a *system*—an observably organized, working ensemble. Any action by one component of the system will bring about a response or reaction from another. For example, in a telephone system, receivers are linked to other telephone receivers and signals are transmitted. Urban systems also exist, in which various points within a city or connecting cities are linked by highway, railway, and other transportation and communication networks. An open system, such as an entire telephone communication network, is one in which the relationships between the components can be altered or influenced by other components. A closed system, such as an intercom within a building that is not linked to the outside, or a city subway, cannot be affected by external components. A space system is an interlocking mechanism or relationship involving both site characteristics and situation characteristics. Stated differently, it is an assemblage of units united by some form of regular interaction or interdependence.

Scale is an important concept in geography in that it involves levels of spatial generalizations (see also the Introduction, p. 14). What is important in a household may or may not be important in a community; what is important in a community may or may not be important in a region; what is important in a region may or may not be important in a nation; what is important in a nation may or may not be important in international affairs. As the universe of phenomena expands, classifications are at higher levels of generalization.

Spatial Order and Linkages, the Principle of Comparative Advantage, and Distance-Decay Functions

Spatial Order and Linkages

The theoretical geographer believes in the existence of a *spatial order,* or rational patterns of activity, which the geographer perceives in the economic environment he is seeking to understand. This spatial order differs from area to area mainly because of differences in *factors of production*—(1) natural resources (or land), (2) labor, and (3) capital (money and farms, factories, machinery, etc., which can produce wealth). The differences may also include (4) government policies, management abilities, and other qualities of *entrepreneurship,* and (5) *varying distances to materials and markets.* A region's endowment of these five considerations may place it in an advantageous or disadvantageous position with respect to other regions of the world.

These differences are offset somewhat by movement of people and goods between and among the world's specialized areas. Such movement, as we have seen in Chapter 7 (especially Fig. 7.1, p. 104), is referred to as linkages. We shall have much more to say about these linkages in Part 3.

The Principle of Comparative Advantage

Because regions differ in endowment of the three factors of production, plus entrepreneurship and distance to materials and markets, each has certain advantages over the others in production. Therefore, it logically would produce those goods or services in which it has an *absolute advantage* over another region—it can produce something more efficiently than another region.

However, some regions have a wide range of physical and human resources, and others are very poor. This is especially true today in the world of developed and developing economies (Fig. 3.4). If a developed region has an absolute advantage in all lines of production while a developing region has an absolute disadvantage in everything, does it follow that the developed region will produce everything and the poor region nothing? No; the answer is that *each region does the best it possibly can.* That line of production in a region associated with the *greatest absolute advantage* over other regions is called its *comparative advantage.* Similarly, that line of production in a region with all disadvantages which represents its *least absolute disadvantage* is called its *comparative advantage.* From these realities comes the doctrine of comparative advantage, which states that *a region will tend to specialize in producing those goods in which it has a comparative advantage, that is, those goods in which its absolute advantage is greatest or its absolute disadvantage is least* (Figs. 11.1 to 11.3).

This very important principle can be applied to the geography of economic activity. In various ways and levels of observation or scale, we shall apply it later in this chapter to models which help us to understand both agricultural and urban land use. It is important to state here that the comparative advantage may involve either *site* or *situation.* Site advantages, which earlier in this book we have called vertical relationships, refer to internal characteristics—location of a city power plant on a riverfront site, of a farm in a certain climate and associated soil, or of a port in a harbor. The situation, or relative location advantages, involve geographical position with respect to external (horizontal) relationships: our power plant may be downstream near the main consuming centers, or our farm may be nearer a major market, and our port and harbor may be located on the heavily traveled North Atlantic trade route connecting the United States and Canada with Europe. The comparative advantage of a place may refer to either site or situation.

Distance-Decay Function

Geographical features are not distributed evenly over the surface of the earth. For some features, this unevenness may be explained by the *distance-decay curve* or function, which specifies the relationship of variables to distance. In other words, the values of a variable may tend to decrease as distance increases. For example, density of population is very high within a metropolitan area but decreases with increased distance from that area. For those features which are subject to distance-decay, the reasons may be economic or noneconomic. In any case, distance-decay is seldom expressed as a continuously decreasing curve; that is, it seldom results in a gradual and continuous decline in population density with increased distance from metropolitan areas. Instead, the decay function may vary in specific instances—the variations with distance may be erratic—but it will still be discernible (Figs. 11.4 to 11.8). Anything which impedes a variable from an even distribution through space is called an *impedance factor.*

The reasons for distance-decay, and for impedance, may be economic or noneconomic. In either category, an *intervening opportunity* may be a plausible explanation for an impeded distance-decay. If, by way of illustration, a person is traveling a given set of distances, the possibility that an intervening opportunity will occur before he completes any one of those distances increases as the distances increase. For example, if we decide to travel up to 5 miles in order to purchase a shirt, there will be some probability that we can get an equally satisfactory shirt closer than 5 miles. If we travel up to 10 miles to purchase a shirt, our chances of finding one closer than 10 miles would be even greater, and so on, with further increments in distance.

Distance-decay is often examined in geography through the use of the *gravity model,* which is particularly effective when applied to urban conditions (Figs. 11.9 and 11.10). The gravity model tells us that if a small city and a large city are located an equal distance from the place in which we live, we should travel more often to the large city than to the small one. Stated more scientifically, the gravity model tells us that the number of trips from a given center to each of a set of other centers will tend to be proportional to the product of their size and that of the originating center, and inversely proportional to the distance separating each from the originating center.

The *intervening-opportunities model,* first introduced in sociology to explain migration in the United States, indicates that people moving a given distance are responding not necessarily to the size of the population in a given place but rather to the opportunities (Fig. 11.11). This hypothesis can be stated as follows:

the number of persons going a given distance is directly proportional to the number of opportunities at that distance and inversely proportional to the number of intervening opportunities.

Elementary Geography Models of Spatial Structure

Spatial Structure and Rent

Spatial structure. So far we have discussed elements of theory, ideas of measurement and space, and some of the basic concepts which constitute or underlie the geographical theory of economic regions. We shall now attempt to understand some of the simple models of the *spatial structure of economic activities.* By spatial structure we mean the pattern or set of spatial relationships which are maintained by different functional components of the space economy—in other words, their layout or plan. These components have relative locations and also occupy site in space, and can be observed in a map of land use types.

Rent. An important insight into both the relative position and site aspects of economic activity can be gained through an examination of the concept of *rent.* We shall consider here *contract rent, economic rent,* and *geographic rent.*

Contract rent. Contract rent is the payment we make for the right to use something belonging to another person. It is a periodic payment for the use of a durable item belonging to someone else—a room, an apartment, an automobile, a farm, etc. We define it here so that it will not be confused with other types of rent.

Economic rent. *Economic rent* is best defined as the surplus yield of a piece of land over the next best piece of land (Figs. 12.1 and 12.2). As presented by the distinguished economist David Ricardo, that surplus is obtained from the inherent fertility of better land over poorer—a fertility or productivity which, as we have noted, involves site characteristics (or, as noted in the Introduction, vertical relationships).

Geographic rent. Whereas the concept of economic rent results from differences in returns of land that are due to causes other than location, *geographic rent* is due to relative location—to the advantage or disadvantage of distance of a given location over that same location for another purpose, or of another location over a given location for a specified purpose.

In presenting the theories to follow, we shall be making use particularly of economic and geographic rent, and the definitions of each should prove useful to the reader.

The von Thünen model. J. H. von Thünen, who operated an estate in northern Germany in the early part of the nineteenth century, noted that distance from certain key places, especially markets, affected the type of use to which land was put. He formulated a theory in which a given state or country was (1) isolated, with neither foreign trade nor incoming or outgoing migration; (2) composed solely of a large town surrounded by rural area; (3) on a plain which was an isotropic surface—an undifferentiated land area over which everything was held constant; and (4) characterized by marked internal relationships: the town depended upon the plain for its supply of produce and, in turn, supplied the residents of the plain with their wants and needs. In fact, the only variable in von Thünen's model was distance from the central city (Fig. 12.3; see especially explanatory caption).

According to the theory, different crops, and crop and animal combinations, would be grown in concentric circles at increasing distances from the central city— intensively cultivated, high-yield (or highly perishable) items near the city and more extensive agriculture, involving more land per unit of labor or capital, with increased distance from the city. Indeed, the outermost ring involved a very extensive type of stock raising, with emphasis upon wool, butter, cheese, etc. Beyond was uncultivated land that was capable of cultivation if the market price in the city rose sufficiently high above the costs of producing agricultural products and transporting them to market.

The important point about the theory is that it yielded an insight into relative location and transportation cost—an insight into geographic rent, which we have already defined as a surplus return accruing to one piece of land over another piece of land because of its more favorable location (Fig. 12.4). Although von Thünen applied the concept only to agricultural land use, which prevailed in his day, it can also be applied to different uses of land in an urban area. Indeed, we can say that most of the rent in urban regions is geographic rent—that is, is due to its better location of the land in question rather than to inherent fertility or productivity of the site (Figs. 12.5 to 12.12).

The Christallerian model. In this increasingly metropolitan and urban world, the relationship between and among urban places is especially important. In 1933, Walter Christaller wrote a book, *Central Places in South Germany,* in which he founded a theoretical framework for the size and spacing of urban places. He assumed (1) an isotropic surface, (2) an even distribution of rural population, (3) a triangular distribution of population centers, (4) a marketing range for each function, (5) a population threshold for a given function, and (6) constant spatial behavioral parameters of the population. Like von Thünen, Christaller hypothesized as to the impact of distance (transport costs) on the movement of different products—in this case, products obtainable at different central places. Based upon his six assumptions, he postulated: (1) a size hierarchy of central places, ranging from first-order centers (the smallest) to seventh-order centers (the largest); (2) a functional hierarchy of these places, with the low-level services available in the first order and higher-level services in successively higher orders (Fig. 8.3); (3) market areas consisting of regular hexagons that aggregately covered the entire isotropic surface (Figs. 12.13 to 12.20); (4) market areas for lower-level functions that are smaller and located completely or partially within the market areas for higher-level functions, and (5) higher-order central places that are farther apart than lower-order central places.

The hierarchal order, size, and spacing of the centers were determined by their distance (expressed in time and/or cost). Higher-order centers, their range of functions increasing with size, would be farther apart than centers of smaller size, the maximum distance apart being determined by the maximum range of a given service or product.

Although urban networks in the real world do not form perfectly hexagonal patterns, it is true that cities are not all the same size and that larger cities are spaced farther apart than smaller ones. It is also true that a wider range of functions, including those highly specialized functions which people do not need frequently, are found only in the larger places, which are farther apart. Therefore, market areas and the range of a good or service have an impact upon the spacing of centers, and they are also related to *population thresholds,* or the minimum number of people necessary to support a given type of activity. In practice, central-place theory is used today both in understanding and in planning our increasingly urban world.

The Weberian model. Whereas von Thünen and Christaller were concerned with land use in a regional perspective, Alfred Weber, in his *The Theory of Industrial Location* (1909), was interested in the location of an individual manufacturing plant. Weber assumed (1) given locations of raw materials; (2) fixed locations and sizes of individual places of consumption; (3) transportation costs, which he divided into *assembly costs* incurred in transporting raw materials to the point of production and *marketing costs* incurred in transporting the commodity to market; (4) a given dispersal of labor whose supply was not limited and whose costs varied from place to place; and (5) an inelastic demand (a demand which would not change with price) for products. Weber sought to discover the forces that ultimately would be responsible for location of a manufacturing plant. To do this, he first sought a regional location on the basis of transport costs, then adjusted that location for differences in labor costs, and finally added considerations of agglomeration (Fig. 12.24).

Weber divided raw materials into those which are *ubiquitous* (available everywhere) and *localized* (available only in certain places). Furthermore, raw materials which entered into the finished product without any weight loss he considered to be *pure,* and those which lost weight were *gross.* Transportation costs (assembly and marketing costs) were assumed to be a constant function of distance in these simpler early models, although Weber was sensitive to freight rate differences (Fig. 12.21). Assembly costs for ubiquitous raw materials would be zero, because such materials occurred everywhere. On the other hand, assembly costs for localized materials would be important only if production were not located at their site of occurrence. Marketing costs would be zero if the plant were located at the market, but perhaps important if it were near a localized raw material. The closer the plant is to raw materials, the smaller are the assembly costs and the greater the market costs; the closer it is to market, the greater the assembly costs and the smaller the marketing costs. If a plant is located at neither the raw material nor the market, it incurs some assembly and some marketing costs. It is now possible to draw concentric circles around each raw material or market (Fig. 12.21). These concentric circles, lines of equal transport costs, are *isotims.* Weber then introduced the *material index,* which specified the relation between the weight of the localized raw materials and the weight of the finished product. Next, he introduced the distance such weight must be moved, and he called this *locational weight.* Applying locational weights to a hypothetical situation, Weber arrived at a minimum-transport-cost location (Figs. 12.21 and 12.22).

If a plant is located at a site other than that of minimum transport costs, it is possible, through the use of *isodapanes,* lines of equal transportation costs above the minimum (Fig. 12.23), to calculate what that amount will be and where such sites will be located on the isotropic surface.

One attraction away from the minimum-transport-cost location might be labor, which Weber assumed to differ from place to place. In order to pull the plant away from a minimum-transport-cost location, the savings in labor must exceed (or at least equal) the additional transport costs incurred. Beyond a certain line, which Weber termed the *critical isodapane,* savings in labor cost offset the increased transportation costs; outside it, they do not. Hence, within the critical isodapane, firms will be labor-oriented; outside it, they will be transport-cost-oriented.

Agglomeration economies may also be important in the selection of a location for a plant. These result from decisions or influences from the person deciding the plant location. They may involve such considerations as (1) labor economies, (2) the development of subsidiary industries and services, or (3) infrastructure. Thus, a number of firms may make use of a common labor pool for certain purposes; or they may be interdependent as to product, with the finished material of one serving as an input to another; or they may share infrastructure (highways, railway or port facilities, water supply lines, fire service, insurance, etc.). To make use of agglomerative economies, advantages should exceed liabilities of transport cost (Figs. 12.24 and 12.25).

Later work. The theories of von Thünen, Christaller, and Weber, although formulated in the nineteenth and early twentieth centuries, are still important to today's conditions. Particularly in the past quarter-century, several modifications and refinements have been added, but these have not changed materially the underlying assumptions and resulting postulates of the theories themselves. Professors Hoover, Ohlin, and Isard have made especially important contributions. Isard, following Ohlin and Hoover, developed a twofold classification of economies resulting from the relative location of firms:

1 *Localization economies:* those realizable by firms in a single industry at a single location as a result of the expansion of total output of that industry at that location.

2 *Urbanization economies:* those realizable by all firms in all industries at a single location as a result of the enlargement of the total economic size (population, income, output, or wealth) of that location for all industries taken together.

Interindustry flow matrix: input-output tables. Linkages not only connect areas; they also connect activities or groups of activities. In the early 1930s, Professor W. Leontief derived an interindustry flow matrix which shows flows from sector to sector in a given economy, and can be applied at differing intensities or levels of agriculture (p. 201). It can show linkages from sector to sector in all or selected primary, secondary, or tertiary activities, in different degrees of detail. Although not a theory, it provides an excellent means for assessing recent and current conditions, and even for comparing different economies as to internal sectoral components and flows. This matrix has in no small measure resulted from the digital computer.

PART 3
Sectoral and Spatial Aspects of Primary, Secondary, and Tertiary Activity

Part 3 is, in effect, a series of case studies of primary, secondary, and tertiary activity. We shall give detailed attention to conditions in the United States, appraise conditions in Canada, and briefly review other selected key producing and consuming countries. The purpose of these case studies is to provide actual examples against which to test many of the ideas presented in Part 2.

Approach and Method

Approach

In an examination of the chapter titles of Part 3, the reader will note that the commodities selected do not cover the entire range of all commodities produced. The purpose of selection is to provide insight into specific kinds of primary, secondary, and tertiary activity. Accordingly, in Chapters 14 to 18, we shall be treating commodities which pass through all stages of activity from primary to secondary to tertiary. All or part of the products in question in these chapters originate in a different primary activity. Wheat products (Chap. 14) originate in agriculture; meat products (Chap. 15) originate in grazing and agriculture; fish products (Chap. 16) originate in commercial fishing; forest products (Chap. 17) originate in commercial forestry, and iron and steel (Chap. 18) originate in mining. In Chapter 19, we shall look at the motor vehicle industry, which receives its incoming materials chiefly from other manufacturing rather than from primary activity and processes them through several stages before selling vehicles to the consumer. (These stages include making repair parts for use once the vehicle has been sold and driven and is in need of repair.) In Chapter 20, we shall examine the petroleum industry as a source of both fuel and raw materials. In Chapter 21, we shall shift the emphasis to urbanization, since so many of our activities take place in urban environments—and more will be located there in the future.

Method

In keeping with our discussion in Part 2, we shall first employ the methods of description, measurement, and classification that are common to the institutional and theoretical approaches. We shall look at primary, secondary, and tertiary stages of selected economic activity and at linkages connecting these stages. Furthermore, each examination will not be restricted to the traditional geographic, or spatial, viewpoint, but will include a cross reference of sector and space. We shall rely heavily upon cartography, as may be noted in Figures 14.1 to 14.7. The reader will note that the upper half of each figure contains sectoral conditions, and the lower half contains spatial conditions. The progression from primary to secondary to tertiary stages may be grasped by turning the pages. In succeeding chapters, different primary and secondary activities will be treated. However, because tertiary activity consists to a large extent of wholesale and retail trade that is very closely associated with the distribution of population and with wholesale and retail outlets, the same spatial conditions are reproduced in the tertiary stage for all the commodities, although the sectoral description varies with each chapter.

Also in keeping with the methodology explained in Part 2, an institutional and a theoretical explanation is offered for each pattern of primary, secondary, and tertiary activity, and for subdivisions of each of these where they are relevant.

Description, Measurement, and Classification of Information

In describing, measuring, and classifying the economic activity responsible for the selected commodities, we shall be making intensive use of available source materials, including published descriptions, long-standing classifications, and the census materials that are periodically renewed. The census data will play a key role in our discussion because they provide an element of measurement that is otherwise unobtainable. Consequently, we shall be relying upon the United States Census of Agriculture, Census of Manufacturing, Census of Transportation, Census of Wholesale Trade, and Census of Retail Trade. Data abstracted from these various sources are presented in the sectoral portions of the key illustrations (see, for example, Figures 14.1 to 14.3).

Measurement criteria and terminology. In assessing the importance of the three stages of activity and of the subdivisions within each, we shall use a number of criteria. Perhaps the most universally accepted one is *employment,* which indicates the actual number of personnel at work, whether self-employed or hired, in a given activity. This criterion is widely used because it can be applied with reasonable validity to primary, secondary, and tertiary stages and to subdivisions within each. A second criterion which is also important is *value of shipment.* Its significance lies in the fact that not only can it be used to assess each of the activities, but it also suggests the increase in value as commodities move from primary to secondary to tertiary stages. The value of shipment is, as the term implies, the monetary worth of a given commodity at the completion of a stage of activity.

In manufacturing, a number of additional criteria are in general use and will also be employed in this book. These are the *costs of labor,* the *costs of incoming materials,* and the *value added* in the manufacturing process. The meanings of the first two terms are obvious. Value added is calculated by subtracting from the final shipment value the costs of raw materials (usually the main item) and also the costs of energy, agents of manufacture, subcontract work, and lesser items. The term can be applied to a given producing unit or to a variety of producing units.

Other official terms relate to the producing units themselves. The word *establishment* is used to refer to a given producing unit, whether a farm in agriculture, a manufacturing plant, or a retail or wholesale store. The term *function* is used to refer to the nature of economic activity performed by the establishment. The word *industry* refers to a collection of establishments engaged in a generally similar function. The word *firm* refers to administrative organization, whether managed by an individual, a company board, or a public or private corporative arrangement. A firm may have jurisdiction over one or more establishments in one or more industries.

Census code. It is important to understand that original census information is not disseminated haphazardly by the United States government, but is presented in a format that has been set down by the U.S. Office of Management and Budget.[1]

Especially in the sections on manufacturing, we shall be making intensive use of appropriate census materials, and hence it is important to understand the official classification. The term *digit detail* is used in this classification, with the fewer digits indicating the coarse, more general categories, and additional digits denoting subdivisions. For example, all manufacturing is classified into the following two-digit-detail categories:

[1] U.S. Office of Management and Budget, *Standard Industrial Classification Manual,* 1972.

20 Food and kindred products

21 Tobacco manufactures

22 Textile-mill products

23 Apparel and other finished products made from fabrics and similar materials

24 Lumber and wood products except furniture

25 Furniture and fixtures

26 Paper and allied products

27 Printing, publishing, and allied industries

28 Chemicals and allied products

29 Petroleum refining and related industries

30 Rubber and miscellaneous plastics products

31 Leather and leather products

32 Stone, clay, glass, and concrete products

33 Primary metal industries

34 Fabricated metal products, except ordnance, machinery, and transportation equipment

35 Machinery, except electrical

36 Electrical machinery, equipment, and supplies

37 Transportation equipment

38 Professional, scientific, and controlling instruments; photographic and optical goods; watches and clocks

39 Miscellaneous manufacturing industries

19 Ordnance and accessories

Subdivisions within each two-digit detail include a further classification, which is shown below for the two-digit detail officially listed as "20":

201 Meat products

202 Dairy products

203 Canned and preserved fruits, vegetables, and seafoods

204 Grain-mill products

205 Bakery products

206 Sugar

207 Confectionery and related products

208 Beverages

209 Miscellaneous food preparation and kindred products

A still further refinement, the four-digit detail, involves specific industries. Within the "201" category, these are classified as follows:

2011   Meat-packing plants

2013   Sausages and other prepared meat products

2015   Poultry and small-game dressing and packing

Still a further refinement, the five-digit detail, indicates subdivisions within industries. These will not be used in this book.

Because our interest is in explaining the distribution of industries (four-digit detail) rather than industry groups (two- and three-digit detail) or subdivisions (five-digit detail), the classifications we shall be citing in the chapters to follow are almost invariably the four-digit detail.

National averages and norms. Also in later chapters we shall be referring from time to time to the labor force of the United States engaged in primary, secondary, or tertiary activity. (See Figure 1.3.)

In addition, especially in manufacturing, we shall be comparing the inportance of a given industry with that of all manufacturing with regard to labor force, value of shipments, and value added in manufacture. For the reader's information, as of 1970 (estimated), those actual figures for the United States were:

Manufacturing labor force: 19,241,000

Value of all shipments in manufacture: $630,710,000,000

Value added in manufacture: $298,276,000,000

Finally, we shall refer frequently in our manufacturing assessment to the per cent of overall value of shipments from a given industry that is accounted for by the value added in manufacture. We shall make this comparison between that industry and the overall national average. The reader will note from the data above that, for the United States as a whole, the value added by manufacture accounted for about 47 per cent of the value of shipments.

Key classifications. *Manufacturing.* An important insight into locational and horizontal relationships of manufacturing may be obtained through classification of labor and incoming materials as percentages, respectively, of value of shipments. Two leading authorities in industrial analysis have so classified the manufacturing of the United States, using data from the Census of Manufactures.[2] Their classification is as follows:

Low-labor-cost industries: labor costs represent 9 per cent or less of the value of shipments.

Medium-labor-cost industries: labor costs represent 10 to 20 per cent of the value of shipments.

High-labor-cost industries: labor costs represent over 20 per cent of the value of shipments.

Low-materials-cost industries: materials costs represent 49 per cent or less of the value of shipments.

Medium-materials-cost industries: materials costs represent 50 to 59 per cent of the value of shipments.

High-materials-cost industries: materials costs represent 60 per cent or more of the value of shipments.

As we shall see in specific cases discussed in the chapters to follow, the relative importance of labor or materials in the value of a finished product may or may not have an impact on location of a manufacturing establishment or industry, depending upon circumstances of the decision at hand.

Agriculture. Another classification, referring to the primary activity of agriculture, will be of use in succeeding chapters. This consists of a detailed map of agricultural types and regions (Fig. 5.1). The criteria upon which it is based are explained in Chapter 5.

Summary

In review, our approach in the chapters to follow will be to describe, measure, and classify both sectoral and spatial aspects of selected economic activity and then attempt to give a brief institutional and theoretical explanation of the location of each aspect. Finally, in Chapter 21, we examine in some detail the importance of urban conditions to the location and functioning of economic activity, particularly in the developed market economies.

[2] E. B. Alderfer and H. E. Michl, *Economics of American Industry*, McGraw-Hill Book Company, New York, 1957, pp. 10-11.

Chapter 14

Wheat Products

In this chapter we shall be interested in the geography of the activities responsible for wheat and its products, which originate in agriculture.

The United States

Wheat is important to all three stages of activity in the economy of the United States. It occupies a substantial portion of all harvested agricultural acreage and constitutes at least a noteworthy portion of all manufactured products. It is a significant item of wholesale and retail trade, partly because of its volume and partly because it is an important item of daily food consumption and animal feed products. Its importance in the tertiary sector lies not only in domestic consumption but also in exports.

Figures 14.1 to 14.7 indicate the primary, secondary, and tertiary stages of economic activity associated with the output and eventual retail sale of wheat and its products. The figures also show substages of secondary activity (manufacturing) and both sectoral and spatial linkages connecting the various stages and substages. Before proceeding further, the reader is encouraged to study carefully this series of diagrams and maps, as well as similar illustrations in the other chapters of Part 3, as these provide a very important insight into the subject matter of each chapter.

Primary Activity

Description, measurement, and classification. Figure 14.1 shows certain sectoral and spatial considerations of importance in wheat production as an agricultural activity in the United States.

Sectoral considerations. The major function performed in the primary sector of wheat production is the provision of raw material for the nation's grain mills. The process is simple and well known: through agricultural activity, the actual growing of wheat. The United States is a major wheat producer, responsible for approximately 15 per cent of all the world's output and ranking behind the Soviet Union and slightly ahead of China. These three nations account for essentially one-half of the world's annual wheat production. Although the size of producing unit varies, not only with degree of specialization in wheat but also with location in the United States, a substantial number of such units are large and tend to concentrate upon wheat only. The industry is capital-intensive, involving few actual producing units and very heavy capital investment. Hence the percentage of all farm operators engaged in wheat growing is very small—an estimated 6 to 7 per cent of all farms (slightly under one-half of the 13 per cent devoted to all cash grains, including wheat, corn, barley, sorghum and lesser grains). However, wheat accounts for between 16 and 18 per cent of the harvested acreage of all crops in the United States, and its annual sales value amounts to between 7 and 8 per cent of that for all the leading crops. Trends are toward even larger and fewer producing units, increasing capital investment, and declining labor. Between the early 1930s and the late 1960s, the man-hours required per acre of production were reduced from 8.8 to 2.9. Conversely, the size and capital investment of each production unit are rapidly increasing. In Kansas, the average farm size has increased from 241 acres at the turn of the century to over 600 acres in 1970; in South Dakota, from 363 to over 1,000 acres; and in Montana, from 886 to over 2,500 acres. Investment in equipment often exceeds $50,000 or even $100,000 per farm. Most farmers use their own equipment for plowing, harrowing, and planting, and they may or may not own combines for threshing. An increasing amount of harvest is taken by professionals with very modern machinery who commence summer activity in Texas during May and gradually work their way north, ending in September in Montana or even in Canada.

Spatial considerations. As shown in Figure 14.1, wheat is grown in widely different sections of the United States, but is concentrated in the western half of the country and particularly in the Great Plains. A winter wheat (planted in the fall and harvested in mid- or early summer) is produced especially in the southern portion of the Great Plains, but also at selected areas elsewhere. A spring wheat (planted in the spring and harvested in the late summer or early fall) is grown generally in the higher latitudes. Overlapping these classifications are hard and soft wheat. The hard wheat, used primarily for bread, is a specialty of the semiarid country to the west, and the soft wheat, destined chiefly for pastries and crackers, is cultivated in the more humid eastern section.

Vertical relationships. We consider here that vertical relationships are those at any given point between the commodity produced and key elements of the physical environment involved in the production. In Part 2, we have also termed these site relationships. For agriculture, considerations of climate and soil are especially significant. Some of these relationships can be considered constraints, where excesses of physical environmental conditions discourage production. Although wheat can be grown in a wide variety of physical conditions, it cannot be grown in deserts except under irrigation. The arid climatic restriction is the only serious one it encounters in the United States. However, in Canada and in tropical areas, it meets additional extremes of cold on the one hand and excessive moisture on the other, to which it cannot be easily adapted. In the United States, a second important consideration regarding climate is that the hard wheat, which yields bread flour, can be grown with success only in the less humid climates of the West.

In brief review, the major production of wheat in the United States is in the Great Plains, in association with semiarid and neighboring climatic classifications (Fig. 2.3), and in a brown steppe and neighboring soils. A smaller amount, destined particularly for the pastry market, is produced in the humid continental warm-summer climate and associated soil types there (Figs. 2.7 and 2.8).

Horizontal relationships. These are linkages, that begin in the primary stage and carry the wheat forward into the secondary stage. Strictly speaking, they begin with the emptying of threshed wheat from the combine into the waiting truck and with the transfer by that vehicle either to a granary on the farm itself or, as is more generally the case, to country and terminal elevators located at railway or centralized trucking points beyond the boundaries of the producing unit. If the wheat is carried by the farmer's own trucks, it can be considered a projection of primary activity into the secondary and tertiary stages. If, as is frequently the case, it is transferred by a common carrier, such transfer becomes more logically an aspect of the tertiary activity. We shall discuss these relationships more fully on pages 226 to 230.

Sectorial and spatial considerations: types of farming. There are four major areas of production on which the United States depends for most of its wheat supply. These are the so-called winter-wheat belt, the spring-wheat belt, the Palouse country of the states of Washington and Oregon, and the humid Northeast. The first three of these, accounting for nearly 75 per cent of the annual output, are dominated by commercial grain farming practices. The winter-wheat belt and Palouse area are relatively monocultural—i.e., utilized primarily for growing the one crop only. The spring-wheat belt is far less monocultural. Sizable amounts of barley, oats, flax, wild hay, and still other crops are raised there in competition with wheat. In all three areas, wheat which is grown without irrigation is subject to periodic drought and crop failure. Also in all three areas, some wheat is grown under irrigation and in association with other crops such as alfalfa, sugar beets, and horticultural products. The soft wheat of the eastern United States is grown on smaller holdings under mixed farming conditions, in association, and usually in rotation, with legumes (including soybeans) and pasture grasses, as well as corn, oats, barley, tobacco, cotton, and still other crops. Per-acre yields are slightly above those of the West, but the specialized uses of soft wheats and the higher unit costs of production act to restrict the output.

Explanation. The preceding section has been intended to give the reader an insight into sectoral and spatial considerations, both individually and in their interaction, with respect to the agricultural production of wheat. We have noted that this production is concentrated in particular portions of the United States, sometimes as a specialized product and sometimes as a component of a more diversified agricultural economy. Both the institutional approach and the theoretical approach should offer us some insight into the location of this economic activity. It should be borne in mind that our concern is especially with location and

that demand, supply, and transportation costs or time may affect that location.

Institutional explanation. *Cultural taste.* An extremely important consideration with respect to demand is cultural taste. The inhabitants of Europe, and their offshoots in various parts of the world including North America, have a centuries-old reliance upon products of wheat, just as their counterparts in eastern and southern Asia have a reliance upon products of rice. Cultural taste is therefore an important, and often unappreciated, aspect of the location of wheat growing in the United States. If we, as a people, generally preferred rice or some other cereal to the bread products based upon wheat, without doubt less wheat would be grown in this country.

As mentioned previously, the importance of hard wheat for bread, another aspect of cultural taste, is significant because this commodity is consumed in far larger quantities than pastries. The hard winter and hard spring wheat types have a high protein content, ranging between 10 and 16 per cent, and a gluten which is sufficiently elastic to retain gas in the final loaf of bread. Soft wheat, on the contrary, has a protein content of between 7 and 10 per cent and a weaker gluten. The protein content separating bread wheat from pastry wheat is approximately 12.5 per cent.

Supply aspects mesh effectively with those of demand. In brief, the hard wheat, which is most in demand because of its use in bread, can be grown only under semiarid conditions. Although the production of wheat has long been significant in the United States, the varieties brought to this country by the early settlers were generally soft wheat and would not have been adapted easily to commercial conditions that emerged in the nineteenth and twentieth centuries. Indeed, it was not until the introduction of Turkish hard red winter wheat into the Great Plains of North America in the 1870s, an introduction coinciding surprisingly with actual settlement of that part of the country, that the Great Plains' potential for supplying this needed commodity was fully realized.

Variations in human decisions. A second institutional explanation lies in the variation of human decisions concerning growing different agricultural commodities under different physical environmental

WHEAT PRODUCTS

Primary Activity

**Sectoral
Considerations**

1. **Function and Process**
   - A. Function: agricultural production of wheat
   - B. Process: fall or spring planting; summer or early fall harvest

2. **Significance**
   - A. Per cent of farms and ranches in all U.S. types of agriculture in cash grains (data not available for wheat only):   **13%**
   - B. Per cent of all U.S. harvested acreage in wheat: **16–19%**
   - C. Per cent of value of all U.S. harvested crops in wheat: **7–8%**

**Spatial
Considerations**

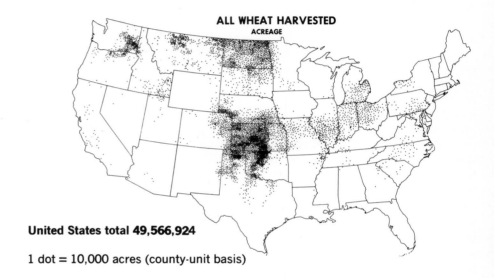

ALL WHEAT HARVESTED
ACREAGE

United States total 49,566,924

1 dot = 10,000 acres (county-unit basis)

Figure 14.1 Sector-space considerations, wheat products, primary stage. In this and all similar figures in Part 3, the sectoral aspects are at the top of the page, and the spatial aspects below. Note four areas of wheat growth: (1) the winter wheat belt of Kansas and neighboring states; (2) the spring wheat belt of North Dakota and neighboring states; (3) the Palouse country of eastern Washington and Oregon, extending into Idaho, and (4) the more humid eastern states, especially south of the Great Lakes but also farther south. The first three produce mainly hard wheat, and the last mainly soft wheat. (U.S. Bureau of the Census)

Sectoral Considerations

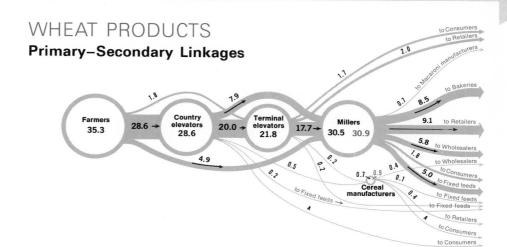

WHEAT PRODUCTS
Primary–Secondary Linkages

Spatial Considerations

Figure 14.2 Primary-secondary linkages, hard and soft wheat, domestic and export flows. Sectoral aspects are shown in volume index numbers. Grain moves from country elevators to terminal elevators, the latter frequently located at grain mills or export ports. In the spatial section, hard wheat flows are at the top and soft wheat flows at the bottom. Arrows indicate optimum patterns rather than recorded movement. Dots are at general places of origin and destination, rather than specific cities (except for export ports). (Drawings after information from the U.S. Department of Agriculture, the spatial aspects from Economic Research Service Technical Bulletin No. 1444)

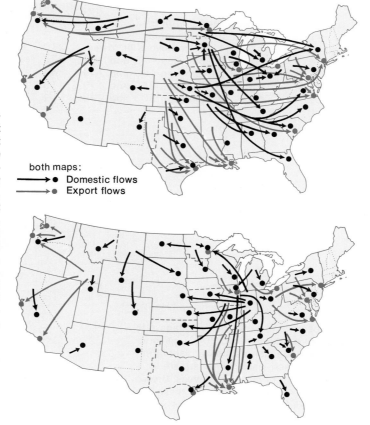

both maps:
→● Domestic flows
→● Export flows

WHEAT PRODUCTS

Secondary Activity
Substage One: Flour and Other Grain-Mill Products (SIC 2041)

1. **Function and Process**
   - **A.** Function: conversion of wheat into flour and bran; *no weight loss involved*
   - **B.** Process: grinding

2. **Significance**
   - **A.** Per cent of all U.S. manufacturing employment: 0.10%
   - **B.** Per cent of value, all U.S. manufacturing shipments: 0.44%
   - **C.** Per cent of value added in all U.S. manufacturing: 0.18%

Sectoral Considerations

3. **Major Inputs**
   - **A.** Per cent of labor costs (all employees) in final shipment value: 5.81%
   - **B.** Per cent of materials costs in final shipment value: 80.01%

4. **Number and Size of Establishments**
   - **A.** Total number: 541
   - **B.** Size categories
     - 1 4 employees or fewer: 210
     - 2 Between 5 and 99: 276
     - 3 Between 100 and 249: 44
     - 4 Between 250 and 499: 9
     - 5 Between 500 and 999: 2

Spatial Considerations

Figure 14.3 Sector-space considerations, substage one (flour and other grain-mill products—SIC 2041), secondary activity. Each brown dot is a manufacturing plant hiring 249 or fewer employees, and each black square is a similar establishment with 250 or more employees. Brown numbers show plants of 249 or fewer where these are too dense to be plotted, and black numbers show plants with 250 or more.

WHEAT PRODUCTS
Linkages: Substage One–Substage Two and Tertiary

Sectoral Considerations

Spatial Considerations

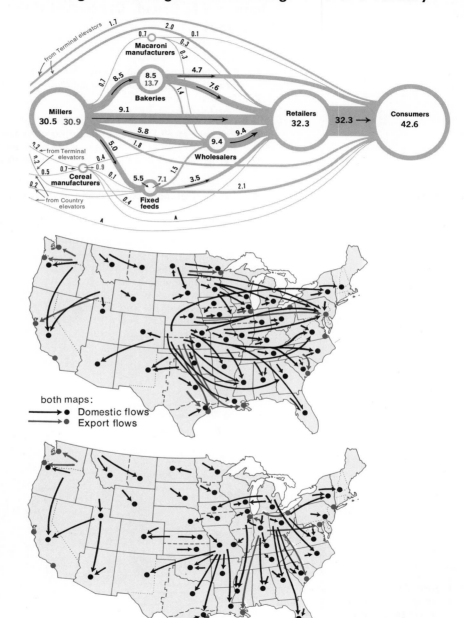

both maps:
→ ● Domestic flows
→ ● Export flows

Figure 14.4 Secondary linkages (hard and soft wheat flour from substage one to substages 2A and 2B, and secondary-tertiary linkages). Sectoral considerations are a continuation from Figure 14.2. Spatial arrows are optimum rather than recorded flows. Hard wheat flour is at the top; soft wheat flour at the bottom. (Op. cit. Figure 14.2)

WHEAT PRODUCTS

Secondary Activity
Substage 2A: Bread, Cake, and Related Products
(SIC 2051)

Sectoral Considerations

1. **Function and Process**
   A. Function: conversion of flour into bread and cake; *no weight loss, but other materials added; final product very perishable*
   B. Process: oven baking

2. **Significance**
   A. Per cent of all U.S. manufacturing employment: 1.14%
   B. Per cent of all U.S. manufacturing shipments: 0.91%
   C. Per cent of value added in all U.S. manufacturing: 1.05%

3. **Major Inputs**
   A. Per cent of labor costs (all employees) in final shipment value: 27.71%
   B. Per cent of materials costs in final shipment value: 46.04%

4. **Number and Size of Establishments**
   A. Total number: 4,042
   B. Size categories
      1 4 employees or fewer: 1,594
      2 Between 5 and 99: 1,753
      3 Between 100 and 249: 487
      4 Between 250 and 499: 158
      5 Between 500 and 999: 42
      6 Over 1,000: 8

Spatial Considerations

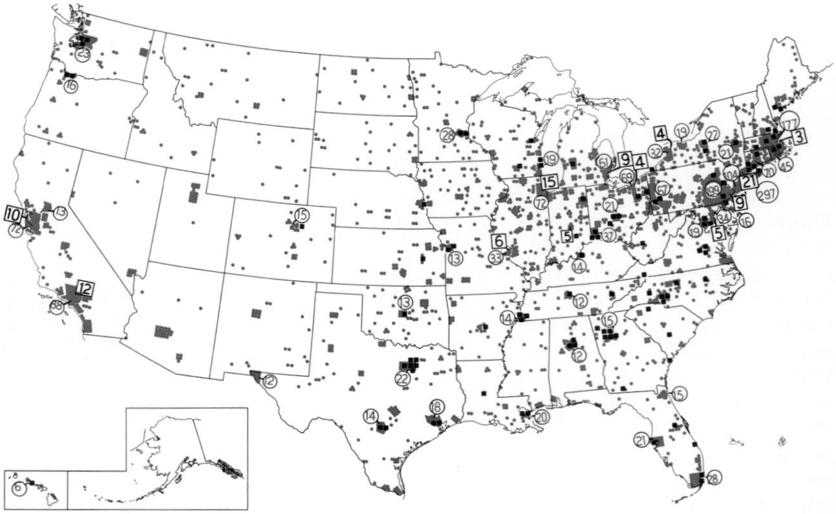

Figure 14.5 Secondary activity, substage 2A (bread, cake, and related products—SIC 2051). Symbols are explained in Figure 14.3.

WHEAT PRODUCTS

Secondary Activity
Substage 2B: Cookies and Crackers (SIC 2052)

Sectoral Considerations

1. **Function and Process**
   - **A.** Function: conversion of flour into cookies and crackers; *no weight loss; final product perishable*
   - **B.** Process: oven baking

2. **Significance**
   - **A.** Per cent of all U.S. manufacturing employment: 0.21%
   - **B.** Per cent of all U.S. manufacturing shipments: 0.24%
   - **C.** Per cent of value added in all U.S. manufacturing: 0.28%

3. **Major Inputs**
   - **A.** Per cent of labor costs (all employees) in final shipment value: 18.38%
   - **B.** Per cent of materials cost in final shipment value: 45.73%

4. **Number and Size of Establishments**
   - **A.** Total number: 348
   - **B.** Size categories
     1. 4 employees or fewer: 72
     2. Between 5 and 99:   192
     3. Between 100 and 249:   45
     4. Between 250 and 499:   14
     5. Between 500 and 999:   19
     6. Over 1,000:   6

Spatial Considerations

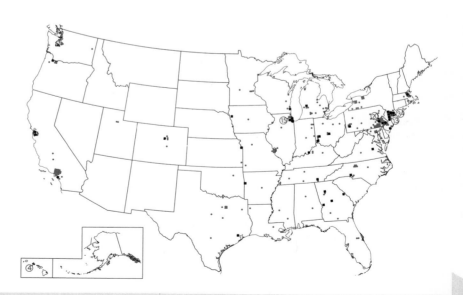

Figure 14.6 Secondary activity, substage 2B (cookies and crackers—SIC 2052). Symbols are explained in Figure 14.3. These products are less perishable than those in Figure 14.5. Has this affected plant location?

WHEAT PRODUCTS
Tertiary Activity

1. **Function and Process**
   A. Function: wholesaling and retailing of bread, cake, cookies, etc. (retailing emphasized here; see also Figure 14.4)
   B. Process: contact with customers in establishments (grocery stores, retail bakeries, etc.)

2. **Significance**
   A. Per cent of all U.S. retail labor force in retail bakeries (selling only; excludes 12,703 establishments in baking and selling)   0.11%
   B. Per cent of value of all U.S. retail sales: 0.07%

3. **Number and Size of Establishments**
   A. Total number: 2,931
   B. Size categories
      1 5 employees or fewer: 2,274
      2 Between 6 and 49 employees: 653
      3 Between 50 and 99 employees: 4

Spatial Considerations

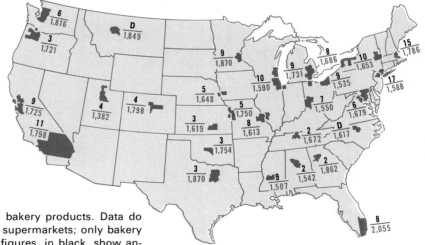

Figure 14.7 Tertiary activity, bakery products. Data do not include grocery stores and supermarkets; only bakery outlets are shown. Numerator figures, in black, show annual per capita retail sales, in dollars, of bakery products within selected standard metropolitan statistical areas (for definition, see glossary). Denominator figures, in brown, give annual per capita retail sales for all commodities sold retail. "D" means that data are not disclosed by the U.S. Census Bureau, and "NA" means that data are otherwise not available. Note variation among SMSAs in expenditures on bakery products, total retail products, and proportion of bakery products to total. (Keep in mind, however, that grocery and supermarket outlets are not shown.)

conditions. In the more humid eastern portion of the country, a variety of crops can be, and are, grown. Consequently, the individual farmer has a wide range of choice each year as to which crops he will or will not grow. On the other hand, with increasing aridity, many of the crops with which wheat competes in the humid East cannot be grown, except under limited areas supplied with irrigation. The range of possible choices therefore is more limited in the West. Even there, however, some choice exists, and human beings do not always make such choices in a fully rational manner—if, indeed, we can define a rational manner. Some will plant sorghum rather than wheat simply because they like to plant sorghum.

Government policy. A third and very important institutional explanation involves government policy, especially at the federal level. This influence has been, and continues to be, manifested in various ways. During the settlement of the Great Plains in the latter nineteenth and early twentieth centuries, the federal government gave large areas of land adjoining desired routes to railway companies to encourage rail construction and subsequent settlement. The actual initial location of settlement, and of wheat growing, hence was affected. At the present time, the federal government both enters into international agreements regarding sale of wheat and also provides some domestic subsidies for sale of wheat internationally below domestic prices; in some instances it makes outright donations of wheat in times of stress to specified developing countries. Hence the volume of wheat grown, and indirectly the location determined by market conditions, is affected by these export negotiations. Finally, in a land-bank program designed to remove marginal land from production—and, by coincidence, much of the wheat-producing land is marginal because of periodic drought —the federal government has encouraged either the continuous fallowing (plowing and cultivating, but not planting) of this land or returning it to natural grass. This policy also has affected the sizes of the producing areas, if not their specific location. These are only a few examples of the many federal programs that affect both the size and location of wheat-producing areas.

Theoretical explanation. As we have discussed, all spatial specialization and therefore all land use spe-

cialization can be explained in terms of the doctrine of comparative advantage. We saw that comparative advantage in the case of land use appears in the form of differential rent yields from using land for different purposes. We also saw that there are two kinds of comparative advantage: first, advantages arising from peculiarities of site—that is, advantages internal to a segment of space or a region—and second, advantages arising from the location of the segment of space or the position of the region relative to other areas—that is, its external relationships with other areas.

In the case of land use, we have seen that David Ricardo and Heinrich von Thünen embodied these two types of comparative advantage in their theories of rent. Ricardo stressed that the origin of economic rent is to be found in the fertility of the soil. On the other hand, von Thünen stressed that the origin of geographic rent is to be found in the advantages that a piece of land in a favorable location has over other land. Hence, Ricardo emphasized inherent physical advantages, while von Thünen emphasized locational advantages, which are, of course, expressed in terms of transportation costs. It is important to keep in mind that essentially these are advantages for a particular type of land use or a particular crop in a particular region. We require both these sources of comparative advantage to arrive at our elementary but nonetheless unequivocal explanation of the location of wheat production. It will remain a *general* explanation, however, and must be modified in the light of the institutional details and peculiarities which apply to any *particular* region of wheat specialization.

Wheat is grown on the more arid periphery of the agricultural land use in the United States, as it generally is in the major wheat-specializing regions of the world. In terms of the two types of comparative advantage, we have first the Ricardian site advantages. Wheat regions in arid areas constitute more profitable land use than the more intensive mixed farming, which is generally more profitable under humid conditions; however, wheat production (alone) could not compete with mixed farming in humid regions because of its low yield per acre. Yet, it is a more intensive and more profitable form of land use than livestock ranching, which occurs in areas with more arid conditions. In terms of comparative advantages arising from location, we find that wheat has a low response to distance; that is, the transportation-cost function is more gently sloped than in many other forms of agricultural production. Wheat transported in bulk and requiring no special conditions such as refrigeration can be transported long distances without lowering the dollar yield to the farmer below that which he would receive under other forms of land use. We have seen that the yield of a unit of land is the value of its output (price times quantity) minus costs of production, which include transportation costs.

We may make a few final remarks on the intensity of agricultural land use. Production of agricultural outputs, like most types of production, is accomplished by combining inputs of different kinds. These are traditionally divided into three categories: land, labor, and capital. Agriculture is said to be *intensive* when large quantities of labor and/or capital are applied to a unit area of land. We say that the capital-land ratio or labor-land ratio is high. This results in high outputs per unit of land because little land relative to other factors is used. On the other hand, if a lot of labor has been used, the output per unit of labor will tend to be relatively low. In terms of *extensive* agriculture the same reasoning applies, with relatively low labor-land ratios and low output per unit of land. In the case of intensive agriculture, the aim of factor (land, labor, capital) combinations is to economize on land, while in extensive agriculture the aim of such combinations is to economize on labor, capital, or both. The specialized agricultural regions are characterized by extensive forms of agricultural production economizing on both labor and capital *per unit of land*. The comparative advantages for this form of agriculture relative to other forms lie in its ability to economize labor by substitution of capital (machinery). Specialized wheat production in semiarid and arid portions of the United States is extensive agriculture, whereas mixed crop and livestock farming farther east is more intensive.

In this general regard, the zones of von Thünen's model provide even a casual observer with some insight as to intensity of land use in the United States as it affects, and reflects, wheat growth. If we consider the highly urbanized effective area of this country including Chicago, St. Louis, Washington, D.C., and Boston, and all urban places in between, as von Thünen's "city,"

we find the more intensive land use, the mixed crop and livestock farming including some horticulture—and soft wheat growing—near this "city." Farther away—perhaps in von Thünen's fourth and fifth rings—are the winter and spring wheat belts. Still farther from the "city"—corresponding to von Thünen's sixth ring—is extensive commercial grazing.

Horizontal Linkages: Primary to Secondary Stages

Figure 14.2 shows both sectoral and spatial aspects of the movement of grain to flour mills and to ports of export. The reader will note that most of the grain moves initially to country elevators, frequently on the farmers' own trucks and sometimes on commercial carriers. These elevators almost invariably are located on railway lines, and most of the grain moves directly by rail or by combined rail and water to terminal elevators which forward the grain either to flour mills or to ports of overseas shipment. Slightly more than two-thirds of each annual harvest is either consumed domestically or placed in storage, and one-third is exported. (These are general figures; the annual ratio of exports to production ranges from 1:10 to 1:2.) The grain may be transferred from rail to water—to transport systems serving either the Great Lakes, the nation's inland and coastal waterways, or both. As we shall see later in this chapter, the Great Lakes transportation is especially important.

With respect to media, the truck tends to be very active in short-haul service, especially from farm to country elevator, but it also provides some service for longer distances. The rail lines, or combined rail and water facilities, are especially important in the longer-range movement of the grain.

Secondary Activity

Description, measurement, and classification. As we have mentioned, once the wheat leaves the producing unit, it moves to country elevators and terminal elevators, and from there is taken either to grain mills for processing (and then to bakeries for still further processing) or directly to export terminals. We are concerned in this section with the grain mills and bakeries.

In U.S. Office of Management and Budget nomenclature, which has been adopted officially by the Bureau of the Census, we are interested in the production of flour and other grain-mill products (SIC 2041); in bakery products of bread, cake, and related commodities (SIC 2051); and in cookies and crackers (SIC 2052). We shall refer to the production of flour as *substage 1* of this secondary activity, and to the production of both types of bakery products as *substage 2*.

Substage 1: sectoral considerations. Function and process. The function performed in the first substage of the manufacture of wheat products is the conversion of wheat into flour and bran. An important aspect of this function is that essentially no loss in weight is involved; almost the full amount of incoming raw materials is converted into finished products. The process is known as *gradual reduction,* in which the grain is put through a succession of fluted rollers and then through a sifting operation. This is repeated as long as necessary, with the distance between the rollers gradually decreased. Through this process, the kernel of the grain is gradually separated from the outer husk to the degree that is actually desired. Complete separation is possible, resulting in flour that is perfectly white, or in varying amounts of the outer husk, known as bran, being left in the flour.

National importance. As is shown in Figure 14.2, the milling of flour and other grain-mill products is not an extremely important activity of the secondary sector in the United States. It accounts for essentially $\frac{1}{10}$ of 1 per cent of all manufacturing employment, slightly less than $\frac{1}{2}$ of 1 per cent of all manufacturing shipments, and slightly less than $\frac{2}{10}$ of 1 per cent of the value added in all manufacturing in the United States.

By Aldefer and Michl criteria, the flour and other grain-mill-products industry in the United States is low in terms of labor costs (5.81 per cent), but very high in terms of materials costs (80 per cent; see Fig. 14.3 and p. 214). Value added in manufacture is only about 20 per cent of final shipment value, as compared with a national average of about 47 per cent (p. 214). Thus, the flour and other grain-mill-products industry can be said to be very low in terms of labor costs, very high in terms of materials costs (which are both inputs to the industry), and very low in terms of value added

(which is an output of the industry). It is important to state once again that essentially no materials are lost in the manufacturing process, so that nearly all the products from the primary sector are converted into manufactured products. As we shall soon see, all these considerations are important in an explanation of the location of the industry.

Size of establishment. Yet another insight into the location of manufacturing can be obtained through an examination of the size of establishment. (*Establishment* here refers to specific *factories,* not *firms.*) Of the 541 establishments engaged in the production of flour and other grain-mill products, 210 employ fewer than 4 personnel, 486 employ fewer than 100, and 539 employ fewer than 500. This is definitely a small-business type of industry.

Substage 1: spatial considerations. The location of manufacture of flour and other grain-mill products, together with the value of shipments, is shown in Figure 14.3. There is a general location of the industry in the western half of the United States manufacturing belt, with a tendency toward concentration, especially of the larger plants, in well-known key cities such as Minneapolis and Chicago. In addition, there is a projection into the eastern half of the manufacturing belt, especially in the Buffalo area of New York State. Also, there is important production in the state of Kansas, again concentrated especially within and near the major metropolitan areas. Finally, on the West Coast, where a growing market exists in the form of a rapidly expanding population, there is an important concentration of this activity in California and also in Washington. Within the heart of the intermontane area, Utah is an outstanding producer.

Substage 2: sectoral considerations. Function and process. Substage 2 involves two types of bakeries: (1) those which produce bread, cake, and related products which are quite perishable (substage 2A) and (2) those which produce cookies, crackers, and other products which do not become stale quickly (substage 2B). The main function performed by both is the conversion of flour, with certain additives, into the various bakery products. As is apparent in Figures 14.5 and 14.6, neither is an extremely important industry in the United States when considered in terms of manufacturing employment, the value of shipment, or value added in manufacture. The production of bread, cake, and related products is a high-labor-cost industry but is low in terms of materials costs, and thus it is the reverse of the flour-milling industry. The bakeries producing cookies and crackers are intermediate in terms of labor costs, but are also low in terms of materials costs. For both industries, the value added in manufacture is more than 50 per cent of the final shipment value, thus exceeding the United States national average of about 47 per cent.

The production of bread, cake, and related products takes place in a total of 4,042 establishments, nearly all of which employ fewer than 500 workers apiece. Indeed, more than one-third employ fewer than 5 personnel per establishment, and nearly five-sixths employ fewer than 100. Only 50 of the entire 4,042 employ more than 500.

There are far fewer establishments producing cookies and crackers—a total of only 348. Again, these are mostly small businesses, as shown in Figure 14.6.

Substage 2: spatial considerations. The distribution of bakeries producing bread, cake, and related products is relatively close to that of the population itself, although there tends to be a rather high concentration in the eastern half of the manufacturing belt—a slightly higher concentration than is warranted on the basis of population alone.

A generally similar pattern is evident in the location of plants producing cookies and crackers.

Explanation. *Milling of flour and other grain-mill products. Institutional explanation.* The institutional explanation for the location of the milling of flour and other grain-mill products is found especially in the historical background of the industry and in government-approved practices within the industry in the establishment of freight rates.

The production of flour from grain is, of course, a historically old process, which until recently was carried out with comparatively crude grindstones instead of modern techniques and which was used to produce flour from locally grown grain for local sale. As long as the product was chiefly a soft wheat utilized for consumption in the immediate vicinity and as long as the United States was in a period of settlement which involved pressing back the frontier rather than one of economic maturity, the industry was characterized by tiny establishments generally distributed in accordance with the population. However, as we have mentioned, the introduction of new types of hard wheat into the Great Plains in the latter part of the nineteenth century resulted in the possibility of specialization in establishments making bread-type flour and producing for sale in the rapidly expanding eastern portions of the country. This was soon followed by the introduction of the gradual-reduction process of milling, and so the stage was set for the conversion of the industry into its present form of small and intermediate-sized establishments, located strategically on routes of shipment from the raw material to the ultimate market.

A critical consideration here is that of freight rates. We have already mentioned that these do not, in fact, vary with distance, but are affected by value, stage of manufacture, weight, etc. In addition, *in-transit* freight-rate privileges in the United States allow a raw material which is processed en route to final market to go forward to its ultimate destination at raw-material rates for the entire journey, even though it is processed at some point along the route. However, no backhaul—a flow of goods back toward the initial starting point at a geographic angle of less than 90° from the direction of the original goods movement—can be involved. Thus a plant receiving wheat from Kansas can locate in Kansas City and forward the flour eastward to the bakeries and forward the animal feeds to the Northeast, East, and Southeast to the dairy and cattle-fattening areas of the United States, and it can receive the in-transit freight-rate privileges for both types of shipment. As we have seen, the final market for flour and grain-mill products comprises bakeries, on the one hand, and feed-mill plants and wholesalers, on the other.

The impact of both historical background and in-transit freight-rate privileges is shown in the present location of the nation's flour-milling industry. In Kansas and Minnesota, there is an orientation to both raw materials and markets. In Chicago, Buffalo, and other key places in the heavily populated manufacturing belt, there is an orientation to markets and raw materials, as is also true of the establishments in California, Washington, and Utah.

Still another explanation lies in a combination of physical environmental conditions and institutional factors. The Great Lakes transportation system, which recently became a Great Lakes–St. Lawrence Seaway transportation system (pp. 112 to 113), long has played a key role in the shipment of grain products because, as we have seen in Chapter 7, the movement of bulk products by lake vessel is extremely economical. In lesser measure, the inland and coastal waterways also play a role. Thus, as we have stated, there exist key break-of-bulk points from rail to water transfer at the western end of the lakes (Duluth and Chicago, for example), where grain is transferred to the lake vessels, and key break-of-bulk points from water to rail transfer at the eastern end (Buffalo). There is a strong tendency for milling operations to be located at such places. This situation is not necessarily associated with in-transit freight-rate privileges and probably would exist even without them.

Theoretical explanation. The theoretical explanation of the location of flour-milling installations can be found in Weberian location theory since the general pattern tends to follow that of minimum-transportation-cost location. We obtained from our review of Weber the postulate that the pull of a localized raw-material input tends to be proportional to the weight loss of that raw material. That is, "pure" materials exert little or no influence on the location of manufacturing plants utilizing them, while "gross" materials exert a pull to their location, the strength of which increases as the amount of weight loss increases.

Since milling involves no weight loss, these secondary production installations are located at all points on routes between raw-material sources and market locations, with break-of-bulk points being especially attractive. Some raw-material locations also coincide with market locations. There is also a low ratio of labor costs to materials costs, and hence we do not have any low-labor-cost sources exerting a strong-enough influence to pull the industry away from minimum-transport-cost locations. Also, scale economies are not of great significance in milling relative to transportation costs on output; therefore, as we would expect, the industry is characterized by many small and intermediate-sized plants.

The comparative-advantage factors which will influence our theoretical location of secondary activity again consist of site and relative-location advantages. In terms of our Weberian model, factors which determine location are transportation costs on both inputs and outputs; and secondly, on the advantages of agglomeration which would tend to pull the location of a plant away from its minimum-transport-cost location. As there are no radically significant economies of scale to be achieved in the milling of wheat, we would expect transportation costs to be dominant in determining the location of milling capacity.

We also saw in Weberian analysis that the greater the weight loss on localized raw materials, the stronger the pull on the location of the plant. There is no significant weight loss associated with the process of converting wheat to flour, and hence the pull of wheat-producing regions would not be more significant than the pull of the market. However, we have seen in the previous discussion that much milling is located in the western half of the manufacturing belt, with concentrations in Minneapolis and Chicago and metropolitan areas in Kansas. These locations represent convenient collection points for aggregation of wheat from dispersed production on farms. These are in fact raw-material locations or minimum-cost raw-material assembly points from a diverse set of individual centers. That the pull of the localized raw materials is not overwhelmingly dominant in the case of milling locations is shown by the shift of much capacity to the eastern markets; thus Buffalo now has the largest concentration of milling capacity in the United States.

Bakery-products industries. *Institutional explanation.* The chief institutional explanation for the location of both bread, cake, and related-products industry, on the one hand, and the cookie and cracker industry, on the other, is that both are important in the daily diets of almost every person, and their location is very closely associated with population distribution. Where there is a variance, it is due mainly to perishability of product. Hence there is a tendency for the cookie and cracker plants, which are much fewer in number, with products less perishable than bread or cake, to be located in a pattern that is somewhat out of adjustment from that of population distribution.

Bakeries of bread and cake, which are perishable products, long have been referred to in manufacturing assessments of the institutional school as *ubiquitous* because they are located generally in accordance with population distribution. Some practitioners assume that 10 per cent of the manufacturing labor force can be set aside as associated more or less with these ubiquitous industries, so that the remainder of the United States labor force can be assessed in terms of its unique characteristics—tendency of manufacturing to specialize—rather than its universal elements.

Theoretical explanation. There are few inherent economies of scale or advantages of agglomeration in the technology of bread and cookie production. The market for these products is atomistic; that is, it correlates closely with the distribution of population. The third factor of importance here is that the range of these goods is low.[1] Given these three factors alone, we would deduce that manufacturing consists of small-scale establishments, the distribution of which shows little deviation from the distribution of population.

As pointed out in the previous institutional explanation, bakery products are perishable and are required frequently by householders, restaurants, etc.; production therefore tends to follow closely the distribution of population. This perishability of product and the short-term periodicity of purchase restrict the range of the goods, and hence they are low-order products in a Christallerian functional ranking. As higher-order central places have all those functions which lower-order centers have, we find plants producing bakery products throughout the entire range of central places, the industry comprising essentially small businesses.

As we said, bread and cookies have in their technology of production few inherent economies of scale or advantages of agglomeration. Such economies, when they occur, produce advantages from the concentration of production at a few points. As we have seen, these advantages must exceed the increased transportation costs which are incurred from concentration. In the case of bakery products, we may observe that not only are scale economies relatively small, but also trans-

[1] Moreover, it is a low-order good in the functional hierarchy.

portation costs are high. Apart from the perishability factor, the market for these products is atomistic, tending to increase rapidly the transportation costs to markets. However, we may also note that establishments producing bakery products vary greatly in scale depending on whether they are located in small towns or large cities. This is a result of market density and is thus a transport advantage rather than a technical scale economy. Finally, in contrast to milling. the bakery-products industry has a relatively high ratio of labor cost to materials cost, and thus material sources may be expected to exert less locational pull than labor and market locations.

Tertiary Activity

By definition (p. 4), tertiary economic activity includes all that is not primary or secondary. Therefore, with respect to Part 3 of this book, it refers to all transportation (except that by trucks belonging to farmers, carriers belonging to manufacturing establishments, etc.), as well as wholesale and retail trade. For this reason, tertiary activity began to play a role in our assessment immediately after the primary stage and continued to do so in following stages.

Horizontal linkages. We have already noted the sectoral and spatial aspects of the movement of grain from primary to secondary activity. We are concerned here particularly with the movement from flour mills to bakeries and export ports, from flour mills to prepared-feed mills, and from flour mills directly to wholesalers and retailers, as well as with the movement of bakery products to wholesalers and retailers. All this is shown diagrammatically in Figure 14.7, and no additional explanation is necessary.

Wholesale and retail trade outlets. There are three ultimate markets for flour-mill products in the United States: (1) the internal human population, (2) the internal animal population, and (3) ports of export.

Between two-thirds and three-fourths of all wheat consumed domestically in the United States is in the form of bakery products, with a very small fraction—less than 2 per cent—in the form of rolled wheat, macaroni, and other specialized foods. The retail sale of such products usually is in grocery stores, ranging in size from huge suburban or downtown supermarkets to small convenience stores. A substantial portion also is sold, either directly or via sales trucks, from the producing bakeries. Only a small portion of bakeries concentrate on retail trade alone. Per capita sales from these, for selected standard metropolitan statistical areas, are shown in Figure 14.7. The wide range of sales from such places is due to a number of causes, but especially to competition from grocery stores and producing bakeries. Although the data therefore do not

show total bakery-product consumption, they do reveal, or at least suggest, rather differing shopping habits in different parts of this country. Most bakeries are small, with fewer than three employees, but the larger establishments, with ten or more employees, account for over two-thirds of sales in the United States.

Both the institutional and the theoretical explanations of the location of retail outlets of bakery products stem from product perishability and customer convenience. The general need for a convenient bakery is well known and has been treated in institutional literature. In theoretical terms, this need helps to explain the

Figure 14.8 Growth and distribution of wheat in Canada. Note the flows toward both coasts for export. What locational explanations discussed in the section on the United States are applicable here? (After Figure 9.20, Tomkins and Hills, *A Regional Geography of North America,* published by W. J. Gage Company Ltd. and reprinted by permission of Gage Educational Publishing Ltd.)

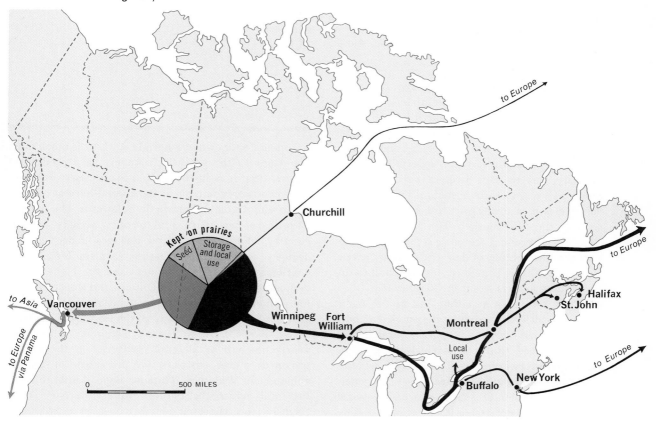

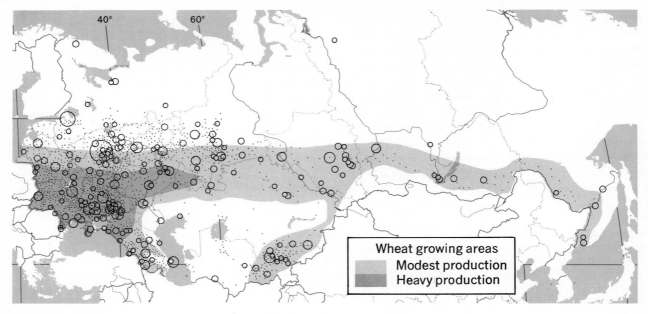

Figure 14.9 Growth areas and domestic market areas of wheat in the Soviet Union. (Base map as in end map showing population and urbanization, from *Oxford Economic Atlas of the World,* 4th ed., p. 65)

urban hierarchy (although, paradoxically, this commodity is sold at all levels in the hierarchy).

Between one-sixth and one-fourth of all wheat products consumed domestically in the United States is used for animal and poultry feed. Such consumption may be of the entire wheat grain, especially that of poorer quality, but usually involves only the outer husk, which, as we have seen, is sold on the market as bran. Sometimes it is mixed with other grains before being sent to the feed market. The location of the wholesalers of this product therefore is found in association with the distribution of dairy cattle, beef cattle, hogs, and poultry in the United States. We shall examine some of these aspects again in Chapter 15.

Except for terminals at either end of the Great Lakes system, which are active in the service of both domestic and foreign markets, no port of foreign shipment in the United States is exclusively a grain-receiving or grain-forwarding center. Instead, whether located on the East, South, or West Coasts, shipment of grain is one dimension of a series of activities which conglomerately act to determine the location and function of the port facilities.

Canada

In Canada, as shown in Figure 14.8, wheat is much more important to the domestic economy as a product of export, than it is in the United States. Between two-thirds and three-fourths of the annual harvest of Canada is sent abroad, primarily in bulk form. The pattern of primary, secondary, and tertiary activity of that country, and the horizontal linkages, reflect a high degree of regional specialization, with the largest production in the Prairie provinces and the highest level of domestic consumption in Ontario and Quebec, where more than two-thirds of the population of the country is located. A second flow is from the Prairies to the West Coast, particularly to British Columbia. All in all, nearly one-half of all grain produced in the Prairie provinces moves eastward for processing or further shipment in Winnipeg, Thunder Bay, Montreal, Halifax, and across the border, Buffalo in New York. Slightly more than one-fourth moves westward, especially to Vancouver, for domestic and foreign use, and most of the remainder is stored, retained for next year's seed crop, or used for feed in the Prairie provinces. As in the United States, bakeries and tertiary activity are associated particularly with the leading metropolitan areas and ports of export.

An interesting dimension to the Canadian export trade is the role of the Great Lakes–St. Lawrence Seaway system and the interplay between eastbound movements of grain and westbound movement of iron ore. The ports of Baie Comeau and Sept-Îsles, located on the downstream estuary of the St. Lawrence River, have become important rendezvous centers for lake vessels, which can carry grain downstream as far as the first of these ports; the grain is then stored in huge terminal elevators for shipment overseas by ocean vessel. Iron ore from Quebec fields is then loaded on the same lake vessels at Sept-Îsles and proceeds up the St. Lawrence and Great Lakes system to the United States and Canadian ports. This two-way movement of bulk cargo, in vessels which are extremely economical on a ton-mile basis, is proving increasingly successful.

The Soviet Union and China

In the Soviet Union, the distribution of the consuming population, the areas of primary growth, and the major milling centers are much more closely concentrated within a single area—the Ukraine—than is true in the United States and Canada (Fig. 14.9). The major grain mills also are found in this area.

In China, there is also a conspicuous spatial overlap between the areas of production and the distribution of population; the major exception is that China's effective area of heavy population concentration includes not only the major wheat-growing area but also a sizable southeastern portion of the country, where wheat is not grown (Fig. 14.10).

Although it would be presumptuous to attempt either an institutional or a theoretical explanation of the location of primary, secondary, and tertiary activity in these countries without full investigation, the forces which we have mentioned with regard to the United States and Canada appear also to be at work here. These include the evolution of population growth in key areas of the country, transportation costs, government policies, the natural environmental limitations of wheat growth, and the importance of human decision—here usually expressed as government policy—concerning wheat versus competing crops.

A final statement with respect to both countries is important: Because of the vagaries of Asian monsoon weather, either country may experience periodic but intensive drought, scarcely equaled in other wheat-growing areas of the world. In these times, both countries become significant wheat importers; conversely, in the "good" years, they may become exporters. Although this fact does not necessarily affect the location of primary, secondary, or tertiary activity in either country, it decidedly affects the functions performed at each of these stages, especially the annual acreage of primary activity and the import and export functions of some tertiary activity.

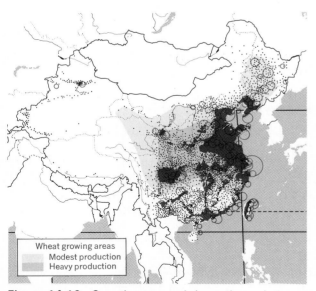

Wheat growing areas
Modest production
Heavy production

Figure 14.10 Growth areas and domestic market areas of wheat in China. (Base map as in end map showing population and urbanization, from *Oxford Economic Atlas of the World,* 4th ed., p. 65)

Chapter 15

Meat Products

In this discussion of meat products, we shall be treating a raw material that originates within the primary activity of grazing, and we shall follow the production process through the secondary and tertiary stages. Meat products, as cited in the United States Census of Manufactures (SIC 2011), includes not only beef (60 per cent of all meat products), but also pork (37 per cent), veal (1.6 per cent), and lamb (1.4 per cent). However, we shall concentrate on the production of beef and pork, inasmuch as these are the overwhelmingly dominant products in the industry.

The United States

Meat products not only are critical but also are increasing in significance as items of consumption in the United States, whether measured on a basis of per capita or overall consumption. Despite a 60 per cent increase in domestic production between 1950 and 1970, imports rose in the decade of the 1960s and in the early 1970s. The United States produces more than one-fourth of all beef and veal in the world for which data are available and nearly one-fourth of all meat from swine. No other nation approaches the United States in beef output, although China probably raises and consumes more swine.

Primary Activity

Description, measurement, and classification. ***Sectoral considerations.*** The function of the primary sector in meat production is the provision of live cattle (through commercial grazing and agriculture) and of live hogs (through agriculture alone) for slaughter in the secondary stage. The processes of commercial grazing and of agriculture are relatively similar, except that the forage grasses utilized in grazing are normally natural and are only occasionally, if at all, reseeded, fertilized, or otherwise improved by man. Commercial grazing, as we have seen in Chapter 5, is basically an exploitation of natural forage, whereas agriculture involves at least periodic planting of that forage and of crops which may be used in the fattening process of both cattle and hogs.

Figure 15.1 contains some sectoral data indicating the importance of meat production in grazing and agriculture in the United States. Over 580,000 ranches and farms are involved in this activity. They constitute nearly 18 per cent of all such units in the country, and the value of meat products sold from ranches and farms amounts to essentially one-third the value from all agriculture in the United States.

The increasing efficiency and capital intensiveness of the primary stage of this activity are indicated in a recent thirty-year trend, which shows that the man-hours invested per 100 pounds of meat produced have been reduced by nearly 50 per cent for beef and more than 50 per cent for pork.

Spatial considerations. Cattle. Some 60 per cent of the beef cattle that ultimately are slaughtered in the United States are born in the seventeen western states, and the remainder in widely scattered parts of the East, almost totally excluding only the northernmost portion (Fig. 15.1).

Cattle breeds increasingly are the heavy beef types—Aberdeen-Angus, Hereford, Shorthorn, etc. In the South, where high temperatures, insects, and diseases discourage these breeds, increasingly successful efforts have been made to cross them with Zebu (Brahman) and other low-latitude cattle. The result has been a distinctly new breed, known by various names, which produces satisfactory meat and is competing with the Angus, Hereford, and other traditional breeds which are still present in large numbers in the South.

Animals born on open range are usually transferred to feedlots at ages ranging from twelve to thirty months. A few, however, are slaughtered while "grass-fat"—when they are at the peak of condition from grazing on the range. In either case, most are shipped from the grass country.

Although the fattening of cattle in feedlots is still considered a farming operation, the existence of professionally managed feedlots, in some instances accommodating many thousands of cattle and engaged only in the fattening process, is increasingly common. Technically, this can be considered an initial stage of manufacture, although officially it is still classified as agriculture.

Feedlot practices are trending toward rapid fattening of younger animals, when more pounds per unit of feed are realized than at later ages. The animals are in small enclosures, exercise very little, and merely gorge themselves on blended feeds that include corn, soybeans, alfalfa, clover, grass, hay, cotton meal, sorghum molasses—and even, in some instances—fish meal and chicken manure!

Swine. As shown in Figure 15.1, the production of swine in the United States is concentrated rather sharply within the central portion of the country, with Iowa producing nearly one-fourth of the national total and Illinois and Indiana jointly producing nearly another one-fourth. Like production of beef, this industry involves an increasing degree of specialization, frequently in units producing swine only. Breeding animals are very carefully selected, and conditions of growth are closely controlled. As with cattle, the animals are kept in confinement for their entire lives and are shipped to the slaughterhouses when they have reached optimum size, usually while less than one year old.

Sectoral and spatial considerations. Types of farming. We have mentioned that 60 per cent of the cattle ultimately killed for beef in the United States are born in the seventeen western states, and the remainder in widely scattered sections of the East. A comparison of Figures 5.1 and 15.1 will indicate that in the West cattle are associated primarily with commercial livestock ranching; in the East they are associated primarily with the growth of feed grains and livestock, general farming, and dairy farming, the latter in the southern portion of the dairy belt, where male calves may be either killed in the first few months of life as veal or allowed to mature to beef. The concentration of the swine-producing industry is heavily within the feed-grain and livestock section, with the swine comprising most of the livestock so produced.

Vertical and horizontal relationships. The vertical relationships are mainly those of association, at any given point, with climatic and soil conditions. These can be inferred from a comparison of Figures 2.3 and 2.7 with Figure 15.1. Clearly, the semiarid climates and their associated soil types are conducive to grazing in the West, while the desert climate and associated soil types are not, except under irrigation. Although the map is too general to reveal it, there is a strong tend-

BEEF AND PORK PRODUCTS

Primary Activity

1. **Function and Process**
    A. Function: agricultural production of beef and pork for meat, leather, and products*
    B. Process: (for beef) commercial grazing and/or agriculture; (for pork) agriculture (see text, pp. 235 and 246)

2. **Significance**
    A. Per cent of farms and ranches in all U.S. types of agriculture and grazing: 18%
    B. Per cent of value of all U.S. farm products sold: 30%

COWS, OTHER THAN MILK COWS, INCLUDING HEIFERS THAT HAVE CALVED
NUMBER

United States total **24,751,452**

1 dot=5,000 head (county-unit basis)

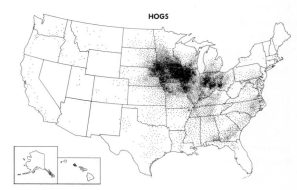

HOGS

United States total **67,949,259**

1 dot = 10,000 head (county-unit basis)

Figure 15.1 Sector-space considerations, beef and pork products, primary stage. Location of beef cows indicates places of beef origin. (U.S. Bureau of the Census)

*Some data sources also include lamb and veal, but these have been excluded by careful estimate in calculations for this book.

BEEF AND PORK PRODUCTS

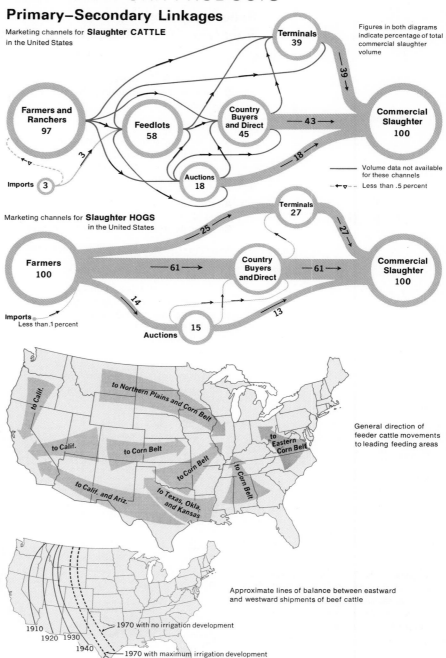

Primary–Secondary Linkages

Marketing channels for **Slaughter CATTLE** in the United States

Figures in both diagrams indicate percentage of total commercial slaughter volume

Terminals 39

Farmers and Ranchers 97

Feedlots 58

Country Buyers and Direct 45

Auctions 18

Imports 3

Commercial Slaughter 100

— 43 →

— 18 →

— 39 →

3

Volume data not available for these channels

Less than .5 percent

Marketing channels for **Slaughter HOGS** in the United States

Farmers 100

Terminals 27

Country Buyers and Direct

Commercial Slaughter 100

Auctions 15

Imports — Less than .1 percent

— 25 →

— 61 →

— 61 →

— 27 →

14

13

General direction of feeder cattle movements to leading feeding areas

to Calif.
to Northern Plains and Corn Belt
to Calif.
to Corn Belt
to Corn Belt
to Eastern Corn Belt
to Corn Belt
to Calif. and Ariz.
to Texas, Okla. and Kansas

Approximate lines of balance between eastward and westward shipments of beef cattle

1910 1920 1930 1940

1970 with no irrigation development

1970 with maximum irrigation development

Sectoral Considerations

Spatial Considerations

Figure 15.2 Primary-secondary linkages, beef and pork products. In sectoral flows, note different arrangements for cattle and hogs, especially the absence of feedlots for hogs. Many cattle begin their lives on the Great Plains and are shipped east or west for fattening and/or slaughter. The western market area is growing—in demand and size of supply zone. Movement of hogs (not shown) is mainly from farms (Fig. 15.1) to slaughterhouses (Fig. 15.3). (After information and illustrations supplied by U.S. Dept. of Agriculture)

BEEF AND PORK PRODUCTS

Secondary Activity
Substage One: Meatpacking Plants (SIC 2011)

Sectoral Considerations

1. **Function and Process**
   - **A.** Function: conversion of cattle and swine into beef, pork, and products
   - **B.** Process: slaughtering, butchering, chilling, canning, freezing, etc.; *some weight loss*

2. **Significance**
   - **A.** Per cent of all U.S. manufacturing employment: 0.88%
   - **B.** Per cent of value, all U.S. manufacturing shipments: 2.79%
   - **C.** Per cent of value added in all U.S. manufacturing: 0.84%

3. **Major Inputs**
   - **A.** Per cent of labor costs (all employees) in final shipment value: 8.01%
   - **B.** Per cent of materials costs in final shipment value: 86.12%

4. **Number and Size of Establishments**
   - **A.** Total number: 2,697
   - **B.** Size categories
     1. 4 employees or fewer: 1,170
     2. Between 5 and 99: 1,213
     3. Between 100 and 249: 169
     4. Between 250 and 499: 84
     5. Between 500 and 999: 30
     6. Over 1,000: 31

Spatial Considerations

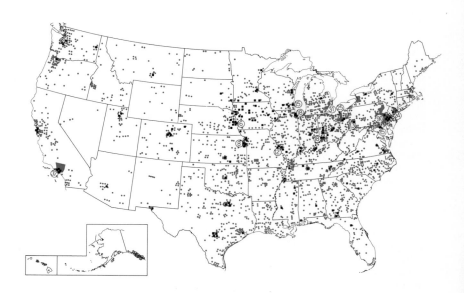

Figure 15.3 Sector-space considerations, beef and pork products, substage one (meatpacking plants—SIC 2011), secondary activity. See Figure 14.3 for explanation of symbols.

BEEF AND PORK PRODUCTS

Substage One—Tertiary Linkages

Sectoral Considerations

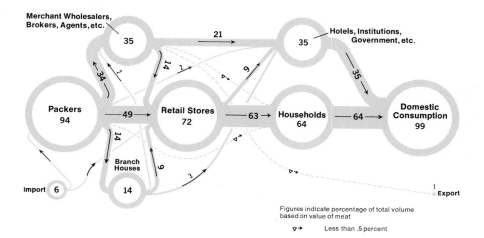

Spatial Considerations

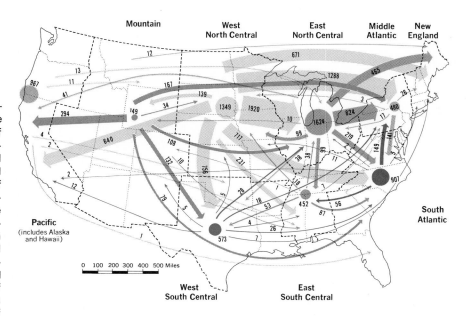

Figure 15.4 Linkages, substage one—tertiary stage. Note that the main consumers of meat products are hotels, restaurants, institutions, etc., and private households. Spatial movement is in thousands of tons, among U.S. Census Bureau divisions. Note that the largest flows are from slaughterhouses in the West North Central and East North Central census divisions to places farther east or west. (Sectoral information from U.S. Dept. of Agriculture; spatial linkages calculated from U.S. Census of Transportation)

Tertiary Activity—Meat

**Sectoral
Considerations**

(For sectoral information, see Fig. 15.4, sectoral considerations.)

**Spatial
Considerations**

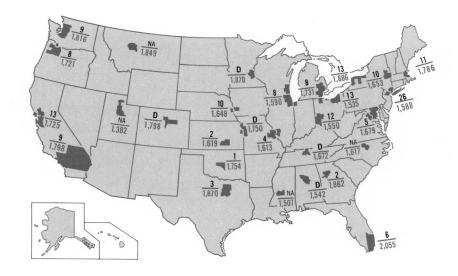

Figure 15.5 Sector-space considerations, beef and pork (meat) products, tertiary stage. For explanation of symbols, see Figure 14.7.

BEEF AND PORK PRODUCTS
Secondary Activity
Substage Two A: Leather Tanning and Finishing (SIC 3111)

Sectoral
Considerations

1. **Function and Process**
   - **A.** Function: conversion of hides and skins into leather; *no significant weight loss*
   - **B.** Process: tanning

2. **Significance**

A. Per cent of all U.S. manufacturing employment:	0.15%
B. Per cent of all U.S. manufacturing shipments:	0.15%
C. Per cent of value added in all U.S. manufacturing:	0.12%

3. **Major Inputs**

A. Per cent of labor costs (all employees) in final shipment value:	21.41%
B. Per cent of materials costs in final shipment value:	62.98%

4. **Number and Size of Establishments**

A.	Total number:	519
B.	Size categories	
	1 4 employees or fewer:	146
	2 Between 5 and 99:	286
	3 Between 100 and 249:	57
	4 Between 250 and 499:	25
	5 Between 500 and 999:	4
	6 Over 1,000:	1

Spatial
Considerations

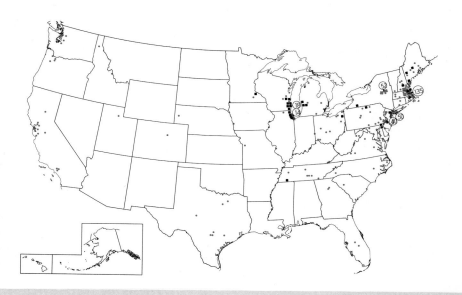

Figure 15.6 Sector-space considerations, beef and pork products, substage two A (leather tanning and finishing—SIC 3111). For explanation of symbols, see Figure 14.3. Why the concentration of plants along the eastern and western margins of the manufacturing belt?

241

BEEF AND PORK PRODUCTS

Linkages, Substage Two A–Two B—Tertiary

Geographic division of origin	Tons (000)	Per cent of goods movement by means of transport			
		Rail	Motor carrier	Private truck	Other & unknown
U.S.	874	9.2%	59.6%	27.8%	3.4%
New England	191	1.6	87.8	7.3	3.3
Middle Atlantic	166	3.9	91.6	0.3	4.2
East N. Central	84	20.3	57.9	19.7	2.1
West North Central	138	—	10.6	89.1	0.3
South Atlantic	79	4.2	57.3	23.3	15.2
East South Central	169	27.7	32.1	40.0	0.2
Rest of U.S.	47	na*	na	na	na

*na = not available.
Source: United States Census of Transportation, 1967.

Sectoral Considerations

Spatial Considerations

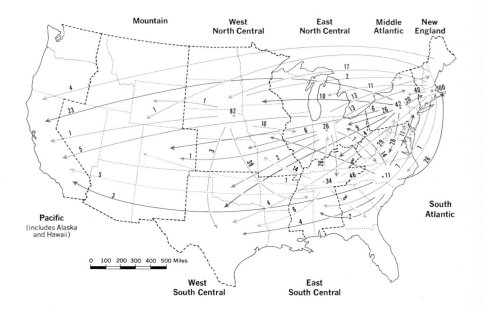

Figure 15.7 Linkages, substage two A to substage two B and to tertiary. Arrows show movement, in thousands of tons, of leather and leather products (except clothing) among Census Bureau divisions. Note the small volume compared with Figure 15.4.

BEEF AND PORK PRODUCTS

Secondary Activity
Substage Two B: Production of Footwear, Except Rubber (SIC 3141)

1. **Function and Process**
   - **A.** Function: conversion of leather into footwear
   - **B.** Process: cutting, shaping, sewing, gluing; some loss of weight and material; much hand work

2. **Significance**
   - **A.** Per cent of all U.S. manufacturing employment: 1.02%
   - **B.** Per cent of value, all U.S. manufacturing shipments: 0.49%
   - **C.** Per cent of value added in all U.S. manufacturing: 0.58%

Sectoral Considerations

3. **Major Inputs**
   - **A.** Per cent of labor costs (all employees) in final shipment value: 30.04%
   - **B.** Per cent of materials costs in final shipment value: 44.66%

4. **Number and Size of Establishments**
   - **A.** Total number: 951
   - **B.** Size categories
     1. 4 employees or fewer: 124
     2. Between 5 and 99: 254
     3. Between 100 and 249: 220
     4. Between 250 and 499: 283
     5. Between 500 and 999: 63
     6. Over 1,000: 7

Spatial Considerations

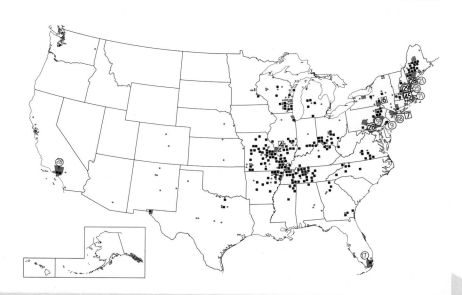

Figure 15.8 Sector-space relationships, substage two B (footwear, except rubber—SIC 3141). For explanation of symbols, see Figure 14.3. Why the concentrations?

BEEF AND PORK PRODUCTS

Linkages, Substage Two B–Tertiary

Sectoral Considerations

Geographic division of origin	Tons (000)	Per cent of goods movement by means of transport			
		Rail	Motor carrier	Private truck	Other & unknown
U.S.	409	3.9%	61.2%	27.0%	7.9%
New England	201	3.8	85.4	1.2	9.6
Middle Atlantic	34	0.1	91.9	3.2	4.8
East North Central	94	5.3	17.2	74.0	3.5
West North Central	23	0.6	51.2	47.7	0.5
East South Central	38	8.2	19.1	63.2	9.5
Balance of U.S.	19	na*	na	na	na

*na = not available.
Source: United States Census of Transportation, 1967.

Spatial Considerations

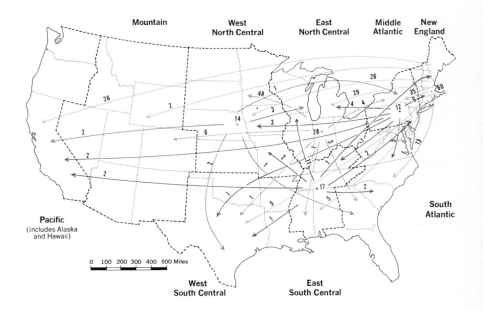

Figure 15.9 Linkages, substage two B to tertiary. Arrows show movement, in thousands of tons, of footwear (except rubber) among Census Bureau divisions.

BEEF AND PORK PRODUCTS
Tertiary Activity—Shoe Stores

1. **Function and Process**
   - **A.** Function: wholesaling and retailing of footwear, except rubber (retailing emphasized here)
   - **B.** Process: contact with customers in establishments (stores), or via mail orders

2. **Significance**
   - **A.** Per cent of all U.S. retail labor force in footwear, except rubber:

        1.15%
   - **B.** Per cent of value of all U.S. retail sales:

        0.94%

3. **Number and Size of Establishments**
   - **A.** Total number:

        20,600
   - **B.** Size categories
     1. 5 employees or fewer: 14,559
     2. Between 6 and 49 employees: 5,990
     3. Between 50 and 99 employees: 46
     4. Over 100 employees: 5

Sectoral Considerations

Spatial Considerations

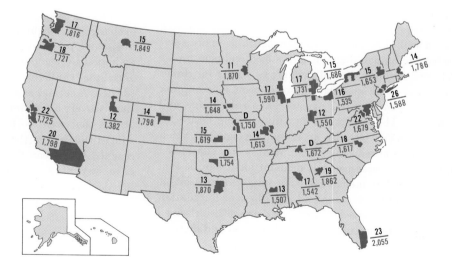

Figure 15.10 Sector-space considerations, tertiary stage, shoe stores. Department stores and other diversified outlets are not included. For explanation of symbols, see Figure 14.7.

ency for beef-cattle grazing to be restricted in semiarid climates to areas too dry for the growing of wheat. Except for the problems of excess heat and moisture, which have been offset by the development of special breeds, as has been previously described, there is no special limitation to the growing of beef cattle in the East and South, and hence there is a very wide distribution of animals there.

The concentration of swine in the feed-grain and livestock agricultural region, with the humid continental long-summer and neighboring climates and their associated prairie, chernozem, and gray-brown soils, is not the result of a severe constraint in the physical environment. Swine can be produced in a very wide range of physical conditions, although they do not thrive under excess heat. The explanation for this concentration is in the historical background and the shift in market prices, as we shall see.

Institutional explanation. Although meat consumption is an extremely inefficient way of converting the "grow power" of farm land into calories—an acre of land will yield only about one-eighth as many calories for the human diet if it grows feed and pasture for beef production as it will if it grows wheat for direct human consumption—the volume of meat consumption in the United States is, as we have seen, large and expanding. This indicates not only a rising desire for meat in the diet but also an expanding demand, which is desire plus purchasing power. Meat is now considered sufficiently a necessity that demand for it can be said to be somewhat inelastic—to an important extent, it will continue to be purchased regardless of fluctuation in price. In recent years, domestic demand has risen so fast and so consistently that a substantial and increasing share is now being supplied by imports.

The very size of this demand signifies that, unless there exists some kind of constraint for meat production, meat could be produced with profit throughout a wide range of agricultural types and regions in the United States. We have noted that the only definite constraints are desert conditions in the West (overcome by irrigation, where available) and a combination of excessive heat and moisture conditions in the South.

Cattle. In the location of the primary stage of the production of cattle for beef, we are concerned with grazing and agriculture. As with wheat, cultural taste is an important consideration in the current location of beef-cattle production. Also as with wheat, man has eaten beef for all recorded time, and there is evidence that he will continue to do so in the foreseeable future. The volume of consumption thus depends in part upon a historically derived taste for meat.

Historical background also provides a further explanation of the current location of the primary stage. As we have seen, cultural heritage from northwestern Europe included use of animals for both beef and dairy purposes, and these were introduced into the eastern United States at the time of settlement. However, when settlement reached the Great Plains, it encountered another culture, this one from southern Europe. The settlement of Latin America, including Mexico, by Spain had resulted in a transplant of the hacienda to this part of the New World. Many of these large estates had become well established in Texas by the early part of the nineteenth century, when settlers from the eastern United States were gradually pushing westward. Conflicts between the two cultures did not prevent an exchange of insight regarding certain cultural attributes—and, partially as a result, the large ranch became an important component of the Great Plains during and after the conflicts between the United States and Mexico. A second aspect of this cultural exchange was the discovery of longhorn cattle, descendants of Spanish breeds that were both on the haciendas and running wild at the time settlers from the eastern United States reached the Great Plains. Although such cattle later gave way to Angus, Hereford, and similarly refined breeds during the economic maturity of the twentieth century, they played a vital role in the development of the beef-cattle industry in the early days because they had adapted well to the environment of their day. Thus, a ranching practice had been developed by the Spanish culture, and by way of Mexico, it first encountered westward-moving settlement from northwestern Europe in the nineteenth century. The stage was set for present-day commercial livestock ranching.

Whereas interaction between cultures helps to explain the current location of commercial livestock ranching in the West, the production of beef in the eastern and southern portions of the country is traceable to the mixed farming practices of northwestern Europe.

Again it is important to mention government policy

as an institutional force with respect to this particular activity. Very rigid import regulations control the movement of live cattle across the borders of the United States, and there also exist certain regulations regarding the movement of chilled or processed beef. Another aspect of government policy, previously mentioned in Chapter 14, "Wheat Products," involves encouraging the conversion of marginal wheat-growing land back to natural grasses. This process of conversion is of benefit to cattle producers and tends to extend the geographic area of grazing activity. Still another government practice is that of allowing grazing in national forests and in certain federally owned grazing districts. Again, such a policy fosters this economic activity.

The location of cattle feeding and fattening lots is becoming increasingly important as a consideration in its own right. In historical background, cattle were at one time slaughtered in substantial numbers while grass-fat, i.e., in reasonably good physical condition, usually in the fall, as a result of a summer's grazing. However, the emergence of the specialized feed-grain and livestock area in the upper Mississippi valley resulted in a production of corn and related grain which could fatten the animals much more satisfactorily than grass alone. The slaughterhouses that were in operation during the latter part of the nineteenth century were located mainly in that feed and livestock area, between the source of range cattle to the West and the markets to the East. As the finishing of cattle became a specialized activity in itself, feedlot operators began to locate in an advantageous position in relation to the source of grass-fat cattle; the grain, hay, and other commodities, needed in the fattening operation; and the slaughterhouses. As a result, there was a strong tendency for such specialized operators to concentrate on the fringe of the slaughterhouse area, particularly in Chicago, Omaha, Kansas City, and other large metropolitan areas. Some of the larger operations are also found nearer the source of the raw materials, where sufficient grain is grown under irrigation so that feed is available and frequently where there is a sufficient regional market to justify the operation.

Swine. The institutional aspects of cultural taste and demand which are responsible for the location of the beef industry can also be applied to the location of the hog industry in the United States. However, the geographic concentration of this industry very strongly

into a few states in the upper portion of the Mississippi and Ohio River valleys is appreciably the result of a long-standing cultural tradition involving swine in a rotation crop and animal economy that has been inherited from northwestern Europe. The emergence of corn and soybeans as key crops in this area, almost simultaneously with increased hog production, is a case study of a happy combination of products in time and space. Clearly, the climate and soils of this area could produce a much wider range of crops and animals than now are found there. The historical explanation lies principally in a demand for pork that has been historically high and continues to be important and in the location of this area in overlap with the highly populated northeastern portion of the United States, which is the principal market for the finished product.

Production and transportation costs; market prices. Although the historical background of an economic activity can never be overlooked in assessing its current location and essential functions and linkages, we should never lose sight of current conditions and change. For both beef cattle and swine, the constant interplay between production and transportation costs, on the one hand, and market prices, on the other, is an important force in their economic geography. These are further considered by the farmers, ranchers, and other decision makers with reference to similar costs and prices of alternative livestock and/or crops. Thus the institutions of the market, and of transportation, are significant. Here, especially, there is a decided overlap into theoretical explanation.

Theoretical explanation. Production of both cattle and swine can be considered a footloose activity since it does not involve any rigid locational requirements and can take place under a wide variety of conditions. In the United States, some beef production occurs in almost all agricultural areas throughout the East, South, and Middle West, but the comparative advantages for large-scale specialized beef production are greatest in the western Mountain states on the semiarid periphery of cultivation.

Ricardian comparative advantages for beef production in the West produce large units of extensive land use where the main source of animal fodder is direct grazing. In these areas wheat cultivation could not compete with specialized beef production as in the winter and spring wheat belts farther east. Hence, though rent yields are low per unit area in beef production, they are higher than could be accrued from alternative land uses.

In a von Thünen context, his classic model relegated such extensive land use to the periphery (Fig. 12.3), with a low rent yield but a compensating low slope to a relatively flat transportation-cost function. However, recent tendencies toward the processing of animals by stall feeding in more accessible areas, as in the case of dairy farming, are increasing.

In the case of swine, strong *in situ* comparative advantages accrue to production in the upper Mississippi and Ohio valley region, as well as transportation or accessibility advantages. Strong backward and forward linkages have developed—backward linkages to corn and other feeds and forward linkages to processing industries and markets.

Horizontal Linkages: Primary to Secondary Activity

Product flows of both cattle and swine from areas of production to those of slaughter are shown in Figure 15.2. As with wheat, the truck is especially important as a short-haul carrier, up to 500 miles, and rails tend to be more important beyond that point. However, the truck can be used as a satisfactory long-haul carrier; as we shall see, it has been partially responsible for a shift within the United States of the slaughtering industry. Movement by lake vessel and shallow-draft barge is insignificant because of the perishability of live animals. In this activity, time is an important ingredient of cost. Animals must be fed and watered; hence it is important that they reach the market as fast as possible after the time of loading, and water vessels move too slowly for this purpose.

Secondary Activity

Description, measurement, and classification.
In general, meat is responsible for slightly more than 80 per cent of the ultimate value of factory shipments from the meat-products industry; hides, for slightly less than 10 per cent; and miscellaneous by-products, for the remainder. In U.S. Office of Management and Budget nomenclature, the three-digit detail of meat products (SIC 201) is subdivided into the following four-digit-detail categories: meat-packing plants (SIC 2011), establishments producing sausages and other prepared meat products (SIC 2013), establishments producing poultry, and wholesale small-game dressing and packing (SIC 2015). The hides move forward to the leather tanning and finishing industry (SIC 311) and then on to a series including the production of industrial leather belting and packing (SIC 312), boot and shoe cut stock and findings (SIC 313), footwear except rubber (SIC 314), leather gloves and mittens (SIC 315), luggage (SIC 316), handbags and other personal leather goods (SIC 317), and leather goods not elsewhere classified (SIC 319). In this section, we shall be concerned with three of these industries, all at the four-digit detail: meat-packing plants (SIC 2011), leather tanning and finishing establishments (SIC 3111), and footwear except house slippers and rubber footwear (SIC 3141). This selection is intended to show the progress through the various substages without becoming an encyclopedic accounting of all such substages.

Substage 1: meat-packing plants (SIC 2011). Sectoral considerations. The function of meat-packing plants is to transform live cattle and hogs into the products mentioned above. The process is an age-old one of slaughtering, butchering, and preserving meat and other products. For cattle, only about one-half the weight of the live animal emerges as a dressed carcass; for hogs, the percentage is slightly higher. However, substantial portions of the by-products are retained for use in pet food, as components of various medicines and drugs, etc.

In national importance the industry has a rather curious position. It provides less than 1 per cent of all manufacturing employment, but accounts for nearly 3 per cent of all manufacturing shipments. The value added in manufacturing is quite low—less than 1 per cent (Fig. 15.3). As to its major inputs and outputs, the industry is low in labor costs and very high in materials costs, but involves a very low percentage of value added to final shipment value (compare Fig. 15.3 with Alderfer and Michl criteria on p. 214 and with the national average of final shipment value on p. 214). A total of 2,697 establishments are involved, of which some 43 per cent hire 4 employees or fewer, and 45 per cent hire between 5 and 99 employees. However, 30 establishments each hire more than 250 employees, and four leading companies (*firms,* not *establishments*) account for more than one-fourth of the value of all shipments.

Spatial considerations. Figure 15.3 shows the location of these meat-packing plants in the United States and the value of shipments. In the eastern portion of the country, the concentration within Iowa, Nebraska, and Minnesota, and the somewhat reduced but nevertheless significant production in neighboring states to the east, is quite apparent. Much of the heavily populated Northeast, except for New England, is worthy of mention in meat-packing. In the South, except for Texas, the activity is not very intense. This pattern is repeated in the West, although there are concentrations of high activity in California, Colorado, and, in lesser measure, Washington.

Substage 2: leather tanning and finishing (SIC 3111). *Sectoral considerations.* The function of leather tanning and finishing is to transform hides and skins into finished leather. Hides come from large animals such as cattle and horses and usually weigh from 25 to 75 pounds each. Skins come from smaller animals, such as calves, pigs, lambs, and goats, and usually weigh less than 25 pounds apiece. The leather from hides is destined particularly for such heavy uses as shoe soles and belting, and that from skins for a wide variety of specialized uses requiring light and soft leather.

Separate processes are involved in the tanning of hides and skins, even though the same function is being performed. Hides are processed mainly in tannic acid, in operations requiring up to six months. Skins are tanned by way of a mineral process, especially using chrome salts or related products. Less time is required than for hides, but more capital equipment and a higher degree of labor skill are necessary.

The industry is very small, containing only 519 establishments, which aggregately account for a tiny fraction of all manufacturing employment, shipments, and value added (Fig. 15.6). Furthermore, it is a small-establishment industry, with the majority of plants employing fewer than 100 employees, and only one hiring more than 1,000. Although it is high as to both labor and materials costs, value added as a per cent of final shipment is less than the national average.

Spatial considerations. The available data show the leather tanning and finishing industry to be concentrated in the northeastern region of the United States as designated by the Bureau of the Census, especially in the New England and the Middle Atlantic divisions. A lesser output is in the East North Central division of the North Central region (Fig. 15.6), with a noteworthy production in the South as a region and a very modest output in the West.

Substage 3: shoes, except rubber (SIC 3141). *Sectoral considerations.* The function of this stage of manufacture is to transform the leather from hides (for soles) and skins (for upper portions) to shoes. Although highly mechanized, the process requires careful supervision of the machines, and in some instances actual hand cutting, so that much labor is necessary. Because of this, more than 1 per cent of all manufacturing employment in the United States is in this particular industry, although the value of all manufacturing shipments is less than $1/2$ of one per cent, and the per cent of all value added in manufacturing is less than $6/10$ of 1 per cent. A total of 951 establishments are engaged in this production, with most employing between 5 and 499 workers (Fig. 15.8). It is a very high labor-cost industry, but is low in terms of materials costs. Partly because of the high labor cost, the value added is a rather resounding 55 per cent of final shipment value, as compared with the national average for all manufacturing of 47 per cent.

Spatial considerations. Like leather processing, this industry is concentrated in the eastern portion of the manufacturing belt, especially in the New England and Middle Atlantic divisions. Again, as in leather processing, there is a spillover into the East North Central division and relatively modest production in other parts of the United States.

In the case of both the leather tanning and finishing industry and the production of leather shoes, location does not conform to either the current market distribution or the source of raw materials. An explanation for this skewing of location is not immediately apparent upon inspection of maps alone. Perhaps our institutional and theoretical approaches can shed some light on this.

Institutional explanation.

Meat-packing plants in the United States tend to be located at some point along the route from the initial raising of the animal under either grazing or agricultural circumstances to ultimate markets which conform to geographic distribution of population. The larger slaughterhouses are located very critically between national sources of supply and demand, and the smaller ones appear to be equally critically situated with respect to regional and local sources of supply and demand.

These three levels of observation—local, regional, and national—are important in an examination of both historical and current forces at work on location of the meat-packing industry. As has been true in the past, the local producer seeks local supply and slaughters for himself and a minor market in the immediate vicinity. The regional producer, usually involving companies rather than individuals, follows the same general pattern but on a broader regional scale, usually involving a major metropolitan area or city and its trading territory. National producers have very complex linkage relationships to supply and demand forces involving the entire country.

At one time, meat production was largely in the hands of the local producers. By the mid-nineteenth century, it had become an intermixture of local and regional producers. Only in the latter part of the nineteenth century and in the twentieth century did national production by large corporations become significant. As the economy of the United States matured into a truly national system, these firms grew at the relative expense of the local and regional producers.

An important technological advance, the advent of the refrigerated car, enabled the national corporation to move effectively into the forefront of production between 1875 and 1900. With that development, secondary aspects of beef production—but not pork production—changed in locational emphasis. It was possible for large terminal slaughterhouses to become established, especially in Chicago, but also in St. Louis, Kansas City, and, in lesser measure, Omaha. These slaughterhouses were located sufficiently close to the market so that the freshly killed beef could be forwarded by refrigerated cars, but they were also suffi-

ciently close to raw materials so that they could serve the cattle country. In addition, most of the centers were important break-of-bulk points where railway trains were regrouped or where there was a transfer from railway to another type of carrier. Chicago, especially, was a leader in this regard, being a city where railroads of different corporations and different freight classification territories came together. It was logical for slaughterhouses to be located in such metropolitan areas at this time.

However, with changing economic conditions and rapidly developing new technology, a further shift occurred in the location of manufacturing. In Chicago, the stockyards declined and were essentially closed out as operations on a national scale. The advent of a large and efficient motor truck, that could carry both livestock and refrigerated meat products, allowed a more flexible movement of both live animals and meat to centers located more advantageously between the major areas of supply and demand. The loss of weight in the slaughtering process and the problem of keeping animals alive and healthy before slaughter encouraged the shift of the industry towards the raw materials. An even more current trend is location of slaughterhouses near regional feedlots, away from large urban places such as Kansas City or Omaha. Fattened cattle are shipped to intermediate-size slaughterhouses (employing 500 to 1,000 persons), and the meat is taken by refrigerated truck to markets as distant as New York City. Different conditions of labor supply, wage differentials, fringe benefits, and degree of unionization were important forces in this shift.

Meanwhile, the rapid growth of population in the western states of the mainland United States, especially in California, meant a sizeable regional market. California and neighboring states, long established as cattle raisers, over the years have directed their animal supply to western regional markets which have become so large that they now are receiving some slaughter animals from the Mountain West and Texas.

The primary institutional and historical factors which are important to understand in assessing the current location of the meat-processing industry in the mainland United States are the interplay of production and transportation costs, on the one hand, and market prices, on the other, as modified by changing technology and shifting population.

In a way, the same forces have been at work in the leather tanning and shoe industries. The concentration of these in New England was in large measure historical development, inasmuch as the need, know-how, and raw materials were brought from Europe by the earliest settlers. Such manufacturing was important in New England, and especially so in the vicinity of Boston, prior to and during the nineteenth century. The Middle Atlantic division also was an active producer. Only during the twentieth century has an effective diffusion taken place from those divisions. The industry is growing in the western half of the manufacturing belt and on the West Coast, and we therefore logically can anticipate an expansion there because of the increasing size of markets and proximity to raw and processed materials.

Theoretical explanation. Slaughtering animals for meat consumption marks the beginning of the secondary processes of meat-packing (and by-product activities), whether the meat is to be sold fresh or is to be frozen or canned. There is considerable weight loss on the raw material—approximately 45 per cent—and hence there is a tendency to locate near its sources. These sources of raw material are not the original ranches, but areas of beef fattening. Therefore, the concentration in fattening areas of feed grains represents the least-cost location in a Weberian framework, in terms of both weight loss and differential transportation rates. Moreover, the market for meat products is dispersed throughout urban centers.

In the case of the shoe and leather industries, the raw material consists largely of hides. These industries are not materials-oriented, as there is no significant weight loss involved. In New England and the Middle Atlantic states, they are located near major markets. The inputs to these industries therefore involve relatively low materials costs but high labor costs, in both relative volume and unit costs of skilled labor. We would expect, therefore, that the minimum-transportation-cost location would be at the market location, as "pure" raw materials cannot bind production to their location. Skilled labor has been built up in New England and the Atlantic states, and therefore isodapanes would follow fairly closely the isotims around the market centers in the East.

These industries consist of smaller-scale operations, as there are few economies of scale to be achieved. In many cases, rapidly altering fashions place a premium on the flexibility of output changes, and therefore small-scale, more adaptable operations are characteristic.

Subsequent Linkages and Tertiary Activity

In terms of tertiary activity, little can be added by way of description, measurement, classification, or explanation to what has been stated in previous chapters and is shown in Figures 15.4, 15.5, 15.7, 15.9, and 15.10. Internal markets are high for meat and leather products. Wholesaling and especially retailing of all aspects of this industry tend to be associated geographically with the distribution of population. Meat now can be preserved through freezing, and leather is not perishable; thus storage over a long period of time is possible with no loss in value. These aspects facilitate a tendency for location of tertiary activity in a general relationship with population distribution.

In this chapter we have followed the meat-products industry from animal production to final consumption, along with the linked industries of leather and shoe production. Meat as a commodity is designated in economic terminology as a *superior good*. This means that as incomes rise, while more of all commodities tend to be purchased, expenditures on meat consumption increase more than proportionately. In other words, meat has a positive income elasticity of demand, and hence we can predict that more of our future food budgets will be spent on meat, especially beef; thus the production of beef animals will continue to increase.

Shoes and other leather goods for consumer demand occupy a similar position to that of meat in that they are low-order goods in the retail hierarchy, although their periodicity of purchase is larger, and hence the density of these retail outlets tends to be less than those for meat. As previously noted, the retail grocery function occurs in the lowest-order central places, but specialized shoe and clothing retail functions tend to be of a somewhat higher order. Such specialization, of course, precludes clothing retail at the general store. Thus our postulates from the Christallerian model of threshold and range of goods assist in explaining the distribution of these tertiary activities.

Specialized meat retailing, i.e., the butcher shop,

is disappearing under the pressure of scale economies accruing to the supermarket, and specialized shoe retailers may disappear similarly because of competitive scale advantages of the large department store.

CANADA

The pattern of meat production in Canada is remarkably similar to that in the United States. A substantial number of beef animals are raised on the Great Plains, and some of them are shipped both eastward and westward for fattening and ultimate slaughter. Hogs are produced in the general farm area. The slaughterhouses in Canada are oriented more sharply toward the larger metropolitan markets than is the case in the United States, with Toronto, Montreal, Winnipeg, and Vancouver containing a large number of such processing plants. As in the United States, the country's leather industry is concentrated especially in the eastern portion, and the explanations for this are not unlike those already advanced for the United States.

Chapter 16

Selected Forest Products

Forest-products industries involve exploitation of un-domesticated forests. The growth of timber in woodlots and the production of tree crops planted by man are here considered agriculture.

Our concern in this chapter is with the obtainment of raw timber, commonly known as *roundwood,* and selected derivatives. On the world scene, the Soviet Union is the leading producer, accounting for more than 18 per cent of the total cut; the United States follows closely with more than 15 per cent. Brazil, China, and Canada are next in rank, each supplying between 5 and 8 per cent.

The United States

Primary Activity

Description, measurement, and classification. The territory now lying within the continental United States (excluding Alaska and Hawaii) is believed once

to have contained more than 900 million acres of forest —an amount exceeding the current reserves of all other nations except the Soviet Union and Brazil. With certain exceptions, almost the entire portion of the country east of the Mississippi was forest-covered, as was much of the mountainous and coastal country of the West. Conifers and deciduous trees were to be seen in substantial stands, for this part of the world is in the middle latitudes, where trees of both categories are frequently present and often intermingled (Fig. 5.5).

Approximately one-third of this original forest acreage has been converted to other uses; some 600 million acres are still in forests. Now that Alaska and Hawaii are in the Union, reserves of all forest land total some 777 million acres. These constitute over 8 per cent of the world's total reserves. Over three-fourths are considered productive, and nearly nine-tenths of the productive forests are considered accessible. Thus, over two-thirds of the United States' reserves now are thought to be both productive and accessible—i.e., to be commercial forest. About 8 per cent of this commercial forest is officially classified as old-growth saw timber—virgin stands with trees large enough and numerous enough to be exploited as lumber. The remaining 92 per cent is made up of either second-growth saw timber or of trees too small to be used for lumber but at least partially useful as pulpwood, mine pitprops, and diverse other products.

The actual timber volume of conifers in the nation's currently exploitable forests exceeds that of hardwoods by a ratio slightly in excess of 2:1.[1] Conifers constitute more than 95 per cent of the reserves in the West and Alaska, somewhat less than 50 per cent of the reserves in the South, and slightly over 20 per cent of the reserves in the Northeast. Species of oak, hickory, maple, beech, birch, and other hardwoods dominate conspicuously in the Northeast and moderately in the South, but are insignificant in the West and in Alaska. The Douglas fir, ponderosa pine, and lodgepole pine are the leading conifers of the West; the loblolly, shortleaf, longleaf, and slash pine are the leading conifers of the South; and varieties of spruce, fir, and pine make up most of the small amount of conifers in the Northeast.

Sectoral considerations. We shall consider logging camps and logging contractors (SIC 2411); sawmills and planing mills, general (SIC 2421); veneer and plywood establishments (SIC 2432); pulp mills (SIC 2611), and paper mills, except building paper (SIC 2621). We shall consider logging camps and logging contractors to be primary, and the remainder to be substages of secondary, activities. This is in contrast to the official classification of the U.S. Office of Management and Budget, which considers all these activities to be secondary. However, the function performed in logging consists of felling trees and reducing them to logs for shipment to sawmills. The process ranges from a highly automated peeling and subsequent clipping of timber under optimum conditions in developed areas, to use of chain saws in those same developed areas where trees have more branches and conditions for more automation are not so satisfactory, to a higher ratio of hand labor in the less developed areas. The activity is therefore as much an exploitation of natural conditions as grazing or agriculture, and hence it is here considered primary.

There are very many logging camps and contrac-

[1] Alaska's coastal forests are included in this estimate.

tors in the United States—16,334, according to the 1967 Census of Manufactures. More than 13,000 of these are very small, engaging fewer than 5 employees each; some 3,000 employ between 5 and 99 persons, and only 41 employ more than 100. Although we consider the activity primary, data exist for comparing it with all manufacturing (Fig. 16.1). It is a comparatively minor industry, whether considered in terms of employment, value of shipment, or value added. Its internal conditions, again compared with overall manufacturing, reveal that it is high in terms of labor costs, intermediate in terms of materials costs, and slightly above the national average in value added as a per cent of final shipment value. This last figure is especially interesting, since primary activities as a whole are not considered to add substantial value to initial materials in comparison with secondary or tertiary activity.

Spatial considerations. Because of the very large number of logging camps in the United States, a dot map of the distribution is not so informative as a map of value added (Fig. 16.1). Here we see a predominance of the Pacific states, with Oregon, Washington, and California ranking in that order. The South as a region is important, with nearly all states worthy of mention as producers. The heavy population pressure in the Northeast has taken its toll in forest growth, and much of the production of that area is from its open areas.

Sectoral and spatial considerations. Current and projected exploitation. Existing and anticipated consumption of roundwood in the United States is shown in Figure 16.2. By the year 2000, total roundwood consumption is expected to be 60 per cent above the current level—an increase resulting largely from population growth—with per capita consumption remaining almost constant. However, there will be changes in the composition of consumption, with pulpwood and, in lesser measure, veneer logs being used in higher proportion and such cruder materials as fuel wood declining.

Ownership. Some 92 per cent of commercial forest land in the South and 81 per cent in the North is privately owned, in contrast to only 32 per cent in the West (Fig. 16.3). Furthermore, small private holdings are especially numerous in the South and North in

FOREST PRODUCTS INDUSTRIES

Primary Activity: Logging Camps and Contractors (SIC 2411)*

Sectoral Considerations

1. **Function and Process**
   - **A.** Function: exploitation of natural forest products; *much weight loss.*
   - **B.** Process: cutting and initial preparation of trees in natural habitat

2. **Significance**
   - **A.** Per cent of all U.S. manufacturing employment: 0.36%
   - **B.** Per cent of value, all U.S. manufacturing shipments: 0.26%
   - **C.** Per cent of value added in all U.S. manufacturing: 0.26%

3. **Major Inputs**
   - **A.** Per cent of labor costs (all employees) in final shipment value: 23.03%
   - **B.** Per cent of materials costs in final shipment value: 52.87%

4. **Number and Size of Establishments**
   - **A.** Total number: 16,334
   - **B.** Size categories
     - 1   4 employees or fewer: 13,120
     - 2   Between 5 and 99 employees: 3,173
     - 3   Between 100 and 249 employees: 34
     - 4   Between 250 and 499 employees: 2
     - 5   Between 500 and 999 employees: 5

Spatial Considerations

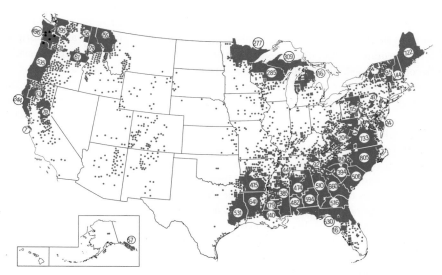

Figure 16.1 Logging camps and contractors (primary activity, SIC 2411). For explanation of symbols, see Figure 14.3. This is an activity with numerous but small establishments, located near naturally growing forest timber and near timber which can be grown by agriculture.

*Although this is here classified as primary activity, data sources in the U.S. Office of Management and Budget classify it as secondary, and hence the comparison with secondary activity.

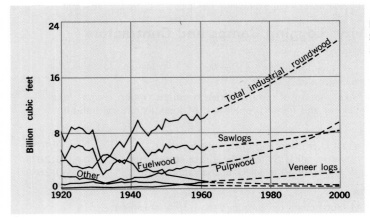

Figure 16.2 Roundwood consumption in the United States. (After data from *Timber Trends in the United States,* GPO, Washington, D.C., 1965)

contrast to the West, where corporations own more than one-half of all private commercial forest land.

Reserves, regional exploitation, and trends. The Pacific Coast states (including Alaska and Hawaii) contain the largest reserves of actual saw timber in the United States, followed by the South and the North (Fig. 16.4). However, trees will grow rapidly in the humid subtropical climate of the South—much more so than elsewhere—because of the warm temperatures and copious precipitation there. Current practices in the South increasingly are to plant and harvest these trees as agriculture rather than merely to exploit them as forest products. Therefore, we can expect the South to become increasingly important as a supply area for all three categories—pulpwood, saw logs, and veneer logs—that are in greatest demand.

Institutional and historical explanation. Particularly for cultures which matured in northwestern Europe and continued in various parts of the world as colonial offshoots from that area, the tree has played a critical role in daily living. Clearing of the forest for agriculture has both enabled the spread of population and provided raw materials for construction of housing, furniture, and other needs, as well as fuel for both production and space heating. Thus, at the outset of exploitation, the sources of supply and demand were in essentially the same position. As populations increased in numbers and technology advanced, reserves of standing timber were decimated well in advance of

dense populations, and the land thus cleared was used primarily for agriculture. Two interesting trends are outstanding in the United States' record of tree cuttings: (1) excessive exploitation and (2) migration. The excessive rate at which the United States used up its forests has been emphasized frequently. Even today, we have not shown a mature wisdom in timber use. Too often, the land occupied by the initial settlers was not diverted fully to other uses, but was partially abandoned to the elements. Second-, third-, or fourth-growth forests, many of them scraggly and untended, have reappeared on such land, and some have contributed to a declining harvest.

Migration resulted in both a retreat of the forest and an advance of settlement. In the early part of the twentieth century the forest cutters turned their attention to the rich reserves of virgin timber in the West, the output of which rose during the twentieth century from about one-tenth of the nation's wood in the early 1900s to nearly one-half at mid-century. In the late 1960s and 1970s, production began to decline, partly because of recognition of a wood shortage in the West, although as we have seen, most of the saw-timber reserves still are in that area. This recognition—accompanied by government policy—was largely the result of public action, and most of the western forests were placed under the protective custody or control of the federal government.

Thus we see the institutional explanation of both past and present logging to be a close relationship, both sectoral and spatial, between supply and demand.

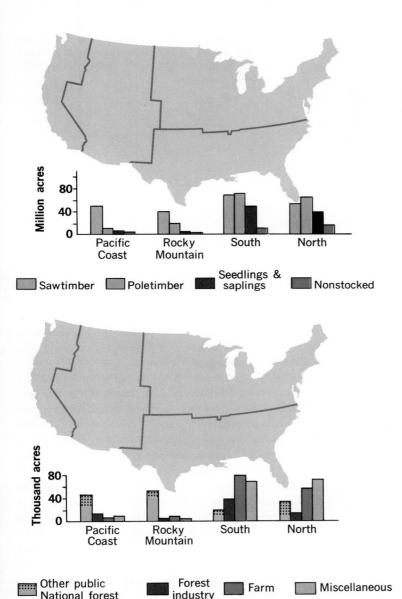

Figure 16.3 Ownership of commercial forest land in the United States. Land belonging to the forest industry, farm, or miscellaneous categories is privately owned. (After data from *Timber Trends in the United States*, GPO, Washington, D.C., 1965)

Rather belatedly, government policy has been important, especially in the establishment of national forests and national parks, augmented in some instances by state and local reserves, to prevent catastrophic exploitation. Still more recently, as we shall see later in the chapter, substitution of other products for forests products has been important in reducing a demand which otherwise would have been even higher than it now is.

By slowing the amount of exploitation, this action has affected the relative importance of the various areas of exploitation, which compete with one another to supply existing demand at current market prices.

Theoretical explanation. Much of our discussion in Chapter 14, "Wheat Products," is of relevance to our present discussion of the primary production of forest

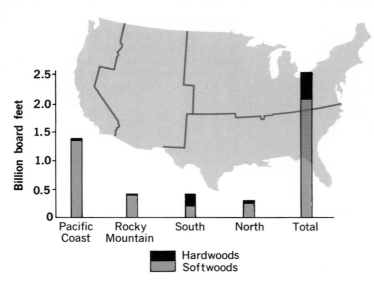

Figure 16.4 Distribution of saw timber in the United States. (After data from *Timber Trends in the United States*, GPO, Washington, D.C., 1965)

products. The reader will find that much of the theoretical explanation of the location of this type of activity is based on the land-use theories of Ricardo and von Thünen. In the von Thünen model the rent-bid function for any type of land use is determined by the transportation costs of the product. Those products which have a low slope to their rent-bid function are relatively insensitive to transportation costs and are pushed to peripheral areas of low accessibility. It is interesting to note that von Thünen placed wood production in a location of relatively high access—i.e., his second zone (see Fig. 12.3)—as this bulky, low-value product cannot bear high long-distance transport costs. Hence, in von Thünen's original model, wood had a high and steeply sloped rent-bid function, which could not possibly explain the present location of forest products. On the other hand, the wilderness surrounding the isolated state more closely approximates the present distribution of the large concentrations of forest resources, but it should be remembered that they were outside the range of economic exploitation in von Thünen's model.

In Ricardo's model, less fertile land yields lower rent; similarly, less profitable land use is relegated to less fertile areas. Tree growth is characteristically slow and represents a fairly low value of output per unit area; hence annual dollar yields per unit area are low. The better land is therefore cleared for high-yield land uses such as intensive rotational agriculture, and less profitable tree cultivation is pushed out. In addition, as we have seen in the von Thünen case, it is also pushed out to less accessible areas.

Returning to the Ricardian differential-fertility model, areas of relatively high accessibility but low inherent fertility for many types of agriculture may offer comparative advantages for sylvaculture. This appears to be the case in the sandy soil areas of the southeastern United States. Sandy soils of poor fertility for agriculture are utilized for tree growth because of the comparative advantage of this type of land use. The comparative advantage in terms of rent yields is further augmented by the climate, which promotes rapid tree growth relative to northern areas. Species of southern pine utilized for kraft-paper production can be planted and reach the required stage of maturity within twelve to twenty years. This area has therefore become important for tree cultivation.

Secondary Activity

Description, measurement, and classification. As we have mentioned, four of several secondary activities in the forest-products industries have been selected for closer examination in this chapter: sawmills and planing mills, general; veneer and plywood establishments; pulp mills; and paper mills except for building paper. In the United States, more than 60 per cent of all roundwood is destined for dimension lumber or veneer, nearly 30 per cent for pulpwood, and the small remainder for fuel wood, other industrial wood, or mine pitprops (the structuring inside underground mines).

Substage 1: sawmills and planing mills, general (SIC 2421). *Sectoral considerations.* The function performed by sawmills and planing mills is reduction of roundwood to dimension lumber of various standardized lengths and widths. The process involves cutting with saws, usually huge rotary blades, and planing with mechanized equipment. With respect to four-digit-detail activity, it is comparatively important when measured by employment, accounting for approximately 1 per cent of all manufacturing. It is less so when considered by value of shipments and value added, in each case being responsible for $6/10$ of 1 per cent. The industry is high in labor costs and intermediate in per cent of materials cost to final shipment value. Its value added as a per cent of final shipment value is just slightly below the national average (Fig. 16.5).

There are about two-thirds as many sawmills and planing mills as logging camps and contractors. Again, this is a small-establishment type of industry, with only slightly more than 300, from a total exceeding 10,000, employing more than 100 persons, and only 8 employing over 1,000.

Spatial considerations. If the sawmills and planing mills of the United States absorbed all the roundwood produced in the country, the location of the two activities might be expected to coincide closely, inasmuch as logs are both bulky and heavy and hence more costly to ship than dimension lumber or plywood. However, as we have seen, the nation's pulp and paper industry absorbs nearly one-third of the overall output of logging camps and contractors, so that the distribution of sawmills is not quite the same as that of logging camps. Sawmill and planing-mill products generally are not so important in those parts of the country where pulp mills are particularly numerous (compare Figs. 16.4, 16.5, and 16.10). Thus we find that New England and the Pacific Coast do not supply as high a percentage of the nation's sawmill and planing-mill products as of its pulpwood, whereas the East South Central region,

the West South Central region, and the Mountain West are much more important producers of the former than of the latter.

Substage 2A: veneer and plywood establishments (SIC 2432). *Sectoral considerations.* Roundwood from logging camps goes to veneer and plywood establishments, as well as to sawmills and planing mills and to pulp mills (Fig. 16.6). The function of the veneer and plywood industry is to reduce roundwood to thin strips, usually no thicker than $1/8$ inch. The process of producing both veneer and plywood begins with turning the log against knives which peel it into even strips. For veneer, these strips are usually hardwood and are glued or otherwise fastened to the exterior surfaces of various kinds of furniture or are put to similar uses. Plywood, which usually comes from softwood trees, is glued together, with the grain of each strip at right angles to the grain of the strips above and below, into sections ranging upward in thickness from less than $1/4$ inch. More than 50 per cent of such plywood is used in home construction.

The industry is of relatively minor importance when compared with the national average for all manufacturing with regard to employment, value of shipments, or value added (Fig. 16.7). It is a high-labor-cost industry, medium to high in materials cost, and slightly below the national average in terms of value added as a per cent of final shipment value. Only 667 plants are engaged in the activity, and most of these hire between 5 and 249 employees.

Spatial considerations. One would expect a concentration of this activity in areas where coniferous softwoods predominate—and one finds it there. Oregon and Washington are both significant producers, and California is not unimportant. The South is also outstanding as a region, with the South Atlantic division contributing effectively and the East South Central and West South Central regions noteworthily. The East North Central region of the Northeast is the only significant producer, and its product here is partially veneer produced from hardwood.

Linkages to tertiary activity. These linkages, shown in Figures 16.8 and 16.9, are discussed in further detail on page 270.

FOREST PRODUCTS INDUSTRIES

Secondary Activity
Substage One A: Saw Mills and Planing Mills
(SIC 2421)

1. **Function and Process**
   - **A.** Function: conversion of roundwood (logs) into dimension lumber; *some weight loss involved*
   - **B.** Process: sawing, usually with band saws

2. **Significance**
   - **A.** Per cent of all U.S. manufacturing employment: 1.01%
   - **B.** Per cent of value, all U.S. manufacturing shipments: 0.61%
   - **C.** Per cent of value added in all U.S. manufacturing: 0.63%

3. **Major Inputs**
   - **A.** Per cent of labor costs (all employees) in final shipment value: 24.87%
   - **B.** Per cent of materials costs in final shipment value: 56.12%

4. **Number and Size of Establishments**
   - **A.** Total number: 10,271
   - **B.** Size categories
     1. 4 employees or fewer: 5,697
     2. Between 5 and 99 employees: 4,258
     3. Between 100 and 249 employees: 241
     4. Between 250 and 499 employees: 49
     5. Between 500 and 999 employees: 18
     6. Over 1,000 employees: 8

Sectoral Considerations

Spatial Considerations

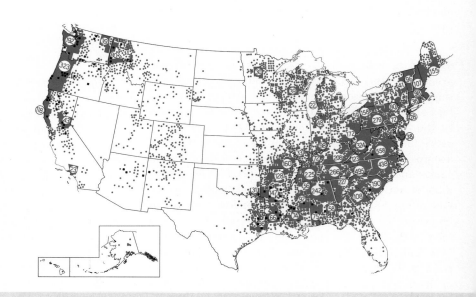

Figure 16.5 Sector-space considerations, substage one A (saw mills and planing mills—SIC 2421). For explanation of symbols, see Figure 14.3. How do these establishments compare in number, size, and location with logging camps and contractors (Fig. 16.1)?

FOREST PRODUCTS INDUSTRIES

Linkages, Substage One A–Tertiary

Geographic division of origin	Tons (000)	Per cent of goods movement by means of transport				
		Rail	Motor carrier	Private truck	Water	Other & unknown
U.S.	38,714	51.7%	11.5%	28.8%	7.9%	0.1%
South Atlantic	3,221	22.2	9.5	68.1	—	0.2
East South Central	2,800	29.9	11.3	58.8	—	—
West South Central	3,392	49.7	20.2	29.9	—	0.2
Mountain	4,995	77.9	12.3	9.8	—	—
Pacific*	20,925	58.0	10.1	17.2	14.5	0.2
Rest of U.S.	3,381	na†	na	na	na	na

*Excluding Alaska and Hawaii.
†na = not available.
Source: United States Census of Transportation, 1967.

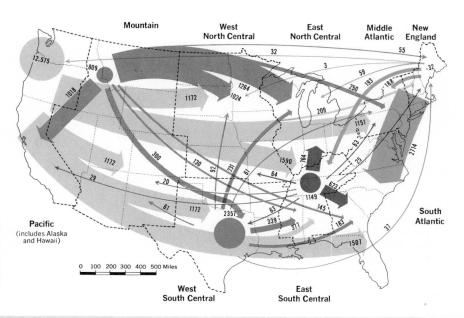

Figure 16.6 Linkages, substage one A—tertiary activity. For explanation of symbols, see Figure 15.4. Note the overwhelming movement toward the eastern United States.

FOREST PRODUCTS INDUSTRIES

Secondary Activity
Substage One B: Veneer and Plywood (SIC 2432)

1. **Function and Process**
   - A. Function: conversion of roundwood (logs) into thin sections, then into veneer and plywood; *little weight loss*
   - B. Process: peeling, polishing, gluing

2. **Significance**
   - A. Per cent of all U.S. manufacturing employment: 0.32%
   - B. Per cent of value, all U.S. manufacturing shipments: 0.35%
   - C. Per cent of value added in all U.S. manufacturing: 0.26%

3. **Major Inputs**
   - A. Per cent of labor costs (all employees) in final shipment value: 24.92%
   - B. Per cent of materials costs in final shipment value: 59.53%

4. **Number and Size of Establishments**
   - A. Total number: 667
   - B. Size categories
     1. 4 employees or fewer: 66
     2. Between 5 and 99 employees: 355
     3. Between 100 and 249 employees: 172
     4. Between 250 and 499 employees: 61
     5. Between 500 and 999 employees: 12
     6. Over 1,000 employees: 1

Sectoral Considerations

Spatial Considerations

Figure 16.7 Sector-space considerations, substage one B (veneer and plywood—SIC 2432). For explanation of symbols, see Figure 14.3. Why the clustering of larger establishments in the Northwest and South?

FOREST PRODUCTS INDUSTRIES

Linkages, Substages One A and One B–Tertiary

Sectoral Considerations

Geographic division of origin	Tons (000)	Per cent of goods movement by means of transport			
		Rail	Motor carrier	Private truck	Other & unknown
U.S.	12,227	71.1%	12.4%	16.2%	0.3%
New England	79	47.8	30.2	22.0	—
Middle Atlantic	127	19.9	42.4	36.9	0.8
East North Central	1,472	32.6	26.4	40.9	0.1
South Atlantic	1,006	21.3	25.6	53.0	0.1
East South Central	766	58.1	30.5	11.2	0.2
West South Central	333	69.5	7.6	22.9	—
Pacific*	8,024	85.7	6.4	7.5	0.4
Rest of U.S.	420	na†	na	na	na

*Excluding Alaska and Hawaii.
†na = not available.
Source: United States Census of Transportation, 1967.

Spatial Considerations

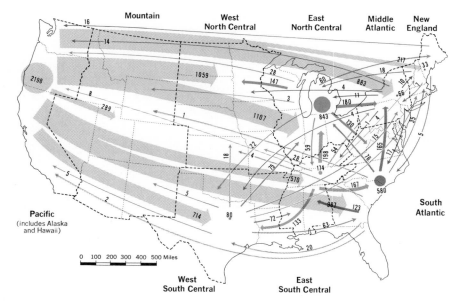

Figure 16.8 Linkages, substage one A and substage B—tertiary activity. For explanation of symbols, see Figure 15.4. Why the heavy movement to the South as well as to the Northeast?

FOREST PRODUCTS INDUSTRIES
Tertiary Activity

Sectoral Considerations

1. **Function and Process**
   A. Function: wholesaling and retailing of lumber, plywood, and other building materials (retailing emphasized here)
   B. Process: contact with customers in establishments (stores) or via mail orders

2. **Significance**
   A. Per cent of all U.S. retail labor force in retailing of lumber and other building materials: 2.01%
   B. Per cent of value of all U.S. retail sales: 2.53%

3. **Number and Size of Establishments**
   A. Total number: 23,966
   B. Size categories
      1 5 employees or fewer: 13,528
      2 Between 6 and 49 employees: 10,195
      3 Between 50 and 99 employees: 191
      4 Over 100 employees: 52

Spatial Considerations

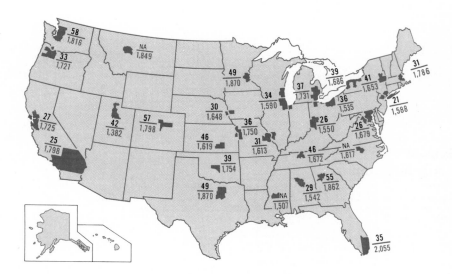

Figure 16.9 Sector-space considerations, tertiary stage— lumber, plywood, and other building materials. For explanation of symbols, see Figure 14.7. Some diversified retail outlets are not included.

Substage 2B: pulp mills (SIC 2611). It is misleading to classify pulp mills as a separate substage behind veneer and plywood because most of the raw materials for pulp mills comes directly from the logging camps and contractors, and not by way of sawmills and planing mills or veneer and plywood establishments. (This is a major problem in classification; in geography, as elsewhere, our classifications sometimes embarrass us with their logic, so that we must explain them or finesse them in a subjective way.) When pulpwood enters into the pulp mill, it has been cut into standard lengths of 6 to 8 feet and peeled of bark.

Sectoral considerations. The function of pulp mills is the extraction from wood of *cellulose,* a substance found in the cell walls of the fibrous portions of many kinds of plant life. Cellulose is available in cotton, corn, sugar cane, wheat, bamboo, and many other botanical forms, including wood, which is the primary commercial source. On the average, cellulose accounts for about 56 per cent of the weight of growing timber. It almost invariably occurs in *lignin,* an imperfectly understood combination of compounds which bind the cellulose fibers together, and with *pentosan,* a complex combination of carbohydrates. The extraction of the cellulose from wood is known as *pulping,* and we are interested at this point in the mills specializing in this aspect of manufacture.

The pulping process can be either *mechanical* or *chemical.* In the mechanical process, the pulpwood is ground into small fragments, which either are forwarded directly to an associated paper mill or are stored in bulk for subsequent shipment and papermaking operations. The mechanical process produces cheap paper, especially newsprint.

Three chemical processes generally are recognized: the *sulfite,* the *sulfate,* and the *soda.* The first two are used most commonly. All involve the chemical cooking of wood which has been ground into chips, the major objective being the removal of lignin and pentosan. The sulfite process, which is an acid reaction, is particularly effective on spruce and most other softwoods except pine, the resins of which are not removed by this process. The sulfate and soda processes are alkaline in reaction, the difference between them being appreciably a matter of the amount of sulfur present in the cooking

solution. They can utilize a variety of softwoods. Besides its use in production of high-quality papers, the sulfate process is generally important for the production of kraft, usually brown, wrapping paper, most of which in the United States comes from the pulp of the southern pine.

Pulp produced chemically is of a much higher cellulose content than that produced mechanically, and consequently it forms papers that are smoother, stronger, and more durable. However, its ratio of yield to input is less than that of mechanical pulp, which, as we have seen, consists largely of ground-up pulpwood. After removal from the pulping machines, chemically produced pulp may or may not be bleached, depending upon its ultimate use. Subsequently, it is forwarded to the papermaking machinery, either in the same building or many miles away.

A *semichemical* process of pulping involves partial treatment of pulpwood utilizing any of the three chemical processes described above and subsequent mechanical action. The resulting pulp is intermediate between chemical and mechanical pulp in quality and is higher in yield than chemical pulp but lower than mechanical pulp. It is used mainly for the making of cardboard and wrapping paper.

This is a small industry, however measured. The per cent of manufacturing employment is extremely low, and the value of its manufacturing shipments and the value added in the manufacturing process are almost as low. By Alderfer and Michl criteria, its ratios of both labor and materials costs to final shipment value are at the intermediate level in comparison with all manufacturing in the United States. Its value added as a per cent of manufactured shipment value is slightly lower than that for all manufacturing in the country. Only 61 plants are engaged entirely in this activity, and they range surprisingly in size, with 32 employing fewer than 100, and 29 employing more than 100 (Fig. 16.10). Other plants, not shown in Figure 16.10, produce both pulp and paper.

Spatial considerations. We have indicated the importance of softwoods for cheaper kinds of paper and of both hardwoods and softwoods for more expensive papers. The distribution of pulp mills in the United States reflects these various activities. Unfortunately, since so few plants are involved, the output from the various states cannot be given because of the census disclosure rule, which stipulates that information cannot be published which may reveal an excessive insight into a given producer. However, we do note that the South and the far West are the outstanding producers, in that order, with New England rating rather heavily.

Substage 2C: paper mills, except building paper (SIC 2621). *Sectoral considerations.* The function of paper mills is obvious—the further processing of pulp into actual paper. We have anticipated some of the actual processes in the discussion of pulping. Pulp may come from the pulping section of an integrated operation, or it may be shipped varying distances from a pulp mill. Wastepaper, collected from urban areas and elsewhere, may be added at this time. In the United States, about one-third of all incoming material to the paper mill is such waste, and the remaining two-thirds is wood pulp. The paper mill begins its process with a beating operation, which involves the mechanical rolling of pulp under water, so that the cellulose fibers break up and intermesh still further than when they were at the pulp stage. Dyes, chalk fibers, and other substances designed for special purposes may be added during this beating operation. The product is then refined, so that the density of the slushy material that it has now become is more even and the fiber lengths more or less uniform. The slush then enters and actual papermaking machines, where it is poured evenly over a series of continuously moving belts, pressed, dried, sized, sometimes *calendered* (passed over huge rollers with glossy surfaces so that it becomes "slick"), and finally rolled into huge cylinders for shipment. The slick paper is desired by the so-called slick magazines, and an even higher gloss can be obtained if a coat of fine clay is added before calendering (Fig. 16.11).

This industry is more important to the national economy than that of pulping, employing nearly $7/10$ of 1 per cent of all manufacturing workers and accounting for an even higher percentage of all manufacturing shipments and of the value added to all manufacturing. It is high as to labor costs and intermediate as to materials cost, and its value added exceeds the national average as a per cent of final shipment value. A total of 354 establishments were at work in this industry in

1967, and their size ranged from very small to very large. Except for the 21 smallest establishments, an effectively large number are found at each of the various categories of employment size used in this book (Fig. 16.11). Of the grand total of establishments, 247 were not integrated in any way with the pulp mill, and 107 were so integrated. In some instances, more than one paper mill was integrated with the same pulp mill.

Spatial considerations. The geographic location of paper mills is especially concentrated in the Northeast of the United States, whether considered by actual number of units or by value added. The East North Central division is a particularly heavy producer, but the New England and Middle Atlantic divisions are also important. The South is also a very important producer, but the West is not nearly as significant in the production of this commodity as in the production of lumber products.

Institutional explanation. We reserved an explanation of the location and linkages of the various substages of secondary activity in forest-products industries until after we have seen the basic sectoral and spatial features of each because all are so intertwined functionally that their explanation sometimes is found in their linkages.

Historical factors. We mentioned previously the historical importance of wood to man as a fuel and as a source of material for the construction of houses, tools, and a variety of other necessities and luxuries. We stressed particularly its role in northwestern Europe, which, in its primeval stage, is known to have been heavily forested. The historical background for the use of roundwood for dimension lumber and fuel has been simple in the sense that resources which initially were near at hand were cut away both for their use and for purposes of clearing the land initially for agriculture and subsequently for urban settlement.

Making paper from plant fiber is a very old art—at least 2,000 years old. It may well have been a Chinese discovery, and knowledge of it may have filtered slowly from China to the Middle East, to southern Europe, to northern Europe, and finally to European colonial empires. Not until the fifteenth century, however, did paper exceed vellum (animal skin, especially lambskin) as a writing material. Cheap as well as quality paper soon came to be known, and by the time of European colonization, papermaking had been heavily integrated into European culture and soon was carried overseas by the colonists. The first paper mill in the United States, for example, was constructed in Germantown, Pennsylvania, in 1690.

Prior to the invention of papermaking machinery in 1799, the making of paper was appreciably a hand operation, dependent upon rags for fibers. Mechanical production, however, resulted in a demand for new sources of fiber, and wood was one of the first to be given serious attention. By 1850, the early imprints of today's pulp and paper industry had made their appearance, and subsequent developments involved technological improvements and expansion of capital equipment. Modern machinery can produce paper in continuous sheets at a rate of over 20 miles per hour.

The peeling of logs into veneer and plywood is a very late technological development, which has reached the height of significance only in the twentieth century.

Market prices and transportation costs. The present geographic location of the various stages of the forest-products industry can be effectively understood by envisaging the obtainable forests as only slowly replaceable and therefore retreating in successive waves of exploitation, each farther from ultimate markets than its predecessor. These markets for both dimension lumber and paper are mainly large populations and hence urban areas. The location of the various stages of production therefore can be expected at some point along the route from raw materials to market.

With gradual regrowth of new timber in the cut-over land and, more recently, with the actual planting of trees through agricultural practice in large tracts—especially under humid subtropical climate, where a tree can grow to minimum pulp size in twelve years and minimum log size in twenty years—the exploitation moves back again to the sites that are nearer the ultimate market, and so the cycle begins anew.

Of the various stages of manufacture, we have seen that the actual logging operations must be at the site of the raw materials. Since those materials are cut away with use, logging camps are forever on the move, choosing the sites which are most advantageous in view of current prices and transportation costs.

Sawmills must be located very carefully with respect to both raw materials and markets, inasmuch as the incoming product is roundwood, which is both bulky and heavy. Sawmills will tend to locate very near the logging camps, unless a favorable means of transport, such as a river, can be utilized to link the two. The same can be said of pulp mills and veneer and plywood establishments, which, like sawmills, consume roundwood. Also, logs must not be permitted to become too dry because they will crack and be ruined for lumber or veneer purposes. If they are not to be used fairly soon, they must be stored—or shipped—in water.

The location of paper mills is something else again, especially in that a substantial share of their incoming materials—in the United States, about one-third—is wastepaper, which is present in largest quantities in urban areas. Location near urban areas, or in excellent transportation juxtaposition to such areas, thereby assures not only a good position regarding market but also an ample supply of important imcoming material. Since pulp can be packed into bulk bales, which are comparatively light and of a rectangular size that is easily packed into a cargo carrier, it is therefore relatively economical to transport to the paper mill. Thus we can anticipate a tendency for paper mills to locate nearer to markets.

Where a site is so advantageous as to be in a favorable position regarding both incoming pulpwood and markets, that site may well be selected.

Theoretical explanation. Secondary production involves sawmills and planing mills, veneer and plywood production, and pulp and paper mills. In the case of the first two types of activities, there occur significant Weberian weight reductions on raw-material inputs; i.e., these inputs, in Weberian terms, are "gross" materials. Hence, processing installations are pulled toward the localized raw materials rather than toward market locations.

As discussed earlier in this chapter, pulp and paper production involves many different types of processes according to the nature of the product, ranging from kraft packing paper, through newsprint, to fine book and specialized types of paper. However, even though the industry is characterized by such diversity, we can make some general conceptual observations on the forces influencing its location. Two factors are of im-

FOREST PRODUCTS INDUSTRIES

Secondary Activity
Substage One C: Pulp Mills (SIC 2611)

Sectoral Considerations

1. **Function and Process**
   A. Function: conversion of roundwood (short logs) into wood pulp; *no weight loss*
   B. Process: chipping, grinding, sometimes chemical action, mechanical intertwining of fibers

2. **Significance**
   A. Per cent of all U.S. manufacturing employment: 0.07%
   B. Per cent of value, all U.S. manufacturing shipments: 0.13%
   C. Per cent of value added in all U.S. manufacturing: 0.12%

3. **Major Inputs**
   A. Per cent of labor costs (all employees) in final shipment value: 17.12%
   B. Per cent of materials costs in final shipment value: 55.23%

4. **Number and Size of Establishments**
   A. Total number: 61
   B. Size categories
   1   4 employees or fewer: 16
   2   Between   5 and   99 employees: 16
   3   Between 100 and 249 employees: 7
   4   Between 250 and 499 employees: 13
   5   Between 500 and 999 employees: 6
   6   Over 1,000 employees: 3

Spatial Considerations

Figure 16.10 Sector-space considerations, substage one C (pulp mills—SIC 2611). For explanation of symbols, see Figure 14.3. The maps show pulp mills only, and not pulp and paper mills; this is why there are so few.

FOREST PRODUCTS INDUSTRIES

Secondary Activity
Substage Two C: Paper Mills, Except Building Paper (SIC 2621)

1. **Function and Process**
   A. Function: conversion of wood pulp into paper (sometimes in establishments integrated with wood pulp mills); *no weight loss*
   B. Process: either mechanical or chemical, depending upon end product (see text, p. 266)

2. **Significance**
   A. Per cent of all U.S. manufacturing employment: 0.71%
   B. Per cent of value, all U.S. manufacturing shipments: 0.87%
   C. Per cent of value added in all U.S. manufacturing: 0.90%

3. **Major Inputs**
   A. Per cent of labor costs (all employees) in final shipment value: 23.67%
   B. Per cent of materials costs in final shipment value: 52.34%

4. **Number and Size of Establishments**
   A. Total number: 107* 247† 354
   B. Size categories:
      1 4 employees or fewer: — * 21† 21
      2 Between   5 and   99: 3* 90† 93
      3 Between 100 and 249: 9* 75† 84
      4 Between 250 and 499: 23* 43† 66
      5 Between 500 and 999: 39* 13† 52
      6 Over 1,000 employees: 33*   5† 38

*Integrated with pulp mill.
†Not integrated with pulp mill.

Sectoral Considerations

Spatial Considerations

Figure 16.11 Sector-space considerations, substage two C (paper mills—SIC 2621). For explanation of symbols, see Figure 14.3.

269

portance in the siting of mills: first, an adequate water supply and, second, the pollution characteristics of the industry. The iron and steel industry is by far the largest industrial consumer of water, and the pulp and paper industry is the second largest. Pulp- and paper-mill sites therefore must be at points where there is adequate water supply. In terms of pollution, water pollution occurs as a result of heated and waste effluence, and noxious fumes also are emitted. These factors tend to keep mill sites away from major urban locations; however, since it is only in relatively recent years that social sensitivity to industrial pollution has developed, such considerations are more significant in new mill sitings, with older mills already occupying urban locations making technical changes in the hope of meeting recent pollution regulations.

As we have seen, pulp and paper mills occur both in integrated installations and separately. Pulp mills tend to be raw-material-oriented because the transport costs on pulpwood are high (there exists a low ratio of value to weight) relative to transport costs on pulp. There is, however, no significant weight loss in the pulping processes, and hence, as pulpwood may be considered closer to a Weberian "pure" raw material than a "gross" raw material, there is no strong pull to this input on the basis of weight loss alone.

Keeping the above siting observations in mind, we can say that paper mills as separate entities tend to be market-oriented. Again, pulp, the localized raw material, is a pure raw material imparting the whole of its weight to the finished product. As water and filler, etc., are used in papermaking in addition to pulpwood, the material index of paper is probably equal to unity. On this basis, isodapanes developed from isotims constructed around raw-material sources and the market location would be elliptical, with the long axis of the ellipse represented by the transportation route joining raw-material sources with the market location.

Tertiary Activity

The construction industry is a very substantial consumer of the products of sawmills and planing mills and of plywood; the furniture industry, of veneer; and the printing and publishing industry, of paper. An important aspect of tertiary activity for these products,

therefore, is wholesaling, carried on either by independent firms or by branch plants of manufacturing firms. Those establishments selling lumber products tend to be located favorably with respect to ultimate population, especially the heavier sections of population increase, where residential and other construction is particularly active. Printing establishments may well have their own pulp mills, paper mills, pulp and paper mills, and wholesaling arrangements. Or, as we have said, they may purchase from independent wholesalers. In any case, there is a tendency for such wholesalers to be located favorably with respect to their own markets. Those markets, in turn, may well be publishing firms, which, although they serve the general public, produce a commodity which is fairly high in value relative to weight and can stand the cost of appreciable shipment to the market (Fig. 16.12).

The tertiary stages hence are largely market-oriented activities. Like most tertiary production, they are labor-intensive relative to raw materials; this is especially true in the case of furniture making and printing activities. Printing utilizes technical labor inputs that are obtainable only in the larger urban centers, and these also constitute the major markets for printed outputs such as books, magazines, and newspapers. Because of the immediacy of the consumption of newspapers, they must, at least for major sales volumes, be produced in, or adjacent to, major markets. Printing is therefore a higher-order function in a Christallerian hierarchy.

The role of export and import to the various stages of manufacture of the selected wood products varies with the product. The United States is a modest net exporter of roundwood, especially saw logs and veneer logs, and a net importer of pulpwood. It is more than noteworthy as an importer of dimension lumber and sawn wood, plywood, veneer, pulp, and especially newsprint. Most of the supply comes from Canada. In location, this means particular significance for ports on the Great Lakes–St. Lawrence system and along the Atlantic and Pacific seaboards which receive and send those commodities. These concepts are outlined in some detail in the next section of this chapter, and can be understood more clearly in an examination of Figure 16.13, where the relative positions of the United States and Canada are shown.

FOREST PRODUCTS INDUSTRIES

Linkages, Substages One C and Two C to Tertiary

Geographic division of origin	Tons (000)	Per cent of goods movement by means of transport				
		Rail	Motor carrier	Private truck	Water	Other & unknown
U.S.	25,370	71.9%	22.7%	3.0%	2.2%	0.2%
New England	4,183	76.6	21.6	1.2	0.1	0.5
Middle Atlantic	4,400	49.8	44.9	5.2	—	0.1
East North Central	4,332	64.0	29.6	6.1	—	0.4
South Atlantic	3,139	82.0	11.7	1.2	5.1	—
East South Central	3,420	79.0	12.6	1.7	6.7	—
West South Central	1,367	88.7	5.5	3.2	2.4	0.2
Pacific†	3,284	77.8	15.6	2.2	4.2	0.2
Rest of U.S.	1,245	na*	na	na	na	na

*na = not available.
†Excluding Alaska and Hawaii.
Source: United States Census of Transportation, 1967.

Sectoral Considerations

Spatial Considerations

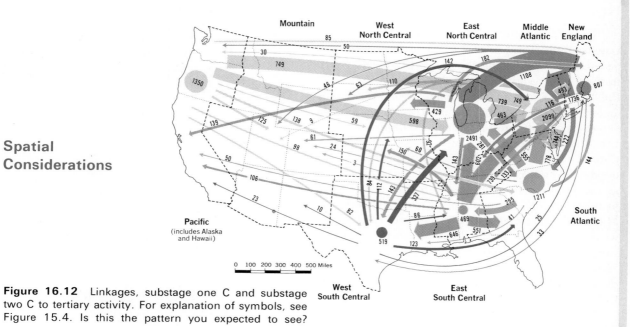

Figure 16.12 Linkages, substage one C and substage two C to tertiary activity. For explanation of symbols, see Figure 15.4. Is this the pattern you expected to see?

271

Canada

Canada produces far less roundwood than the United States—some 5 per cent of the world's annual cut, as compared with more than 15 per cent for the United States. In disposition, slightly more is made into pulpwood and correspondingly less into saw logs, veneer logs, etc. Rather surprisingly, less is used for fuel than in the United States, although the amount is very small for both countries.

Canada exports very little in the way of saw logs, but does send a small proportion of pulpwood—some 2 per cent of its total cut—out of the country, especially to the United States, and an almost equally small percentage of dimension lumber is exported. However, nearly one-third of all wood pulp and nearly 70 per cent of all paper and paperboard are exported. The largest item of export is newsprint, of which over 95 per cent is exported, mostly to the United States. Directly or indirectly, exports from Canadian forests account for about one-fourth of that country's total exports.

Primary, Secondary, and Tertiary Activity

Description, measurement, and classification. Canada ranks third in the world in both total and accessible forest—behind the Soviet Union and Brazil in the first category and behind the Soviet Union and the United States in the second. Significantly, the amount of forest considered inaccessible in Canada exceeds accessible forest by an approximate ratio of 5:3. Like those in the Soviet Union, about four-fifths of Canada's forests are coniferous, and the remainder are deciduous (Figs. 5.5 and 16.13). Coniferous stands reach across the country longitudinally, fringed on the south in relatively low latitudes by deciduous trees in the Maritimes–St. Lawrence–Great Lakes area and at somewhat high latitudes in the Prairie provinces. There are very few deciduous trees in the Mountain and Pacific West. Over one-half of the total forest land is in the three provinces of Quebec, British Columbia, and Ontario, and nearly one-fourth is in Quebec alone.

About 91 per cent of the productive forests of Canada are in the possession of the Crown, and 9 per cent are owned by corporations and individuals, with some 3 per cent of the overall total in private woodlots. Most of the Crown land is administered by the provincial governments, and only a small portion by the federal government. A right to cut timber has been granted on some 23 per cent of all Canadian productive forest land.

In the early 1970s, some 3,700 sawmills of varying size were in operation in Canada, receiving roundwood from an even larger number of logging camps and contractors. As in the United States, there is a strong tendency to be raw-material-oriented, unless inexpensive water transportation is available for floating the logs from the original site of felling to a mill site located

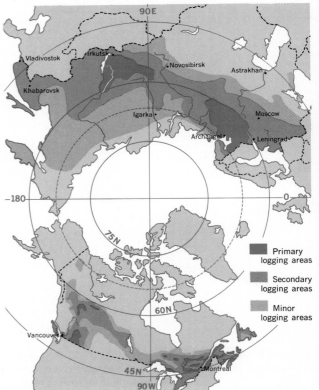

Figure 16.13 Areas of forest exploitation in Canada and the Soviet Union. [Data for Soviet Union after Robert M. Bone, "The Soviet Forest Resource," *The Canadian Geographer,* **10** (2): 106, 1966. Data for Canada compiled by text authors from various sources]

closer to market. This is particularly true in the western provinces. In the east, where the sites of raw materials and markets are in closer juxtaposition, a distinctive orientation is less discernible.

As of the early 1970s, there were 40 pulp mills, 45 paper mills, and 77 pulp and paper mills in Canada. Of these, 61 were in Quebec, 40 in Ontario, and 29 in British Columbia.

Explanation. Both the institutional and the theoretical explanations of the present location of the various stages of economic activity in Canada are generally similar to those previously given for the United States. One force which has been particularly strong with respect to Canada but which does not have a counterpart in the United States is the pull of exports; hence much of the industry, especially in Quebec and the Maritimes and along the north shores of the Great Lakes, is oriented not so much to a domestic Canadian as to an export market, in which the United States plays a major role. The market attraction, therefore, is shifted geographically to accommodate the force of such export.

The Soviet Union

We have mentioned that the Soviet Union is the leading producer of forest products and that it contains nearly 20 per cent of the world's total forest reserves and a slightly higher percentage of all accessible forests. These immense reserves include both coniferous and deciduous species, with the former occupying 80 per cent of the forest-covered area, and the latter 20 per cent.

All forests in the Soviet Union are national property, and administrative policies and procedures have varied sharply from time to time. The forests have been classified into three groups for purposes of administration and utilization. Group I involves forests in which there is very little exploitation. Stands are felled only where their usefulness for other purposes declines noticeably. These include nurseries, green belts, resorts, sanctuaries, shelter belts, and analogous categories.

Occupying less than 3 per cent of the land of the Soviet Union, such forests contain some 5.5 per cent of the stands of timber. They are found in various parts of the country, but generally in correspondence with population density. Group II contains exploited forests in which the cut-growth ratio must be carefully regulated. Commercial cutting is allowed except for a strip some 4 miles wide along either bank of the Volga and certain rivers. Group II stands make up some 8 per cent of all forest area, contain about 5 per cent of all timber, and are found especially in the central and southwestern portion of the European section of the country. Group III involves all other forest lands in the Soviet Union —some 85 to 90 per cent (accounts vary) of the remaining area and stand. Nearly all actual extraction now comes from Group III, the reserves of which are so large that a cut-growth balance is not a major consideration. Indeed, many of the older trees in this forest are overdue for harvest and are deteriorating in quality because of age.[2]

The main product from Soviet forests is softwood, of which most is in the Asian section of the country. Inasmuch as the primary direction of demand, both domestic and foreign, is from the west, the country faces a significant problem of distance between supply and demand. Although such north-south rivers as the Ob, Yenisei, and Lena allow some movement of logs by water toward the Trans-Siberian and associated railways, nearly two-thirds of all timber shipment is by rail—an expensive operation in which there is strong competition with other semifinished and processed materials that also move by rail.[3] As a partial result, sites of actual timber exploitation in the Soviet Union are in the European section of the country to a greater degree than is desirable in terms of the overall distribution of reserves. Over 50 per cent of the harvest is in the European section (excluding the Ural Mountains), and slightly less is in the Asian section (including the Urals).

[2] For details, see A. D. Bukshtynov, *Forest Resources of the U.S.S.R. and the World,* Ministry of Agriculture, U.S.S.R., Moscow, 1959. (English translation published by the National Science Foundation and the U.S. Department of Agriculture, 1960; see especially pp. 35ff.)

[3] Robert M. Bone, "The Soviet Forest Resources," *The Canadian Geographer,* **10**:94–116 (especially 96–97), 1966.

Only about 40 per cent of the wood cut in the Soviet Union is destined for saw logs and veneer logs, and only 7 per cent for pulpwood. Nearly 25 per cent is used as fuel, nearly as much for miscellaneous industrial purposes, and almost 5 per cent for mine pitprops. The major difference between conditions of utilization in the Soviet Union and in the United States is a higher proportion of the wood used as fuel and a correspondingly lower proportion for saw logs, veneer logs, etc.

The distribution of pulp mills reflects the strong orientation to raw materials that we have seen in Canada and the United States, despite the fact that the profit motive is at least theoretically lacking in the Soviet Union, and matters of cost and price should not play so vital a role as in countries where the private sector is significant. Combined pulp and paper plants and paper plants tend to be oriented especially toward internal markets.

Brazil

We are treating Brazil briefly in this chapter not only because it is a major producer and consumer but also because it exhibits an entirely different set of priorities from those of the more developed countries in terms of use. Nearly 90 per cent of all the annual Brazilian cut is used for fuel, and most of the remainder for saw logs, veneer logs, etc. Only a tiny fraction is manufactured into pulp. In Brazil, the strip of tropical rain forest along the southeastern coast is especially prominent as a supply area to nearby dense populations, although there is an increasing tendency toward reliance upon the enormous reserves of the interior. A very small amount of sawn wood is exported, but essentially all the very sizable annual harvest—between 7 and 8 per cent of the world's total exploitation—is utilized at home, mainly for fuel.

Chapter 17

Products From Fishing

The United States and Canada are comparatively minor producers and consumers in a worldwide fishing industry that more than tripled in volume between 1950 and 1970. The United States currently produces less than 4 per cent of this overall catch, and Canada less than 2 per cent. Inasmuch as the interest of this book is chiefly in the reasons for location of primary, secondary, and tertiary stages of economic activity as seen in the United States and, in some measure, Canada, we shall carry on during this chapter with our examination of these two countries. However, we shall give some attention to other nations which are heavy producers. (For a review of leading nations, see Fig. 17.1.)

The Physical And Biological Environments

Our general discussion of the world's physical and biological environments in Chapter 2, while containing a number of descriptions and classifications of those con-

ditions in the world, does not provide specialized information for better understanding of commercial fishing. That fishing is usually separated, in terms of physical and biological conditions, into freshwater and saltwater categories.

Fresh Water

Nearly two-thirds of the world's freshwater fish are taken in eastern and southern Asia. A substantial portion of these is raised in shallow ponds, flooded fields, and inlets and are fed artificially. Technically, this type of activity is agriculture rather than fishing, and the natural environment does not play so crucial and direct a role as it would if the fish were forced to fend for themselves. Where fish are not "domesticated" but are caught from waterways and water bodies, the natural environment assumes a more direct and commanding role. It is not, however, excessively restrictive. Freshwater fish are taken in the tropics, in the middle latitudes, and in the high latitudes. The north-south range of their global distribution is thus as extensive as that

275

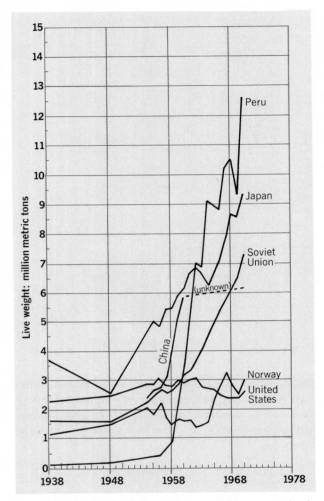

Figure 17.1 Catch of the six largest fishing countries in the world. (After FAO, *Yearbook of Fishery Statistics*) News sources indicate that Peru's catch has dropped sharply since 1970 because of overfishing.

of agriculture, and in the Northern Hemisphere, at least, it is more so.

Specific natural conditions vary, of course, with locality. However, most freshwater fish are taken in shallow rivers and streams. Even in larger and deeper water bodies, such as the Great Lakes, they are caught chiefly in the shallows, where most of their food occurs. The relationship of freshwater fish to water temperature, food supply, and other relevant conditions is not markedly unlike that of maritime fish, which we shall consider in succeeding paragraphs.

Salt Water

Nearly three-fourths of the earth's surface is covered with water, of which the oceans constitute all but a fraction. Inasmuch as the oceans contain myriads of living organisms, they might be expected to provide man with far more raw materials than they do now. In fact, their potential is largely unknown. We are certain, however, that the life they contain is very unevenly distributed, both horizontally and vertically. This is true both of *pelagic* life, which tends to inhabit the surface waters, and of *demersal* life, which tends to inhabit the ocean floors, especially in shallow waters.

Plankton. Fish, like organisms, must receive nourishment in order to exist. A clue to their world distribution thus lies in the location of their sources of nourishment. A basic source is *plankton*—tiny, sometimes microscopic, forms of plant and animal life drifting passively in the water.[1] The animal forms of plankton are called *zooplankton,*[2] and the plant forms, *phytoplankton*. The live forms of the former feed upon the latter, and both are food for small fish, which are eaten by still larger fish, thus creating a *food-supply chain* to the largest forms of oceanic zoological life. Of course, the chain is not always a continuum; some large as well as small fish and sea-dwelling mammals eat the plankton directly,[3] and there are many other exceptional cases. Nevertheless, the supply of plankton—more specifically, of phytoplankton—is a highly critical factor in determining the number of fish which can exist in both oceanic and fresh water. Even more important is the annual rate of phytoplankton *growth,* which acts as a control to the annual fish increase, for obviously no more fish can exist than can be fed. The Malthusian doctrine appears to be appropriate even to fish!

Sunlight and certain nutrient substances and gases are basic requirements to the existence of phytoplankton. Water temperature is also important. Although varying with latitude and season, sunlight tends to penetrate effectively the upper 250 to 300 feet of oceanic

[1] A few fish feed on higher forms of plant life growing in shallow water, but their numbers appear to be small.
[2] The term *zooplankton* is sometimes used to include fish eggs as well as the actual organisms.
[3] Among these are some whales and sharks.

waters, and live phytoplankton are not found extensively at lower depths. Nitrates, phosphates, carbon, and other necessary plant nutrients are derived appreciably from decaying plant and animal tissues which sink to lower levels. The phosphates, particularly, accumulate there. A portion of these nutrients is brought continuously to the zone of sunlight penetration by upwellings, currents, river and stream discharges (which themselves contain additional nutrients), and other forms of water circulation. Thus they are made available to the phytoplankton. In shallows, such as continental shelves, water movements are especially effective in providing nutrients to the plankton, for the distance of water movement there is not great. The two most necessary gases, carbon dioxide and oxygen, are usually present in the upper water levels and hence are available to the phytoplankton. Limitations imposed by temperature, while recognized, are as yet not well known. Temperature differences do not appear to limit commercial fishing excessively as an activity, for fish are caught in latitudes ranging from the tropics to the subpolar areas.

Phytoplankton thus are concentrated primarily in shallow waters overlying continental shelves. In addition, they appear to be present but unevenly distributed in the surface waters of oceans, being more numerous where upwellings and ocean currents bring nutrients to the zone of sunlight penetration. The mixing of warm and cold currents adds to the effectiveness of the circulation and to the plankton supply, for each type of current contains its own mixture of nutrients, gases, and other requirements of phytoplankton existence.

The growth of phytoplankton appears to go on at all times of the year, but varies in intensity with the season at higher latitudes because of differing rates of efficiency of water penetration by sunlight at different times of the year. During winter the phytoplankton count is low in these latitudes, and the nutrients accumulate. With early spring comes a "burst" of phytoplankton, which thrive on the stored nutrient supply. In late spring the zooplankton and other predators "graze" the phytoplankton excessively, and the numbers of the latter diminish. Nutrients accumulate once again, and coincidentally many of the zooplankton die or are consumed. In the late fall the phytoplankton suddenly become numerous again, although less so than in the preceding spring.

In contrast, tropical phytoplankton appear to experience little, if any, seasonal fluctuation in growth.

Zooplankton exist both with the phytoplankton and at slightly lower depths in the water. In the latter case, they feed from phytoplankton and other residue which have sunk beneath the zone of sunlight penetration.

Despite its seasonal fluctuation at intermediate latitudes, the plankton supply per unit of water appears to be more plentiful there than in the tropics. However, the supply is not uniformly distributed in either intermediate or tropical latitudes. Instead, it is notably abundant over continental shelves and other shallows, in ocean currents, and near upwellings of undersea water. It appears to be most abundant where these features are combined.

Plankton, shoals, and fish. Feeding directly or indirectly upon plankton, the world's saltwater fish are most numerous in the shoals underlain by continental shelves. For many demersal varieties, cod, rosefish, hake, haddock, halibut, flounder, and others,[4] the type of ocean floor is also an important consideration. Most demeral fish feed directly from invertebrates, which, in turn, feed from the food-supply chain leading eventually to plankton. However, most invertebrates shun soft ocean bottoms of mud and muck, choosing instead the harder floors. Hence demersal fish are more numerous where the shoals are made up of hard materials (Fig. 17.2). The pelagic varieties—herring, pilchard, anchovies, menhaden, mackerel, tuna, and others—may migrate much farther from the shallows in their search for food, but even they appear to be in most plentiful supply over or near continental shelves (Figs. 17.3 and 17.4).

On the basis of existing knowledge, therefore, we can say that the world's maritime fish are abundant in the vicinities of continental shelves and in the active ocean currents and upwellings, notably where currents of differing temperatures come together. They are most numerous in places satisfying all three of these requirements. Moreover, *schools* of fish tend to occur most often in these last-named places of optimum conditions; here it is possible to drop a net and bring up a catch dominated by a single fish type. In other places the fish

[4] Including the majority of crustaceans and mollusks.

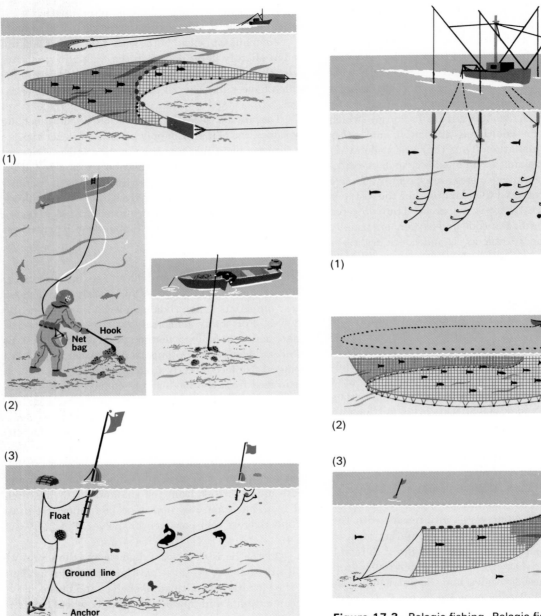

Figure 17.2 Demersal fishing. Demersal fishing is the taking of marine life from the ocean floor: (1) trawling the ocean floor; (2) lifting sponges, either by diving or by hooking from a boat; (3) sinking baited hooks to the ocean floor to catch halibut. (After *Commercial Fishing Gear*, U.S. Fish and Wildlife Circ. 48)

Figure 17.3 Pelagic fishing. Pelagic fishing is the taking of marine life from water levels above the ocean floor (cf. Figure 17.2): (1) trolling for salmon; (2) purse seining for menhaden; (3) using gill nets. The three drawings are self-explanatory except for gill netting, in which fish become entwined by their gills in the net and are taken from the water when the net is withdrawn. (After *Commercial Fishing Gear*, U.S. Fish and Wildlife Service Circ. 48)

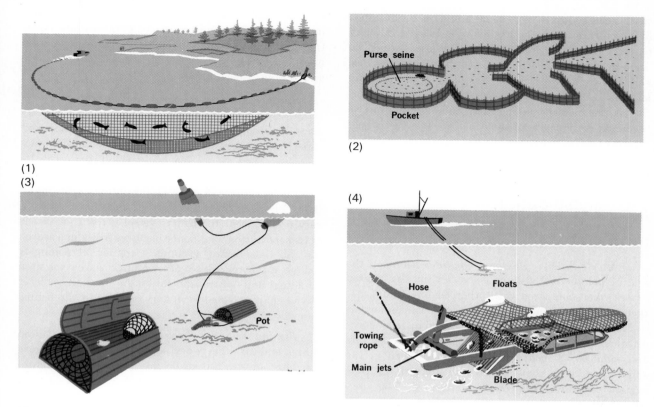

Figure 17.4 Fishing near the shore. This involves both demersal and pelagic fishing, but especially the former. (1) A haul seine; (2) a sardine weir; (3) lobster pots; (4) a hydraulic surf clam dredge. (After *Commercial Fishing Gear,* U.S. Fish and Wildlife Service Circ. 48)

appear to be not only reduced in number but also more diversified as to genera, species, etc. Nets dropped here will yield a leaner and more heterogeneous harvest.

Plankton, Fish, and the Human Diet

We have noted in previous chapters that eating meat is a very inefficient method of converting natural foods into human muscular and mental energy. As yet we can only estimate the efficiency of using fish toward the same end. Estimates show that only about 1 ton of fish is produced for every 1,000 tons of plankton made available in the oceans. For certain larger fish, the efficiency is even less. The loss is due appreciably to inefficiencies in the oceanic food-supply chain. Each fish which eats plankton or another fish utilizes only a part of its food to build flesh. If that fish is consumed by another fish and it, in turn, is eaten by another, much food value is lost in converting the plankton at the bottom of the food-supply chain to the fish which man eventually catches and eats. Obviously, it would be far more efficient for man to eat plankton directly, and experiments toward this end are being conducted. Doubtless one reason we have not given the matter more serious consideration is that the present inefficiency is not felt as financial loss. Man has essentially no capital investment in the food-supply chain of ocean life and is not so sensitive to losses there as he would be, for example, in agriculture, where he has invested heavily in many parts of the world. Furthermore, the losses which do occur in the ocean are hidden beneath the water surface and thus are not so easily appraised as those which are more intimately a part of man's daily living. Nevertheless, the inefficiencies do exist, and only now are we becoming truly aware of them.

Description, Measurement, and Classification

The United States

Primary activity. *Sectoral considerations.* If the role of commercial fishing is modest in the United States when compared with other leading fishing nations in terms of tonnage catch, it is even less important to the national economy when measured by labor force or value of product. Only about 13,000 vessel operators and some 60,000 boat operators are involved in the activity, and only about 200,000 are engaged, full time or part time, directly in commercial fishing.[5] This compares with more than 3 million farm operators and employees and nearly 19 million in manufacturing. The value of the annual fish catch in the United States is nearly $600 million, compared with about $40 billion for all agricultural products sold and about $600 billion for all manufactured products. This particular case study is concerned with a minor economic activity when measured in traditional terms. One reason for the low rank, which also exists in Canada, is that neither country has developed worldwide fishing fleets, as have Japan, the Soviet Union (both of which we shall discuss in this chapter), and a number of countries in northwestern Europe.

Interestingly, about one-half of the total annual fish catch in the United States is for human consump-

[5] A vessel is of 5 registered tons or more. Such fishing vessels account for about three-fourths of the country's annual catch. The 60,000 boats (of less than 5 registered tons each) are manned chiefly by part-time fishermen, who aggregately account for the remaining one-fourth. Approximately 110,000 operators and employees are directly engaged in activities taking place on the vessels and boats, and 90,000 in shore activities.

tion, and the remainder is used for animal feed, bait, fertilizer, and other miscellaneous purposes. The country produces less than one-half of its total annual needs, importing the remainder from Canada, Japan, and various other sources.

Spatial considerations. Like the primary stages in forest-products industries and mining, the primary stage of fishing involves exploitation of an undomesticated component of the physical and biological environments. The actual place of exploitation—the location of the primary activity itself—therefore is constantly shifting in a search for optimum raw materials. Especially for commercial fishing, this mobility is very pronounced; the fishing vessel is itself an article of transportation, and hence it moves freely in a search for the best fishing grounds. Commercial fishing is unique in this regard. No other primary activity is sited on actual units of transportation. As we shall see later in the chapter, some secondary activity in the fishing industry also is carried out in such units.

Fishing regions. Fish landings for the United States and all other world areas are shown in Figure 5.4. Most of the fish taken are from the continental shelves along the Pacific, Gulf, and Atlantic Coasts. A substantial share is within the 3-mile offshore limit over which the United States asserts jurisdiction.[6] However, much fishing is carried on, and has been for years, in the Grand Banks in the North Atlantic, which is outside the jurisdiction of any nation.

The various fishing regions are distinguished not only by differing volumes of catch but also by specialization of product, all of which are well known. Salmon

[6] An offshore limit consists of the waters immediately adjacent to a coast under the jurisdiction of the nation controlling that coast. The citizens of that nation have exclusive fishing rights there. If foreigners are allowed to fish, they do so only under special license. Beyond the jurisdiction limit, oceans may be fished without restriction.

However, there is no uniform, generally accepted outward limit to territorial waters. The United States currently claims jurisdiction over a 3-mile limit, and Canada over 12 miles. Both nations claim some additional distance for purposes of certain fishing, jurisdiction over petroleum and other minerals, and other circumstances. Some nations claim rights to waters as far as 200 nautical miles from their coasts. To date, attempts to arrive at international agreement on the seaward limit of sovereignty have not been successful. A 12-mile limit is gaining in general acceptance and may become standardized.

and tuna are predominant in Pacific waters; shrimp, in the Gulf of Mexico and the South Atlantic; oysters, crabs, and clams, in the Chesapeake Bay area; clams and flounder, in the Middle Atlantic; and flounder, lobster, whiting, and cod, in New England (and, of course, menhaden, a trash fish which accounts for nearly one-third of the weight of all fish taken in the United States, at less than 5 per cent of all value).

Inland waterways and water bodies are comparatively unimportant whether measured by volume or value (Fig. 5.4).[7] Recently, the introduction of salmon varieties to the Great Lakes from the Pacific Coast has stimulated both commercial and sports fishing there.

Secondary activity. *Sectoral considerations.* The functions performed as secondary activity in the United States are the processing of fresh, frozen, and packaged fish and seafood (SIC 2036) and the preparation of fish meal, which does not have a separate manufacturing census classification (Fig. 17.5). The fresh-fish industry is very small in terms of employment, shipment value, and value added in manufacturing. In comparison with all other industries, by Alderfer and Michl criteria, it is intermediate in labor costs but high in materials costs. The value added as a per cent of final shipment value is considerably below that for all manufacturing in the United States. Only 497 establishments are recorded in this industry, and most employ fewer than 100 workers.

Spatial considerations. As might be expected, the industry is located along the coast, particularly in New England and the Middle Atlantic states. The sparse densities in the South and on the Pacific Coast are due mainly to the fact that the shipment of fresh fish under refrigeration directly to wholesalers and retailers is

classified as fishing rather than processing and hence does not appear in Figure 17.5.

Tertiary activity. Fresh fish is sent immediately into retail markets, which serve the population densities of the northeastern United States. Per capita consumption of fish products is considerably higher in the New England and Middle Atlantic divisions of the Northeast than in the East North Central regions and other parts of the interior of the country. An increased tendency to market frozen or canned seafood has resulted in large per capita consumption inland, but the figure is yet substantially below that of the coastal areas.

Canada

Sectoral considerations. Although smaller than that of the United States, Canada's fish catch is much larger relative to the national economy. The catch has been increasing, but employment declined during the 1960s from nearly 80,000 to fewer than 70,000 directly engaged in the taking of fish, and from more than 20,000 to 18,000 in processing plants. About 5,000 vessels and 30,000 smaller boats are involved in the actual fishing operation. More than 150 species of fish and shellfish are taken, but the leading species are generally similar to those taken in the previously described Atlantic and Pacific Coasts and the Great Lakes of the United States. The total market value of all Canadian fisheries products is approximately 375 million dollars; nearly three-fourths of these products are exported, chiefly to the United States but also to northwestern Europe and elsewhere.

Spatial considerations. The Canadian fishing industry depends not only upon the continental shelves and inland waterways but also, in greater measure than the United States fishing industry, upon the Grand Banks of the North Atlantic (Fig. 5.4). A higher percentage of the fishing fleet is therefore made up of larger vessels—and, indeed, the Canadian official designation of a vessel is a craft of at least 10 gross tons, rather than 5, as designated by the United States. The larger fishing vessels are capable of leaving the immediate continental shelves and going into the open oceans, especially the Grand Banks. They are known in fishing

[7] A dimension recently added to the production of fish from the interior of the United States is actually agriculture rather than fishing. This is fishpond culture, which is now progressing beyond experimentation efforts. In Arkansas the yield from fishponds exceeds that from the Mississippi River fisheries by a ratio of more than 2:1, and in Missouri by a ratio of 4:1. South Dakota also appears to be interested in this new type of agriculture. Catfish, carp, and buffalo fish are the leading varieties. If harvested as fingerlings, they are used as bait or to stock new ponds. If harvested as adults, they are processed like any other commercial catch.

PRODUCTS FROM FISHING
Secondary Activity: Fresh, Frozen, Packaged Fish and Seafood (SIC 2036)

1. **Function and Process**
   - **A.** Function: conversion of recently-caught fish and other seafood into edible form; *some weight loss*
   - **B.** Process: butchering, freezing, canning, etc.

2. **Significance**
   - **A.** Per cent of all U.S. manufacturing employment: 0.11%
   - **B.** Per cent of value, all U.S. manufacturing shipments: 0.09%
   - **C.** Per cent of value added in all U.S. manufacturing: 0.06%

3. **Major Inputs**
   - **A.** Per cent of labor costs (all employees) in final shipment value: 13.84%
   - **B.** Per cent of materials costs in final shipment value: 70.63%

4. **Number and Size of Establishments**
   - **A.** Total number: 497
   - **B.** Size categories
     1. 4 employees or fewer: 123
     2. Between 5 and 99 employees: 332
     3. Between 100 and 249: 25
     4. Between 250 and 499: 11
     5. Between 500 and 999: 6

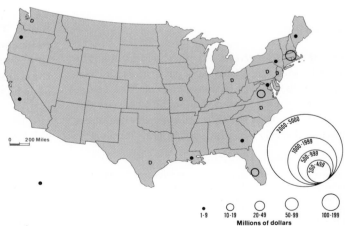

Figure 17.5 Sector-space considerations, secondary activity (processing of fresh, frozen, or packaged fish and seafood—SIC 2036). Circles show value added (see Glossary) by state. "D" means "information not disclosed."

parlance as *offshore* vessels, in contrast to *onshore* craft, which are never far from their home ports.

Slightly more than 50 per cent of the total Canadian catch is taken to Atlantic ports, somewhat more than one-third to Pacific ports, and the remainder within and along the Great Lakes and inland waterways. The actual species taken in each region are generally similar to those previously described for the United States. The geographic distribution of the canning industry in Canada, like that of the United States canning industry is concentrated especially within and near the landing ports. Although there exists no very sizable domestic market in the Atlantic and Pacific regions, this deficiency is offset partly by the fact that much of the product is exported soon after the initial landing of the fish. These various ports are in a good position for the export trade to the United States and Western Europe.

Peru

Sectoral and spatial considerations: Present. Peru may be thought of as the Horatio Alger of commercial fishing, having risen from almost no production in 1938 to its present commanding position of producing nearly 20 per cent of the world's output. Such meteoric growth, fascinating in itself, becomes scientifically interesting when we begin to probe structure-space relationships.

The industry is basically simple in structure. About four-fifths of the catch involves anchovies, a pelagic fish only a few inches long which thrives so close to the shore that most fishing craft—purse seiners—put out in the morning and return in the evening. Capital equipment in actual fishing—the 1,500 purse seiners and their sparse equipment—is small. A typical boat is not over 60 feet long and has a designated carrying capacity of 50 metric tons or less, although many are loaded to almost double that capacity. Peruvian carpenters construct the boats of wood (of which, however, only a part is from Peruvian forests). Shipyards offer no credit to buyers, but financing usually can be arranged from the firm supplying the motor. (This firm, in turn, usually is based in the United States or France.) Once on shore, the anchovies are made into fish meal in some 125 processing plants that frequently are not factories in

the usual sense of the word in this very arid climate, but involve a few pieces of machinery fastened to a concrete slab. Other species of fish, notably the bonito, also are caught, especially for canning and subsequent export, but even these canneries are simple and inexpensive to construct and maintain.

Production has been notably heavy in the vicinity of Chimboate, a port on the north coast which has risen from a village of 5,000 population to a metropolis of 100,000. Another important landing port is Callao, the outport for Lima. Activity is on the rise at still a third port, Végueta. In the early 1970s, some 15,000 workers were engaged in fishing, and 20,000 in fish processing, in Peru.

The industry is in readjustment after an initial boom. As so often occurs in a mushrooming infant industry, marginal producers dominated the early phases of growth. Readjustment began, particularly in processing plants, in the early 1960s. In 1963, there were 175 fish-meal plants in Peru. By 1965, there were 125. Meanwhile, foreign investors, knowledgeable in economies of scale, recently have been buying into what has been essentially a Peruvian-owned industry (aside from capital financing of the boats, as explained above). Some one-sixth of all 1965 direct investment in Peru involved capital from the United States, and additional investment has come from Europe. These trends have continued into the 1970s.

Sectoral and spatial considerations: Future. However, the industry offers promise of permanence, if excessive exploitation of the supply source can be avoided. About one-third of the catch is exported as fish meal. The industry now is vital to Peru; fish meal makes up about one-fourth of all exports, exceeding appreciably outflows of copper and cotton. The basic question of continuity, however, has not yet been resolved because no one knows exactly under what conditions or at what rate the anchovies reproduce.

A related question involves yet another industry of Peru, the long-standing guano industry. This fertilizer, from the droppings of millions of birds that feed on the anchovies, will be lost, as will the birds themselves, if the anchovies are fished excessively. Clearly, studies must be made—and soon—to establish the limits of tolerance with which this new and thriving fishing industry can function without seriously endangering man's relationship with the natural environment or with alternative activities.

As this book goes to press, there is increasing evidence that Peruvian fishing has upset the ecological balance on the adjacent continental shelf: the anchovies are dwindling in supply and the fishing industry is declining.

Japan

Sectoral and spatial considerations: Present. Commercial fishing in Japan, which produces nearly 14 per cent of the world's catch, is very unlike that in Peru in many respects. Demonstrated stability is perhaps the most important difference. Japan has been the leading commercial fishing nation for more than a quarter of a century, whereas Peru's status as a major fishing nation was attained recently and may be only temporary. Japan gradually has increased capital investment in the industry over these many years, despite heavy losses during World War II, whereas Peru's investment has come only recently. Most Japanese investment is domestic, as is that of Peru, but the share of foreign investment in the South American country is growing much more rapidly than that in Japan. Most of the newer Japanese investment is in offshore vessels capable of ranging the high seas, whereas Peruvian investment continues in small, coastwise craft. Japanese production is almost entirely for domestic consumption, whereas fish products are Peru's leading export (Figs. 17.1 and 5.4).

In structure and geographic distribution, Japanese fishing still is largely an industry of small operators dispersed throughout more than 3,000 coastal villages in all four major islands and many smaller islands as well. Some 90 per cent of the 225,000 fishing enterprises account for only about 12 per cent of the annual catch. These, obviously, are the small operators; the remaining 20,000 enterprises account for about 88 per cent of the catch. The larger enterprises, located prevailingly in coastal ports rather than villages, are increasing in relative importance. The number of operating firms, as well as the total labor force in fishing, declined noticeably in the 1950–1970 period, during which time the total catch rose.

Open-ocean fishing is on the increase, both relatively and absolutely. In 1955, the high seas accounted for less than 4 per cent of the country's total fish catch, whereas by 1970 the figure was 25 per cent of a catch that was over 25 per cent higher. Meanwhile, the catch by coastwise craft that range only into shallow water declined by essentially the same percentages as the gains registered by the larger vessels. Despite an important but aggregately minor increase in aquaculture in shallow seas and inland waters, Japan is looking increasingly to the high seas to supply her growing need for animal protein.

In terms of specific categories of fish taken, freshwater fish are very minor; nearly all fish consumed in Japan comes from the oceans and seas. Leaders among the ocean fish include mullet, cod, hake, herring, mackerel, tuna, bonito, redfish, and anchovies. Mixed and unidentified fish are also of marked and growing importance. Mollusks, particularly the squid and clam, rank high among demersal sea life taken in shallow water. The oyster, cultivated under aquaculture, also is significant—for food as well as pearls.

Sectoral and spatial considerations: Future. Japanese fishermen range over most of the world's oceans, but especially the Pacific Ocean on either side of the equator. Emphasis upon the high seas implies both a widening of the range of fishing and more intensive use of waters now being fished. Somewhat less than one-fifth of the catch is exported, and a small amount is imported. This activity can be expected to continue, subject to constraints of resource depletion and international agreement.

The Soviet Union

Sectoral and spatial considerations: Present. The Soviet Union also is increasing her dependence upon the world's oceans to feed a growing population which has not been supplied adequately from domestic agriculture. The country now catches more than 10 per cent of the world's annual harvest. At least one-third, and possibly as much as 40 per cent, of the total annual per capita consumption there of animal protein comes from fishery products. Freshwater fish are important, accounting for somewhat under one-tenth of the total

Soviet catch. Small fish—herring, sardines, anchovies, etc.—are extremely important in that catch, accounting for over 40 per cent. Cod, hake, and herring make up over 20 per cent. Redfish are prominent among the remainder. Unlike Japan, the Soviet Union does not catch many mixed and unidentified fish, one reason being that the primary Russian fishing grounds are in the North Atlantic Ocean, the Barents Sea and the North Pacific Ocean rather than in tropical waters, where mixed and unidentified fish are numerous. Greatest yields are obtained from the Norwegian Sea (mostly herring), the Barents Sea (mostly cod), and the North Atlantic (over one-half cod and haddock, but important amounts of herring and perch). Among the leading fishing ports are Murmansk on the Barents Sea, Archangel on the White Sea, Leningrad on the Baltic Sea, Nikolayevsk and Vladivostok on the Pacific Coast, Astrakhan and Baku on the Caspian Sea, Kerch on the Black Sea, and Yeisk on the Sea of Azov.

Sectoral and spatial considerations: Future. Current plans stress a continued emphasis on commercial fishing, especially off western Greenland, eastern North America, and the eastern North Atlantic, as well as the more active use of other, unspecified waters. A Soviet Union–Cuban fishing base now exists in Havana, and Soviet trawlers are beginning to exploit warmer regions of the Atlantic Ocean.

An important feature of open-ocean fishing by both the Soviet Union and Japan is the floating cannery, which is, in effect, a factory ship supplied in terms of raw materials by the smaller fishing vessels and in terms of energy and finished-product transfer by commercial vessels plying to and from the port from which the vessel operates—or a closer port, if, as illustrated in the immediately preceding paragraph, appropriate arrangements can be made. The obvious advantages of this type of operation derive from the fact that like the initial fishing vessel or boat, this stage of activity is actually located on a transportation unit, and hence an enormous mobility is possible that simply cannot occur with equal facility in other kinds of economic activity.

The future of fishing by the Soviet Union, now that its activity has been expanded into the open oceans, is similar to that previously described for Japan.

Explanation

Institutional Explanation

In both sectoral and spatial terms, the fishing industry of the world is rather simple, whether viewed at primary, secondary, or tertiary levels of activity or of connecting linkages. Very little has been done to apply specific theories to the fishing industry, partly because of the severity of the physical environmental constraint, which limits much of the world's fishing to the continental shelves and inland waterways and water bodies, and partly because of the mobility of the vessels, which enables the primary stages of that activity—and, in recent years, some secondary stages—to move about freely. Even the location of the onshore phases of the industry, which are manifested as secondary activities in the form of canneries and processing establishments and as tertiary activities in the form of wholesaling and retailing outlets, is the result of a very definite need to be near the landed fish, which are highly perishable. Hence there is a strong orientation in terms of physical location to the fish-landing ports. If this orientation can be coupled with a regional or national location near a high-density population which consumes the fish, so much the better. The advent of techniques of canning, refrigerating, and freezing has enabled the industry to be located some distance from its ultimate market—a condition which was not very feasible when fish were sold fresh or were subjected to crude and rather costly preservation techniques of smoking, drying, or curing.

Because of its unique features, particularly mobility and the constraints set by the physical environment, the industry does offer an interesting case study documenting our abstractive drawing in the Introduction (p. 15)—namely, the existence of a zone of actual conditions, another of economic feasibility, and a third of overall possibility. We have examined actual conditions and have seen that some nations, especially the Soviet Union and Japan, plus some others in northwestern Europe that have not been discussed, maintain fishing fleets which have extended their zones of actual conditions to all oceans of the world, thereby reaching out to include not only the total zone of economic feasibility but also that of overall possibility. For other countries, such as the United States and Canada, actual conditions still are restricted more or less to continental shelves, nearby fishing banks, and inland waterways, although the potential exists for widening their zones of actual conditions and economic feasibility in the same way as Japan and the Soviet Union have done.

If, however, these nations were to engage upon such a policy, and particularly if others were to follow suit, the net result could well be a general overfishing—an excess for which compensation would be necessary either by cutting back overall exploitation or drastically increasing the supply of fish in the open ocean. Indeed, the Stockholm Conference on the Environment, held in June 1972, has indicated that such measures are now necessary.

Theoretical Explanation

As we have seen, the main fishing areas for both pelagic and demersal commercial fishing activities are restricted largely to the continental shelves in temperate climates. This is a natural condition which, although influenced by man to some extent, is not determined by his actions. However, given this natural condition, we are concerned with making some theoretical observations which will contribute to our understanding of the location and volumes of commercial catches. While in some types of fishing large factory ships are utilized, the dominant types of fishing vessels are relatively small, as there are few economies of scale in boat construction and operation; in addition, short periods at sea with rapid return of catch are more economical. The problem therefore resolves itself into optimizing between transport costs (distance traveled), size of catch (boat scale), and speed of delivery. These factors together will determine a fairly limited search range, size of catch, and time at sea.

The secondary stage of fish production, namely, fish processing, concerns largely canning and freezing activities. The following points are significant in this context: First, a large weight loss is involved in processing in the case of both freezing and canning, and second, while many small fishing ports are located along all coasts, a large proportion of the catch going to these small ports, since it is small in overall volume, is consumed mainly as fresh fish domestically and in restaurants immediately adjacent to the small ports. On the other hand, at larger ports the volume of catch is significantly greater, and thus they provide a raw-material basis for factory location. Finally, these ports constitute a break-of-bulk point between the source of raw materials and the ultimate markets, and thus they are in an economical location with respect to secondary activities.

In the tertiary stage of commercial fish production the following points are especially important: First, since fresh fish is highly perishable, the range of distribution is limited, and hence the major port of the market is restricted to coastal locations where fish is landed, and to their immediate hinterlands. Second, the canning and freezing processes increase the durability of the product, and hence its range, so that catches on the East, West, and Gulf Coasts can be marketed in the interior.

Fish and fish products are low-order goods and can be obtained, especially when frozen or canned, throughout the entire spectrum of the central-place hierarchy. As the range of these goods is seldom greater than a few miles or a few city blocks, the threshold to support their retail trade in terms of the volume of purchasing power is relatively low.

Chapter 18

Iron and Steel

This chapter is an inquiry into the mining of iron and certain other metals with which it is alloyed in steel making. It is a critical chapter for two reasons: First, it introduces the reader to mining as a primary stage of economic activity. Second, it is a case study—at primary, secondary, and tertiary stages—of one of the largest and most dynamic activities in the technically advanced or developed nations, and in many of the developing ones as well. We shall examine here the mining and manufacturing of iron and selected alloy metals. In Chapter 19 we shall carry the examination further into activities which depend heavily upon the steel mills for incoming materials.

Natural Environmental Conditions

Iron is among the most plentiful of substances in the earth's outer crust, comprising over 5 per cent of all leading elements and exceeded only by oxygen, silicon,

and aluminum. However, techniques of recovering iron are not so efficient as those for recovering copper, lead, zinc, and some other metals—at least when measured in dollars and cents. An iron content of about 20 per cent is now considered absolute minimum if an iron deposit is to be developed as an ore. In contrast, the metal content of copper need amount only to less than 1 per cent, under certain conditions, to be considered commercially exploitable.

Minerals. Of the many iron-bearing minerals, only four contain sufficiently high concentrations of the metal to be regarded as substantial commercial sources. These are *magnetite, hematite, limonite (göthite),* and *siderite.* Their salient features are outlined in Table 18.1. The first three are by far the leaders in iron content. Magnetite, it will be noted, contains the highest iron percentage. When pure, it is combined with only one other element, oxygen. Hematite also contains only iron and oxygen, with the proportions of the two elements slightly different from those in magnetite. Limonite contains the same two elements plus water, and

TABLE 18.1
LEADING IRON-ORE MINERALS

Mineral	Chemical composition	Approximate per cent of iron content when pure[*]
Magnetite	Fe_3O_4	72
Hematite	Fe_2O_3	70
Limonite (göthite)	$2Fe_2O_3 \cdot 3H_2O$	60
Siderite	$FeCO_3$	48

[*]The percentage of iron as found in nature varies markedly; however, the very best ores seldom contain more than 65 per cent. Calculated from various sources.

siderite the same two plus carbon. Only in extremely rare situations do any of these minerals occur in the pure state. Usually they are mixed with minor amounts of aluminum, manganese, phosphorus, sulfur, or other elements and are compounded into a matrix of non-metallic materials. As found in nature, an ore of 65 percent iron content is a high-quality ore; most have 55 per cent or less.

Natural processes of concentration. Several quite different natural processes are known to be responsible for raising the iron content of a rock deposit. Some involve the action of water, either at the surface or underground. By way of illustration, an ore bed may have been laid down as a sedimentary rock and not altered subsequently, so that today it can be mined in much the same general way as a coal seam. Other processes may take place in the absence of water;

TABLE 18.2
IRON-ORE RESERVES AND RESOURCES OF THE WORLD
(IN MILLIONS OF TONS)

Region	(1) Reserves of ore (long tons)	(2) Potential ore (long tons)	(3) Total resources (long tons)	(4) Reserves of recoverable iron (Fe) (short tons)
United States	10,494[*]	96,353	106,847[*]	2,000
Canada	35,727	87,988	123,715	11,730
Mexico, Puerto Rico, Central America	573	198	771	380
South America	33,561	57,478	91,039	18,330
Europe	20,964	12,598	33,562	8,530
U.S.S.R.	108,755	190,740	299,495	>31,000
Africa	6,693	24,113	30,806	3,380
Middle East, Asia, and Far East[†]	17,027	53,344	70,371	11,160
Australia, New Zealand, New Caledonia	16,535	VAST	> 16,535	10,210
Total	250,329	>522,812	>773,141	>96,720

[*]Including 3 billion tons of taconite and 600 million tons of recoverable iron (Fe) estimated by the authors.
[†]Exclusive of the Asian part of the U.S.S.R.
Source: U.S. Bureau of Mines, *Mineral Facts and Problems, 1970,* p. 297.

magmatic materials high in ferrous content may have been brought together by gravity action before they solidified to become part of the igneous rock in which they occur today as an ore. Also, more than one process may have been involved. It is not uncommon for iron-bearing materials, however initially laid down, to have been enriched by selective removal of some of their nonferrous components by the chemical or mechanical action of water. As a result of these and still other processes, iron deposits as found today may be either bedded (stratified) or massive and may be located either near the surface or at varying levels underground. The shallow ores, if present in substantial amounts, lend themselves excellently to modern large-scale methods and machinery.

Extent and distribution of reserves. Although there must exist a definite limit to the amount of fugitive minerals, man has not yet been able to find such a limit in the world as a whole for any given material. As his methods and tools have improved, he has been able to derive more and more of wanted materials from matrices once considered worthless. This is particularly true of iron, which, as we have noted, is known to be present in substantial quantities in much of the earth's outer crust. Who is to say how much of this remains to be exploited, since it occurs, albeit in lean proportions, in so many places?

Despite the improbability of arriving at a firm estimate, it is desirable to appraise the iron content of the more obvious concentrations of iron ore. Several such appraisals have been made, and one of the most recent is presented in Table 18.2. This table is the latest in a series of reserve estimates that have changed rapidly during the past decade. One reason for the changes is that iron is present in so many parts of the earth's surface. Another is that new reserves are discovered rather frequently. Of course, the table is basically an estimate, although by experts. Columns 1 and 4 are most important, with column 1 showing the estimate of known reserves, and column 4 the iron content of those reserves. In these terms, the Soviet Union is especially fortunate, as are Canada and Australia. Brazil, not shown in the table, possesses the largest share of the reserves indicated for South America, followed by Venezuela. Although iron is a fugitive re-

source, not easily replaceable in the natural state (it can, of course, be recycled when its use is ended as a manufactured product), the known world reserves are very large relative to known production: there is enough known iron to last for nearly three hundred years at current rates of production and consumption.

The United States

Primary Activity

Description, measurement, and classification: sectoral and spatial considerations. *Function and process.* Mining, in this case of iron ore, is the removal of a desired material from the earth's lithosphere. Strictly speaking, this function ends with the act of removal from the natural state, although, as we shall soon see, some additional operations may be included.

The processes of mining involve both *underground* and *open-pit operations,* plus *beneficiation.* As the terms imply, underground mining necessitates the driving of a tunnel, usually accompanied by the sinking of a shaft, while open-pit mining is the taking of ore that lies at or near the surface of the earth, after the removal of overburden. At one time, underground mining was practiced at depths exceeding only a few hundred feet, but open-pit techniques, the result of improved technology, have enabled man to gouge huge holes in the earth, sometimes more than 2,000 feet deep. These techniques are now favored over underground methods, especially because of economies of scale realized with efficient technology.

Initial milling processes of *agglomeration* and *concentration* now are found at or near both open-pit and underground mines. Agglomeration involves the combining of fine particles into lumps, or pellets, which can survive the fiery heat of blasts in steel furnaces—heat which would send many of the original fine particles up the furnace chimneys or disintegrate them, thus causing them to be lost. This process does not necessarily raise the proportion of iron to the total mass of ore, but merely enables the blast furnaces to recover more efficiently the iron which is already present. Concentration, on the other hand, involves the removal of

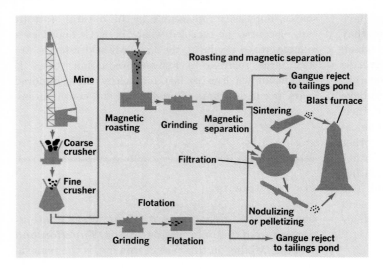

Figure 18.1 Two processes of iron-ore beneficiation: roasting and magnetic separation, and flotation. Because they have certain steps in common, these concentration processes are shown here in the same graph. They are, however, distinct processes.

many unwanted materials and the resulting enrichment of the ore before it enters the furnaces (Fig. 18.1).[1] It not only increases the efficiency of furnace operation but also reduces transportation costs from concentration plant to factory by removing waste before shipment. Much of the output of concentration plants is also agglomerated before shipment. The term *beneficiation* is being used increasingly to refer to both these processes, although some authorities use it to mean only concentration. In its broadest interpretation, beneficiation denotes any process other than mere transportation that increases the value of ore after it is mined but before it is smelted.

We have seen in Table 18.2 the estimated distribution of world reserves of iron ore. Those in the United States have been further estimated as shown in Table 18.3.

The United States produces more than 12 per cent of all iron ore, and it consumes some 20 per cent. Three

important trends with geographic implications are evident in the iron-ore-mining industry of the United States: (1) increased use of foreign ores, (2) increased dependence upon beneficiated lower-quality domestic ores, and (3) small but definite regional adjustments in location of mining activity. At present there are some one hundred operating iron-ore mines in the United States, of which ninety are open pit and the remainder underground. Because of the capital-intensive nature of such activity, employment is but a tiny fraction of the labor force in all mining, itself less than 1 per cent of the national labor force. As is evident in Figure 18.2, future demand of the United States is expected to be supplied more and more from foreign ores, especially in Canada and South America, despite a rising domestic output. In the late 1940s, 1950s, and early 1960s, much United States capital was invested in foreign iron-ore mining, notably in Canada, South America, Australia, and Africa. Nor has this investment ceased. Henceforth, domestic mining will compete with these and still other operations supported abroad by domestic capital. Some of these operations can make use of direct-shipping ores that do not need beneficiation and thus can be produced without the added cost of this processing stage.

Until recently, commercial use of low-quality ore (20 to 35 per cent metal content) was not feasible. In the early 1950s, however, processes were developed for such commercial use, and by 1980 these low-quality ores

[1] Iron ore of 51.5 per cent or higher iron content and 10 per cent or lower silica content is known in the trade as *direct-shipping ore,* which need not be concentrated before being charged into a blast furnace. It may be agglomerated, however, in order to maximize recovery of the very fine material.

Usable iron ore includes all direct-shipping ore plus output from beneficiation plants (except those located directly at iron and steel mills). *Crude* iron ore is mined but unbeneficiated ore. The difference between the two may be substantial: domestic output of usable ore in the United States ranges from one-half to two-thirds the output of crude ore.

TABLE 18.3

IRON-ORE RESERVES AND RESOURCES OF THE UNITED STATES
(IN MILLIONS OF LONG TONS)

	Reserve ore	Potential ore	Total resources
Lake Superior region:			
Minnesota	1,814	38,581	40,395
Michigan	405	17,224	17,629
Michigan and Wisconsin	36	18,996	19,032
Wisconsin		49	49
Total	2,255	74,850	77,105
Northeastern region:			
New York	21	932	953
Pennsylvania	79	5	84
New Jersey		16	16
Maine		317	317
Total	100	1,270	1,370
Southeastern region:			
Alabama	2,848	2,366	5,214
Georgia	52	2,015	2,067
Tennessee	50	1,453	1,503
Virginia		492	492
Mississippi	16		16
Total	2,966	6,326	9,292
Central Gulf region:			
Texas	174		174
Missouri	305	4	309
Oklahoma	1	1	2
Louisiana	162		162
Total	642	5	647
Central-Western region:			
Montana	66	283	349
South Dakota		493	493
Colorado	7	98	105
Utah	446		446
New Mexico	124	15	139
Wyoming	444	274	718
Total	1,087	1,163	2,250

(*Continued on next page*)

TABLE 18.3 (*Continued*)

	Reserve ore	Potential ore	Total resources
Western region:			
Arizona	103	439	542
Nevada	168		168
California	156	1	157
Oregon	3	1	4
Washington	6	2	8
Total	436	443	879
Alaska	8	11,272	11,280
Hawaii		1,024	1,024
Grand total	7,494*	96,353	103,847

*Exclusive of large reserves of taconite ores, for which data are not available for publication. It is believed by the authors that a minimum of 3,000 million tons of these taconite ores have been proven as a source of ore for beneficiation plants which are in operation or under construction.
Source: U.S. Bureau of Mines, *Mineral Facts and Problems, 1970,* p. 298.

may well supply over two-thirds of all domestic production and account for nearly the whole output from the Lake Superior vicinity (Fig. 18.3).

Some regional adjustments in mining also have taken place during the past decade. The South, notably the Birmingham, Alabama, district, which until recently was a national supplier of some importance, has declined both relatively and absolutely. Scattered sites in western and northeastern states have become correspondingly more active. At present, over 75 per cent of the country's iron ore comes from the famed Lake Superior ranges, nearly 20 per cent from dispersed sites west of the Mississippi River, and most of the remainder from New York, Pennsylvania, and New Jersey (Fig. 18.3).

Lake Superior ranges. Production of iron ore near the western and southern margins of Lake Superior has been the subject of so many articles, both scholarly and popular, that it has by now become almost legendary. Nearly as well known are the six ranges from which nearly all the ore is taken: the renowned Mesabi and the smaller Marquette, Menominee, Gogebic, Cuyuna, and Vermilion ranges (Fig. 18.3). Output, as available, is shown in Table 18.4. The Mesabi, Cuyuna, and Vermilion ranges are situated generally west of Lake Superior, near the lakehead ports of Superior, Duluth, and Two Harbors; the Marquette range is in northern Michigan; and the Gogebic and Menominee ranges are shared by Michigan and Wisconsin. Since 1854, these six ranges have accounted for well over 3.5 billion tons of iron ore, and the Mesabi alone has supplied over 2.7 billion tons. Hematite is the primary mineral taken from all six ranges, and magnetite

Figure 18.2 Major sources of United States iron ore.

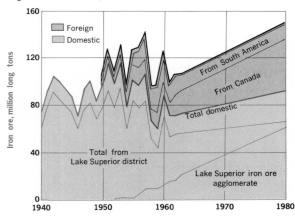

IRON AND STEEL PRODUCTS
Primary Activity

Sectoral Considerations

1. **Function and Process**
   - **A.** Function: extraction and beneficiation of iron ore; *much weight loss*
   - **B.** Process: open-pit and some underground mining; removal of waste and some pelletizing through beneficiation (see Figure 18.1)

2. **Significance**
   - **A.** Per cent of all U.S. mining labor force: 3.64%
   - **B.** Per cent of value, all U.S. mining shipments: 3.52%
   - **C.** Per cent of all U.S. mining establishments: 0.53%

Spatial Considerations

3. **Number and Size of Establishments**
   - **A.** Total number: 146
   - **B.** Average size (number of employees) per establishment: 158

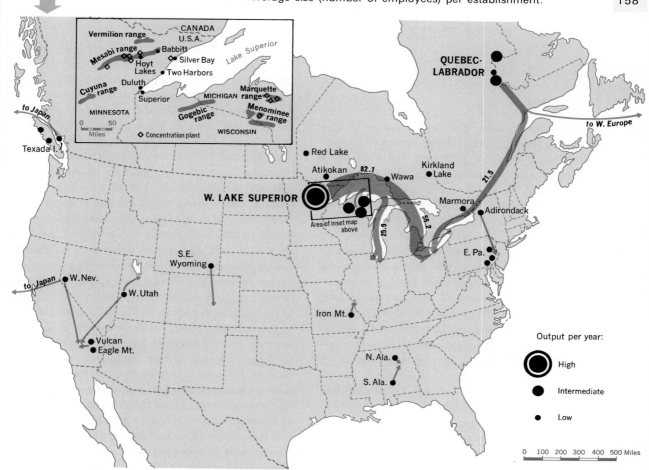

Figure 18.3 Sector-space considerations, primary stage of iron-ore production, and primary-secondary linkages. (After information from U.S. Bureau of Mines)

TABLE 18.4

U.S. IRON ORE MINED AND SHIPPED BY RANGES, GREAT LAKES ORIGINATING AREA, 1971 (GROSS TONS)

Range	Mine production	Shipments
Cuyana	*	*
Marquette	21,481,084	9,108,303
Menominee	5,375,787	2,706,446
Mesabi	129,741,992	48,985,154
Other Great Lakes	*	*
Total	159,389,781	61,775,560

*Figures included in total to avoid use of individual company data.
Source: American Iron Ore Association.

ranks second. The former accounts for well over 90 per cent of the Lake Superior ore, and the latter for nearly all the remainder.

Lake Superior ores. The ores occur at shallow depths in the Mesabi range, seldom exceeding 200 feet and almost never exceeding 1,000 feet. The width of the mineralized zone here is not generally over 3 miles, but its length is well in excess of 100 miles. The central portion and upper levels of this range once contained high-grade deposits, most of which have been mined. Along the margins and beneath this better ore are very substantial reserves of *taconite,* which here is made up of hematite and some magnetite mixed in comparatively lean proportions largely with hard, nonmetallic materials. It is the taconite of this and other Lake Superior ranges which contains the sizable inferred amounts of iron with which the United States is usually credited in international comparisons. Its metal content is low, varying from 20 to 35 per cent, but reserves are substantial, notably at Mesabi.

The better ores of the other five fields, like those at Mesabi, are of direct-shipping quality. Some taconite also occurs at the two ranges in Michigan, where it is known as *jasper.* The Cuyuna ores are somewhat unique in that they contain manganese in amounts approximating 5 per cent of their total bulk. Like those of the Mesabi, these Cuyuna deposits are at comparatively shallow levels, whereas most of the ores in the other ranges are at appreciable depths. Open-pit mining predominates in the Mesabi and Cuyuna ranges, and underground mining in the others.

Beneficiation of ore other than taconite. Commercial beneficiation of ore other than taconite is said to have commenced in Minnesota as early as 1907 and in some eastern states even earlier. In 1940, beneficiation was initiated on a general scale in the Lake Superior region, as well as in other producing fields in the nation. Minnesota ores, particularly, were subjected to the process, and now more than 80 per cent of the state's crude iron ore other than taconite is concentrated before shipment. A smaller portion is agglomerated, but not concentrated.

Beneficiation of taconite. Successful commercial beneficiation of taconite dates back only to the late 1940s, and active processing to the mid-1950s. The process is more complex, partly because taconite is much harder than most other ore and because the wear on the machinery is much greater. Also, it is more difficult to separate the iron from the gangue (unwanted) materials. Most of the serious problems associated with its beneficiation, however, appear to be either solved or within reach of solution. The advent of the process is marking the dawn of a new era—more accurately, the continuance of an old era—in the Lake Superior mining region. With the depletion of better iron ore there in the face of a rising national demand for iron and steel, serious attention was given to developing iron-ore fields in foreign countries as well as to upgrading some of the remaining Lake Superior deposits. Both movements have acquired momentum. The increasing importance of foreign ores, which we shall discuss in more detail later, is an accomplished fact, and the United States no longer depends almost exclusively upon domestic sources. However, the long-elusive technique of beneficiating domestic taconite is also an accomplished fact, and it would appear that the Lake Superior region will continue to be a vital source area for the nation's iron ore. Essentially all Lake Superior ore, whether taconite or not, now is beneficiated before smelting, and over one-half is agglomerated.

Other mining sites. The one-fourth of the country's domestic iron ore obtained at places other than the Lake Superior ranges is secured at scattered places. Sites in Wyoming, Utah, northern Missouri, and other states west of the Mississippi River supply respective regional levels, which amount to somewhat less than one-fifth of national demand. Most of this ore is beneficiated prior to smelting. A series of mines in eastern Pennsylvania, New Jersey, and New York, plus another group in the Adirondacks of northern New York, account for less than 5 per cent of domestic consumption. All this ore is beneficiated before smelting. The Birmingham, Alabama, district, once second only to Lake Superior, now is a minor source of ore (Fig. 18.3).

Institutional explanation. We are interested here in the reasons for the present location of iron-ore mining in the United States. Because understanding that location involves the supply as well as the demand, at this point we can offer only a few suggestions; we shall return later, after describing the location of the iron and steel complexes of the country, to a more thorough explanation.

Reserves, historical background, and technology. We mentioned previously that mining as an economic activity is oriented to sites of available ore. Because, as we have seen, iron is present in the earth's crust in varying amounts, averaging about 5 per cent, this particular resource is therefore somewhat unusual in its rather general availability. However, as has been noted, only recently has it become economically feasible to exploit fields of 20 per cent iron content, and prior to the 1950s it was not feasible to utilize, for large-scale exploitation, fields of less than 30 per cent iron content. Therefore, the very existence of large reserves of ore is an important determinant of the location of mining activity. Such reserves are not widely distributed in the world, but are restricted to a very few sites, and as we increase the minimum iron content that might be considered to constitute an ore from 20 to 30 to 40 to 50 per cent, or even higher, such fields become progressively fewer in number and usually more erratically distributed over the earth's surface.

In the United States, only the Lake Superior region has large known reserves of iron ore. Fortunately, these are at shallow depths and are located coincidentally near cheap inland waterway transportation and in good relationship to domestic markets. Both production and transportation costs are relatively low. All other reserves of the country, although their iron content usually is higher than in the Lake Superior region, are either sufficiently low in quality or otherwise sufficiently expensive to mine that, when production costs are added to those of transportation, they tend to serve only regional markets.

Historical background provided a large, accessible market. The United States and Canada were settled mainly on their respective eastern coasts, and their frontiers—with exceptions—gradually moved west. Most of the people and the internal demand for iron and steel products stems today from an overall effective area bounded by Chicago, St. Louis, Baltimore, New York City, Boston, Montreal, Toronto, and Windsor–Detroit.

Without rapidly developing technology, however, the reserves of the Lake Superior region could not be utilized efficiently today. In this instance, the research resulting in technological advances that enabled use of the taconites was heavily subsidized by the iron-ore companies as the reserves of the higher-quality ores diminished. The research was successful. Science—or, more accurately, technology—did provide.

Government policy. An interesting aspect of the development of the taconite deposits in the Lake Superior region has been the role of government policy—in this case, of the state of Minnesota. Of the several taxes which were assessed against the mining companies of that state, the most severe was an ad valorem tax against the exploitable minerals in the ground.

This tax discouraged taconite development because of the very substantial amounts of the substance known to exist. Taconite could not be taxed as long as it was not considered to be commercially exploitable. Once classified as an ore, the very large taconite reserves would be taxed at rates so high that the companies interested in exploiting taconite did not feel they could afford to develop those reserves. In 1941, the state legislature enacted a new law under which production rather than reserves was taxed, and the actual commercial development of taconite began immediately.

Now that the United States is searching abroad for iron ore, the policies of nations possessing the ore, and of the United States federal government, are increasingly matters of concern to the private sector of the United States that is largely responsible for actual development. Especially important are export and import tariffs and quotas, policies of internal regulations, and policies affecting transportation costs.

Transportation costs. In Chapter 7 we discussed the relative costs per ton-mile of transporting bulk cargo by various media, and we indicated that the vessel designed for the Great Lakes–St. Lawrence Seaway system is one of the least expensive in the world. Over 98 per cent of the ore from the Lake Superior region of the United States moves to its ultimate destination by way of a combination of land and water routes. The lakehead port of Superior forwards well over one-third of this outgoing ore, and Duluth and Two Harbors each accounts for an additional one-fourth (Fig. 18.3). Escanaba, Silver Bay, Marquette, Taconite Harbor, and Ashland, are among the lesser, but still noteworthy, iron-ore-forwarding ports.

The preference of shippers for the rail-water route is not difficult to understand upon examination of relative transportation costs. Recently, total charges for transporting a ton of iron ore from the Mesabi range to Pittsburgh by rail amounted to approximately $10.23, while the rail-water charges were $6.60. In another comparison, all-rail charges for moving a ton of iron ore from Mesabi to Chicago were $5.41 and rail-water charges were $3.65. Even these figures do not reveal the very low cost of Great Lakes transportation: of the $6.60 total charge per ton for the land-water haul between Mesabi and Pittsburgh, $4.42 involved overland hauls (Mesabi to lake port, about 50 miles, and Lake Erie port to Pittsburgh, about 120 miles), whereas $2.18, including loading and unloading charges, involved the approximate 1,000-mile haul from the lakehead ports to lower Lake Erie!

Recently, a proposal has been made to construct a pipeline that would carry iron-ore slurry from Mesabi to Chicago, at a transport cost competitive with, or even slightly favorable to, rail-water costs.

Theoretical explanation. Our theoretical explanation of the mineral industry sector or primary sector of the iron and steel industry is concerned largely with the substitution between transport costs and production costs. These costs, as noted in Chapter 11, can be referred to as costs associated with site and costs associated with relative location. As pointed out in this chapter, the tendency in this sector of the mineral industry is to mine leaner ores and at more remote locations. Hence technological change has been associated with offsetting the economic consequences of those developments.

The economic impact of relative location is translated into transportation costs by the volume or tonnage to be transported and the distance. The tonnage transported is further dependent upon the grade of ore and recovery rate, more low-grade ore having to be transported for a given level of output. Theoretically, therefore, the process of beneficiation moves the production point closer to the market and therefore reduces the disadvantage of more remote deposits.

With respect to mining lower-grade ores, techniques to economize the production costs—such as open-pit mining—can be viewed as altering the site qualities (internal characteristics) of mine locations.

Horizontal Linkages: Primary To Secondary

Figure 18.3 shows the sectoral and spatial movement of iron ore from mine and beneficiation plant to smelter in the United States. Domestic movement, chiefly from the Lake Superior ranges to lower lake ports, is self-explanatory. Foreign imports amount each year to a minimum of one-third, and a maximum of one-half, of all consumption, depending upon the size of domestic inventories. Canada supplies nearly one-half of all imported iron concentrates of ore, with most of the remainder coming from Brazil, Venezuela, and other Latin American countries, plus Liberia.

Almost 20 per cent of all steel is made in the United States. The processing of iron ore and other ferrous metals, and the products derived therefrom, involves very numerous and complex operations, entering wholly or partially into a wide variety of finished products. The secondary stages of ferrous-metal recovery, with which we are concerned in this chapter, are themselves comprehensive: The U.S. Office of Management and Budget, in its category "Primary Metals Industry" (two-digit-detail 33), lists 7 three-digit-detail breakdowns and 24 four-digit-detail classifications. To simplify matters for this chapter, we shall examine blast furnaces (including coke ovens) plus steelworks and rolling mills (SIC 3312); cold-rolled steel-sheet, steel-strip, and steel-bar-making establishments (SIC 3316); and steel foundries (SIC 3323). Since commodities do not always flow through these various substages consecutively, we shall here label them substages 1, 2A, and 2B.

Secondary Activity

Substage 1: blast furnaces and steel mills (SIC 3312). *Sectoral considerations.* The function performed by this substage is the conversion of iron ore and beneficiated concentrates into *pig iron, wrought iron,* and various grades of *steel.* Pig iron is secured when the ores and concentrates are subjected to a smelting operation that removes most of their impurities. Essentially all iron-smelting operations use coke as a fuel, and some carbon thus passes from the coke to the molten metal. (However, as we shall see, not all steelmaking processes require coke.) Because of the presence of the carbon, which may range from 3 to 5 per cent of the total mass, pig iron is very brittle and difficult to work when solidified. If the carbon is removed by refining, the product becomes wrought iron, which is much more workable but too soft for most purposes. Most steel is produced by first withdrawing the carbon and other impurities from pig iron and subsequently re-adding the carbon in carefully measured amounts. Low-carbon steels contain 0.8 per cent or less of the element, and high-carbon steels between 0.8 and 2 per cent. Manganese usually is added also, even in nonalloy steels. To other steel, known as alloy steel, are added manganese (in larger amounts than in nonalloy steel), nickel, chromium, vanadium, and other metals which combine readily with iron and carbon and may be used to obtain such special qualities as resistance to abrasion or corrosion under specific conditions. Low-carbon steel is utilized especially for structural purposes, and high-carbon and alloy steel for machinery, tools, etc. Most pig iron is processed in *blast fur-*

naces, and most steel in *basic oxygen, open-hearth, electric,* or *bessemer* units.

The blast furnace. About 96 per cent of iron ore consumed in the United States is smelted in blast furnaces. Three per cent is sent directly to steel furnaces, and the remainder goes into miscellaneous uses.

Blast furnaces are huge, barrel-like cylinders, up to 100 feet high and usually between 25 and 30 feet in diameter, lined with firebrick (Fig. 18.4). Charges of iron ore and/or concentrates, then of limestone, and then of coke are inserted continually at the upper section, and the charges gradually fuse as they sink toward the bottom of the furnace. Temperatures at the top are about 400°F, and those at the bottom are over 3000°F. Average daily pig-iron capacity per furnace ranges from 250 to over 2,000 short tons.

Figure 18.4 A modern blast furnace. Coke, iron ore or concentrate, and limestone are inserted at the top in successive layers, and molten iron and slag are withdrawn at the bottom.

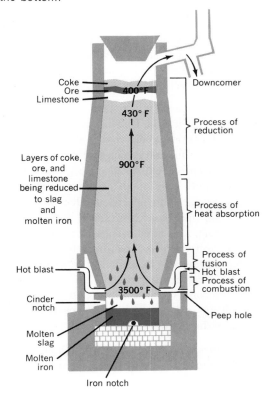

In the actual conversion of ore into metal, carbon from the coke combines with oxygen from the ore to form a gas which is withdrawn at the top of the furnace, so that the resulting iron drops to the bottom of the furnace, where it is withdrawn in a molten state. The iron ore placed into the furnace usually is at least of direct-shipping quality (51.5 per cent or higher). Each ton of iron ore requires approximately ⅓ ton of coke and 1/10 ton of limestone. Modern technology is decreasing the ratio of both coke and limestone. In blast-furnace operations, a substantial amount of flue dust is produced, which contains some iron. The initial recovery of all iron present in the ore is about 93 per cent, but between 4 and 5 per cent goes up the chimneys in flue dust, which is later recovered; thus the actual recovery rate of metallic iron in the ore is about 97 per cent.

Technological improvements have included (1) careful regulation of the amount and composition of each batch of ore placed in furnaces; (2) raising the temperature, pressure, and oxygen content of the blast; (3) powdering some of the coke or, alternatively, using natural gas to raise temperatures at key places; and (4) increasing the use of beneficiated ore. It is estimated that beneficiation and use of oxygen in the blast have doubled the capacities of some blast furnaces, excluding other changes in technology.

Other techniques of pig-iron manufacture. In Norway, Sweden, Finland, Italy, Japan, and some other countries or localities where coal is scarce and hydroelectricity is plentiful and cheap, electric furnaces have partially replaced blast furnaces in pig-iron manufacture. They require only about one-half as much coke as the blast furnaces, for electricity does much of the actual heating. Open-hearth furnaces, designed chiefly for making steel, also have been used to produce iron. Even in the United States, open-hearth furnaces smelt some 4 per cent of all ore, and electric furnaces smelt less than 0.2 per cent. Experiments are also being conducted in the conversion of iron ore to metal without actual smelting—a process which is expected to be less costly than reduction.

Wrought-iron manufacture. Although pig iron may be used for products made by casting (pouring of molten

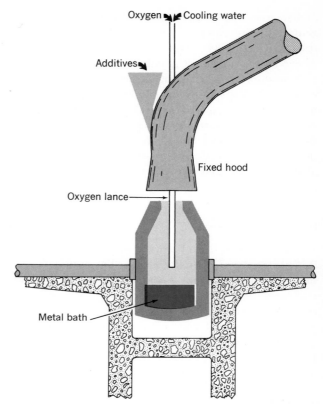

Figure 18.5 A basic oxygen converter. The oxygen is forced through the metal from the top.

metal into a mold), it is not malleable. Wrought iron, on the other hand, can be pounded and forged into a variety of shapes, does not rust easily, can be magnetized with an electric current, and possesses several other qualities rendering it useful in a variety of ways. Its manufacture is appreciably a hand operation surprisingly similar to methods of two or more centuries ago. A batch of molten pig iron is placed upon an open hearth near a flame. A workman known as a *puddler,* using a long rake, manipulates the molten iron, exposing different portions to the flame until the carbon content is essentially burned out—a condition signified when the mass becomes pasty. Deprived of its carbon, the iron is subjected to rolling and other processing. Recent efforts at mechanizing wrought-iron production have met with some success.

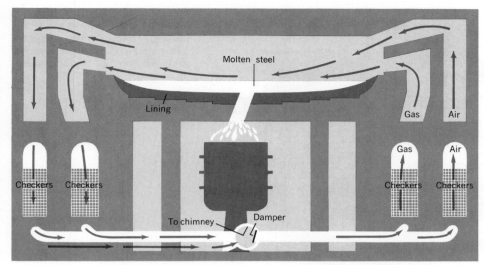

Figure 18.6 An open-hearth furnace. Modern open-hearth furnaces use not only air but also basic oxygen, which is forced in jets across the shallow pan of molten steel.

Movement of iron. About 90 per cent of all iron from blast furnaces is forwarded to steel mills, and 10 per cent is used as iron only.

Basic oxygen process. Oxygen in air has been used in steelmaking. Recently, commercial oxygen has become available at a sufficiently reduced cost so that it, too, can be used more actively. To a degree, it is used in all steelmaking processes, usually mixed with air or moisture. During the past quarter century, however, a new method, known as the *basic oxygen process* and sometimes called the *Brassert process,* was developed in Austria (Fig. 18.5). In this new method, the equipment consists essentially of a large, kettlelike converter which holds the molten pig iron. A jet of oxygen is directed from above upon the molten iron at the center of the container. The jet stream quickly oxidizes the metal upon which it is focused, causing an increase in weight. The now heavier liquid sinks, reacts chemically to oxidize some of the molten pig iron with which it comes in contact at lower levels, and at the same time is replaced at the surface by more molten iron to be processed. The basic oxygen converter can take scrap up to as much as one-fourth of its total charge and can process iron of intermediate phosphorus content (0.1 to 2 per cent). It also removes other impurities satisfactorily. Most units now in use hold 30 to 250 tons and process a charge in ten to twenty minutes. Since it makes steel equal in quality to open-hearth steel, since it is faster than any other process, and since it requires only small capital investment, the basic oxygen process offers promise of active competition. This process has gained rapid acceptance and now accounts for more than one-half of all steel made in the United States.

Open-hearth furnace. The open-hearth furnace has been preferred by many steelmakers because (1) individual units can be constructed to handle very large amounts of metal, (2) it readily accepts scrap as well as pig iron, and (3) it accepts phosphoric and sulfuric ores, which the bessemer converter (described below) cannot process. Made of steel and brick, the hearth is broad but not deep; a batch of molten metal poured into it will spread rather thinly and expose a substantial upper surface (Fig. 18.6). Over this surface pass preheated air and gas, and the carbon and other impurities of the metal thus are oxidized. The direction of the air current is reversed periodically to increase the efficiency of the impurity removal. Recently oxygen has been substituted for air in some units. Both basic and acid

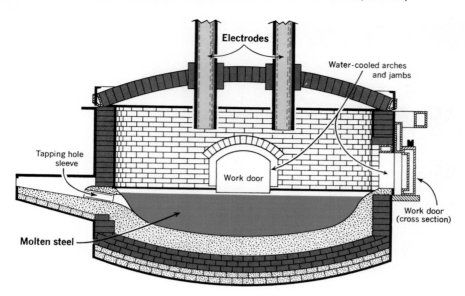

processes are employed. As in bessemer converters, the difference is essentially in the material with which the furnace is lined. Open-hearth furnaces have been built with individual capacities ranging from 10 to 600 tons of steel, with the average unit capable of working 200 to 300 tons at one time. It usually takes between eight and twelve hours to process a single charge. Once the leading process for steelmaking, the open-hearth method has rapidly declined in use, especially during the past decade, so that it now is responsible for only about one-third of all steel in the United States.

Electric furnace. We have noted that electric furnaces are used to produce small amounts of pig iron. A rather similar unit is used to make steel (Fig. 18.7). The sole contribution of the electric current appears to be very high and even heat—at least 3000°F in pig-iron manufacture and 2800°F in steel production. The furnace is usually cylindrical. In the arc type, an electric current passes through the molten pig iron from terminals usually suspended from the top. In the induction type, the current passes through a series of coils which create a magnetic field about a crucible containing the molten iron. Average units have capacities of 100 tons, although some now are twice that size. They process pig iron in three to five hours and scrap iron in five to eight hours, the length of processing time varying with the size of the batch. Chiefly because of

the accuracy with which their temperatures can be regulated, electric furnaces are excellent for making alloy steels and are also efficient utilizers of scrap. However, they are in close competition with open-hearth furnaces, the temperatures of which can be regulated with increasing exactness. Some 15 per cent of all steel produced in the United States is made with this process.

The bessemer converter. The bessemer converter consists essentially of a large container in which air or oxygen is blasted from the bottom through the molten pig iron which it contains. Its capacity ranges from 15 to 60 tons, and processing takes only ten to twenty minutes. By combustion, the oxygen in the blast simply burns out the carbon, silicon, manganese, and certain other troublesome impurities, such as sulfur and phosphorus. The original bessemer converter, lined with sandstone or some other siliceous material capable of absorbing basic impurities, cannot process pig iron of higher than 0.10 per cent phosphorus. It is still used in some plants, where it is known as the *acid bessemer converter.* A variation in its use involves lining the converter with limestone or some other basic material which can neutralize phosphorus present in rather large amounts—2 per cent or higher of total charge content. This is known today as the *basic bessemer process* or *Thomas process.* Unfortunately, neither technique is effective on pig iron with a phosphorus content of 0.1 to 2 per cent, and much of the world's pig iron falls within this range. The bessemer converter is also at a disadvantage in modern technology in that it can accept essentially no scrap, which is an important ingredient in the world's steel industry. Today, this process is minor in United States production.

The role of scrap. An important and growing consideration in steel production in the United States and elsewhere is reuse of iron and steel that has already been manufactured or has been wasted in manufacture, rather than reliance entirely upon the mined product. In the United States, approximately 1 ton of scrap is consumed for every 2 tons of iron in ore. The electric furnace is particularly effective in the processing of scrap iron and in mixing it with new iron. The basic oxygen and open-hearth processes are less so. Some scrap is recovered in the actual iron- and steelmaking process. This is called *home, revert,* or *runaround* scrap. Still other scrap is purchased from establishments which fabricate iron and steel products. This is known as *prompt* industrial scrap. Finally, other scrap is purchased from outside sources. This is usually known as *obsolete* scrap—old machines, automobiles, ships, etc. Home and prompt industrial scrap tend to be recycled quickly into the furnaces, and obsolete scrap acts as a cushion against periods of short supply in pig iron or prompt industrial scrap.

Continuous casting. Some 10 per cent of the United States annual steel is now further processed by *continuous casting.* This action involves taking molten steel directly from a furnace and converting it into desired shapes for ultimate use, thus avoiding the intermediate step of forming the molten steel into ingots and then later reheating them to form these desired shapes. This new technique was first introduced in the United States in 1963, a decade after it appeared in Europe.

Other sectoral data. Production of iron and steel is a major industry in the United States, accounting for nearly 3 per cent of all manufacturing employment and for more than 3 per cent of all shipments and value added (Fig. 18.8). Despite the heavy capital investment, it is a high-labor-cost industry, but is only intermediate in materials costs. The value added as a per cent of final shipment value is slightly below that of all manufacturing in the United States. The industry contains 329 establishments. These tend to be large: only 39 hire fewer than 5 employees, and more than 100 account for over 1,000 employees per establishment.

Spatial considerations. Figure 18.8 shows the distribution of blast furnaces, steelworks, and rolling and finishing mills in the United States and the value added by state (where these data are published). Over one-third of the plant capacity of the United States is located along the shores of the lower Great Lakes—chiefly at Chicago in Illinois; East Chicago and Gary in Indiana; Dearborn, River Rouge, and Trenton in Michigan; Toledo, Lorain, and Cleveland in Ohio; Erie in Pennsylvania; and Buffalo, Lackawanna, Tonawanda, and North Tonawanda in New York. These are scattered, but they merit a common classification because all are at, or very near, lower lake ports that are not close to iron or good coal, but depend largely upon Great Lakes transportation to bring the iron and upon land transportation to bring the coal. Equally important, they are near markets within the nation's manufacturing belt.

Within a radius of 80 miles of Pittsburgh is another group of blast furnaces with an aggregate capacity nearly equal to that along the lower Great Lakes. Some thirteen of these are in the immediate vicinities of Pittsburgh and Youngstown, and many of the others are along the upper Ohio River. This is an older producing district than the Great Lakes ports, and some equipment here is obsolescent and even obsolete.

Eastern furnaces involve eight sites in Pennsylvania, one (Baltimore at Sparrows Point) in Maryland, one (Troy) in New York, and one (Everett) in Massachusetts. All in all, these provide more than one-eighth of the nation's capacity. In the South, seven Alabama plants account for one-twelfth. The remaining furnaces are scattered rather widely throughout the country.

Locational trends. The geographic distribution of blast furnaces is undergoing some change, with lower Great Lakes and eastern seaboard sites gaining at the relative expense of some inland locations. Considered areally, this change involves different rates of growth—with faster establishment of new works in

IRON AND STEEL PRODUCTS
Secondary Activity: Substage One—Blast Furnaces, Steel Works, and Rolling and Finishing Mills (SIC 3312)

Sectoral Considerations

1. **Function and Process**
   - **A.** Function: conversion of iron ore (direct shipping, pelletized, concentrated) into iron and steel products; *substantial weight loss*
   - **B.** Process: smelting, adding of desired ferro-alloys

2. **Significance**

A. Per cent of all U.S. manufacturing employment:	2.75%
B. Per cent of all U.S. manufacturing shipments:	3.48%
C. Per cent of value added in all U.S. manufacturing:	3.39%

3. **Major Inputs**

A. Per cent of labor costs (all employees) in final shipment value:	22.35%
B. Per cent of materials costs in final shipment value:	56.05%

4. **Number and Size of Establishments**

A.	Total number:	329
B.	Size categories	
	1 4 employees or fewer:	39
	2 Between 5 and 99:	74
	3 Between 100 and 249:	38
	4 Between 250 and 499:	40
	5 Between 500 and 999:	36
	6 Over 1,000:	102

Spatial Considerations

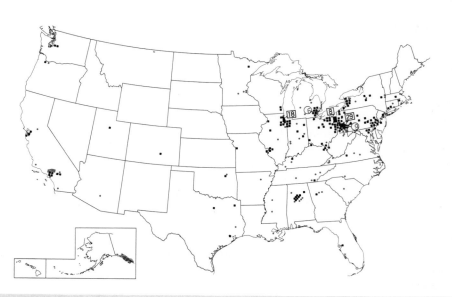

Figure 18.8 Sector-space considerations, iron and steel products, secondary activity, substage one (blast furnaces, steel works, and rolling and finishing mills—SIC 3312). For explanation of symbols, see Figure 14.3.

IRON AND STEEL PRODUCTS

Secondary Activity: Substage Two A—Production of Cold-rolled Sheet, Strip, and Bars (SIC 3316)

Sectoral Considerations

1. **Function and Process**
   - **A.** Function: conversion of steel into sheets, strips, and bars; *little weight loss*
   - **B.** Process: mainly molding and rolling

2. **Significance**
   - **A.** Per cent of all U.S. manufacturing employment: 0.10%
   - **B.** Per cent of all U.S. manufacturing shipments: 0.18%
   - **C.** Per cent of value added in all U.S. manufacturing: 0.10%

3. **Major Inputs**
   - **A.** Per cent of labor costs (all employees) in final shipment value: 14.91%
   - **B.** Per cent of materials costs in final shipment value: 74.85%

4. **Number and Size of Establishments**
   - **A.** Total number: 107
   - **B.** Size categories
     1. 4 employees or fewer: 7
     2. Between 5 and 99: 53
     3. Between 100 and 249: 18
     4. Between 250 and 499: 17
     5. Between 500 and 999: 11
     6. Over 1,000 employees: 1

Spatial Considerations

Figure 18.9 Sector-space considerations, substage two A, secondary activity (production of cold rolled sheet, strip, and bars—SIC 3316). For explanation of symbols, see Figure 14.3.

IRON AND STEEL PRODUCTS
Linkages, Steel Works and Rolling Mill Products to Other Secondary and Tertiary

Sectoral Considerations

Geographic division of origin	Tons (000)	Per cent of goods movement by means of transport				
		Rail	Motor carrier	Private truck	Water	Other and unknown
U.S.	113,521	52.9%	35.9%	3.6%	7.5%	0.1%
New England	696	20.1	74.8	4.0	1.0	0.1
Middle Atlantic	31,411	53.6	31.9	3.5	10.9	0.1
East North Central	51,705	50.7	42.6	2.6	4.1	—
West North Central	1,222	60.4	30.6	9.0	—	—
South Atlantic	10,534	47.0	30.8	2.0	19.7	0.5
East South Central	8,673	77.9	16.5	1.9	3.1	0.6
West South Central*	2,808	29.8	23.9	21.9	24.4	—
Mountain	2,469	na*	na	na	na	na
Pacific†	4,003	39.7	52.4	7.5	—	0.4

*Movement by transport not available.
† Excluding Alaska and Hawaii.
Source: United States Census of Transportation, 1967.

Spatial Considerations

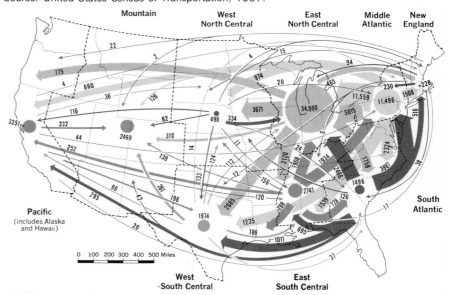

Figure 18.10 Linkages, substages one and two A, to other secondary, activities and to tertiary activity. For explanation of symbols, see Figure 15.4.

IRON AND STEEL PRODUCTS

Secondary Activity: Substage Two B—Steel Foundries (SIC 3323)

1. **Function and Process**
   - **A.** Function: conversion of molten steel into desired shapes; *little weight loss*
   - **B.** Process: casting into molds;

2. **Significance**
   - **A.** Per cent of all U.S. manufacturing employment: 0.35%
   - **B.** Per cent of all U.S. manufacturing shipments: 0.21%
   - **C.** Per cent of value added in all U.S. manufacturing: 0.30%

3. **Major Inputs**
   - **A.** Per cent of labor costs (all employees) in final shipment value: 40.24%
   - **B.** Per cent of materials costs in final shipment value: 34.10%

4. **Number and Size of Establishments**
   - **A.** Total number: 296
   - **B.** Size categories
     1. 4 employees or fewer: 21
     2. Between 5 and 99: 116
     3. Between 100 and 249: 76
     4. Between 250 and 499: 44
     5. Between 500 and 999: 27
     6. Over 1,000 employees: 12

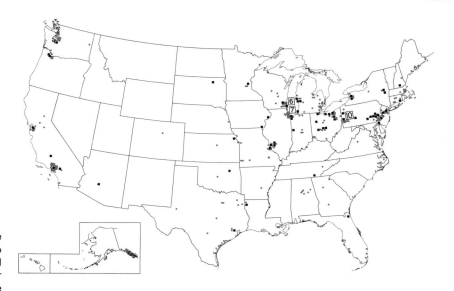

Figure 18.11 Sector-space considerations, substage two B, secondary activity (steel foundries—SIC 3323). For explanation of symbols see Figure 14.3.

IRON AND STEEL PRODUCTS

Linkages, Iron And Steel Castings To Tertiary

Geographic division of origin	Tons (000)	Per cent of goods movement by means of transport				
		Rail	Motor carrier	Private truck	Water	Other and unknown
U.S.	12,556	31.5%	49.8%	17.6%	0.6%	0.5%
New England	84	7.9	75.5	16.5	—	0.1
Middle Atlantic	1,615	35.3	56.1	8.4	0.1	0.1
East North Central	5,283	23.3	55.1	21.2	0.2	0.2
West North Central	341	24.3	61.8	13.4	—	0.5
South Atlantic	834	38.9	53.7	7.2	—	0.2
East South Central	3,267	42.2	40.5	15.8	0.5	1.0
West South Central	334	1.4	22.0	75.9	0.4	0.3
Mountain	188	na*	na	na	na	na
Pacific†	610	40.8	44.2	8.4	6.2	0.4

*Movement by transport not available.
†Excluding Alaska and Hawaii.
Source: United States Census of Transportation, 1967.

Sectoral Considerations

Spatial Considerations

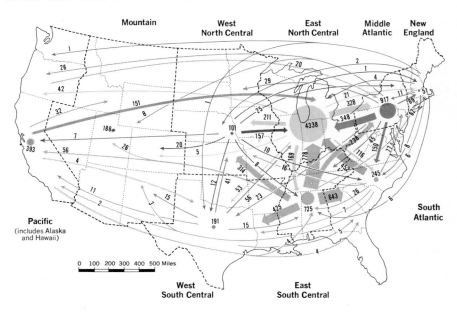

Figure 18.12 Linkages, substage two B–tertiary. For explanation of symbols, see Figure 15.4.

306

some areas than in others—rather than an outright shift of furnaces from one site to another.

Changing technology in the making of steel involving rapidly increasing reliance upon the basic oxygen process at the comparative expense of open-hearth and bessemer units could mean a major shift in location. The basic oxygen process does not require a heavy capital investment compared with the open-hearth process, and therefore it might be logical to expect a major regional shift of the U.S. steelmaking industry with this new technological and sectoral change. Another force which might also be responsible for a shift of the industry is the increased reliance upon foreign ores with the decline in the reserves of the choicest domestic ore.

Rather surprisingly, however, there was no major redistribution of the U.S. iron and steel industry within the decade of the 1960s and in the early 1970s. Instead, most of the basic oxygen units have been installed in existing locations, with a particularly heavy rate of installation in the Pittsburgh–upper Ohio region, where older steel mills, many of them smaller open-hearth units and bessemer units, have become obsolete. We shall return to this topic later in this chapter.

Substage 2A: Cold finishing of steel shapes (SIC 3316). *Sectoral considerations.* This is one of several relatively small industries which, in flow of materials, is situated between establishments producing steel and those utilizing it for various types of finished products, some of which will be described in Chapter 19. As the name implies, these establishments are engaged mainly in the rolling, in a cold process, of steel sheets, strips, bars, shapes, and other finished steel from purchased hot-rolled products. Some are a part of iron making and steelmaking, as described in the discussion of substage 1 above. Those which are described here are engaged entirely in the one function and are classified as such by the U.S. Office of Management and Budget. The process involves the passing of the various forms through rollers under different shapes and pressures resulting in products within fine limits of tolerance. As is shown in Figure 18.9, the industry is minor in comparison with the iron and steel industry, whether measured by employment, value of shipment, or value of all manufacturing in the United States. It is an interme-

diate-labor-cost industry, but is high in materials costs. The value added is small in comparison with that for all manufacturing for the United States and in comparison with the value added by blast furnaces and steel mills. Only slightly more than 100 establishments are engaged in the activity, and most hire between 5 and 99 employees (Fig. 18.9).

Spatial considerations. Geographic distribution of this activity conforms rather closely to that of blast furnaces and steel mills, particularly the lower Great Lakes production sites and those of the upper Ohio River and Pittsburgh area (Fig. 18.9).

Substage 2B: Steel foundries (SIC 3323). *Sectoral considerations.* Again, as the name implies, this activity involves the manufacturing of steel castings—a process whereby molten steel is poured into forms of a desired shape and the steel is thus hardened into that shape. This is also a small industry, but one in which labor costs are very high relative to final shipment value and in which materials costs are comparatively low. The value added as a per cent of final shipment value is a surprising 65 per cent, in comparison with the national average of all manufacturing of 47 per cent. Nearly 300 establishments are engaged in the activity, and again we see a pattern of small establishments, with the largest number employing between 5 and 99 workers (Fig. 18.11).

Spatial considerations. Like the cold-rolled steel-products industry, this activity is concentrated heavily within the East North Central and Middle Atlantic divisions of the United States, where most of the nation's steel is also produced. The map of value added in Figure 18.11 is self-explanatory in this regard.

Horizontal Linkages—Secondary to Tertiary; Tertiary Activity

Nearly all the demand for steel, iron, and initial fabricated products thereof stems from sources inside the United States—especially industries engaged in general construction and in the manufacture of transportation facilities, machinery and equipment, and containers. We shall examine some of these in Chapter 19. An important consideration here is that these various markets are not final consumer markets and hence are more to be found in the location of the key manufacturing industries and the general construction activity of the country than in the distribution of population and urban units as such (Figs. 18.10 and 18.12).

Explanation: Secondary and Tertiary Activity

Why has the iron and steel industry, and its various components, located in its present sites? Both the institutional and the theoretical explanations can provide some insight.

Institutional explanation. *Historical background.* Colonization of the United States took place during an early stage in the development of iron and steel technology. Small blast furnaces were known, operated by charcoal. The bessemer and open-hearth converters were not to be invented until 200 years later. Interest in iron manufacture was shown by some colonists almost immediately upon arrival; the Virginia Company, for example, built a furnace on the James River in 1621, but this soon was destroyed by Indians. Some twenty years later, however, a successful furnace began operation in Lynn, Massachusetts. By 1775, the iron output of this almost independent nation was about 30,000 tons. During the nineteenth century, the industry grew rapidly. By 1860, only the United Kingdom was outproducing the United States, and thirty years later even that nation had been bypassed.

At the outset the United States, like Europe of its day, used charcoal as fuel. In the nineteenth century, anthracite began to be substituted for charcoal—a technique which, although never practiced widely in Europe, gained such acceptance in the United States that by the outbreak of the Civil War anthracite was responsible for twice as much of this country's iron as was charcoal. Meanwhile, Europe shifted almost exclusively to coke in its blast furnaces, and the United States followed suit after the Civil War.

This meant a shift of the industry from eastern locations to western Pennsylvania and eastern Ohio, where the very extensive deposits of high-grade bituminous coking coal in the Appalachian region became the mainstay of fuel supply. At this time, more than four

times as much coal was necessary per ton of iron ore than is needed today. Later, when the Lake Superior iron ore began to be utilized, new plants were established at current locations along the lower Great Lakes. During the twentieth century, the lower lake sites grew at rates exceeding those in Pittsburgh and Youngstown. On the Atlantic seaboard, some new plants were constructed and existing ones were enlarged, mainly to accommodate a larger share of foreign ore. Meanwhile, iron and steel operations in the South, notably at Birmingham, Alabama, had grown to their present modest proportions; those in the West, also modest in size, achieved their present status in the twentieth century.

Because a very large amount of coke and limestone was necessary per unit of finished iron, the coalfields, especially, were important attractions to the industry. Later, with the discovery of the Lake Superior ranges in favorable juxtaposition to the Great Lakes shipping system, with technology increasing and freeing the industry, and with a heavy demand for coke and coal, location at present sites on the lakes became economically feasible. The westward extension of population in the ultimate market, which is still continuing, was another force favoring the regional location of the industry in its present sites.

Current decisions not to shift the pattern drastically with the advent of the basic oxygen process appear to be the result of two forces. On the one hand, population change seems to be stabilizing somewhat for the nation as a whole, and there appears to be some evidence that the northeastern United States, including New England and the Middle Atlantic and East North Central divisions, will continue to have the heaviest demand for the product. A second consideration is industrial inertia. Once an industry is established in a given location, with sizable capital investment, it is very reluctant to move from that location unless there are compelling reasons for such a move.[2]

Transportation costs and freight rates. The sensitivity of the United States iron and steel industry to markets is partially the result of comparatively high

[2] See especially Allan Rodgers, "Industrial Inertia: A Major Factor in the Location of the Steel Industry in the United States," *Geographical Review,* **42**:56–66, 1952.

freight rates on finished steel products—rates which on a ton-mile basis sometimes are as high as three times those for pig iron or coal. At one time, these domestic freight rates for steel were calculated as if steel were manufactured in Pittsburgh. This was the so-called Pittsburgh-plus system. Thus a Chicago steel-plant manager selling to a Chicago buyer necessarily added freight charges which would have been assesed if the product had been made in Pittsburgh. If he sold the steel in Pittsburgh, he found it necessary to absorb the cost of shipment to that city. Needless to say, Pittsburgh did not object to this arrangement, but many of the other steel-manufacturing cities did. Between 1924 and 1948, a multiple point basing system was substituted for Pittsburgh-plus, but in 1948 this too was abandoned. Now steel is shipped f.o.b. (free on board) from the factory of its production. Although many authorities feel this change of policy has favored steel producers other than those in Pittsburgh, Youngstown, and the vicinity, a sizable portion of the industry was constructed there because of the earlier freight-rate conditions and remain there today.

Theoretical explanation. Viewed from an analytical perspective we can classify the iron and steel industry in the United States according to three basic types of location, and this classification accounts in large measure for most other regions of production. Iron and steel centers are found at market sites such as those on the eastern seaboard, at raw-material sites of iron ore and coal, and at break-of-bulk points. We shall review these types of location largely in Weberian terms of minimum-transport-cost location and in terms of agglomeration.

Weber pointed out that raw-material and transport costs are the most important factors in influencing the distribution of manufacturing, and he concluded that the location of manufacturing is determined by the ratio of the weight of the localized raw materials to the weight of the product. Labor can draw industry away from its minimum-transport-cost location when savings in lower labor costs are greater than the extra transport costs involved. He also discussed the agglomerating tendency of industry, resulting from the economies which industries achieve by concentrating in a single area.

Canada

Description, measurement, and classification: Sectoral and spatial considerations. Canada exports between one-sixth and one-seventh of its annual production of iron ore—a production amounting to more than 6 per cent of the world total. Nearly two-thirds goes to the United States, and most of the remainder to the Common Market. Paradoxically, the country also imports some 20 per cent of its annual consumption, mostly from the United States but also from Brazil.

The sites of mining, export, and domestic processing are shown in Figure 18.13. The ore fields in Quebec are the main sources of supply, aggregately responsible for more than two-thirds of all Canada's iron-ore output. As shown, most of this ore is exported. Steel production is concentrated particularly in Ontario, notably Hamilton, with other important centers at Montreal and Quebec and near Vancouver in British Columbia.

Explanation. Both the institutional and the theoretical explanation for the location of Canada's iron and steel industry are focused upon two important points: foreign demand for most of the iron ore and the concentration within key metropolitan areas of domestic demand. The importance of transportation costs is critical in understanding both sets of patterns. Movement of iron ore from Quebec and Newfoundland-Labrador is a comparatively recent innovation, the first ore having been shipped in 1954. The key transportation considerations here are the 357-mile railway to Sept-Isles from this field and another from Gagnon, Quebec, 200 miles to the southwest.[3] A third site, at Wabush, on the Newfoundland-Labrador boundary, also has become an important producer. The short rail haul to the lower St. Lawrence ports, whence transfer is possible to both lake vessels and oceangoing vessels (see p. 112), means comparatively inexpensive combined land-water

[3] Trevor Lloyd, "Iron Production in Quebec Labrador," in Richard S. Thoman and Donald Patton (eds.), *Focus on Geographic Activity*, McGraw-Hill Book Company, New York, 1964, pp. 85–92.

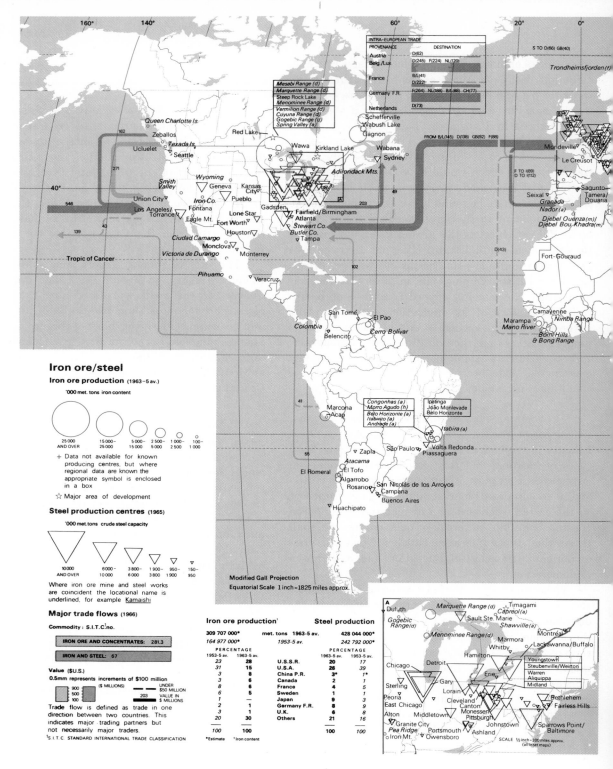

Figure 18.13 World view of production, transfer, and consumption of iron ore and steel. (After *Oxford Economic Atlas of the World,* 4th ed., p. 43)

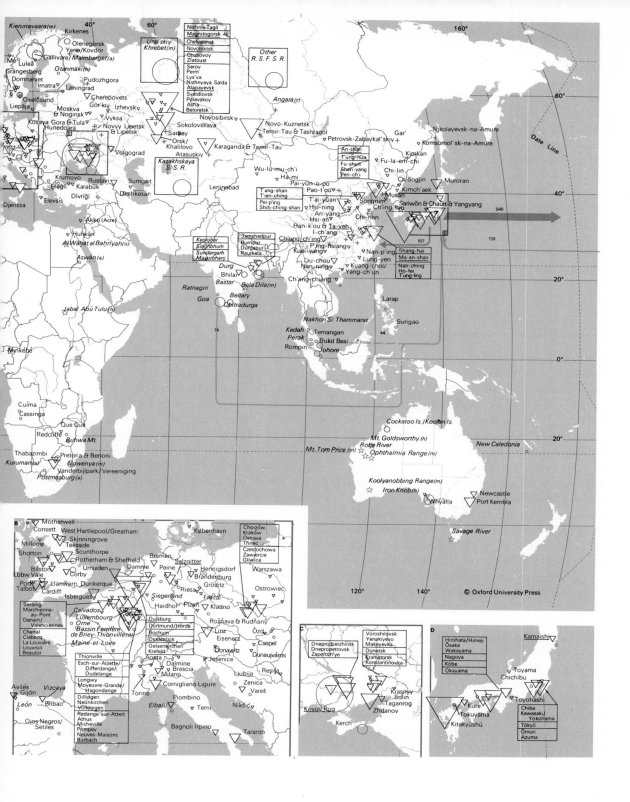

shipping costs, inasmuch as most of the ore moves by lake or coastwise vessel.

Location of a major share of the steel industry in Hamilton, Montreal, and other key urban centers is a historical development which is related appreciably to the population density of each historical period. By the beginning of the twentieth century, both a blast furnace and a steel mill had been installed in Hamilton, and another company was located there in 1913. At present, of the forty-one establishments engaged in the production of iron and steel in the country, essentially all are located in close association with the major metropolitan areas, which, directly or indirectly, form the primary domestic market.

The Soviet Union

Description, measurement, and classification: Sectoral and spatial considerations. The Soviet Union is now the world's largest producer of iron ore (more than 25 per cent of the world output), pig iron (more than 20 per cent), and steel (more than 20 per cent). It has achieved this strong position in the past fifty years, and especially in the past twenty-five, so that much of its productive capacity is comparatively new. Furthermore, the location of this production has been carefully planned by the state in this centrally planned economy. Thus, we have at once a case study involving new production regions, new technology, and centrally planned decision making. Furthermore, much of the existing plant was destroyed during the German invasion of the European section of the Soviet Union in World War II, so that new industry could indeed be based upon recent locational decisions.

Yet the Soviet iron and steel industry has rebuilt heavily in the European portion of the country, secondarily in the Urals, and at a more or less third level of intensity in Soviet Asia. The patterns of current iron-ore mining and steel production are shown in Figure 18.13. The Ukraine, long a site of iron and steel production, is now receiving increasing attention. The primary source area for iron ore is at Krivoj Rog, where deposits of hematite and some magnetite are obtained. The iron content averages 50 per cent or somewhat less in a

discontinuous belt about 35 miles long and 2 miles wide. Poorer ores exist on the margins of the core area, so that the total field can be said to be some 80 miles in length and 4 miles in width. Most of the better ores have been mined, but substantial reserves of ore contain 30 to 36 per cent iron. Integrated blast furnaces, steel furnaces, and rolling mills are found in the vicinity at the cities of Krivoj Rog, Dnepropetrovsk, Dneprodzerzinsk, and Zaporozje. Two hundred miles to the east are the steel-producing cities of the Donets River basin: Donetsk (Doneck), Jenakijevo, Kramatorsk, Makejevka, Ždanov, and lesser centers. To the south and across the sea of Azov is another fully integrated plant at Kerch (Kerč') on the Crimean peninsula. The Donets and Krivoj Rog regions produce more than one-half of all iron ore, nearly one-half of all pig iron, and almost as high a share of the steel made in the Soviet Union. Integrated complexes of Krivoj Rog and Ždanov are expanding. Volgograd, to the east, is significant.

No other iron-ore mining area of the Soviet Union has been brought into productivity more rapidly than the Urals. Production there before the 1917 revolution was less than 2 million metric tons per year. By 1945, with the Ukraine largely in German hands, nearly 70 per cent of all Soviet iron ore came from the Urals. In the 1970s, the area continues to supply huge quantities of ore, about one-third of the national total. Once very active, the Magnitogorsk iron ores are nearing depletion, and supplies are coming increasingly from Kustanai, 200 miles to the southeast. Farther northward in the Ural Mountains, mines at Uralśkije Gory serve the Urals field complex. That complex is located in an industrial region which extends latitudinally for about 600 miles and longitudinally for over 300 miles. Among the more prominent iron and steel centers are Magnitogorsk, Chelyabinsk (Čelábinsk), Ňiznij Tagil, Alapajevsk, and other centers. The Urals region now accounts for over one-third of the country's iron ore and pig iron and for slightly more of its steel.

A grouping of cities in the latitudinal center of the European section of the Soviet Union, including Moscow (Moskva), Cherepovets (Čerepovec), Leningrad, Vyksa, Gorkij, and neighboring places are receiving increasing attention in the Soviet Union, partly because of their general proximity to the huge Kursk iron-ore deposits, which are located about half way between

Moscow and the Donets region. Recoverable deposits there have an iron content of 30 to 40 per cent and lie at depths as shallow as 200 feet. The problem with this industrial area is a shortage of coal, of which some must be shipped from the Kuznets basin in Soviet Central Asia. For this reason, a substantial number of plants in this area are steel centers, rather than fully integrated operations. This is especially true of the larger plants.

In Soviet Central Asia, the Kuznets region has been developed by the various five-year plans of the Soviet Union, especially during the past quarter century. The Kuznets basin has excellent supplies of coal, but is short of an ample supply of iron ore, much of which must be shipped from the Kazachskaja S.S.R. Important steel-producing centers include the integrated facilities at Novokuznetsk (Novokuzneck) and the steel furnace at Novosibirsk. The Kuznets region now produces only about 7 per cent of the nation's iron and less than 10 per cent of its steel. Recently, the Karaganda area has expanded in steel production (Fig. 18.13).

Locational trends. In terms of population density, the European section of the Soviet Union has been, and still is, the major source of demand. Furthermore, most of the iron ore which is exported moves into centrally planned countries immediately to the west of the Soviet Union. Much of the demand in the Ukraine declined temporarily when the Germans invaded this area, so that the Urals and Asian fields gained. This gain was augmented by the desire of central planning authorities to develop Soviet Central Asia, the far east, and the far north. Plans in the late 1950s and early 1960s revealed such efforts to develop the Asian portion of the Soviet Union. However, planning in the mid-1970s indicates an understanding of the realities of market demand, even in a centrally planned economy. Particular attention is being paid once again to the Ukraine, to the central European area around Moscow, and to the Urals-Kuznets.

Explanation. Whether we are concerned with the institutional or the theoretical explanation, it is necessary to examine transportation costs and distances if we are to understand trends in the location and functioning of the iron and steel industry of the Soviet Union. The country has no inland system of inexpensive lake-vessel transport such as exists in the Great Lakes–St. Lawrence Seaway system of North America. Most rivers there are north-south oriented, whereas the primary direction of commodity movement is east-west. Railways move most of the heavy freight for long distances. Given the historical development of the Soviet Union, which emphasized growth of the European portion, the country has not been successful in overcoming the magnetism of market demand of this effective area. True, it was possible to bring the Urals into production by long-term investment without expectation of early return or amortization, but this region is located in relatively close proximity to the heavy population pressures of the Ukraine, Moscow, Leningrad, and other sections of the effective part of the country. It is also true that the Kuznets area has been developed to the degree that it has some national prominence. A substantial portion of its finished product, however, serves regional, rather than national, demand. Thus a centrally planned, profit-free economy has been very attentive to existing market demand and transport costs in planning and implementing its iron and steel industry.

The Common Market

Description, measurement, and classification: Sectoral and spatial considerations. If the Soviet Union is the largest single nation in terms of production of iron ore, iron, and steel, it is exceeded by the nine-nation Common Market in the last two of these categories. This group, which appears to be evolving toward the status of a single nation, is responsible for nearly 12 per cent of all iron ore and for more than 23 per cent of all iron and all steel.

France is the leading supplier of iron ore, responsible for some two-thirds of all that is produced in the Common Market. Most of this comes from the historically famed Minette iron-ore fields in northeastern France and in Luxembourg (Fig. 18.13, large circle). Essentially all other supplies of iron ore in the Common Market are small in reserves, lean in quality, and rather widely distributed in location. The United Kingdom utilizes its rather poor and scattered fields for about one-half of its domestic demand, and West Germany depends upon its even leaner fields for approximately one-fourth.

West Germany is the leading producer of both pig iron and steel. It is followed by France, the United Kingdom, and Belgium in the pig-iron output and by the United Kingdom, France, Belgium-Luxembourg, and Italy in the production of steel. The famed Ruhr River district (Fig. 18.13, Duisburg, etc.) is responsible for the overwhelming portion of this iron and steel output—a production which is located over the Ruhr coalfields. A smaller productive capacity is situated in the Saar coalfields nearby, and other output is rather widely scattered in West Germany. In the United Kingdom, the facilities also are located on coal: on the eastern, southern, and western margins of the Pennines Mountains, in the Scottish Lowlands of the north, and along the southern fringe of the Welsh peninsula to the southwest. In France, facilities are located especially on and near the Minette iron-ore field and along the coal deposits of the Meuse River that extend across from the Sambre coalfield of Belgium-Luxembourg.

Explanation. The production of pig iron and steel in Europe is located overwhelmingly on either coal or iron ore. This is particularly true of the Minette iron-ore field of France, of the Ruhr and Saar coalfields of Germany, and of the Sambre-Meuse coalfields of Belgium, Luxembourg, and France. Indeed, the entire area can be considered a single iron- and steel-producing region, the north-south axis of which extends for approximately 250 miles. In the United Kingdom, also, coal has long attracted the iron and steel facilities, with the imported iron ore supplied by way of relatively handy seaports in this comparatively small island. Both areas depend to some degree upon scrap—West Germany and France for approximately 20 per cent, and the United Kingdom for nearly 40 per cent—and upon imports of iron ore from Sweden and elsewhere.

The explanation for the location of the iron and steel facilities thus is first and foremost an early orientation to coalfields, at which time a very high ratio of coal to iron was necessary in the smelting process. As we have seen, that ratio now has declined, and still is declining, but industrial inertia—the propensity to use existing facilities even when they sometimes are obsolete or to rebuild at existing sites—has tended to encourage continuity of these locations. As to efficiency of function, which is another key interest of economic geographers in economic activity, government policy has played a very critical role. For years, the governments in France and West Germany found cooperation difficult, and during the past century their differences have erupted into three major wars and a number of lesser conflicts. The United Kingdom, while involved in some of these conflicts, looked primarily away from Europe toward an empire and later commonwealth to supply needed materials and markets for its iron and steel industry as well as its other activity.

Only during the past quarter century has a cooperative movement of northwestern Europe come into a meaningful context. The formulation of the initial six-member Common Market in the late 1950s, and the acceptance of three additional members in the early 1970s, has meant that, at long last, economic activity with splendid reciprocal access and an equally favorable potential for effective linkages might, in fact, come into being. Government policy therefore has been reversed in the past century from that of a narrow nationalism that weakened the natural linkages between and among the various producing areas and their ultimate markets to that of an international cooperation which, to date, has been surprisingly successful, despite adverse cross-currents that still remain.

Japan

Japan deserves mention in this chapter if only because of its outstanding volume of production, considering that it is an island nation, essentially without good supplies of either iron ore or fuel. Producing only a token amount—less than $2/10$ of 1 per cent—of the world's iron ore, this country is responsible for over 16 per cent of all pig iron and of all steel. In 1946, Japan had been so thoroughly destroyed by bombing that it had only 500 thousand tons of steelmaking capacity. Twenty-five years later it had essentially a capacity of 100 million tons, of which more than 80 per cent was based upon the basic oxygen process. Heaviest plant concentrations are in coastal cities in Kyushu and southern Honshu, with lesser works in northern Honshu and southern Hokkaido. This is an industry in

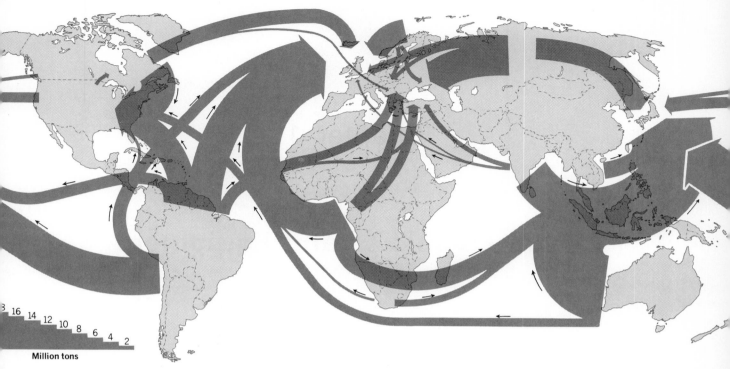

Million tons

Figure 18.14 Estimated world trade in iron ore (iron content) in 1980.
(After Fig. 22 in Gerald Manners, *The Changing World Market for Iron Ore, 1950–1980,* Baltimore, Johns Hopkins Press for Resources for the Future, 1971, p. 318)

which inexpensive labor is applied to a highly efficient, modern technology to produce a commodity destined for overseas as well as domestic consumption. Clearly, the most important locational force is the pull of the seaports, which supply so much of the ore and coal and forward the substantial portion of finished material.

World Trends

Although this chapter is focused mainly upon the United States and Canada, a look at world trends is revealing. A recent book implies these trends for the entire industry by assessment of changing demand for iron ore.[4] Between 1964 and 1980, trade in iron ore (measured by iron content only) is expected to increase

[4]Gerald Manners, *The Changing World Market for Iron Ore, 1915–1980,* The Johns Hopkins Press for Resources for the Future, Inc., Baltimore, 1971.

from 110 million metric tons to 250 million and to rise proportionately from less than 40 per cent of all consumed iron in ore to more than 46 per cent. Australia will become an extremely important supplier, especially to Japan (Fig. 18.14). Latin America will probably increase its supplies to the United States, Western Europe, and Japan, as will Canada (especially to the United States and Western Europe). Western Africa will ship more and more of this product to Western Europe and Japan, and to Eastern Europe as well. The Soviet Union will increase its shipments, notably to Western Europe.

Perhaps the most important conclusion is implied rather than stated in the map of future world iron-ore trade: that trade is to become much more international than is now the case, with both institutional and theoretical explanations applied increasingly at the global, rather than the national or economic community levels of observation.

Chapter 19

Motor Vehicles and Equipment

The making of motor vehicles involves the putting together of some 15,000 semifinished and finished materials into completed units. Steel is an important component of the automobile, and in a sense, the motor vehicle industry can be considered a further substage of steelmaking. However, so many other semiprocessed materials are utilized in this industry that it is best considered a separate economic activity.

The United States is the leading producer and consumer of motor vehicles, especially passenger cars, and is responsible for about 30 per cent (measured by number rather than size of units) of the world total. The European Economic Community now produces nearly 40 per cent of all such cars, and Japan about 15 per cent. Both the European and the Japanese cars tend to be smaller than those made in the United States. Japan produces nearly one-third of all commercial vehicles, the United States about one-fourth, the European Economic Community approximately one-fifth, and the Soviet Union slightly more than one-tenth. Canada accounts for some 4 per cent of all passenger and commercial vehicles.

The United States

Some 69 per cent of all natural rubber, 62 per cent of all synthetic rubber, 60 per cent of all reclaimed rubber, 51 per cent of all lead, 46 per cent of all sheet steel, 34 per cent of all zinc, 32 per cent of all strip steel, 29 per cent of all bar steel, 28 per cent of all alloy steel, 16 per cent of all types of steel, 14 per cent of all stainless steel, 11 per cent of all nickel, 8 per cent of all aluminum, 8 per cent of all copper, and 2 per cent of all cotton consumed in the United States are accounted for by the nation's motor vehicle industry. These figures suggest the importance of this industry in the United States as a consumer of raw materials and semiprocessed goods. It is also impressive in terms of demand, as reflected in the nation's tertiary sector: Some 24 per cent of all retail sales, 17 per cent of all wholesale trade, and 17 per cent of all service trade other than retail or wholesale are attributable to motor vehicles.[1]

[1] *1971 Automobile Facts and Figures,* Automobile Manufacturers Association, Inc., 1971, p. 42.

These figures do not include the substantial number of employees in the public sector—those who plan highways, collect taxes, sell licenses, etc.—who are indirectly tied to the motor vehicle industry. Whether or not wisely, this economic activity is a keystone to both the society and the economy of the United States and, certainly when measured by numbers, is much more important to this country than to any other.

Primary Activity

As indicated in the list of products consumed, the motor vehicle industry of the United States stimulates a number of different primary activities in various portions of the world. Indeed, at one time, when natural rubber was in short supply and synthetic rubber had not yet been produced actively, some of the large automobile corporations maintained their own plantations in the tropics. Today, in the involved systems of interlocking ownership and directorates, some of the companies have interests in mining and other primary activities in various parts of the world. However, samples of these primary activities have been treated elsewhere in this book, and we can consider here that the automobile industry essentially begins at the secondary, or manufacturing, stage.

Secondary Activity

Specifically, in U.S. Office of Management and Budget terminology, the classification "motor vehicles and motor vehicle equipment" is listed at the three-digit detail. Under that heading, we have selected a number of four-digit activities for careful review: motor vehicles and passenger-car bodies (SIC 3711), truck and bus bodies (SIC 3713), motor vehicle parts and accessories (SIC 3714), and truck trailers (SIC 3715). Although, to be consistent in the book, we shall refer to these as substages, each tends to be somewhat separate and not necessarily a stage in an ongoing series. This is particularly true of the manufacture of motor vehicle parts and accessories, an industry which produces materials either to be added on after manufacture or to be used as repair parts during the ten years or more of the life of the automobile.

Substage 1A: Motor vehicles (SIC 3711). *Description, measurement, and classification. Function and process.* The generally familiar process of motor vehicle assembly, if the plant is fully integrated, is that as shown in Figure 19.1. Where the overall process is not fully integrated within a single plant, as is increasingly the case, the final assembly operation may occur in a separate place located only a few miles away, or many thousands of miles away, from the remainder of the process. A significant recent change in the process has been the addition of the computer, especially in the selection of various types, colors, and shapes of parts for the specific automobiles. As a result, automobiles need no longer go down the assembly line in rows of similar styles and models, but can be varied as to style and type in accordance with specialized requests received from dealers.

Sectoral considerations. The production of motor vehicles (SIC 3711) is responsible for nearly 1.7 per cent of all manufacturing employment, nearly 5 per cent of all manufacturing shipments, and slightly less than 3 per cent of the value added in all manufacturing (Fig. 19.2). As we have stated previously, this is a major industry in the United States economy. Furthermore, it tends to be a large-establishment industry, with 72 of the total number of 181 establishments hiring more than 1,000 employees each. Paradoxically, it also is a small-establishment industry, with a total of 78 plants hiring fewer than 100 employees each. However, more than 90 per cent of the value added in manufacture is accounted for by the large establishments. By Alderfer and Michl criteria, the industry is low in labor costs and high in materials costs. However, its value added as a per cent of final shipment value is only 27 per cent, compared with the national average of some 47 per cent.

Spatial considerations. The distribution of motor vehicle plants in the United States is well known. More than one-third of the value added is concentrated in Michigan, especially in Detroit and its environs. Neighboring Ohio, Indiana, Wisconsin, and Illinois also are important. Farther removed are important facilities in New York, California, Missouri, and Georgia, as well as lesser production in a number of states. We stated earlier that the facilities located away from Michigan

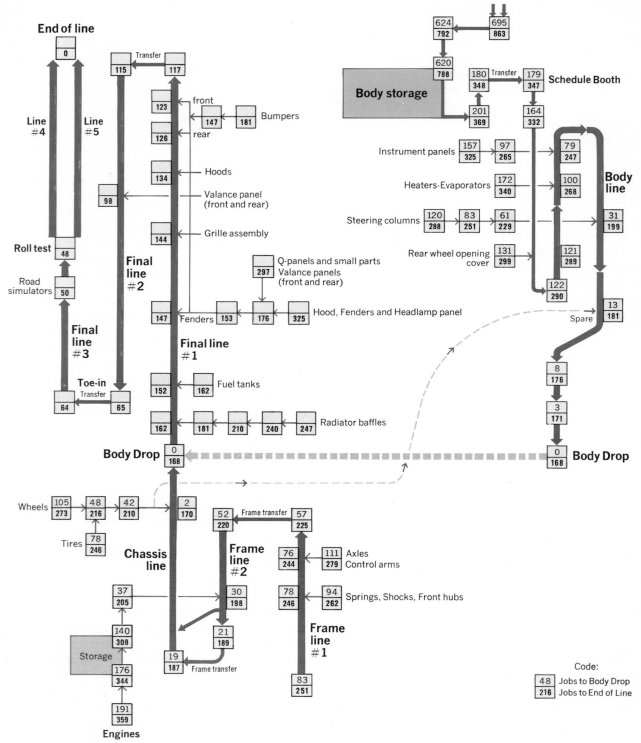

Figure 19.1 Assembly flow chart of the Pontiac Motor Division, General Motors Corporation. (After information supplied from GMC)

tend overwhelmingly to be engaged in final assembly operations, with the initial stages of manufacture concentrated within and near Detroit.

Substage 1B: Motor vehicle parts and accessories (SIC 3714). *Description, measurement, and classification. Function and process.* The function of this industry is to produce necessary repair parts and accessories for motor vehicles. The processes vary sharply because of the wide range of end-product materials, but they tend to be only semiautomated and to be produced in a large number of comparatively small establishments (Fig. 19.3).

Sectoral considerations. This is a surprisingly large and active manufacturing industry, actually accounting for more manufacturing employment than the motor vehicle industry itself (1.88 per cent of all manufacturing employment, as compared with 1.66 per cent for all motor vehicles manufacture). The value of shipments, however, is less than one-half that of the motor vehicle industry, and the value added by manufacturing is somewhat more than three-fourths that of the motor vehicle industry. Production of parts and accessories is a very high-labor-cost industry, with labor responsible for nearly one-fourth of the final shipment value. It is, however, low in costs of materials, which account for only slightly more than 50 per cent of the value of final shipment. The value added by manufacturing is nearly 50 per cent of final shipment value—a high figure when compared with some 47 per cent for all manufacturing in the nation as a whole. Establishments are small but numerous, with most of them employing between 5 and 99 workers and almost as many employing fewer than 5.

Spatial considerations. Despite the nature of its function and process, the small size of its establishments, and the decentralized market for its final product, the motor vehicle parts and accessories industry is geographically concentrated in the same general area as that producing motor vehicles. Michigan alone is responsible for more than 40 per cent of the value added in the industry, with neighboring states, especially Ohio and New York, key producers.

Substages 1C and 1D: Manufacture of truck and bus bodies and truck trailers (SIC 3713, 3715). The salient data on these two activities are shown in Figures 19.5 and 19.6. Each is much less important, whether measured in terms of employment, value of shipment, or value added, than the making of motor vehicles or of motor vehicle parts and accessories. Geographically, as measured by value of shipments, they are not so concentrated in Michigan as the motor vehicles industry, but tend to be located in neighboring states and in the Middle Atlantic region.

Tertiary Activity

Oriented to domestic markets. As we all know, the sale of motor vehicles in the United States is by way of dealerships, which have contractual arrangements with the major manufacturing firms. Accessories and parts generally are sold also through the same dealerships, although these are augmented by a wide range of independent firms, mail-order houses, etc. There are now slightly more than 25,000 dealers in the United States which handle the domestically made motor vehicles. In addition, there are now more than 12,000 dealers selling foreign makes, including many dual dealerships that sell both domestic and imported vehicles. All in all, more than 7 million passenger cars of domestic origin and between 1 and 1.5 million cars of foreign origin are sold in the United States each year (Figs. 19.4, 19.7, 19.8).

For obvious reasons, including frequent checkups and service, the automobile dealers tend to be market-oriented and to be geographically distributed in general accordance with population density. This is also true, in lesser measure, of distributors of parts and accessories, which can be somewhat more concentrated than the dealers themselves and can rely upon mail-order trade. The sale of truck and bus bodies and trailers tends to be oriented to smaller motor vehicle manufacturers and hence is as much a secondary as a tertiary activity. In some comparatively rare instances, truck and bus trailers may be sold to final consumers to augment existing equipment, in which case the activity is classified as a wholesale action to a user rather than to a producer. In any case, the market for these two

MOTOR VEHICLES AND EQUIPMENT

Secondary Activity: Substage One A—Motor Vehicles (SIC 3711)

Sectoral Considerations

1. **Function and Process**
   - **A.** Function: assembly of motor vehicles
   - **B.** Process: mainly assembly line, especially in final stages (see Figure 19.1)

2. **Significance**
   - **A.** Per cent of all U.S. manufacturing employment: 1.66%
   - **B.** Per cent of all U.S. manufacturing shipments: 4.89%
   - **C.** Per cent of value added in all U.S. manufacturing: 2.80%

3. **Major Inputs**
   - **A.** Per cent of labor costs (all employees) in final shipment value: 9.89%
   - **B.** Per cent of materials costs in final shipment value: 73.13%

4. **Number and Size of Establishments**
   - **A.** Number: 181
   - **B.** Size categories
     - 1 4 employees or fewer: 33
     - 2 Between 5 and 99: 45
     - 3 Between 100 and 249: 11
     - 4 Between 250 and 499: 10
     - 5 Between 500 and 999: 10
     - 6 Between 1,000 and 2,499: 19
     - 7 Over 2,500 employees: 53

Spatial Considerations

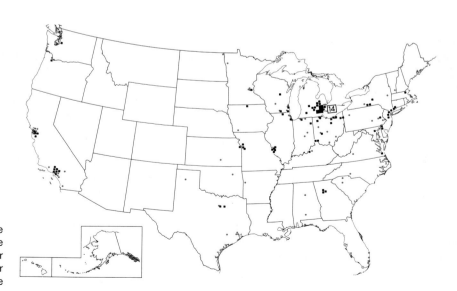

Figure 19.2 Sector-space considerations, substage one A, secondary activity (motor vehicles—SIC 3711). For explanation of symbols, see Figure 14.3.

MOTOR VEHICLES AND EQUIPMENT

Secondary Activity: Substage One B—Motor Vehicle Parts and Accessories (SIC 3714)

Sectoral Considerations

1. **Function and Process**
   - **A.** Function: manufacture of spare parts and of accessories
   - **B.** Process: mainly assembly line or hand operations (varies with size of establishment)

2. **Significance**
   - **A.** Per cent of all U.S. manufacturing employment: 1.88%
   - **B.** Per cent of all U.S. manufacturing shipments: 2.08%
   - **C.** Per cent of value added in all U.S. manufacturing: 2.17%

3. **Major Inputs**
   - **A.** Per cent of labor costs (all employees) in final shipment value: 24.86%
   - **B.** Per cent of materials costs in final shipment value: 51.12%

4. **Number and Size of Establishments**
   - **A.** Total number: 1,674
   - **B.** Size categories
     1. 4 employees or fewer: 579
     2. Between 5 and 99:   720
     3. Between 100 and 249:   153
     4. Between 250 and 499:   87
     5. Between 500 and 999:   55
     6. Over 1,000 employees: 80

Spatial Considerations

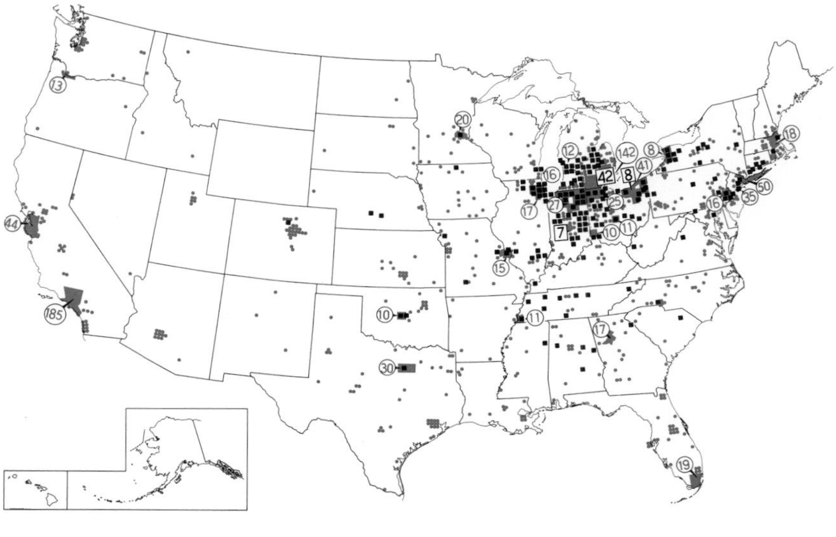

Figure 19.3 Sector-space considerations, substage one B, secondary activity (motor vehicle parts and accessories —SIC 3714). For explanation of symbols, see Figure 14.3.

MOTOR VEHICLES AND PARTS

Linkages, Substages One A and One B to Tertiary Activity

Geographic division of origin	Tons (000)	Per cent of goods movement by means of transport			
		Rail	Motor carrier	Private truck	Other and unknown
U.S.	35,629	57.5%	37.2%	4.7%	0.6%
Middle Atlantic	2,831	46.8	53.0	—	0.2
East North Central	26,617	60.7	33.4	5.4	0.5
West North Central	2,188	64.6	34.8	0.2	0.4
South Atlantic	1,921	37.7	60.8	1.4	0.1
Rest of U.S.	2,072	na*	na	na	na

*Movement by transport not available.
Source: United States Census of Transportation, 1967.

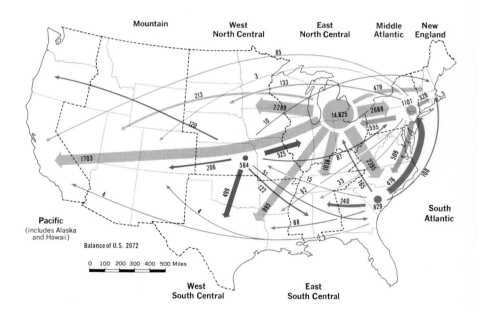

Figure 19.4 Linkages, substages one A and one B to other secondary and to tertiary. For explanation of symbols, see Figure 15.4.

MOTOR VEHICLES AND EQUIPMENT
Secondary Activity: Substage One C—Truck and Bus Bodies (SIC 3713)

Sectoral Considerations

1. **Function and Process**
   - **A.** Function: manufacture of truck and bus bodies
   - **B.** Process: mainly hand and semi-assembly line operations

2. **Significance**
   - **A.** Per cent of all U.S. manufacturing employment: 0.15%
   - **B.** Per cent of all U.S. manufacturing shipments: 0.12%
   - **C.** Per cent of all value added in all U.S. manufacturing: 0.12%

3. **Major Inputs**
   - **A.** Per cent of labor costs (all employees) in final shipment value: 27.21%
   - **B.** Per cent of materials costs in final shipment value: 53.30%

4. **Number and Size of Establishments**
   - **A.** Total number: 641
   - **B.** Size categories
     1. 4 employees or fewer: 175
     2. Between 5 and 99: 401
     3. Between 100 and 249: 41
     4. Between 250 and 499: 12
     5. Between 500 and 999: 10
     6. Over 1,000 employees: 2

Spatial Considerations

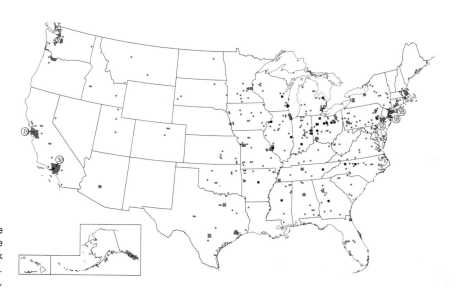

Figure 19.5 Sector-space considerations, substage one C, secondary activity (truck and bus bodies—SIC 3713). For explanation of symbols, see Figure 14.3.

MOTOR VEHICLES AND EQUIPMENT
Secondary Activity: Substage One D—Truck Trailers (SIC 3715)

1. **Function and Process**
   - **A.** Function: manufacture of truck trailers
   - **B.** Process: mainly hand and semi-assembly line operations

2. **Significance**
   - **A.** Per cent of all U.S. manufacturing employment: 0.11%
   - **B.** Per cent of all U.S. manufacturing shipments: 0.12%
   - **C.** Per cent of value added in all U.S. manufacturing: 0.10%

3. **Major Inputs**
   - **A.** Per cent of labor costs (all employees) in final shipment value: 20.6%
   - **B.** Per cent of materials costs in final shipment value: 62.44%

4. **Number and Size of Establishments:**
   - **A.** Total number: 179
   - **B.** Size categories
     - 1 4 employees or fewer: 37
     - 2 Between 5 and 99: 88
     - 3 Between 100 and 249: 24
     - 4 Between 250 and 499: 21
     - 5 Between 500 and 999: 6
     - 6 Over 1,000 employees: 3

Spatial Considerations

Figure 19.6 Sector-space considerations, substage one D, secondary activity (truck trailers—SIC 3715). For explanation of symbols, see Figure 14.3.

Linkages, Substages One C and One D To Tertiary Activity

Sectoral Considerations

Geographic division of origin	Tons (000)	Per cent of goods movement by means of transport				
		Rail	Motor carrier	Private truck	Water	Other and unknown
U.S.	896	57.9%	26.4%	14.3%	0.4%	1.0%
Middle Atlantic	85	8.1	55.7	35.9	0.3	—
East North Central	147	44.6	39.3	14.5	0.3	1.3
Pacific*	275	66.9	25.6	5.5	1.0	1.0
Rest of U.S.†	389	na†	na	na	na	na

*Excluding Alaska and Hawaii.
†Movement by transport not available.
Source: United States Census of Transportation, 1967.

Spatial Considerations

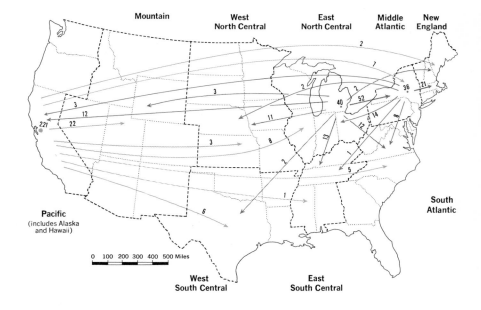

Figure 19.7 Linkages, substages one C and one D to other secondary and to tertiary. For explanation of symbols, see Figure 15.4. Note the rather heavy movement from the Pacific division to the eastern half of the country—offset, at least partially, by westward shipments from the East North Central and Middle Atlantic divisions.

MOTOR VEHICLES AND EQUIPMENT

Tertiary Activity

1. Function and Process

A. Function: wholesale and retail distribution

B. Process: mainly contact with customers at automotive retail establishments

2. Significance

A. Per cent of all U.S. retail labor force: 9.66%

B. Per cent of value of all U.S. retail sales: 17.99%

3. Number and Size of Establishments

A. Total number, excluding gasoline stations: 105,500

B. Size categories

1 5 employees or fewer: 64,918

2 Between   6 and 49: 33,157

3 Between 50 and 99: 2,615

4 Over 100: 664

5 Not operated entire year: 4,146

**Spatial
Considerations**

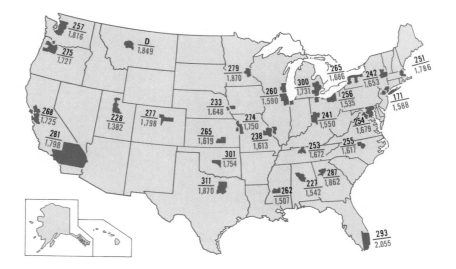

Figure 19.8 Sector-space considerations, tertiary activity (motor vehicles and equipment). For explanation of symbols, see Figure 14.7. Includes sales of new and used cars (numerator figures).

commodities tends to be firms rather than individuals, and their geographic orientation to population density is less explicit than that of the sale of motor vehicles.

Involving Foreign Trade. With respect to exports and imports, some 4 per cent of the passenger cars manufactured in the United States, and more than 10 per cent of commercial vehicles, are sent into foreign markets, especially into Western Europe and Canada. All in all, United States automotive exports of cars, trucks, and buses amount to more than 1.5 billion dollars each year. However, total automotive exports reach more than 4 billion dollars, the important difference being supplied by parts, tires, and related materials.

Even more startling is the sale of foreign cars in the United States, which increased from 6.1 per cent of all automobiles in 1965 to more than 15 per cent in the early 1970s, excluding shipments from Canada. Wholesaling and shipping arrangements for both the exported and imported automobiles tend to be made by firms of their manufacture. Dealerships are established, respectively, in foreign markets by the United States firms, or in the domestic markets by foreign firms, in much the same manner as has been described above for domestic arrangements.

Explanation: Secondary and Tertiary Activity

Institutional explanation. *Historical background.* Although considered a prime example of modern technology, the motor vehicle is very much rooted in the past. One account of its development begins in 1678, with the use of the cylinder and the piston to pump water.[2] Later came the steam engine, the self-propelled vehicle, interchangeable parts, toll roads, time and motion studies, and crude gasoline-powered buggies. In 1899, in Lansing, Michigan, the Olds Motor Works was established. This is reputed to have been the first United States factory devoted solely to car manufacture. In 1909 came the famed Model T of Henry Ford, and by 1913 the output of the "Tin Lizzie" reached 1,000 vehicles a day. In that same year, used cars began to compete actively with new ones. By 1925, more closed than open automobiles were being made,

and the groundwork for today's automobile industry was laid. In 1973, the last convertible was made by Ford Motor Company; future cars will be closed (occasionally with sun roofs).

In locational terms, the key consideration regarding the institutional-historical background of the United States automobile manufacturing industry is that it evolved from an earlier, horse-drawn-buggy era in which sites were concentrated in Michigan. It has continued in the Michigan area, partly because of industrial inertia and partly because the location is advantageous in terms of transport costs for both incoming materials and finished products.

Corporate structure. The "Big Three" of the automobile industry—General Motors, Ford, and Chrysler—supply about 96 per cent of the value of the domestic automobile market. General Motors alone accounts for about one-half of the market, and Ford for over one-fourth. Because of the volume and far-flung national and global distribution of their operations, these corporations are able to maximize economies of scale which smaller competitors cannot. Such economies reach beyond the production of automobiles: General Motors, for example, turns out some forty products including diesel locomotive engines, refrigerators, spark plugs, and radios. Each of the other passenger-car producers has at least one nonautomotive division.

Plans for decentralization. The cost of shipping a finished automobile by rail is at least twelve times as high as that of shipping the various parts in a knocked-down form ready for final assembly.[3] Therefore, some final assembly operations are performed in special plants situated not far from the nation's 25,000 dealers selling domestically made automobiles. As we have noted, the dealers have located with an eye to potential markets. The migration of the nation's population to cities and towns has meant an increased clustering tendency on the part of many dealer establishments, with such clusters especially prominent in the large metropolitan areas. This attraction of dealers to urban markets and of final assembly plants to dealers has meant some decentralization in the final assem-

---

[2] Merrill Denison, *The Power to Go,* Doubleday & Company, Inc., Garden City, N.Y., 1956, pp. 13–18.

[3] Neil P. Hurley, "The Automotive Industry: A Study in Industrial Location," *Land Economics,* **35**:1–14, 1959.

bly plants of the nation's automobile industry from the Michigan area to the vicinity of urban and a few rural markets. This decentralization is not due entirely to final market considerations. It is as well a shift toward large numbers of people to provide a *combination* of market, labor, raw and semiprocessed material, and still other advantages. The labor force of the automobile industry, for example, is composed to a surprising degree of unskilled or semiskilled workers, for many operations of the industry are at least semiautomated. Where sizable populations exist, such labor is easily available. We have noted the wide range of semiprocessed materials required by the industry and these are most easily available in large manufacturing areas, which attract a variety of industries.

Summary. In brief review, the institutional-historical explanation of the location of those components of the automobile industry which we have examined in this chapter is as follows: The industry began in and around Detroit, where the manufacture of horse-drawn buggies had become a thriving activity. The addition of motors to such buggies was an easy adaptation. A very large number of small firms and establishments characterized the infant stages of the industry, but these were reduced with competition to the Big Three and lesser competitors. Location decisions increasingly have become major corporate decisions. However, the freight-rate structure and population distribution have had an effect upon the location of some final assembly plants, so that the industry has become somewhat decentralized and diffused—but only slightly so.

Theoretical explanation. *Secondary activity.* Unlike the production of several other commodities previously discussed, motor vehicle and equipment production has no primary stage, but may be viewed as a substage of iron and steel production, discussed in the preceding chapter. Our theoretical explanation is therefore concerned only with secondary and tertiary production. Secondary production has been divided into four substages according to their respective SIC groupings.

Motor vehicle production is characterized by strong scale economies, which result, as discussed in Chapter 12, in lower unit costs of production as the scale of output increases. Hence, as we would expect, the industry comprises a few large plants. Because of massive capital requirements, entry into the market is highly restricted, and smaller enterprises over the industry's relatively short history have become integrated into the present few representative companies. This large-scale capital-intensive requirement has the further effect of making fixed costs a significant proportion of total costs and thus produces a strong tendency toward so-called industrial location inertia.

In the fabrication process there are significant Weberian weight reductions, and hence, as we would expect, the few large plants are dominantly raw-material-oriented rather than market-oriented. Labor costs represent a fairly small proportion of total costs relative to raw-material inputs, and hence there is no tendency for the industry to move to areas of cheap labor and away from minimum-transportation-cost locations. This rationale applies also to substages 1C and 1D, with the Atlantic states also providing proximity to raw-material inputs.

Assembly takes place at both production installations and in separate assembly plants at market locations. Several factors are important here: (1) Transportation costs for assembled products are significantly greater than those for parts; (2) separate assembly plants are located only at points in, or adjacent to, the largest markets; and (3) transportation costs increase rapidly as the market changes from a single large market to many small dispersed market locations. Assembly, in a theoretical sense, therefore would tend to represent a locational distribution which followed a minimum-transportation-cost location between two different market distributions. These market distributions are, on the one hand, large, concentrated market centers (assembly divorced from production) and dispersed smaller markets (assembly integrated with production).

Substage 1B in automotive production—namely, parts and accessories—can be discussed in terms of our theory concerning three basic concepts: external economies of linkage, scale economies, and skilled labor inputs. Parts- and accessories-producing units are located adjacent to automotive production plants, but consist of small establishments and utilize a high value of labor inputs. External economies of scale result when a large concentration of plants producing the same type of product and linked products locate in the same area. A division of labor develops in the linked industry, allowing plants to engage in the production of highly specialized outputs. These specialist plants, by supplying several firms with the same products, can both develop a high level of technical expertise and achieve some scale economies from a large volume of output. This would not be possible if the automotive-producing plants provided their own requirements internally. Moreover, with large-scale concentration, a specialized labor force tends to develop, which it would not do in the absence of large-scale industrial concentration. This latter is logically an external economy of scale which accrues to a plant locating in a particular area, and it has little or nothing to do with its own scale of operation.

Tertiary activity. A very substantial amount of tertiary activity in automobile production is accounted for by retail dealerships, of which there are approximately 25,000 handling domestically manufactured cars and slightly less than half that number specializing in imports. In a Christallerian functional hierarchy, sales of new cars would not be expected to appear in first- or second-order central places, as population thresholds and hence income thresholds would be insufficient to support this specialized activity. Since automobiles are a relatively high-cost good and are purchased infrequently, we would expect the market range to be quite great. Hence, on this basis we would deduce that dealerships would be located in higher-order central places significant distances apart.

Sales of automobiles, however, involve not only the initial transaction but also after-sales servicing. This service function would tend to restrict the range over which it could be provided, as there is a premium on prompt and frequent servicing availability. From this we would deduce that dealerships would tend to locate closely throughout space and therefore would be found even in lower-order central places. Hence, dealership distribution tends to represent an equilibrium condition between more distant locations to achieve necessary sales thresholds and a dense distribution to meet the restricted after-sales servicing range.

Canada

Canada has no internally owned manufacturing plants of whole automobiles, and indeed the entire transportation industry is 85 per cent owned from abroad. Nevertheless, the manufacture of motor vehicles alternates with the manufacture of pulp and paper as the largest contributor to Canadian manufacturing in terms of value added. Final assembly plants of the United States' Big Three, for selected models, are to be found in Canada, as are plants owned by American Motors and by Volvo of Sweden. Most of these are in Ontario, with the Swedish plant in Halifax, Nova Scotia.[4] The Ontario locations tend to be in accord with the thesis of the geographer D. Michael Ray that ownership of branch plants in Canada tends to be highest in those areas near the headquarters of the investing firm and to experience decay with increasing distance from those headquarters.[5] The concentration in Ontario thus could reflect proximity to Michigan. It also reflects a market orientation to effective demand in Canada—a concentration of substantial numbers of people with high per capita purchasing power.

Government policy has affected the pace of activity and linkage relationships of the Canadian firms. One such policy is the Canada–United States Agreement on Automotive Products, ratified in 1965, which provides for the removal of tariffs and other hindrances to trade in motor vehicles and parts between the two countries. The plan is intended to provide access to markets in the United States for Canadian motor vehicle and component producers. Canadian production and export of vehicles increased as a result of the plan, and the pact was brought under review in the early 1970s, when trade

[4] A Renault final assembly plant near Montreal ceased operations in July 1972 because costs of final assembly operations were too high, compared with those in France. To enter the United States duty-free under the 1965 Automotive Agreement, such automobiles needed to have at least 50 per cent Canadian content, a provision which increased overall delivery costs to the United States market by 30 per cent. *Toronto Globe and Mail,* May 16, 1972, p. B1.

[5] D. Michael Ray, *Dimensions of Canadian Regionalism,* Canadian Department of Energy, Mines and Resources, Ottawa, 1971. See also D. Michael Ray, *Market Potential and Economic Shadow,* University of Chicago, Department of Geography Research Paper 101, 1965.

relationships of the United States with a number of trading partners were being subjected to careful reassessment. Despite such an incentive, Canadian automobile output amounts to less than 5 per cent of that of the world, and the internal market continues to attract a substantial number of automobiles produced in Western Europe and Japan as well as final assembly of automobiles from the United States. Another government policy affected the location of an automobile plant—in this case, federal incentives for the Volvo plant to locate in Halifax, Nova Scotia. This is an interesting effort to insert a fast-growth industry into a slow-growth area. However, such reduced production costs as can be allocated to lower wages of labor are more than offset by the high cost of transportation of the finished vehicles to Ontario, Quebec, and other market concentrations within Canada.

The European Economic Community

The traditional dominance of the United States in the production as well as consumption of automobiles is now being seriously challenged by the nine-nation European Economic Community. In some respects, that dominance is being not only challenged but also superseded: The Economic Community now produces more automobiles than the United States—a number exceeding 40 per cent of the world's total, compared with slightly more than 30 per cent for the United States. West Germany, which alone accounts for more than one-half as many automobiles as the United States, is the leader in this output, followed by France, Italy, and the United Kingdom. Interestingly, a very substantial portion of these automobiles are produced for export: in West Germany, approximately 55 per cent; in France and the United Kingdom, about 43 per cent; and in Italy, more than 36 per cent. The growing domestic market for automobiles is increasingly important, and the Community and other nations of Western Europe appear to be on the verge of an "automobile explosion" not unlike that experienced by the United States in the first half of the twentieth century.

In commercial vehicles, the substantial production by the European Economic Community—nearly 20 per cent of the world's total—is destined in larger measure for domestic rather than foreign markets. The percentage of exports of these vehicles varies from 22.5 per cent in France to 56.5 per cent in West Germany.

Production is largely by domestic, privately owned firms, although in some countries the state shares ownership with the private firms. Branch plants of United States corporations also are very much in evidence. In West Germany, the Volkswagen firm accounts for about one-half of the nation's automobile production. In the United Kingdom, British Motor Corporation is the largest single manufacturer of automobiles. The output in France is divided mainly among the government-owned Renault corporation and three private firms: Citroën, Peugeot, and Simca (the last, however, is owned by Chrysler in the United States). In Italy, the Fiat corporation is easily the leader. Meanwhile, branch plants of the United States corporations are conspicuous in West Germany, the United Kingdom, and France.

Partly because it includes so many industries, Western Europe has no focal automobile complex to match that of Detroit. Production in Western Europe is overwhelmingly within the EEC countries. Individual plants may be found in such large cities as Bremen, Cologne, and Düsseldorf in West Germany, and yet the leading Volkswagen plant is at Wolfsburg, until recently a very small town on the Mittelland Canal east of Hanover. Analogous dichotomies in locations concerning large and small urban centers can be seen in France and the United Kingdom. Because Western Europe is relatively small in physical size, highly populated, and yet sensitive to overseas markets, we can isolate only with difficulty its specific geographic orientation with respect to its automobile industry. Certainly existing markets and market potential, both domestic and foreign, are important considerations in the location of individual plants.

Japan

Japan has become an outstanding producer of both passenger cars and commercial vehicles. In passenger cars, it is now third in the world, exceeded only by the

United States and West Germany, and soon may exceed the latter. Japan is the world's leading producer of commercial vehicles, exceeding the United States and all individual nations of the European Economic Community, although it in turn is exceeded by the EEC as a whole. Japanese firms have traditionally been quite independent of foreign investment, and the two largest, Toyota and Nissan motors, sharing about 56 per cent of the country's total automobile production, are continuing as independents. However, three smaller corporations are merging, respectively, with the Big Three corporations of the United States, so that the United States now has some economic ownership of the Japanese motor vehicle industry.

The largest Japanese domestic plants are located in Tokyo and the nearby centers of Yokohama and Kawaguchi. The country is building some overseas final assembly plants in southeastern Asia and Latin America and is negotiating for similar plants in the United States and Canada.

The Soviet Union

The Soviet Union is a comparatively modest producer of automobiles, being responsible for less than 2 per cent of the world's production. However, it makes nearly 10 per cent of all commercial vehicles, and among individual nations is exceeded only by Japan and the United States. The output of motor vehicles in the Soviet Union is mainly in the Moscow-Gorkij area, with other plants near centers of steel production in the Ukraine, the Urals, and the Kuznets.

Chapter 20

Petroleum and Natural Gas

Petroleum and natural gas are important to the geography of economic activity for several reasons. First, particularly in the United States, they are key sources of energy, which, as we have discussed in Chapter 8, is so critical a factor in making possible both the increase and the diffusion of the processes of *producing* goods and services. Second, as we have discussed in Chapter 7, petroleum products are significant as a source of energy in the transportation revolution, which has enabled efficient economic *distribution* of the goods and services, once they are produced. Third, they reflect primary, secondary, and tertiary stages of activity and are worthy of note as sources of employment in each stage. Finally, they provide a substantial amount of materials which go forward as semiprocessed inputs into other activities such as the chemical industry.

Petroleum and Petroleum Products

Natural Occurrence

Although in Chapter 2, we mentioned briefly the natural occurrence of minerals, our treatment there was focused on solid minerals and did not enable the reader to appreciate the aspect of the physical environment associated with petroleum and natural gas.

Petroleum and natural gas as substances. Petroleum and natural gas are composed of varying mixtures of the elements carbon and hydrogen, plus certain minor additional elements. Whether, in a specific instance, the materials in question occur as gases, liquids, or waxy solids depends largely upon the carbon-hydrogen ratio. The term *petroleum* is usually applied only to the liquid materials, some of which contain gases and solids in solution or suspension, and these may be light, medium, or heavy. When the lighter oils are distilled or evaporated, either naturally or by man, the residue is usually a compound of hydrocarbons known as *paraffin*. Further distillation often results in another hydrocarbon arrangement called *asphalt*. Petroleum with a predominantly paraffin base tends to be lighter in color and vaporizes at a lower temperature than petroleum that is primarily asphaltic. These terms, as many readers are aware, are retained throughout the industry, being applied often at service stations where motor oil is purchased. Still other oils are of *mixed base,* containing both paraffin and asphalt.

Derivation. Like coal, petroleum and natural gas are generally believed to have been derived from organic sources and occur today in complexes of sedimentary beds. The details of their origin, however, are somewhat different from those of the origin of coal.

As migrant materials. In truth, we are less certain about the origin of petroleum and natural gas than we are about the origin of coal, largely because they have not always existed in, or necessarily near, the places where they now are found, but have moved slowly, as the millenniums have passed, through porous rocks from their nebulous places of origin to the places where they now are gathered. If we knew more about those places of origin, we could be more specific in theorizing about the derivation of the materials which have migrated from them.

Declining concept of inorganic origin. It was once thought that petroleum originated wholly from chemical reactions within the upper rocks of the earth's crust, with such reactions possibly intensified by volcanism and/or by the action of underground water. Most available evidence, however, does not support this view.

Concept of organic origin. It now appears that petroleum and natural gas may well have been created through the chemical alteration of plant and animal life, especially plankton, that once were buried in deep muck underlying brackish waters. When the muck was covered by other sediment, it was compressed. Eventually, in partial response to the compressive forces, the droplets of petroleum moved away, activated either by the natural gas that had formed in the initial stages of alteration or by water. If nearby rock beds were sufficiently porous, the hydrocarbon droplets entered them and traveled through them until encountering some sort of impenetrable barrier to migration. If overlying rocks and underlying materials were likewise impenetrable, the petroleum and gas gathered within the pores of the rock through which it had traveled—awaiting, as it were, exploitation by man.

Characteristics of traps. Places of accumulation of petroleum and natural gas are usually referred to as *traps*. Essentially all these are found in sedimentary rocks, and hence the association of petroleum and natural-gas extraction with such strata (Fig. 20.1). They may occur at any depth at which the sedimentary rocks are found. Oil has been discovered at depths exceeding 25,000 feet below the land surface of the drilling vicinity and theoretically may occur in sandstones to a depth of 65,620 feet.[1] However, nearly all current production is at depths from 1,000 to 20,000 feet. Usually the gas migrates to the highest levels in the trap, with the petroleum at lower levels. Petroleum can exist without natural gas, and vice versa.

Potential and existing reserves. *Petroleum.* Inasmuch as petroleum is a liquid migrant that has accumulated rather haphazardly in the earth, the areas of its occurrence and the amount of its reserves cannot be determined with the same reliability as those of a solid, sedimentary material like coal. Instead, its potentialities are expressed in terms of *sedimentary basins* of possible accumulation, and its reserves in terms of *petroliferous areas* of known occurrence.

Sedimentary basins. The peculiarities of petroleum formation more or less have restricted its global extent to places of rather deep accumulation of quasi-distributed sedimentary rocks. Certain types of landforms and rock structures therefore can be expected to be non-

[1] Peter R. Odell, *An Economic Geography of Oil,* G. Bell & Sons, Ltd., London, 1965, p. 8.

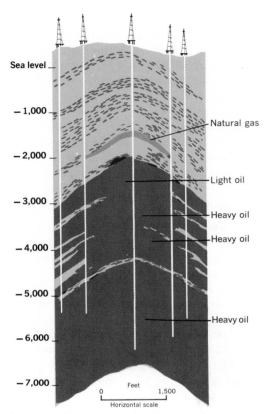

Figure 20.1 Petroleum and natural gas in an anticlinal formation near Los Angeles. This is an unusually rich deposit. Anticlines are only one of a number of traps in which underground petroleum and natural gas accumulate. The two are seen here in the same trap, with the gas above the petroleum. This is typical where petroleum and natural gas occur together, but they do not always do so. (After drawing by Decius as reproduced by Powers, AIME, in Alan M. Bateman, *Economic Mineral Deposits,* Wiley, New York, 1950, p. 664)

petroliferous; youthful mountains and igneous shields, for example, are usually without substantial petroleum. Thus most of the world's high mountains and its shields of surfacing igneous materials are considered nonpetroliferous.

Considered by continent, the world's sedimentary basins are most widespread in Asia, North America, and tropical South America, with Europe, Africa, and Australia not so well endowed.

Considered by nation, the Soviet Union and the United States, in that order, contain the most extensive sedimentary basins (but not necessarily *proved* reserves). Brazil, Canada, China, Argentina, and Australia also have interesting possibilities.

Petroliferous areas. Proved reserves of petroleum are shown in Table 20.1. These. like the sedimentary basins of which they are a part, are uneven in distribution, and the amounts of the actual reserves cannot be detected or even inferred from maps of their global extent. The known reserves of any commodity actually are to be viewed only as working inventories at a certain time under given assumptions—and this is particularly true of petroleum, the search for which is continuous and active. The known reserves of one year may vary appreciably from those of another with the development of a single major field or series of fields.

Having taken due caution, we can now note that the nations around the Persian Gulf in the Middle East aggregately control the largest known reserves in the world. Of other nations, the United States and the Soviet Union are the leaders, and Venezuela is more than noteworthy (Fig. 20.2).

Adequacy. Unlike those of coal, known reserves of petroleum are sufficient to last for less than half a century at the current consumption and production rates. The short-term outlook is not so gloomy as the foregoing statement would suggest, however, as new pools are being discovered constantly, and existing pools now are being used more efficiently through improved techniques of recovery, refining, and consumption. Nevertheless, the long-range outlook is not promising, and it may happen that within the life-span of some of the younger readers of this book, substitute sources of petroleum (such as oil shale) or sources of energy other than petroleum will be utilized more generally. Indeed, we may return again to coal as a major energy source, or possibly rely more heavily upon nuclear energy. Geothermal energy (obtained by tapping water heated naturally underground, or by forcing water down to be warmed by hot rocks, then usually putting it through turbines to create electricity) or solar energy (obtained by intensifying the sun's heat, usually also for turbines) also are excellent alternatives which are not used up with use.

Oil shale. As suggested by the name, oil shale was once mud and/or clay impregnated with organic re-

TABLE 20.1
WORLD PROVED RESERVES OF CRUDE OIL, DECEMBER 31, 1968

Area, country	Proved reserves (billions of barrels)*	Per cent of world total reserves
Western Hemisphere:		
United States†	30.7	6.7
Venezuela	15.5	3.4
Canada	8.4	1.9
Mexico	5.5	1.2
Other	7.8	1.7
Middle East:		
Saudi Arabia	77.0	16.9
Kuwait	69.0	15.2
Iran	54.0	11.9
Iraq	28.0	6.2
Abu Dhabi	18.0	4.0
Neutral Zone	15.0	3.3
Other	9.8	2.2
Africa:		
Libya	30.0	6.6
Algeria	7.0	1.5
Other	7.6	1.7
Europe:		
U.S.S.R.	40.0	8.8
Other	2.8	.6
Far East:‡		
China	15.0	3.3
Indonesia	8.8	1.9
Other	2.4	.5
Oceania	2.5	.5
World total	454.8	100

*One barrel equals forty-two United States gallons.
† The United States also contained 8.6 billion barrels of natural-gas liquids.
‡ Includes 100 million barrels of condensate.
Source: U.S. Bureau of Mines, *Mineral Facts and Problems, 1970,* p. 156. Exploration for both petroleum and natural gas in the North Sea, the Arctic shores of Canada and the United States, and a broad area around Indonesia appears to be successful in each area and may result in rather dramatic changes in some of the data reported in this table.

mains. As is true in the formation of petroleum, these deposits congealed and were compressed with the passage of time and the addition of overlying beds, but the organic matter remained largely as a part of the newly formed shales. It is in this form that oil shale is mined and processed, with the ultimate yields including not only oil but also gas and fixed carbon. Experiments in recovering the oil are now well past the pilot-plant stage.

The United States has been particulary well endowed with this natural resource, and other parts of the world are known to have sizable reserves (Table 20.2). Known reserves of oil shale are well in excess of those of petroleum.

Tar sands. In the vicinity of Canada's Athabaska River, east of the Rockies, is a series of sandy surface-level deposits impregnated with organic matter at varying stages of transition into petroleum, including some reserves of the end product. Estimates do not agree as to the total amount of these reserves, but it is not inconsiderable.

The United States

The United States produces nearly one-fourth, and consumes about one-third, of all petroleum produced in the world. Therefore, it can serve as a particularly

TABLE 20.2
ESTIMATED SHALE-OIL RESOURCES* IN SHALES AS RICH AS 10 GALLONS PER TON OR RICHER (IN BILLIONS OF BARRELS)†

Area	Known resources
United States	4,060
South America	800
Asia	104
Africa	100
Europe	76
Australia and New Zealand	1
World total	5,141

*In-place oil.
† Based on U.S. Geological Survey Circular 523, 1965.
There are large deposits of oil shale in Saskatchewan and Manitoba. Deposits of oil shale are known to exist in New Brunswick, Newfoundland, Nova Scotia, Ontario, and Quebec in Canada.
Source: U.S. Bureau of Mines, *Mineral Facts and Problems, 1970,* pp. 189–190.

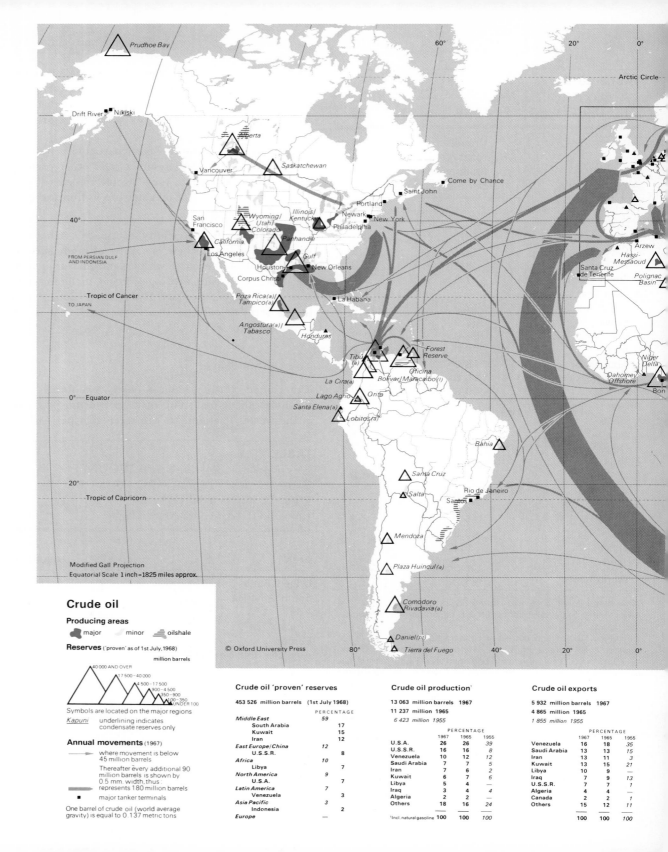

Crude oil

Producing areas

major   minor   oilshale

Reserves ('proven' as of 1st July, 1968)

million barrels

40 000 AND OVER
17 500 – 40 000
4 500 – 17 500
900 – 4 500
350 – 900
100 – 350
UNDER 100

Symbols are located on the major regions

Kapuni   underlining indicates condensate reserves only

Annual movements (1967)

where movement is below 45 million barrels

Thereafter every additional 90 million barrels is shown by 0.5 mm. width, thus : represents 180 million barrels

■ major tanker terminals

One barrel of crude oil (world average gravity) is equal to 0.137 metric tons

Modified Gall Projection
Equatorial Scale 1 inch = 1825 miles approx.

© Oxford University Press

Crude oil 'proven' reserves

453 526 million barrels (1st July 1968)

	PERCENTAGE
Middle East	59
South Arabia	17
Kuwait	15
Iran	12
East Europe/China	12
U.S.S.R.	8
Africa	10
Libya	7
North America	9
U.S.A.	7
Latin America	7
Venezuela	3
Asia Pacific	3
Indonesia	2
Europe	—

Crude oil production[1]

13 063 million barrels 1967
11 237 million 1965
6 423 million 1955

	PERCENTAGE		
	1967	1965	1955
U.S.A.	26	26	39
U.S.S.R.	16	16	8
Venezuela	10	12	12
Saudi Arabia	7	7	5
Iran	7	6	2
Kuwait	6	7	6
Libya	5	4	—
Iraq	3	4	4
Algeria	2	2	—
Others	18	16	24
[1]Incl. natural gasoline	**100**	**100**	*100*

Crude oil exports

5 932 million barrels 1967
4 865 million 1965
1 855 million 1955

	PERCENTAGE		
	1967	1965	1955
Venezuela	16	18	35
Saudi Arabia	13	13	15
Iran	13	11	3
Kuwait	13	15	21
Libya	10	9	—
Iraq	7	9	13
U.S.S.R.	7	7	1
Algeria	4	4	—
Canada	2	2	1
Others	15	12	11
	100	**100**	*100*

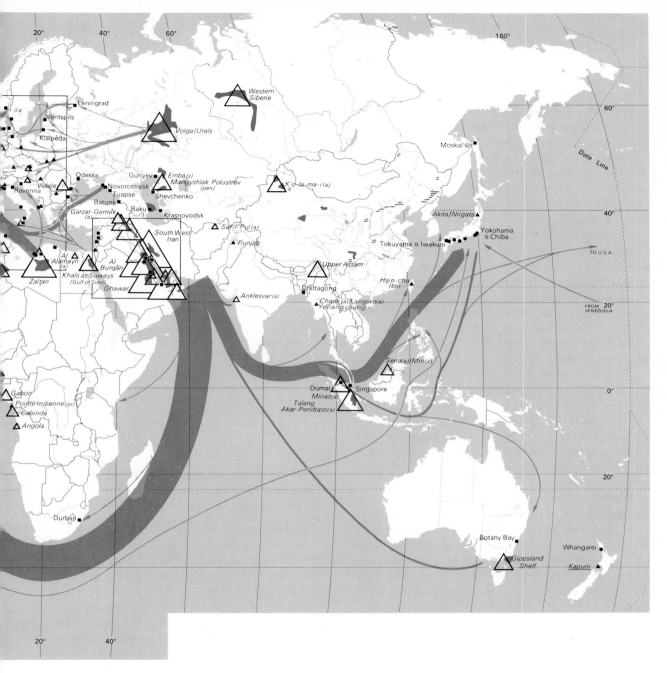

Crude oil imports

5 942 million barrels 1967
4 869 million 1965
1 862 million 1955

	PERCENTAGE		
	1967	1965	*1955*
Japan	13	10	*3*
Italy	11	10	*7*
U.K.	9	10	*11*
France	9	9	*10*
Germany F.R.	9	9	*3*
U.S.A.	7	9	*16*
Neths. Antilles	5	6	*17*
Netherlands	4	4	*5*
Canada	3	3	*5*
Others	30	30	*23*
	100	100	*100*

Figure 20.2 A world view of crude oil recovery. (After *Oxford Economic Atlas of the World,* 4th ed. p. 35)

apt case study for primary, secondary, and tertiary stages of activity regarding this resource.

Primary Activity. *Sectoral considerations.* *Function and process.* More than is true of other primary stages we have examined this stage on petroleum and natural-gas liquids[2] involves search as well as exploitation. In contrast to forest products and fishing, and even iron ore, where the major concentrations are reasonably well known, petroleum, over the ages, has flowed through the rocks, occurs at varying depths, and hence is extremely difficult and costly to find. Processes of exploration are very complex and modernized. This is especially true of those which indicate possible reserves when the science of geophysics has been applied. Sound waves from explosions touched off at the earth's surface pass through various rock layers with different frequency and intensity and are recorded on seismographs. These recently have been adapted to marine operations as well.

Despite these advances, however, the actual location of petroleum and natural gas depends upon the drilling of test holes. Between 15,000 and 30,000 test holes are drilled in the United States each year, of which approximately 15 per cent are successful wells and the remainder are dry holes. About 8 per cent of "wildcatting" operations, in which drilling is done on the basis of hunch, are successful.

Once the petroleum has been discovered, it is subject to the function of actual recovery. We have mentioned that the petroleum may be found at depths exceeding 25,000 feet, but that most production ranges from depths of 1,000 to 20,000 feet. At one time, recovery involved pumping the oil or associated natural gas that occurred near each well and the drilling of numerous wells to be sure a field was efficiently exploited. However, new processes involve the injection of water, gas, air, steam, or other fluids or gases into oil reservoirs so that the petroleum or natural gas is forced toward the well and hence recovered. This and other techno-

[2]Some natural gas either occurs as a liquid or becomes a liquid in the early stages of processing. In the industry it is treated as a petroleum product rather than a natural-gas product and is formally recognized in most data records at the processing stage, although it exists in some quantities in the natural state. In either case, it is called natural-gas liquids.

TABLE 20.3

PRIMARY-SECTOR COSTS IN THE PETROLEUM INDUSTRY IN THE UNITED STATES (IN MILLIONS OF DOLLARS)

Category	
Exploration	2,396
Development	2,316
Production	2,645
General and administrative overhead not reported elsewhere	701
Drilling and production platforms	147
Total	8,205

Exploration costs include leasing, geologic and geophysical operations, drilling of exploratory wells including the completion of successful wells, and installing wellhead connections. Development costs follow discovery of an oil pool and include outlays for roads, for equipping the discovery well beyond the wellhead for production, for drilling additional wells including dry holes, for equipping productive wells, and later for secondary recovery installations. Production costs include costs for pumping or lifting, labor, field supervision, repair, maintenance and other direct overhead, production or severance taxes, and ad valorem taxes on producing properties and other property and equipment used in producing operations.
Source: U.S. Bureau of Mines, *Mineral Facts and Problems, 1970,* p. 164.

logical improvements have constantly raised the level of efficiency of crude-oil recovery by approximately 0.5 per cent per year since World War II.

Other sectoral considerations. The costs involved in the primary sector of this activity are suggested in Table 20.3. There is a surprisingly even distribution of exploration, development, and production costs. Significantly, the total costs of this stage amount to nearly 40 per cent of the value of shipments of all petroleum products emerging from refineries in the United States.

The primary stage is an active employer of persons, hiring nearly twice as many employees as the secondary, or refining, stage. By the early 1970s, approximately 275,000 persons were engaged in exploration, development, production, and associated functions in the primary stage. However, all stages are experiencing a reduction in labor force. In the fifteen years between 1956 and 1971, the employment in the primary stage decreased nearly 15 per cent, while production of petroleum increased by 30 per cent and that of natural gas by 91 per cent.

Spatial considerations. The distribution of production of crude oil and natural-gas liquids in the United States is shown in Figure 20.2. Natural-gas liquids now account for about one-sixth as much of the total output as crude oil alone, and the output is increasing at an average annual rate of 7 per cent per year—twice that of crude oil. The current dominance of Texas of both products is apparent from the map, as is the importance of Louisiana.

The discovery of oil in 1968 near Prudhoe Bay in arctic Alaska is a significant find and may well change the overall pattern of production/distribution of petroleum in the years ahead.

Linkages: Mainly primary to secondary. Linkages to petroleum refineries in the United States and all other areas of the world are shown in Figures 20.2 and 20.3. The reader will note that, for the first time, foreign oil enters the scene, inasmuch as many United States refineries process such oil, as well as that produced domestically. We touched upon the importance of mode of carrier in these linkages in Chapter 7. Recent technological developments tending to lower the cost of transporting crude oil include highly automated large-diameter, thin-walled pipeline systems made of high-strength steel, as well as larger tankers and barges. Better methods of internal insulation and better external protective coatings also have been developed. Generally, pipelines transporting crude materials tend to be larger in diameter than those carrying finished products. One of the most important of these will be the new 800-mile 48-inch pipeline designed to carry crude oil from the north slope area of Alaska to the ice-free port of Valdez, in southern Alaska, where it will be shipped to the West Coast of the United States. This line will eventually have a capacity of 2 million barrels per day.

We have mentioned that the United States consumes nearly one-third of all petroleum products in the world, but produces only about one-fourth. Import linkages, particularly to the refineries along the East and Gulf Coasts, are shown in Figure 20.2. Only about 55 per cent of such imports are crude oil, the remainder being mainly residual fuel oil. As is shown in the map, the primary source countries are Venezuela, Canada, and the Netherlands Antilles.

Secondary Activity. *Sectoral considerations.* *Function and process.* The function of this activity is reduction of crude oil into motor and aviation gasolines, distillate fuels, liquefied petroleum gases, jet fuels, kerosene, and petroleum coke. These energy sources account for approximately 90 per cent of the products from the United States refineries. The remaining 10 per cent are used primarily for materials entering the petrochemical industry and for asphalt, road oil, solvents, coke, lubricants, waxes, and other products.

Refining is a semiautomatic, almost endless process, which, although it involves several stages, tends to take place at a single site. Older, more elementary methods of distillation have been replaced by methods which permit not only the recovery of desired products but also their recovery (within limits) in desired percentages of finished products. Moreover, essentially all the crude petroleum ultimately is utilized, and there is almost no waste.

Other sectoral considerations. As is shown in Figure 20.4, the petroleum-refining industry of the United States is especially important in that it accounts for 3.63 per cent of all manufacturing shipments. It is less significant as a source of value added and is especially minor in per cent of all manufacturing employment. Being capital-intensive, it allocates a very small percentage of final shipment value to labor costs, but a high percentage to materials costs—which, as we have seen, are subjected earlier to very high costs of exploration, development, and primary production (Table 20.3). Its value added as a per cent of final shipment value is slightly less than one-half of the national average. More than one-half of its 437 establishments employ fewer than 100 workers, and 80 find work for fewer than 5. However, these data should not be misinterpreted, inasmuch as the industry is very capital-intensive and each employee accounts for a very large daily output of finished product. The industry is highly automated and computerized.

Spatial considerations. In at least two respects, the refining technology mentioned above is significant

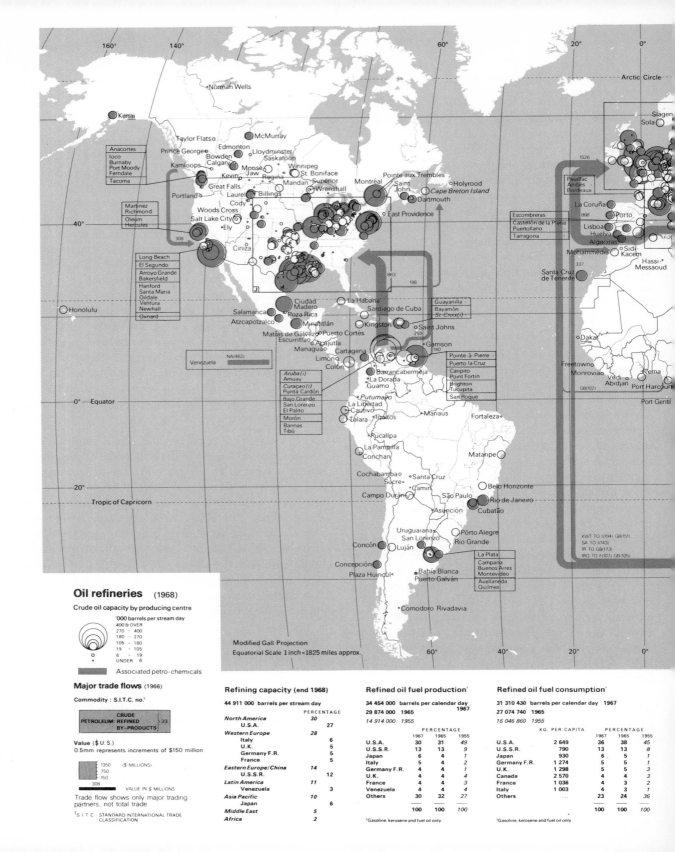

Oil refineries (1968)

Crude oil capacity by producing centre

'000 barrels per stream day
- 400 & OVER
- 270 – 400
- 180 – 270
- 105 – 180
- 19 – 105
- 6 – 19
- UNDER 6

Associated petro-chemicals

Major trade flows (1966)

Commodity : S.I.T.C. no.[1]

CRUDE PETROLEUM: REFINED BY-PRODUCTS 33

Value ($ U.S.)
0.5mm represents increments of $150 million

1350
750
150 ($ MILLIONS)
308 VALUE IN $ MILLIONS

Trade flow shows only major trading partners, not total trade

[1] S.I.T.C. STANDARD INTERNATIONAL TRADE CLASSIFICATION

Modified Gall Projection
Equatorial Scale 1 inch = 1825 miles approx.

Refining capacity (end 1968)

44 911 000 barrels per stream day

	PERCENTAGE
North America	30
U.S.A.	27
Western Europe	28
Italy	6
U.K.	5
Germany F.R.	5
France	5
Eastern Europe/China	14
U.S.S.R.	12
Latin America	11
Venezuela	3
Asia Pacific	10
Japan	6
Middle East	5
Africa	2

Refined oil fuel production[1]

34 454 000 barrels per calendar day 1967
29 874 000 1965
14 914 000 1955

	PERCENTAGE		
	1967	1965	1955
U.S.A.	30	31	49
U.S.S.R.	13	13	9
Japan	6	4	1
Italy	5	4	2
Germany F.R.	4	4	1
U.K.	4	4	4
France	4	4	3
Venezuela	4	4	4
Others	30	32	27
	100	100	100

[1] Gasoline, kerosene and fuel oil only

Refined oil fuel consumption[1]

31 310 430 barrels per calendar day 1967
27 074 740 1965
16 046 860 1955

	KG. PER CAPITA	PERCENTAGE		
		1967	1965	1955
U.S.A.	2 649	36	38	45
U.S.S.R.	790	13	13	8
Japan	930	6	5	1
Germany F.R.	1 274	5	5	1
U.K.	1 298	5	5	3
Canada	2 570	4	4	3
France	1 036	4	3	2
Italy	1 003	4	3	1
Others	...	23	24	36
		100	100	100

[1] Gasoline, kerosene and fuel oil only

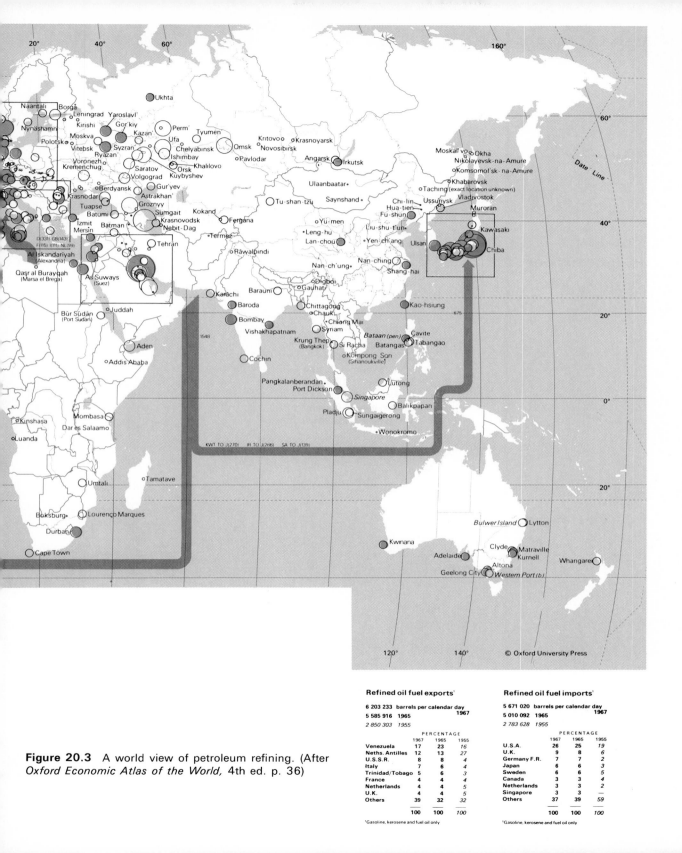

Figure 20.3 A world view of petroleum refining. (After *Oxford Economic Atlas of the World,* 4th ed. p. 36)

Refined oil fuel exports[1]

6 203 233	barrels per calendar day		**1967**
5 585 916	1965		
2 850 303	*1955*		

	PERCENTAGE		
	1967	1965	*1955*
Venezuela	17	23	*16*
Neths. Antilles	12	13	*27*
U.S.S.R.	8	8	*4*
Italy	7	6	*4*
Trinidad/Tobago	5	4	*3*
France	4	4	*4*
Netherlands	4	4	*5*
U.K.	4	4	*5*
Others	39	32	*32*
	100	**100**	*100*

[1]Gasoline, kerosene and fuel oil only

Refined oil fuel imports[1]

5 671 020	barrels per calendar day		**1967**
5 010 092	1965		
2 783 628	*1955*		

	PERCENTAGE		
	1967	1965	*1955*
U.S.A.	26	25	*19*
U.K.	9	8	*6*
Germany F.R.	7	7	*2*
Japan	6	6	*3*
Sweden	6	6	*5*
Canada	3	3	*4*
Netherlands	3	3	*2*
Singapore	3	3	*—*
Others	37	39	*59*
	100	**100**	*100*

[1]Gasoline, kerosene and fuel oil only

© Oxford University Press

PETROLEUM AND NATURAL GAS
Secondary Activity: Petroleum Refining (SIC 2911)

1. **Function and Process**
   - **A.** Function: conversion of petroleum into products (mainly gasoline and fuel oil); *no weight loss*
   - **B.** Process: mainly chemical separation and addition

2. **Significance**
   - **A.** Per cent of all U.S. manufacturing employment: 0.55%
   - **B.** Per cent of all U.S. manufacturing shipments: 3.63%
   - **C.** Per cent of value added in all U.S. manufacturing: 1.81%

3. **Major Inputs**
   - **A.** Per cent of labor costs (all employees) in final shipment value: 4.75%
   - **B.** Per cent of materials costs in final shipment value: 77.28%

4. **Number and Size of Establishments**
   - **A.** Total number: 437
   - **B.** Size categories
     1. 4 employees or fewer: 80
     2. Between 5 and 99: 168
     3. Between 100 and 249: 81
     4. Between 250 and 499: 52
     5. Between 500 and 999: 34
     6. Over 1,000 employees: 22

Sectoral Considerations

Spatial Considerations

Figure 20.4 Sector-space considerations, secondary activity (petroleum refining— SIC 2911). For explanation of symbols, see Figure 14.3.

PETROLEUM AND NATURAL GAS

Linkages, Secondary To Tertiary

Sectoral
Considerations

Geographic division of origin	Tons (000)	Per cent of goods movement by means of transport				
		Rail	Motor carrier	Private truck	Water	Other and unknown
U.S.	404,721	5.3%	9.8%	4.0%	80.8%	0.1%
Middle Atlantic	42,966	4.4	10.0	2.0	83.6	—
East North Central	33,182	11.4	40.4	9.9	37.5	0.8
West North Central	7,290	19.3	44.3	18.3	18.1	—
South Atlantic	4,000	9.6	8.0	12.0	70.4	—
West South Central	248,872	4.1	3.8	1.7	90.4	—
Mountain	7,337	18.4	55.8	25.7	—	0.1
Pacific*	39,133	3.7	10.2	7.4	78.7	—
Rest of U.S.	21,941	na†	na	na	na	na

*Excluding Alaska and Hawaii.
† Movement by transport not available.
Source: United States Census of Transportation, 1967.

Sectoral
Considerations

Spatial
Considerations

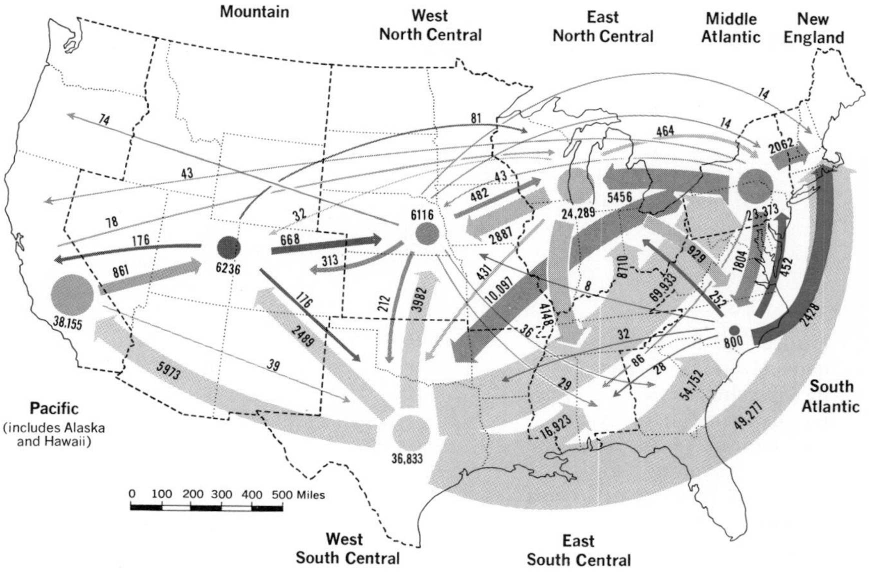

Figure 20.5 Linkages, secondary-tertiary activity. For explanation of symbols, see Figure 15.4. Movement by pipeline is not shown.

PETROLEUM AND NATURAL GAS
Tertiary Activity

1. **Function and Process**
   A. Function: retail sale of gasoline, engine oil, and other petroleum products, and automobile supplies
   B. Process: customer contact in establishments

2. **Significance**
   A. Per cent of all U.S. retail labor force: 6.13%
   B. Per cent of value of all U.S. retail sales: 7.32%

3. **Number and Size of Establishments**
   A. Total number: 216,059
   B. Size categories
      1   5 employees or fewer: 174,931
      2   Between   6 and 49:   24,889
      3   Between 50 and 99:   105
      4   Over 100 employees: 12
      5   Not operated entire year: 16,122

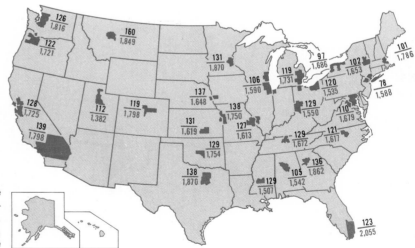

Figure 20.6 Sector-space considerations, tertiary activity (gasoline service stations). For explanation of symbols, see Figure 14.7. Note the high percentage of labor force and retail sales in this activity. Why the sharp difference in annual per capita sales in New York City and Los Angeles?

to the sector-space relationships in economic geography: (1) The efficiency of technology results in almost negligible waste, and so it is relatively easy to ship either crude petroleum or finished products, and refineries therefore tend to be located near either markets or raw materials, and (2) the small size of the labor force associated with the industry signifies that it is a minor source of employment and that relatively few settlements and only sparse populations are directly dependent upon it.

The actual distribution of the refineries and the linkages to tertiary activity are shown in Figures 20.4 and 20.5. The largest output is located near the raw materials and at break-of-bulk points along the Gulf Coast. Additional locations are near markets, inasmuch as the cost of shipping the petroleum products and gas is low and almost no waste material is included. The California region, where heavy production and consumption coincide, and the Atlantic Coast, where markets predominate, contain very important locational sites. As Alaskan production begins to be more active, we can expect the California and other West Coast locations to expand accordingly.

Secondary to tertiary linkages. The heaviest movement of petroleum and petroleum products is from producing fields in Texas, Louisiana, and neighboring states, such as Oklahoma and Kansas, to the core of the manufacturing belt in the Northeast. A secondary pattern is from the same area of origin to consumers on the periphery of the manufacturing belt in the South, Middle West, and North. A third movement is from southern California to places of consumption on the West Coast. A fourth is from east to west—either overland or via the Panama Canal.

In addition to the broad patterns mentioned in the preceding paragraph, a very substantial movement of refinery products is to local markets, particularly within those of large metropolitan areas in which many refineries are located. Too small to show on a map of the whole nation, these movements make up a significant share of overall movement of petroleum products from refinery to tertiary demand.

Partly because of the importance of local delivery, as mentioned above, about 42 per cent of all refined products move to tertiary sources by motor carrier, whereas 29 per cent move by pipeline, 26 per cent by watercraft, and approximately 3 per cent by railroad. (These figures differ sharply from U.S. Census Reports in Figure 20.5, which show only broad, interdivisional movements and not local and smaller regional deliveries.) Trends in this pattern appear to favor the pipeline, which is now replacing the motor carrier in delivering to air terminals, where demand for jet fuel is geographically concentrated into single points and is increasing.

A virtual network of pipelines serves almost every part of mainland United States. Individual lines range in diameter from 6 to 48 inches. There is a tendency for the smaller lines to accommodate petroleum products and for the larger ones to accommodate crude petroleum. The primary route pattern is from places of production to those of consumption. From Gulf of Mexico sources, this pattern is not directly to the East Coast, but is in the form of an arch, going northward to the west part of the manufacturing belt and then transecting that belt in an east-west direction.

Most of the water movement is by coastwise tanker, although some barge freighting occurs. The primary direction of such movement is from the Gulf South to shores of the Middle Atlantic states.

Somewhat less than 3 per cent of petroleum products from the United States are exported, whereas almost no crude petroleum is exported. Japan, Canada, and Mexico are the leading recipients.

Tertiary activity. About 90 per cent of the petroleum products consumed in the United States produce energy in the form of heat and power, and the remainder are used for raw materials, especially in petrochemicals, asphalt, road oil, solvents, coke, lubricants, waxes, and miscellaneous products. Significantly, more than one-half or more of all petroleum products are used for transportation, more than one-fifth for household and commercial fuel, and nearly one-tenth for industrial purposes. Gasoline still constitutes about three-fourths of all the fuels used in transportation, although, with the changeover from the piston engine to jet aircraft, the demand for jet fuel has increased both absolutely and proportionately. Jet fuel is primarily of the kerosene type, somewhat similar to that used in the old kerosene lamps.

The spatial distribution of the tertiary activity of the United States strongly reflects distribution of the population (Fig. 20.6). The retail sale of gasoline, which is by far the largest form of demand, is reflected spatially in the thousands of retail service stations found in metropolitan areas, other large and small urban places, and rural settlements. Wholesale distributors to these stations are located predominantly in the nation's metropolitan areas, particularly at break-of-bulk points along pipeline or waterway routes. Distributors of fuel for household, commercial, and industrial use also are found particularly in the large metropolitan areas, where motor vehicle carriers move the product to the final demand. A similar pattern may be observed with respect to service to the airline industry, although, as we have noted previously, pipelines are tending to replace motor carriers in moving the product to some airports.

The actual sites of demand for petroleum consumed in electricity generation, and in the making of petrochemicals and other products which have petroleum materials as a substantial input, are located somewhat erratically throughout the country and are not in as close harmony with population distribution as the primary sources of demand treated above.

Institutional explanation. *Historical recency.*

Slightly more than a century has passed since completion of E. L. Drake's oil-well undertaking at Titusville, Pennsylvania, on August 27, 1859. This sizable industry, with value of shipments at an intermediate level among all those in the United States of comparable classification by the U.S. Office of Management and Budget, is a product of modern times. It is not afflicted with the industrial inertia that characterizes both the establishments and the firms of many of the older, usually slow-growth industries. Therefore, whether considered in terms of technological apparatus, administrative organization, or transport efficiency, this industry had the benefit of several centuries of an industrial revolution before it came into existence. It is therefore a highly efficient, well-organized, capital-intensive industry, with inherent advantages in both the social and economic milieus of which it is a part, including government policy and the favorable conditions of the physical and biological environments.

Transportation efficiency. We have mentioned that crude petroleum is utilized almost entirely in manufacture and contains essentially no waste products. Furthermore, being a liquid, it lends itself admirably to a bulk means of transfer, whether by vessel, pipeline, or overland or air carrier. Parenthetically, the same comment can also be made about the production process, in which the liquids flow through and between one manufacturing stage to another, finally to emerge as other liquids or gases (plus a few solids).

Corporate structure. Partly because of its historical recency, this industry is administratively centralized: the largest eight companies control nearly 60 per cent of the entire petroleum-refining industry in the United States. Furthermore, these same companies own, either directly or through subordinates, many of the pipeline facilities for carrying both crude petroleum and petroleum products. Decisions concerning the locations of key sites of production and of facilities for distribution are made prevailingly by a very few corporate boards under conditions previously described (pp. 142 to 143).

Government policy. One of the most significant government programs which affects domestic petroleum operations and prices is the limitation of imports. The United States became a net importer of petroleum in 1948, and in 1955 a Trade Agreement Extension Act was passed, in which the President initiated a voluntary import control program for curtailing oil imports if they reached the level that would appear to impair the national security. The program consisted basically of requesting companies to restrict imports to recommended levels. This program was not fully successful, and in 1959 it was superseded by a program imposing mandatory controls, administered by the U.S. Department of the Interior.

Other United States programs affecting location include research carried on by the U.S. Bureau of Mines; pollution control, particularly involving the offshore drilling and marine transportation of petroleum; exploratory work by the U.S. Geological Survey, including activities in the continental shelves; and the leasing of federal lands for the exploration of oil and gas.

These various government programs tend to affect

sectoral, rather than spatial, aspects of the petroleum industry in the United States. However, their net result does mean a differential impact on amount of production in key refineries and different strengths and weaknesses in linkages connecting primary to secondary to tertiary stages. They therefore do have an impact upon the overall network—not so much upon the pattern as upon the intensity of activity within and between component units.

Theoretical explanation. *Primary activity.* Studies of petroleum utilize advanced theoretical concepts and techniques of analysis. These techniques and theory apply probability analysis to decision making, risk, and uncertainty. We shall not concern ourselves at this stage with such analysis, but shall point out some basic concepts that will enhance our understanding of this type of economic activity.

In Chapter 10 it was proposed that the location of any form of economic activity can be explained in terms of the necessary and sufficient conditions for its existence at a particular location. In the case of petroleum and natural gas, a necessary condition for production is of course that the gas or petroleum exists at the location. It is important to remember, however, that this is not a sufficient condition for production. For production to take place, deposits must be economically exploitable.[3] In order to ascertain that the sufficient conditions are fulfilled, we need to know a great deal of detailed information about the *quality, quantity,* and *accessibility* of the deposits. Marginally inferior deposits such as oil shales become less marginal as techniques of production improve. Smaller quantities that may have been considered uneconomic at a given time may be exploited by secondary recovery methods. Accessibility has two aspects: access to the wellhead or nearness to the surface (a site quality), and access to the market (a situation quality). Accessibility is again

a function of price and technical progress. At present, depths greater than 20,000 feet tend to be marginal in profitability, while deposits undersea, formerly inaccessible, are now economically accessible even at considerable ocean depths as a result of technical development of deep-sea oil rigs.

As previously pointed out, the primary production of petroleum and natural gas includes exploration, development, and production. Exploration requires a high level of technical ability and is a high-cost activity. Reserves are closely related to expenditures on exploration, at least up to the point where some threshold of knowledge is obtained about an area.[4] Obviously, exploration will take place only where there is some positive probability that petroleum exists, for example, in gently folded sedimentary regions. If we assume that exploration will increase where the probability of success is greatest and, further, that the chances of success are greatest where the intensity of exploration is greatest, we shall have some idea of why the distribution of world reserves is as it is.

Secondary activity. In the secondary stage of production, i.e., petroleum refining, there is little or no weight loss—and hence, in a Weberian sense, a material index close to unity—and thus there exists no strong pull to the production end. Moreover, crude petroleum is easily transported over water by supertanker or over land by pipeline. Also, refining is a capital-intensive process requiring only small inputs of highly skilled technical labor. In a theoretical sense, therefore, there is a natural pull toward market locations. Reinforcing this pull to the market location are Weberian agglomeration economies or external economies to the industry with existing infrastructure and linked industries such as chemical processing.

Tertiary activity. The first part of this chapter emphasized that over one-half the value of petroleum products is consumed in the transportation sector and that retail sales of gasoline constitute the largest form of demand. As gasoline stations are the outlets through which such demand is met, we shall restrict our conceptual observations to their locations.

[3] It is useful for the purposes of analysis and theory to distinguish between *resources* and *reserves.* All known occurrences of petroleum constitute petroleum resources; those which are economically exploitable constitute petroleum reserves. Hence reserves are a class of resources. Both petroleum resources and petroleum reserves are continuously changing over time. Resources are largely a function of exploration expenditures, while reserves are largely a function of price and techniques of production.

[4] It is not surprising that world reserves have continued to increase and are now greater than ever recorded.

The market for the product of a gas station may be viewed as linear rather than as an area, and all stations on a line may be considered in some measure to be competitive. Other things remaining the same, the density of gas stations will tend to be proportional to the volume of traffic traversing any given length of highway. As the density of traffic increases, the volume of demand will provide the necessary income thresholds to support more gas stations. Traffic volumes increase at intersections, and stations concentrate at these locations. As time costs are involved in movement, compulsory stopping points, such as at stoplights, will tend to attract stations.

Gas stations on opposite sides of a highway at a given point will be in competition, and a station may try to capture some of the market of the opposite station. In order to do this, price advantages, superior service (such as clean rest rooms), or "gifts" (drinking glasses, for example) must be offered in at least a sufficient quantity to induce drivers to take the extra time and risk involved in crossing the highway. In the case of a divided highway, each gas station has a directional monopoly.

To some extent we may draw the theoretical explanation for gas-station location from the intervening-opportunities model. At first glance we might assume that if all gas stations on a strip of highway offered identical prices and service, then the probability of passing up a given station would be zero. However, on a trip, the extra distance to the next gas station has to be covered anyway. If we introduce price differences and the fact that the demand for gas is dependent also on how much one has in the tank, things become a little more complicated. In order to avail oneself of a low price, one has to have less than a full tank. What constitutes a low price in the eyes of the purchaser depends upon how low he expects the next station's price to be, the state of his tank at the first station and the distance to the next. It may be reasonable to assume that on any long stretch of highway, empty tanks would occur randomly distributed throughout its length. A gas station's captured market is therefore that strip of highway beyond itself where drivers expect to run out of gas. Distances between stations may be posted, or drivers may have to guess. Gas stations may be expected to locate further apart where distances are posted, than where they are not.

Canada

Two important factors are involved in even a brief assessment of petroleum refining in Canada: (1) Measured by value of shipments, it is fourth in rank of importance among forty industries classified by Statistics Canada, exceeded only by motor vehicles, pulp and paper mills, and slaughtering and meat processors, and (2) it is owned almost entirely by corporations of the United States.

In view of the substantial reserves of both crude petroleum and oil shale and Athabaska tar sands in Canada, the pattern of development results appreciably from the policies of the corporations which have developed the petroleum fields to date, as further conditioned by policies of the Canadian government and the United States. Most of the fields occur in the province of Alberta, with pipeline networks reaching to the east and west. In addition, Venezuela supplies a portion of Canadian demand, some of the petroleum moving by way of Portland, Maine, through a tandem pipeline series to refineries in Montreal. This is entirely inbound crude petroleum. The Canadian government regulates movement of petroleum from its own western fields and from abroad. (General reference, Figs. 20.2 and 20.3.)

The Soviet Union

Petroleum production in the Soviet Union has risen nearly sevenfold since 1950 and now accounts for about 16 per cent of the world total, ranking behind only the United States. The facilities of production are state-owned (Figs. 20.2 and 20.3).

For a number of years, the leading producing field was Baku, near the point of entry of the Caucasus Mountains into the Caspian Sea. A second very important producing area has been opened up especially during the past quarter century, and this has been given much attention recently. Known as the Second Baku, this area really is a series of fields situated to the southwest of the Ural Mountains along the Volga River.

The rapid growth in Soviet production is due mainly to activity in the Second Baku area, which has increased its output more than eleven times since 1950. It now accounts for more than three-fourths of all petroleum recovered in the Soviet Union. The Baku fields account for less than one-eighth, and the remaining sources are small and scattered, with the island of Sakhalin in the Pacific Ocean of noteworthy importance. Pipelines link major producing fields and markets.

Venezuela

Third among individual producing nations, Venezuela currently accounts for about 10 per cent of the world's total petroleum output. The leading fields are in and along the margins of Lake Maracaibo and to the east near the mouth of the Orinoco River (Fig. 20.2). Nowhere is production far from the sea, which is fortunate, since most the of the petroleum is exported. Both crude petroleum and refined products are shipped, the latter having been processed either in one of the several refineries within or near the fields of extraction or in one of the few but large refineries on the nearby Dutch-owned islands of Aruba and Curaçao in the Netherlands Antilles.

Companies from the United States, the United Kingdom, and the Netherlands are represented in the country, with nearly three-fourths of both reserves and output controlled by United States firms.

The Middle East

Although the petroleum wealth of the Middle East has been suspected for some time and initial extraction was begun at about the turn of the twentieth century, full knowledge of the immensity of the reserves and full-scale exploitation of them have developed only during the past quarter century.

Extraction. About one-fourth of the world's extracted petroleum comes from the very sizable fields in the Middle East. Iran, Saudi Arabia, and Kuwait each export betweeen 6.5 and 7.5 per cent, and Iraq exports about 4 per cent.

The fields tend to be in two clusters (Fig. 20.2). The largest cluster fringes the southwestern, western, and northern portions of the Persian Gulf, whereas the lesser one is almost entirely in Iraq, not far from the Tigris River valley in the upper portion of the country.

Refining. The Middle East contains twenty-six refineries which aggregately amount to about 7 per cent of all non-Communist refining capacity and about 17 per cent of the capacity of the United States alone. In short, most of the petroleum that is extracted in the Middle East is shipped in crude form to refineries located near the markets. Middle Eastern refineries are located either at oilfield sites or at ports of trans-shipment from pipelines to ocean vessels (Fig. 20.3).

Ownership. The petroleum belongs to the nations within whose boundaries it occurs. These countries, however, being less developed, initially allowed exploitation by private companies of the United States, the United Kingdom, France, the Netherlands, and, later, Japan and Italy under concessions in which about one-half of the net profits (actually, at the outset, even less) went to the owning country and the remainder to the companies. Exploitation is still being practiced by these firms, but under drastically revised "working rules." Older concessions have been, or are being, changed as to these rules. In early 1973, for example, Iran acquired full control over all operations there, including ownership of installations, with management shared between the country and the companies. More recently, one American oil firm has agreed to allow Iran to own one-half interest in the company's refining and marketing operations in New York State, in return for an assured supply of crude oil and other provisions. Other Middle Eastern countries are demanding altered working relationships in analogous situations. Because of the enormous supplies of petroleum in the Middle East—supplies not only necessary for growing energy demands for North American and European markets but also important geopolitically in the sense that they are desired by other leading political powers—it is likely that the nations owning the oil will continue sequentially to alter the "working rules" of exploitation into the foreseeable future.

Other Production and Potential Outside Centrally Planned Economies

Current production of crude petroleum and some petroleum products, varying from country to country, is found in Libya (6.7 per cent of the world total), Algeria (2.3 per cent), Indonesia (1.6 per cent), and a series of minor producers in various parts of the world. Conditions in each, while unique, offer no major new insight

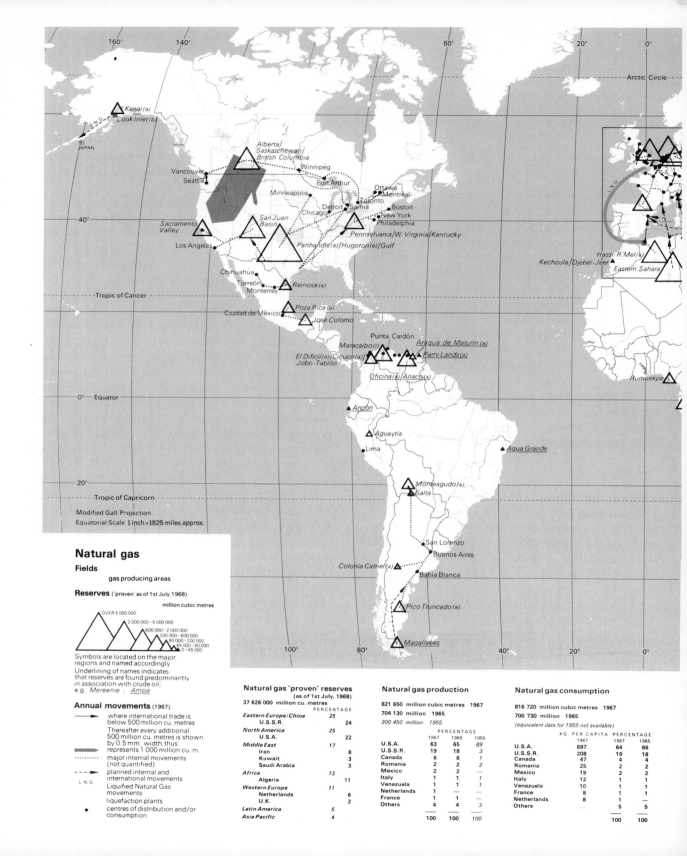

Natural gas

Fields

gas producing areas

Reserves ('proven' as of 1st July, 1968)

million cubic metres

OVER 5 000 000
2 000 000 – 5 000 000
600 000 – 2 000 000
200 000 – 600 000
90 000 – 200 000
45 000 – 90 000
0 – 45 000

Symbols are located on the major
regions and named accordingly
Underlining of names indicates
that reserves are found predominantly
in association with crude oil:
e.g. *Mereenie* : *Ampa*

Annual movements (1967)

→ where international trade is
below 500 million cu. metres

Thereafter every additional
500 million cu. metres is shown
by 0.5 mm. width, thus
represents 1 000 million cu. m.

···· major internal movements
(not quantified)

– – – planned internal and
international movements

L N G Liquified Natural Gas
movements

▲ liquefaction plants

• centres of distribution and/or
consumption

Modified Gall Projection
Equatorial Scale 1 inch = 1825 miles approx.

Map labels:
Kenai (a)
Cook Inlet (b)
TO JAPAN
Alberta/Saskatchewan/British Columbia
Winnipeg
Vancouver
Seattle
Port Arthur
Minneapolis
Ottawa
Montréal
Detroit
Toronto
Sarnia
Boston
Chicago
San Juan Basin
New York
Philadelphia
Sacramento Valley
Pennsylvania/W. Virginia/Kentucky
Los Angeles
Panhandle (a)/Hugoton (a)/Gulf
Chihuahua
Torreón
Monterrey
Reinosa (a)
Ciudad de México
Poza Rica (a)
José Colomo
Punta Cardón
Maracaibo (i)
Araqua de Maturin (a)
El Dificil (a)/Cicuco (a)
Parry Lands (a)
Jobo-Tablón
Oficina (i)/Anaco (a)
Ancón
Aguaytia
Agua Grande
Lima
Monteagudo (a)
Salta
San Lorenzo
Buenos Aires
Colonia Catriel (a)
Bahía Blanca
Pico Truncado (a)
Magallanes
Hassi-R'Mel (a)
Kechoula/Djebel-Jeer
Eastern Sahara
Rumuekpe

Natural gas 'proven' reserves
(as of 1st July, 1968)

37 626 000 million cu. metres

	PERCENTAGE
Eastern Europe/China	25
U.S.S.R.	24
North America	25
U.S.A.	22
Middle East	17
Iran	8
Kuwait	3
Saudi Arabia	3
Africa	13
Algeria	11
Western Europe	11
Netherlands	6
U.K.	2
Latin America	5
Asia Pacific	4

Natural gas production

821 650 million cubic metres 1967
704 130 million 1965
300 450 million 1955

	PERCENTAGE		
	1967	1965	1955
U.S.A.	63	65	89
U.S.S.R.	19	18	3
Canada	6	6	1
Romania	2	2	2
Mexico	2	2	—
Italy	1	1	1
Venezuela	1	1	1
Netherlands	1	—	—
France	1	1	—
Others	4	4	3
	100	100	100

Natural gas consumption

816 720 million cubic metres 1967
700 730 million 1965

(equivalent data for 1955 not available)

	KG. PER CAPITA	PERCENTAGE	
	1967	1967	1965
U.S.A.	697	64	66
U.S.S.R.	208	19	18
Canada	47	4	4
Romania	25	2	2
Mexico	19	2	2
Italy	12	1	1
Venezuela	10	1	1
France	8	1	1
Netherlands	8	1	—
Others	...	5	5
		100	100

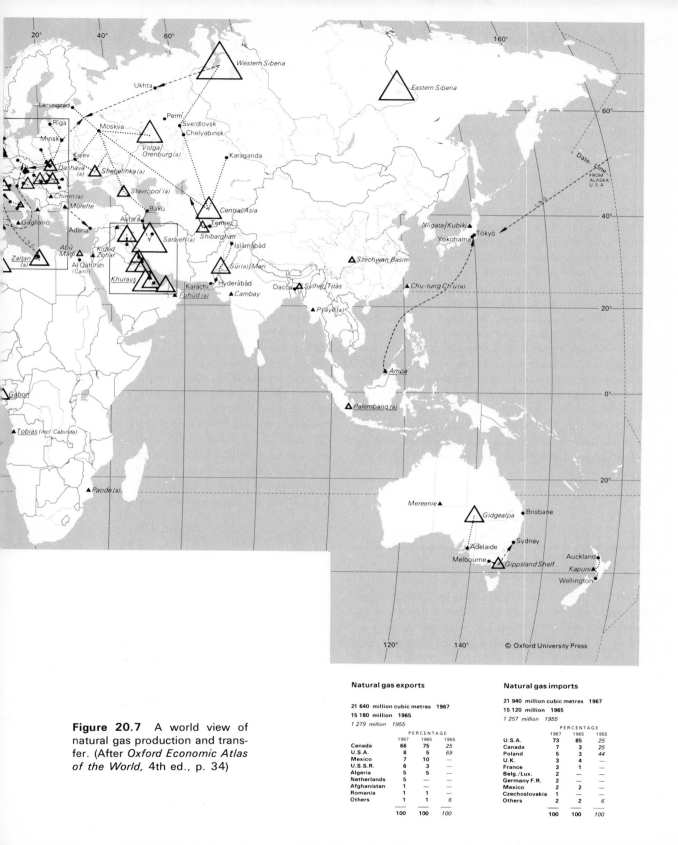

Figure 20.7 A world view of natural gas production and transfer. (After *Oxford Economic Atlas of the World,* 4th ed., p. 34)

Natural gas exports

21 640 million cubic metres 1967
15 180 million 1965
1 279 million 1955

	PERCENTAGE		
	1967	1965	*1955*
Canada	66	75	*25*
U.S.A.	8	5	*69*
Mexico	7	10	—
U.S.S.R.	6	3	—
Algeria	5	5	—
Netherlands	5	—	—
Afghanistan	1	—	—
Romania	1	1	—
Others	1	1	*6*
	100	100	*100*

Natural gas imports

21 940 million cubic metres 1967
15 120 million 1965
1 257 million 1955

	PERCENTAGE		
	1967	1965	*1955*
U.S.A.	73	85	*25*
Canada	7	3	*25*
Poland	5	3	*44*
U.K.	3	4	—
France	3	1	—
Belg./Lux.	2	—	—
Germany F.R.	2	—	—
Mexico	2	2	—
Czechoslovakia	1	—	—
Others	2	2	*6*
	100	100	*100*

© Oxford University Press

into the location and functioning of this activity. Potential production that is not included in the previous discussion is especially high in the North Sea, where national jurisdiction is divided among the United Kingdom, Norway, Denmark, West Germany, the Netherlands, and Belgium. Substantial reserves of both petroleum and natural gas have been, and are being, discovered there. Initial, conservative estimates place the amount of petroleum at some 10 billion barrels, or more than 2 per cent of the world's supply (excluding oil shale and tar sands). Natural gas is also present in substantial quantities. The primary advantage of this field is in its close access to the huge market of the European Economic Community and lesser countries of Western Europe. The major disadvantage is the physical location, well away from shore in the North Sea, and the severe storms encountered there much of the year, where winds sometimes approaching 100 miles an hour whip up waves 75 to 100 feet high. These conditions not only render difficult the obtaining of the petroleum from the relatively shallow sea (generally 150 to 400 feet high) but also increase the danger of a major petroleum leakage and pollution of the many shores adjacent to the North Sea. Transportation of both petroleum and natural gas is, or soon will be, both by pipeline along the floor of the water and by water carrier.

Administrative Arrangements

Major Companies

Outside the United States and centrally planned countries, eight very large, integrated corporations are responsible for over 80 per cent of crude petroleum production, 71 per cent of refining capacity, 35 per cent of tanker ownership, and about 70 per cent of the marketing facilities of petroleum products.[5] Five of these are United States companies: Exxon, Gulf Oil, Mobile Oil, Standard Oil of California, and Texaco. One is British: British Petroleum Corporation (BP), 51

[5] Peter R. Odell, *An Economic Geography of Oil*, G. Bell & Sons, Ltd., London, 1965, p. 28.

per cent of which is owned by the national government. One is French, also jointly owned by the national government and private shareholders: Compagnie Française des Petroles (CFP). One is owned by British and Dutch interests: Royal Dutch–Shell. Each is a separate corporation, but they sometimes engage in joint efforts for specific purposes. This is especially true in the Middle East, where, for example, the Kuwait Petroleum Company is a BP-Gulf operation.

Professor P. R. Odell suggests that these eight companies, with aggregate holdings in several fields and aggregate outlets in North America, Western Europe, and elsewhere, have a rather wide margin of flexibility in developmental decision making. He considers three factors especially important: (1) Because of their desire to return to private investors as high a profit as possible, the corporations may, for example, be unwilling to abandon capital equipment in a field that has become a marginal producer; (2) since there are political as well as economic implications of the presence of the petroleum industry in countries where royalties, tariffs, etc., on oil account for a substantial portion of national income, a company's decision to increase or decrease prodution may have serious political repercussions; and (3) since the grade and quality of crude petroleum vary so much from field to field, decisions concerning extraction must always be made with this variation in mind as well as the possible political and economic implications of the development of a new field.[6]

Independent Companies

The "Big Eight" produce a smaller share of the world's petroleum than they did fifteen years ago. Rising competition has come from independent companies, particularly in the United States, which until recently produced almost wholly for the domestic market. Many of these companies expanded initially to secure new supplies of oil, but quickly saw advantages in marketing abroad as well. Other companies—the government-owned Italian Ente Nazionale Idrocarburi (ENI) and some Japanese firms, especially—also have become much more active.

[6] Ibid.

Nationalism

Still a further element affecting the administrative arrangements in petroleum recovery is a feeling of nationalism in certain oil-endowed countries that wish to use their resources for their own populations. In countries where nationalism is especially strong—for example, Mexico, Brazil, Argentina, Morocco, Algeria, Tunisia, Egypt, Iran, Iraq, Libya, and Indonesia—agonizing decisions must be made concerning the admission of foreign capital. Inasmuch as political power is not always stable in some of these countries, policies may vary sharply from one regime to another, and foreign investors, fearful of losing their capital through expropriation, may become wary. Occasionally, knowledge of large proved reserves of a resource such as oil in a given country will offset the wariness of foreign decision makers, and investment will occur despite the risk.

Natural Gas

The obtainment of natural gas is sufficiently similar to that of petroleum so that the activity merits only passing mention in its own right. Natural gas is becoming increasingly important, especially in the United States and the Soviet Union, as a substitute for petroleum in the production of energy and power (Fig. 20.7). In the United States, the average annual rate of increase in demand for natural gas is essentially 7 per cent, and natural gas now supplies approximately 35 per cent of the country's energy requirements. Nearly two-thirds of the world's natural gas is produced in the United States. Some 90 per cent of the natural gas obtained at the wells is marketed; the remainder is either reinserted into the ground to obtain more gas or burned up at the wells. Industrial demand accounts for nearly one-half of the total; space heating of homes and commercial buildings, for approximately one-third; production of electricity, for about one-sixth; and the driving of compressors in pipelines, for most of the remainder.

Less than 2 per cent is used as a raw material for other manufacturing. Demand is especially high in areas of primary production—Texas and Louisiana, which produce nearly three-fourths of the country's natural gas—and in the manufacturing belt of the Northeast. A pipeline network has been, and is being, completed to more heavily populated parts of the country. About one-third is consumed in Texas, Louisiana, and Oklahoma, and much of the remainder in California. A small amount of the United States supply is imported from Canada, which now produces more than 5 per cent of the world's natural gas.

The Soviet Union now produces and consumes some 20 per cent of the world's natural gas. Production and consumption there have risen sharply since 1950 and are expected to rise even further. The northern Caucasus accounts for about one-fourth, the Ukraine for less than one-fourth, the Second Baku for somewhat less than one-fifth, Soviet Central Asia for one-eighth, and other places for smaller amounts. Pipelines link the leading fields with places of heavy consumption. Some movement by railway tank car and watercraft also occurs. Preliminary negotiations call for ocean shipping of natural gas in liquefied form from the Soviet Union to the United States.

We have mentioned the importance of natural-gas reserves in the North Sea, from which pipelines are being laid to Scotland in the United Kingdom; pipelines also are planned through the Netherlands and Belgium to Paris, and may be extended to other Western European countries.

Both the institutional and the theoretical explanations of the petroleum industry apply also to the natural gas industry. From the total perspective of economic geography, however, a consideration as important as location is conservation. Existing and projected reserves may well carry us through the twentieth century, but there seems little evidence that a long-run dependence upon this very convenient but scarce fuel will be possible. Our sharply increased dependence upon it signifies that, at a time when we should be substituting logic for expediency in the use of scarce commodities, we have not yet learned to do so.

Chapter 21

The Urban Region

A textbook in economic geography, particularly if it is concerned mainly with the United States and other developed market economies, would be incomplete without at least one chapter specifically devoted to metropolitanization and the urban region. True, we have referred to urban places from time to time in this book: we noted in Chapter 1 (especially Fig. 1.4) the increasing tendency for the world's population to live in metropolitan areas and other large urban places. In Chapter 8, we introduced the concept of an urban hierarchy, in which very large urban places offer a wide range of economic functions and establishments; we also noted that with decrease in the size of an urban center, the range of both functions and establishments also decreases, as does the territory served by each. In that same chapter we suggested that secondary and tertiary activity tend to be located near large concentrations of people, which usually are found in urban places, whether because of the markets, the labor supply, more easily available energy, or such amenities as transportation, communication, and indoor recreation.

Both the institutional approach and the theoretical approach to geography, as explained in Part 2, involve a sensitivity to the urban unit, whether as a nucleus of the functional or nodal region (the more traditional concept) or as a component of an urban network that is, in turn, part of a spatial structure and system (the more theoretical concept). The theories of von Thünen, Weber, and Christaller all refer, explicitly or indirectly, to the importance of markets, as expressed in concentrations of people, and of transportation costs or time relative to those markets in locating primary, secondary, and tertiary activity (Chapter 12 and all accompanying figures). Nontheoretical approaches to understanding the location of such activity also involve a careful consideration of urban places.

In short, urbanization is a phenomenon which is with us, and will be with us increasingly in future decades and generations. It contains a wide range of secondary and tertiary activity which has not been explicitly discussed in this book—such newer industries as chemicals and computer technology, as well as such traditional industries as cotton and woolen textiles. As we shall see shortly, urban places contain essentially all the tertiary activity of the United States except that specifically engaged in transporting goods to and from primary and secondary stages and in keeping the budgetary records for such stages. Urbanization is particularly important to economic geography and modern regional planning in that it offers both (1) employment, either locally or within commuting range, and (2) a general living environment for most people.

Employment

Tertiary activity accounts for a substantial and increasing share of the labor force in nearly all countries, and especially so in such developed market economies as the United States. In Chapters 14 through 20, we discussed examples of primary and secondary activity, plus transportation and wholesale and retail trade. All in all, these five categories account for about 60 per cent of the United States labor force. Not covered in that group are federal, state, or local government activities; establishments offering various personal services, such as hotels, movie theaters, and medical offices; establishments concerned with finance, insurance, and real estate; and a variety of other tertiary establishments which are found in urban places. These tertiary activities have not been treated in preceding chapters because they are not directly associated with the progression of goods from primary to secondary to tertiary stages. Indeed, these activities do not in themselves deal with goods at all; they involve professional and personal services. Such services are not directly related to the production of goods, but exist because of the efficiency of activities that do produce goods. Economies which are highly efficient in goods production now can afford an increasing number of services which are not directly related to such production but which could not exist without that efficiency. The very efficiency of goods production—especially the substitution of capital for labor in the production process—has meant relatively fewer people employed in primary and secondary activity, and in goods-producing tertiary activity, and more and more employed in those tertiary activities devoted to services.

This generalization is illustrated in Table 21.1,

TABLE 21.1

LABOR-FORCE BREAKDOWN OF SELECTED STANDARD METROPOLITAN STATISTICAL AREAS (IN PER CENT OF TOTAL)

Industry	Los Angeles–Long Beach	New York	St. Louis
Construction	5	4	5
Manufacturing	27	21	29
Transportation	3	5	5
Communications, utilities, and sanitary services	3	4	3
Wholesale trade	5	5	5
Retail trade	16	15	16
Finance, insurance, and real estate	6	10	5
Business and repair services	5	5	3
Personal services	4	4	4
Health services	6	6	6
Educational services	7	7	7
Other professional and related services	5	6	4
Public administration	5	6	6
Other	3	2	2

Source: U.S. Census of Population, 1970.

which shows the distribution of activity in three different standard metropolitan statistical areas (SMSAs) of the United States—Los Angeles–Long Beach, St. Louis, and New York. The reader will note that manufacturing and retail trade both tend to be significant employers of people in most of the SMSAs, but that a wide range of other tertiary activities, most of them service-oriented, are present.

Trends

The increasing tendency for people to live in large urban places of the United States is shown in Table 21.2. More than two-thirds of the population of this

Names shown on map above are of major cities in areas selected for Figs. 14.7, 15.10, 16.9, 19.8, and 20.6.

Small numbers on map refer to list below, of all other Standard Metropolitan Statistical Areas:

1 Lewiston-Auburn
2 Portland
3 Manchester
4 Lawrence-Haverhill
5 Lowell
6 Fitchburg-Leominster
7 Worcester
8 Springfield-Chicopee-Holyoke
9 Pittsfield
10 Brockton
11 New Bedford
12 Fall River
13 Providence-Pawtucket-Warwick
14 New London-Groton-Norwich
15 Hartford
16 Meriden
17 New Britain
18 Waterbury
19 New Haven
20 Bridgeport
21 Norwalk
22 Stamford
23 Utica-Rome
24 Syracuse
25 Binghamton
26 Paterson-Clifton-Passaic
27 Jersey City
28 Trenton

29 Atlantic City
30 Vineland-Millville-Bridgeton
31 Wilmington
32 Scranton
33 Wilkes-Barre-Hazelton
34 Allentown-Bethlehem-Easton
35 Philadelphia
36 Reading
37 Lancaster
38 Harrisburg
39 York
40 Altoona
41 Johnstown
42 Erie
43 Pittsburgh
44 Youngstown-Warren
45 Akron
46 Canton
47 Steubenville-Weirton
48 Wheeling
49 Lorain-Elyria
50 Mansfield
51 Toledo
52 Lima
53 Columbus
54 Springfield
55 Dayton
56 Hamilton-Middletown
57 Bay City

58 Saginaw
59 Flint
60 Ann Arbor
61 Jackson
62 Lansing
63 Muskegon-Muskegon Heights
64 Grand Rapids
65 Kalamazoo
66 South Bend
67 Gary-Hammond-East Chicago
68 Fort Wayne
69 Lafayette-West Lafayette
70 Anderson
71 Muncie
72 Indianapolis
73 Terre Haute
74 Evansville
75 Rockford
76 Davenport-Rock Island-Moline
77 Peoria
78 Bloomington-Normal
79 Champaign-Urbana
80 Springfield
81 Decatur
82 Green Bay
83 Madison
84 Racine
85 Kenosha

86 Duluth-Superior
87 Fargo-Moorhead
88 Sioux Falls
89 Sioux City
90 Waterloo
91 Dubuque
92 Cedar Rapids
93 Des Moines
94 Lincoln
95 St. Joseph
96 Springfield
97 Topeka
98 Louisville
99 Lexington
100 Huntington-Ashland
101 Charleston
102 Richmond
103 Newport News-Hampton
104 Norfolk-Portsmouth
105 Lynchburg
106 Roanoke
107 Memphis
108 Knoxville
109 Chattanooga
110 Asheville
111 Greensboro - Winston-Salem - High Point
112 Durham
113 Charlotte
114 Fayetteville

115 Wilmington
116 Greenville
117 Columbia
118 Charleston
119 Augusta
120 Macon
121 Savannah
122 Columbus
123 Albany
124 Jacksonville
125 Tallahassee
126 Orlando
127 Tampa-St. Petersburg
128 West Palm Beach
129 Ft.Lauderdale-Hollywood
130 Pensacola
131 Huntsville
132 Gadsden
133 Tuscaloosa
134 Montgomery
135 Mobile
136 Biloxi-Gulfport
137 Little Rock-North Little Rock
138 Pine Bluff
139 Fort Smith
140 Shreveport
141 Monroe
142 Baton Rouge
143 New Orleans

144 Lafayette
145 Lake Charles
146 Tulsa
147 Lawton
148 Wichita Falls
149 Sherman-Denison
150 Texarkana
151 Tyler
152 Waco
153 Austin
154 San Antonio
155 Houston
156 Beaumont-Port Arthur-Orange
157 Galveston-Texas City
158 Corpus Christi
159 Brownsville-Harlingen-San Benito
160 McAllen-Pharr-Edinburg
161 Laredo
162 Amarillo
163 Lubbock
164 Abilene
165 San Angelo
166 Midland
167 Odessa
168 El Paso
169 Tacoma
170 Spokane
171 Salem

172 Eugene
173 Boise
174 Billings
175 Santa Rosa
176 Vallejo-Napa
177 Sacramento
178 Stockton
179 Modesto
180 San Jose
181 Salinas-Monterey
182 Fresno
183 Bakersfield
184 Santa Barbara
185 Oxnard-Ventura
186 Anaheim-Santa Ana-Garden Grove
187 San Diego
188 Reno
189 Las Vegas
190 Ogden
191 Provo-Orem
192 Colorado Springs
193 Pueblo
194 Phoenix
195 Tucson
196 Albuquerque
197 Honolulu
198 San Juan
199 Mayagüez
200 Ponce

Figure 21.1 The 200 largest standard metropolitan statistical areas of the United States. (U.S. Census Bureau)

TABLE 21.2

METROPOLITAN POPULATION BY
SIZE CLASS, 1970

Metropolitan area population	Number of areas	Population (millions)	Population increase, 1960 to 1970 (in 1970 boundaries)	
			Number (millions)	Per cent increase
All areas	243	139	20	14
2 million or more	12	52	6	12
1 million to 2 million	21	28	6	27
500,000 to 1 million	32	22	3	18
250,000 to 500,000	60	20	3	16
Under 250,000	118	17	2	14

Note: If we compare the population of metropolitan areas as defined in 1970, there is an increase of 26 million people. However, if we look at growth occurring within fixed metropolitan boundaries as defined in 1970, as in this table, there is an increase of 20 million. The latter figure does not reflect increases due to territorial extension of 1960 areas or the growth of additional areas to metropolitan status between 1960 and 1970.
Source: Population and the American Future: The Report of the Commission on Population Growth and the American Future, Government Printing Office, Washington, 1972, p. 26.

country is contained in 243 standard metropolitan statistical areas. Furthermore, each category is growing at a rate the same as, equal to, or exceeding the national average, except the largest.[1] The two groups which have grown most rapidly are those between 1 million and 2 million and between 500,000 and 1 million.

If we disallow acquisition of territory by annexation, nearly three-fourths of this growth was accounted for by natural increase, and slightly more than one-fourth by net in-migration (immigrants from abroad as well as migrants from nonmetropolitan portions of the United States, less any emigrants leaving the United States and any people moving from large urban places to rural territories or small urban places).

Associated with this phenomenon of overall metropolitan growth has been a slow growth, and in some areas an actual decline, of populations of central cities

within metropolitan areas. Indeed, of the twenty-one central cities of the United States with a 1960 population of 500,000 or more, fifteen lost population during the following decade. Most people who left the central cities moved to suburbs or to country places within commuting range of a modern metropolitan area.

The Future Urban Region

Whereas in 1900 the urban population represented only 40 per cent of the United States total, by 1970 it represented nearly three-fourths. The movement of people from rural to urban conditions has been fast and dramatic. Such people are moving largely into metropolitan places, which by the year 2000 are expected to contain some 85 per cent of the United States population, as compared with about 71 per cent in 1970.[2]

[1] This is understandable, in view of the size of the populations of the largest category and the way in which rates of growth are calculated. If, for example, we were to add one person to a given base of ten people, the rate of growth would be 10 per cent. If we added one person to a population base of 100, we would obtain a growth rate 1 per cent. If we added one person to a population of 1,000, we would obtain a growth rate of $\frac{1}{10}$ of 1 per cent.

[2] Although there are certain exceptions, an urban place in the United States is generally considered to be one with 2,500 inhabitants or more. A standard metropolitan statistical area (SMSA) contains a core city (or more than one core city) totaling 50,000 or over, plus adjacent counties (or, in New England and parts of Pennsylvania, townships) which are judged to be a part of the metropolitan area.

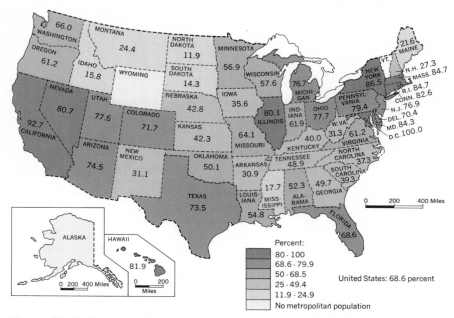

Figure 21.2 Per cent of United States population living in standard metropolitan statistical areas, by states, 1970. (Commission on Population Growth and the American Future)

Figure 21.3 Urban regions of the United States expected by the year 2000. (Commission on Population Growth and the American Future)

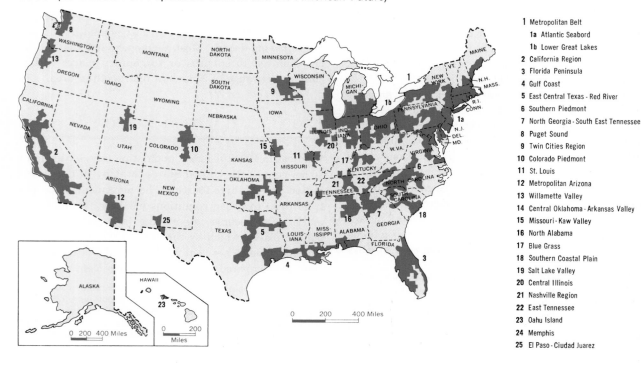

1 Metropolitan Belt
  1a Atlantic Seabord
  1b Lower Great Lakes
2 California Region
3 Florida Peninsula
4 Gulf Coast
5 East Central Texas - Red River
6 Southern Piedmont
7 North Georgia - South East Tennessee
8 Puget Sound
9 Twin Cities Region
10 Colorado Piedmont
11 St. Louis
12 Metropolitan Arizona
13 Willamette Valley
14 Central Oklahoma - Arkansas Valley
15 Missouri - Kaw Valley
16 North Alabama
17 Blue Grass
18 Southern Coastal Plain
19 Salt Lake Valley
20 Central Illinois
21 Nashville Region
22 East Tennessee
23 Oahu Island
24 Memphis
25 El Paso - Ciudad Juarez

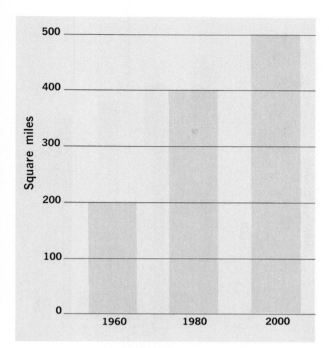

Figure 21.4 Expanding area of urban regions of the United States. Each urban region is occupying, and expected to occupy, much more space than at present. (Commission on Population Growth and the American Future)

Figure 21.1 shows the standard metropolitan statistical areas in the United States at this time. Figure 21.2 shows the per cent of the United States population, by state, living in those standard metropolitan statistical areas. Figure 21.3 shows the projected boundaries of those areas by the year 2000 which are conceived as urban regions. Figure 21.4 shows the expanding area of an average urban region in the United States—an expansion which is expected to more than double in terms of land use by the year 2000. The future importance of metropolitanization to the United States is clear, not only in terms of future provision of employment, but also in terms of future occupance of increasing amounts of land. When we consider the implications of additional open space needed for the residents, both within and near the metropolitan region, and the residential requirements for people who commute to work in metropolitan regions, we understand more thoroughly the importance of metropolitanization in our future.

Environmental Impact

We indicated in the opening chapter that economic geography involves concern not only with the location of economic activities, and the interaction between and

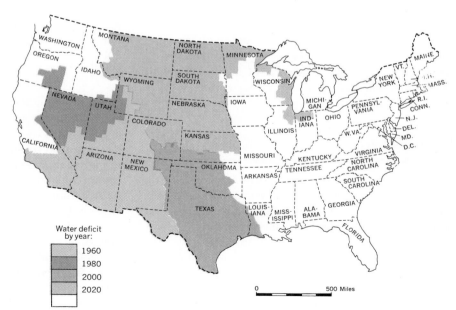

Figure 21.5 Water deficits existing or expected in the United States, by regions, for years specified. (Commission on Population Growth and the American Future)

Water deficit by year:
1960
1980
2000
2020

among such activities, but also with the interaction involving the physical and human environments. National concern for environmental impact is reflected in the National Environmental Policy Act of 1969, especially Section 102.[3] Under this act, all federal agencies are required to include environmental-impact assessments in their future programs and projects, utilizing an interagency approach. *Environment* is interpreted as meaning the human as well as the physical setting. The act has been supported by judiciary decisions and hence appears well on the way to becoming policy.

We are all aware, from knowledge of our home communities, of the importance of landforms, water availability, climate, and other physical environmental features in metropolitan growth. Increasingly, now that our production and transportation have benefited from technology (both invention and innovation), we are able to consider the location of economic activity in physical and also cultural circumstances which aggregately can be said to constitute a desirable "quality of life." That quality involves conservation—wise use for our time and the foreseeable future—of the full range of natural and human resources within which economic activity occurs. It includes the full range of physical and cultural circumstances, which have been explained in the Introduction and earlier chapters of this book. Two considerations, selected by a recent Presidential Commission on Population Growth and the American Future, are shown in Figures 21.5 and 21.6. These involve (1) possible water deficits in certain portions of the country and (2) an assessment of air pollution, with alternative solutions.

Significance for Planning

Any sound approach to regional planning in a modern, developed market economy cannot ignore the overwhelming significance of urban places, especially metropolitan areas. We shall have much more to say about this topic in Part 4. At this time we shall only raise a flag: The metropolitan region is with us, and cannot be conveniently overlooked in planning our future.

[3] See especially Gilbert F. White, "Environmental Impact Statements," *The Professional Geographer*, **24**:303–309, 1972.

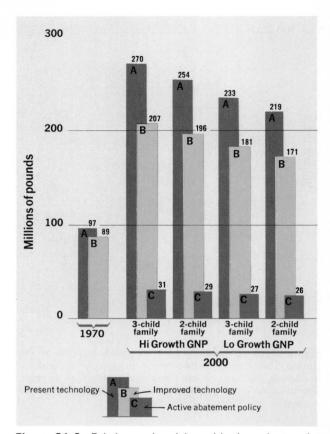

Figure 21.6 Existing and anticipated hydrocarbon emissions in the United States, under high growth and low growth assumptions. (Commission on Population Growth and the American Future)

However idyllic the rural landscape may appear when we drive to the country for an outing, the efficiency of present-day economic activity depends in appreciable measure upon economies of scale which are derived only in metropolitan conditions. Whether we like it or not, the metropolitan area is a fact of life. We may alter its structure and make it more livable, but we cannot destroy it entirely, unless we wish to return to conditions which, after a brief experience with them, we almost certainly would find unsatisfactory. Indeed, as we shall see in Part 4, one of the first and most important considerations in meaningful regional planning is the network (hierarchy) of urban places and connecting linkages.

PART 4
Economic Geography
and
Regional Planning

The preceding parts of this book have all been preliminary to Part 4. In the Introduction, we examined various approaches to the study of the geography of economic activity, stressing a general breakdown into institutional and theoretical schools of thought. In Part 1, we looked at the real world through description, simple measurement, and classification. In Part 2, we elaborated upon the institutional and theoretical approaches, stressing both their distinctive and their mutual aspects. In Part 3, through case studies, we traced selected commodities through some primary, secondary, and tertiary stages of economic activity and appraised the linkages connecting each set of stages. In our effort to understand the intricate details of these various stages (and not, as may be inferred, to emphasize the accomplishments of a single nation), we have focused attention upon conditions in the United States, examining in a general review analogous conditions elsewhere, especially in neighboring Canada.

In this part, we pass through the threshold from *understanding* and possible *prediction* to *planning.* At the outset, it is important to distinguish between research, which provides understanding and possible prediction, and planning; these are very different forms of activity. They are particularly different with respect to ends, or objectives. A research specialist cannot in all conscience merely select a particular end or objective on the basis of emotional bias and set out to prove it correct or incorrect. The process of scientific reasoning, whether inductive or deductive, proceeds independently from the *wishes* of the scientist carrying out a particular piece of research. Of course, scientific research is directed toward solving a particular problem, but we cannot alter logical, scientific reasoning, or depart from scientific findings, in order to obtain proof or disproof.

Scientific research therefore presents its findings in scientific statements. Now there is a strict definition of a scientific statement: *A scientific statement is one which can be proven or disproven only on the basis of empirical evidence.* What we have said previously applies again here—*The scientist is concerned with what is and not with what ought to be.* What ought to be involves *value judgments,* which the scientist may not introduce as scientific statements. He or she may, of course, have strong personal opinions about many things, but he or she must always separate personal conviction from results achieved on the basis of scientific evidence. It is here especially that research differs from, and yet necessarily precedes, the planning process.

However, in all candor, we must raise again a difference in opinion as to the nature of science. In its strictest sense, science is "Commissarish" in Koestler's terms (see p. 140). This interpretation appeals especially to the theoretical-deductive school of thought in geography. Interpreted more broadly as an objective search for truth, it admits to some of the "Yogi" perspective, which the institutional-historical school finds acceptable.

It is important to emphasize that both approaches and methods contribute enormously to the understanding and prediction which are vital to the planning process. The institutional-historical approach, with its emphasis upon the study of reality as it has actually developed in a given place at a given time, provides an insight otherwise unobtainable into specific places or groups of places that may be called regions—and, in the final analysis, none of these regions is exactly duplicated anywhere else on the face of the earth. The theoretical-deductive approach, with its emphasis upon universals, hypotheses, theories, and models, provides an enormous insight into worldwide behavior of a wide range of activity, so that the conditions of a specific region are considered not in isolation, but against a worldwide background of universal experience and findings from which more valid conclusions can be drawn.

As will be explained in detail in the next two chapters, both authors of this book have had the opportunity to contribute to a planning process involving the initiation of a regional planning and development program for the province of Ontario in Canada. Our experience there led us to conclude that the background research for a given region could be conducted successfully by geographers (and scholars from other disciplines) who favored the institutional-historical approach and whose interests were particularly focused upon a given set of circumstances in a given region. However, it was not only useful but also necessary to provide a second set of efforts from the theoretical approach—from persons who were specialists in transportation, urbanization, environmental perception, and other areas where the theoretical-deductive approach has yielded good results and who could advise, stimulate, and otherwise provide a common denominator of universals that could prevent the institutional-historically oriented research teams from becoming excessively isolated from generally accepted truths.

The approach to planning, therefore, is by way of research—research drawn from both the institutional-historical and the theoretical-deductive viewpoints. We shall discuss the methods in greater detail in Chapter 22, in which we examine the planning process. We can say at this point that planning involves more than objective search and predictions. It also involves *value judgments of what ought to be.* The basic question asked by the planner is: What combination of social, economic, political, physical, and related conditions should be treated in each area under consideration, and ultimately in the world, and how should each of these be treated? The importance lies not only in the question but also in the fact that it must be asked over and over again with the passing of time and the focusing of attention upon different sets of conditions and places. The range of information necessary for adequate planning is essentially the same as that in economic geography, given the definition set forth in the

Introduction to this book. That range includes all available data that might contribute to an improved quality of life, which is the ultimate goal of modern planning. As in economic geography, the range includes not only economic information but also cultural and physical information that may be important to the quality of life. Furthermore, as will be emphasized in Chapter 22, such data should be made available at a very fine spatial grid—city blocks in urban areas and units smaller than townships in rural areas—so that people and planners can have a wide range of data to use in setting down and revising the regional boundaries that are so essential to the planning process.

Chapter 22

Research and the
Planning Process

The Planning Process

Planning requires three categories of input. First, the planner must know the *goals* he or she wishes to achieve; he or she must have a set of *objectives*. Second, he or she must prescribe a set of *policies* through which these goals or objectives can be achieved. And finally, he or she must recommend ways and means of *implementing* the policies.

In countries which elect their governments, public planning is further, and continuously, subject to two very important practical constraints: (1) acceptance by people and (2) the interest, financial resources, and jurisdiction of the organization responsible ultimately for a plan.

The successful realization of each goal or objective and the successful relationships among people, governments, and planning ultimately depend upon a basic foundation of fundamental research. It is here that research and planning meet.

Planning is therefore a *process* involving a contin-

uous reexamination of objectives and means in view of continuously changing events. On the one hand, because man began to plan his activities when reasoning replaced instinct in his existence, the roots of this process are so deeply embedded in history as to be scarcely distinguishable. On the other hand, planning as a modern idea is not yet thoroughly understood—certainly not in practice—because of the extreme complexity and rapid change that characterize the modern world. Like geography, planning involves a *structure* (a set of sectors) which is *located in space* on this earth, *related to time,* and *subject to interaction,* both at a specific time and with change in time. The successful planner recognizes an interplay involving structure, space, and time.

Planning and Development

The word *development* is increasingly being considered both synonymous with, and yet distinct from, *planning.* We have described planning as the establishment of logical goals or objectives, and of the means for their attainment, and we have indicated that planning is a process appraising not only current conditions but also change. We can consider here that *change* is alteration from existing conditions, whether favorable or unfavorable; *growth* is increase, whether favorable or unfavorable; and *decline* is decrease, whether favorable or unfavorable.

At one time, development was considered merely to reflect existing conditions that changed more or less haphazardly. However, in this age of heightened awareness of our various environments, development now is being used increasingly to mean *planned and implemented change, whether growth or decline.* (Presumably, planned change is favorable, or advantageous.) From this point forward, therefore, we shall use the word *planning* to imply the *initiation and activation of the overall planning and development process* and the word *development* to imply the *result.*

Levels of Observation (Scale)

We mentioned previously the importance of levels of observation, or scale, as applied to scientific research. Those levels also are important in planning. Two important concepts are *aggregative* and *disaggregative* planning and development.

Aggregative planning and development. We can consider planning to begin at the level of individuals, and of individual homes, and to aggregate upward in scale through the family; the multifamily unit, including the private company; the municipality; the large corporation; the state or province; the nation; and international groups. As long as the perspective is from the smaller unit looking upward toward the larger, we can consider this to be *aggregative planning, or microplanning.* This is the planning with which most cities and towns are keenly concerned, inasmuch as it includes local zoning of land for various levels of residential, commercial, street, or other uses. Indeed, this is the type of activity outside centrally planned countries that most people believe all planning to be. It is, of course, important. But it is only one aspect of the overall process.

Disaggregative planning and development. Another viewpoint which is extremely important is the *disaggregative,* or *macroplanning,* perspective. Here the view is that of a large political or social unit looking downward toward all the subdivisions, including communities and rural places, under its particular jurisdiction or influence. An important distinction between disaggregative and aggregative planning is also *scale,* with disaggregative planning and development involving large areas and general conditions, and aggregative planning involving smaller areas and very specific conditions. The level of separation is usually considered to be that of the large urban unit, notably the metropolitan area, which must plan both aggregatively and disaggregatively.

Because it may involve the spatial impact of enormous budgets of state, provincial, and federal governments and of large corporations, disaggregative planning can affect communities very decidedly, however subtly. Most regional planning is disaggregative in nature.

Need for harmony. Because of their differing perspectives, aggregative and disaggregative planning may clash. The danger of this is heightened with the appearance of strong personalities representing either viewpoint. However, in the long run, the two must be in general harmony, with the more detailed specific recommendations of the aggregative plan in working relationship with the "woof and warp" recommendations of the disaggregative plan.

The Planning Region

We mentioned previously the importance of the homogeneous and the functional regions in the interpretation of geography, especially economic geography (pp. 128 to 131). We also noted that these regions can be observed at different levels and that their boundaries do not neatly coincide, but overlap into complex patterns, depending upon the type of classification for which each regional type is used.

The planning region is related to both these types in the same way that planning and development are related to research: it reflects subjective views as to what should be, rather than being merely a classification, based upon scientific research, of what now exists. Therefore, we should not consider the planning region to be similar to the homogeneous or functional regions because the planning region is not a research tool, but a planning and development tool, always reflecting the viewpoint and interest of the organization which is responsible for a particular planning process. However, the planning region should be based upon some form of logic, and part of that logic is based upon research—either upon the homogeneous or the functional region, the latter frequently involving urban systems and hierarchies. Planning and research regions are therefore related, as is demonstrated by the illustrations to follow.

Delimitation by watershed. Traditionally there are two major approaches to the delimitation of planning regions. One, a classic example of which is the famous Tennessee Valley Authority in the United States, is delimitation by river basin. The fundamental purpose of the planning in such a case usually is the conservation of the ecological balance of the area, i.e., the wise use of resources, both for our time and for the foreseeable future. Because waterways are critical to that balance—indeed, providing its geographical configuration in arid and semiarid areas and in other places where man has not settled densely—the watersheds of river basins can be considered logical planning boundaries for this purpose. That they are acceptable as boundaries is shown by the fact that the TVA experiment has been duplicated in various other parts of the world, almost always using watersheds of river basins as boundaries. Since the watershed is homogeneous in the sense that it is a specific part of a river-basin system, and uniform in the sense that it is a definite physical feature, this type of planning-region delimitation can be considered an example of drawing planning boundaries on the basis of the homogeneous region as used in research.

Delimitation by urban systems. However, in an urbanized or rapidly urbanizing area, planning by river-basin watershed is inadequate. The reason is simple: A mature system of urban places is an efficient, modern, *functional organization of space.* As we have seen, this organization takes the form, more or less, of hierarchy, with the smaller urban places and their immediate trading territories situated generally within the influence of the larger urban places, and these in turn within areas of influence of still larger urban places. A metropolitan area—or, sometimes, a conurbation of two or more metropolitan areas into a megalopolis—is at the highest level in each hierarchy. Taken together, these urban places and their trading areas comprise an intricate pattern based upon a working relationship of a minimum distance between centers and a minimum population to be served by each center. In brief, no minimum distance should be so small, or no population so small, that the center cannot continue to exist at its particular level in the hierarchy. Ideally, the resultant pattern takes the form of a series of hexagons, with each angle of a hexagon forming a nucleus of a yet smaller hexagon. In a modern, highly urban, and still urbanizing area, the locational planning boundaries can be placed most logically between zones of influence or urban places so that the entire zone of influence of any given place is not intersected by a planning boundary.

To be sure, this approach means recognizing the urban places and their zones of influence as they exist *on the earth's surface,* and not according to an idealized model. It is also true that waterways have an effect upon the location of urban places, and will continue to do so because of their importance as sources of water supply and sewage removal. *However, except in very dry places, where river floodplains tend to define sharp boundaries between intensively used land and very extensively used land, or in areas with very sparse populations, the geographic locations of waterways and river basins should be considered subordinate to the locations of cities and their trading areas—of human organization of space—in setting the boundaries of a planning region.* This is true even if the major concern of planning is preserving the ecological balance, since a majority of people now live in urban places, where the danger of upsetting that balance may be the greatest. The delimitation of planning regions by urban systems and their respective trading areas is an excellent example of the utilization of the research functional region and of an urban system in the setting down of boundaries for a planning region.

Importance of the interest of the jurisdictional unit. Again, however, it is necessary to stress the importance of the interest and the area of jurisdiction of the unit responsible for a given planning process, whether that unit is public or private. Ideally, the boundaries of a planning region should not seriously intersect any jurisdictional boundary lines of the unit responsible for the actual planning. We are thus confronted with a dilemma of attempting to draw boundaries based, on the one hand, upon functional or homogeneous research planning regions—especially upon urban places and their trading areas—and, on the other hand, upon political boundaries. This is a difficult dilemma. Its solution is never easy and is always found in the context of the individual circumstances in a given area.

The Growth Point

Important to the concept of a planning region in this time of rapid urbanization is the idea of a *growth point.* A regional economy does not exist by accident, or in isolation, but is structured geographically on key urban places which can be called *growth points.* This is particularly true in modern, highly urbanized areas, but it is also true in less developed parts of the world where extensive rural activities predominate, for even these activities depend in large measure upon a market center. In its simplest sense, a growth point can be considered an urban place capable of growth under specified conditions. Such growth may be either *self-sustained* or *assisted* to varying degrees. In this book, the term *growth point* refers to the general concept, whereas *growth pole* is used to refer to those large places—usually metropolitan or larger areas—which are the keystones of national growth; *growth center* is used to refer to those smaller urban places which are the foundation of regional growth. By and large, growth centers tend to transmit impulses from the growth pole to smaller places. For this reason, the growth-point approach to regional planning is particularly effective within a range of 100 miles from each growth pole or very large growth center. Growth centers in more re-

mote places usually either are oriented to primary industries or are highly specialized as to both secondary and tertiary activities—i.e., they cater to high-value-low-bulk manufacturing and to such services as can function there.

The growth-point idea is of relatively recent origin and has been ascribed to the French scholar Francois Perroux.[1] It is employed in one of several forms in the planning of most developed countries, and in many of the less developed ones as well. For the rapidly expanding urban areas, the immediate suburbs are often referred to as *overspill* growth points, and places some distance from the suburbs, to which activity is diverted to prevent excessive congestion at the core, are called *interceptor* growth points.

The recognition of systems of urban places, functionally related to one another, enables not only the geographic structuring of those parts of an area which are growing spontaneously but also the provision of assistance to slow-growth areas through the tapping of the dynamic energy of their fast-growth counterparts. In this idea more than any other lies the hope of redressing the heavy imbalance of population and economic growth which is now concentrating in the world's metropolitan areas and larger urban places, and of shifting some growth into nearby places which may not have quite so many economic advantages but which have total assets—economic, social, political, and physical—that may be equal to, or perhaps greater than, those of the major metropolitan areas.

Growth points thus can be identified by (1) their geographic position (particularly within networks of transportation and communication), (2) their functional role in the regional and national economies, and (3) their potential for growth. Much of the present literature on growth points is concerned with the growth potential of points more or less as abstractions —not unlike von Thünen's isolated state—and not with public policy. However, in truth, contributions from the public sector are vital to a growth point, even in economies where private enterprise plays an extremely important role, and is paramount in socialist and other centrally planned economies. Government budgets (for roads, water supply, health, education, etc.) are on-

[1] Francois Perroux, "Note sur la notion de 'pole de croissance,'" *Economie Appliquée,* 1955.

going; and although they may change in volume from year to year, they can be expected to continue indefinitely. Therefore, a growth-point policy which is based upon careful evaluation of the regional impact of annual governmental expenditures is a permanent one, and any growth point selected by such a government will expect continuous input of assistance through the normal channels of government operation. Hence, in government policy, the growth point is viewed somewhat differently from the way it is seen in the traditional academic exercise on the topic: a growth point tends to be a center selected by a government for permanent assistance, and will exist permanently as long as that government maintains its interest.

Basic Structure

As we noted earlier in the chapter, the structure of the planning process can be considered in terms of three basic categories of input: (1) *goals* or *objectives,* (2) *policies* by which these goals or objectives can be achieved, and (3) ways and means of *implementing* the policies.

Planning goals or objectives. Selection of the goals or objectives of a plan necessarily must be preceded by fundamental analysis of the resources and the needs of the area under consideration. To be of maximum use to the planner, that analysis must be based upon scientific research. It is here, particularly, that the realms of researcher and planner overlap: the researcher provides conclusions from scientific analysis, and the planner uses these conclusions, plus his value judgments, as a basis for recommending and implementing policies. Such analysis can take one of two forms and ideally should involve both: (1) trend studies, including projections into the future, and (2) simulation models.

Trend studies. Although the basic decisions in planning may be intended to offset current trends, it is important to have a clear knowledge of those trends, if for no other reason than to know what to counteract. Because we are concerned with both relative and absolute differences in trends of different parts of an area, it is important that all data reflecting trends be assembled into very small geographic parcels—ideally, on

a block-by-block basis within urban areas and, at the most, on a township-by-township basis in rural areas. The data should involve the widest possible range of information concerning the welfare of the region—not only the usual census materials relating to size, growth rate in overall numbers, proportion of male and female residents, urban and rural characteristics, ethnic groups, etc., but also changes in labor forces; capital investment; income; building construction; transportation and communication; investment; terrestrial, hydrogeologic, and atmospheric conditions; carrying capacities and pollution levels of land, water, and air; and still other data. In brief, the trend studies should involve the widest possible range of data, applied to a very fine geographic "mesh," so that the researcher is able to see clearly the nuances of change as these are applied to both structure and space. Furthermore, trends need to be related to a central norm, which can provide a common denominator for comparison. That central norm can be the average or mean for a larger unit—perhaps a state, a region, or an entire nation—which contains the various areas under consideration. In practical terms, this larger unit may well be the area of jurisdiction of the political unit responsible for the particular planning operation.

A successful trend study should cover a sufficient amount of time for a meaningful interpretation—a half century in broad, descriptive terms, including the most recent fifteen-year period (with particular attention to the last five years, noting technological and related changes) in detailed analysis. A specific projection into the future for at least fifteen years, again always comparing the past trends of each small data-reporting unit with those of the overall area under consideration, is vital. A general projection over an additional ten years or more is useful, but always subject to later refinement.

Model simulation. Another approach to the analysis of needs and resources of a region that is coming into increasing use is the utilization of simulation models. Like trend studies, these depend heavily upon the availability of a wide range of data on a fine geographic mesh. Different types of models may be constructed for different purposes. Some may be an attempt to simulate the total functioning of an economy, and others an attempt to emphasize, say, the transportation aspects of that overall functioning. Some may be highly theoretical, and others may be more nearly applied. To date, one of the most widely accepted models has been the Leontiff input-output tables which indicate, for each area of consideration, the movement of goods from each sector of an economy to all other sectors and to final demand (see p. 201). Efforts have been made recently to translate this sectoral model into a fine spatial mesh so that the relationship between structure and space will be clear with respect to the flow of goods from the primary, secondary, and tertiary activities within one small area (say, a county) and to such activities in other small areas. The use of models, in both economic geography and planning, is only in the embryonic period and can be expected to become more important. (See also Chapter 12.)

Geocoding. The reader will note that both the analyses mentioned above require a wide range of data, assembled and released not only for very large areas, such as states or nations, but also for very small areas, such as counties or townships or even city blocks. Effective regional planning necessarily depends upon the availability of a wide range of data for small as well as large geographic areas. For most parts of the world, data are not available in sufficient quantity or range or in a fine-enough geographic mesh to make possible the kind of fundamental research which must precede the other two steps of an effective regional planning or regional development program. In several countries, experimentation is now going on with the gathering and storing of data on a point-by-point basis—i.e., using individual addresses or individual residences—and the publication of such data on the basis of standardized grids, which would be smaller in densely populated, complex urban areas and larger in the more sparsely populated rural areas. However, the grids would be compatible—the larger ones could be disaggregated into the smaller ones, and the smaller ones could be aggregated into the larger ones—so that a comparison of information with change in time could be possible. Such objective data gathering and reporting—utilizing objective grids rather than any type of political boundaries such as a municipality or township—are especially important to the researcher in that they provide for objective reporting. Just as changes in the mercury level of a thermometer indicate alteration in temperature, so would the data obtainable from a standardized grid reveal, over a period of time, changes in that grid from, say, rural to urban conditions.

Policy recommendation. Once an insight has been gained into the resources and needs of an area being planned, the time has come for policy recommendations. This step, too, depends upon a substantial background of research, although here the research tends to be more subjective and to involve a substantial measure of value judgments. Also at this time, priorities are established as to the relative intensities of the various needs recognized in the area under consideration and to the sequence and relative weights to be given to development of various human and natural resources. Inasmuch as the financial cost of providing the optimum conditions almost invariably will exceed the available funds, careful selection also will be made from among the various alternatives, including the amount of financial assistance to be allocated to each policy. Finally, because we live in a time of rapid change, it is necessary to distinguish between specific recommendations, which usually apply to short-term conditions, and general recommendations, which usually can be expected to affect long-range conditions.

Implementation. Just as an idea is of little value until it is communicated to, and judged by, other minds, so is a plan of little value until it is implemented or acted upon. Successful implementation depends heavily upon sound initial planning involving not only the anticipated consequence of each short- and long-term recommendation but also popular acceptance and financial viability. General acceptance by the population for which the planning is being carried out and by the decision makers, public or private, ultimately responsible for the implementation is critical. Therefore, an important aspect of implementation involves the art of politics, whether applied to a government body or a private corporation. Because plans involve expenditure, they must anticipate a return of benefits to costs—usually a favorable return, but always a carefully calculated one. There are various ways of calculating benefit-cost ratios. Invariably, these involve the assignment of positive or negative numerical values for anticipated benefits and costs, whether social, economic, or environmental, over a specified period of time. These two points—acceptability and viability—often bypassed or assumed in classroom studies of planning, can make or break the implementation of a plan.

A Planning Schedule

Although planning is a process, it must involve a schedule with specific bench-mark target dates for achievement of selected goals. It must also involve short-term as well as long-term considerations. There are, of course, as many schedules as there are planning organizations, and no two planners would necessarily agree on the exact nature of a given schedule. However, we shall present here the schedule which was adopted officially by a public agency, the government of Ontario in Canada, for its initiation of a regional planning program in the 1970s.

Ontario's plan was envisaged as both short term and long term, with specific objectives to be reached within a ten-year period (some within five years) and longer objectives to be reached over a thirty-year period. Because data are always necessary both to project objectives and to test them when the target year has been reached, the time periods were the decennial census years, which in Canada are 1971, 1981, 1991, 2001, etc. For specific objectives, five-year time periods, also verifiable in more restricted censuses, were 1976, 1986, 1996, etc. Recommendations were to be specific for the 1976 and 1981 periods and increasingly general for the 1986, 1991, 1996, and 2001 periods.

The administrative structure of the government of Ontario's program is very complex, involving local citizen groups, which were aggregated into broader regional councils; provincial civil servants in field offices; staffs of all departments and agencies cooperating in the program; staffs of selected offices in the federal government; and regional and municipal governments. The program therefore, is designed to achieve a maximum degree of overall coordination.

Regional Goals

Ontario has been divided into ten planning regions, and goals were selected for each region. The selection of such goals was the culmination of the first phase, the *analysis phase,* of a threefold approach to regional development in Ontario, the other two phases being *policy recommendation* and *policy statement and implementation.* In recognition of the importance of research to this particular portion of the planning process, the analysis involved seven steps: the identification of provincial goals, the review of past growth trends and the creation of such models as could exist on the basis of existing data, the carrying out of social and economic base studies for each region, the examination of present and potential land use, the examination of the impact of technology upon present and anticipated conditions, the consideration of possible growth points, and the selection of regional goals (Fig. 22.1).

Identification of provincial goals. We have mentioned previously that the general goals of the planning process cannot be established successfully without giving careful consideration to the interest of the organization responsible for the planning process. In this particular case, the organization was the province of Ontario, whose overall interest and goals were indicated in a white paper, *Design for Development.*[2] Those goals were stated in general terms as "motherhood goals," which are difficult to define and measure specifically but which nevertheless stand as general guidelines for the planning operation. In the case of the government of Ontario, the goals were threefold: (1) the encouragement of each region to its social, economic, political, and environmental potential; (2) the discouragement of excessive misuse of the physical environment; and (3) the coordination of activities of all provincial agencies, plus careful and close liaison with subprovincial and federal agencies and the private sector, in realizing the first two goals. The first two can be considered logical planning goals; the third, a means rather than a goal, was included because of its overall importance to the planning process.

[2] *Design for Development,* Government of Ontario, Toronto, 1966.

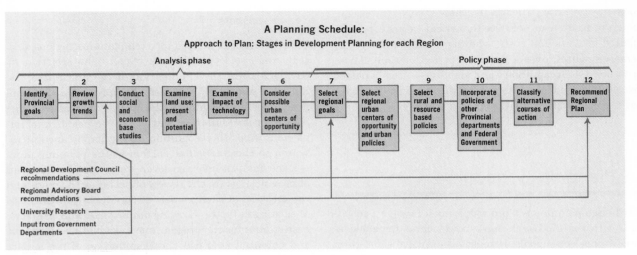

A Planning Schedule:
Approach to Plan: Stages in Development Planning for each Region

Figure 22.1 The planning schedule used in Ontario. Regional goals stemmed from analysis of needs and resources, including substantial input from the people and from universities and other professional sources. These goals were reexamined after the analysis report was submitted to popular review and formed the first step in policy formulation. The policy phase, too, was referred to the people, and actual policy programs emerged after completion of the twelve steps shown above. As usual it was necessary in practice to alter these steps in specific regions to fit the time and space requirements of that region—to mesh with existing conditions. Centers of opportunity are growth points.

Assessment of provincial conditions. The second step was in fact a series of steps, all of which were designed to examine the overall condition of the entire province and to arrive at a better understanding of the conditions to be treated. It involved a comprehensive statement from the regional development councils and other citizens groups as well as professional bodies concerning the major problems in the various regions and in the province, a review of growth trends for the province as a whole, and the selection of such models as could be utilized on the basis of available data. In addition, careful assessment was made of all existing research by all departments and agencies, both at the provincial government level and in selected federal, regional, and local offices. A comprehensive university research program was initiated to assist in assessing the broader provincial problems and in examining specific conditions which emerged.

Trend study. For the trend study, sixty-three indicators of social, economic, and environmental change were selected for a trend period of fifteen years or the nearest available time for which data could be had. The data were gathered for the smallest geographic unit for which they were available, which all too often proved to be nothing smaller than counties. They then were compared with the average provincial trend of that particular indicator over the specific year period. Individual maps were made of the overall provincial trend and of five categories of trends in the reporting units: high, intermediately high, provincial average, intermediately low, and low. For the first time in its history, this province had a review of changing conditions with the provincial average as a common denominator. Thus it was possible to reinforce intuitive judgment with numerical evidence (Figs. 22.2, 22.3, and 22.4).

Models. In recognition of the importance of key urban places for the implementation of the Ontario program, gravity models of population and economic potential were constructed for the province as a whole, with particular emphasis upon those key urban places which might serve as logical growth points. A second series was equally important; the government of Ontario had developed an overall input-output study for the province as a whole, but had not expressed this information regionally. The second model broke down these provincial sectoral requirements into county requirements, thus providing for each county of Ontario an assessment of all goods and commodities entering counties and being exported from them, thus making it possible to understand what might be called "county economies."

Social and economic base studies for each region. With the completion of the first two steps, a general understanding emerged not only of the past trends as revealed by the selected indicators but also of the opinions of both private and professional people concerning the needs and resources of each region and the potential for growth points as presented by selected models. However, it was still necessary to gain a more intimate insight into the social and economic conditions of each of the ten planning regions. This was done through careful review of these conditions as revealed by the overall provincial trend study and also through special field work carried out by research teams employed by the government of Ontario.

Land use study. A comprehensive examination was made of all land use in Ontario, with emphasis upon three aspects: existing land utilization, the potential for alternative uses of land in terms of its inherent physical capacity for such uses, and the possible impact of alternatives in demands upon the land, especially from urban, recreational (including tourist) sources, and primary industries, especially agriculture. Examination of present use was on a broad regional scale, rather than a micro scale. It resulted in a mosaic for each region, as well as for the province as a whole, of current utilization. The inherent physical capacity of the environment was considered in terms of (1) each of the primary industries, (2) recreation, and (3) urban uses. Demand was evaluated particularly in terms of (1) that expected from each urban unit in the province, whether increasing or decreasing; (2) that anticipated from open-space and recreational requirements of Ontario's residents, plus a rising tourist industry; and (3) the needs

of primary activities, particularly agriculture and forest products, which must have large amounts of land for suitable production.

Impact of technology. The planner must be constantly aware of technological change, anticipated as well as current. Much technological change includes not only the invention of new machines and electronic equipment but also the derivation of new processes and methods of production or service which may or may not be based upon those new machines or equipment. In this day of rapid change, the planner must be particularly sensitive to a new change which might drastically alter both the short-range and the long-range potential of his plan. For example, the experimental land vehicle, which is supported by a cushion of air or a reverse magnetic thrust and travels along a prescribed route at speeds up to 250 miles an hour, could clearly alter the concept of commuting to and from a major center and therefore could offset seriously any plan based upon older, slower means of public transportation. A careful examination of the impact of technology upon anticipated conditions is necessary at a fairly early stage of analysis.

Alternative growth points. Because the government of Ontario had selected the growth-point strategy, it was necessary to consider in detail the potential of all existing cities for various categories of growth points—whether found in expanding or contracting regions and whether considered to be overspill, interceptor, or stimulation growth points. For each urban place that might possibly qualify as a growth point, the following aspects were considered: present size; past rate of growth; past rates of growth of tertiary, secondary, and primary activities; location with respect to the present urban systems network; present size and past rates of population growth of the trading area of each center plus present sizes and past growth tendencies of primary, secondary, and tertiary activities in each trading area; and present transportation, water supply, sewage disposal facilities, educational institutions, and other infrastructure and the relative costs of adding to these. Finally, models of urban growth potential were developed in terms of current populations and in terms

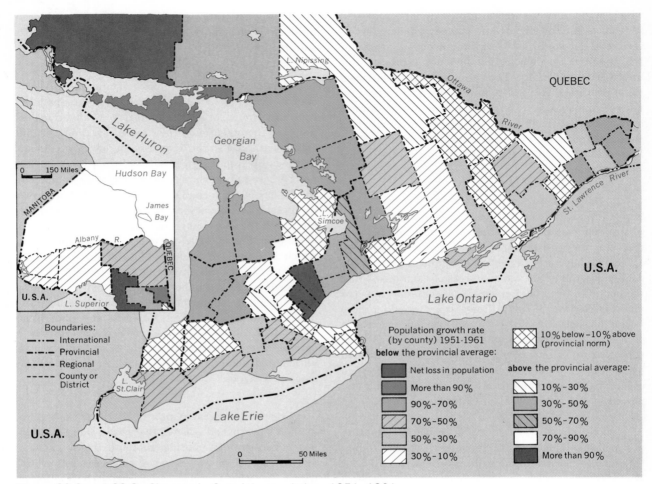

Figure 22.2 and 22.3 Changes in Ontario's population, 1951–1961, and 1961–1966. Note the trends: no net loss in the earlier decade, but a net loss over a substantial area in 1961–1966. The heavy growth is in or near metropolitan areas—Toronto, Kitchener-Waterloo, London, Hamilton—whereas losses generally are in places remote from these large metropolitan zones. (Government of Ontario)

of possible alternatives of overall population distribution that might result from specific policy decisions.

Selection of regional goals. Whereas general provincial goals could be specified at the outset, regional goals could result only from a careful assessment of overall provincial conditions and trends, and of regional conditions, as revealed by the steps previously described. Therefore, the selection of regional goals was postponed to the end of the analysis phase.

Public review. For each of the ten planning regions, analysis reports were completed on the basis of the steps previously described. These were publicly released and subjected to intensive community-level discussion and review before being considered as possible policy.

Policy Recommendation

Upon the completion of discussion concerning the analysis reports of each region and the receipt of reactions

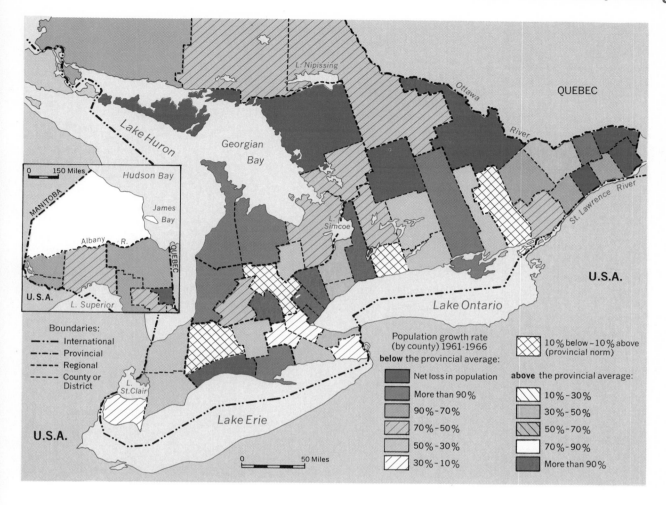

Population growth rate (by county) 1961-1966

below the provincial average:

- Net loss in population
- More than 90%
- 90%-70%
- 70%-50%
- 50%-30%
- 30%-10%

10% below-10% above (provincial norm)

above the provincial average:

- 10%-30%
- 30%-50%
- 50%-70%
- 70%-90%
- More than 90%

and suggestions from the public at large and from all interested professional agencies, Ontario proceeded into a second phase, which involved recommendation of specific policies. This phase involved six steps; the first of these overlapped specifically, and all the others generally, with the steps in the preceding phase (Fig. 22.1).

Selection of regional goals. Although regional goals had been suggested in the analysis phase, they were selected in the initial stage of the policy-recommendation phase, with the benefit of the suggestions that had been received by way of public review. Those goals were based fundamentally upon policies that might relate to the various types of change encountered

in the analysis phase. Where growth was experienced, and was considered favorable, the regional goals were focused particularly upon the geographic structuring of such goals into identifiable urban communities and other conditions associated with such a goal. Where a region appeared to be static or in decline, value judgments were made concerning the desirability of stimulation, or possibly of encouraging the out-migration of population, and the regional goals logically were based upon those conditions. As might be expected, no particular region was in either total expansion or total decline, but they were all experiencing nuances of each, and the recommended policy was tailored to those nuances as well as to the overall regional goals.

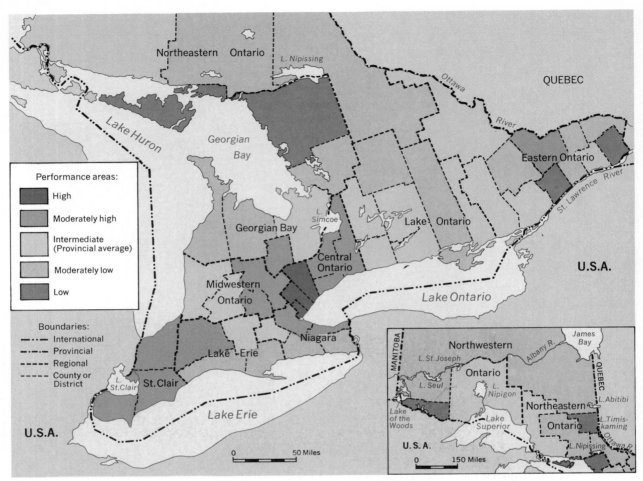

Figure 22.4 Overall performance in Ontario as shown by sixty-three indicators of population and economic change. Policies were based appreciably on this map and on Figures 23.2 and 23.3, especially if trends were expected to continue. The planners asked: should these trends continue—and, if not, what alternatives should be recommended? (Government of Ontario)

Selection of growth points and urban-oriented policies. In the analysis phase, consideration was given to all possible candidates for growth points in each region. In this early stage of the policy-recommendation phase, selection was made of the growth points and the policies that would be associated with such points, particularly in view of the regional goals that now had become firm. Again, the nature of the growth point depended strongly upon the goals for each particular region.

Selection of rural and resource-based policies. Inasmuch as regional planning and development is a process involving the entire spectrum of human and natural considerations, it is not necessarily limited to urban conditions, although the strong impact of urbanization is recognized. Rural and resource-based policies involved particularly (1) conservation, or the wise use, for our time and the foreseeable future, of the land, water, and air; (2) reservation of sufficient open space and recreational land to accommodate the growing population; and (3) all important suggestions concerning possible assistance to ethnic groups living on special reservations, especially the native Indians and Eskimos, many of whom were oriented to rural rather than urban ways and appeared inclined to remain so.

Incorporation of policies of all departments and agencies. Although there was constant liaison between the various departments and agencies of the provincial government and representatives of local and regional government on the one hand and the federal government on the other, a specific step was provided in the policy recommendation phase to ensure that all possible suggestions for liaison would be incorporated into the policy recommendations to follow.

Alternative courses of action. For each region, alternative courses of action were based upon four possibilities: (1) continue present trends; (2) encourage out-migration from the more remote areas of the province; (3) encourage rapid expansion of the more remote areas, with massive financial investment; and (4) encourage a moderate expansion of key places in the remote areas, thereby offsetting excesses of population decline, and harness those places as effectively as possible to key growth poles and growth centers of the fast-growing areas. Each of these recommendations carried certain connotations concerning the projected size and location of growth points, or urban-oriented policies, and of rural and resource-based policies.

Selection of regional plan. From all preceding steps, and with specific reference to the immediately foregoing step, a specific plan was arrived at concerning the definite growth points to be selected for each region and the urban- and rural-oriented policies to be associated with each region. The details of these recommendations will be presented in Chapter 23.

Public review. As in the analysis phase, the policies recommended for each region were published in a report that was circulated throughout various communities of the region and subjected to large numbers of discussions by both public and private groups so that its contents could be clearly understood and commented upon before the third and final phase—that of policy statement and implementation.

Policy Statement and Implementation

The completion and public review of the analysis and policy-recommendation reports marked the first two stages in a meaningful regional planning and development program. This analysis was followed by a statement of policy and recommended implementation procedures for each region. That policy usually involved some changes as a result of public discussions, but was strongly influenced by all preceding effort. Implementation was to be brought about less by the allocation of special funds than by an ongoing, continuous examination of the regional impact of all normal provincial budgetary expenditures. That implementation took five forms:

1   The location of specific government facilities which themselves offer employment opportunities. With governments and government-oriented activities employing an increasingly large number of people, the location of these facilities could mean rather substantial employment and regional and community impact. Involved in this assessment of the location was the critical matter of centralization and decentralization, geographically as well as administratively, of government operations. This clearly was a philosophical as well as a developmental question.

2   The location of government facilities which provide infrastructure, i.e., the means for the private sector as well as individuals and public groups to carry on with their own pursuits. Included in this term were arterial highways, railways, master water and sewer lines, power lines, lines of communication, and serviced land. All these are usually grouped under the term *physical* or *hard* infrastructure. However, infrastructure also includes education and health facilities, housing, museums, theaters, and other features which affect man's social and mental well-being. These are usually called *social* infrastructure.

3   Normal grants, both *conditional* (containing certain specifications for expenditure) and *unconditional* (without such specifications), on the part of a province or the federal government to local government. These ranged widely, but for obvious reasons could be considered additional means of implementing regional development recommendations, particularly where regional or local government assumed part of the responsibility for planning.

4 Direct incentives to the private sector. These usually were financial incentives—tax relief, loans, grants, or other monetary inducements—for the purpose of achieving both structural and spatial objectives of a regional development program. Again, these ranged widely in practice as to kind and degree.

5 Land use controls. Governments with experience in regional development of densely populated areas have found that measures of direct land use control may be necessary, depending upon circumstances. Such measures may involve incentives or regulations—carrots or sticks—with the precise nature of each varying in accordance with the conditions to be treated. Certainly the carrot approach is the more agreeable and is preferable if its ratio of benefit to cost is acceptable.

Chapter 23

Case Studies In Regional Development

Whereas in Chapter 22 we examined the planning process, in this chapter we shall discuss three specific efforts toward regional development—one in Canada, one in the United States and one in the United Kingdom. The reader will note that our interest is not in the total planning and development process, but in disaggregative development as described in Chapter 22, implemented at the regional level of observation. Our concern will be with overall goals, means and measures adopted to achieve those goals, and degree of success in goal achievement.

The Province of Ontario

The province of Ontario is one of the most recent political units outside the centrally planned economies to give serious consideration to regional development. Chapter 22 presents a review of the planning procedures initially utilized.

In Ontario, as in the United States and many other countries, the economy is a mixture of public and private initiative and enterprise, and the adoption of an overall regional planning program there necessarily was sensitive to the total range of such viewpoints. Also, the initiation of a regional planning and development process where none had existed was an exercise not only in the planning process but also in constant discussion, assessment, and other testing of public opinion so that development proposals would meet general acceptance. Both authors of this book have been active in the Ontario regional development program.

Goals

As we have seen, the initial goals of Ontario's *Design for Development,* published in a white paper in 1966, were (1) the encouragement of each of Ontario's ten development regions to its social, economic, political, and environmental potential; (2) the discouragement of excessive misuse of the physical environment; and (3) the coordination of activities of all provincial agencies, plus careful and close liaison with subprovincial and federal agencies and the private sector, in realizing the first two goals (Fig. 22.1).

Regional potential. *Refinement of goals.* The first goal is important yet ambiguous: What is "regional potential"? Does it imply an optimum size of population for each region? An optimum level of living on a per capita basis? An optimum size of infrastructure—whether such physical infrastructure as highways, water supply, and sewage lines or such social infrastructure as facilities for health and education? In combination with the second goal, does it imply an optimum way and degree of regional use of the physical environment? Equally important, if there can be agreement on these general questions, how can they be translated into quantitative measures so that science can be brought to bear in the planning process?

The trend studies, the second step in the analysis phase of Ontario's regional development program (pp. 372–374), provided insight into sixty-three indicators of the social, economic, and environmental change for which data were available. Inasmuch as data were gathered for the smallest unit possible, the overall trends in that unit could be compared with the provincial average rate of change and with other general indices, including national trends, to provide a greater measure of insight into ongoing conditions. These trend studies revealed (1) a rapid and increasing rate of movement from rural to urban, especially metropolitan, places in the province (Figs. 22.2, 22.3, and 22.4); (2) for those metropolitan places, a very rapid rate of growth, combined with some urban sprawl; and (3) a slight tendency toward a widening gap in levels of living between the faster-growing and the slower-growing sections of Ontario. In brief, some of the major regional development problems were found to be associated with the very rapid trend toward urbanization and metropolitanization.

This question of metropolitanization was important not only in itself but also in its general implications. Is there an optimum size of an urban or metropolitan unit at each place in the hierarchy—a size above or below which disadvantages outweigh advantages? This question has been surveyed at great length in the literature of economics, planning, geography, and related disciplines and has evoked a very wide range of professional and lay opinions. Large sizes may be less costly, on a per capita basis, in the provision of physical infrastructure, such as highways, sewers, water mains, etc., and small sizes less costly in the provision of social infrastructure, such as school and health facilities. A substantial number of professionals view a size of 200,000 to 500,000 as optimum. However, other experts take the position that there is no major optimum size and that economies of scale will continue to accumulate if an urban unit, regardless of size, is carefully planned so that subordinate communities retain individual identity, involving easy access to decision-making headquarters by all citizens of that community and also involving good service to the citizens by that community's government.

Furthermore, the question is not merely an internal one of urban size, considered from the viewpoint of the municipality itself. It also involves the welfare of all people in the area for which development is being planned—in other words, people living outside the major urban places but within their respective zones of influence, or trading areas.

After careful consideration, it was decided that within the greater goal of encouragement of each region to its potential, there would be subordinate goals of (1) reducing the trend toward concentration of people compactly within the very large urban places and (2) at the same time reducing the social and economic inequities among the economic regions. It was realized that the achievement of these two subordinate goals, if carefully planned and developed, would result in simultaneous alleviation of the major problem associated with each because higher levels of income were found to exist within the major metropolitan areas and large urban places to which people were moving in considerable numbers. Therefore, if populations could be dispersed somewhat more evenly and if incomes—plus social infrastructure, such as health and education, and physical infrastructure, such as highways, and water supply, and sewage lines—could be distributed more evenly, not only would the two subordinate goals be realized, but major steps also would have been taken toward achievement of the main goal, that of encouraging each region to its potential.

Means. The ultimate means of achieving these goals involved the ongoing expenditures of the provincial government—of all departments and agencies, including those concerned with health and education, economics, transportation, and the physical environment—plus the results of negotiation and persuasion with the federal government, regional and local government, and the private sector. In other words, the ultimate means were both financial and political.

Measures. It was recognized at the outset that the process of urbanization, in Ontario as elsewhere, is definite and essentially irrevocable. Measures to alleviate excesses of population concentration within the metropolitan and urban places and their immediate suburbs were not designed to counteract the urbanization trends. *Instead, they were designed to consider the full implications of the zones of influence surrounding each major urban place. In other words, the program envisaged simultaneous and planned development not only of metropolitan and urban cores and suburbs but also of adjacent metropolitan regions.* It was recognized that in secondary activity, certain types of low-bulk, low-weight, but high-value commodities could be manufactured as advantageously within centers located as far as 90 miles away from a metropolitan core as within the metropolitan area. Also, certain tertiary activities, such as regional offices of government departments, selected education and other social institutions, and some personal and professional services, could be located in centers somewhat removed from the metropolitan core. The specific measures taken to encourage a more even distribution of population in Ontario therefore involved a more complete use of the metropolitan region and encouragement of new employment into selected regional centers rather than the metropolitan core and suburbs.

The encouragement of some economic activity away from metropolitan cores and suburbs into metropolitan regions would also serve to achieve the second of the subordinate goals—the reduction of social and economic inequities among regions—because the higher incomes of metropolitan and other large urban cores and suburbs would be diffused into adjacent regions.

Growth points: primate and linked centers. The synchronized development of a metropolitan or urban region involves carefully orchestrated relationships between metropolitan areas, their immediate suburbs, and the outlying regional centers. The concept adopted for this purpose was that of *primate-* and *linked-*center relationship, with the primate center considered to be the metropolitan core and suburbs, and the linked center to be the regional urban place depending upon the primate center (Fig. 23.1). In some instances, the linked center would provide housing for a person who commuted daily to and from the primate center. However, the announced policy was to encourage selected economic activity, as described in the preceding paragraph, from the primate to the linked centers. The entire network of primate and linked centers therefore would constitute the basic economy of the metropolitan or urban region to be developed.

Growth points: the strategic center. If the dispersion of population throughout a metropolitan or urban region could be successfully accomplished, what could be done for the territory beyond immediate access to metropolitan areas? By and large, these were the areas within the province which were being depopulated the most rapidly (Figs. 22.2 to 22.4). Two answers appeared feasible: (1) This trend toward depopulation should not be altered significantly unless there appeared to be, either presently in existence or in the foreseeable future, the potential for an economic base that would support populations of specified sizes, and (2) no economic activity should be encouraged into such a remote area unless that activity either (*a*) fulfilled a fundamental service role, such as governmental jurisdiction over resources, or (*b*) showed evidence of economic viability without continuous public subsidy.

It was recognized that, except for selected recreational and primary activities, the major hope of offsetting the comparatively rapid decline of populations in remote areas was to be found in urban places. However, because many existing urban places depended upon agriculture or other primary activities which were declining, it would not be feasible to offer support to all such places. Instead, certain places were chosen which had a demonstrated potential for continuity and perhaps for growth. These were designated *strategic centers*. Where that potential lay in a diversified economic base, such centers were classified into the *strategic A*

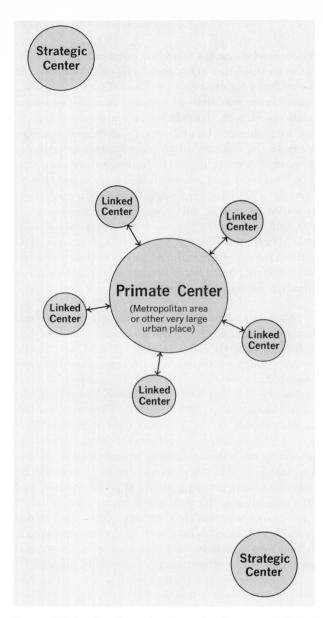

Figure 23.1 A schematic view of primate and linked centers. The zone of immediate influence of a metropolitan area can be planned along with the area itself, so that orderly change occurs simultaneously within the core, suburbs, and zone of influence. Meanwhile, territory beyond the zone of immediate influence is served by strategic centers, whose activities are geared to the needs of such remote territory. In the future, with improved technology and other changes, some of the more remote territory might be added to the zone of metropolitan influence, and some may be withdrawn from that zone.

category, and a wide range of physical and social infrastructure was encouraged there. Centers which were dependent upon a single activity, usually a primary activity, but which evidenced a reasonable expectation of continuity for the next thirty years were classified as *strategic B* centers and infrastructure was made available cautiously, if at all, to such places.

Many of the native Indian reserves of Ontario lay in the outlying, less developed areas of the province which were experiencing depopulation. Because such reserves were fixed in location, and because their populations were of different viewpoints as to whether to remain on the reserves or to integrate with the society and economy of the remainder of the province, they were treated as special cases, which indeed they were and are. For those native Indians wishing to remain on the reserves, the encouragement of handicraft and cooperatives appeared to be a logical first effort. For those wishing to leave the reserves, ways and means were being developed to encourage such action.

Conservation of physical resources. The regional approach to the conservation of physical resources in the Ontario development program was attempted through two general efforts: (1) careful assessment of land use and (2) a heightened awareness of the constant need to regulate and evaluate the volume and quantity of water and air available for different purposes. The first of these measures is described in step 4 of the analysis phase, as presented in Chapter 22 (p. 372). It involved (1) an inventory of current land uses at a macro level, (2) an evaluation of alternative uses in terms of the physical capacity of the land, and (3) an evaluation of alternative sources of demand for land at specified future year periods. The second was carried out through specific measures of departments and agencies responsible for regulation of the environment, but was coordinated with the provincial regional development program. It was recognized that this objective was not disassociated from that of regional social and economic potential, inasmuch as a redistribution of population would affect markedly the volume and intensity of the use or misuse of the physical environment.

Coordination. This goal was, in truth, a means, but was listed as a goal for purposes of internal empha-

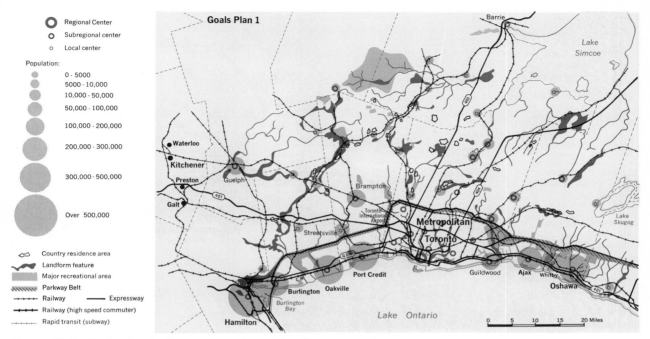

Figure 23.2 Goals Plan 1 of a transportation study of Toronto and environs that preceded regional development planning in that province. Goals Plans 2, 3, and 4 are shown in succeeding illustrations. In addition, low-density and high-density (population) trends were projected for the area. The Toronto-Centered Region concept (Fig. 23.6) stemmed in part from this earlier work and in part from assessment of economic and social needs as shown in the steps of Figure 22.1. (Government of Ontario)

sis. It was achieved through an elaborate committee structure, which has been described briefly in Chapter 22 (p. 371). Although a full coordination of all human efforts and woes is a physical impossibility, a certain measure of unanimity was achieved in understanding and realizing the full impact of a coordinated regional development program.[1]

Pilot studies. The initial efforts at development of Ontario were focused upon (1) Toronto and its adjacent Toronto-Centered Region and (2) Northwestern Ontario.

[1] A more detailed review of Ontario's goals and of the entire regional development program is available in Richard S. Thoman, *Design for Development in Ontario: The Initiation of a Regional Planning Program,* Allister Typesetting and Graphics, Toronto, 1971.

The Toronto-Centered Region. A concept for the development of the Toronto-Centered Region was released for public discussion in 1970 and was adopted as a progress report in 1971. It is shown in Figure 23.6, preceded by alternatives proposed earlier (Figs. 23.2 to 23.5). In recognition of the goals of encouraging regional social and economic potential and conservation, the Toronto-Centered Region was divided into three zones. Zone 1, along the lakefront, was the zone of expected growth. Within metropolitan Toronto and to the west, that growth was to be discouraged somewhat, mainly by providing amenities for growth elsewhere. It was also to be carefully regulated geographically into identifiable communities, each of which would be separated from the other by a substantial green area (Fig. 23.6). To the east in zone 1, where trend growth has not been

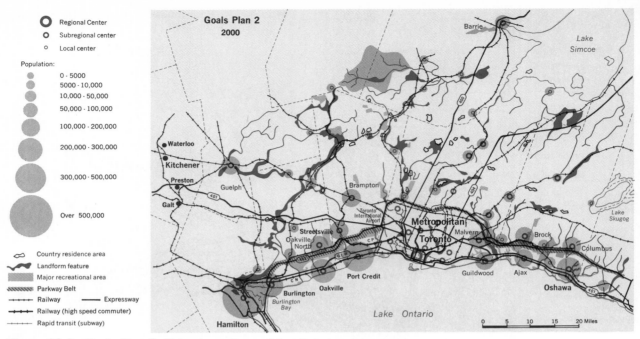

Figure 23.3 Goals Plan 2. This plan, plus outlying linked centers to stimulate change throughout the Toronto-Centered Region, eventually formed the major inputs to the final concept (Fig. 23.6). (Government of Ontario)

Figure 23.4 Goals Plan 3. (Government of Ontario)

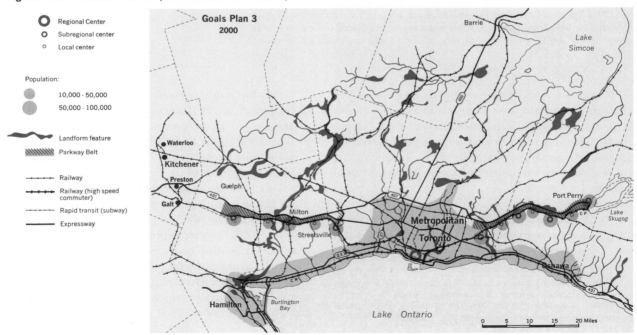

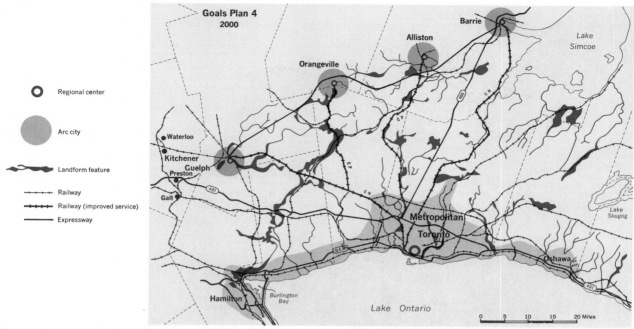

Figure 23.5 Goals Plan 4. (Government of Ontario)

high and is expected to remain low under normal conditions, more activity would be encouraged through a combination of the five measures of implementation indicated on pages 377–378. Zone 2 would be primarily a land bank—maintained as green as possible and as devoid of urban growth as possible. Existing communities would not be encouraged to expand rapidly, but would be expected to continue to grow in the future at rates not exceeding those in the past. Zone 3 would be an area of expansion—normal in the west in the vicinities of Hamilton and Kitchener-Waterloo and encouraged to the north and the east in the vicinities of Barrie and Midland and of Port Hope and Cobourg.

All in all, it was estimated that by the year 2001, some 8 million people would be living in the Toronto-Centered Region, with slightly less than 5.7 million in zone 1, less than 400,000 in zone 2, and approximately 2 million in zone 3 concentrated within the three linked-center vicinities of Hamilton and Kitchener-Waterloo to the west, Barrie and Midland to the north, and Oshawa, Port Hope, and Cobourg to the east. In 2001, the developed Toronto-Centered Region is expected to

have a slightly lower percentage of Ontario's population than it would have contained if there had been no plan. However, those people will be rationally located within the Toronto-Centered Region, rather than jammed into the Toronto metropolitan core and suburbs, and will be experiencing a greater degree of economic and social equity than would have been the case had there been no plan. This will be true particularly of inhabitants of those peripheral growth points designed for stimulation and of commuters to and from those growth points who live even beyond the boundaries of the Toronto-Centered Region.

Northwestern Ontario. Whereas the Toronto-Centered Region offered challenges in terms of structuring spontaneous growth and stimulating slow growth, as well as conservation of the physical setting, Northwestern Ontario is largely a remote, slow-growth area in which some communities are declining. However, the permanent future of the region does not appear to be one of decline. It is located upon Canada's major east-west route connecting the Prairie provinces and British

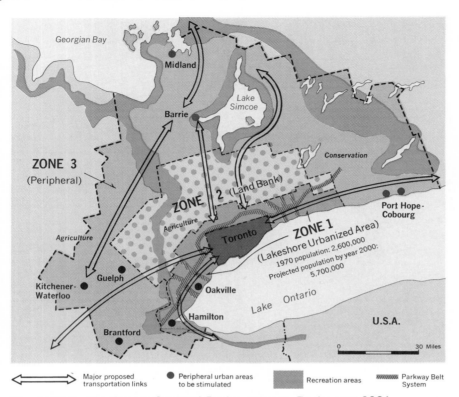

Major proposed transportation links ● Peripheral urban areas to be stimulated ▒ Recreation areas ▨ Parkway Belt System

Figure 23.6 The Toronto-Centered Region concept. By the year 2001, some 5.7 million people are expected to live in Zone 1, 400,000 in Zone 2, and nearly two million in Zone 3, concentrated in three nodes located to the west (Hamilton, Brantford, Guelph, Kitchener-Waterloo); to the north (Barrie, Midland); and to the east (Oshawa, not shown, at the eastern margin of Zone 1, plus Port Hope and Cobourg, and Peterborough, located to the north of Port Hope and Cobourg). Where growth is spontaneous, it will be structured spatially by the Parkway Belt System, which will both connect and separate specific centers. Where growth is slow, it will be stimulated, if agreed upon generally, by new nodes to the north and east. Zone 2 is essentially a land bank. The Toronto-Centered concept is intended to optimize use of both human and natural resources. No attempt is made specifically to limit growth, because growth is regarded as a national issue. With so much land, Canada's problems involve adequate channeling of growth and related change into suitable places. All communities in Goals Plan 2 (p. 384) are included in this concept, plus some others not shown. (Government of Ontario)

Columbia with Ontario, Quebec, and the East. The route involves not only unbroken rail, land, and air linkages but also access to the world's oceans through the upper lakehead port of Thunder Bay (formerly Fort William and Port Arthur) and smaller ocean ports. Furthermore, the potential for recreation and the pri-

mary activities of mining and lumbering is excellent.

The region is one of a sparse, slowly growing population (Fig. 23.7). With nearly 60 per cent of all the land area of Ontario, this region contains only 3.2 per cent of the inhabitants. Its growth rate is less than 1 per cent per year, compared with more than 2 per cent for the province as a whole. The region is highly urban, with nearly one-half of its inhabitants living in the metropolitan area of Thunder Bay. An additional 37 per cent live in four centers of fewer than 10,000 each located in the western portion of the region—Kenora, Fort Francis, Dryden, and Atikokan. Over one-tenth of the population is of native Indian descent, and most of the Indian peoples live in isolated settlements widely dispersed in the region.

Standards in education, health, and social services were found to be lower in Northwestern Ontario than in the province as a whole. Provision of adequate housing also was a serious problem. Inadequate transportation and communication resulted in the isolation of some urban centers and rural populations.

The economy was based largely upon mining, pulp and paper, and tourist industries, supplemented by transportation and storage industries. The regional

Figure 23.7 The spatial framework for proposed growth in Northwestern Ontario. Growth points with suitable potential (Primate and Strategic "A") are to be given more infrastructure (highways, serviced land, sewers, etc.). Other growth points will receive certain incentives, but only if there is clear evidence of growth potential. This proposal was sponsored by both the federal and Ontario governments. (Government of Ontario)

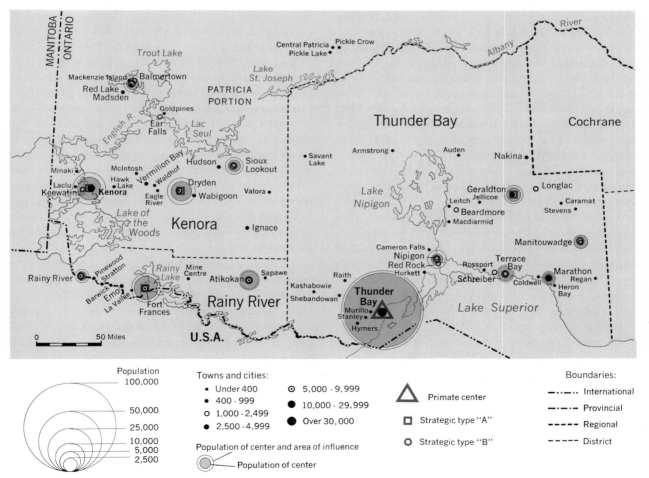

economy was found to be highly dependent upon external demand, especially from the United States, for pulp, newsprint, and minerals, as well as for much of the total demand for recreational services.

Pollution of some of the waterways and water bodies, especially from the pulp and paper and mining industries, was found to be a serious problem in some localities. For the region as a whole, however, with its comparatively sparse population and unaltered natural conditions, the conservation of the physical setting did not yet pose as serious a problem as in the Toronto-Centered Region to the south.

To offset undesirable social and economic conditions and trends, certain centers were designated for specific attention (Fig. 23.7). Thunder Bay, the only metropolitan area in the region, was considered a primate center, where selected secondary and tertiary activity was to be encouraged. Because this was in a slow-growth region in its entirety, no linked centers were designated. At this critical stage of the region's existence, development objectives focused upon stimulating the growth of the metropolitan region. To be successful, such stimulation would need to be within the core and immediate suburbs of Thunder Bay, rather than within urban places located in the trading territory, or metropolitan region. For the remainder of Northwestern Ontario, four centers were chosen as strategic A centers, where diversified activities were encouraged. These were the three previously mentioned centers of Kenora, Dryden, and Fort Francis, plus Geraldton, located to the northeast of Thunder Bay. Each was selected not only because of its diversified economy, but also by virtue of its strategic location with regard to existing and future populations of Northwestern Ontario. In addition, eight strategic B centers were selected to carry on with their present specialties of mining and forestry.

A total of sixty-nine recommendations of a regional development nature were made for this region, most of them involving the primate or strategic centers mentioned previously, and all of them involving continuous expenditures of the provincial budget. In addition, special recommendations involved the native Indian communities.

The future. Ontario's regional development program is in its early stages. However, there appears to be evidence of sincere efforts toward implementation of a program which has the advantages of both comprehensiveness and continuity—comprehensiveness in that it is a development program for the entire province, involving the entire provincial budget, cooperation with federal and lower levels of government, and the private sector; continuity in that it has become an umbrella program for assessing regional implications of each annual budget and, because budgets appear each year, carries the implication of long-range planning.

Precedent

Although regional planning and development within the province of Ontario is in an advanced stage in comparison with similar efforts in the United States and Canada, it is based upon precedent in various parts of the world. The comprehensive approach to development, in which attention is given not only to social and economic conditions but also to careful use of the physical setting, has been indigenous to such efforts in the centrally planned countries. The comprehensive approach of those countries has been sensitive not only to specific processes and events associated with social and economic conditions but also to processes and events in the physical environment and to an overlap between the social and economic processes on the one hand and the physical processes on the other. (This is not to say, however, that all problems associated with excesses of environmental exploitation and with social and economic inequity have been eliminated there.) An important aspect of the experience of the centrally planned countries, especially the Soviet Union, has been the use of the *complex,* or cluster of naturally affiliated industries and related activities, in the planning of existing activity and the development of new areas. (Note the relationship of the complex to Weberian agglomeration.) For example, an iron and steel plant can attract and support substantial numbers of fabricating mills and finished-products plants, which bring together not only steel but also related components. When a new area of the Soviet Union is to be developed, it is carefully considered in terms of such complexes, as well as the potential of the physical setting.

Experience in northwestern Europe has provided even more appropriate models for planning in the United States and Canada than has that in the centrally planned economies, inasmuch as most countries in northwestern Europe are democracies. Nearly every country of continental Europe now has some kind of regional development program, most involving efforts to decentralize economic activity on at least a modest scale and to reduce social and economic inequities which are found there, even in the smallest countries. However, efforts in the United States and the United Kingdom have contributed substantially to the planning experiment now being carried out in Ontario.

The United States: The Tennessee Valley Authority

The United States has long been planning in piecemeal fashion for various parts of the country, including efforts in the 1960s to identify and assist areas of slow growth and to set aside certain regions, such as Appalachia, for specific attention to their unique problems. However, it was the Tennessee Valley Authority, established in the early 1930s, that initiated regional planning on a grand scale in the country.

Historical and Geographical Background

Historical review. Within the short span of less than two centuries, the Unted States has been forced by circumstances largely beyond its control to review man's relationship with his fellow man and with his physical setting. The task has not been easy. The creation of an embryonic nation along the Atlantic coastline, the westward expansion and a frontier mentality that included the fallacious certainty of manifest destiny, the acquisition of such enormous tracts as the Louisiana Purchase and the present state of Alaska for sums that today are trivial—these and related circumstances were part and parcel of an outlook wherein expansion was thought to be inevitable and natural resources, including land, to be almost without end. Yet, by the early portion of the twentieth century, the frontier had essentially disappeared in the mainland

United States, and initial efforts had been made in the conservation of natural resources, which had been recognized even then to be limited in both quantity and quality. In the early 1900s a growing conservation movement, focused especially upon resources, made an embryonic impact upon the land. National parks, forests, and grazing lands—most of them located in the West, where some public land was still available for such purposes without complex legal procedures—were set aside before they all were forfeited to human greed and lack of foresight. It was not until the early 1930s, however, that the general thoughts of conservation began to be considered more seriously on a regional basis. It was not until the creation of the Tennessee Valley Authority that such thoughts were translated into action.

Geographical conditions. Some parts of the United States had suffered more than others, because of either excessive exploitation or neglect, in the onrush of the country into so-called modern conditions. Nowhere was this misuse and neglect more obvious than in the mountains of Appalachia, where many of the trees had been removed and not satisfactorily replaced, agriculture had been initiated but continued desultorily and in some cases abandoned, and mines had been dug and, particularly in the search for coal, were giving way to surface stripping operations which are so fatal to the landscape. Perhaps worst of all, recurring floods destroyed properties annually in the stream and river valleys, where most of the people lived. The people, many of whom were living under hardship conditions that were inherited through generations and augmented by the Depression of the 1930s, could not look forward to any dramatic change in the conditions that had become a way of life. Many had no electricity, no running water, and no modern conveniences in dwelling units that were in many cases substandard.

However, even a short review of the conditions of that day should not be entirely negative. The humid subtropical climate in which the Tennessee River valley is located is hospitable to human habitation; the rainfall is abundant and evenly distributed throughout the year, and many of the natural resources, although excessively used and despoiled, were and are renewable. Others, although not renewable, were and are still present in substantial reserves. The floods could be controlled by proper engineering procedures, and new electricity could be created, both from the water and from coal and other nearby sources, which could raise living standards. Most important of all, the provision of social infrastructure—education, health, and a more positive outlook on life—was and is a definite possibility here, as elsewhere in the world.

Creation of the TVA

The Tennessee Valley Authority was one of a number of experiments begun in the early days of the New Deal of President Franklin D. Roosevelt. Like many of these experiments, it was considered rash. From the outset, TVA made a key contribution to modern planning in its concept of multipurpose planning and development. Whereas prior to TVA—and, regrettably, this is still the case—planning had been piecemeal, in the Tennessee Valley Authority it was to be regarded as comprehensive for the area under concern.

Goals

On April 10, 1933, President Roosevelt said, "It is time to extend planning to a wider field, in this instance comprehending in one great project many states directly concerned with the basin of one of our greatest rivers."[2] He proposed that TVA "be charged with the broadest duty of planning for the proper use, conservation and development of the natural resources of the Tennessee River drainage basin and its adjoining territory for the general social and economic welfare of the nation."[3] Later he said, "The original legislation . . . was intended to raise . . . standards of life by increasing social and economic advantages in a given area."[4] Here is clear evidence of a resource-oriented program which, however, was not to overlook the human condition.

Major objectives. The major objectives of the Tennessee Valley Authority were flood control, creation of electric power, and improvement of navigation. The

Tennessee River long had been subject to almost annual flooding, resulting in catastrophe and loss of life and property on a scale seldom experienced anywhere in the United States today. Electric energy was not available in many rural areas and was expensive in many of the urban places. Navigation by modern barges, requiring a 9-foot minimum draft, was impossible along the entire main section of the river. All three of these objectives, together with some lesser objectives, were to be met through the establishment of a system of dams—nine along the main channel and more than twenty across tributary streams and valleys. This system of dams was designed to accomplish all three of the major objectives. Floods would be controlled by carefully regulating water levels during rainy periods—releasing the waters of tributaries into larger rivers sequentially rather than all at once, as though there never would be a flood crest. The system was designed more or less like a computerized traffic system on major highways and freeways, releasing pressures continuously rather than allowing them to build to a crisis. The same dams would create enormous quantities of electric power, which would be sold at a very low rate. Two objectives would therefore be accomplished: (1) the provision of more electricity to the region and to the nation and (2) the establishment of a "yardstick" for assessing appropriate charges to consumers of electric power. Navigational objectives were to be met through the establishment of a system of locks on the nine dams on the main channel, allowing passage of rivercraft upstream as far as Knoxville (Fig. 23.8).

Other objectives. In any multipurpose program, goals become merged. Some other objectives which, when viewed against the perspective of time, may be judged as important as the three mentioned above also were a part of the TVA program. The reduction of excesses of soil erosion became an important objective of the program as the extent of this process came to be recognized. The provision of more adequate recreational facilities, combined with reforestation, became an additional objective. The production of fertilizer and the demonstration of its appropriate use on farms, thereby increasing the efficiency of agriculture, was yet another. Inasmuch as the construction of one of the major dams, the Norris Dam, was in a rural area, a

[2] C. H. Pritchett, *The Tennessee Valley Authority,* Russell and Russell, New York, 1971 (first published by The University of North Carolina Press, Chapel Hill, 1943), p. 116.
[3] Ibid.
[4] Ibid.

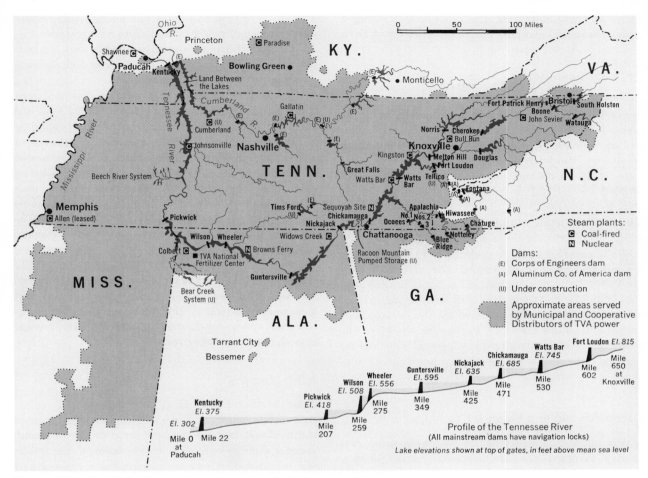

Figure 23.8 The TVA. The territory of actual jurisdiction is the Tennessee River basin, which extends from Virginia and North Carolina to the Ohio River. TVA jurisdiction does not extend to the Cumberland River in northern Tennessee. However, the influence of TVA extends beyond the river basin of its jurisdiction, especially to areas served by distributors of electric power created by TVA, shown in the map. Most planning regions today are delimited by human organization of space, usually cities and dependent territory, with river basins receiving an important but secondary ranking. The main objectives of TVA involve the physical setting—flood control, excessive erosion, etc., plus generation of electricity and navigation. Important but secondary objectives involve planning for orderly arrangement and change of human occupance.

model town—Norris—was constructed at that site, thereby furthering progress in the planning and development of new towns in the United States. Where educational facilities needed to be moved because they would be flooded by a lake once the dam was built, care was given, in cooperation with local officials, to build model schools which were centralized, in contrast to the small, one-room schoolhouses that had existed previously. All these objectives, plus others which emerged during the actual planning program, were part of TVA.

Regional Delimitation

Because of the nature of the major goals of the Tennessee Valley Authority, the primary boundaries for the region followed the watershed of the Tennessee River and its tributaries, excluding territory beyond those tributaries. However, in practice, different boundaries were set up for different activities. Thus, for purposes of flood control and navigation, the watershed boundaries were essentially maintained. For the sale of electric power, whether to municipalities or cooperatives which came into existence mainly to distribute such power to rural areas, the boundaries were substantially beyond the basin itself. Indeed, the actual Tennessee Valley Authority Act referred not only to the valley itself but also to "such adjoining territory as may be related to or materially affected by the development consequent to this act. . . ."[5] In practice, therefore, the watershed became more or less a general guideline for regional delimitation, rather than a hard line circumscribing all activities.

Administrative and Financial Arrangements

A very interesting aspect of the Tennessee Valley Authority involved the administrative arrangements, where there initially was grave danger of overlapping authority of various federal departments and agencies, as well as jurisdictional disputes with state and local governments. The relationship with federal groups was resolved by giving TVA rather complete authority for various responsibilities concerning both major and lesser objectives. In practice, TVA worked closely with the federal agencies normally responsible for the various objectives. Furthermore, care was taken at the outset, and has continued to be maintained, in relationships with state and local government. TVA recognized the jurisdiction of these respective groups, but exerted strong efforts to cooperate, especially by providing services. Particularly in the generation and distribution of power, however, the Authority maintained

[5] Ibid., p. 134.

a nearly complete autonomy, discharging this responsibility through power boards of its own creation.

Relationships with the private sector were less harmonious, especially at the outset. A major apprehension grew within the private power industry, which tended to charge its customers rates between five and eight times as high as those charged by TVA. An inherited concern on the part of private enterprise regarding government activity thus was heightened by the use of government power sales as a yardstick for determining appropriate charges to the consumer. Private enterprise maintained that TVA rates were possible only in a publicly supported, multipurpose program where revenues accruing from one purpose could be allocated as subsidies to another—a privilege which single-purpose power companies did not have.

Financing of TVA was by independent budget, directly available from the federal government. However, the Authority was never considered the beneficiary of a continuous federal subsidy, but was required to amortize this investment through the sale of power, navigation charges, and other sources of income.

Achievements

Prior to World War II, TVA was regarded mainly as a daring experiment in planning the physical environment and, in lesser measure, the social environment. Despite some objections and some failures, it generally was recognized to have been successful in achieving its initial objectives. However, the advent of national wartime responsibilities, including the development of nuclear power, resulted in the establishment of new nuclear facilities in the TVA area, the introduction into the valley of manufacturing which consumed large amounts of electricity, and other changes which aggregately forced an emphasis upon a creation of power and energy more or less at the expense of the other purposes. Indeed, the demand for energy became so large that production of energy from coal exceeded that from hydroelectric sources—and lately TVA has been accused, because of its large demand for coal to be used in electricity generation, of encouraging excesses of strip mining both within and outside the valley.

Like many experiments, TVA now has become a part of the mainstream of life in the United States. Yet, at least in terms of its three major objectives and the technology involved in reaching them, it has been copied in various parts of the world, including the centrally planned countries. In its day, it was a major effort in regional planning. From the vantage point of today, however, we can see that it did not provide nearly enough emphasis upon social and economic conditions. Insufficient attention was given to urban needs and to the relationships among urban places, which some authorities now prefer to call "urban systems." This was true of the delimitation of the region as well as the major objectives of the program. These deficiencies, however, do not offset the resounding achievements of the program, especially when viewed in a time perspective of more than four decades.

The TVA also was an achievement in that it introduced comprehensive and effective regional planning into the United States. Less centralized administrative efforts have occurred along a number of river basins in succeeding years and decades—none, however, as thorough as TVA. In the early 1960s, there appeared federal programs to identify and assist temporarily small areas of economic stress, followed in the late 1960s and early 1970s by semicomprehensive and long-range programs administered by the Appalachian, New England, Atlantic Coast, Ozarks, Great Lakes, and Four Corners Regional Commissions. In the areas served by these commissions, highways and other infrastructure have been stressed, as have growth points. Some states also have planning agencies. We must say, however, that regional planning in the United States is not taken as seriously as it is in Canada, the United Kingdom, Western Europe and, of course, the centrally planned economies.

The United Kingdom: Greater London

At about the same time that regional planning was being introduced in the United States, it was also being considered seriously in the United Kingdom. A milestone in such development was reached in the period 1930–1933, with the completion of the Land Utilisation Survey, covering England, Wales, and Scotland at a scale of 6 inches to 1 mile. As was true of TVA in the United States, the emphasis of the survey was upon use of the physical setting rather than upon human needs and resources. Even earlier, in 1909, a Town and Country Planning Act had been introduced, but it did not become truly effective until superseded in 1947 by a much stronger act, which required each county to prepare a factual survey and a plan for future development based upon that survey.

Meanwhile, beginning in 1928, there was recognition of the importance of planning for economic and social conditions, viewing these as disaggregative development from the perspective of the federal government rather than as aggregative development from the perspective of each individual municipality. In recognition of the decline in mining employment, an act was passed to encourage migration of unemployed miners to jobs in more prosperous areas, especially to the southeast. However, in the early 1930s, emphasis began to be placed upon the creation of employment within the slow-growing areas, rather than on encouraging out-migration. The Special Areas Act of 1934 set aside four regions of Great Britain—in the northeast, southern Wales, western Cumberland, and central Scotland, where unemployment was especially high—as special areas to be given financial assistance. The initial emphasis was upon the provision of infrastructure, particularly transportation, sewage facilities, power, and communication. Subsequently, in 1937, under an amendment to the act, loans were made to industrial firms which would move to special areas (Fig. 23.9).

The Greater London Plan

Goals. Meanwhile, plans were being made to distribute populations more evenly, especially within the areas of influence of metropolitan regions. London was singled out for particular attention and, in 1943 and 1944, a plan was prepared for the development of Greater London (Fig. 23.10). The specific objective of the Greater London plan was to reduce the urban concentration and congestion within the city of London and its suburbs. Four zones were recognized within the London area:

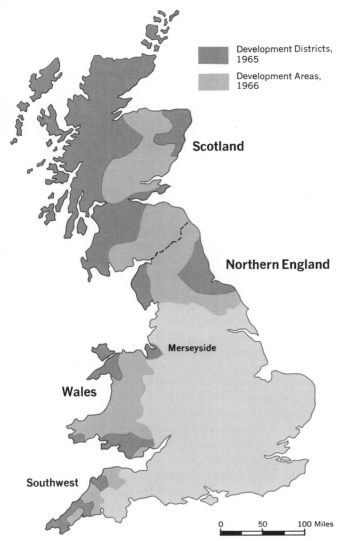

Figure 23.9 Development districts and areas of the United Kingdom. The two concepts refer to two different pieces of legislation and can be interpreted jointly by the reader to refer to areas in the United Kingdom judged to be lagging economically.

1   An inner urban zone, from which population and industries would be encouraged to migrate outward and in which no new economic activity, including certain types of tertiary activity, would be permitted.

2   A suburban ring, in which there would be no further additions of residential or industrial uses.

3   A green belt, in which no development would be permitted.

4   An outer ring, which would receive the overspill of population and economic activity that normally would have gone to the London core area and suburbs.

To encourage this decentralization, a total of eight new towns were established within, or adjacent to, the

Figure 23.10   Four zones of Greater London: inner urban, suburban ring, green belt, outer ring. Population and industries are encouraged to leave the first; no further development for industrial or residential purposes is allowed in the second; no development is allowed in the third; overspill and intercepter activities, both economic activity and residences, are encouraged in the fourth. (After Ashok K. Dutt, "Regional Planning in England and Wales: A Critical Evaluation," *Plan: Journal of the Town Planning Institute of Canada,* 1970)

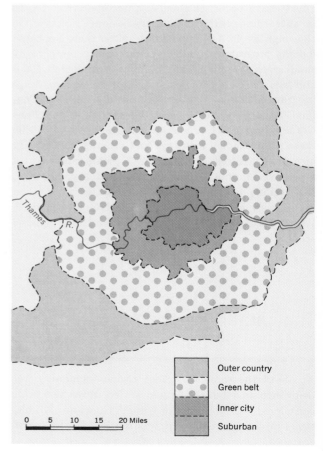

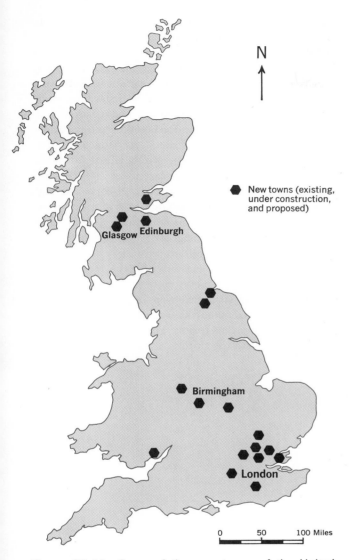

territory covered by the Greater London plan, and some twenty existing towns within the southeast were encouraged to expand (Fig. 23.11).

Achievements. The Greater London plan has succeeded so efficiently in reducing the population of both the inner core and the suburbs that questions are now being raised as to whether a complete lack of growth in those two zones is wise. The identity of the green belt has been retained with reasonable success, and the stimulation of the new towns and existing towns in the outer zone also has gone forward effectively. Most of the new inhabitants of this periphery commute to work in zones 1 and 2.

However, the overall plans for regional development in the United Kingdom have not met with as much success. Despite massive efforts to retain economic activity in the slow-growth areas, populations there have continued to decline, and the social and economic inequities between these areas and the more prosperous and faster-growing ones remain rather pronounced. However, it has been strongly argued that, were it not for programs designed to rationalize both population density and social and economic inequities in the United Kingdom, these differences would be much greater than they now are.

Appraisal of the Planning Experience in Ontario, the United States, and the United Kingdom

The planning experience under discussion in this chapter involved nearly half a century of effort. During that period, planners not only were coming to grips for the first time with the implications of planning and development on a broad regional scale but also were faced with changing goals in the planning process. Perhaps because of the closing of the frontier in the United States and the more heavily settled portion of Canada, we placed an earlier priority, as we now see the historical record, upon conservation of the physical environment and physical resources in our planning efforts.

Figure 23.11 Some of the new towns of the United Kingdom. The symbols refer only to new towns, not to older centers, some names of which are shown for general identification. Some of the new towns are for dormitory purposes only, housing commuters who work in nearby metropolitan areas. Others include economic activity which has been encouraged to locate there, and eliminates the need for commuting. The "new town" concept is subject to differing interpretation in the United Kingdom, and other maps show additional centers, all in the general vicinity of those shown here. The new town movement is essentially an effort to move people away from urban cores and immediate suburbs, usually to "exurbs" just beyond. (See the outer ring of Figure 23.10)

This led to what can be interpreted today as an error in the regional delimitation for planning processes in that emphasis was placed upon watershed boundaries and upon physical resources only. However, now that we have come to view the conservation movement in human as well as natural environmental terms, we see the importance of recognizing human organization of space, whether in understanding, planning, or developing the region. Thus, drawing regional planning boundaries on the basis of trading areas of urban places appears to be a logical approach; considering the total range of human values as well as physical environmental conditions also is important in the modern planning process.

A key question in the planning process concerns the degree to which the artificial actions and judgments of a plan, designed by a relatively few people, should interfere with the very wide range of individual judgments, both private and public, that normally affect the location and functioning of economic activity. This question is particularly appropriate with regard to the magnetic attraction of large urban places for economic activity. One school of thought maintains that econ-omies of scale and optimum social and physical conditions can be realized regardless of the size of the metropolitan region and that proper planning and development involves merely geographic structuring of growth which is more or less spontaneous. Another school maintains that, particularly regarding social values, the liabilities of metropolitan and urban congestion cannot be easily understood, and certainly cannot be measured, but nevertheless are very much in existence. This school would make strong efforts, at public expense, to decentralize and deconcentrate economic activity more or less evenly over a landscape, although allowing for the forces of urbanization and the urban network within this deconcentration. Still a third school recognizes the magnetism of urbanism, but maintains that an appropriate answer is deconcentration of some economic activity into the region immediately adjacent to a metropolitan or urban core and suburbs, but still within the zone of influence—a carefully orchestrated, simultaneous development of core, suburbs, and adjacent region. The authors of this book tend to agree with the third of these three alternatives.

Glossary

Absolute advantage The production advantage a region may have, measured in terms of such relevant inputs as labor and capital.

Action space That spatial area throughout which an individual functions or interacts.

Administrative / political principle The central-place system of Christaller which provided most efficient administration, each center being closer to one center of the next higher order by which it was administered, so that no subdivision of centers occurred. (This is sometimes referred to as the *K-7 network*.)

Agglomeration economies The reduction of unit cost in output experienced by firms or establishments when they concentrate in a single place.

Allometric growth A growth relationship in which the size of each of the parts of a system is closely related to the size of all other parts or the whole system.

Anisotropic surface A segment of the earth's surface which is assumed to vary in some way or ways throughout its aerial extent.

Assembly costs Transport costs in assembling all inputs of materials to a production point.

Assumption A condition introduced as a possible truth on which to base a theory. (This is sometimes referred to as a *premise*.)

Axiom An assumption accepted as unquestionably true.

Bilateral trade The movement of goods between only two regions or nations.

Buridan's ass A situation of indeterminancy introduced into philosophy by the fabled ass or donkey between two bales of hay.

Central-place theory Geographic theory relating size, spatial distribution, and functions of settlements in a system.

Ceteris paribus A Latin phrase meaning "holding all other things constant." It is used to enable us to discuss what would happen if we allowed only some factors to change.

Classification A logical ordering and grouping of observations.

Closed system A system in which the relationships between and among the components in an ensemble cannot be altered or influenced by other components.

Comparative advantage The greatest absolute advantage of a region or a country's economy over its least absolute advantage. (*See also* index, David Ricardo.)

Complementarity   A necessary condition for economic interaction, in that in one place there exists a demand for a good or service which is capable of being supplied by another place. (*See also* index, Stouffer and Ullman.)

Consumer good   A product made for consumption and used up with use. Examples: candy, clothing.

Contract rent   The periodic payment for use of someone else's property.

Cost space   A dimension of operational space in which the cost variable is the dimension on which measurements are made.

Critical isodapane   That isodapane which represents increased transport costs equal to the savings of labor costs from points of cheap labor supply.

Cultural dualism or pluralism   The side-by-side existence of two or more recognizable cultures in a given area.

Deduction   A process of arriving at logical conclusions from a set of assumptions; hence, reasoning from the general to the particular.

Demersal   Life at or near the floors of lakes, continental shelves, etc.

Developed economy   An economy which has achieved a high level of output per worker and hence enjoys a high level of consumption of goods and services per person.

Development   Planned change. (*See* **planning** for further explanation.)

Diffusion   The gradual movement, over time, from one place to another, or one series of places to others, of a new thought or practice.

Digit detail   The code used by the United States Office of Management and Budget, and by official agencies in many other countries and in the United Nations, to classify functions producing goods and services. (For further explanation, *see* pp. 213–214.)

Diminishing returns   The condition which exists when, in successively applying equal amounts of one or two factors of production (land, labor, capital) to the remaining factor or factors, an added application yields a lesser increase in production than its predecessor.

Discontinuous space   Space in which the continuity is broken in some way, whether by interstices, sudden changes in value, or other causes.

Distance-decay   The negative impact of distance upon the flow of information, goods, or services, or upon fixed features in space. Interaction or influence is usually relatively easy when cause and effect are close together in space, but is less efficient with increased distance separating one from the other.

Distance-decay curve   A downward sloping curve or line joining coordinates of distance and the values of a selected variable.

Ecology (and economic geography)   Those aspects of the interaction of man and the physical setting pertaining to the location and functioning of economic activity.

Economic base; basic-nonbasic activities   The economic base of an area (community, region, country, etc.) comprises those economic activities which are mainstays of support. *Basic* economic activities are those which attract income to the community, region, country, etc., by sale of goods and/or services beyond the boundaries of that area. A *nonbasic* activity merely facilitates flow of currency, goods, and/or services within that area. There are differing ratios of basic to nonbasic activities in different areas; but a rule of thumb which some specialists follow is that employment of one additional person in a basic activity provides for employment of one additional person in a nonbasic activity.

Economic feasibility   The sound financial capacity, at a given time and place and under given technological and other conditions, to carry out an idea, project, or program, such as the opening of a new mine or the construction of a new city.

Economic reality   Economic conditions, in this book spatially expressed, as these actually exist at a given time.

Economic rent   The excess returns accruing to a factor of production because of its specificity or limited supply.

Economies of scale   Savings in costs per unit of production, transportation, exchange, etc., usually through use of larger and more efficient machinery, tools, or methods.

Effective area   "Where the action is"—usually an urban place or group of urban places where key decisions are made for a larger area. An effective area usually is densely populated, but may or may not be functionally or nodally arranged.

Empirical observation   Observation made through sensory mechanisms—hearing, tasting, smelling, etc.

Employment   Number actually at work as employees of an establishment, firm, activity, etc.

Endogenous factor   A factor with values determined entirely within a system.

Establishment   A producing unit—a farm, factory, store, etc.

Exchange   Actual transfer, usually involving money, of goods and/or services.

Exogenous factor A factor which is outside the system yet which may have some effect on the system.

Explanation The answering of questions by employing logical reasoning from observation.

Final demand vector That column in an input-output table which shows the values of completed goods for consumption.

Firm The administrative unit responsible for managing establishments which, in turn, carry out functions. A corporation and a private company may be called firms.

Fixed factors of production Those factors which cannot be increased in a short-run period.

Flora The vegetative cover, domestic or wild, of the earth.

Friction of distance The negative impact of distance, reflected in freight charges for goods, long-distance charges for telephone calls, expenditure of human or animal energy in walking, etc., that affects flows of goods, information, and people from place to place. (*See also* **distance-decay**.)

Function The economic activity, including production or transport of goods and/or services, performed by establishments. Agriculture, manufacturing, and retail trade are examples of functions.

Functional order The assumption that central-place functions can be arranged in an orderly sequence, with low-order functions (providing such daily necessities as bread and gasoline) found in numerous establishments, and with higher-order functions (providing goods of a more specialized nature) in fewer, more widely spaced establishments. (*See also* Fig. 8.3.)

Generalization A statement about a set of things or events which tends to be true about that set but may not be true about any of the things or events individually.

Geographic model A formal statement of theory purporting to explain spatial relationships between and among factors.

Geographic rent The excess return or yield of a piece of land over another piece of land which results purely from its more favorable location.

Gravity model In geography, a human interaction model having a structure similar to the equation in physics expressing gravitational force. (*See also* pp. 176–178.)

Gross raw materials Those raw materials which suffer weight reduction when being combined into a final product.

Growth points, growth centers, growth poles Terms referring to foci of growth in either abstract or actual space—increasingly, to actual space. Growth points are those key nodes in an urban network which may affect other urban places as well as rural areas, and are hence fundamental to either normal or planned change. *Growth point* refers to the general concept; *growth pole* to large metropolitan places of national importance that originate development impulses; *growth center* to places of intermediate size that transfer impulses from the growth poles to the outlying areas.

Heuristic criteria The values of a model in serving to guide empirical research.

Hinterland The territory upon which a seaport depends strongly for subsistence, and which, in turn, depends upon the port. Some scholars use this term as synonymous with *trading area,* which refers to zone of retail and/or wholesale influence; some do not. The original German meaning is ''behind land'' or ''land behind,'' implying a seaport association. (*See* pp. 93–94.)

Horizontal integration The merging of two or more firms making the same product to achieve greater economies of scale per unit of output.

Horizontal relationships The linkage flows from economic activity to other activities, and from area to area. (*See also* Fig. 7.1.)

Hypothesis An initial idea which constitutes an educated guess as to the explanation of an event.

Impedence factor A factor which causes a variable to decline over distance; a factor impeding a variable from having an even distribution throughout space.

Indeterminacy A word used to refer to situations which can be stated only in probabilistic terms.

Induction A method of reasoning from observed facts, or from the particular to the generalization. (*See also* **deduction**.)

Input-output table A table or matrix showing the volumes of flows between and among producing sectors for both intermediate and final production use. (*See* index, W. Leontief; *see also* p. 201.)

Intermediate goods Goods in demand for which the production process is incomplete.

Intervening opportunity Any opportunity which can satisfy a demand in space closer to an origin than can another point also capable of satisfying that demand. (*See also* index, Stouffer and Ullman.)

Isochrone A line representing equal travel time from a given point.

Isodapane A line joining all points which involve the same increase in transport costs over the minimum-transport-cost location.

Isotim A line representing equal travel cost from a given point.

Isotropic surface A segment of the earth's surface which is assumed to be the same throughout its extent.

Jargon Technical terminology or characteristic idioms used in a particular area of knowledge.

Less developed economy (underdeveloped economy) An economy which as yet has not achieved a high level of output per worker and does not enjoy a high level of consumption of goods and services per person.

Level of observation (scale) Perspective at which a situation is viewed. For example, in geography, conditions may be seen at the level of the individual, city block, neighborhood, city, metropolitan area, state, nation, group of nations, world.

Levels of development Degrees of efficiency on the parts of economies in the provision of goods and services. (*See also* **less developed economy** and **developed economy**.)

Lex parsimoniae The law of minimum effort which applies the conservation of energy to human spatial systems.

Linkages Ties of interactance between and among activities and areas. (*See* Fig. 7.1. *See also* **horizontal relationships**.)

Localized raw materials Raw materials occurring only at a fixed number of points throughout a region.

Location quotient The percentage of employees of a given area working in a selected manufacturing activity compared with that area's percentage of all manufacturing. Location quotient can also be used in assessing primary and secondary activity. Its purpose is to show degree of specialization by an area in a given activity.

Locational variable A variable which changes through space.

Locational weight The weight which has to be moved in a region, including the sum of the raw materials and the final product.

Marginal land That land from which the value of its yield is just equal to the cost of producing that yield.

Marketing costs Transport costs for distributing outputs to markets from the point of production.

Marketing principle The central-place system of Christaller which maximized market opportunities for any central place with three centers of the next higher order central place lying equidistant from any given order of central place. (This is sometimes referred to as the *K-3 network*.)

Marketing range of a good The maximum distance over which a good can be marketed from a given location.

Material index The ratio of the weight of the localized raw materials to the weight of the finished product.

Multilateral trade A system of regional or national trading relations in which exports and imports between any two regions need not balance, as they can be offset by imports from and exports to other regions in the system, which involves more than two regions or nations.

National income, national product The value, at current prices, of all goods and services produced by the domestically owned components of a national economy. Technically, *income* refers to wages, salaries, and profits, whereas *product* refers to all goods and services sold. However, the two should add up to the same figure. *Gross* national income or product does not include allowance for depreciation, whereas *net* national income does include such allowance. *Gross domestic product* refers to the total value of all goods and services produced in a country, regardless of the national source of origin of the capital financing such production. Usually gross national product exceeds gross domestic product, especially in the developed economies; but in some countries, such as Kuwait, the gross domestic product can considerably exceed the gross national product.

Necessary condition A condition which must be fulfilled in order for an event to occur; therefore, this condition is met in all cases of occurrence of the event.

Objective probability An estimate of the likelihood of an event's occurring, based on numerical calculation of the factors which determine that likelihood.

Occam's razor The scientific rule that assumptions should not be increased unnecessarily.

Open system A system in which relationships between components in an ensemble can be altered or influenced by other components.

Operational space A space in which dimensions are measured in realistic or operational magnitudes such as time and cost or effort. (*See also* **economic feasibility**.)

Order of center The position a settlement occupies in a central-place system, on the basis of its size of population. Many scholars now accept orders ranging from first- through seventh-order centers. (*See also* Fig. 8.3.)

Ore A portion, however small, of the earth's surface

containing enough of a desired material that mining or quarrying is economically possible, feasible, or taking place.

Outlying area ''Where the action ain't.'' An outlying area contains little or no population, and is usually governed from an effective area.

Pattern of occupance The total imprint of man and his works upon the natural setting of an area. *Urban occupance* reflects an urban dominance; *rural occupance,* a rural dominance.

Pelagic life Life at or near the water surface of lakes, oceans, etc.

Plankton Tiny, sometimes microscopic, life. *Zooplankton* is animal life; *phytoplankton* is plant life.

Planning A process involving a continuous reexamination of goals and means, in view of continuously changing events. *Microplanning* applies the process to small areas, such as portions of cities. *Macroplanning* applies the process to larger areas, such as networks of metropolitan and other urban places and their zones of influence. Microplanning is mainly aggregative (aggregating upward from the viewpoint of the individual, household, neighborhood, city, etc.), whereas macroplanning is disaggregative (disaggregating downward from state or national capitals, etc.). Ultimately, for a given area, microplanning and macroplanning must be in harmony. (*See also* **levels of observation.**)

Population threshold The size of population necessary to support a given function or activity. (The term can also refer to establishments.)

Postulate A truth resulting from reasoning logically from a set of assumptions.

Prediction A final stage of the scientific method involving forecasting of events on the basis of known facts and logical reasoning.

Primary economic activity Activity transforming a natural object into something to be either consumed directly or further processed. The five recognized primary activities are agriculture, grazing, mining and quarrying, forest industries, and fishing/hunting.

Producer good A product used to make other products, such as a factory or a tool-making machine.

Pure raw materials Materials which enter into a final product without any weight loss.

Qualitative information Information which cannot be reduced to numerical form but is often treated by statements in terms of ordinal magnitudes. (*See also* **quantitative information.**)

Quantitative information Information which can be stated in numerical form and values. This information can be in *cardinal* form, in which values can be both measured and ordered (e.g., the basic number system), or in *ordinal* form, in which the values can be ordered but not measured (e.g., shades of color).

Quaternary economic activity Tertiary activity requiring a high level of professional training and high capital investment, such as financial services. (Not universally accepted; *see* index, Gottmann; *see also* **primary, secondary, tertiary activity.**)

Region A portion of the earth's surface delimited because of some unifying criterion or criteria, and not simply set aside for mere convenience. A *homogeneous or formal* region may be applied to either cultural (wheat belt) or natural (Rocky Mountains) features. A *functional or nodal* region consists of a point of focus and lines of linkage to outlying territory, and is usually applied only to cultural (city-trading area; capital-state or nation) features. A *planning region* is an area set aside for planning purposes and usually involves dependence upon functional region criteria, because both the functional region and planning involve organization of space. (*See also* pp. 128–131, 366–368.)

Regional development The achievement of planned change in a region. (*See also* **planning, region, levels of observation.**)

Science A method of studying facts and events regardless of the subject matter in which those facts and events are classified.

Secondary economic activity Activity which further processes materials received from the primary stage. Examples are manufacturing, construction, utilities. (*See also* **primary, quaternary, tertiary activity.**)

Site All the internal characteristics of a defined area. (*See also* **vertical relationships.**)

Situation The relative location of a place—i.e., its location relative to other places.

Size hierarchy of central places The arrangement of settlements in a hierarchy based on population size.

Space distortion A condition in which a variable measuring space exhibits different rates of change.

Space inversion A condition in which space measured in two dimensions (e.g., distance and time) results in points having opposite spatial relationships on those dimensions.

Space system Any assemblage of objects united by some form of regular interaction in which the space occupied by the component parts is significant and/or the interaction between the component parts is a first-order characteristic of the system.

Spatial constant An element showing no variation throughout space.

Spatial elasticity The change in values of a variable with distance from a selected origin. The rate of change also may be shown.

Standard Metropolitan Statistical Area (SMSA) As officially defined by the United States Office of Management and Budget, a SMSA contains a core city or twin cities with at least 50,000 inhabitants, plus such adjacent entire counties (or, in New England and a few other parts of eastern United States, townships) as are officially added. (*See* Fig. 21.1.)

Strong assumption An assumption of least generality (i.e., one which requires many qualifications for acceptance in its stated form).

Subjective probability Conjecture; an estimate of likelihood, based on nonquantitative or intuitive opinion.

Subsistence income The minimal income necessary to maintain a unit of labor in production.

Sufficient condition As defined by example: it is necessary for a substance to be sweet if that substance is sugar; but, since the substance may be honey, sweetness is not a sufficient condition for the substance to be sugar. (*See also* **necessary condition.**)

Surrogate variable A variable which substitutes for another variable.

System; systems analysis A system is a functional unit comprising a series of interrelated functional subunits. An automobile is a system, made up of these and other subsystems: cooling, electrical, braking, etc. The automobile, in turn, may become part of a still larger traffic system. Systems analysis attempts to resolve a system into its parts and to explain and predict their motions and consequences.

Tautology The restatement of the same question in a different way and, at the same time, the use of it as an explanation.

Tertiary economic activity Activity which either (1) distributes materials produced in primary or secondary activity stages (e.g., retail or wholesale trade), or (2) provides services (transportation, government work, teaching, etc.) that could not exist in such large quantities without marked efficiency in primary and secondary activity. (*See also* **primary, secondary, quaternary activity.**)

Theory A logical statement of the possible explanation of an event. A theory consists of a hypothesis, a set of assumptions, and derived postulates.

Threshold See population threshold.

Time space A dimension of operational space in which the time variable is the dimension on which measurements are made.

Topology A branch of mathematics concerned with transformations of geometric configurations; "rubber sheet geometry."

Traffic principle The central-place system of Christaller which minimized traffic links joining the greatest number of people, each center being equidistant between two centers of the next highest order. (This is sometimes referred to as the *K-4 network.*)

Transfer earnings The earnings which a factor of production (land, labor, capital) can obtain in its next best alternative use.

Transferability A necessary condition for economic interaction, meaning that a good is capable of being economically transported between two places. (*See also* index, Stouffer and Ullman.)

Ubiquitous raw materials Raw materials occurring at all points in an area.

Urbanized area As officially delimited by the U.S. Office of Management and Budget, the densely populated and highly urban section of a metropolitan or other urban place. It differs from SMSA in that it includes only strictly urban conditions. (*See also* **Standard Metropolitan Statistical Area.**)

Value added In manufacturing, the final shipment value of a product less costs of raw materials, energy, agents of manufacture, and lesser functions of the manufacturing process.

Variable One element in a group of factors that can take on different magnitudes within that group.

Variable factors of production Those production factors which can be readily increased in a short-run period.

Vertical integration The integration of two or more firms to achieve efficiency in production and distribution of goods. A manufacturing firm may purchase a retail firm to provide an outlet for its own goods.

Vertical relationships The on-site associations, such as interactions between and among geologic structure, landforms, slopes, soil types, vegetation, climate, and land use; not to be confused with **vertical integration,** above.

Weak assumption An assumption of great generality (i.e., one which requires few or even no qualifications for acceptance in its stated form).

Bibliography

Introduction

Ballabon, M. B. "Putting the 'Economic' into Economic Geography," *Economic Geography,* **33**:217–223 (1967).

Boyce, R. B., and W. A. V. Clark. "The Concept of Shape in Geography," *Geographical Review,* **54**:561–572 (1964).

Chisholm, M. *Geography and Economics,* London, Bell, 1966.

Eliot Hurst, Michael E. *A Geography of Economic Behavior,* North Scituate, Mass., Duxbury Press, 1972.

Haggett, Peter. *Geography: A Modern Synthesis,* New York, Harper and Row, 1972.

Lloyd, Peter E., and Peter Dicken. *Location in Space: A Theoretical Approach to Economic Geography,* New York, Harper and Row, 1972.

Lukerman, F. "On Explanation, Model and Description," *Professional Geographer,* **12**:1–2 (1960).

Morrill, Richard L. *The Spatial Organization of Society,* Belmont, California, Wadsworth Publishing Company, 1970. (Excellent bibliography.)

Spate, O. H. K. "Quantity and Quality in Geography," *Annals of the Association of American Geographers,* **50**:377–394 (1960).

The Science of Geography. Report of the *Ad Hoc* Committee on Geography, Earth Sciences Division, National Academy of Sciences–National Research Council, Publication 1277, Washington, D.C., 1965.

Thoman, Richard S. "Some Comments on *The Science of Geography,*" *Professional Geographer,* **17**, No. 6: 8–10 (1965).

Watson, J. W. "Geography: A Discipline in Distance," *Scottish Geographical Magazine,* **71**:1–13 (1955).

Part 1

Alexandersson, Gunnar. *Geography of Manufacturing,* Englewood Cliffs, N.J., Prentice-Hall, 1967.

Berry, Brian J. L. *Geography of Market Centers and Retail Distribution,* Englewood Cliffs, N.J., Prentice-Hall, 1967.

Bryson, Reid A., and John E. Kutzbach. *Air Pollution,* Resource Paper No. 2, AAG Commission on College Geography, Washington, D.C., 1968.

Chisholm, Michael. *Rural Settlement and Land Use,* London, Hutchinson University Library, 1968.

Davis, Kingsley. *World Urbanization, 1950–1970,* Berkeley, University of California Institute of International Studies, vol. 1, 1969; vol. 2, 1972.

Dormstadter, Joel. *Energy in the World Economy: A Statistical Review of Trends in Output, Trade, and Consumption Since 1925,* Baltimore, Md., Johns Hopkins Press for Resources for the Future, Inc., 1971.

Eliot Hurst, Michael E. "Transportation and the Societal Framework," *Economic Geography,* **49**:163–184 (1973).

Eliot Hurst, Michael E. (Editor). *Transportation Geography: Comments and Readings,* New York, McGraw-Hill, 1974.

Garrison, W. L. "Fragments on Future Transportation Policy and Programs," *Economic Geography,* **49**:95–102 (1973).

Gregor, Howard F. *Geography of Agriculture: Themes in Research,* Englewood Cliffs, N.J., Prentice-Hall, 1970.

Guyol, Nathaniel B. *Energy in the Perspective of Geography,* Englewood Cliffs, N.J., Prentice-Hall, 1971.

Hare, F. K., and C. I. Jackson. *Environment: A Geographical Perspective,* Ottawa, Government of Canada Department of Environment Geographical Paper No. 52, 1972.

Hayami, Yujiro, and V. W. Ruttan. *Agricultural Development: An International Perspective,* Baltimore, Md., Johns Hopkins Press, 1971.

Kenyon, James B. "Elements in Inter-Port Competition in the United States," *Economic Geography,* **46**:1–24(1970).

Kneese, Allen V., Sidney E. Rolfe, and Joseph W. Harned (Editors). *Managing the Environment: International Economic Cooperation for Pollution Control,* New York, Praeger, 1971.

Knox, Francis. *The Common Market and World Agriculture: Trade Patterns in Temperate-Zone Foodstuffs,* New York, Praeger, 1972.

Korten, David C. *Planned Change in a Traditional Society: Psychological Problems of Modernization in Ethiopia,* New York, Praeger, 1972.

Mayer, Harold M. "Some Geographic Aspects of Technological Change in Maritime Transportation," *Economic Geography,* **49**:145–156 (1973).

Nulty, Leslie. *The Green Revolution in West Pakistan: Implications of Technological Change,* New York, Praeger, 1972.

Ohlin, B. *Interregional and International Trade,* Cambridge, Mass., Harvard University Press, 1933.

Smith, R. H. T., and A. M. Hay. "A Theory of the Spatial Structure of Internal Trade in Underdeveloped Countries," *Geographical Analysis,* **1**:121–136 (1969).

Stutz, Frederic P. "Distance and Network Effects on Urban Social Travel Fields," *Economic Geography,* **49**:134–145 (1973).

Sun Nai-Ching, and Michael C. Bunamo. "Competition for Handling United States Foreign Cargoes: The Port of New York's Experience," *Economic Geography,* **49**:156–162 (1973).

Taaffe, Edward J., and Howard L. Gauthier, Jr. *Geography of Transportation,* Englewood Cliffs, N.J., Prentice-Hall, 1973.

Taaffe, Edward J., Richard Morrill, and Peter Gould. "Transport Expansion in Underdeveloped Countries: A Comparative Analysis," *Geographical Review,* **53**:503–529 (1963).

Thoman, Richard S. *Free Ports and Foreign-Trade Zones,* Cambridge, Maryland, Cornell Maritime Press, 1956.

Thoman Richard S., and Edgar C. Conkling. *Geography of International Trade,* Englewood Cliffs, N.J., Prentice-Hall, 1967.

Thoman, Richard S., and Donald J. Patton (Editors). *Focus on Geographic Activity: A Collection of Original Studies,* New York, McGraw-Hill, 1964.

Tuan, Yi-Fu, "Ambiguity in Attitudes Toward Environment," *Annals of the Association of American Geographers,* **63**:411–423 (1973).

Vance, James E., Jr. *The Merchant's World: The Geography of Wholesaling,* Englewood Cliffs, N.J., Prentice-Hall, 1970.

White, Gilbert F., David J. Bradley, and Ann U. White. *Drawers of Water: Domestic Water Use of East Africa,* Chicago, University of Chicago Press, 1972.

Part 2

Ackerman, E. A. "Where Is a Research Frontier?" *Annals of the Association of American Geographers,* **53**: 429–440 (1963).

Alonso, W. "A Theory of the Urban Land Market," *Papers and Proceedings of the Regional Science Association,* **6**:149–157 (1960).

Alonso, W. *Location and Land Use: Toward a General Theory of Land Rent,* Cambridge, Mass., Harvard University Press, 1964.

Applebaum, W., and S. B. Cohen. "The Dynamics of Store Trading Areas and Market Equilibrium," *Annals of the Association of American Geographers,* **51**:73–101 (1961).

Bachi, R. "Standard Distance Measures and Related Methods for Spatial Analysis," *Papers and Proceedings of the Regional Science Association,* **10**:83–132 (1963).

Beckmann, M. J. "City Hierarchies and the Distribution of City Size," *Economic Development and Cultural Change,* **6:**243–248 (1958).

Beckmann, M. J. *Location Theory,* New York, Random House, 1968.

Beckmann, M. J., and J. C. McPherson. "City Size Distribution in a Central Place Hierarchy: An Alternative Approach," *Journal of Regional Science,* **10:**25–33 (1970).

Berry, Brian J. L., and H. G. Barnum. "Aggregate Relations and Elemental Components of Central Place Systems," *Journal of Regional Science,* **4:**35–68 (1962).

Bertalanffy, L. von. *General System Theory,* New York, Braxiller, 1968.

Bracey, H. W. "English Central Villages: Identification, Distribution and Functions," *Lund Studies in Geography, Series B, Human Geography,* **24:**169–190 (1962).

Brown, L. A., J. Odland, and R. G. Golledge. "Migration, Functional Distance and the Urban Hierarchy," *Economic Geography,* **46:**472–485 (1970).

Bunge, W. *Theoretical Geography,* Lund Studies in Geography, Series C, 1966.

Burton, I. "The Quantitative Revolution and Theoretical Geography," *Canadian Geographer,* **7:**151–162 (1963).

Carrothers, G. A. P. "An Historical Review of the Gravity and Potential Concepts of Human Interaction," *Journal of the American Institute of Planners,* **22:**94–102 (1956).

Chiou-Shuang, Yan. *Introduction to Input-Output Economics,* New York, Holt, Rinehart and Winston, 1969.

Chorley, R. J., and P. Haggett (Editors). *Models in Geography: The Madingley Lectures for 1965,* London.

Christaller, W. *Central Places in Southern Germany* (translated by C. W. Baskin), Englewood Cliffs, N.J., Prentice-Hall, 1966.

Curry, L. "Quantitative Geography," *Canadian Geographer,* **11:**265–279 (1967).

Curry, L. "The Geography of Service Centres within Towns: The Elements of an Operational Approach," *Lund Studies in Geography, Series B, Human Geography,* **24:**31–54 (1962).

Curry, L. "The Random Spatial Economy: An Exploration in Settlement Theory," *Annals of the Association of American Geographers,* **54:**138–146 (1964).

Davies, W. K. D. "Centrality and the Central Place Hierarchy," *Urban Studies,* **4:**61–79 (1967).

Dunn, E. S. *The Location of Agricultural Production,* Gainesville, University of Florida Press, 1954.

Friedrich, C. J. *Alfred Weber's Theory of the Location of Industries,* Chicago, University of Chicago Press, 1929.

Gale, S. "Explanation Theory and Models of Migration," *Economic Geography,* **49:**257–274 (1973).

Getis, A. "The Determination of the Location of Retail Activities with the Use of a Map Transformation," *Economic Geography,* **39:**14–22 (1963).

Golledge, R. G., and D. Amadeo. "On Laws in Geography," *Annals of the Association of American Geographers,* **58:**760–774 (1968).

Golledge, R. G., G. Rushton, and W. A. V. Clark. "Some Spatial Characteristics of Iowa's Dispersed Farm Population and Their Implications for the Grouping of Central Place Functions," *Economic Geography,* **42:**261–272 (1966).

Golledge, R. G., R. Briggs, and D. Demko. "The Configuration of Distances in Interurban Space," *Proceedings of the Association of American Geographers,* **1:**60–65 (1969).

Greenhut, M. L. *Plant Location in Theory and Practice: The Economies of Space,* Chapel Hill, University of North Carolina Press, 1956.

Greenhut, M. L. "Size of Markets versus Transport Costs in Industrial Location Surveys and Theory," *Journal of Industrial Economics,* **8:**172–184 (1960).

Hagerstrand, T. "Migration and Area: Survey of a Sample of Swedish Migration Fields," in D. Hannerberg, T. Hagerstrand, and B. Odeving (Editors), *Migration in Sweden: A Symposium, Lund Studies in Geography, Series B, Human Geography,* **13:** 27–158 (1957).

Haggett, P. *Locational Analysis in Human Geography,* London, Edward Arnold, 1965.

Hall, A. D., and R. E. Fagen. "Definition of System," *General Systems,* **1:**18–28 (1956).

Hall, P. (Editor). *Von Thünen's Isolated State,* London, Pergammon, 1966.

Hamilton, F. E. I. "Models of Industrial Location," in R. J. Chorley and P. Haggett (Editors), *Models in Geography,* London, Methuen, 1967, pp. 361–424.

Harris, C. D. "The Market as a Factor in the Localization of Industry in the United States," *Annals of the Association of American Geographers,* **44:**315–348 (1954).

Harvey, D. W. "Theoretical Concepts and the Analysis of Agricultural Land Use Patterns in Geography," *Annals of the Association of American Geographers,* **56:**361–374 (1966).

Hoover, E. M. *The Location of Economic Activity,* New York, McGraw-Hill, 1948.

Huff, D. L. "A Topographical Model of Consumer Space Preferences," *Papers and Proceedings, Regional Science Association,* **6**:159–173 (1960).

Isard, W. *Location and Space-Economy: A General Theory Relating to Industrial Location, Market Areas, Land Use, Trade and Urban Structure,* Cambridge, Mass., M.I.T. Press, 1956.

Isard, W., D. F. Bramhall, G. A. P. Carrothers, J. H. Cumberland, L. N. Moses, D. O. Price, and E. W. Schooler. *Methods of Regional Analysis: An Introduction to Regional Science,* Cambridge, Mass., M.I.T. Press, 1960.

Janelle, D. G. "Central Place Development in a Time-Space Framework," *Professional Geographer,* **20**: 5–10 (1968).

Kain, J. F. "The Journey-to-Work as a Determinant of Residential Location," *Papers and Proceedings, Regional Science Association,* **9**:137–159 (1962).

Karaska, G., and D. Bramhall. *Location Analysis for Manufacturing,* Cambridge, Mass., M.I.T. Press, 1969.

Lee, T. R. "Perceived Distance as a Function of Direction in the City," *Environment and Behavior,* **2**:40–51 (1970).

Lowrey, R. A. "Distance Concepts of Urban Residents," *Environment and Behavior,* **2**:52–73 (1970).

Lynch, K. *The Image of the City,* Cambridge, Mass., M.I.T. Press, 1960.

Mayfield, R. C. "Conformation of Service and Retail Activities: An Example in Lower Orders of an Urban Hierarchy, in a Lesser Developed Area," *Lund Studies in Geography, Series B, Human Geography,* **24**:77–90 (1962).

Morrill, Richard L. "Simulation of Central Place Patterns over Time," *Lund Studies in Geography, Series B, Human Geography,* **24**:109–120 (1962).

Morrill, Richard L. "The Development and Spatial Distribution of Towns in Sweden: An Historical-Predictive Approach," *Annals of the Association of American Geographers,* **53**:1–14 (1963).

Peet, J. R. "The Present Pertinence of von Thünen Theory," *Annals of the Association of American Geographers,* **57**:810–811 (1967).

Saarinen, Thomas F. *Perception of Environment,* Resource Paper No. 5, AAG Commission on College Geography, Washington, D.C., 1969.

Schaefer, F. K. "Exceptionalism in Geography: A Methodological Examination," *Annals of the Association of American Geographers,* **43**:226–249 (1953).

Scott, Allen J. *An Introduction to Spatial Allocation Analysis,* Resource Paper No. 9, AAG Commission on College Geography, Washington, D.C., 1971.

Stouffer, S. A. "Intervening Opportunities: A Theory Relating Mobility and Distance," *American Sociological Review,* **5**:845–867 (1940).

Stutz, F. P. "Distance and Network Effects on Urban Social Travel Fields," *Economic Geography,* **49**:134–144 (1973).

Thomas, E. N. "Towards an Expanded Central Place Model," *Geographical Review,* **51**:400–411 (1961).

Thünen, J. H. von. *Der Isolierte Staat in Beziehung auf Landwirtschaft und Nationalokonomie,* Hamburg, 1875. (*See also* J. R. Peet, above.)

Tobler, W. R. "Geographic Area and Map Projections," *Geographical Review,* **53**:59–78 (1963).

Toulmin, S. *The Philosophy of Science,* London, 1953.

Warntz, W. *Toward a Geography of Price,* Philadelphia, University of Pennsylvania Press, 1959.

Warntz, W., and D. Neft. "Contributions to a Statistical Methodology for Areal Distributions," *Journal of Regional Science,* **2**:47–66 (1960).

Webber, J. J. "Empirical Verifiability of Classical Central Place Theory," *Geographical Analysis,* **3**:15–28 (1971).

Wolpert, J. "The Decision Process in Spatial Context," *Annals of the Association of American Geographers,* **54**:537–558 (1964).

Part 3

Alexander, J. W. "The Basic-Nonbasic Concept of Urban Economic Functions," *Economic Geography,* **30**:246–261 (1954).

Applebaum, William. *Shopping Center Strategy: A Case Study of the Planning Location and Development of the Del Monte Center, Monterey, California,* New York, International Council of Shopping Centers, 1970.

Berry, Brian J. L. *Theories of Urban Location,* Resource Paper No. 1, AAG Commission on College Geography, Washington, D.C., 1968.

Borchert, John R. "America's Changing Metropolitan Regions," *Annals of the Association of American Geographers,* **62**:352–373 (1972).

Calef, W. *Private Grazing and Public Lands: Studies of the Local Management of the Taylor Grazing Act,* Chicago, University of Chicago Press, 1960.

Chakravarti, A. K. "Green Revolution in India," *Annals of the Association of American Geographers,* **63**:319–330 (1973).

Chisholm, M., and P. O'Sullivan. *Freight Flows and Spatial Aspects of the British Economy,* New York, Cambridge University Press, 1973.

Forrester, J. W. *Urban Dynamics,* Cambridge, Mass., M.I.T. Press, 1969.

Fuchs, V. R. *Changes in the Location of Manufacturing in the United States since 1929,* New Haven, Conn., Yale University Press, 1962.

Harvey, David. *Society, the City, and the Space-Economy of Urbanism,* Resource Paper No. 18, AAG Commission on College Geography, Washington, D.C., 1972.

Hewes, Leslie. *Suitcase Farming Frontier: A Study in the Historical Geography of the Central Great Plains,* Lincoln, University of Nebraska Press, 1973.

Hidore, J. J. "The Relationship between Cash-Grain Farming and Land Forms," *Economic Geography,* **39**:84–89 (1963).

Higbee, E. C. *Farms and Farmers in an Urban Age,* New York, Twentieth Century Fund, 1963.

Hoyt, Homer. *According to Hoyt: Fifty Years of Articles,* Washington, D.C., Homer Hoyt, 1966.

Hutchinson, Sir Joseph. *Farming and Food Supply: The Interdependence of Countryside and Town,* Cambridge, Cambridge University Press, 1972.

Kenyon, J. "On the Relation between Central Function and Size of Place," *Annals of the Association of American Geographers,* **57**:736–750 (1967).

Kerr, D. "Some Aspects of the Geography of Finance in Canada," *Canadian Geographer,* **9**:175–192 (1965).

Linge, G. J. R., and P. J. Rimmer (Editors). *Government Influence and the Location of Economic Activity,* Canberra, Australian National University, Research School of Pacific Studies, Research Publication HG/5, 1971.

Manners, Gerald. *The Changing World Market for Iron Ore, 1950–1980,* Baltimore, Md., Johns Hopkins Press for Resources for the Future, Inc., 1971.

Mayer, Harold M. *The Spatial Expression of Urban Growth,* Resource Paper No. 7, AAG Commission on College Geography, Washington, D.C., 1969.

Mayer, Harold M. "Urban Nodality and the Economic Base," *Journal of the American Institute of Planners,* **20**:117–121 (1964).

Mayer, Harold M., and Richard C. Wade. *Chicago: Growth of a Metropolis,* Chicago, University of Chicago Press, 1969.

Muller, Peter G. "Trend Surfaces of American Agricultural Patterns: A Macro-Thünenian Analysis," *Economic Geography,* **49**:228–242 (1973).

Murphy, Raymond E. *The Central Business District,* Chicago, Aldine Atherton, 1972.

Pred, A. "Industrialization, Initial Advantage, and American Metropolitan Growth," *Geographic Review,* **55**:158–189 (1965).

Pred, A. "The Concentration of High Value-Added Manufacturing," *Economic Geography,* **41**:108–132 (1965).

Pred, A. "The Intrametropolitan Location of American Manufacturing," *Annals of the Association of American Geographers,* **54**:165–180 (1964).

Revzan, David A. *A Marketing View of Spatial Competition,* Berkeley, University of California School of Business Administration, 1971.

Roepke, Howard G. *Readings in Economic Geography,* New York, John Wiley and Sons, 1967.

Rugg, Dean S. *Spatial Foundations of Urbanism,* Dubuque, W. C. Brown, 1972.

Schrader, L. F., and G. A. King. "Regional Location of Beef Cattle Feeding," *Journal of Farm Economics,* **44**:64–81 (1962).

Semple, R. Keith. "Recent Trends in the Spatial Concentration of Corporate Headquarters," *Economic Geography,* **49**:309–318 (1973).

Smith, Bruce W. "Analysis of the Location of Coal-Fired Power Plants in the Eastern United States," *Economic Geography,* **49**:243–250 (1973).

Standard Industrial Classification Manual, 1972. Washington, D.C., U.S. Office of Management and Budget, Government Printing Office, 1972.

Ullman, E. L., and M. F. Dacey. "The Minimum Requirements Approach to the Urban Economic Base," *Papers and Proceedings of the Regional Science Association,* **6**:175–194 (1960).

Weaver, J. C., L. P. Hoag, and B. L. Fenton. "Livestock Units and Combination Regions in the Middle West," *Economic Geography,* **32**:237–259 (1956).

Yaseen, L. C. *Plant Location,* New York American Research Council, 1960.

Part 4

Ayal, Eliezer B. (Editor). *Micro Aspects of Development,* New York, Praeger, 1973.

Burchell, Robert, with James W. Hughes. *Planned Urban Development: New Communities American Style,*

New Brunswick, N.J., Center for Urban Policy Research, Rutgers University, 1972.

Brewis, T. N. *Regional Economic Policies in Canada,* Toronto, MacMillan, 1969.

Bryson, Reid A., and John E. Kutzbach. *Air Pollution,* Resource Paper No. 2, AAG Commission on College Geography, Washington, D.C., 1968.

Chisholm, Michael, and Gerald Manners (Editors). *Spatial Policy Problems of the British Economy,* New York, Cambridge University Press, 1971.

Commission on Regional Aspects of Development, International Geographical Union. *Proceedings,* vols. 1 and 2, Toronto, Allister Typesetting and Graphics, 1974.

Cumberland, John H. *Regional Development: Experiences and Prospects in the United States of America,* Paris and The Hague, Mouton, 1971.

Friedmann, John. *Urbanization, Planning, and National Development,* Beverly Hills, California, Sage Publications, 1973.

Friedmann, John, and William Alonso (Editors). *Regional Development and Planning,* Cambridge, Mass., M.I.T. Press, 1964.

Gauthier, Howard L. "The Appalachian Development Highway System: Development for Whom?" *Economic Geography,* **49**:103–108 (1973).

Gertler, L. O. (Editor). *Planning the Canadian Environment,* Montreal, Harvest House, 1968.

Gould, Peter R. *Spatial Diffusion,* Resource Paper No. 4, AAG Commission on College Geography, Washington, D.C., 1969.

Hagerstrand, T., and A. R. Kuklinski (Editors). *Information Systems for Regional Development: A Seminar, Lund Studies in Geography, Series B, Human Geography,* 1971.

Hansen, Niles M. (Editor). *Growth Centers in Regional Economic Development,* New York, Free Press, 1972.

Hansen, Niles M. *Intermediate-Size Cities as Growth Centers: Applications for Kentucky, the Piedmont Crescent, the Ozarks, and Texas,* New York, Praeger, 1971.

Hansen, Niles M. *Location Preference, Migration, and Regional Growth: A Study of South and Southwest United States,* New York, Praeger, 1973.

Hewitt, Kenneth, and Ian Burton. *The Hazardness of a Place: A Regional Ecology of Damaging Events,* Toronto, University of Toronto Department of Geography Research Publication No. 6, 1971.

Hodge, Gerald. *The Identification of Growth Poles in East-ern Ontario,* Toronto, Government of Ontario Department of Treasury and Economics, 1966.

Hodge, Gerald. "Urban Systems and Regional Policy," *Canadian Public Administration,* **9**:181–193 (1966).

Kuklinski, A. (Editor). *Growth Poles and Growth Centres in Regional Planning,* Paris and The Hague, Mouton, 1972.

Kuklinski, A., and R. Petrella. *Growth Poles and Regional Policies: A Seminar,* Paris and The Hague, Mouton, 1972.

Lefeber, Louis, and Mrinal Datta-Chaudhuri. *Regional Development Experiences and Prospects in South and Southeast Asia,* Paris and The Hague, Mouton, 1971.

Lewis, Peirce F., David Lowenthal, and Yi-Fu Tuan. *Visual Blight in America,* Resource Paper No. 23, AAG Commission on College Geography, Washington, D.C., 1973.

Mihailovič, Kosta. *Regional Development Experiences and Prospects in Eastern Europe,* Paris and The Hague, Mouton, 1972.

Morrill, Richard L., and Ernest H. Wohlenberg. *The Geography of Poverty in the United States,* New York, McGraw-Hill, 1971.

Mumphrey, Anthony J., and Julian Wolpert. "Equity Considerations and Concessions in the Siting of Public Facilities," *Economic Geography,* **49**:109–121 (1973).

O'Neill, Helen B. *Spatial Planning in the Small Economy: A Case Study of Ireland,* New York, Praeger, 1971.

Ray, D. Michael. *Dimensions of Canadian Regionalism,* Ottawa, Government of Canada Department of Energy, Mines and Resources Geographical Paper No. 49, 1971.

Regional Plan Association. *The Office Industry: Patterns of Growth Location,* Cambridge, Mass., M.I.T. Press, 1972.

Rothblatt, Donald N. *Regional Planning: The Appalachian Experience,* Lexington, Books, 1971.

Smith, David M. *The Geography of Social Well-Being in the United States,* New York, McGraw-Hill, 1973.

Thoman, G. Richard. *Foreign Investment and Regional Development: The Theory and Practice of Investment Incentives, with a Case Study of Belgium,* New York, Praeger, 1973.

Thoman, Richard S. *Design for Development in Ontario: The Initiation of a Regional Planning Program,* Toronto, Allister Typesetting and Graphics, 1971.

Wood, W. D., and Richard S. Thoman (Editors). *Areas of Economic Stress in Canada,* Kingston, Queen's University Industrial Relations Centre, 1965.

Index

Page numbers in *italic* indicate illustrations.

THE WORLD'S POLITICAL UNITS

Greenland

United States
(Alaska)

Canada

United States

British
Honduras

Haiti

Dominican Republic

Mexico

Cuba

Puerto Rico

Guatemala

Honduras

Jamaica

El Salvador

Nicaragua

Tobago

Trinidad

Costa Rica

Venezuela

Guyana

Panama

Surinam

French Guiana

Colombia

Ecuador

Brazil

Peru

Bolivia

Paraguay

Chile

Argentina

Uruguay

Falkland Islands